Information Systems in Business
An Introduction

Information Systems in Business
An Introduction

James O. Hicks, Jr.
Virginia Polytechnic Institute and State University

West Publishing Company
St. Paul   New York   Los Angeles   San Francisco

COPYRIGHT © 1986 By WEST PUBLISHING COMPANY
50 West Kellogg Boulevard
P.O. Box 64526
St. Paul, MN 55164-1003

Printed in the United States of America

Library of Congress Cataloging-in-Publication Data

Hicks, James O.
Information systems in business.
Includes index.
1. Management information systems. I. Title.
T58.6.H488 1986   658.4'038   85-26474
ISBN 0-314-93188-0

Intext Photo Credits:

Chapter and Module Credits
PART I Opening Photo Courtesy of NCR Corporation. **Chapter 1 Opening Photo** Courtesy of Digital Research Inc. **Fig. 1–13** Courtesy of Sorcim Corporation. **Fig. 1–14** Copyright Lotus Development Corporation 1985. Used with permission. **Chapter 2 Opening Photo** Courtesy of Hewlett-Packard Company. **Figs. 2–2, 2–3, 2–7, 2–9, and 2–10** From "Personal Computers, " by H.D. Toong and A. Gupta.
Credits Are Continued Following the Index

Copyediting: Deborah Annan
Text illustrations: Anco/Boston
Composition: Graphic Typesetting Service
Cover: Design Team/Paul Konsterlie
Color gallery design: Wendy Calmenson

Contents

Chapter 3

Management Information Systems 70

Chapter 4

Systems Concepts 92

Part Two: Developing User Applications

Chapter 5

System Analysis

Chapter 6

System Design and Implementation

Chapter 7

Application Development by Users 170

Part Three: Computer Resources 197

Chapter 8

The Central Processing Unit and Storage Devices 198

Chapter 9

Data Entry and Information Response　　234

Chapter 10

System Software　　266

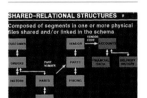

Chapter 13

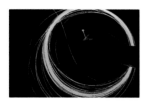

Distributed Data Processing and Office Automation 354

Part Four: Information Systems, Management, Society and You 397

Chapter 14

Managing the Information-System Resource 398

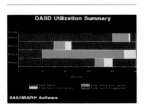

Color Galleries

Preface

The computer age has become the information age. In my twenty-year career as a computer operator, system analyst, information systems consultant, and information systems educator, one fact is clear: business people who successfully apply computers are not primarily interested in computers. They are most concerned with their needs for information and how to build computer-based information systems to meet those needs. A business person who does not have a basic understanding of the tools and techniques for determining his or her information needs, and how to transform these needs into computer software, will never apply computers successfully. Business people are interested in how to put the computers to work, and how to build and use information systems.

These observations led me to write *Management Information Systems: A User Perspective,* which was published in 1984. The success of that textbook indicates that there are many educators who agree with the premises of that text. Thus, I was eager to write a text with similar premises, but designed primarily for the introductory course.

The Approach of the Text

This text emphasizes how to effectively use computer technology rather than simply cite the technology itself. An introduction to information systems concepts early in the text builds a framework for understanding computer information systems, and demonstrates the importance of determining business information needs before being concerned with the technical aspects of hardware, data storage, operating systems, and the like. Any good system analyst will tell you that in building information systems it is most important to first determine information needs before being concerned with computer hardware. Yet, most introductory textbooks cover computer hardware first, and then discuss analyses of information needs later in the text. This approach misleads students into believing that computer hardware is the most important part of information systems. The danger of this approach is demonstrated by the large amount of computer hardware, especially personal computers, that are gathering dust through lack of use. Their purchasers simply did not have a clear understanding of how they would use them before they were purchased. They were more concerned with computer hardware than how to effectively use the hardware.

Many educators have told me that the reason most textbooks concentrate on hardware first is because it is interesting to students. I think this is true. Full color pictures of hardware and discussions of the speed with which the hardware can operate are certainly interesting. But, how useful will this information be to you once you graduate and attempt to apply this knowledge to business problems? The hardware that you studied will likely be obsolete then.

There is a better way to generate interest and to provide you with skills that will be useful to you now and throughout your career. Hands-on use of the personal computer will be more useful to you than looking at color photos of computer hardware. After covering introductory material in Chapter 1, this text covers personal computers in Chapter 2. You can immediately put the personal computer to work learning BASIC programming, the disk operating system, word processing, electronic spreadsheets, and/or data-base management systems. There is more than ample material in the two appendices and the *Educate-Ability Student Manual* supplement to provide you with hands-on experience on the personal computer. BASIC programming, the disk operating system, WordStar, Lotus 1-2-3, SuperCalc3, and dBASE II/III are covered in Appendices A and B. The very easy-to-use integrated package, *Ability,* which has word processing, electronic spreadsheet, data base, graphics, and communications capabilities is covered in the *Educate-Ability Student Manual.*

Hands-on use of the personal computer not only will provide you with the skills to use this most important tool, but it has another equally important contribution in this text. All computers, from the largest supercomputers to personal computers, have many characteristics in common. As we study these characteristics, we will use personal computers to illustrate them. As you use PCs, you will literally be able to see and feel these characteristics of computers.

A very important trend in information systems is the use of computers without programming. This trend is often called application development by end users. It has been estimated that by 1990 over 80 percent of the business use of computers will be through application software that was developed by end users rather than system analysts and programmers. As you use the personal computer in this course you will be making your first steps towards application development by an end user. This text emphasizes how you can put the computer to work without programming, and places less emphasis on computer programming.

Determining business information needs and developing information systems is largely a process of dealing with and managing complexity. If you are to be successful in applying computers to anything other than trivial tasks, you must have the tools for analyzing information needs in an orderly and structured fashion. The easiest and yet most powerful tool for dealing with information system complexity is the structured system development life cycle. Its tools, such as data flow diagrams, data dictionaries, and pseudocode, are easy to learn. Yet, they are useful any time you need tools to help you understand an information system, regardless of how simple or how complex that information system may be. These tools are useful not only when you are developing information system applications through writing programs, but they are also useful with the newer techniques used in application development by end users.

Features of the Text

Each chapter and module within the text contains the following features to assist in your understanding of the material covered.

1. An outline provides an overview of the topics discussed in the chapter or module.
2. A prologue discusses a specific organization or person with a question or a problem concerning the topics covered in the chapter or module. These,

along with the *Thinking About Information Systems,* help to relate the material to real life situations.

3. Two small cases per chapter, called *Thinking About Information Systems,* encourage you to consider real world applications of the concepts covered in the chapter. Typical topics include: the relationships between the application backlog and application development by end users; is it better to choose the hardware or software first when buying a PC?; and should the introduction of PCs be controlled by central computer departments?

4. Each chapter and module contains two *PC User Tip*s. These provide practical personal computer information which you can use immediately. Typical topics include "How to Get Free Software," "Help! I Just Erased the Only Copy of My File," "Making Your Printer Do Some Fancy Fontwork," and "Word Processing Accessories."

5. The page margins throughout the text contain definitions of new and unfamiliar terms that are used in the chapter text. Learning the terminology of information systems is important in understanding it. In addition to these margin definitions, the text contains a particularly complete glossary of information systems terms. You should use it regularly as you read this text.

6. At the end of each chapter and module a summary of the key points discussed in the chapter is provided along with a list of key terms covered.

7. The last feature in each chapter and module is a self-quiz on the concepts covered with ten completion and ten multiple-choice questions. Often instructors use these types of questions on exams. You should use these self quizzes to test your understanding of the material covered.

In addition to the features of each chapter, the text contains a real-world application of personal computers at the end of each part. These show in detail how PCs are being used to solve business problems.

The eight color photo essays in the text cover a particular information systems topic through the use of color photos. One of these photo essays will take you on a tour of a large computer center. Another will show you the process of buying and setting up a personal computer. The others are equally interesting.

There are two appendices at the end of the text. Appendix A provides an introduction to BASIC programming using personal computers or the DEC VAX computers. Appendix B provides hands-on instruction for MS-DOS, WordStar, LOTUS 1-2-3, SuperCalc3, and dBASE II/III.

Supplements to the text include a Study Guide authored by Robert M. Brown. This study guide provides detailed outlines, additional questions, and other materials to assist you in mastering the material in the text.

Some instructors will decide to use *Educate-Ability,* or another integrated package, to give you hands-on experience with integrated software. If you use *Educate-Ability,* your instructor will tell how to obtain your copy of *Educate-Ability. Educate-Ability* is the student version of *Ability,* an integrated package with word processing, spreadsheet, graphics, database, and communications capabilities. *Educate-Ability* has *Ability*'s full capabilities except that it limits spreadsheet and file sizes. Even with these limitations you can learn all the capabilities of *Ability* and perform some very useful work with the educational version. For example, you can write papers or letters up to ten pages in length. *Educate-Ability* runs on the IBM PC, PC XT,

PC AT, all the IBM compatible computers running PC or MS-DOS 2.0 or later. To accompany your *Educate-Ability* software you will want to purchase from your bookstore a copy of the *Educate-Ability Student Manual.*

An application disk containing BASIC, LOTUS 1-2-3, SuperCal3, dBASE, WordStar, and Ability application exercises can also be obtained through your instructor.

Overview of the Text Contents

The text contains 16 chapters divided into 4 parts. These chapters cover the topics which I consider to be the most important in a first course in information systems. A certainty in the information systems area is that instructors differ on the material that each feels should be covered in this course. Therefore, the text provides four modules that cover topics which some instructors may want to include in the course. In fact, some instructors will not cover all the chapters in the text. This built-in flexibility will allow your instructor to tailor the course to your specific needs.

Part One covers the fundamentals of information systems including such topics as personal computers and management information systems concepts. Part Two is devoted to covering the methods that are used to apply computers to business information needs. You will find that you can understand these approaches to developing applications without an indepth understanding of computer hardware and software which is covered in Part Three under Computer Resources. Part Four covers how information systems resources are managed and the relationships between information systems, society, and you. The four modules cover the history of the computer industry, programming languages, decision support systems, and computer system evaluation and acquisition.

As you read this text you will see that users must be directly involved in the process of developing information systems. In fact, research has shown that the most successful information systems are those where there is a direct heavy user involvement in development and maintenance of those systems. A business professional simply cannot afford to take the attitude that knowledge of information systems is not necessary, and consequently leave application development entirely to information systems professionals. Only you know what information you need from a system. If you do not understand information systems it will be impossible to translate this need for information into an operational information system. I am sure you will find these an enjoyable and useful course. In fact if you master the material in this course and apply it now and when you begin your career, I think that you will find this course to have been the most useful of any taken in your collegiate program.

Acknowledgements

A textbook of this type is produced not only by the author but by a team of individuals. There are numerous clerical, proofreading, and research tasks necessary to produce a textbook. Several individuals have made contributions in one or more of these areas including Jeannie Christian, Kihyun Do, Jennifer Vance, Janet Tolley, and George Krusen. Others have made more specific contributions to this text. I would like to thank Jack Cathey and Bob Phillips for their assistance in developing Appendix B and the PC User Tips, Tom Harvey for his photo research and assistance in developing the photo galleries, and Roy Smith for his help in developing the Thinking About Information Systems cases. A particularly important person in developing this book has been Phyllis Neece, whose typing and word processing skills were indispensable in completing the manuscript. I am also thankful for the environment at Virginia Polytechnic Institute and State University that encourages the commitment and provides the support to projects of this duration and size.

Numerous professors at other institutions were most helpful in providing review and criticism of the manuscript in its development stages. These include: James Adair, Bentley College; Jack Baroudi, New York University; Warren J. Boe, University of Iowa; Eli Boyd Cohen, California State University-Sacramento; William R. Cornette, Southwest Missouri State University; Marilyn J. Correa, Polk Community College; John DaPonte, Southern Connecticut State University; Sharon Hill, Prince Georges Community College; John A. Kelder, Cerritos College; James E. LaBarre, University of Wisconsin-Eau Claire; Murray Levy, West Los Angeles College; Richard W. Manthei, Joliet Junior College; Tom Murray, Lynchburg College; Shailendra Palvia, Kent State University; Leonard Presby, William Patterson College; Douglas V. Rippy, University of Dayton; Patsy C. Smith, Georgia State University; Sandra Stalker, North Shore Community College; H. Ray Souder, Northern Kentucky University; Robert Tesch, University of North Carolina, Greensboro; and James Wynne, Virginia Commonwealth University. Many of their ideas have been included in the book.

Finally I am grateful to my family for the support and encouragement they gave me in this project. The support of an author's family is crucial during the long hours that are necessary to produce a book of this type. My family has contributed to this project in many ways. These contributions are important and I am grateful.

To my wife Eva
and my son Kevin

Part One

Information Systems Fundamentals

Chapter 1

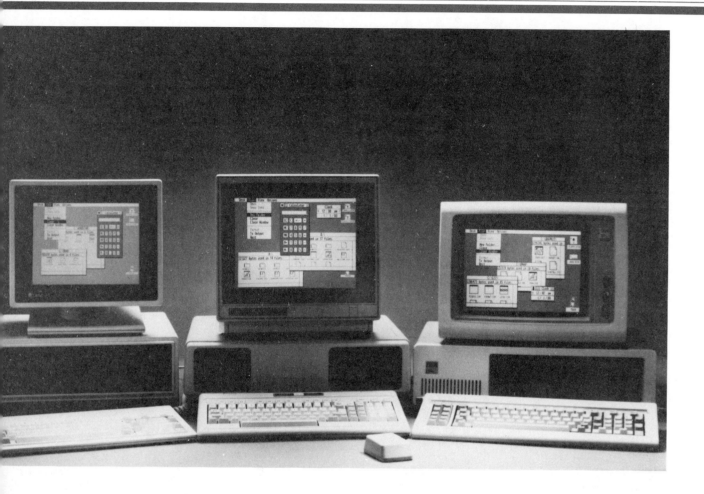

An Introduction to Computers

CHAPTER OUTLINE

PROLOGUE

Many schools are requiring that their students buy a personal computer. Others are providing personal-computer labs for students. Gaining computer literacy has become a top priority of students. Organizations of all sizes are putting the computer to work. It seems like everybody is using the computer! What is this machine that has caused such a revolution in our society? But more important, how can you put it to work for you? You will find answers to these questions in this chapter.

Introduction

The premier invention of this century is the computer. In a relatively short time it has affected many areas of our lives. For example, computers help control our automobiles, act as challenging adversaries in electronic games, make possible very sophisticated medical diagnostic tools such as the computerized axial tomography (CAT) scanner, and even act as an ideal matchmaker through computerized dating services. But most important, computers have had a tremendous impact on the way information is processed within organizations. Although information has been processed manually throughout history, modern management information systems would not be possible without the computer.

In the first section of the chapter we will explore the capabilities and characteristics of this machine we call a computer, then present a brief overview of a computer system, and look at how a computer stores and processes data. In the final section of the chapter we will turn our attention to the most practical and important topic: how to put the computer to work for you.

What Is a Computer?

Definition

A **computer** can be defined as an information processor that is able to perform substantial computation, including numerous arithmetic or logical operations, without intervention by a human operator. The term *substantial* in this definition is open to wide interpretation. Is a pocket calculator that performs a series of statistical computations without human intervention a computer? It may or may not be. In recent years the distinction between calculators and computers—particularly programmable calculators—has become quite blurred.

Characteristics and Capabilities

A computer should have the following characteristics and capabilities (see Figure 1–1).

1. *Is electronic.* A computer operates by the movement of electronic pulses through circuits rather than by the mechanical movement of parts. This characteristic is essential to the speed of modern computers. Electronic pulses flow through the circuits of today's computers at roughly half the speed of light (about six inches in a billionth of a second). This is incredibly fast compared with mechanical movement. Certainly a computer could be designed and built based on mechanical movement; however, such a machine would be useless because of its slow speed.

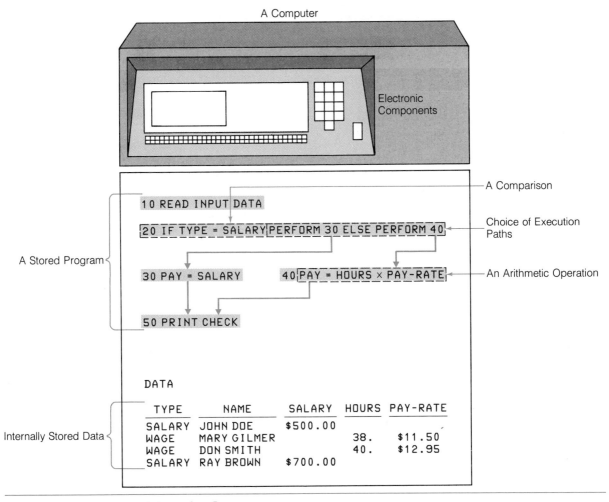

FIGURE 1–1 Capabilities of a Computer

Both the program and data are stored internally within the machine. The program is executed in order by statement number, starting with statement 10, until a branching statement is encountered. Statement 20 is a branching IF statement. If the type is equal to salary, then statement 30 is performed. If the type is not equal to salary, then statement 40 is performed.

2. *Can perform arithmetic operations.*   A computer must be able to add, subtract, multiply, and divide.
3. *Can compare.*   The ability to compare one piece of information with another (to determine whether they are equal, whether one is less than the other, and so on) is essential to the operation of a computer. Comparison operations are also called logical operations.
4. *Has internal storage and retrieval of data.*   Today's computers have vast capabilities for storage and retrieval of data. Some computers can store several million characters of data within their central processing unit.

program
A set of instructions for the computer to follow.

execution
To run a computer program.

execution path
The specific set of program instructions used by the computer.

payroll program
A computer program that prepares checks to pay employees and maintains payment information.

5. *Can execute a **stored program**.* A computer can internally store (or hold) the instructions for operations to be performed on data. This set of instructions for a particular computer run is called a **program.**

6. *Has choice of alternative, execution paths* within a program. A computer can choose (or branch) among different sets of program instructions based on the values of the input data. For example, in a *payroll program* one series of instructions would be executed if the employee is paid according to hours worked. A different series would be executed if the employee is paid a fixed salary. Therefore, the course of execution of a program may vary substantially based on the input data that the computer is examining.

Although all these items are important, the two most crucial are that computers are electronic and that they can execute stored programs. Prior to the computer there were machines, such as the mechanical calculator, that would perform arithmetic operations, and there were many ways to store and retrieve information, including filing cabinets. However, the electronic basis for the computer gives the computer incredible speed and accuracy while the stored program enables this speed and accuracy to occur without human intervention. Essentially, humans are exceedingly slow compared with the flow of electronic pulses.

Stored Programs

A stored program gives the computer three advantages: (1) it enables the computer to operate at electronic speeds, (2) it provides tremendous reliability, and (3) it makes the computer general-purpose. The electronic speed of the computer would be of little value if not for the stored program. For example, let's assume an operator had to sit at a computer and enter manually an instruction for each step to be performed, such as an addition, subtraction, or comparison. Obviously, such a machine would be of little more use than a basic pocket calculator. The speed of the machine would be limited by the speed of the person operating it. Furthermore, the person would be making decisions on what sequence of operations would be executed next. This certainly would decrease the *accuracy* and *reliability* of such a machine because of the potential for human error.

accuracy
A quality held by that which is free from error.

reliability
A quality held by that which is dependable and can be trusted.

Once a computer program has been written to perform a task and has been thoroughly checked so that all errors have been removed, the computer will execute it with extreme accuracy and reliability—producing results with essentially no error. Many experts would argue that this ability to capture human decision making and processing capabilities in a computer program is by far the most significant contribution of computers. In essence, once a task that was previously performed by humans has been accurately captured in a computer program, the computer will continuously perform the task with very high accuracy and reliability. In other words, society no longer has to train people to perform that task. Humans are free to perform tasks of which computers are not capable. This is indeed revolutionary. We have long had machines and animals—such as tractors, horses, automobiles, and lawnmowers—that lighten the burden of manual labor. However, the computer is the first machine that relieves us of the intellectual burden of storing, processing, and retrieving data and of making decisions based on the data.

The stored-program capability makes the computer general-purpose in that the stored program can be changed. A single computer can be used for many different tasks. These tasks may be as varied as data processing; editing, formatting, and typing the contents of this book; and controlling robots that weld the parts of an automobile body.

Computers are truly revolutionary machines. Because of the dramatic decrease in their cost, they are being used in many facets of daily life. To function in today's society and especially in the business world you must develop not only a computer literacy, but also the ability to use the vast potential inherent in a computer. It is the primary goal of this text to develop your ability to understand and use computer technology.

Overview of a Computer System

In this and the next two sections we look at the basics of computer systems, storage, and processing of data. Later chapters will cover these concepts in more depth. Figure 1–2 shows an overview of a computer system. All computer systems have four categories of devices: *input, processing, storage,* and *output.* As we discuss these devices we will illustrate them with the *personal computer* system shown in Figure 1–3.

Input Devices

There are many types of input devices, the most widely used being a keyboard with an attached *cathode-ray tube (CRT).* Optical scanners, voice-recognition devices,

input
Data being received (or to be received) into a device or into a computer program.

processing
To perform operations on data.

storage
The process of retaining data, program instructions, and output in machine-readable form.

output
The information produced by a computer from a specific input.

personal computer
A computer small enough to be placed on a desktop and designed to be used by one person who possesses very little, if any, programming knowledge.

cathode-ray tube (CRT)
An electronic vacuum tube, such as a television picture tube, that can be used to display data or graphic images.

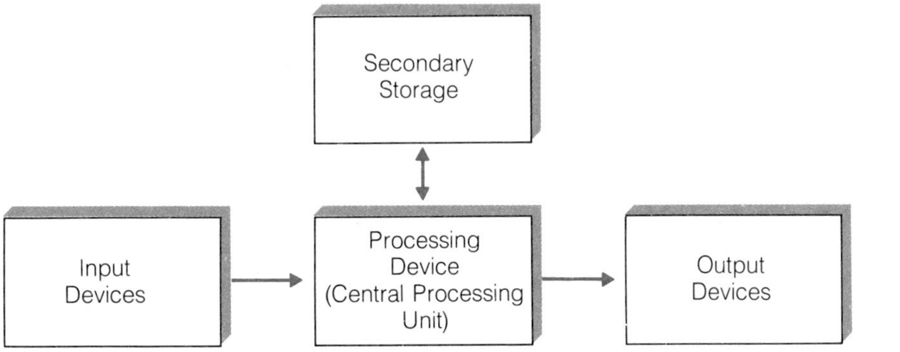

FIGURE 1–2 Overview of a Computer System
Data and programs are moved back and forth between primary storage (within the central processing unit) and secondary storage, as they are needed for execution of programs.

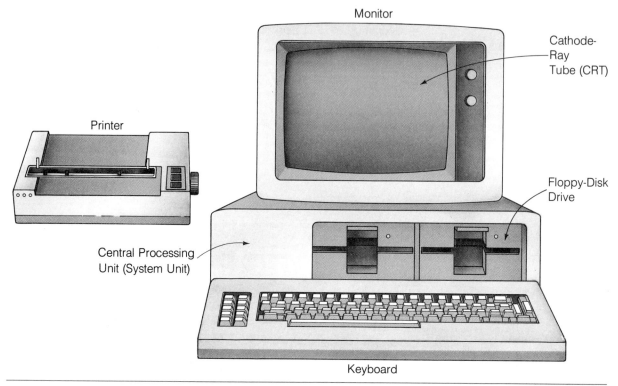

FIGURE 1–3 A Personal-Computer System

Although the monitor is sometimes called a cathode-ray tube (CRT), technically the CRT is only a part of the monitor.

and various devices that read magnetically coded tape or disk are other examples. Many of these devices overlap into two or more of the four categories; for example, CRT terminals are both input and output devices.

Central Processing Unit

The processing role in a computer system is performed by the **central processing unit (CPU).** The CPU is the centerpiece of a computer system; strictly speaking, it is the computer. Its function is to interpret and execute the instructions of the program. Thus the CPU in effect controls the complete computer system. As shown in Figure 1–4 the CPU has three components: the control unit, the arithmetic-logic unit, and primary storage. The **control unit** decodes program instructions and directs other components of the computer to perform the tasks specified in the program instructions. Arithmetic operations such as multiplication, division, subtraction, and addition are performed by the **arithmetic-logic unit.** This unit also performs logical operations such as comparing the relative magnitude of two pieces of information. **Primary storage** stores the program instructions that

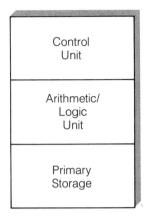

The Central Processing Unit

FIGURE 1–4   The Central Processing Unit

A central processing unit on a personal computer is often called the system unit.

are currently being executed and also stores data while they are being processed by the CPU.

Secondary Storage

Secondary storage is used for relatively long-term storage of data. The most widely used secondary-storage media are magnetic disks, such as *floppy disks* used in personal computers, and magnetic tapes. The bulk of information used by a computer application is stored in secondary storage but must be transferred to primary storage before it can be processed by the CPU. Therefore information is continually being read into and written out of primary storage during the execution of the program. The data not being used by the CPU are stored in secondary storage. The main differences between primary and secondary storage are that primary storage is a part of the CPU, allows very fast access to data, is *volatile,* and is more expensive than secondary storage.

Output Devices

Output devices record data either in forms humans can read, such as printouts, or in machine-readable forms such as magnetic disks and tapes. Output devices include a wide variety of printers which use different technologies—such as impact, print chains, ink jets, and laser imaging—to produce print. Other examples of output are voice output as well as graphics terminals which display information directly in graphic form, such as bar charts and line graphs. Many of the types of input and secondary storage already discussed (such as magnetic tape, disk, and CRT terminals) also serve as output devices or media. Figure 1–5 illustrates the input, processing, secondary storage, and output devices typically used in a medium-to-large computer system.

floppy disk
A data-storage medium, used in small computers, that is a 3½-, 5¼-, or 8-inch disk of polyester film covered with a magnetic coating.

volatile storage
Computer storage that loses the data and/or programs stored in it when the electricity to the computer is turned off.

Food Town is a medium-sized grocery chain located in the eastern seaboard states. John Wilson, the chief executive officer of Food Town, has become very concerned about the information he gets from his data-processing system. He knows that a large amount of data is gathered and stored in company disk and tape files. All of the company's accounting systems, such as accounts payable, accounts receivable, and payroll, are computerized. In addition, the company has computer-based inventory-control systems, personnel systems, and sales/marketing systems. Wilson presents his problem as follows: "With all this information being collected and stored, why can't I get better management-information reports? My assistant should be able to sit down at a terminal and pull information from these various systems and integrate it in a way that would be meaningful. Sure I can get information from the personnel system or from the payroll system, but whenever I need information from two or more of these systems, it seems to involve a major undertaking. More often than not, by the time I get the information, a decision has already been made and the information is not used. These computers just don't help me a great deal in my decision making." Does Wilson have a valid point? Is it possible to provide the type of information he is requesting?

How Does a Computer Store Data?

The Data Hierarchy

Listed here in ascending order of complexity are the components of the data hierarchy in an information system:

semiconductor
A solid crystalline substance, such as silicon, that has a conductivity greater than good insulators but less than good conductors such as metal.

1. Bit
2. Byte
3. Field or item
4. Record
5. File or data set
6. Data base

This is called a data hierarchy because data bases are composed of files, files are composed of records, and so on. Figure 1–6 illustrates the relationships among these components of the information-system data hierarchy.

semiconductor storage
Storage that uses semiconductor electronic circuits to represent bits of data. Currently most semiconductor storage is integrated circuits (often called chips). These chips contain miniaturized electronic circuits that have been reproduced photographically onto silicon wafers.

Bit   The term **bit** is short for binary digit. It can assume either of two possible states and therefore can represent either a 1 or 0. In secondary storage a bit typically represents data through the positive or negative polarity of an electrical charge on a magnetic recording medium such as tape or disk. *Semiconductor storage* is usually used for primary storage. In semiconductor storage a bit is represented by an electrical circuit that is either conducting or not conducting electricity.

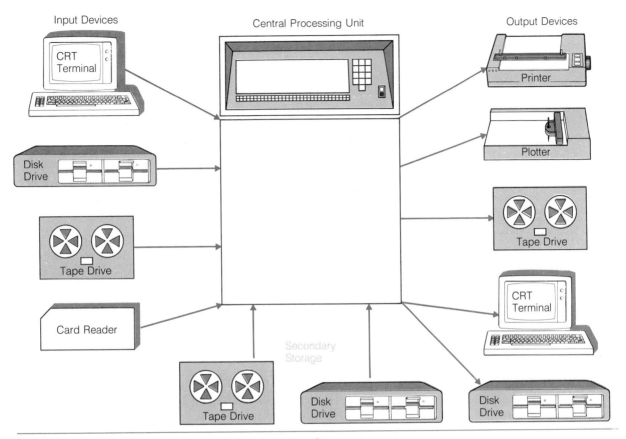

FIGURE 1–5   A Medium-to-Large Computer System

There is a large variety of input and output devices for computers, (see chapter 9). Only the most common ones are shown here.

Byte   The ability to represent only binary digits (bits) in a computer system is not sufficient for business information processing. Numeric and alphabetic characters as well as a wide variety of special characters such as dollar signs, question marks, and quotation marks, must be stored. In a computer system, a character of information is called a **byte.** A byte of information is stored by using several bits in specified combinations called **bit patterns.** One widely used bit pattern for personal computers and data communications is the American Standard Code for Information Interchange (ASCII); see Figure 1–7. ASCII uses seven bits to represent one character. Each 1 or 0 corresponds to a single bit.

Field or Item   The next level in the data hierarchy is a field or item of data. A **field** or **item** of data is one or more bytes that contain data about an *attribute* of an *entity* in the information system. An entity in a payroll system is an individual

attribute
A characteristic or property that an entity has.

entity
A subject on which data is kept in an information system.

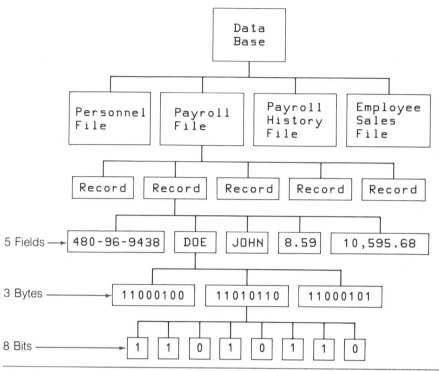

FIGURE 1–6   The Data Hierarchy

Data bases contain files, files contain records, records contain fields, fields contain bytes, and bytes contain individual binary digits or bits. Ultimately all data are represented through bits that have values of either 1's or 0's.

employee. Attributes are the employee's name, pay rate, and so on. The hourly rate is a field or item of data. Figure 1–8 shows a payroll record with typical fields of data.

Record   A **record** is a collection of fields relating to a specific entity. For example, the payroll record shown in Figure 1–6 contains fields of data relating to a specific employee. An analogy can be made between a computer-based record and an individual folder in a manual file (see Figure 1–9). A folder in a payroll file may contain much the same information as a record in a computer-based payroll file. The field that identifies a record from all other records in a file is the **record key.** For example, the record key in a payroll record is usually the employee's social security number because it is different for each employee.

File   A **file** is a collection of related records. For example, the collection of payroll records for all employees in a company is a payroll file. The concept of a

Character	ASCII Bit Pattern
A	1000001
B	1000010
C	1000011
D	1000100
E	1000101
F	1000110
G	1000111
H	1001000
I	1001001
J	1001010
K	1001011
L	1001100
M	1001101
N	1001110
O	1001111
P	1010000
Q	1010001
R	1010010
S	1010011
T	1010100
U	1010101
V	1010110
W	1010111
X	1011000
Y	1011001
Z	1011010
0	0110000
1	0110001
2	0110010
3	0110011
4	0110100
5	0110101
6	0110110
7	0110111
8	0111000
9	0111001

FIGURE 1–7 The ASCII Coding Scheme

A coding scheme is a bit pattern that uses bits in specified combinations to represent characters. Only a portion of the ASCII coding scheme is shown here. The complete coding scheme is covered in chapter 11.

computer file is very similar to a manual file in a filing cabinet, as illustrated in Figure 1–9.

Data Base A **data base** consists of all the files of an organization, structured and integrated to facilitate update of the files and retrieval of information from them. The term has often been used rather loosely. Technically a data base consists of the files that are part of a *data-base management system*. However, data base is often used to refer to all the files of an organization.

data-base management system
A computer program that stores, retrieves, and updates data that are stored on one or more files.

Payroll Master-File Record

First Name, Middle Initial
Last Name
Street Address
City/State
Zip Code
Social Security Number
Sick Leave Eligibility Date
Effective Date of Salary Increase
Date of Birth
Department Number
Hourly Rate
Sick Hours
Overtime Earnings
Regular Earnings
Federal Tax Year-to-Date
Marital Status
Number of Dependents
Total Voluntary Deductions Year-to-Date
FICA Year-to-Date
State Tax Year-to-Date
City Tax Year-to-Date
Net Earnings Year-to-Date

FIGURE 1–8   Sample Data Fields in a Payroll Master-File Record

The term master file often refers to the file that stores relatively permanent data. This payroll master file would be updated whenever employee paychecks are produced.

PC USER TIP   Naming Files

As you become a more frequent computer user, the number of files you will have to keep track of will grow sharply. Careful naming of these files will make it easier for you to recall what is in them and will also help when you are trying to group files. For instance, a dozen files that all had to do with an accounting project could have file names that begin with "AP" (for Accounting Project). A worksheet file in this group might be named APCHART.WKS. The WKS file extension tells you that the file is a LOTUS 1-2-3 worksheet file, and the AP tells you that the file deals with your accounting project. The CHART in the file name might stand for CHART OF ACCOUNTS. Many software packages today, including DOS, give you the ability to sort your files (or at least the directory of those files) in alphabetical order, or in order by file extension. If you had a hundred files, a sort of this type would place all your AP files together in the listing. You could also copy all of the AP files to another disk by using a DOS wildcard command such as COPY AP*.* B:. This would copy all files that start with the letter AP on the current disk to the B: disk. Remember, a little thought invested at the creation of a file and its name could save you a lot of time in the future.

Finding Data in a File

There are basically two types of file organization: those which allow sequential access to the data and those which allow direct access. With a **sequential-access file,** records must be read in the same order as they were written to the storage

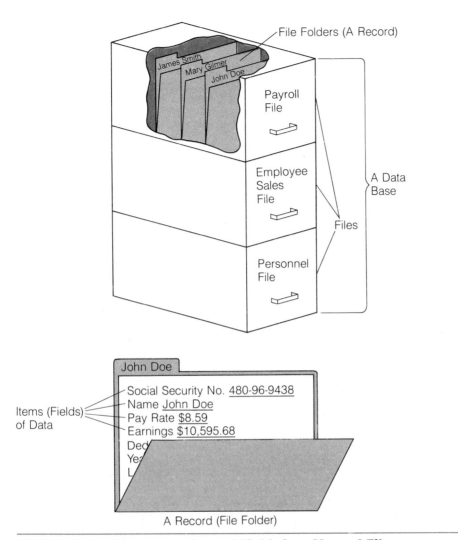

File Folders (A Record)

James Smith
Mary Gilmer
John Doe

Payroll File

Employee Sales File

Personnel File

A Data Base

Files

John Doe

Items (Fields) of Data

Social Security No. 480-96-9438
Name John Doe
Pay Rate $8.59
Earnings $10,595.68
Ded
Ye
L

A Record (File Folder)

FIGURE 1–9   Files, Records, and Fields in a Manual File

A computer file is analogous to a manual file drawer. Computer records are analogous to individual file folders within a drawer. Computer items of data are analogous to the data items contained in a file folder. Thinking of data storage in this manner will help you remember the way information is stored in a computer system.

media. The computer begins searching for a record by examining the first record in the file and then sequentially examining the next record and so on until the required record is located. Certain storage media like magnetic tape will allow only sequential access to data. In order for a record to be found on a reel of magnetic tape, the tape must be read sequentially, beginning with the first record.

On the other hand, a **direct-access file** allows immediate direct access to individual records in the file. There are several techniques used to accomplish direct-access file organization; these will be discussed in more depth in chapter 11. Magnetic disks, such as floppy disks, are by far the most commonly used devices for storing direct-access files. Direct access file organization must be used whenever the application requires immediate access to individual records. It is widely used today whenever the computer configuration includes CRT terminals which display management information on demand.

Thinking About Information Systems 1–2

Western University is a large university with a well-respected engineering college. All the departments within engineering and many departments in other colleges do a large amount of funded research. The manager of each research project is called a principal investigator (PI). In addition to assuring that the research is done properly, the PI must be sure that the funds expended on a research project do not exceed the funds allotted for the project. Outside sponsors of research such as the National Science Foundation and the Department of Defense will not cover over-expenditures on these projects. Funds to cover over-expenditures come directly from the university budget. Therefore, before committing to additional expenditures on a project, such as graduate assistants or equipment, the PI must be sure that there is enough remaining budget to cover the expenses.

The university has a central accounting system that allows a PI to retrieve the current budget balance through online computer terminals. Many academic departments in the university do not trust the central accounting system. Thus they use various methods—from manual ledgers to microcomputer-based systems—to maintain separate accounting systems. Other departments feel that the central system is perfectly adequate and therefore do not expend funds maintaining their own systems. The major complaint of those who do not trust the central system is one of timeliness of data. All commitments to expend resources, such as purchase orders for equipment, are executed through manual forms that are processed through several administrative departments before being entered into the central accounting system on a daily basis. Often it takes four to five days for these expenditure commitments to be reflected in the central-accounting-system files. The vice president of finance of the university is considering a policy that would prohibit departments of the university from maintaining their own accounting systems. Should departments be allowed to maintain their own accounting systems? Does the central system need improvements? If so, what would you suggest? Would a simple policy prohibiting departmental accounting systems be successful?

How Does a Computer Process Data?

Batch Processing

queries
Requests for information from a file.

With **batch processing,** changes and *queries* to a file are stored for a period of time, and then a processing run is made periodically to update the file and to produce responses to the queries. Batch runs can be made on a scheduled basis,

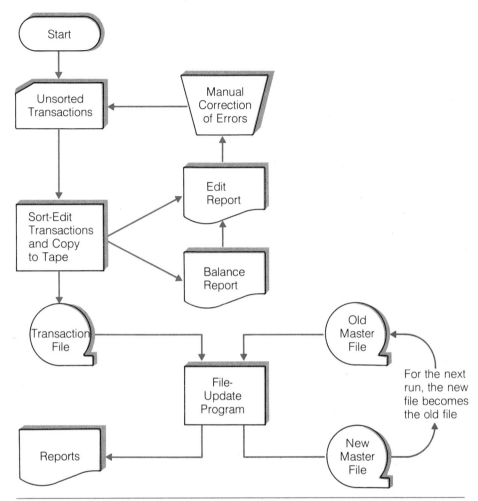

FIGURE 1–10 Batch Processing with Sequential Tape Files

Changes used to update a master file are called transactions. Since the records are stored sequentially on the master file (usually in ascending order by the record key), the transactions are sorted in this same order prior to updating. In the file-update program, records are read off the old master file simultaneously with changes read off the transaction file. The old master-file records are updated and then written to the new file.

such as daily, weekly, or monthly, or they can be made on an as-required basis. Batch processing with a sequential file stored on magnetic tape is illustrated in Figure 1–10. Figure 1–11 illustrates batch processing with a direct-access file stored on disk.

Immediate Processing

In **immediate processing,** transactions are processed to update the file immediately or shortly after a real-world event occurs (see Figure 1–12). Information-

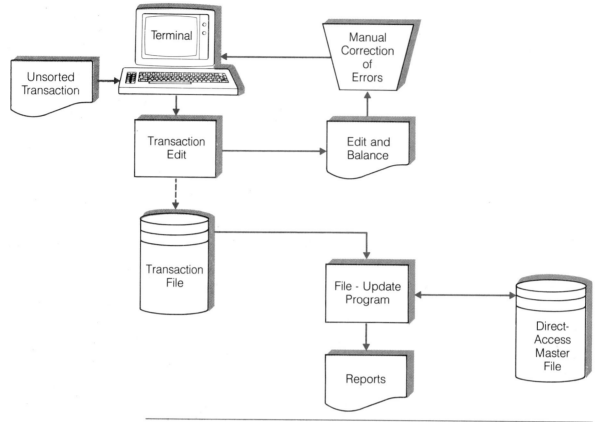

FIGURE 1–11 Batch Processing with a Direct-Access File

In this example the master file as well as the transactions used to change the master file are stored on a direct-access file. These changes are held until a periodic file-update is run. During the update run, the records in the master file are read into the file-update program. Each record is changed and then is written back to the same physical location it occupied before the change. This is called in-place updating.

processing applications that use immediate processing are often called **realtime applications.** A realtime application can immediately capture data about ongoing events or processes and provide the information necessary to manage them. An airline-reservation system is an example of a realtime application.

Realtime systems must have realtime files that are updated immediately after the event occurs. Consequently, at any point in time, the data in realtime files should accurately reflect the status of the real-world variables they represent. For example, when a customer reserves a seat on an airline flight, the reservations agent keys in that fact and the inventory of nonreserved seats on the flight is immediately changed to reflect one less available seat. Immediate processing requires direct-access files, since immediate processing with sequential files would be impractical because of the time required to search for individual records. Batch processing, on the other hand, can occur with either sequential- or direct-access files. Chapter 11 will cover these concepts in more depth.

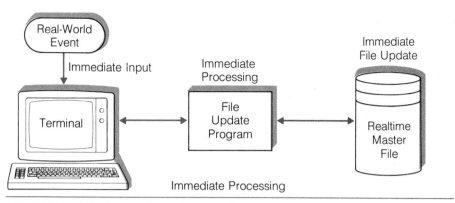

Immediate
File Update

Immediate Input

Immediate
Processing

Real-World
Event

Terminal

File
Update
Program

Realtime
Master
File

Immediate Processing

FIGURE 1–12 Immediate Processing

As real-world events occur, the realtime master file is updated immediately. When processing errors occur an error message is displayed on the terminal for immediate correction by the terminal operator.

How to Put the Computer to Work for You

Now that we understand the essential concepts concerning computers and the ways information is stored and processed, let's look at how you can put the computer to work for you. It is much easier than you may imagine. There are only two ways to do it. You can use computers without writing programs or you (or someone else) can write the necessary programs to perform the tasks you want done. The smart approach is the first one—use computers without writing programs, if possible. Writing programs can be a time-consuming, labor-intensive process. But if your computer needs are unique, writing programs may be the only alternative.

Putting the Computer to Work Without Programming

There is a very strong movement toward this approach to using computers. Personal computers (PCs) have been an important contributing factor in this movement. Large numbers of PCs have been sold, and naturally the buyers want them to perform useful work. But no computer performs work without programs. If programs have to be written for all the individual tasks that users want performed, where would all those programs come from? It has been estimated that if we wrote specific programs for all the tasks performed on computers, by the year 1990 we would need more programmers than the total population of the United States! Fortunately there is a better way. The four most typical ways to apply the computer without programming are word processing, electronic spreadsheets, data-base management systems, and preprogrammed application packages.

Word Processing In both your academic and professional careers you will continually need to convey your thoughts in writing. Your writing skills will be one of the crucial factors determining your future success. Computers can help you develop these skills. People who teach writing find that the use of word-processing software typically improves student grades by one letter grade.

What can word-processing programs do for you? Most important, they store your writing on computer files. This allows you to make extensive revisions with minimal retyping. Any good writer will tell you that refinement through revisions is the secret to good writing.

Excellent word-processing programs are available for PCs. Three of the most popular are **Wordstar**, **Word**, and **Word Perfect**, but there are many other very good ones. There are even programs that will indicate when you have made spelling, punctuation, and style errors. Errors such as subject/verb disagreements are highlighted. Some programs can even tell you when you have used redundant, verbose, unclear, cutesy, or pompous language!

We will cover word processing in more depth in chapter 13; also, in Appendix B we will cover hands-on use of Wordstar.

Electronic Spreadsheets   If a situation calls for little input data but requires complex calculations, often the quickest and easiest way to accomplish this on the computer is to use an electronic spreadsheet. Although the electronic spreadsheet originated with personal computers, most computers now support such programs. Two that are widely used on personal computers are **SuperCalc** and **Lotus 1–2–3**. These programs allow users to build a spreadsheet that has **rows** and **columns** on the computer display screen. Figure 1–13 illustrates a SuperCalc electronic spreadsheet. As you can see, each column is labeled by an alphabetic digit and each row by a numeric digit. Any intersection of a row and column on the spreadsheet is called a **cell.** The **cell address** is the column letter and the row number in which the cell is located. For example, the top left cell of a spreadsheet is cell A1.

Think of a spreadsheet as a very large piece of ruled paper on your desk (see Figure 1–14). You can enter data or formulas in cells on this spreadsheet. Each cell has its own address, identifying the row and column in which it is located. Some programs allow users to build very large spreadsheets. For example, Lotus 1–2–3 allows 256 columns and 2,048 rows. If each cell in such a worksheet were ¼-inch high and 1-inch wide, the entire worksheet would be more than 21-feet wide and approximately 42-feet high! Of course, no CRT screen would show all of that worksheet. Most spreadsheets display about 20 rows and 8 or 9 columns on a screen. The user can move around the worksheet in order to view particular parts of it on the screen, as shown in Figure 1–14.

Any cell within the worksheet may contain alphabetic titles (labels), numeric values, or formulas. For example, in Figure 1–13 the cells in column A contain labels or titles. Cell B4 contains a constant 1,000 and B6 a constant 300. Spreadsheet cells may also contain formulas that calculate a number based on the values contained in other cells in the spreadsheet. For instance, in Figure 1–13 the cell B8 would contain the formula B4 + B6. This formula tells the spreadsheet program to sum the values in B4 and B6 and place the result in B8, where the formula is stored. Formulas in spreadsheet cells can be as complex as a user's courage will allow. Almost any formula using addition, subtraction, multiplication, division, or exponentiation, no matter how complex, can be entered into a spreadsheet cell.

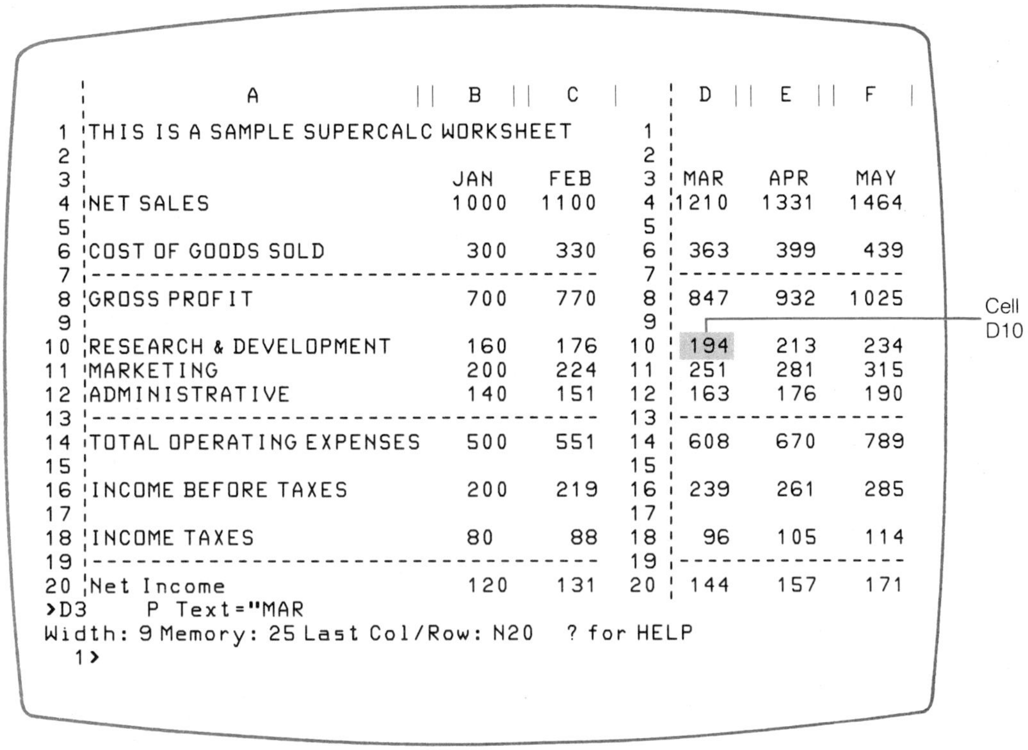

```
                  A              ||  B  ||  C  |      |  D  ||  E  ||  F  |
  1 ¦THIS IS A SAMPLE SUPERCALC WORKSHEET        1 ¦
  2 ¦                                            2 ¦
  3 ¦                         JAN    FEB         3 ¦ MAR    APR    MAY
  4 ¦NET SALES               1000   1100         4 ¦1210   1331   1464
  5 ¦                                            5 ¦
  6 ¦COST OF GOODS SOLD       300    330         6 ¦ 363    399    439
  7 ¦-----------------------------------         7 ¦-----------------
  8 ¦GROSS PROFIT             700    770         8 ¦ 847    932   1025
  9 ¦                                            9 ¦
 10 ¦RESEARCH & DEVELOPMENT   160    176        10 ¦ 194    213    234
 11 ¦MARKETING               200    224        11 ¦ 251    281    315
 12 ¦ADMINISTRATIVE          140    151        12 ¦ 163    176    190
 13 ¦-----------------------------------        13 ¦-----------------
 14 ¦TOTAL OPERATING EXPENSES 500    551        14 ¦ 608    670    789
 15 ¦                                           15 ¦
 16 ¦INCOME BEFORE TAXES      200    219        16 ¦ 239    261    285
 17 ¦                                           17 ¦
 18 ¦INCOME TAXES             80     88         18 ¦ 96     105    114
 19 ¦-----------------------------------        19 ¦-----------------
 20 ¦Net Income              120    131        20 ¦ 144    157    171
 >D3      P Text="MAR
 Width: 9 Memory: 25 Last Col/Row: N20    ? for HELP
    1>
```

Cell
D10

FIGURE 1–13   An Electronic Spreadsheet

Electronic spreadsheets have quickly become the most widely used software for personal computers. In fact, they are largely responsible for the personal computer becoming so popular among managers.

Electronic spreadsheets are most useful in a situation with relatively little data input but with complex calculations. They are also very handy when a user wants to see how sensitive a final answer is to input data changes (see Figure 1–15). The figure shows a loan-repayment schedule prepared on an electronic spreadsheet. A skilled user of spreadsheets could put this application on a microcomputer in less than an hour. The user can input varying values for principal amount of the loan, monthly interest rate, and number of monthly payments. This allows the user to see the impact of changes in these input values on the monthly payment. In addition, the spreadsheet is set up to show the amount of each payment that is applied to the interest and how much is going toward paying off the loan.

Figure 1–15 is a relatively simple spreadsheet application where the user can change only three input values. Much more complex spreadsheets are being constructed today. For example, Figure 1–16 is a spreadsheet used by a real-estate company to evaluate whether to invest in the construction of apartment buildings. Figure 1–17 provides a list of variables that could be varied to reveal to the real-estate company the impact on the after-tax cash flow.

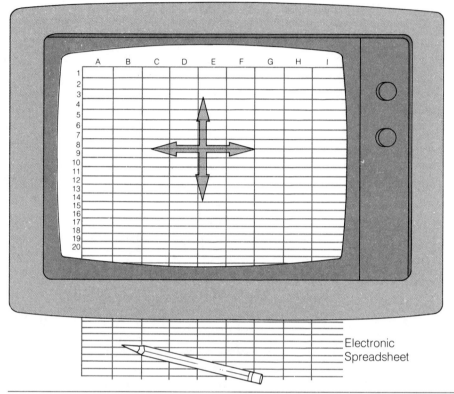

Computer
Display
Screen

Electronic
Spreadsheet

FIGURE 1–14 Cells in an Electronic Spreadsheet

The computer display screen acts as a window to the spreadsheet, enabling the user to
see any part of a very large spreadsheet stored in the computer's memory.

PC USER TIP   Backup Your Data Diskettes

If important data are being kept on a diskette it is necessary to make backup copies of the related files. This is done so that no data is lost in the event a diskette is damaged or accidently erased. There are two general ways to copy a group of files from one diskette to another: an exact copy of the diskette can be made or all the files on a diskette can be copies to a new diskette one by one. The disk copy approach (e.g. The DOS DISKCOPY command) is quicker than the file copy approach when there are a large number of files involved. The file copy approach (e.g. the DOS COPY*.* X: command) is quicker

if the number of files is small. Additionally, the file copy approach is less likely to result in errors because it works around bad spots on the diskette. If a backup diskette is not made on a scheduled basis then the backup copy should have the date of the backup on it. You should rotate your backup and working diskettes to prevent excessive wear on one or the other. It is inevitable that a personal computer user will lose, damage, or erase an important file. Being prepared for this will ensure that the loss is an inconvenience and not a catastrophe.

```
                  LOAN REPAYMENT SCHEDULE
PRINCIPAL AMOUNT OF THE LOAN          $8,000.00 ⎞
                                                 ⎟  These variables
MONTHLY INTEREST RATE                     1.00%  ⎬  can be changed
                                                 ⎟  by the user
NUMBER OF MONTHLY PAYMENTS                   24  ⎠

MONTHLY PAYMENT                          $376.59
```

PAYMENT NUMBER	REMAINING PAYMENTS	BEGINNING BALANCE	INTEREST PAYMENT	REDUCTION IN PRINCIPAL
1	23	$8,000.00	$80.00	$296.59
2	22	$7,703.41	$77.03	$299.55
3	21	$7,403.86	$74.04	$302.55
4	20	$7,101.31	$71.01	$305.57
5	19	$6,795.73	$67.96	$308.63
6	18	$6,487.10	$64.87	$311.72
7	17	$6,175.39	$61.75	$314.83
8	16	$5,860.55	$58.61	$317.98
9	15	$5,542.57	$55.43	$321.16
10	14	$5,221.41	$52.21	$324.37
11	13	$4,897.04	$48.97	$327.62
12	12	$4,569.42	$45.69	$330.89
13	11	$4,238.52	$42.39	$334.20
14	10	$3,904.32	$39.04	$337.54
15	9	$3,566.78	$35.67	$340.92
16	8	$3,225.86	$32.26	$344.33
17	7	$2,881.53	$28.82	$347.77
18	6	$2,533.76	$25.34	$351.25
19	5	$2,182.51	$21.83	$354.76
20	4	$1,827.74	$18.28	$358.31
21	3	$1,469.43	$14.69	$361.89
22	2	$1,107.54	$11.08	$365.51
23	1	$742.03	$7.42	$369.17
24	0	$372.86	$3.73	$372.86

FIGURE 1–15   Loan-Repayment Schedule on an Electronic Spreadsheet

One of the features that gives a spreadsheet its power is the ability to copy formulas from one part of the spreadsheet to another. For example, in this spreadsheet, after the user entered the formulas in order to calculate the numbers across the row where payment no. 2 appears, these formulas were copied into all cells for payments nos. 3 through 24. Thus all the numbers shown for payments 3 through 24 were automatically calculated without the user having to enter either formulas or numbers.

Electronic spreadsheets are an extremely important tool for today's computer users. For this reason Appendix B provides you with an introduction to Lotus 1–2–3 and SuperCalc.

Data-Base Management Systems   Let's now examine how easy it is to implement simple applications on a data-base management system without program-

APARTMENT CONSTRUCTION SPREADSHEET
22-Apr-85

SIZE IN SQ. FT.	6000	CONSTRUCTION COST	$240,000
VACANCY RATE	5.00%	LOT COST	$20,000
COST/SQ. FT.	$40.00	INT. ON CONSTRUCTION	$9,441
MARGINAL TAX RATE	40.00%	CLOSING COSTS	$3,000
APPRECIATION RATE	5.00%	LEGAL FEES	$2,000
PERCENT DOWN	20.00%	LANDSCAPING COST	$15,000
LOAN INTEREST RATE	14.25%	TOTAL INVESTMENT	$289,441
MGT & MAINT COST	10.00%	DOWN PAYMENT	$57,888
LOAN TERM (YEARS)	15	NO. OF UNITS	6
LOAN PMT. PER MO.	$3,122.67	AVG RENT/UNIT	$462
RETURN ON CASH FLOW	8.99%	RENT ESCALATION	5.00%
		RENT/INVESTMENT	11.50%

YEAR	GROSS RENT	CASH OUTFLOW	DEPRECIATION PERCENT	TAX SAVINGS	AFTER TAX CASH FLOW	CASH + EQUITY INCREASE	PROPERTY VALUE
0					($57,888)	($57,888)	
1	$31.621	$40,634	5.56%	$7,802	($1,210)	$18,436	$303,913
2	$33,202	$40,792	5.56%	$6,938	($652)	$20,456	$319,108
3	$34,863	$40,958	5.56%	$6,004	($92)	$22,618	$335,064
4	$36,606	$41,133	5.56%	$4,991	$464	$24,935	$351,817
5	$38,436	$41,316	5.56%	$3,892	$1,013	$27,420	$369,408
6	$40,358	$41,508	5.56%	$2,698	$1,548	$30,091	$387,878
7	$42,376	$41,710	5.56%	$1,397	$2,063	$32,966	$407,272
8	$44,494	$41,921	5.56%	($22)	$2,551	$36,064	$427,636
9	$46,719	$42,144	5.56%	($1,572)	$3,003	$39,408	$449,017
10	$49,055	$42,378	5.56%	($3,269)	$3,408	$43,022	$471,468
11	$51,508	$42,623	5.56%	($5,130)	$3,755	$46,937	$495,042
12	$54,083	$42,880	5.56%	($7,175)	$4,028	$51,183	$519,794
13	$56,787	$43,151	5.56%	($9,426)	$4,211	$55,796	$545,783
14	$59,627	$43,435	5.56%	($11,907)	$4,285	$60,817	$573,073
15	$62,608	$43,733	5.56%	($14,647)	$4,228	$66,292	$601,726
16	$65,739	$6,574	5.56%	($17,678)	$41,486	$71,573	$631,813
17	$69,026	$6,903	5.56%	($18,862)	$43,261	$74,852	$663,403
18	$72,477	$7,248	5.56%	($20,104)	$45,125	$78,295	$696,573
19	$76,101	$7,610	0.00%	($27,396)	$41,094	$75,923	$731,402
20	$79,906	$7,991	0.00%	($28,766)	$43,149	$79,719	$767,972

FIGURE 1–16   A Spreadsheet for Evaluating Apartment Investments

A person who knows the variables involved in apartment investments and also knows how to use an electronic spreadsheet can easily construct a spreadsheet of this type, which could prove invaluable. The spreadsheet shows both the after-tax cash flow and the percentage return on that cash flow. The return is equivalent to interest that would be earned on the money invested in the apartments. ( ) in this figure indicate a negative number.

ming. If an application consists of keeping records in a file, updating those records periodically, and producing relatively simple reports from the data in the file, a data-base management system can be used by a nonprogrammer to quickly implement the application.

To illustrate this, let's assume a manager of a department in a business wishes to keep a file containing a record for each employee who works in the department. In the records he wants to store the employees' names, the dates they were hired,

Size in Square Feet
Vacancy Rate
Cost/Square Foot
Marginal Tax Rate
Appreciation Rate
Percent Down
Loan Interest Rate
Management and Maintenance Cost
Loan Term (Years)
Lot Cost
Closing Costs
Legal Fees
Landscaping Costs
Number of Units
Rent Escalation
Rent/Investment

FIGURE 1–17   Values to Be Varied for Spreadsheet Shown in Figure 1–16

Users of the spreadsheet can vary any of these values in order to see the impact that such a change would have on after-tax cash flows and the return on cash flow. This kind of analysis is called what-if analysis. The user is obtaining answers to questions like: what if the vacancy rate were 10 percent instead of 5 percent?

their office and home phone numbers, their birthdates, and their spouses' names. He wants to store birthdates because he plans to send birthday cards to employees each year. Also, he is not very good at remembering names, so he will store the employees' spouses' name. He would like two reports displaying all the data in the file: one in sequence by employee's last name and a second one in sequence by employee's birthdate. We will use **dBASE II** to illustrate the implementation of this application. First we must enter the structure of the file. Figure 1–18 illustrates the structure of the file we created. We had to give the file a name and give each field a name, indicate whether the field was ***character data*** or ***numeric data,*** and indicate the length of the field. Next, we entered the data to the file. Figure 1–19 illustrates an input screen for entering the employee data. Then, we told dBASE II the characteristics of the report we wished to generate. Figure 1–20 illustrates the building of a report with dBASE II. Once a report form is entered all we have to do is tell dBASE II to generate the report, using the command REPORT FORM EMPBDATE. The report that dBASE II generated is illustrated in Figure 1–21.

To generate a report in order by employee last name, we first enter a report form similar to the one in Figure 1–20. In fact the only difference would be the name of the report. We tell dBASE II to sort the file in order by name and then enter the report command again. The report generated is shown in Figure 1–22. A skilled user of dBASE II could in less than an hour implement this application, including entering the data shown in the illustration.

Application Packages   Quite often users purchase a set of computer programs designed to accomplish the requirements of a particular application. Many busi-

character data
Data on which arithmetic calculations will not be done.

numeric data
Numbers on which arithmetic calculations will be performed.

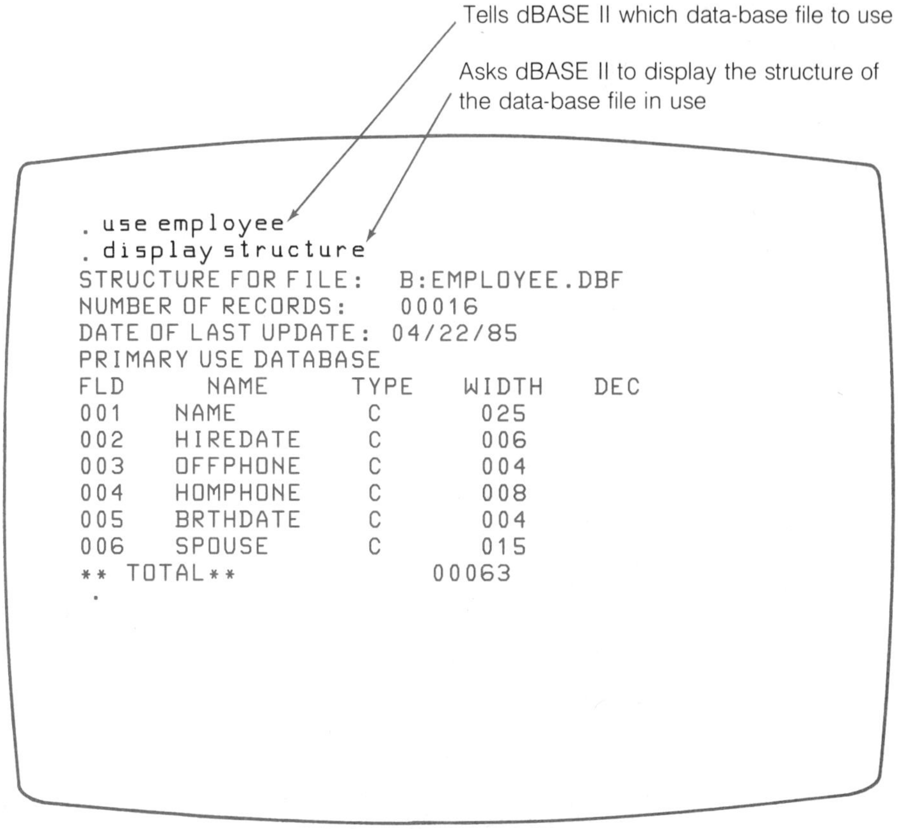

Tells dBASE II which data-base file to use

Asks dBASE II to display the structure of the data-base file in use

```
. use employee
. display structure
STRUCTURE FOR FILE:   B:EMPLOYEE.DBF
NUMBER OF RECORDS:     00016
DATE OF LAST UPDATE:  04/22/85
PRIMARY USE DATABASE
FLD       NAME       TYPE      WIDTH      DEC
001       NAME        C         025
002       HIREDATE    C         006
003       OFFPHONE    C         004
004       HOMPHONE    C         008
005       BRTHDATE    C         004
006       SPOUSE      C         015
** TOTAL**                      00063
   .
```

FIGURE 1–18   Structure of the Employee File

nesses have very similar information requirements. This is especially true among firms in the same industry. For example, all drugstores have a need to keep an inventory of prescription drugs, reorder the drugs when the supply gets low, keep records (by customer) of prescriptions filled, and print labels to go on individual prescription bottles. Such systems can be readily purchased. They often include not only the software for the system, but also the computer itself; it is offered as a complete package. Unless the drugstore has a unique requirement, it would be substantially less expensive to buy the software than to write the programs.

Many of the computing applications required in the accounting function of a business are available as software that can be purchased. For example, all businesses that sell to customers on a credit basis have a need for accounts receivable. Keeping up with who owes the business money, and how much, is a very standard accounting application. Software packages to perform this application are readily available. Figure 1–23 illustrates output from such a package.

The purpose of this chapter is only to inform you of the wide availability of application packages that can be purchased. In Module D we discuss evaluation of purchased software in more detail. Evaluation is a very important process to go through when buying software.

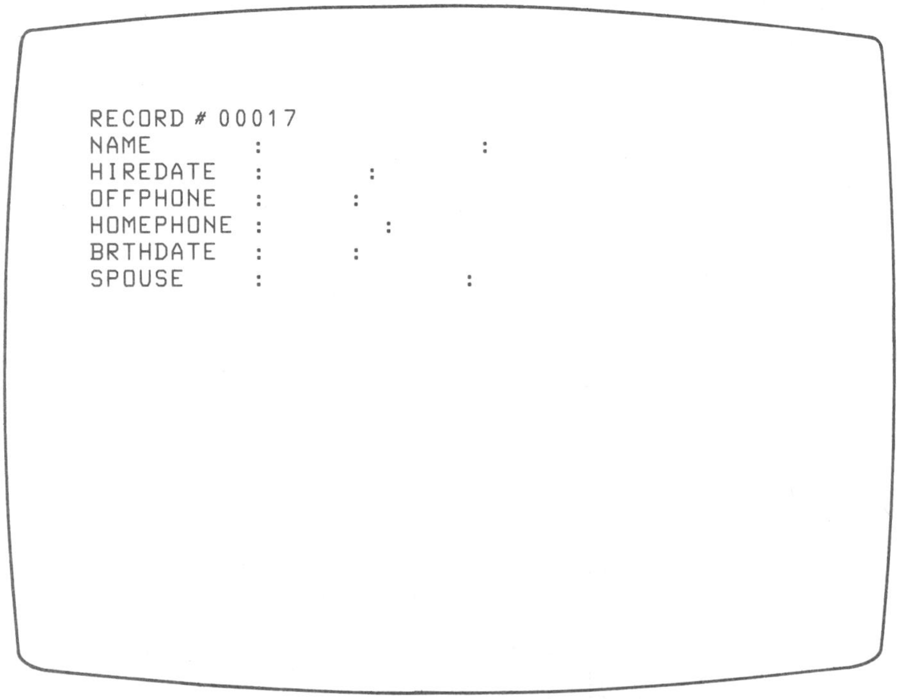

```
RECORD # 00017
NAME        :                    :
HIREDATE    :              :
OFFPHONE    :         :
HOMEPHONE   :            :
BRTHDATE    :         :
SPOUSE      :                 :
```

FIGURE 1–19   dBASE II Input Screen for Entering Employee Data

Each data item is entered between the two colons. Once the last data item is entered, in this case spouse, dBASE II will display an input screen for record no. 18.

Finally, it should be pointed out that this has been a very brief overview of the topic of using computers without programming. We cover this topic in more depth in Chapter 7.

If you are planning a career in the design and implementation of computer-based information systems, is it better to have an educational background in computer science or in management information systems (MIS)? A typical computer-science curriculum emphasizes the technological aspects of computing, whereas a typical MIS curriculum emphasizes business and how computers are used in the business area. Take one side of this argument and support your position.

Thinking About Information Systems 1–3

Putting the Computer to Work by Writing Programs

If your use for a computer is unique, and many are, it will be necessary to write programs. These programs will be tailormade to fit your specific requirements.

This command causes dBASE II to create a report

The width of a report column and the field name to be printed in it

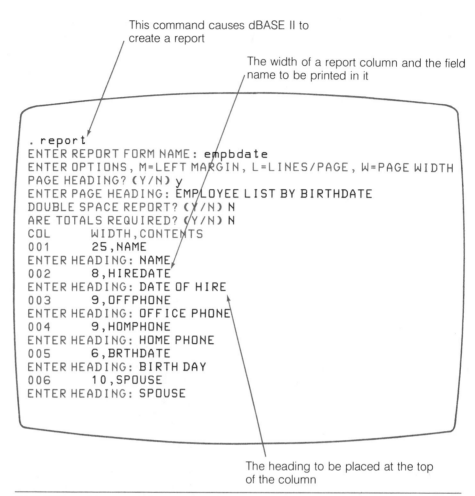

```
. report
ENTER REPORT FORM NAME: empbdate
ENTER OPTIONS, M=LEFT MARGIN, L=LINES/PAGE, W=PAGE WIDTH
PAGE HEADING? (Y/N) y
ENTER PAGE HEADING: EMPLOYEE LIST BY BIRTHDATE
DOUBLE SPACE REPORT? (Y/N) N
ARE TOTALS REQUIRED? (Y/N) N
COL      WIDTH,CONTENTS
001      25,NAME
ENTER HEADING: NAME
002       8,HIREDATE
ENTER HEADING: DATE OF HIRE
003       9,OFFPHONE
ENTER HEADING: OFFICE PHONE
004       9,HOMPHONE
ENTER HEADING: HOME PHONE
005       6,BRTHDATE
ENTER HEADING: BIRTH DAY
006      10,SPOUSE
ENTER HEADING: SPOUSE
```

The heading to be placed at the top of the column

FIGURE 1–20   Entering a Report Description to dBASE II

In this report we have decided to let dBASE use its standard (default) left margin, lines per page, and page width since we did not enter anything for these options.

Developing computer applications through programming can be time consuming. Furthermore, computer programs are not as easily changed after they are completed as are other approaches, such as electronic spreadsheets. For these reasons it is important to carefully analyze and document your information needs before beginning to write a program.

system analysis
The process of studying an information requirement to determine precisely what must be accomplished and how to accomplish it.

When your computer processing needs are simple you may in the future do the *system analysis* and programming yourself. However, most users rely on professional system analysts and programmers to develop the more complex programs.

Whether you plan to write programs in the future or not, you should have a general understanding of how programs and information systems are developed.

```
PAGE NO. 00001
04/22/86
                            EMPLOYEE LIST BY BIRTHDATE

            NAME            DATE OF   OFFICE    HOME       BIRTH    SPOUSE
                            HIRE      PHONE     PHONE      DAY

    FIRST, I. M.            610101    0001      552-0001   0101     IRMA
    TRESS, MATT            830503    7632      552-9742   0106     ALDA
    CABOODLE, KIT ANNE     720712    9876      552-6789   0201     CURT
    MAID, TAYLOR          820715    1000      552-2000   0209     HARRY
    LIFE, ALMA            850907    3423      552-6775   0309     LARRY
    HIGHWATER, HELEN      540809    0091      552-1907   0406     JOE
    SETTERA, ED           751205    1264      552-6732   0423     MARY
    SHARALIKE, SHARON     850130    9051      552-0382   0501     FRED
    DERHODE, JAUN MOREFORE 831023   5676      552-4385   0607     JANE
    ZON, HANS             841209    5623      552-8791   0717     BARBARA
    ERDBUNS, BUD          760807    1287      552-9845   0924     ELIZABETH
    TOTTLER, T.           780921    1423      552-8294   1005     ALFRED
    WANNAKRACKER, POLLY   690801    4352      552-4938   1115     SAM
    BREAKER, J. L.        840501    8642      552-0978   1209     TOM
    AYRE, CLAIRE D.       860208    9834      552-5683   1223     BOB
    THYME, JUSTIN         790309    9537      552-4973   1231     LISA
```

FIGURE 1–21   Employee List by Birthdate

This process, called the **system development life cycle** is covered in chapters 5 and 6.

There are a number of reasons the system development life cycle needs to be understood; the most important are as follows:

1. Even when you develop computer applications without programming you have to define your information-processing requirements and decide how to implement them on the computer. Certain systems-analysis and design techniques used in developing computer programs can also be most helpful in developing applications without programming. For example, good programs are written in separate **modules** that work together. Such programs are much easier for people to understand. Good spreadsheets are also built in terms of modules so as to improve clarity. Many users with no knowledge of program design concepts have built huge spreadsheets that have become useless because no one could understand how to use them.

2. A general knowledge of the system development life cycle is valuable when you convey your information requirements to professional system analysts

program module
A small identifiable unit of program statements that performs one program task.

```
PAGE NO. 00001
04/22/86
                              EMPLOYEE LIST

        NAME                DATE OF    OFFICE     HOME       BIRTH      SPOUSE
                            HIRE       PHONE      PHONE      DAY

AYRE, CLAIRE D.             860208     9834       552-5683   1223       BOB
BREAKER, J. L.             840501     8642       552-0978   1209       TOM
CABOODLE, KIT ANNE          720712     9876       552-6789   0201       CURT
DERHODE, JAUN MOREFORE      831023     5676       552-4385   0607       JANE
ERDBUNS, BUD                760807     1287       552-9845   0924       ELIZABETH
FIRST, I. M.                610101     0001       552-0001   0101       IRMA
HIGHWATER, HELEN            540809     0091       552-1907   0406       JOE
LIFE, ALMA                  850907     3423       552-6775   0309       LARRY
MAID, TAYLOR                820715     1000       552-2000   0209       HARRY
SETTERA, ED                 751205     1264       552-6732   0423       MARY
SHARALIKE, SHARON           850130     9051       552-0382   0501       FRED
THYME, JUSTIN               790309     9537       552-4973   1231       LISA
TOTTLER, T.                 780921     1423       552-8294   1005       ALFRED
TRESS, MATT                 830503     7632       552-9742   0106       ALDA
WANNAKRACKER, POLLY         690801     4352       552-4938   1115       SAM
ZON, HANS                   841209     5623       552-8791   0717       BARBARA
```

FIGURE 1–22   Employee List by Name

and programmers. You will be much better equipped to decide whether or not the proposed design of your computer system will meet your needs.

Do you, as a user, need to learn to write programs for a computer? Many would say no. They would argue that there are several ways to apply the computer without programming. Others would argue that to be computer literate (that is, to understand computers), you should have some exposure to programming. Currently there is no clear answer to this question. The appendices and supplements to this text offer **hands-on exposure** to both the BASIC programming language and the most popular methods of using computers without programming—electronic spreadsheets, word processing, and data-base management systems.

One thing is clear though. You can be sure that hands-on exposure to the computer—whether it be with or without programming (or both)—will be an extremely valuable first step in developing the computer skills you will need in your career.

Many users are putting the computer to work through the personal computer. We will examine this most widely used computer in the next chapter.

REPORT NO AR6315
RUN DATE 10/31/8X
COMPANY AA

ACCOUNT	NAME	FUTURE DUE	CURRENT DUE	1-30	31-60	PAST DUE 61-90	91-120	OVER 120	OUTSTANDING RECEIVABLES
784612	WYGANT DISTRIBUTORS, INC.	HARTWELL ROAD		JUPITER HILLS	DE	19702-2614			
	MR. W. RAMSDEN								
	AVG. DAYS-36 CR/LMT-3500								
ACCOUNT TOTAL:		652.19	1,125.64	294.81	108.45				2,181.09
		30%	52%	13%	5%				
799426	ZELLER COMPANY	124 MILLBROOK RD		EAST GALLANT	AL	36902-1157			
	MR. P. GORHAM								
	AVG. DAYS-63 CR/LMT-1000								
ACCOUNT TOTAL:				456.24	178.26	312.49			946.99
				48%	19%	33%			
GRAND TOTAL****									
	SALES TERRITORY: 01A	1,576.72	16,459.32	9,621.14	1,164.91	447.56	78.60	120.41	29,468.66
		5%	56%	32%	3%	2%	1%	1%	
	DISTRICT CR MGR: BB	6,482.19	39,412.80	24,562.44	2,051.23	2,114.86	594.60	403.19	75,621.31
		8%	52%	31%	3%	4%	1%	1%	
	REGIONAL CR MGR: WF	10,398.65	98,714.37	52,114.71	5,662.17	3,729.29	1,700.68	1,288.74	173,608.61
		6%	57%	30%	3%	2%	1%	1%	
	COMPANY TOTAL:	26,042.03	256,622.13	107,781.58	12,715.25	7,520.12	3,918.45	2,542.60	417,142.16
		6%	62%	25%	3%	2%	1%	1%	

FIGURE 1–23   Output from an Accounts-Receivable Package

An aged trial balance provides information about the overdue amounts that customers owe a firm. For example, in this figure Wygant Distributors, Inc. owes the firm $652.19 that is due in the future, $1,125.64 that is currently due, $294.81 that is 1 to 30 days past due, and $108.45 that is 31 to 60 days past due.

Summing Up

☐ The premier invention of this century is the computer. In a relatively short time it has affected many areas of our lives.

☐ A computer can be defined as a data processor that can perform substantial computation, including numerous arithmetic or comparison operations, without intervention by human operators.

☐ The primary capabilities or characteristics of a computer are that it must be electronic, be able to perform arithmetic and comparison operations, have internal storage and retrieval of data, have the ability to execute a stored program, and have the ability to modify the execution of a program stream during execution.

☐ The electronic basis for the computer gives the computer incredible speed and accuracy while the stored program enables this speed and accuracy to occur without human intervention.

☐ Stored programs have three advantages:

1. They enable the computer to operate at an electronic speed.
2. They provide very high reliability.
3. They make the computer general-purpose.

☐ Any computer system has four categories of devices: (1) input devices, (2) processing devices, (3) storage devices, and (4) output devices.

☐ The processing role in a computer system is performed by the central processing unit (CPU). Its function is to interpret and execute the instructions of the programmer.

□ A computer system has two types of storage: primary storage and secondary storage. Primary storage is contained within the CPU and is used to store programs and the data they use during execution. Secondary storage is used for relatively long-term storage of data outside the CPU.

□ The components of the information-system data hierarchy, in order of complexity, are: (1) bit, (2) byte, (3) field or items, (4) record, (5) file, and (6) data base.

□ In batch processing, changes and queries to a file are stored for a period of time and then a processing run is made periodically to update the master file, produce scheduled reports, and produce responses to queries.

□ In immediate processing, transactions are processed to update files immediately or shortly after a real-world event occurs.

□ One type of application that uses immediate processing is a real-time system. A real-time application can immediately capture data about ongoing events or processes and provide the information necessary to manage them. An airline reservation system is a real-time system.

□ There are two ways to apply the computer—without and with writing programs.

□ The four most typical ways to apply the computer without programming are word processing, electronic spreadsheets, data-base management systems, and preprogrammed application packages.

□ Word-processing programs allow the user to make extensive revisions with minimal retyping.

□ Electronic spreadsheets allow users to quickly apply the computer to problems that have a small volume of input, but involve complex calculations.

□ If an application consists of keeping records in a file, updating those records periodically, and producing relatively simple reports from the data in the file, a data-base management system can be used without programming to quickly implement the application.

□ Many information requirements can be met by application software that is available through purchase.

□ Usually users write programs when there are unique information requirements; otherwise they rely on software that already exists.

Key Terms

computer	bit	direct-access file
stored program	byte	batch processing
program	bit patterns	immediate processing
central processing unit (CPU)	field *or* item	realtime applications
control unit	record	using computers without
arithmetic-logic unit	record key	programming
primary storage	file	word processing
secondary storage	data base	WordStar
output devices	sequential-access file	Word

Word Perfect
electronic spreadsheets
SuperCalc
Lotus 1-2-3
rows
columns
cell

cell address
data-base management system
dBase II
character data
numeric data
application package

using computers with
  programming
queries
system development life cycle
module
hands-on exposure

Self-Quiz

Completion Questions

1. The two most important characteristics of computers are that they are electronic and that they can execute _____ .
2. A computer system has four categories of devices: input devices, _____ devices, _____ devices, and output devices.
3. The _____ decodes program instructions and directs other components of the computer to perform the tasks specified in the program instructions.
4. A _____ is one or more bytes that contain data about an attribute of an entity in the information system.
5. A _____ consists of all the files of an organization, structured and integrated to facilitate update of the files and retrieval of information from them.
6. There are basically two types of file organization: _____ -access file organization and _____ -access file organization.
7. Under _____ processing, transactions are processed to update the file immediately or shortly after a real-world event occurs.
8. The typical ways to apply the computer without programming are word processing, _____ , data-base management systems, and preprogrammed application packages.
9. Any intersection of a row and column on the spreadsheet is called a _____ .
10. The process of developing programs and information systems is called the _____ .

Multiple-Choice Questions

1. Which of the following is not one of the characteristics of a computer?

a. electronic
b. external storage
c. stored program
d. program modification at execution
e. all of the above are characteristics

2. The CPU (central processing unit) consists of:
a. input, output, and processing
b. control unit, primary storage, and secondary storage
c. control unit, arithmetic-logic unit, and primary storage
d. input, processing, and storage
e. none of the above

3. Which of the following is not an advantage of stored programs?
a. provide reliability
b. reduce operational costs
c. enable the computer to operate at electronic speeds
d. make the computer general-purpose
e. all of the above are advantages

4. All of the following are examples of input devices except:
a. COM
b. CRT
c. optical scanners
d. voice-recognition devices
e. all of the above are input devices

5. Which of the following is not true of primary storage?
a. It is a part of the CPU.
b. It allows very fast access to data.
c. It is relatively more expensive.

d. Information must be transferred to primary storage before it can be processed.

e. All of the above are true.

6. What is the control unit's function in the CPU?

   a. to decode program instructions
   b. to transfer data to primary storage
   c. to perform logical operations
   d. to store program instructions
   e. none of the above

7. The ascending order of a data hierarchy is:

   a. bit—byte—record—field—file—data base
   b. byte—bit—field—record—file—data base
   c. byte—bit—record—file—field—data base
   d. bit—byte—field—record—file—data base
   e. none of the above

8. Which of the following is not true of immediate processing?

   a. It is often used in realtime applications.
   b. It can occur with either sequential or direct-access files.
   c. It can be used in an airline-reservation system.
   d. Transactions are processed shortly after a real-world event occurs.
   e. All of the above are true.

9. Electronic spreadsheets are most useful in a situation where relatively _____ data must be input, and (but) _____ calculations are required.

   a. little; simple
   b. large; simple
   c. large; complex
   d. little; complex

10. Which of the following statements is true?

   a. The smart approach to using computers is to write programs.

b. Knowledge of the system development life-cycle is not important to operators who use computers without programming.

c. Hands-on exposure to the computer is not helpful to those who write programs.

d. Personal computers have been an important contributing factor in the movement toward using computers without programming.

e. None of the above is true.

Answers

Completion

1. stored programs
2. processing, storage
3. control unit
4. field
5. data base
6. sequential; direct
7. immediate
8. electronic spreadsheet
9. cell
10. system development cycle

Multiple-Choice

1. b
2. c
3. b
4. a
5. e
6. a
7. d
8. b
9. d
10. d

Chapter 2

Personal Computers

CHAPTER OUTLINE

PROLOGUE

Recently a happy senior student entered my office and with contagious elation stated that she had received the job offer she wanted. There are obviously many ingredients in the mixture of a successful job search, but she was absolutely convinced that the deciding factor was her knowledge of how to apply personal computers. I have even had students who have taken with them, on an interview trip, floppy disks containing work they have performed in school. They pull out the disks in the middle of the interview and show the potential employer their personal-computer skills. They usually get the job. In this chapter our objective is to increase your knowledge of personal computers.

Introduction

Currently the fastest growing segment of the computer market is personal computers. Just as the industrial revolution of the nineteenth century opened up large markets for inexpensive, mass-produced goods, the personal-computer industry today is broadening the information-processing market through inexpensive and easy-to-use systems. **Personal computers** (PCs) are *microcomputers* designed to be operated by one user possessing very little, if any, programming knowledge. Often PCs are called microcomputers; but the term *personal computer* is more commonly used.

Personal computers make enormous computing power available to people from all walks of life. Consequently, both the number of users and the variety of applications are growing rapidly. Whether the application is mundane like balancing your checkbook or novel such as composing a symphony, the personal computer effectively serves the needs of the nonprogrammer. It is this versatility and user friendliness that promises to help the small personal computer prevail in its struggle against today's *minicomputers* and *mainframes*.

Certainly, the personal computer as a separate topic is important. However, it is also a very good vehicle for introducing you to computer hardware and software. It is small, nonthreatening, and easily understandable. It may be more than user-friendly, it may be user-seductive!

In this chapter we will explore the hardware components of a typical personal computer. This will be followed by a discussion on software. The software is what makes the personal computer useful, as with all computers; and the software available for PCs is particularly rich and varied. We will then talk about things to consider when buying personal-computer hardware and software.

Many people have bought personal computers for their homes. However, the market for PCs in homes has not been as large as expected. We will explore some of the reasons for this. Personal computers have not been without their problems and challenges; these challenges will also be discussed. Finally, we will look at some of the future directions of the personal-computer industry.

One of the objectives of this chapter is to give you an introduction to the vast potential for applications of the personal computer. The appendices of this book contain an introduction to BASIC language, as well as discussions on widely used spreadsheets, word processing, and data-base packages. In addition, this text is accompanied by the *Educate-Ability Student Manual*. **Ability** is an easy-to-use integrated package containing spreadsheet, wordprocessing, data base, graphics, and communication capabilities. The educational version of Ability is free to any school using this text. If you have access to a personal computer you will enhance your knowledge of personal computers and their use by developing an application of your own using BASIC, one of the packages covered in the appendices, or Ability. That sentence is not strong enough. If I were a student and I did not have access to a personal computer *I would find a way to gain access to a personal computer* and learn how to apply it in my intended career!

---

microcomputer
The smallest of computers, typically used by one person at a time.

minicomputer
A midsize computer generally used in midsize or smaller organizations by several users at the same time.

mainframe
The large computer system found in large organizations and used by many people at the same time.

The Hardware of a Personal Computer

The System Unit

A figure from chapter 1 has been repeated here (see Figure 2–1) to refresh your memory of the components of a personal-computer system. These components are also shown in schematic form in Figure 2–2. Let's take a look inside the *system unit*.

The heart of a personal-computer system is a microprocessor. A **microprocessor** is a central processing unit (CPU) contained on a semiconductor chip. As you can see from Figure 2–2, a microprocessor, like any computer CPU, contains an arithmetic-logic unit, control units, and various registers (memory) for storing small amounts of data. These microprocessor chips, along with their plastic packages, are about three-quarters of an inch wide and three inches long. The microprocessor, primary memory, disk controller, serial interface, and parallel interface are typically a part of the system unit of a personal computer. They are all installed

system unit
The part of a personal computer that contains the central processing unit.

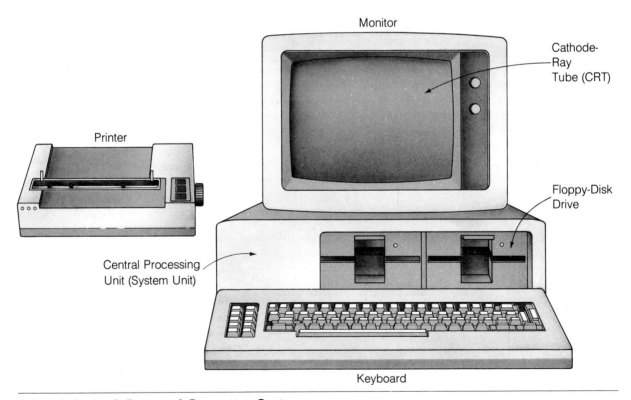

FIGURE 2–1   A Personal-Computer System

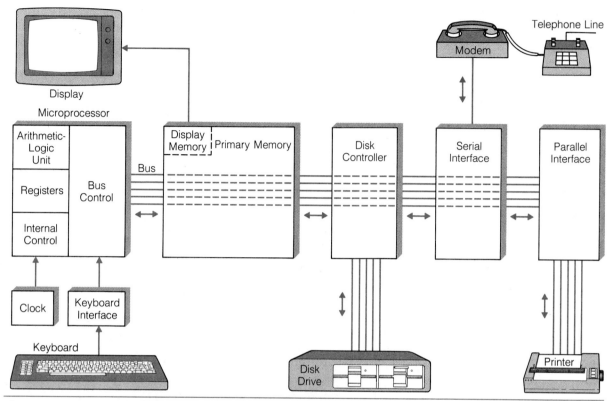

FIGURE 2–2 Hardware of a Personal Computer

The hardware of a personal computer includes devices for processing and storing information and for communicating with the user and other electronic devices. A set of parallel conductors called a bus (*color*) connects the main components. The processing unit, which generally includes not only the microprocessor chip itself but also various auxiliary chips, carries out essentially all calculations, and controls the entire system. Information can be entered into the system through a keyboard. Pressing a key generates a coded signal unique to that key; the code is stored in the display memory and so appears on the cathode-ray-tube display. The primary memory, which consists of semiconductor memory chips, holds programs and data currently in use; it is a random-access memory, meaning that the content of any cell can be examined or changed independently of all the other cells. Disk storage generally has a larger capacity than the primary memory. The interfaces connect the computer to other devices, such as a printer or a modem (which gives access to other computers through the telephone system). In a serial interface, information is transferred one bit at a time; in a parallel interface, multiple conductors carry several bits (in most instances eight) at a time.

on the main circuit board. Figure 2–3 shows a schematic diagram of the main circuit board of the IBM PC. This board often is also called a system board or mother board.

The speed with which a personal computer operates is dependent in part on two characteristics of the microprocessor: its **speed** and its **word size.** Microprocessor speed refers to the number of **machine operations** it performs in a second. Within the last few years microprocessor speeds have increased tenfold—

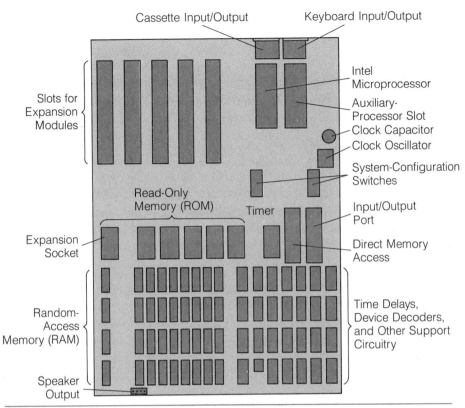

Cassette Input/Output

Keyboard Input/Output

Slots for Expansion Modules

Intel Microprocessor

Auxiliary-Processor Slot

Clock Capacitor

Clock Oscillator

System-Configuration Switches

Input/Output Port

Direct Memory Access

Read-Only Memory (ROM)

Timer

Expansion Socket

Random-Access Memory (RAM)

Speaker Output

Time Delays, Device Decoders, and Other Support Circuitry

FIGURE 2–3 Main Circuit Board of the IBM Personal Computer

The major elements of the main circuit board of the IBM Personal Computer are identified in the drawing above. The size of the board is 8½ by 12 inches. A large number of silicon chips carrying integrated circuits are attached to it; each chip is about a quarter of an inch square and is encased in a rectangular plastic package fitted with electrodes. The chips and elements, such as resisters and capacitors, are interconnected by conductors printed on the board. The microprocessor, the 16-bit 8088 made by the Intel Corporation, has 20,000 transistors and operates at a frequency of almost five million cycles per second. "System programs" are stored permanently in the read-only memory (ROM); random-access memory (RAM) stores programs and data that change from time to time.

to about ten million cycles per second. Although such speeds may seem incredibly high, users are demanding even faster speeds since they do not want to waste time sitting at the keyboard while the microprocessor performs lengthy computations.

Another way to speed up a microprocessor is to increase its word size. The word size of a microprocessor is the amount of information, in terms of bits, processed in one **machine cycle.** The larger the word size the fewer machine cycles required to do a job. Early microprocessors processed 8-bit words in a single machine cycle. Today, 16-bit and 32-bit microprocessors are the most popular. The IBM PC uses a 16-bit microprocessor that operates at a speed of almost five million cycles per second. The IBM PC AT also uses a 16-bit microprocessor, the Intel 80286, that operates at six million cycles per second.

A user can be misled by evaluating the speed of a personal computer solely on the basis of the speed of its microprocessor. Many other factors affect a personal computer's speed, including the efficiency of programs and whether the operator is using hard disk or floppy disk. For example, the PC AT operates from two to three times faster than the original IBM PC, even though its microprocessor is only 20 percent faster.

The primary memory of a personal computer consists of some **read-only memory (ROM)** and some **random-access memory (RAM)**. The ROM contains programs that were built into the computer at the factory and cannot be changed by the user. These programs usually are used very frequently. For example, the programs needed to bring the system up when the power is turned on are often stored in ROM. As the cost of ROM decreases, more and more programs are being placed in ROM, including BASIC language compilers, word processors, and even electronic spreadsheets.

Application programs are usually stored in random-access memory while they are being executed. A typical personal computer used for business purposes would have at least 256 *kilobytes* of RAM. The original IBM PC is expandable to 640K, and the IBM PC AT can be expanded to 3 *megabytes* of RAM. The advantage of having a larger memory is that larger and more powerful programs can be executed. Many personal computers are constructed such that their primary storage may be expanded later by adding **memory modules** if the user's needs increase. These modules are simply plugged into the main circuit board, as shown in the lower left corner of Figure 2–3.

The disk controller, serial interface, and parallel interface shown in Figure 2–2 are all expansion boards that plug into the main circuit board. The slots for expansion boards are shown at the top left of the diagram in Figure 2–3. The IBM PC has five slots for expansion. Many personal computers have expansion slots. These enable a user to configure a PC to meet his or her particular needs. The diagram in Figure 2–2, for example, illustrates a disk controller which allows the machine to use disk drives, a serial interface which is used for telecommunications between two computers, and a parallel interface which is necessary if a printer is to be used with the personal computer. One of the most widely used expansion boards is the memory expansion board, since the main circuit board holds only 256K. Figure 2–4 illustrates a memory expansion board. On the IBM PC, a memory expansion board can hold up to 384K of additional memory. With the 256K that the main circuit board holds, the machine would have the 640K maximum memory allowed on this computer.

Input/Output Devices

The user usually interacts with a personal computer through a **keyboard** and a **monitor screen** (see Figures 2–5 and 2–6). The user types in commands, program instructions, and data. The computer echoes these (displays them on the screen) so that the user can check for errors. During execution of a program the

ROM
Read-only memory, which typically contains programs that can be read and used, but cannot be changed.

RAM
Random-access memory, which stores programs and data that can be quickly changed or read in any conceivable (random) order.

kilobyte
1,024 bytes of memory that will store 1,024 characters of data or programs. Kilobyte is usually abbreviated as K. Therefore, 256K of memory will hold 256 times 1,024, or 262,144, characters of data. In contexts other than computers the word *kilo* or the symbol *K* indicates 1,000. In terms of computers, K is a power of 2 (it is 2^{10} or 1,024) because of the binary nature of computer memory.

megabyte
1,048,576 bytes of memory. A megabyte is often thought of as 1 million bytes, but more accurately it is 1,048,576 bytes, since it is 2^{20} bytes.

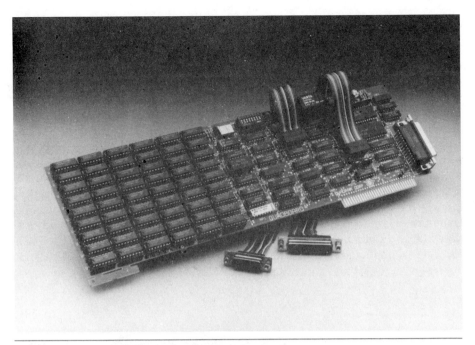

FIGURE 2–4 A Memory Expansion Board

Most memory expansion boards also add other functions, such as a clock/calendar and
additional parallel and serial interfaces (ports).

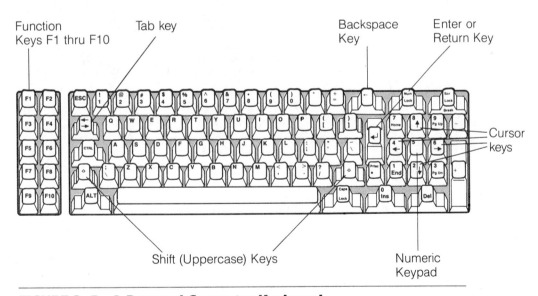

FIGURE 2–5 A Personal-Computer Keyboard

This particular keyboard has been criticized because it has the arrow directional keys on
the numeric keypad (keys 2, 4, 6, and 8). If the operator uses the arrow directional keys
and the numeric keypad simultaneously, he or she must use the shift keys also. This can
be inconvenient.

computer may display instructions or informative messages on the screen, or prompt the user to key in data items. In some cases the program is written such that the final result of the run is also displayed on the screen.

Most personal-computer systems support **color monitors.** Color monitors may be used in a wide variety of applications such as engineering design and business data graphics. Some programmers use bright colors to highlight important information, making it easier to sift through the large quantities of information often generated by a computer.

The most popular secondary-storage media for personal computers are floppy and hard magnetic disks. Most often a **diskette (floppy disk)** is used. Figure 2–7 shows how a floppy disk is read or written to by a disk drive. The diskette rotates inside the square jacket and an electromagnetic head reads or writes data through the head-access slot. When applications involve large programs or large quantities of data, a **hard disk (Winchester disk)** is used. A typical hard disk stores fifty to a hundred times more data than a floppy disk and it rotates much faster, providing quicker access to data. Refer to chapter 8 for a more in-depth discussion of floppy and Winchester disks.

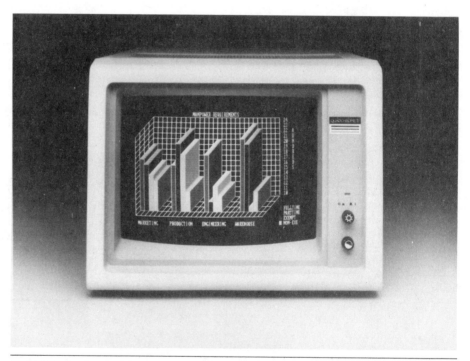

FIGURE 2–6   A Personal-Computer Monitor

Personal-computer monitors are classified as being either monochrome or color. The monochrome monitor is equivalent to a black and white monitor, although the data are usually displayed in either a green or amber color. Color monitors can display a wide variety of colors. They also can display detailed graphics.

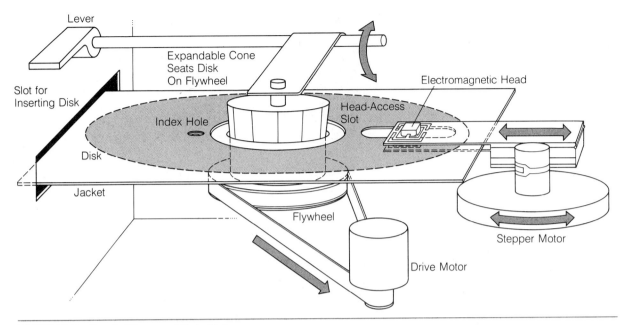

Lever

Expandable Cone
Seats Disk
On Flywheel

Slot for
Inserting Disk

Electromagnetic Head

Index Hole

Head-Access
Slot

Disk

Jacket

Flywheel

Stepper Motor

Drive Motor

FIGURE 2–7   A Floppy-Disk Drive

The floppy-disk system records large quantities of information on a flexible plastic disk coated with a ferromagnetic material. The disk rotates at 300 revolutions per minute in a lubricated plastic jacket. An electromagnetic head is moved radially
across the surface of the disk by a stepper motor to a position over one of the concentric tracks where data are stored as
a series of reversals in the direction of magnetization. The head can read or write: it can sense the magnetic polarity to
retrieve information or impose magnetization to store information. An index mark, whose passage is sensed by a photo-
electric device, synchronizes the recording or reading with the rotation of the disk. This is a schematic drawing of a
double-sided disk made by Qume. There are two gimballed heads, which read and write information on both sides of
the 5¼-inch disk. On each side of the disk some 180 kilobytes of information can be stored in 40 concentric tracks.

Magnetic **tape cartridges** are used for data storage. This tape is similar to the
tape used in stereo music recording. Tape is an inexpensive, *nonvolatile* storage
medium. But its drawback is that data cannot be accessed at random. The computer
has to read every bit of information sequentially until it reaches the desired data.
Currently tape cartridges are used primarily for *backup copies* of data stored on
hard disks.

A large variety of printers are available for use with personal computers. Table
2–1 compares the major types. Figure 2–8 shows one of the most common types,
a **dot-matrix printer.** The printing mechanism of a dot-matrix printer is shown
in Figure 2–9.

Many people prefer to use **daisy-wheel printers,** which produce ***letter-quality*** output. Such output is especially suitable for word processing and mailing
applications. Figure 2–10 illustrates the printing mechanism of a daisy-wheel printer.

nonvolatile
Storage that does not lose
the data and programs
stored on it when the
electricity to the com-
puter is turned off.

backup copy
A duplicate of data or
programs used to restore
the original if it is lost or
destroyed.

letter quality
Printed output that
appears to have been
typed on a typewriter.

FIGURE 2–8 Dot-Matrix Printer

As with most personal-computer printers, the dot-matrix printer is declining substantially in price. Even the lower-priced ones that cost about $250 are very good printers.

Another type of high-quality printer is the laser printer. The better-quality laser printers cost more, sometimes more than the computer itself. However, they are expected to substantially decline in price during the next few years. Their advantages over daisy-wheel printers are that they operate without noise and they are faster.

The near-letter-quality (NLQ) printer is a higher quality dot-matrix printer. By typing more dots or by typing them closer together, NLQ printers can approach the quality of the daisy-wheel printers. They are a good compromise between dot-matrix and letter-quality printers.

TABLE 2–1 Comparison of Personal-Computer Printers

Type of Printer	Price Range (in $)	Speed	Graphics Printing
Dot matrix	250– 900	50– 275 cps[1]	Yes
Letter quality	400– 3,700	12– 90 cps	Usually No
Near letter quality	300– 6,000	8–1320 cps	Yes
Laser	3,400–35,000	8– 28 ppm[2]	Yes

[1]cps is characters per second
[2]ppm is pages per minute

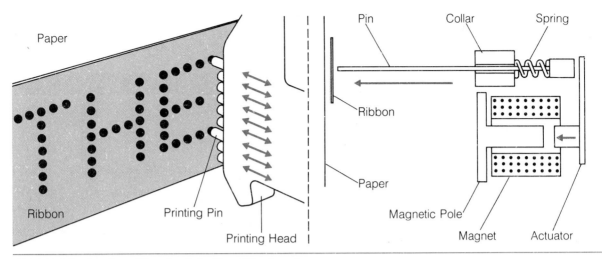

FIGURE 2–9 Dot-Matrix Printing Mechanism

A dot-matrix printer is relatively inexpensive, fast (up to 200 characters per second), and flexible: it can generate compressed, expanded, or bold characters or even graphic images, depending on the commands it receives from the computer. The printing head is a vertical array of pins that are fired selectively, as the head is swept across the paper, to press an inked ribbon against the paper and thereby form a pattern of dots (*left*). Here each capital letter is a subset of a matrix seven dots high and five dots wide; two more pins are available to form the decenders of lowercase letters such as a *p*. The pins are fired by individual solenoids (*right*). The mechanism illustrated here is that of a dot-matrix printer made by Epson America, Inc.

There are many specialized input devices, such as joysticks, light pens, and optical scanners. One of the more widely used is a personal-computer **mouse,** (see Figure 2–11). A wide variety of output devices are also available, including audio output and graphics plotting (see Figure 2–12). A few years ago these devices would have seemed very exotic and may have required complex programming, possibly in assembler language. With today's easy-to-use software, even a novice can create an application using a complex configuration of input and output devices.

Thinking About Information Systems 2–1

The typical advice given to a person seeking to buy a personal computer is to first choose the major software needed and then to choose the hardware that will execute the software. The rationale behind this advice is that software is the most important part of the computer system. If hardware is bought first, a company could end up with a rather restricted choice of software. The Davis Company, however, has been advised to buy hardware first. Its consultant strongly advised the company to buy the IBM PC without considering the software. The consultant's rationale was that IBM will dominate the personal-computer market, that it is a reliable computer manufacturer, and that the IBM PC would have the widest range of business software available. Evaluate the consultant's advice.

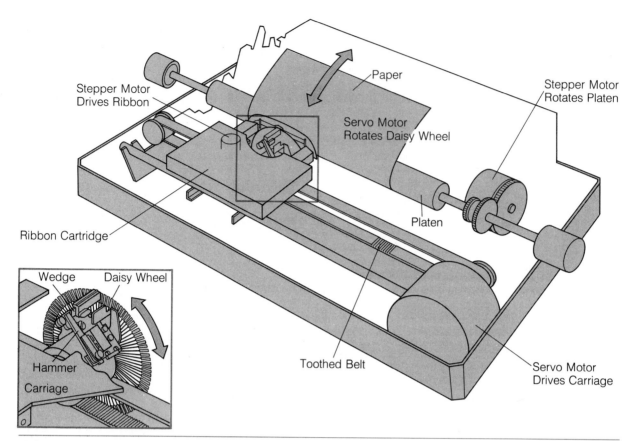

FIGURE 2–10 Daisy-Wheel Printing Mechanism

A daisy-wheel printer produces "letter quality" copy at a rate of from 20 to 55 characters per second. This is a schematic representation of a Qume Corporation printer. The printing wheel has a plastic hub around which are arrayed 96 (in some models 130) radial spokes; a letter number of other symbol is molded into the end of each spoke. In response to signals from the computer, the wheel is rotated either clockwise or counterclockwise to bring the proper symbol into position and stopped; the hammer strikes (with an energy proportionate to the area of the symbol: much harder, say, for a W than for a comma), driving the sliding wedge against the end of the radial arm to press the inked ribbon against the paper; the carriage and ribbon advance as the wheel is spun to bring the next symbol into position.

Data Communications

In chapter 13 we will discuss communication networks for computers in general. However, data communication is an important aspect of many personal-computer systems as well. It allows the operator to share data bases, programs, printers, and other resources with many different users. Typically, a personal computer has a **communications program** that converts data to a standard *protocol*. The converted data are then transmitted through a modem over private or public telephone lines. A **modem** converts the outgoing data from the digital signals that computers use to the analog sound waves that phone lines transmit. When the computer receives data, the same modem converts analog sound waves into digital signals

protocol
A set of rules governing information flow in a communication system. These rules define the format of the message to be sent. See chapter 13.

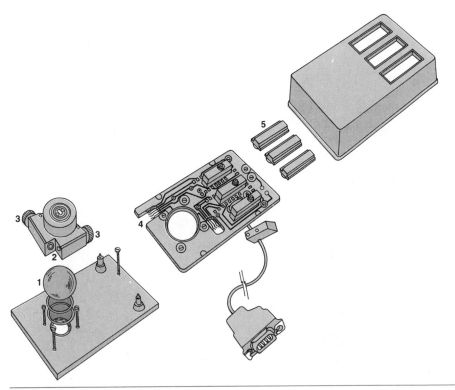

FIGURE 2–11   A Personal-Computer Mouse

Inside the mouse we find a ¾ inch stainless-steel ball (1) As the ball rolls across the desk, it transfers its *x* and *y* movements to two small cylindrical drums (2) resting on the ball at a 90-degree angle to one another. The rolling ball turns the cylinders in proportion to the extent and direction of travel. Connected to the ends of the cylinders are small code wheels (3) coated with alternating stripes of conductive and nonconductive material. As these code wheels turn, they deliver electrical pulses for each incremental rotation of the cylinders. Delicate wire fingers (4) resting on the code wheels decode electrical pulses generated by the conductive stripes, and send them to the computer in a digital form it can read to track the mouse's movement. The three buttons (5) on top are used to select from menues on the screen, edit text, and move symbols.

(see Figure 2–13). Most modems used with PCs transmit data at speeds of 120 or 240 characters per second. A modem is shown in Figure 2–14. A PC modem can also be installed as an internal board in one of the expansion slots on the system board.

Personal computers can also communicate with one another through a local-area network (LAN); see Figure 2–15. LANs also allow several personal computers to share expensive peripheral devices such as hard disks and high-quality printers. Local-area networks will be covered in more depth in chapter 13.

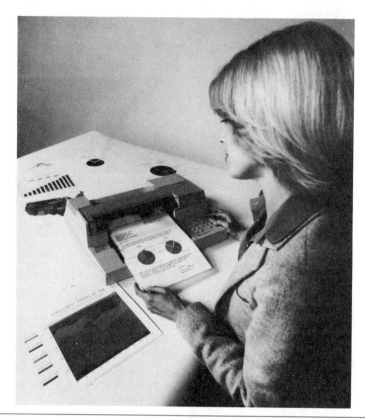

FIGURE 2–12   Microcomputer Graphics Plotter
Very high quality graphics can be produced and printed (in color) through the use of a personal computer.

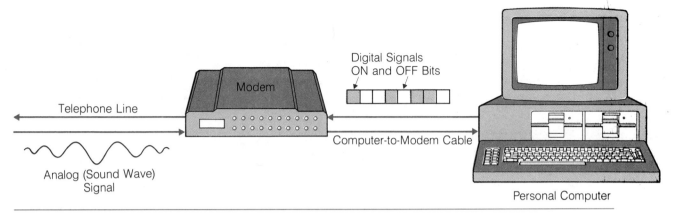

Digital Signals ON and OFF Bits

Modem

Telephone Line

Computer-to-Modem Cable

Analog (Sound Wave) Signal

Personal Computer

FIGURE 2—13   The Conversion of Data with a Modem

Telephone companies are expected to eventually use digital signals to transmit voice. When this occurs, digital computer signals can be transmitted over telephone lines without modems.

FIGURE 2—14   A Modem

This is an external modem. The same modem can be purchased in board form to fit into one of the expansion slots of the computer. The advantage of an external modem is that it can be disconnected and used with other computers. The advantage of the internal modem is that an additional piece of hardware (an external modem) does not have to be transported when the computer is being moved around. Internal modems are often used with portable personal computers.

The Hardware Industry

The advent of the personal computer created a whole new industry. Interestingly enough, the initiative for developing this industry was taken by small, entrepreneurial firms rather than large, established vendors of mainframe computers. The Apple Computer Company produced the first widely-used personal computer in 1977. Its founders, two young college students, built the first Apple personal com-

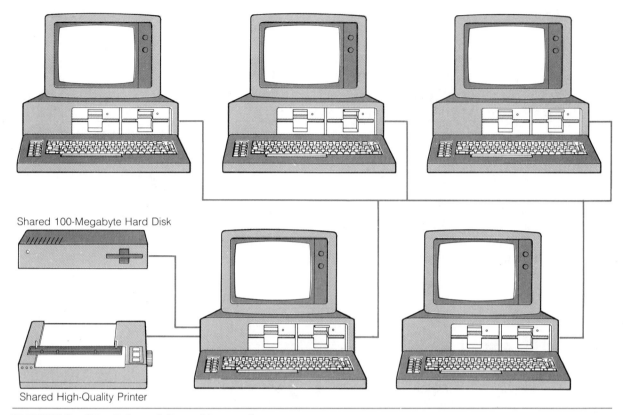

Shared 100-Megabyte Hard Disk

Shared High-Quality Printer

FIGURE 2–15   A Local-Area Network

In the configurations shown, the personal computer to which the hard disk and printer are connected serves as a driver for these devices. This means that the other personal computers communicate with the hard disk and the printer through the driver PC.

puter in a garage. Despite fierce competition from subsequent entrants to the market, Apple has managed to maintain a leading position in the industry. Radio Shack, a manufacturer and seller of electronic products, has used its extensive network of retail outlets to gain a position in the personal-computer industry. IBM, a latecomer to the personal-computer business, has become the dominant vendor in the business market for personal computers. The IBM PC has become a de facto standard for business personal computers. Since its introduction in 1981 many vendors have produced computers that are IBM-PC compatible. One of the most successful models is the Compaq portable PC. IBM's established reputation as the world's largest manufacturer of computers has certainly helped it in achieving this market position. Most observers feel that IBM will continue to dominate the business market for personal computers. However, Apple with its Macintosh computer is attempting to challenge IBM in the business segment of the personal-computer market.

Stiff competition in the personal-computer business has been beneficial to the consumer. Prices have steadily decreased while equipment quality and capabilities have continued to improve. Moreover, manufacturers have been forced to standardize many features like communication protocols and diskette characteristics, in order to appeal to a wider customer base. As with any competitive market, there have been a number of casualties. Some of the smaller vendors have gone out of business, leaving their customers without maintenance support. A buyer of personal-computer equipment should carefully consider the reputation of the supplier before making a major purchase. Purchasing from an unreliable supplier not only could cause the user to lose the investment in computer hardware and software, but also could cause the user to lose customers who were dissatisfied with service resulting from computer malfunction. It is also important for the buyer to determine whether a particular component is **plug-compatible** with the other equipment he or she already has or is likely to acquire.

plug-compatible
A hardware device that can directly replace units produced by another manufacturer.

The Software of a Personal Computer

Businesses are rapidly adopting the personal computer. Small companies are converting their record-keeping to computerized systems, and both large and small firms are using electronic spreadsheets, data-base management systems, word processing, and graphics. The primary reason for this change is the availability of powerful yet inexpensive software packages for personal computers.

General Business Software

Accounting Applications   One of the first systems a business converts to a computer is accounting. Excellent packages are available for general-purpose accounting, including the following:

Accounts Receivable

Accounts Payable

General Ledger

Payroll

These packages are advertised in professional accounting journals. Figure 2–16 shows the output from an accounting software package. Before purchasing such a package, ask the following questions.

1. Are there sufficient accounting controls in the system?
2. Are the various programs integrated so that information which is input once need not be input again for another program?

3. What are the limitations on the number of accounts and transactions the system can process?
4. What level of technical expertise (in terms of both the accounting and the computer) is required to operate the system, and is this expertise available to the business?
5. Will the programs produce flexible management reports that can be easily modified to suit changing business needs?

Financial Management Another important application of personal computers is in financial management. Financial-planning packages can be used to project the financial results of alternative management decisions. The projected financial statements produced for the various alternatives allow management to make informed decisions. One such package is Execucom's IFPS financial modeling program. IFPS was originally designed to be used on mainframes but is now available for PCs. Figure 2–17 illustrates the use of IFPS. Other financial programs focus on problems like stock-portfolio management, stock analysis, capital-project analysis, budgeting, tax planning, and cash management.

Marketing personnel often use programs that generate sales projections. Some packages have powerful **graphics** capabilities like pie charts, bar graphs, and trend lines (see Figure 2–18). These devices can substantially reduce the paperwork that a marketing manager has to do to prepare for a sales meeting. Software packages written for salespeople remove most of the tedium of booking orders. A well-designed order-processing system will price the order, prepare an invoice, update perpetual inventory records, and produce the shipping authorization document. There are also may personal-computer programs that assist in the warehousing and production management functions. These range from inventory management routines to production scheduling to manpower planning.

Electronic Spreadsheets and Data-Base Management We have covered these two types of software extensively in other parts of this text (chapters 1, 12, and Appendix B). However, it is important to point out that the first electronic spreadsheet (VisiCalc) and those which have followed (Lotus 1–2–3) have had a primary role in the phenomenal success of the personal computer. For several years electronic spreadsheets and data-base management software have topped the lists of the best-selling PC software. They are both easy to use and most productive. If you plan a career in business, make it a goal to become proficient in the use of software for electronic spreadsheets, data-base management systems, and word processing.

Word Processing One of the most important uses of personal computers in business is **word processing.** When linked to a high-quality printer, a personal computer can produce excellent reports, letters, and other documents. In addition, it allows the user to, with a few keystrokes, store, edit, and neatly format all these documents. Business people, suffering from a heavy load of paperwork, have welcomed this opportunity to improve productivity. Many good word-processing programs are now on the market. Many are capable of checking the text for spelling

```
                              ACCOUNTS RECEIVABLE
                           SUMMARY AGED TRIAL BALANCE
                              D & G ENTERPRISES INC.
REPORT NO AR6315
RUN DATE 10/31/8X
COMPANY AA
```

ACCOUNT	NAME	FUTURE DUE	CURRENT DUE	1-30	31-60	PAST DUE 61-90	91-120	OVER 120	OUTSTANDING RECEIVABLES
784612	WYGANT DISTRIBUTORS, INC. MR. W. RAMSDEN AVG. DAYS-36 CR/LMT-3500	HARTWELL ROAD		JUPITER HILLS	DE	19702-2614			
ACCOUNT TOTAL:		652.19	1,125.64	294.81	108.45				2,181.09
		30%	52%	13%	5%				
799426	ZELLER COMPANY MR. P. GORHAM AVG. DAYS-63 CR/LMT-1000	124 MILLBROOK RD		EAST GALLANT	AL	36902-1157			
ACCOUNT TOTAL:				456.24	178.26	312.49			946.99
				48%	19%	33%			
GRAND TOTAL****									
	SALES TERRITORY: 01A	1,576.72	16,459.32	9,621.14	1,164.91	447.56	78.60	120.41	29,468.66
		5%	56%	32%	3%	2%	1%	1%	
	DISTRICT CR MGR: BB	6,482.19	39,412.80	24,562.44	2,051.23	2,114.86	594.60	403.19	75,621.31
		8%	52%	31%	3%	4%	1%	1%	
	REGIONAL CR MGR: WF	10,398.65	98,714.37	52,114.71	5,662.17	3,729.29	1,700.68	1,288.74	173,608.61
		6%	57%	30%	3%	2%	1%	1%	
	COMPANY TOTAL:	26,042.03	256,622.13	107,781.58	12,715.25	7,520.12	3,918.45	2,542.60	417,142.16
		6%	62%	25%	3%	2%	1%	1%	

FIGURE 2–16 Sample Printout of an Accounting Package

An aged trial balance provides information about the overdue amounts that customers owe a firm. For example, in this figure Wygant Distributors, Inc. owes the firm $652.19 that is due in the future, $1,125.64 that is currently due, $294.81 that is 1 to 30 days past due, and $108.45 that is 31 to 60 days past due.

and grammatical errors. If your word-processing application involves a large amount of correspondence, be sure to buy a package that includes mailing facilities, like the printing of address labels. A sample printout for a PC-based word processor is shown in Figure 2–19.

Integrated Packages When a business professional is using an electronic spreadsheet, word processor, data-base manager, and graphics program, he or she is often using the same data or text in all of these packages. Moving data from one package to another sometimes can get cumbersome. Consequently, **integrated packages** that combine all four of these functions plus communications software have been developed. Three examples are Xanaro's Ability, Lotus' Symphony and Ashton-Tate's Framework. When these packages were released in the summer of 1984, they were expected to significantly affect the market for *stand-alone* word-processing, electronic-spreadsheet, and data-base packages. The reasoning was that they would give a business person the ability to perform any of the five functions on a common set of data and text. For example, a report could be produced that contained—in an integrated fashion—text, spreadsheets, graphics, and even lists of data. Through the communication package the report could be printed or transmitted to other computers.

Experience has shown that the current integrated packages compromise their functions. For example, the word-processing function of an integrated package may not have all the capabilities of a stand-alone word processor. The same is generally true of the other four functions. Therefore, many personal-computer users continue to use their separate *stand-alone* packages.

stand-alone
Computer hardware or software that operates in an independent and separate manner.

```
        INCOME STATEMENT
                 1985        1986
Revenues      150,000.00  172,500.00
Price            150.00      150.00
Units Sold     1,000.00    1,150.00
Materials Per Unit 57.00       57.00
Materials     57,000.00   65,550.00
Labor per Unit   36.00       36.00
Labor         36,000.00   41,400.00
Cost of Goods Sold 93,00.00 106,950.00
Gross Margin  57,000.00   65,550.00
```

(a) Income Statement

```
\ Income Statement
Columns 1985 thru 1986
Revenues=Price*Units Sold
Price=150
Units Sold=1,000, previous*1.15
Materials per Unit=57
Materials=Materials per Unit*Units Sold
Labor per Unit=36
Labor=Labor per Unit*Units Sold
Cost of Goods Sold=Materials+Labor
Gross Margin=Revenues-Cost
              of Goods Sold
```

(b) IFPS Instructions

Cell:	Contents:	Cell:	Contents:	Cell:	Contents:
A1	Income Statement	B1		C1	
A2		B2	1985	C2	1986
A3	Revenues	B3	+B4*B5	C3	+C4*C5
A4	Price	B4	150.00	C4	150.00
A5	Units Sold	B5	1000.00	C5	+B5*1.15
A6	Materials per Unit	B6	57.00	C6	57.00
A7	Materials	B7	+B6*B5	C7	+C6*C5
A8	Labor per Unit	B8	36.00	C8	36.00
A9	Labor	B9	+B8*B5	C9	+C8*C5
A10	Cost of Goods Sold	B10	+B7+B9	C10	+C7+C9
A11	Gross Margin	B11	+B3-B10	C11	+C3-C10

(c) Electronic-Spreadsheet Contents

FIGURE 2–17 An Income Statement Produced by an IFPS Program

The IFPS instructions to produce the income statement shown in figure 2–17a are illustrated in Figure 2–17b. Notice that with IFPS the user is in effect writing a program to produce the income statement. As illustrated in Figure 2–17c this simple income statement could also be produced through the use of an electronic spreadsheet. The numbers and formulas are placed directly in individual cells without the user having to write a separate program. However, IFPS does perform some tasks that electronic spreadsheets are not currently capable of doing.

Another approach to integration is a package such as IBM's Topview or Microsoft's Windows. These packages run along with stand-alone electronic spreadsheets, word processors, and so on, allowing the user to transfer data and text between stand-alone packages. The screen of the monitor is split into sections called windows. Each window displays part of each stand-alone package (see Figure 2–20).

SALES (IN THOUSANDS)

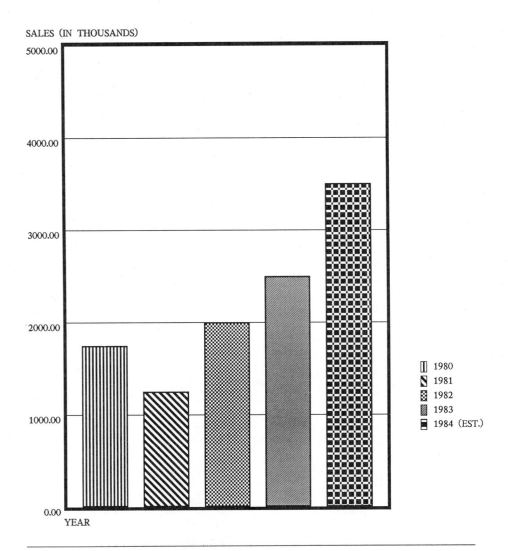

FIGURE 2–18 A Marketing Graph

This graph was printed by a personal-computer laser printer. One of the advantages of a
laser printer is that it can combine graphs and text on the same page.

decision support system
An integrated set of com-
puter tools that allows a
decision maker to interact
directly with computers
to produce and display
information useful in
making decisions.

The personal computer is also playing a central role in the implementation of
decision support systems. Data can be transferred from large, central data bases to
personal-computer storage and subsequently analyzed through the use of tools
such as spreadsheets and graphics. The combination of all the tools available in a
personal computer is often referred to as a personal workstation.

Special-Interest Software

Many industries and professional practices have very special information-processing requirements. Thus special-purpose software packages have been developed. This software is usually advertised in professional and industrial journals and at conventions and conferences. Users can also find special-interest packages by consulting directories such as *Datapro Reports on Microcomputer Software.*

A major market for specialized software is the medical profession. Faced with increasing government regulation and a rapidly changing medical technology, doctors and pharmacists are finding that the computer is ideal for their record keeping.

```
                                        459 North Main Street
                                        Staunton, WV  28013
                                        November 28, 1983




        John W. Bray
        RDM Products Inc.
        3301 West Hampton Avenue
        Blacksburg, VA  24060

        Dear Mr. Bray:

        Thank you for your prompt shipment of the truck parts I
        recently ordered.  I have found your service and parts to be
        of exceptional quality.

        However, in this most recent shipment (Shipping Order No.
        A435-7894) one of the wheel bearings was not the correct
        size.  Since we could not afford to have a truck out of
        service for the time it takes to return the bearing and
        receive a replacement we purchased the bearing from a local
        supplier.  Therefore, I am returning the incorrectly sized
        bearing to you for credit to my account.  If you have any
        questions please contact me at 304-938-2600.

                                  Sincerely,

                                  Ray N. Shea

                                  Ray N. Shea
                                  Shea Trucking Co.
```

FIGURE 2–19 Word-Processing Printout

This letter is being sent to one individual. Word processing is also very useful when you want to send the same letter to many people. All you do is type the letter once, type in the names and addresses, and run the letters. The text can even be individualized so that the addressee's name appears in each letter. The finished letter would appear as if it had been typed individually for that particular addressee.

Gallery 1
Buying and Setting Up a PC

An Entre Computer Center is one of many places where hardware and software for personal computers can be purchased. But, unlike many other retail and discount computer stores, Entre Computer Centers first work to understand a customer's computer needs. In this gallery an Entre customer buys and sets up a personal computer for his business application.

Purchasing the Personal Computer

1 Tom Harvey, a manager at a firm that accepts contracts to supervise the construction of buildings, is having difficulty determining exactly how much of the allotted money for each contract has been budgeted and spent. He is unable to match his figures with the firm's other department's because each department keeps records relating only to its own specific needs. This system seems to work well for every department but Tom's. Tom thinks that a computer would help him to keep track of each account's expenditures and to compare his figures with the other department's.

1

2

2,3 With this in mind Tom goes to a nearby Entre Computer Center to purchase a computer. He tells them that he would like to buy a computer and a project manager software package that he saw in a personal computer magazine.

3

4 Before Tom is shown any hardware or software he is introduced to Connie Vance, an Entre consultant, who analyzes Tom's information requirements. Connie determines that the project management software package is not really appropriate for Tom's needs. She explains that a spreadsheet package may be more useful. It is important to note that the software Tom initially thought to be the right application software for his problem is not really the best solution.

4

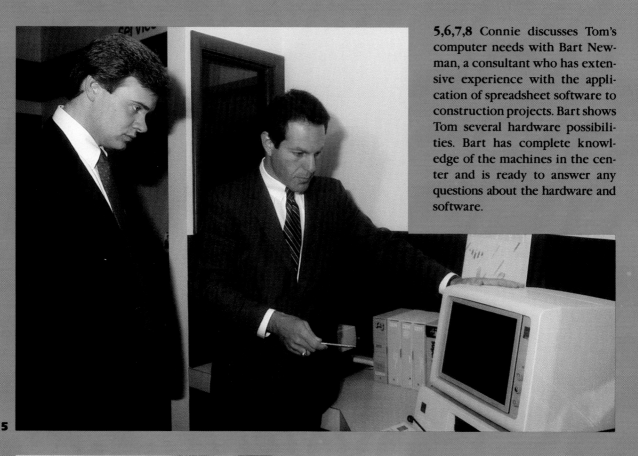

5,6,7,8 Connie discusses Tom's computer needs with Bart Newman, a consultant who has extensive experience with the application of spreadsheet software to construction projects. Bart shows Tom several hardware possibilities. Bart has complete knowledge of the machines in the center and is ready to answer any questions about the hardware and software.

5

6

7

8

9

10

11

12

13

9,10,11 Realizing that Tom often travels to building sites, Bart demonstrates a portable computer.

12 Bart shows Tom a variety of software and how it might relate to his particular business environment.

13 A wide variety of additional books and literature that apply to specific software applications and hardware needs are also available.

14 Once a decision has been made about the hardware and software, Tom enrolls in a class that will teach him to operate his new computer and to use his software effectively and efficiently. The classes are given frequently and are held at the Entre Computer Center or at the client's place of business.

15 Additional instruction is available from a wide variety of videocassettes that allow each individual to work at his or her own pace. The customers are encouraged to use the center's video equipment and machines for learning at their leisure.

16 Specific applications and advanced instruction often call for a one-to-one session. Specially trained employees give individual attention to customers who desire it.

14

15

16

18

17

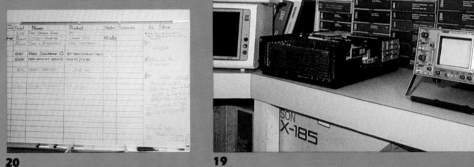

19

20

21

17,18,19 Each Entre Computer Center has facilities and personnel to service hardware should a problem with a machine arise. The trained service specialists attend numerous seminars and classes to ensure that their knowledge and ability are as up-to-date as the machines that they service. If a computer can not be serviced immediately, a similar machine is often loaned until the computer has been repaired.

20 This service "call board" helps to keep all employees informed of the status of each machine in the shop for repair.

21 All models of hardware sold are kept in stock to ensure fast delivery at the time of customer purchase.

Setting Up a Personal Computer

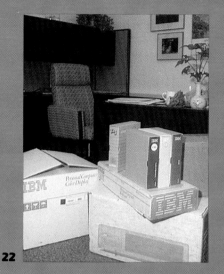

22 After completing his consultation and training sessions, Tom purchases an IBM Personal Computer. Along with the basic IBM software, he plans to use Lotus 1-2-3 spreadsheets to help him with his expenditure summaries.

23 Entre personnel usually set up the new computer and help the customer begin operating it, but Tom has chosen to unpack and set up the PC himself. He feels this will help him understand the computer.

24 After careful instruction from Entre personnel, Tom begins setting up his PC. The cover is easily removed from the computer, exposing the circuit boards and disk drives. It is important to follow the instruction manual carefully.

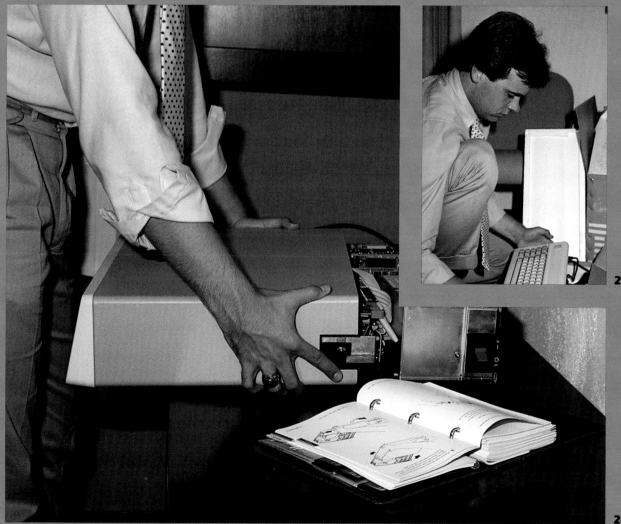

22

23

24

25

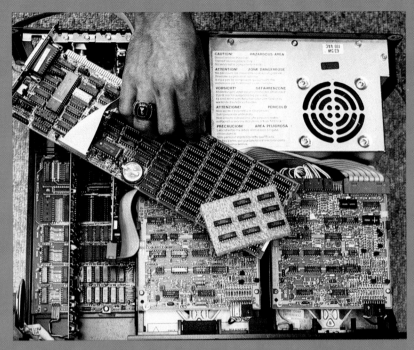

27

26

25,26,27 The memory expansion board can be removed to install additional memory chips that extend the capabilities of the hardware.

28 Tom sets switches inside the housing of the PC for its hardware and memory configuration. He follows the instructions in the documentation for the memory board to set these switches.

29 Once the internal configuration is complete, the monitor and printer are installed simply by plugging their cords into the back of the unit.

30 Continuous feeding computer paper is loaded into the printer.

31 After the machine is properly set up, special diagnostic programs must be run to detect any problems with the hardware. These diagnostic programs ensure proper set up and configuration.

28

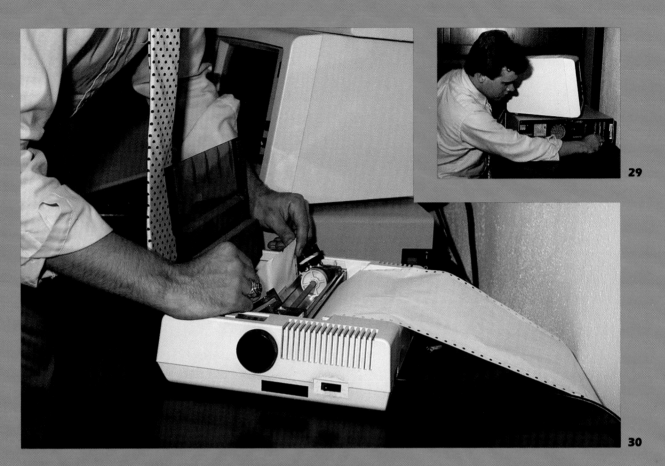

29

30

31

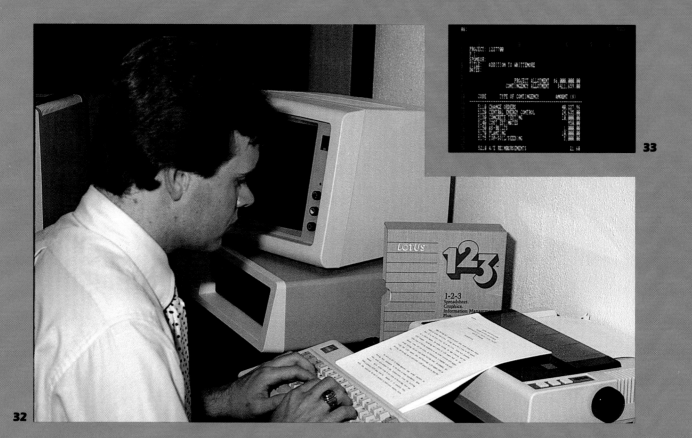

33

34

32 Tom is now ready to install and use his Lotus 1-2-3 software. Lotus 1-2-3- enables him to create schedules and work sheets to summarize his expenditures on various projects.

33,34 With a few simple menu-guided commands, any part of a Lotus 1-2-3 spreadsheet can be printed instantly.

35 Tom can finally compare his Lotus 1-2-3 totals against other records to verify project expenditures.

35

Gallery 2

Using a Fourth Generation Language to Develop an Application

IDEAL™

Fourth generation languages are becoming a very important method for developing business applications. One widely used fourth generation language is ADR/IDEAL, a product of Applied Data Research, Inc., Princeton, New Jersey. This gallery takes you through a demonstration of the use of Ideal to produce an order entry application. On each of the following screens a caption explaining the screen appears in the blue window.

IDEAL™

This is a demonstration of ADR's powerful development system, ADR/IDEAL. In this demo you will see an application developed from start to finish, including how to:

* Create a program
* Define a panel and report
* Write a procedure to:
  -read the data base
  -transmit the panel
  -produce the report
* Compile and run the program

Press F10 to continue...

1

```
IDEAL: MAIN MENU                              SYS: DEM    MENU

Enter desired option number ===)        There are    9 options in this menu:

1. PROGRAM            Define and maintain programs
2. DATAVIEW           Display dataview definitions
3. PDF                Panel Definition Facility
4. RDF                Report Definition Facility
5. PROCESS            Compile, Run, Submit
6. DISPLAY            Display Entities
7. PRINT              Print Entities
8. ADMINISTRATION     Administration functions
9. OFF                End IDEAL Session

        IDEAL can be controlled with simple commands or by using menu
   selections. This is one of the many benefits of IDEAL's workstation
   environment, which also includes features like online HELP, intelligent
   editors, split screen, integrated datadictionary, printing services, and
   online checkout, compilation, and execution services.
                              Press F10 to create a program...
```

2

2 The data view is a definition of the data to be used in the application. The panel definition defines the layout of input screens to be used in the application. Panel is a synonym for CRT screen.

```
=) CREATE PROGRAM ORDERENT
-----------------------------------------------------------------------
IDEAL: PGM IDENTIFICATION     PGM ORDERENT (001) TEST        SYS: DEM FILL-IN

PROGRAM  ORDERENT

Short description  Processing of customer orders.

Description
          An online system for processing customer orders as they are received.
          The quantity ordered and item number are entered.  Based on the item
          number, the item's description and price will be retrieved, and the
          order's total value calculated. _____
_____

      ADR's DATADICTIONARY automatically manages "entities" created in IDEAL,
  such as programs, panels, and reports.  This process is completely
  invisible to the application developer.   IDEAL uses many facilities of
  ADR's DATADICTIONARY as a natural and automatic by-product of the
  application's development.
                      Press F10 to define program resources...
```

3

3 Here the definition and description of the application is entered.

5 The order entry screen or panel is created on this screen by simply typing in the data items between the top and bottom as displayed on the screen.

6 This order entry panel has been set up to accept order number, customer number, order date, and for each item ordered a quantity, item number, item description, price, and amount.

7 This summary screen displays all the data fields that were set up on the previous screen for the order entry panel.

```
=) RESOURCES
----------------------------------------------------------------
IDEAL: PGM RESOURCES          PGM ORDERENT  (001) TEST   SYS: DEM FILL-IN
Specify the dataviews, panels, reports, and programs that this program uses.
DATAVIEW        VER  PANEL     VER  REPORT    VER  PROGRAM   VER  SYS
INVENTORY-ITEM_ PROD ORDERPNL_ 0001 INVRPT_   0001
_____ ____ _____ ____ _____  ____ _____  ____ ___
_____ ____ _____ ____ _____  ____ _____  ____ ___

      This fill-in screen defines all resources to be accessed by the
  program.  This example uses a dataview, panel, and report.
  These relationships are established in the DATADICTIONARY, providing a
  centralized source of information for all resources used by the application.
                      Press F10 to layout the panel...
```

4

➡ EDIT PANEL ORDERPNL

IDEAL: PANEL LAYOUT   PNL ORDERPNL (001) TEST   SYS: DEM FILL-IN

START: ¬   END: ;   NEW: +   DELETE: *   REPEAT: @
....+....1....+....2....+....3....+....4....+....5....+....6....+....7....+....
================================ T O P ================================

================================ B O T T O M ================================

The panel is created by painting the information on the screen just
as you will want it to appear. Textual information can be placed anywhere on the panel. Only two special characters — the "¬" and ";" — are
required in painting a panel.

Press F10 to continue...

5

➡ EDIT PANEL ORDERPNL

IDEAL: PANEL LAYOUT   PNL ORDERPNL (001) TEST   SYS: DEM FILL-IN

START: ¬   END: ;   NEW: +   DELETE: *   REPEAT: @
....+....1....+....2....+....3....+....4....+....5....+....6....+....7....+
============================ T O P ============================

+ORDER+   +CUST. NO.+   +ORDER DATE +   ;

+QTY ITEM NO   ITEM DESC   PRICE   AMOUNT;

+   ; +   ;   ;   +   ;   +   ;

+FILL IN "QTY" AND "ITEM NO" THEN PRESS ENTER;

============================ B O T T O M ============================

Here we have used special characters to lay out the fields as they will
be seen by the end user.

Press F10 to designate panel field names...

6

➡ SUMMARY

IDEAL: FIELD SUMMARY TABLE   PNL ORDERPNL (001) TEST   SYS: DEM FILL-IN

+ORDER+   +CUST. NO.+   +ORDER DATE +   ;
....+....1....+....2....+....3....+....4....+....5....+....6....+....7....+

Seq	Lo	Field name	Attr	I	Len	In.dep	Occ	Comments
1			PSL	X	5			ORDER
2		ORDER-NO	VAL	X		5		
3								CUST. NO.
4		CUST-NO	VAL	X		4		
5								ORDER DATE
6		ORDER-DATE	VAL	X	10			
7			PSL	X	59			QTY ITEM NO ITEM
8								
9								
10								
11								
12								

Panel fields are named on the summary fill-in. Additionally, default
screen attributes, such as highlighting or field protection, may be
modified. Notice that all of the elements contained in the panel are
presented in a single display. More detailed controls, such as editing
and validation checking, can be specified on a second, related menu.

Press F10 to prototype the panel...

7

8 Here we are testing a prototype of the order entry panel by entering some test data.

9 At the top of this screen we see all the data fields for this application along with their type (*x* is character data and *n* is numeric data) and the field length. The number 3.2 indicates that unit price has two decimal places. The bottom of the screen shows how we describe a report to Ideal. In this case we are asking for a summary average unit price and average value on hand to be printed at the end of the inventory report.

```
⇒ FACSIMILE
-------------------------------------------------------------------

ORDER 714830 CUST.NO. 40101 ORDER DATE DEC. 15, 1984

QTY    ITEM NO    ITEM DESC        PRICE        AMOUNT

 3     101000

            FILL IN "QTY" AND "ITEM NO" THEN PRESS ENTER
```

> IDEAL's facsimile feature permits a prototype panel to be displayed and tested. For example, if an alphabetic character is entered into a numeric field IDEAL displays an error message. No procedural code is necessary to run this test.
>
> Press F10 to display the dataview and define the report at the same time...

```
⇒ SPLIT; DIS DVW INVENTORY-ITEM;2 EDIT RPT INVRPT
-------------------------------------------------------------------
IDEAL: DATAVIEW INVENTORY-ITEM                  SYS: DEM      DISPLAY

PANEL FIELD-NAME        TYPE CHRS/DGTS OCCUR
```

> This is a split screen display of the dataview and the detail definition of the report as specified in the resource table. A dataview is a logical view of the data stored in the data base.

```
    ITEM-NO          X       5
    ITEM-DESC        X      20
    UNIT-PRICE       N       3.2
    QTY-ON-HAND      N       5
    QTY-ON-ORDER     N       5
    REORDER-POINT    N       5
-------------------------------------------------------------------
IDEAL: RPT DETAIL DEFN.   INVRPT (001)   FILL-IN   Edit
Field Name,Literal  Sort   Break  Function   Column
Function, or
Arithmetic
Expression
    ITEM-NO
    ITEM-DESC
    UNIT-PRICE                                  S
    QTY-ON-HAND
    VALUE-ON-HAND                               S
```

> Reports are defined by filling in the blanks on the definition screen. You may indicate which fields or calculations to include in the report as well as sorting characteristics, control breaks, and so on.

```
    This completes the report. Press F10 to code the procedure...
```

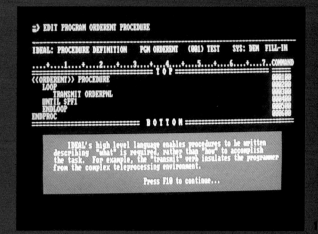

10 A procedure must be set up to process the order panel for each order and produce the report. In the next several screens we will see how this procedure is developed. In this screen we have a loop that transmits or inputs each order through the order panel until the operator presses function key 1.

11 We want to add a FOR EACH construct after the UNTIL statement. This FOR EACH construct will process each item on the order against the inventory data base. To do this we use the intelligent editor.

12 Notice that the intelligent editor has automatically entered all the statements for the FOR EACH construct. All we have to do now is customize them for our application.

13 In this screen we have customized the FOR EACH construct for our application. The FOR EACH construct compares the item number in the inventory data base to the item number on the order panel, calculates the amount of each item, and displays the name of the inventory item on the order panel and produces the inventory report. It also displays a not found message on the order panel if the item number on the order panel does not exist in the inventory data base.

14 We have now completed the description of our application and are back at the main menu of Ideal. We now want to compile our application so we select number five from the menu.

15 The compilation was successful and now we will run the program by again selecting number five from the menu.

16 The report produced by our application.

17 Application generators like Ideal are revolutionizing the ways in which computer applications are developed.

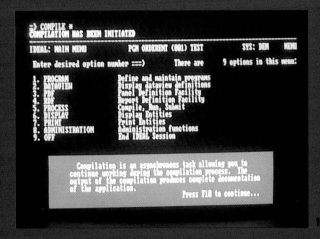

14

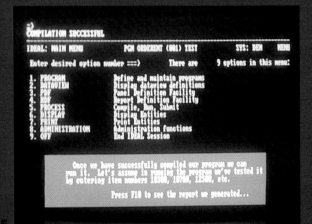

15

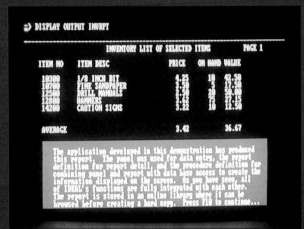

16

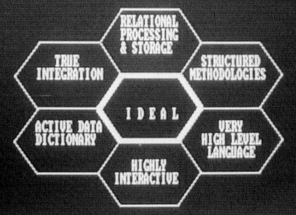

17

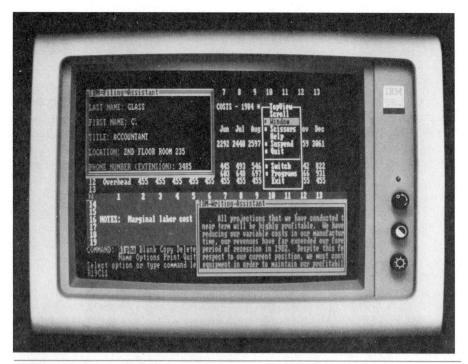

FIGURE 2–20   A Window Package

Four applications are being displayed simultaneously through windows on one screen. In the background a spreadsheet is shown. In the right lower corner a window shows text from the IBM Writing Assistant word processor. In the left upper corner a window shows data from the IBM Filing Assistant, and in the right center of the screen a window shows the Top View menu which is controlling the running of multiple applications.

Applications vary from systems for invoicing patients to data bases for medical-history records. Similarly, lawyers now have their own packages to assist with routine chores like preparing lengthy legal documents and searching data bases for legal precedents. Accountants and auditors are now able to better manage their practices, with the aid of time-keeping and billing programs. There are specialized packages for almost all industries.

Buying Personal-Computer Hardware and Software

Getting Help in Buying a PC System

The computer business is sometimes called the information business, and with good reason. Computers not only perform computations, but they also help us manage large volumes of information. It is interesting though that the machine that assists us in coping with information has caused a flood of information itself. Books, articles, and magazines related to personal computers have proliferated in recent years.

Byte is one of the most widely circulated small-computer magazines. *Infoworld* and *Personal Computing* are also quite popular among users of personal computers. All these magazines carry articles of general interest for business and home users. There are flowcharts and program listings for applications such as managing stock-market investments and playing computer games. The advertisements for software and hardware are an important source of information about products and prices. Also there are magazines that devote themselves to a single, widely used personal computer. For example, *PC Magazine* and *PC Week* cover only the IBM PC and its compatibles. Articles related to personal computers can also be found in various professional periodicals. Journals serving professional groups such as engineers, accountants, and bankers often publish articles describing personal-computer applications in their own areas of expertise.

Finally, to help the user in selecting equipment and designing a system, personal-computer **consultants** are also available. Consultants come from a variety of backgrounds including computer programming, system analysis, marketing, accounting, and engineering. Before selecting a consultant make sure that he or she has a thorough understanding of your application area. One way of checking the credentials of consultants is to talk to their previous customers about the service received. You can find out about personal-computer consultants either through referrals from professional colleagues or by looking in the *Yellow Pages*. Some consultants also give courses in programming and the use of various software packages.

Where to Buy PC Systems

There are several ways to acquire personal-computer hardware and software. Franchised retail chain stores such as Computerland and Entre are major outlets. Owing to their large sales volume they are able to support a staff of technical advisors and maintenance personnel. Since these stores specialize in the computer business, they carry a broad line of products, allowing the customer a wide variety to choose from. Many dealers in office equipment offer business-oriented hardware and software. Electronics stores have also entered the personal-computer business.

There are also many mail-order suppliers of personal-computer systems. A mail-order hardware or software product tends to be less expensive than one bought from a store, but the buyer does assume the extra risk of purchasing a product without testing it. Furthermore, mail-order houses usually offer less personal support than local dealers. It is very important that you test thoroughly any computer hardware or software you may buy, and ask questions about anything that seems unclear. Figure 2–21 provides a checklist for those interested in buying a personal-computer system. Use this checklist to make sure you do not miss some important consideration when making your selection of a PC system. Most buyers will modify this checklist to fit their specific needs.

Two decisions that many PC buyers struggle with are:

Should I buy an IBM or should I buy an IBM-compatible?

Should I buy a portable or a nonportable computer?

Compatibility is desirable if you have an IBM PC at work and plan to take work home. Some people also believe that a large part of all near-future software will be designed for the IBM PC, which makes compatibility attractive. No computer is 100 percent compatible with the IBM PC, owing to the specific read-only memory that comes with the IBM PC. There are, however, levels of compatibility. Several models, such as the COMPAQ computer, are virtually 100 percent compatible. These computers run almost all of the same software and sometimes more software than the IBM PC. If you are willing to accept a compatible, you might save some money and/or wind up with a faster or otherwise superior machine. Read reviews in leading PC publications such as InfoWeek to get an idea of compatibility levels and features.

Portable computers are either luggables or lap-top models. Luggables generally weigh from 25 to 35 pounds and use a regular, though small, CRT display. They are available with floppy and fixed disks and generally have regular-sized keyboards. Lap-top models are about the size of a briefcase and weigh only about 10 pounds. Lap tops usually have the ability to run on a battery pack as well as by wall current, and have smaller, less cumbersome displays. There are reasonably priced LCD and LED displays, but the screens give off too much glare. Gas-driven screens, which are expensive, are much more readable. Lap tops make good use of programs built into read-only memory, since they are too small to house a fixed disk. They also have smaller, less comprehensive keyboards.

Desk-top computers offer larger fixed-disk capacity, larger displays, and a lower price tag. The conclusion you reach will be based on this general trade-off between the power and price of a desk top versus the portability of lap-top and luggable models.

Personal Computers in the Home

Personal computers in the home have a variety of applications, including word processing, entertainment, education, and personal finances. However, the market for personal computers in the home has not been as large as anticipated. It has been found that most people who do not keep financial records manually will not spend the time to keep them on a personal computer either. Quite often a task in financial record keeping, such as balancing a checkbook, is easier to do manually than with a personal computer. But for those who really keep up with their personal financial planning, a PC can definitely be a great help.

The most likely reason a business person purchases a personal computer for the home is to have the same or compatible hardware and software at home as in the office. Having a computer at home means the individual can do the same work at home as he or she does in the office. This is especially true when the home personal computer is linked to a modem, allowing the user to communicate with office computers. Some companies have provided their key employees with portable personal computers so they can use the same machine at home as they use in the office. Portable hard-disk drives are also available that allow the user to move data back and forth from home to the office.

Microcomputing Needs Checklist

When considering the microcomputing needs of your organization, it is important to begin by determining what applications are required. Based upon the requirements of the software you wish to use, hardware decisions can then be made.

The following checklist is intended to aid you in the selection of these microcomputing components. First, it provides you with a list of features and capabilities to consider when selecting software. It then goes on to address hardware requirements, finishing with vendor-related considerations.

Software

1. What problem(s) are you trying to solve?

_____
_____
_____
_____
_____
_____

2. What types of application software do you need?
_____ Electronic Spreadsheet
_____ Word Processing
_____ Budgeting
_____ Project Planning
_____ Project Management
_____ Graphics
_____ Database Management
_____ Query Languages
_____ Electronic Mail
_____ Scheduling
_____ Inventory
_____ Communications
_____ Access to Subscribed-to Databases
_____ Industry-Specific Packages
_____ Custom Software
_____ Other _____

3a. Is integrated software, allowing the transfer of data between packages, needed?
_____ Yes
_____ No

3b. If yes, which packages need to be integrated? Check all that apply.
_____ Spreadsheet
_____ Word Processing
_____ Subscribed-to Databases
_____ Data Downloaded from Mainframe
_____ Other _____

4. Are error-checking capabilities for uploading and downloading data needed?
_____ Yes
_____ No

5. What level of sophistication is the user? The package? (1 = High; 3 = Low)

	User	Package
Package A	_____	_____
Package B	_____	_____
Package C	_____	_____

6. Is hardcopy documentation necessary?
_____ Yes
_____ No

7. Is online help required?
_____ Yes
_____ No

8. What is the development history of the software? (i.e., Have there been several releases indicating product evolution?)
_____
_____
_____

9a. Is it important that the software be compatible with your existing microcomputer software or with other software which is of interest?
_____ Yes
_____ No
_____ Doesn't matter

9b. Who will supply the interface programs that may be needed?
_____ Vendor
_____ Corporate staff
_____ Individual user

10. What types of communication support do you need?
_____ PC to PC
_____ Asynch
_____ Bisynch
_____ SDLC
_____ Local Area Network
_____ PC to Dedicated Word Processor
_____ None
_____ Don't know

11a. Is the software installed and guaranteed?
_____ Yes
_____ No

11b. Is it supported through a "hot line"?
_____ Yes
_____ No

12a. Is education available?
_____ Yes
_____ No

12b. Is it provided by the vendor?
_____ Yes
_____ No

13. What operating system does the software require?
_____ CP/M
_____ MS-DOS
_____ PC-DOS
_____ Unix (Xenix, etc.)
_____ UCSD p-System
_____ Vendor Specific
_____ Other _____

FIGURE 2–21   Checklist for Acquiring a Personal-Computer System

Checklists are very valuable to those interested in acquiring a personal computer or any other computer or software. There are usually so many variables involved in the decision that a checklist is the most practical way of being sure you consider everything that is important to you.

Personal-Computer Challenges

Software Piracy

Most personal-computer software costs in the range of 20 to 500 dollars. Much of this software can be easily copied through the copying facilities of the personal computer. Estimates are that 150 to 200 million dollars of sales are lost to the

Figure 2–21 continued

14. What are the hardware requirements of the software?
Memory _____ K
Microprocessor:
_____ Z80/8080/8085
_____ 8088/8086/80286
_____ 6502/6509
_____ 68000
_____ Vendor Specific
_____ Don't know
Diskettes:
_____ Microfloppies
_____ 5¼
_____ 8 inch
Number of diskette drives:
_____ One
_____ Two
Hard disks;
_____ Yes
_____ If "Yes", what capacity? _____
_____ No
Printer:
_____ Dot Matrix
_____ Letter Quality
_____ Graphics
Terminal:
_____ Alphanumeric
_____ Graphic

Hardware

1. Do you need to be able to expand the memory on your system?
_____ Yes
_____ No

2. Do you need to be able to add peripherals?
_____ Yes
_____ No

3. Do you need a color display?
_____ Yes
_____ No

4a. Do you need graphics capability?
_____ Yes
_____ No

4b. If yes, do you need color graphics?
_____ Yes, immediately
_____ Yes, later
_____ No

5a. Do you need modems?
_____ Yes
_____ No

5b. If yes, what kind?
_____ Direct connection
_____ Acoustic coupler

5c. Will you need intelligent auto-dial capabilities?
_____ Yes
_____ No

6. Will the vendor install the hardware you purchase?
_____ Yes
_____ No

7. Is the hardware maintenance available through the vendor?
_____ Yes
_____ No

8. How long will it take to receive delivery on a system?
_____ One to three weeks
_____ Three to six weeks
_____ Over six weeks

Vendor

1. Are you buying hardware from:
_____ A local supplier
_____ A mail order supplier
_____ Direct sales force

2. How long has the hardware vendor been in the computer business?
_____ Less than one year
_____ One to five years
_____ Five to ten years
_____ More than ten years

3. Is the vendor financially stable?

	Software Vendor	Hardware Vendor	Single Source Vendor
Yes	_____	_____	_____
No	_____	_____	_____

4. Is this a new venture for the hardware vendor?
_____ Yes, first venture in microcomputers
_____ No, part of extensive product line

5. How many hardware service locations are available?
_____ One
_____ Two to ten
_____ 11 to 50
_____ 51 to 100
_____ over 100

6. Is the hardware vendor:
_____ Local
_____ Nationwide

7. How many microcomputer systems has the vendor installed?
_____ None, this is first
_____ Less than 100
_____ 100 to 500
_____ 501 to 1000
_____ 1001 to 10,000
_____ More than 10,000

8. Does the vendor supply and support a full line of peripherals?
_____ Yes
_____ No

9. How long will it take to get service?

	Software	Hardware
Less than 24 hours	_____	_____
24 to 48 hours	_____	_____
More than 48 hours	_____	_____

software industry annually because of this illegal copying. The federal copyright laws prohibit the copying of software since it is copyrighted. Such illegal copying harms the personal-computer software industry. Revenues lost to the industry could have been used in developing better software.

Many software companies use various **copy-protection** schemes to protect their software from copying. These schemes, however, do little to prevent a skilled personal-computer user from copying software. Software copying programs are available whose primary purpose is to enable users to break the software protection schemes. Some companies, such as Lotus Development Corporation, have actively prosecuted those who have illegally copied their software.

When a company has more than one personal computer the software license agreements typically require that a particular copy of software be used on only one machine. For example, if a business has ten PCs, then it must purchase ten copies of the software. Many software companies, however, have discounts that apply when a lot of copies are being purchased. There are also software license agreements that allow software to be used on multiple computers.

Some companies, as an approach to market their software, actually encourage the user to copy their programs. Their hope is that the user will like the software enough to pay them for a copy of the software manual and for periodic updates to the software. PC Write, a word processor, is marketed with this technique.

There is also quite a bit of **public-domain software** available. Such software is not copyrighted and therefore is available to anyone. It is developed and kept up-to-date by the various users of the particular piece of software.

Illegal Access

Throughout our economy there is much information stored on mainframe-computer data bases. These data bases range from public-access data bases (such as the Source and Dow Jones News Retrieval) to private-company data bases, research data bases, and Defense Department data bases. Many of these data bases are linked together through a computer network. If a user gains access to the network, it is relatively easy to access the various data bases on the network.

Personal computers are an ideal device for a person who wishes to gain illegal access to a data base. Such people are known as **hackers;** they just keep hacking away until they gain the desired access.

Many of the data bases have telephone (dial-up) access. First, the hacker obtains the telephone number to access the network or mainframe computer. These numbers are often stored on public-access *electronic bulletin boards* by hackers. Then the hacker simply programs a personal computer to dial the telephone number and systematically try many different password combinations (in a trial and error approach) to find a valid *password.* Once a password has been found, hackers often publicize it among their friends or through an electronic bulletin board. Such a trial and error approach would almost be impossible without a personal computer, since manually inputting many different combinations of passwords would take too much time and effort.

Illegal access to computers, and particularly the destruction of data after the access, is a crime. The FBI usually gets involved in investigating such crimes. However, comprehensive approaches to the prevention of such acts and their detection and prosecution have not been developed.

Managing Personal Computers

Personal computers have certainly brought an increase in productivity to businesses. They allow users to develop, in an efficient and productive manner, applications that fit their particular needs. The laissez-faire (do your own thing) approach to personal computing has kindled the imagination of users; many creative applications have been developed. However, a lack of structure and control in the application of personal computers can result in disasters. For example, recently a number of top-level executives in an oil firm were fired when the company lost several million dollars after it relied on information produced by an electronic

electronic bulletin board
A data base, usually maintained on a single personal computer system, to which other personal computer users may dial into, and either post messages or read the existing messages.

password
A unique string of characters that a user must enter to meet security requirements before gaining access to a data base. The password should be known only to that user.

spreadsheet. The spreadsheet had contained errors and had not been tested properly. It is very easy to introduce errors into electronic spreadsheets, particularly if they are large and complex.

Some feel that the term *personal computer* is inaccurate. The data contained in a firm's personal computers are often very important to the business as a whole and therefore they are not "personal" data. Figure 2–22 lists several personal-computer management concerns. The key to managing personal computers is to provide structure and control without stifling innovation. After several years of experience with personal computers, most companies recognize that the controls necessary to manage mainframe and minicomputers are also often necessary to manage personal computers.

Your data files and programs are important corporate assets—safeguard them!

If data entry processing and other applications formerly run on a mainframe or minicomputer are now run on a microcomputer, have traditional considerations, such as backup, program changes, cross-training, balancing procedures and the like been addressed?

Diskettes are a very portable and fragile medium, the risk of accidental or intentional misuse or destruction of data is very high. Protect the information on these diskettes by preparing duplicate (back-up) copies.

The proliferation of microcomputers means that more and more employees *may* have access to your mainframe's data. Lack of knowledge of EDP operations was once, in itself, a control. More and more computer-literate personnel present a risk. You can't assume employees are unable to access or change centralized data files without permission. Find out!

Microcomputers can be used as sophisticated terminals. They can be programmed to manipulate data received from the centralized computer. Users may also be able to write programs to manipulate data stored in the mainframe. Now, users are programmers.

Many machines mean many applications, thus increasing the possibility that not all are using the same versions of the information. Are decisions being based on obsolete information? All microcomputers that share a common data base should have procedural mechanisms to safeguard integrity of information.

Don't let the relatively inexpensive nature of microcomputer hardware and software delude you; there is a need to properly plan computerized applications.

Your implementation plan should be flexible and as nonbureaucratic as possible. Don't destroy the user's imagination just because planning is introduced.

Document, document, document! Perhaps the most significant weakness of present microcomputer applications is the lack of documentation. Address this issue at the start and stay with it.

Adequately test systems before committing important applications to them. This may sound obvious but adequate testing can avoid time-consuming problems.

Training and cross-training cannot be ignored. Use your documentation in the training process and be sure to stress good internal control procedures.

FIGURE 2–22 Personal Computer Management Concerns

Future Directions of Personal Computers

Personal computers of the future will have increased processing power and greater storage capabilities. All of this will be available at a lower cost. At the same time, networking of personal computers will become more prevalent. Many experts believe that the economics of computing is tending toward the personal computer and away from minicomputers and mainframes. They argue that networks of inexpensive personal computers will be less expensive for a business. A counter to this argument is that minis and mainframes will also greatly improve their cost-performance ratio in the future.

In addition, it has been found that the use of personal computers increases the demand for mainframe computers. Individuals who have never used a computer are introduced to computing through easy-to-use and friendly software on the personal computer. As they become more proficient, they begin to want the capabilities that only the mainframe provides. For example, the mainframe may store large corporate data bases containing information that the PC user would like to periodically **download** to the PC. Once the data are on the personal computer, various analysis tasks using PC software, such as electronic spreadsheets, can be performed. Data can be downloaded from mainframes to personal computers, but it does require mainframe computer resources to do so. Certainly, the ability to move data to and from mainframes and personal computers is going to be important in the future. Many experts believe that data shared widely by users throughout a business will continue to be initially collected and stored on mainframe data bases, which provide efficiency and a controlled environment. Personal computers will download these data for decision-support analysis.

The personal computer is relieving business people of much of the paperwork that is necessary to satisfy accounting, legal, and governmental requirements. This leaves them with much more time and energy for productive work in decision making. The personal computer is providing management with a great deal more analysis and information for decision making than has been practical in the past. These trends are going to continue and accelerate in the future.

download
To move data from a mainframe or minicomputer to a personal computer.

Thinking About Information Systems 2–2

The manager of the Jackson Retail Outlet hired a consultant to establish a personal-computer system that would provide inventory and sales information. The consultant, Jim Lloyd, had recently established his own consulting firm after completing an undergraduate degree at the local university. After waiting four months for his system, the manager of the store approached Jim and wanted to know why the development was taking so long. The manager finally asked Jim what experience he had in consulting. Jim replied that this was his first job, but he had used a spreadsheet package in college. The manager immediately fired Jim, but he had already spent several thousand dollars for the consultant to learn (on the company's time) about a new software product. How could the manager of the store have prevented this fiasco?

Summing Up

☐ Personal computers are the most rapidly growing type of computer system. They are versatile machines that can be used by a person possessing very little computer knowledge.

☐ The CPU of a personal computer is basically evaluated in terms of its speed and word size. The major components of a CPU are the device controllers, arithmetic-logic unit, and primary memory.

☐ A personal computer can support a number of input/output devices, including the following:

Keyboard
Monitor screen
Color monitor
Floppy-disk drive
Hard-disk drive
Cartridge-tape drive
Dot-matrix printer
Daisy-wheel printer
Joysticks
Light pens
Sound-output devices

☐ Personal computers use both floppy and hard disks for secondary storage.

☐ The market for personal-computer hardware is very competitive. Apple, IBM, and COMPAQ are leading suppliers, but there is a large number of other manufacturers selling high-quality equipment as well.

☐ Personal computers communicate over both local-area networks and public telephone lines.

☐ A large variety of packaged software is available for personal computers. The most popular software packages are electronic spreadsheets, word processing, data-base management systems, and integrated packages.

☐ Sophisticated software packages are available for the major business functions like accounting, finance, marketing, and production. Also, special-purpose software exists for various professional practices and other businesses.

☐ In buying a PC, users should first assess their needs for information, select the application software, and then choose the hardware.

☐ Personal-computer equipment and software can be purchased from a variety of sources, including chain computer stores, mail-order stores, and office-supply dealers. Numerous periodicals provide information and ideas about the use of personal computers.

☐ Personal computers can be used in the home for a large number of applications, including personal finances, word processing, and entertainment.

☐ The software industry loses more than 100 million dollars per year to illegal copying. Thus far, a satisfactory solution to this problem has not been implemented.

□ The personal computer has become an ideal tool for people attempting to gain illegal access to mainframe computers.

□ Managers must provide structure and control in the PC environment, without stifling innovation.

□ As personal computers become more powerful and more widely used, the ability to move data between personal computers and mainframes will increase in importance.

Key Terms

personal computer	monitor screen	plug-compatible
microcomputer	color monitor	graphics
Ability	diskette (floppy disk)	word processing
microprocessor	hard disk (Winchester disk)	integrated packages
speed	tape cartridge	consultant
word size	dot-matrix printer	software piracy
machine operation	daisy-wheel printer	copy protection
machine cycle	letter-quality printer	public-domain software
read-only memory (ROM)	mouse	hacker
random-access memory (RAM)	communications program	electronic bulletin board
memory modules	modem	download
keyboard		

Self-Quiz

Completion Questions

1. Microcomputers designed to be operated by one user are called _____ .

2. The heart of a personal-computer system is a _____ , which is a CPU on a chip.

3. The speed with which a personal computer operates is dependent on the speed and _____ of the microprocessor.

4. A _____ converts the outgoing data from the digital signals that computers use to the analog sound waves that phone lines transmit.

5. The _____ has become a de facto standard for personal computers in business.

6. The combination of all the tools available in a personal computer is often referred to as a _____ .

7. A _____ hardware device can directly replace units produced by a different manufacturer.

8. Software packages available for use with personal computers include electronic spreadsheets, data-base management systems, _____ , and graphics.

9. The most popular secondary-storage medium for personal computers is _____ .

10. Some integrated packages split the screen of the monitor into sections, with each section displaying part of each stand-alone package. These sections are called _____ .

Multiple-Choice Questions

1. Which of the following input/output devices is not associated with personal computers?
   a. mice
   b. color monitors
   c. punched cards
   d. dot-matrix printers
   e. optical scanners

2. The word size of a microprocessor refers to:
   a. the number of machine operations performed in a second
   b. the amount of information processed in one machine cycle
   c. the amount of information that can be stored in a byte
   d. the maximum length of an English word that can be input to a computer
3. A typical personal computer used for business purposes would have _____ of RAM.
   a. 4K
   b. 16K
   c. 64K
   d. 256K
   e. 1 megabyte
4. The system unit of a personal computer typically contains all of the following except:
   a. microprocessor
   b. disk controller
   c. serial interface
   d. modem
   e. all of the above are contained
5. The primary memory of a personal computer consists of:
   a. ROM only
   b. RAM only
   c. Both ROM and RAM
   d. memory module
6. The personal-computer industry was started by:
   a. IBM
   b. Apple
   c. Compaq
   d. Atari
   e. Texas Instruments
7. IFPS is a:
   a. financial planning package
   b. electronic spreadsheet
   c. graphics package
   d. data-base management package
   e. integrated package
8. Which of the following magazines covers only the IBM PC and its compatibles?
   a. *Byte*
   b. *PC Magazine*

c. *Personal Computing*
d. *Interface Age*
e. none of the above
9. Which of the following is true concerning personal computers?
   a. They have been most successful in the home.
   b. They decrease the demand for mainframe computers.
   c. The electronic spreadsheet has been a primary reason for their popularity.
   d. Their future is not so bright owing to the improved cost-performance ratio of minis and mainframes.
10. Which of the following professions has not been affected by personal computers?
    a. medical
    b. clerical
    c. accounting
    d. law
    e. all of the above have been affected

Answers

Completion

1. personal computers
2. microprocessor
3. word size
4. modem
5. IBM PC
6. personal workstation
7. plug-compatible
8. word processing
9. magnetic disk
10. windows

Multiple-Choice

1. c
2. b
3. d
4. d
5. c
6. b
7. a
8. b
9. c
10. e

Chapter 3

Management Information Systems

PROLOGUE

Managers see computers as tools for providing information on which to base their decisions. People who are successful with computers know that when developing computer applications they should first focus on their information needs rather than on hardware technology. What they need most is conceptual knowledge about the information requirements of management and the methods for converting these often complex requirements into operational computer software. This chapter will explore concepts of management information systems, and the next four chapters will discuss the methods by which management information requirements are translated into computer information systems.

Introduction

In the last two chapters we developed a basic understanding of what a computer is and how it processes information. Then we examined that most user-friendly of computer systems, the personal computer.

Now we will explore information systems in the same order that managers who successfully employ information systems do. In this chapter we see how management information systems relate to the information needs of management. In chapter 4 we will examine some general systems concepts that apply to any system, computer or otherwise. These will help you immensely in understanding information systems. In chapters 5 through 7 we will see how information needs are analyzed, how these needs are shaped and molded into information-system designs, and finally how these designs are implemented into a working information system.

This chapter could have been titled "Information Systems from the Viewpoint of Managers," which is the essence of management information systems. An information system is a tool that must fit within the framework of the tasks that managers perform. Managers are interested first in how they can put the computer to work, and then in computer technology.

We first explore the relationship between management information systems (MIS) and data processing, including the ways that data-processing applications support an MIS. Then we examine the close relationship between types of decisions that managers make and the information requirements for these decisions. Third, we look at the basic ways an MIS produces information through different types of reports. Fourth, we briefly examine the relationship between the MIS and data-base management systems (DBMS). Perhaps the single most important advancement which has made MIS practical is the software available for data-base management systems. Next, we investigate the relationship between MIS and decision support systems. And finally, we look at the impact of MIS on business.

What Is a MIS?

transaction
A business event such as a sale to a customer. In information systems, the term *transaction* is often also used to refer to any change made in a computer file.

A **management information system** is a formalized computer information system that can integrate data from various sources to provide the information necessary for management decision making. Figure 3–1 illustrates the relationship between data processing and management information systems. The data-processing system supports management information systems. Much of the information that the MIS uses is initially captured and stored by the data-processing system. Data processing is oriented toward the capture, processing, and storage of data whereas MIS is oriented toward using the data to produce management information. The data-processing system performs *transaction* processing. It is very much involved with processing orders, sales, payments on account, and so on. In

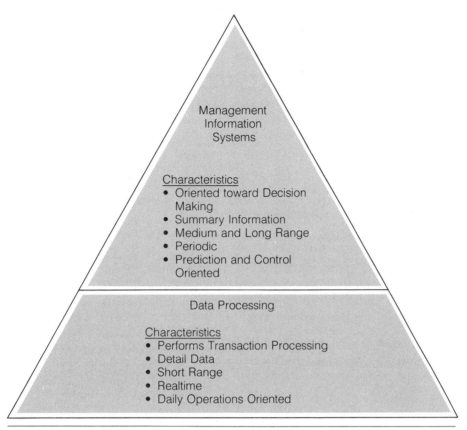

FIGURE 3–1   The Relationship between Data Processing and Management Information Systems

Most firms implement data-processing systems first since processing of transactions with customers is a necessity. As the data are collected through data processing, they also become available to produce the reports required by a management information system.

the course of processing these transactions, the data-processing system collects and stores a large amount of detailed information. This information is the *data base* for the management information system.

data base
A collection of data fundamental to a system.

Objectives, Decisions, and Information

How do we determine what information a manager needs? Information needs are determined by the **decisions** that must be made, which in turn are determined by **objectives.** This relationship between objectives, decisions, and information is illustrated in Figure 3–2.

For example, assume that a company has an objective of increasing its net profit by 50 percent. Decisions would need to be made about which products should be emphasized in order to reach the desired 50-percent increase in profits. Choosing a certain product might require further decisions concerning expansion of plants, or a decision to purchase the product from outside. All of these decisions would be based in part on information from the management information system. As the company moves toward the 50-percent increase in net profit, reports showing how well each product is selling would be crucial. These reports could indicate that a decision should be made to emphasize an alternative product that might be more profitable. This approach to determining the information needs of management is very important to remember, as we will see later when we discuss the development of information systems. The *system analyst* must always keep in mind the decisions and the objectives that the MIS supports.

system analyst
A person whose responsibility is to analyze, design, and develop information systems.

Thinking About Information Systems 3–1

John Gilmer is a senior system analyst for Montgomery Furniture Company. John has been assigned the task of developing an information-system master plan that would govern the future direction of MIS development for Montgomery Furniture. Bill Harmon is manager of the system development office. John reports to Bill. Early one morning they are discussing the basic approach to developing the master plan. John feels that starting with objectives and deriving the decisions to reach those objectives is a waste of time. He believes that in interviews with the company executives the best approach is to ask them what information they need to perform their function. He says to Bill that "executives just don't think in terms of objectives and decisions. It would be very difficult to get them to think in those terms and to take the logical steps from objectives to decisions to information." Furthermore, he feels that he should not suggest various types of information to the executives. He states, "I want to find out what information they feel they need and I don't want to contaminate their requirements with my own opinions." Evaluate John's positions.

Levels of Decision Making

Decisions can be classified as: (1) strategic, (2) tactical, and (3) operational. These levels of decision making also correspond to management levels. Strategic decisions are made by top management; tactical decisions by middle management; and operational decisions by lower-level management. As illustrated in Figure 3–3, all three of these levels of decision making rely on data processing for portions of their information.

Strategic decisions are future oriented and involve a great deal of uncertainty. **Strategic decision making** involves the establishment of objectives for the organization and the long-range plans for attaining these objectives. Decisions regarding the location of plants, and decisions about capital sources and about which products to produce, are examples of strategic decisions.

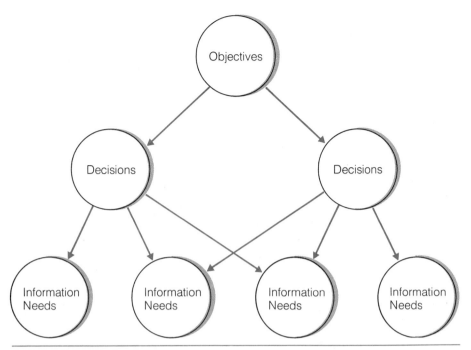

FIGURE 3–2   The Relationship between Objectives, Decisions, and Information Needs

Sometimes it is tempting to think about information needs without first thinking about business objectives and decisions. Such an approach quite often results in information systems that do not meet business needs.

Tactical decision making is concerned with the implementation of the decisions made at the strategic level. This includes the allocation of resources to the pursuit of organizational objectives. Examples of tactical decision making include plant layout, personnel concerns, budget allocation, and production scheduling.

Operational decisions involve the execution of specific tasks to assure that they are carried out efficiently and effectively. These decisions are made primarily by lower-level supervisors. *Standards* are usually preset for operational decisions. Managers and supervisors at this level are expected to make decisions that keep the operation in line with the predetermined standards. Examples of operational decision making include acceptance or rejection of credit, determination of inventory reorder times and quantities, and assignment of jobs to individual workers. Table 3–1 summarizes the characteristics of the three levels of decision making.

Programmable decisions are those decisions for which policy standards or guidelines are already established. For this reason they are often called ***structured decisions.*** These decisions are routine in nature and can be made by reference to previously established policy. An example of a programmable decision is the credit-granting decision based on income, years employed, et cetera of the individual applying for credit. Note that programmable decisions do not necessarily have to be made by a computer-based system. Often these decisions are made by lower-level managers or supervisors. **Nonprogrammable decisions** deal with

standard
An acknowledged guideline or norm against which performance is measured.

structured
That which is highly organized.

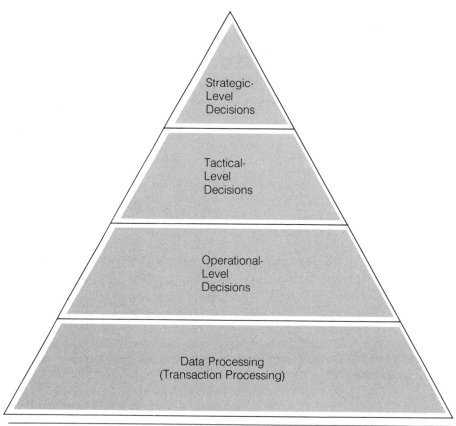

FIGURE 3–3 Levels of Decision Making

Data processing supports these decisions with data that can be further processed to produce information for decision making.

ill-defined and unstructured problems. These decisions are future oriented and contain many variables whose impact on the outcome cannot be quantified. These **unstructured decisions** require highly skilled managers. Examples of such decisions are those regarding plant expansion, new products, and mergers.

In our discussion of levels of decision making, we touched on some of the characteristics of the information required at each level of decision making. Table 3-2 summarizes these characteristics. Most of the entries in this table are self-explanatory. However, we should look closely at some of them, such as the use of *realtime information*. Operational decision making depends heavily on realtime information. For example, your school probably uses a realtime system for course registration. The operational decision to allow you to sign up for a particular class depends on the realtime information of whether the class is full or not. On the other hand, strategic decision making depends much less on realtime information. For instance, one important type of information used at the strategic level is income statements. These statements identify the profitability of plants, products, and so on. Income statements are usually generated at the end of each month. Therefore, they are not realtime. Strategic-level decision making also tends to rely heavily on

realtime information
Information about ongoing events that reflects the status of these events in a completely up-to-date manner.

TABLE 3–1 Characteristics of the Three Levels of Decision Making

	Levels of Decision Making		
Characteristic	*Operational*	*Tactical*	*Strategic*
Problem Variety	Low	Moderate	High
Degree of Structure	High	Moderate	Low
Degree of Uncertainty	Low	Moderate	High
Degree of Judgment	Low	Moderate	High
Time Horizon	Days	Months	Years
Programmable Decisions	Most	Some	None
Planning Decisions	Few	About half	Most
Control Decisions	Most	About half	Few

financial information. Decision makers at this level deal with capital requirements and profitability in dollars. On the other hand, a frontline supervisor is more concerned about the hours worked on a job, the number of orders shipped, the number of defective units produced, and other information of this type.

Management Uses of Information

Management uses information for two purposes: planning and control. **Planning** occurs prior to the execution of any organizational activity. Objectives are established in the planning process. The activities that must occur to reach the objectives are identified, and the resources, such as money, equipment, and labor, necessary to support these activities are allocated. Although planning takes place at all levels

TABLE 3–2 Characteristics of Information Required at Each Level of Decision Making

	Levels of Decision Making		
Information Characteristic	*Operational*	*Tactical*	*Strategic*
Dependence on Computer Information Systems	High	Moderate	Low to Moderate
Dependence on Internal Information	Very High	High	Moderate
Dependence on External Information	Low	Moderate	Very High
Degree of Information Summarization	Very Low	Moderate	High
Need for Online Information	Very High	High	Moderate
Need for Computer Graphics	Low	Moderate	High
Use of Realtime Information	Very High	High	Moderate
Use of Predictive Information	Low	High	Very High
Use of Historical Information	High	Moderate	Low
Use of What-If Information	Low	High	Very High
Use of Information Stated in Dollars	Low	Moderate	High

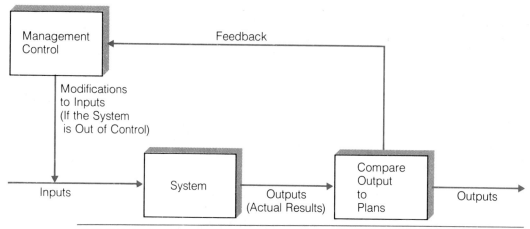

FIGURE 3–4   Management Control

This figure illustrates a system with feedback control. We will cover this concept in more depth in the next chapter, as it is very important to information systems.

of the organization, most of it occurs at the strategic and tactical levels of decision making. Planning depends to a large degree on predictive and external information. Historic information is useful in planning only in that it helps management predict the future.

Control is the process of comparing actual results with the plans identified in the planning process. Figure 3–4 illustrates management control. Let us assume the system shown in this figure is a factory. Management's plan is for the factory to produce $12 million in profit for the year. Inputs to the factory are the factors of production—land, labor, and capital. Output is a net profit. An income statement that compares actual profit to the planned profit provides feedback to management about the performance of the system (factory). If, during the year, management determines that the factory is not likely to reach the $12-million profit goal, this system is out of control. Management would attempt to place the system back in control by making modifications to the inputs. These changes might include reductions in the workforce level, purchase of less expensive raw materials, et cetera.

PC USER TIP   Formatting Disks Ahead of Time

Floppy disks must be formatted before they can be used to store program and data files. Most people format disks as they need them. Unfortunately, this can lead to disaster. It is often discovered that a disk needs to be formatted when a "disk full" error keeps a user from successfully saving a file that he or she has been working on. It is then impossible (with most software) to format a new disk without exiting the current software and losing the file. The best way to avoid this trap is to format some or all of your blank diskettes when you buy them. Putting labels on formatted disks and not on unformatted disks allows you to tell them apart. This simple policy ensures that formatted disks will be ready when you really need them.

A large percentage of the information produced by management information systems is feedback, as shown in Figure 3–4. The information system monitors the system being controlled, compares the system outputs to plans, and provides the feedback information necessary for implementation control.

Qualitative Characteristics of Information

Without quality, information loses its usefulness. A phrase often used to describe the lack of data quality is "garbage in garbage out" (GIGO). This means that unless data meet qualitative characteristics upon input, the information output from the data-processing system will be useless, or garbage. Information must meet four qualitative criteria: relevance, timeliness, accuracy, and verifiability.

Relevance

Information has **relevance** when it is useful in decision making. In other words, if information improves the decision, it is relevant. Obviously, if an airline-reservation agent is making a decision to grant a customer a reservation on a particular flight, the number of empty seats on that flight is relevant information. On the other hand, personal characteristics of the potential customer, such as occupation or sex, generally would not be relevant.

Timeliness

Also, the **timeliness** of information is important. In the context of most management information systems, as information becomes older its value decreases. Generally, lower-level decisions in an organization must have more current and timely information, and as we move up the ladder to higher-level decisions the information can be somewhat older. For example, if we are making the very routine and low-level decision of whether to ship a customer the 150 shirts that were ordered, we must know the number of shirts that we have at the moment. The number of shirts that were available five days or two weeks ago is completely useless information in terms of our decision, so the information is not timely. Conversely, a high-level decision concerning whether to expand a company's capacity for making shirts by building an additional plant would depend partly on the history of shirt sales. Information that is several years old would be useful in this case.

Accuracy

Accuracy refers to information being free of error. The amount of error that we can tolerate is related to other factors, especially timeliness and the dollar value of the decision to be made. If a decision maker must make a decision quickly, a greater degree of error can be tolerated than if he or she has considerable time and resources available to reduce data error. For example, if you smell smoke in your home you are likely to make a quick decision to call the fire department, rather than take the time to establish, without error, the location and actual exis tence of a fire. On the other hand, if you are reconciling your checkbook to a bank statement, you may want to base your decision to call the bank (and accuse people there of making an error) on information that is accurate to the nearest penny.

Verifiability

Verifiability means that the accuracy of information can be confirmed. Information can be verified through comparison with other information that is known to be accurate. Quite often, though, verification is achieved by tracing information to its original source. The term **audit trail** is often used to describe the means by which summarized information can be traced back to its original source. This audit trail is a very important part of any information-processing system. Without this trail it is usually impossible to determine the accuracy of information, therefore bringing into question the usefulness of such information.

In summary, several variables must be considered when designing a management information system. The designer must keep in mind the objectives of the organization, the decisions that must be made, and whether those decisions are of a planning or control nature. The information must be relevant, timely, accurate, and verifiable. In addition, the type of information required depends heavily on the decision level, whether it is operational, tactical, or strategic. Experience has shown that computer information systems are more successful in providing information for control decisions than for planning decisions. They decrease in success the higher the level of decision making. However, we must keep in mind that advancements in manangement information systems are making information systems more applicable to planning and to the higher levels of decision making.

Data or Information Processing?

Data processing has traditionally been defined as the capture, storage, and processing of data used to transform the data into information useful in decision making. Note that a distinction has been made between data and information. **Data** are collected facts that generally are not useful for decision making without further processing. **Information** is directly useful in decision making. It is based on processed data and therefore is the output of a data-processing system. In actual practice, however, this distinction is often difficult to make. One individual's data may be another's information. For example, hours worked by individual employees are certainly information to a frontline supervisor. However, when the decision maker is the president of a company, hours worked by individual employees are simply data that can be further processed and summarized. These summarized data may be information to the president. For these reasons, the trend is to use the term **information processing** rather than data processing.

Types of Reports

We have thus far discussed management decision making and the need for information to support these decisions. But in what form is this information produced? There are four types of computer reports: scheduled, demand, exception, and predictive *reports*.

Scheduled Reports

Scheduled reports are produced on a regularly scheduled basis such as daily, weekly, or monthly. These reports are widely distributed to users and often contain large amounts of information that are not used regularly. As the use of CRTs becomes more widespread, scheduled reports will diminish in importance. Managers will not feel compelled to ask for information on a scheduled listing just in case they may need it in the future—with a CRT the information can be retrieved on demand.

Demand Reports

Demand reports are generated on request. These reports fill irregular needs for information. In the earlier days of computing, the contents of a demand report had to be previously anticipated or there was a delay of often weeks or months in receiving the data. It simply took time to modify programs to produce information that filled unanticipated demands. Today, largely through the *query languages* of data-base management systems, we can fulfill unanticipated demands for information very quickly, often within minutes. This is possible because users and managers themselves can use the query languages to produce reports.

Exception Reports

One of the most efficient approaches to management is the management-by-exception approach. **Management by exception** means that managers spend their time dealing with exceptions or those situations which are out of control. Activities that are proceeding as planned are in control and, therefore, do not need the manager's attention. **Exception reports** notify management when an activity or system is out of control so that corrective action can be taken. Listings that identify all customers with account balances that are overdue are examples of exception reports. Error reports are another type of exception report. **Error reports** identify input or processing errors occurring during the computer's execution of a particular *application*.

Predictive Reports

Predictive reports are useful in planning decisions. They often make use of statistical and modeling techniques such as regression, time-series analysis, and simulation. These reports assist management in answering what-if questions. For example: What if sales increased by 10 percent? What impact would the increase

report
A printing or display of items of information.

query language
A high-level computer language that can be used with minimal training to retrieve specific information from a data base.

application
A specific use of a computer to perform a business task.

have on net profit? The statistical and modeling techniques that produce predictive reports depend largely on historical data. Such data must be readily accessible by the MIS in a form that can be used by the models; otherwise, these models will be of little use to management. Figure 3–5 summarizes the characteristics of the types of reports issued by management information systems.

The MIS and Business Functions

functional area
An organizational unit of a business corresponding to its major duty or activity such as engineering or finance.

A MIS is a federation of **functional information systems.** This concept is illustrated in Figure 3–6. Specialists within each of the *functional areas* such as finance, production, accounting, or engineering are much more familiar with the information requirements of that function than anyone else in the firm. These specialists can design systems to produce the information required to manage their function. The functional information systems interact with one another and often share the same data. As we will discuss in the next section of this chapter, database management systems greatly enhance the ability of these functional systems to share the same data. The important point to remember is that these integrated functional information systems are the MIS.

Thinking About Information Systems 3-2

A typical college of business offers undergraduate majors in several different areas, including management, marketing, finance, accounting, and management information systems. Many of you have already decided on one of these majors. Justify why knowledge from your chosen major would be necessary preparation for a career in system analysis involving the development of computer information systems.

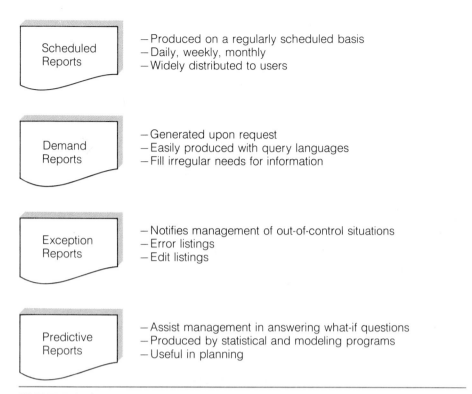

Scheduled Reports	—Produced on a regularly scheduled basis —Daily, weekly, monthly —Widely distributed to users
Demand Reports	—Generated upon request —Easily produced with query languages —Fill irregular needs for information
Exception Reports	—Notifies management of out-of-control situations —Error listings —Edit listings
Predictive Reports	—Assist management in answering what-if questions —Produced by statistical and modeling programs —Useful in planning

FIGURE 3–5   Information-Systems Reports Issued to Management

Although many of these reports are now available on CRTs or video display terminals (VDTs), many managers still prefer reports to be printed out on paper, primarily because of the flexibility and portability of paper.

Each of the functional information systems are, in turn, made up of *application systems,* as shown in Figure 3–6. The accounting information system includes several typical applications. Each application system is also made up of one or more programs. In the payroll system illustrated, there are five programs.

application systems
Computer programs written to perform specific business tasks.

The MIS and Data-Base Management Systems

Data are the central resource of a MIS. Managing this resource is crucial. A **database management system** is a program that serves as an interface between applications programs and a set of coordinated and integrated files called a data base. Prior to the use of DBMS there was little, if any, integration or data sharing among the functional information systems. However, there are many opportunities for these systems to share the same data. For instance, the payroll application within the accounting information system could share data with the personnel information system. Examples of data that could be shared are employee names, addresses, and pay rates.

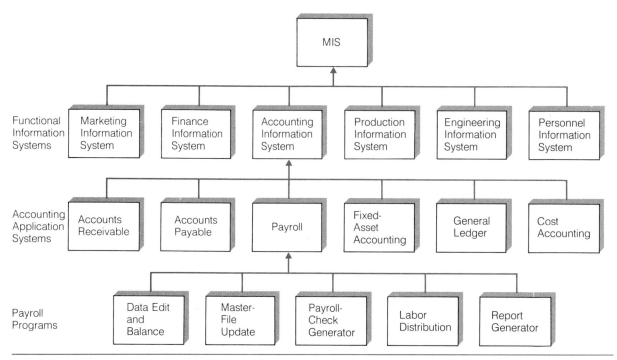

FIGURE 3–6 The MIS as a Federation of Functional Information Systems

Any MIS can be broken down this way into its constituent parts. This hierarchical decomposition of a system is an important tool in understanding complex systems, as we will see in chapter 5.

Data-base management systems are, in effect, an interface between the functional applications and the data base, as shown in Figure 3–7. The DBMS allows the various functional systems to access the same data. The DBMS can pool together related data from different files, such as in personnel and payroll files. The DBMS is perhaps the most important tool in making a MIS possible. We will explore database management systems in more depth in a later chapter.

Decision-Support Systems and the MIS

Management information systems in the past have been most successful in providing information for routine, structured, and anticipated types of decisions. In addition, they have been successful in acquiring and storing large quantities of detailed data concerning transaction processing. They have been less successful in providing information for semistructured or unstructured decisions, particularly

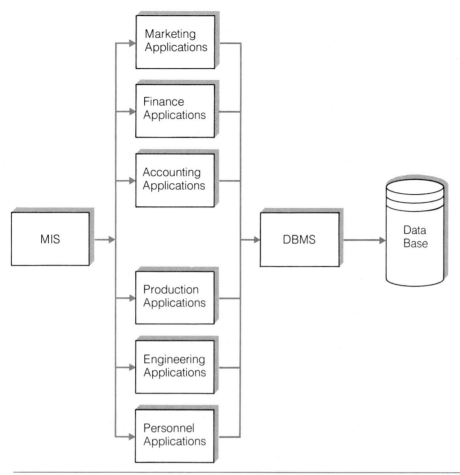

FIGURE 3–7   The Relationship between a DBMS and a MIS

The MIS is made up of individual functional applications such as marketing and finance. These applications in turn use a data-base management system to store and access the data. The data base is stored on disk files.

unanticipated ones. A **decision-support system** provides a set of integrated computer tools that allow a decision maker to interact directly with computers in order to retrieve information useful for semistructured and unstructured decisions. Such decisions might involve plant expansion, mergers, acquisitions, or new products, for example.

A decision-support system is an extension of a MIS. It provides user-friendly languages, data retrieval, data processing, and modeling capabilities for the decision maker's direct use. Many decision makers are now using microcomputers for decision-support purposes. Integrated software in the form of electronic spreadsheets, data-base management, and graphics allows users to react quickly to the changing information needs that usually go along with unstructured decisions.

The Impact of Management Information Systems on Business

All businesses, whether large or small, must perform data processing. They do so either manually or with computers and other devices such as calculators and adding machines. Even the smallest business must perform data processing in order to keep records for income-tax purposes. Law requires that taxpayers keep such records.

Often, though, managers of small businesses depend less on a formal data-processing system and more on informal information sources in making their decisions. Since a small-business manager is very familiar with all aspects of the business, there is less need for a formal data-processing system. As a business grows larger, managers depend much more on data-processing systems for their information. Imagine the managers of General Motors depending on informal sources for information about the operations of the company. Such an approach would be a disaster, since the higher-level managers are not close enough to the day-to-day operations to have readily available the information necessary to make decisions.

Information is truly the lifeblood of a business. A business simply could not service its customers or make higher-level decisions without information to support customer service and decision making. The use of computers in information processing has had several impacts on businesses. Among these are easier business growth, fewer clerical workers, reduced data-processing costs, automation of some decisions, and the availability of different types and greater quantities of information.

Easier Business Growth

Once an information-processing system is installed, most businesses find that they can expand their operations without making substantial changes in the information-processing system. For example, if the information-processing system is designed correctly it should have excess capacity. Therefore, it can easily accommodate a growth in the number of customers, and only small changes (such as the addition of a more powerful central processing unit) or no changes at all would have to be made. Furthermore, a significant factor in the growth of today's large businesses is the existence of computer-based information processing which provides managers with the information to control these very large enterprises.

Fewer Clerical Workers

The use of computers has reduced the need for clerical workers, who in the past did the information processing in a manual system. As the demand for clerical workers has decreased, computers have increased the demand for people who are technically oriented, such as system analysts and programmers. The demand for other workers such as accountants, whose discipline is closely linked with information processing, has also increased.

Reduced Information-Processing Costs

Computers can process information at a much lower cost than humans can. Therefore, the cost of processing information in relation to the amount of output generated from the information-processing system has drastically declined.

Automation of Some Decisions

Many businesses have used the computer to automate certain lower-level decisions. Decisions about when to reorder goods to replenish inventory stocks, or how much fuel to carry on a specific airline flight, are examples of automated decisions.

More and Better Information

Computers have substantially increased the quantity of information available to management. Much of the information now available would have been impossible to obtain with manual systems simply because the amount of calculation necessary to produce the information would have been prohibitive. Examples of this type of information include the output from linear programming, forecasting, and simulation models. Let's consider simulation. With simulation we can build a model (a computer program) of a real-world system (such as an aircraft) through the use of mathematical formulas. The computer, through a large number of manipulations of these mathematical formulas, can simulate the performance of the real-world system, in this case the aircraft. Thus if an aircraft manufacturer is considering developing and producing a new type of passenger aircraft, and is thinking about spending millions or billions of dollars to do so, it would be very useful to have a simulation of that aircraft prior to investing time and money into the project. Fuel consumption and passenger-load factors in relation to specific airline-route structures could be simulated, for example. The information produced from this simulation would enable the manufacturer to judge how profitable such an aircraft would be.

Michelle Short, a senior at a large university, will obtain a degree in decision-support systems in June. She has an interview with a representative from a large southwestern oil company. The interviewer asks Michelle what the difference is between a management information system and a decision-support system. The interviewer then asks how a decision-support system would aid the oil company. Michelle responds by saying that a decision-support system is an extension of a management information system. She says that a decision-support system uses the information captured by the management information system in a variety of decision models. Michelle states that these models usually are established to evaluate risk, to ask what-if questions, and to provide managers with various alternatives for making a decision that will have an impact on the firm's future. She states that the models are useful for problems such as allocating scarce resources or determining future plant capacity. Would you hire Michelle, based on her answer?

Thinking About Information Systems 3–3

Large quantities of information are not always useful to managers. Many managers today suffer from information overload. So much information is available that they have difficulty sorting out and using what is truly relevant. The more sophisticated computer users have designed ways for managers to call up the specific information to be used in specific decisions.

Summing Up

☐ The management information system is a formalized computer information system that can integrate data from various sources to provide the information necessary for management decision making.

☐ Information needs are determined by the decisions that must be made, which in turn are determined by objectives.

☐ Strategic decision making involves the establishment of objectives for an organization and the long-range plans for attaining these objectives.

☐ Tactical decision making is concerned with the implementation of the decisions made at the strategic level.

☐ Operational decisions involve the execution of specific tasks to assure they are carried out efficiently and effectively.

☐ Programmable decisions are those decisions for which policies, standards, or guidelines are already established.

☐ Nonprogrammable decisions are those which deal with ill-defined and unstructured problems.

☐ Management uses information for two purposes: planning and control.

☐ Planning is the establishment of objectives and the activities that must occur to reach these objectives.

☐ Control is the process of comparing actual results with the plans identified in the planning process.

☐ Information is relevant when it is useful in decision making. If a piece of information improves the decision, it is relevant.

☐ Information has time value. In the context of most management information systems, as information becomes older its value decreases.

☐ Accuracy refers to information being free of error. The amount of error that we can tolerate is related to timeliness and the dollar value of the decision to be made.

☐ Verifiability means that the accuracy of information can be confirmed.

☐ Data processing is the capture, storage, and processing of data used to transform the data into information useful to decision makers.

☐ Data are collected facts that generally are not useful in decision making without further processing. Information is based on processed data, and is directly useful in decision making.

☐ Scheduled listings are produced on a regularly scheduled basis such as daily, weekly, or monthly.

☐ A demand listing is generated on request.

☐ Exception reports notify management when an activity or system is out of control.

- Predictive reports assist management in answering what-if questions.
- A MIS is a federation of functional information systems.
- A data-base management system is a program that serves as an interface between applications programs and a set of coordinated and integrated files called a data base.
- A decision-support system provides a set of integrated computer tools that allow a decision maker to interact directly with computers in order to retrieve information useful for semistructured and unstructured decisions.
- The use of computers for information processing has had impact on business in many areas. Among these are: easier business growth, fewer clerical workers, reduced information processing costs, automation of some decisions, and the availability of different and greater quantities of information.

Key Terms

management information system (MIS)
decisions
objectives
strategic decision making
tactical decision making
operational decision making
programmable decisions
structured decisions
nonprogrammable decisions
unstructured decisions
planning
control
relevance
timeliness
accuracy

verifiability
audit trail
data processing
data
information
information processing
scheduled reports
demand reports
management by exception
exception reports
error reports
predictive reports
functional information systems
data-base management system
decision-support system

Self-Quiz

Completion Questions

1. A _____ is a formalized computer information system that can integrate data from various sources to provide the information necessary for management decision making.
2. Decisions can be classified on three levels: strategic, _____ , and operational.
3. _____ decisions are those decisions for which policy standards or guidelines are already established.
4. Management uses information for two purposes: planning and _____ .
5. Information is _____ when it is useful in making a decision.
6. _____ means that the manager spends his or her time dealing with exceptions or those situations which are out of control.
7. _____ assist management in answering what-if questions.

8. A _____ is a program that serves as an interface between applications programs and a set of coordinated and integrated files called a data base.

9. A _____ provides a set of integrated computer tools that allow a decision maker to interact directly with computers in order to retrieve information useful for semistructured and unstructured decisions.

10. _____ decision making involves the establishment of objectives for an organization and the long-range plans for attaining these objectives.

Multiple-Choice Questions

1. The characteristics of strategic decisions include all of the following except:
   a. they are structured
   b. they are future oriented
   c. they have a high level of uncertainty
   d. they are concerned with long-range plans
   e. all of the above are characteristics

2. Which of the following is a tactical decision?
   a. capital-source decision
   b. product decision
   c. plant-location decision
   d. budget allocation
   e. none of the above

3. _____ decisions concern the execution of specific tasks to assure that they are carried out efficiently and effectively.
   a. Tactical
   b. Strategic
   c. Operational
   d. Management
   e. None of the above

4. Which of the following is not true of operational decisions?
   a. concern the execution of specific tasks
   b. primarily made by middle management
   c. usually have preset standards
   d. include acceptance or rejection of credit
   e. all of the above are true

5. Which of the following types of decision making would depend heavily on realtime information?
   a. Strategic
   b. Tactical
   c. Operational
   d. Nonprogrammable

6. Computer information systems are most successful in providing information for:
   a. control decisions
   b. planning decisions
   c. strategic decisions
   d. nonprogrammable decisions
   e. none of the above

7. Which of the following is not one of the qualitative characteristics that information must have?
   a. relevance
   b. retrievability
   c. timeliness
   d. accuracy
   e. all of the above should be met

8. Error reports are an example of:
   a. scheduled reports
   b. demand reports
   c. exception reports
   d. predictive reports
   e. management reports

9. Which of the following is considered to be an interface between the functional applications and the data base?
   a. management information systems
   b. data-base management systems
   c. decision-support systems
   d. data-processing systems
   e. none of the above

10. The use of computers in data processing has had several impacts on businesses. Which of the following is not one of them?
    a. easier business growth
    b. fewer clerical workers
    c. increased data-processing costs
    d. more and better information
    e. all of the above are impacts

Answers

Completion

1. management information system (MIS)
2. tactical
3. Programmable
4. control
5. relevant
6. Management by exception
7. Predictive reports
8. data base management systems (DBMS)
9. decision support system (DSS)
10. Strategic

Multiple Choice

1. a
2. d
3. c
4. b
5. c
6. a
7. e
8. c
9. b
10. c

Chapter 4

Systems Concepts

CHAPTER OUTLINE

PROLOGUE

John Craig recently started work as a programmer in the Management Information Systems Department of the Exxon Corporation. The sheer size of the company continues to amaze him. In the six months he has worked in the Management Information Systems Department he has come to realize that Exxon has some very large and complex information systems. Yet the personnel of the Management Information Systems Department have a very good understanding of these systems. They seem to have a conceptual framework that helps them to quickly understand new and complex information systems. What is this conceptual framework that they call the systems approach? Read on.

Introduction

This chapter contains a general introduction to the concepts of systems. Material of this type is abstract and has broad potential application. The initial section of the chapter offers a rationale for studying this topic. Then systems concepts such as feedback, variety and control, black-box, boundary, input, and output will be described. Familiar examples will be used to reinforce the understanding of the concept.

Both the way data are processed in information systems and the way we develop information systems have many of their roots in the general concepts of systems. In the last two sections of this chapter we will relate general systems concepts to these two very practical concerns.

Why Study Systems?

In education, economic savings can be realized if students master abstract material that has broad potential application. For example, mathematics is studied throughout primary and secondary schools and in the early years of college. Indeed, most students at one time or another are frustrated studying mathematics because of the abstract concepts they are required to master. Math teachers are very familiar with the cry, "Where am I ever going to use this?" However, these skills serve as a basis for study in engineering, agriculture, science, and business.

Most business colleges are organized along the functional lines of finance, marketing, management, management science, information systems, and accounting. Such organizational structures result in specialization and also condition student expectations. Often business students expect material in a business course to increase their ability to address specific business problems in one of these specialties. Therefore, knowledge that is highly transferable and consequently abstract is sometimes viewed unfavorably by students because they fail to see its immediate application in their area of specialization. Basic systems concepts are also abstract in nature. But they are fundamental to understanding how computer information systems are developed and managed.

Systems and **system analysis** are, respectively, a philosophy and methodology for viewing complex wholes at a manageable level of abstraction. It should certainly not be hard to convince someone that the information system of a multinational corporation is a complex entity. Where do we begin to analyze such a system? We may be so overwhelmed with detail that we see the system as being too complex to analyze.

System analysis is a method of dealing with complex systems. By moving to a level of abstraction that contains manageable detail, we can identify and specify alternatives for the design and modification of a system. Assume that the decision process of a student electing to take a course in information systems is to be charted on a flow diagram. Figure 4–1 is a possible representation of the process.

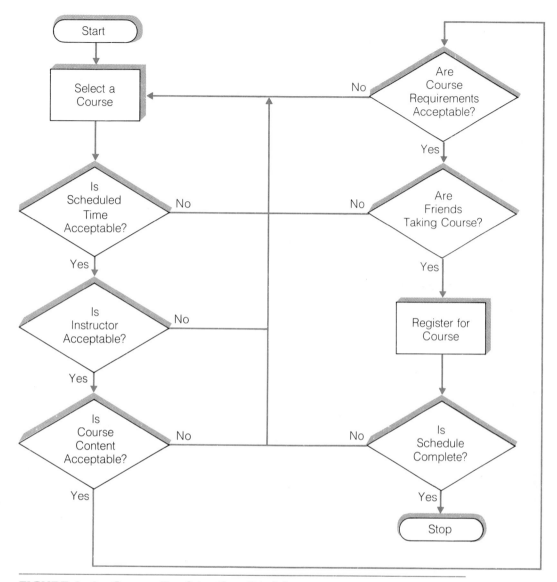

FIGURE 4–1 Course-Registration Decision

This diagram is called a flowchart. It is a tool often used to design and document the steps that a computer program must perform. As you can see, it can also be used to document procedures that are not performed on the computer.

Note that the diagram includes nothing about the mental processes the student employs in making the decision. Even if it were possible to incorporate all that detail, a diagram as large as this book might be needed. A reasonable level of abstraction has been identified; thus the diagram is a workable representation of the decision process. This approach is the basis of system analysis. In addition, educational economy can be realized because the same method can be used to represent and analyze all types of systems.

Another reason for studying systems is that many of their characteristics are similar, and the strategies for analyzing and improving them are therefore similar. The systems approach is used to determine why an automobile is not operating properly. It can also be employed on an information system. In addition, when we begin to view complex phenomena as systems, we can draw analogies between systems that initially might seem unrelated. For example, consider the common characteristics of airline-reservation and course-registration systems.

For these reasons and others that will become evident as the material is mastered, this chapter contains a discussion of systems in an abstract form. Examples are used throughout the presentation so you will be able to see how it is related to business.

Systems

What Is a System?

In the abstract, a system is defined as a set of interacting components that operate within a boundary for some purpose. The boundary filters the types and rates of input and output flows between the system and its environment. The specification of the boundary defines both the system and the environment of the system.

Figure 4-2 provides an overview of a system. The essential concept you should learn here is that a system accepts inputs from its environment and transforms them into outputs which are discharged back into the environment. The items in this figure will be further discussed later in the chapter.

Within the confines of this definition it is possible to conceive of a system within a system. For example, we could view a company as a system and the respective industry as a **suprasystem.** Alternatively, we could define the industry as a system and the company as a **subsystem.** Or we could call the industry a subsystem within the national economy, and the national economy a subsystem within the world economy.

We could view an accounting information system in the same manner. Payroll, accounts receivable, accounts payable, and inventory could be considered subsystems. This relationship is shown in Figure 4–3. Each of these subsystems could be called a system, and the accounting system could be a suprasystem, or a subsystem of the management information system. The fact that the level of abstraction can be adjusted by altering the boundary is one of the major advantages of the systems approach.

Components

Components of a system are units (subsystems) that act in combination with other units to modify the inputs in order to produce the outputs. Components within a system do not have to be homogeneous. For example, a police officer directing traffic at a congested intersection could be viewed as a component of a

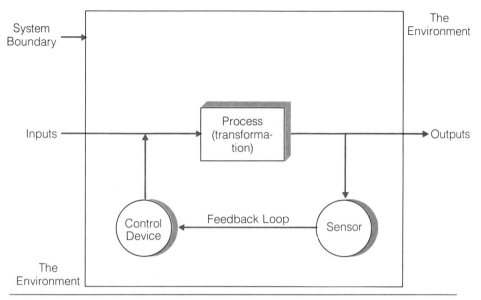

FIGURE 4–2 Overview of a System

These general system concepts provide a conceptual framework that will help you understand all types of systems.

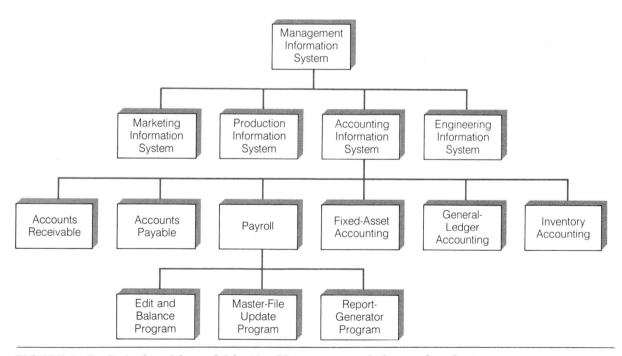

FIGURE 4–3 Relationships within the Management Information System

complex traffic-control system. Signals, signs, lines in the street, and the officer are all components of the system. Systems that control air-traffic and inventory-control systems have many nonhomogeneous components.

Boundary

The **boundary** is the area that separates one system from another. In information systems, the boundary should not be conceived of as a physical skin. It is a region through which inputs and outputs must pass during exchanges with the system's environment. Definition of the boundary of a system is one of the most important steps in systems analysis. C. West Churchman, a leading system analyst, has suggested two questions to be used in determining whether an object is within the boundary of a system.[1] First, can the system analyst do anything about the object in question? Second, is the object important to the objectives of the system? If the answer to both questions is yes, then the object is part of the system.

Assume that a university with a nationally ranked women's basketball team is located in a state with an extensive women's high-school basketball program. The university's basketball coach is considering whether the university should actively recruit and offer scholarships to female basketball players. The alternative is to allow the reputation of the team and the location of the university to be the main factors in attracting outstanding players.

If the objective is to maintain the national ranking of the team, then the answer to the second question is yes. Quality high-school players (the object) are important to the objectives of the system (the university's maintaining national ranking). If the basketball coach decides not to recruit, the answer to the first question is no, and the state high-school basketball program is part of the environment. The boundary of the university women's basketball program lies somewhere between the university and the high-school program. If, on the other hand, the coach decides to recruit, then the high-school program becomes part of the system to maintain an outstanding women's basketball program at the university. Then the boundary is outside the high-school program within the state.

In an accounts-receivable system, if the customer is defined as part of the environment, then the firm has concluded that it cannot influence the time in which the receivable will be paid. However, if the customer is defined as part of the system, then the firm has determined that it can influence the timing of the payment. Cash discounts, credit limits, interest charges, and other collection policies are actions that can be taken to influence the payment of receivables. A similar situation exists in an inventory-control system. If the supplier is considered part of the system, then delivery dates, quantities, and modes of transportation can be influenced by the firm. If the supplier is defined as part of the environment, then the firm cannot influence actions by the supplier.

Environment

The **environment** of a system is defined as anything outside the boundary of the system that influences the operation of the system and cannot be controlled by the analyst. Weather is certainly part of the environment of a vegetable garden. If

[1]C. West Churchman, *The Systems Approach* (New York: Dell Publishing, 1968), p. 36.

a greenhouse with a climate-control system is built over the garden, the boundary of the system has been changed. The environment of the system now includes those systems which supply gas, water, and electricity to the greenhouse.

Inputs

Inputs are the energies taken into the system; they are classified as either maintenance or signal. Maintenance inputs energize the system and make it ready to operate. Signal inputs are the energies to be processed to produce the outputs. Consider a coal-fired electrical generating plant. Maintenance inputs include the electricity necessary to energize the control systems, lubricants for the machinery, and the human input necessary to maintain the system. Signal inputs are the coal used to fire the system and the water that is transformed into steam to power the generators. Electricity and computer programs are the maintenance inputs into a computerized information system. Data are the raw material or signal input processed to produce output from the system.

Outputs

Outputs are the energies discharged from the system into the suprasystem. They are generally classified as products useful to the suprasystem or as waste. The product from the generating station is electric power. Waste includes the steam, smoke, heat, and ash that are discharged into the environment. Modifying some of the waste output so that it goes into a product is one means of improving systems performance. For example, if a greenhouse is built next to the power plant, some of the discharged steam can be used to heat the greenhouse. Industry has used this approach to systems improvement extensively because of the recent emphasis on pollution control. Heat generated by computers and lights is now captured and used for heating some office buildings. CRT screens and reports are examples of the products of an information system. Heat generated by a computer is one of the waste outputs of the system.

The Black-Box Concept

It is often impossible to describe the way a system effects a transformation. It may not be economical to describe a complex system. In some cases, the structure of the transformation may be unknown. There is a limit to the detail humans can practically comprehend and manage.

Under such circumstances, the analyst invokes the **black-box concept.** Rather than describing in detail how the system effects a transformation, the analyst defines the system in terms of inputs and outputs. The black-box concept is based on two assumptions. The analyst assumes that the relationship between the inputs and the outputs will remain stable. In other words, it is assumed that the internal operations of the black box will not change through time. In addition black boxes are assumed to be independent. For example, if a subsystem is described as a black box and it is linked to another black box, then we should be able to predict the output from the combination, given the input. The black-box concept makes it possible for the analyst to enter a hierarchy of systems at any level.

The medical profession uses the black-box concept in diagnosis. Assume you visit a doctor because you have stomach pain. First the doctor evaluates other outputs from the system by taking your temperature, blood pressure, pulse, and respiratory count. She then might evaluate the appearance of the system by examining your eyes, ears, mouth, and skin color. Then she would begin questioning you about your medical history and the inputs you have been placing in the system.

After completing the evaluation, the doctor most likely will suggest some changes in the inputs. She may suggest a change in diet and perhaps some medication. She then evaluates the outputs, especially the pain. If the pain continues, she will alter the inputs again. When the combination of inputs that eliminates the output of pain is found, you are pronounced cured.

In this situation, the doctor has assumed that your body is a black box. Only the inputs and outputs have been considered in your treatment. The situation would have to be very serious before the doctor would consider entering the black box to observe its internal condition. There is much risk involved in opening the black box because infection or other problems might result. Also, there is a considerable economic advantage realized in treating the system as a black box.

Now consider the information system of a large corporation. The system could be analyzed at a very *macro* level if such subsystems as marketing, inventory control, and manufacturing were viewed as black boxes. Another approach might be to look at the inventory-control system. Then the raw materials, work in process, finished goods, and supplies subsystems could be viewed as black boxes. At a more *micro* level, we could consider the supplies inventory-control system, in which case the subsystems for various types of supplies could be seen as black boxes. In this way, the analyst can move back and forth between a macro and micro description of the system. Eventually a point is reached where the black-box concept is invoked. Certainly, when considering an information system, we are not concerned with the molecular structure of the paper used in the system.

macro
Taking a broad, overall view.

micro
Taking a smaller, more detailed view.

Thinking About Information Systems 4–1

Sharon Smith is a new internal auditor for General Motors. During her recruitment she was told that General Motors has one of the most complex and effective cost-accounting systems in the world. She knows that she will be expected to perform audits on this cost-accounting system, and she is very concerned about her ability to understand the system. She feels that it is so large and complex that it will take years to master. Do you think the black-box concept would be of any use to Sharon?

Interface

Interface is a term frequently used in system analysis. The **interface** is the region between the boundaries of systems and also the medium for transporting the output from one system to the input of another system. It does not alter the output of the one system that is input to the other system.

For example, assume that an individual taxpayer and the Internal Revenue Service are systems. The United States Postal Service is then the interface between

PC USER TIP

Data Transfer Between Programs

Data files can be stored in a number of different formats by different application software. Usually there needs to be some type of file conversion in order for two software packages to share or interchange the same data. The producers of application software realize that there is a demand for these conversions and often provide utility programs to perform them. Such utility programs allow data interchange between complimentary software (such as a spreadsheet and data base). They can also provide a way to transfer data files and program files from competing software. Thus, an investment in previously developed applications by the consumer does not become a barrier to upgrading or switching application software.

Lotus 1-2-3 is an application software package that provides for a number of file conversions. To access this feature on Lotus, select the TRANSLATE option on the Lotus Access System Menu. Within the TRANSLATE menu you will be given the following choices:

```
VC to WKS        Translate Visicalc. VC file to LOTUS
                 worksheet file

DIF to .WKS      Translate .DIF data file to LOTUS
                 worksheet file

WKS to DIF       Translate LOTUS worksheet file
                 to .DIF data file

DBF to WKS       Translate dBASE II data file to
                 LOTUS worksheet file

WKS to DBF       Translate LOTUS worksheet file
                 to dBASE II data file

QUIT             Return to LOTUS access system
```

Choosing the .DBF to .WKS option, for instance, will create a worksheet file from a dBASE II data-base file. For each field in the data-base file, a worksheet column will be used. At the top of the column will be placed the field name that you selected when the dBASE II file was created. The column width will be automatically adjusted to equal the field width as defined in the dBASE II data-base file structure. The data themselves will be transferred to the worksheet file, one worksheet row for every data-base record. Character fields will show up as worksheet labels and numeric fields will be translated as worksheet values. This conversion will allow a user to make graphs and perform other functions that are not available in dBASE II. For more information on how to use the LOTUS 1-2-3 TRANSLATE feature, consult your LOTUS 1-2-3 manual or enter the TRANSLATE option from the LOTUS access system and then press the [F1] key for help.

There are a great number of transfer programs available, so before you retype a lot of data in order to move them from one package to another, check out the possibilities of having the transfer done automatically. In some cases no conversion will even be necessary.

the two systems. When two people are engaged in a conversation, air is the interface that transports the sound between them. The interface between two computer systems can be a telephone line or a microwave transmission system.

Feedback

To comprehend how systems survive and adapt to their environment, we must understand the concept of feedback. **Feedback** is a process by which the output of a system is measured against a standard, and any difference is corrected by altering the input. A system with and without a feedback loop is shown in Figure 4–4.

Consider a traffic light that is operated by a timer. Every ninety seconds the light changes, and the direction of traffic through the intersection is altered. Signals of this type often cause traffic jams because they stop traffic on a heavily traveled street when there are no vehicles on the cross street. This is an example of a system without feedback. The performance of such a system could be improved if sensors in the surface of the street were installed. The sensors would indicate when a vehicle was waiting at the intersection. This feedback loop eliminates the problem of the signal cycling when there are no vehicles in the cross street.

Incorporating a memory into the feedback loop also improves system performance. For example, the traffic light's feedback loop could contain a memory that would operate the light at different sequences at various times of the day.

The concept of feedback is very important in an information system. Output from this system is used in decision making. If the output is not relevant to the decisions, then the system is of little use to management. Therefore, it is important that a feedback loop be incorporated into the system to determine the relevance of the output to the decision environment.

standard cost
The amount per unit that an item should cost.

An example of a feedback loop in an information system is the use of *standard costs* in a purchasing subsystem. The signal inputs into the system are the quantities purchased, specifications, identification codes, and actual purchase prices. In the feedback loop, the standard and actual costs for the purchased items are compared. This information can then be forwarded to the purchasing manager, who can take the necessary steps to ensure that the future-purchase costs do not deviate significantly from the standard costs.

In this example, if the standard costs are out of date, the feedback information will be irrelevant in terms of identifying inefficiencies in the purchasing operation. Therefore, one of the necessary maintenance inputs of the system is adjustment of the standard costs in order to keep them current.

Variety and Control

Variety refers to the various deviations from the desired and expected outputs that a system can produce. When these deviations occur the system is out of control. **Control** refers to the exercise of countermeasures to regulate a system so that it produces the desired outputs.

Consider a basketball team that consists of players who never miss a shot, make a bad pass, or commit a foul. It is therefore impossible for this team to lose a game. It might be interesting to play against this team or watch it play once or twice. But interest will quickly decrease. Why watch a team that never loses or makes any mistakes during the game? Because of this team's overall efficiency, there is no variety in the winner of any contest.

If all activities were similar to those of the basketball team, life would be very boring. Indeed, we enjoy basketball and other contests because of the potential

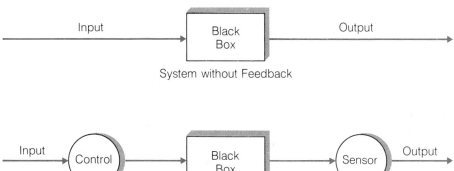

System without Feedback

System with Feedback

FIGURE 4–4 A System With and Without a Feedback Loop

Most systems one way or another have a feedback loop. Otherwise, they would deteriorate to the point where they would not provide the desired output. Imagine a factory that had no quality control!

variety in the outcomes. Even the greatest basketball players miss shots, commit fouls, and make bad passes.

Basketball can be viewed as a game with a generally accepted set of rules that are enforced by officials. The rules state that for a player to advance the ball, it must be passed or dribbled. Body contact is limited, and a defensive player must follow certain rules when guarding an offensive player. For each violation of the rules there is a penalty. When a player walks with the ball, the team loses possession. If one player blocks another, the player is charged with a foul. The offended player can shoot a foul shot, or the team can gain possession of the ball. There is a limit to the number of fouls a player can be charged with before disqualification. For every variety of infraction of the basketball rules, the referees have a countermeasure. This way they can control the game to ensure that in their judgment it is played according to the rules. This is an example of a law developed by Ross Ashby that relates to the control of systems. **Ashby's law of requisite variety** states that to control a system there must be available a number of countermeasures equal to the variety displayed by the output of the system.[2]

For example, if a basketball player commits a foul in getting the ball, and there is no countermeasure (penalty) available to the referee to enforce the rule, the game is out of control. The player can continue to violate the rule. With a countermeasure, the referee can penalize the offending player and control the game.

In the real world, we often develop countermeasures only for those events which have a high probability of occurring. While reading this material, you prob-

[2]H. R. Ashby, *Introduction to Cybernetics* (New York: John Wiley, 1963).

ably do not have a countermeasure for the sudden collapse of the roof of your building. By the same token, you will not count the words in this chapter because you assign an extremely low probability to your instructor asking how many it contains. Indeed, this is how individuals learn to control their environment. Without this filtering process, we could not cope with the variety in our environment.

There are several consequences of the law of requisite variety in dealing with systems. Two basic strategies are available to gain control of a system—decreasing the variety of outputs from the system or increasing the number of counter-measures. When large systems that exhibit a great variety of outputs are being dealt with, Ashby's law gives the analyst a sense of proportion. It may not be feasible for the analyst to obtain the necessary number of countermeasures to gain control over a system. In this situation, the analyst seeks countermeasures for events that have a high probability of occurring or that will produce a large expected loss.

In an inventory-control system, procedures accounting for gold used in a pro-duction process are different from those accounting for metal fasteners with a unit cost of one cent. In a credit-card system, different procedures are employed in evaluating available credit, depending on the amount of purchase. Consider your experience when you purchase an appliance or a piece of jewelry compared with when you purchase a candy bar.

Thinking About Information Systems 4–2

Ruth Kowalski is in a MBA program and is also working as a manager of the product-development department of the Southern Corporation. Currently she is enrolled in a MIS course and has covered the concepts of variety and control. She is particularly interested in these concepts and thinks they make a lot of sense. In fact, she feels she can apply them immediately to her job. She plans to look upon her job as the management of a system. In fact, she feels that she can anticipate most of the variety that will occur within her department. With predesigned controls she believes she will be able to guide the department toward her objectives. Ruth is convinced that this will be her basic philo-sophical approach to management. Do you think that the concepts of variety and control can be the basic underlying theory upon which a manager builds his or her approach to management?

The Steps in Data Processing

Earlier in the book we learned that a computer system has four basic components: input, process, storage, and output. Notice that these components are similar to the components of systems in general that we have covered in this chapter. They also relate directly to the basic steps in data processing, as shown in Figure 4–5. Several data-processing operations occur within each of these steps.

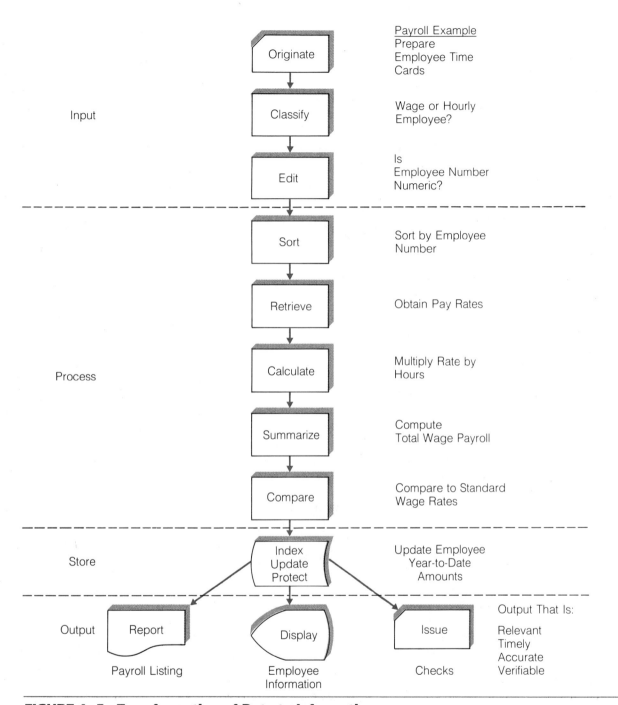

FIGURE 4–5 Transformation of Data to Information

In an information system there are several stages within the input, process, and output steps. An information system is a system because it has inputs, processes, and outputs. With the addition of the storage unit, it has the same components as a computer system, which were covered in chapter 1.

Input

Originate   The occurrence of a business event or transaction often results in the **origination** of data which are input to a data-processing system. For example, your purchase of an airline ticket (the event) causes the origination of data which are input to the airline's reservation system.

Classify   The **classification** of input data is the identification of those data with a certain category. For example, your airline-reservation input data would be classified when the reservation agent identified your flight number and the category of seat you were reserving—either first class or coach.

Edit   Data are **edited** upon input so that errors in the data can be detected. Editing may also occur during the other data-processing steps, but most of it is done at the input stage. There are many different ways to edit data, and a well-designed data-processing system will edit data for all the possible errors that might occur. Upon detection of an error, the individual who is performing the input is given the opportunity to correct the error.

Process

The data-processing operations performed within the process step include sorting, calculating, summarizing, comparing, and retrieving.

key
Within a data record, one or more characters that contains information about the record, including its identification. For example, in a payroll record the record key is usually the social-security number. The social-security number identifies a record as being different from all other records in the payroll file.

Sort   **Sorting** is the arranging of data in some order. Usually it involves the arrangement of a file of records according to *keys,* which are used as a basis for determining the sequence of the records. For example, sorting may be used to arrange the records of a personnel file into alphabetical sequence by using the employee names as sort keys.

Calculate   **Calculation** includes all the standard arithmetic calculations such as add, subtract, multiply, and divide.

Summarize   To **summarize** is to aggregate data into totals or condensations that are more meaningful than the unsummarized data. Therefore, summarization in a data-processing context is usually the addition of arithmetic data into meaningful totals.

Compare   **Comparison** is the process of examining two pieces of information to determine whether they are equal, not equal, or whether one is greater than the other. This is often called logical comparison.

Retrieve   The **retrieval** of information is its movement from secondary storage to the central processing unit so that other processing operations can be performed.

Store

The **storage** step in data processing includes three operations: protect, index, and update. Some people might put the retrieval operation (just discussed) under the store step, since a large part of retrieval is performed by the storage unit in a computer system.

Protect   The **protecting** of stored data is the safeguarding of data from unauthorized erasure, modification, or usage. Protection (or as it is often called, "control") of data systems is becoming a very important area in data processing since such a large amount of sensitive and valuable information is now stored in computer systems.

Index   **Indexing** is the creation and maintenance of pointers and catalogs which indicate the physical storage location of a particular piece of information. Therefore, indexes are often used to find the storage location of a piece of information in a retrieval process. These indexes are the equivalent of a card catalog in a library.

Update   Finally, the **update** operation is the adding, deleting, and changing of stored data in order to reflect new events. For example, when an employee wage rate is increased, the payroll file is updated to reflect the new pay rate.

Output

The output step includes the operation of reporting, displaying, and issuing.

Report   To **report** is to print management information on a hard-copy medium, usually paper.

PC USER TIP   Word-Processing Accessories

To accompany the broad range of word-processing packages on the market, manufacturers have developed a range of accessories to assist in the production of documents. Here are a few of these accessories:

1. Spelling Checker.* This is the most common type of accessory. They are designed to check each word in a document with a dictionary file. If the word is found in the dictionary file, it is assumed to be correct. If the word is not found, it is assumed to be incorrect and is reported to the user. Different products vary in speed, size of the dictionary, ability to add words to the dictionary, ability to "look up" words in the dictionary, sophistication of correcting misspelled words, and the degree of integration with the particular word-processing package. A spelling checker specifically developed for your word processor will provide the best integration, but many stand-alone spelling checkers offer advanced features not available in add-on packages.

2. Thesaurus. Several disk-based thesauruses are now available. These serve the same purpose as their paper counterparts but automate the process of finding synonyms for a word. The user selects the word that is to be looked up, then the program provides a list of synonyms (words with similar meaning) for the chosen word. Again, features such as size and degree of integration vary from product to product.

3. Grammar Checker. Perhaps the most sophisticated accessory is the grammar checker, which is still in early stages of development. Grammar checkers now available can detect such things as side-by-side occurrences of the same word, the use of trite phrases, and incorrect punctuation. Look for new accessories of this type as the power of artificial intelligence is tapped.

*For reviews of two spelling checkers see *PC Magazine,* "A Spelling Checker with a Mind of Its Own," Vol. 3, No. 20, pp. 260–66; and *InfoWorld,* "Review of The Speller," Vol. 6, No. 9, pp. 59–60.

Display A **display** contains similar or perhaps the same information as a report. However, the information appears on a CRT terminal instead of on paper. Most people refer to the information appearing on a CRT as a display rather than a report.

Issue To **issue** is to prepare output documents such as checks, purchase orders, or invoices which are necessary to originate or complete a transaction. In contrast to these documents, a report contains management information that is often summary in nature and is used in controlling the business operation. For example, a weekly listing that contains the total amount of purchase orders issued to various vendors would be a report, whereas the purchase orders themselves would be transaction documents that are issued by the computer.

Systems Theory and Information Systems

General systems theory which we have covered in this chapter is the theory that underlies information systems. It is a very good fit. When we cover system analysis in chapter 5, you will see that we use many of the concepts introduced in this chapter. To deal with complex systems we must use a methodology for breaking these systems into manageable subsystems. This is the basic approach of general systems theory and system analysis.

The information system itself is a subsystem of a firm. It is the subsystem that provides formal information for managing the firm, from the highest levels to the lowest levels of decision making.

In analyzing and designing an information system, an analyst directly uses many of the concepts introduced in this chapter. Drawing the boundary around a proposed information system helps the analyst isolate the problem with which he or she is dealing. The black-box concept is useful in areas where it is not necessary for the analyst to understand the transformation process that is going on. Many information systems, especially accounting-type information systems, are essentially feedback systems for management. These systems produce reports that summarize the results of the firm's operations and allow management to take corrective actions in the firm's inputs in order to change the future outputs. In designing an information system the analyst must constantly keep in mind the concept of variety and control. There are many ways that information systems can get out of control and not function properly. The analyst must anticipate these problems and design countermeasures in the system so as to bring it back in control. For example, an erroneous item number for a material in a manufacturing resources-planning system could cause the wrong material to be ordered, thereby causing the shutdown of the assembly line for a period of time. The system should be designed to detect erroneous item numbers and correct them prior to the ordering of the material.

In summary, it would be a mistake to conclude that the concepts of general systems theory are abstract and therefore not important to a business person. These concepts are the theoretical basis for many of the day-to-day actions taken by information-systems professionals. The usefulness of general systems theory is not limited to information systems. As stated earlier, systems and system analysis are a methodology of dealing with many different kinds of complex problems.

Jack Brand has recently begun work as a programmer/analyst for a large financial company. This week he is enrolled in a training program designed to acquaint new programmer/analysts with the company's methodology for developing computer information systems. The first half-day of the course was spent covering general systems concepts such as boundaries, inputs, outputs, and black boxes. During this part of the course Jack was puzzled about how such abstract concepts could ever be useful in developing new information-system applications or in maintaining existing ones. How would you explain the usefulness of general systems theory to Jack?

Thinking About Information Systems 4–3

Summing Up

☐ In education, economic savings can be realized as students master abstract material that has broad potential application.
☐ Systems and system analysis are a philosophy and methodology for viewing complex wholes at a manageable level of abstraction.
☐ A system is defined as a set of interacting components that operate within a boundary for some purpose.
☐ The boundary is the area that separates one system from another.
☐ The environment of a system is defined as anything outside the boundary of the system that influences the operation of the system and cannot be controlled by the analyst.
☐ Inputs are the energies taken into the system.
☐ Outputs are the energies discharged from the system into the suprasystem.
☐ With the black-box concept a system is defined in terms of inputs and outputs rather than in terms of the transformation that occurs.
☐ An interface is the region between the boundaries of systems, and also the medium for transporting the output from one system to the input of another system.
☐ Feedback is a process by which the output of the system is measured against a standard, and any difference is corrected by altering the input.
☐ Ashby's law of requisite variety states that to control a system there must be available a number of countermeasures equal to the variety displayed by the output of the system.
☐ The four basic steps in data processing are: input, process, storage, and output.
☐ The input operations are origination, classification, and editing.
☐ The processing operations are sorting, calculating, summarizing, comparing and retrieving.

□ The storage operations are protecting, indexing, and updating.
□ The output operations are reporting, displaying, and issuing.
□ General systems theory is the theoretical basis for many of the day-to-day actions taken by information-systems professionals.

Key Terms

systems	interface	compare
system analysis	feedback	retrieve
suprasystem	variety and control	storage
subsystem	Ashby's law of requisite variety	protect
components	originate	index
boundary	classify	update
environment	edit	report
inputs	sort	display
outputs	calculate	issue
black-box concept	summarize	

Self-Quiz

Completion Questions

1. A _____ is a set of interacting components that operate within a boundary for some purpose.
2. The _____ is the area that separates one system from another.
3. Inputs are classified as either maintenance or _____ .
4. _____ is a process by which the output of a system is measured against a standard, and any difference is corrected by altering the input.
5. Ashby's law of _____ _____ states that to control a system there must be available a number of countermeasures equal to the variety displayed by the output of the system.
6. Under the _____ concept, the system is defined in terms of inputs and outputs rather than in terms of how the system effects a transformation.
7. An accounting information system can be viewed as either a _____ of a payroll system or a _____ of the management information system.

8. The _____ of a system is defined as anything outside the boundary of the system.
9. The _____ is the region between the boundaries of systems and also the medium for transporting the output from one system to the input of another system.
10. The input step in data processing includes the operations of origination, classification, and _____ .

Multiple-Choice Questions

1. Which of the following is *not* a characteristic of a system?
   a. operates for some purpose
   b. has homogeneous components
   c. operates within a boundary
   d. has interacting components
   e. all of the above are characteristics
2. The black-box concept is based on the assumption(s) that:
   a. the relationship between the inputs and outputs is stable

b. black boxes are dependent on environments
c. the suprasystem is stable
d. all of the above

3. A medium for transporting the output of a system to the input of another is a (an):
   a. boundary
   b. countermeasure
   c. feedback
   d. interface
   e. none of the above

4. In order for an object to be part of the system, which of the following condition(s) should be satisfied?
   I. The system analyst can control the object.
   II. The object should be independent of other components of the system.
   III. The object should be important to the objectives of the system.
   a. I only
   b. I and II only
   c. I and III only
   d. I, II, and III
   e. none of the above

5. The two classifications of inputs are:
   a. energies and maintenance
   b. maintenance and waste
   c. maintenance and signal
   d. products and waste
   e. none of the above

6. To gain control of a system, two basic strategies are _____ the variety of outputs or _____ the number of countermeasures.
   a. decreasing: increasing
   b. increasing: decreasing
   c. increasing: increasing
   d. decreasing: decreasing

7. The black-box concept:
   a. is invoked by describing a system in terms of inputs and outputs, leaving the transformation process a black box.
   b. assumes that inputs and outputs will remain stable.
   c. assumes that the black box is independent.
   d. 1 and 2 only
   e. all of the above are true.

8. The environment of a system is anything outside the boundary of the system that:
   A. cannot influence the operation of the system.
   B. cannot be controlled by the analyst.
   a. Only A is true.
   b. Only B is true.
   c. Both A and B are true.
   d. Neither A nor B is true.

9. In a coal-fired electrical generating plant, an example of signal inputs includes:
   a. lubricants for the machinery
   b. human inputs
   c. electricity
   d. coal
   e. none of the above

10. Which of the following is a function of the process step of data processing?
    a. protect
    b. index
    c. retrieval
    d. update
    e. none of the above

Answers

Completion

1. system
2. boundary
3. signal
4. Feedback
5. requisite variety
6. black-box
7. suprasystem, subsystem
8. environment
9. interface
10. editing

Multiple Choice

1. b
2. a
3. d
4. c
5. c
6. a
7. e
8. b
9. d
10. c

BMW: PCs in the Fast Lane

By Daniel Ruby

People commonly talk about computers in terms borrowed from the automotive world. One company invites you to take its micro out for a test drive. Another cites the horsepower under the hood of its personal computer.

But at BMW of North America, which proudly refers to its products as "The Ultimate Driving Machines," few people would be tempted to call an IBM Personal Computer "the ultimate computing machine." A better analogy for the PCs cropping up in increasing numbers around the company's Montvale, NJ, headquarters might be one for the new, small pickup trucks—personal workhorses that get the job done.

Without an ostentatious display of style or performance, PCs are transforming dozens of business functions at BMW. From auto-industry-specific needs such as supporting dealers and tracking customer complaints, to standard business functions such as budgeting and personnel tracking, PCs are quietly adding an important measure of management efficiency.

Lean, But Not Mean

Like its cars, BMW's organizational structure is lean, sleek and functional. "New staffing gets much closer scrutiny than new equipment," said John Celenza, assistant controller. In office after office, some of the load that might be carried by a bigger staff is being shouldered by personal computers.

Such a move is appropriate for a company that carved its growing share of the luxury-car market from a difficult history dating back to World War I. Bayerische Motoren Werke AG was founded in 1917 to build aircraft engines. After the Treaty of Versailles prohibited Germany from producing aircraft, BMW began building first motorcycles and then automobiles.

Between the wars, the company prospered with its touring and sports cars. But by 1945, it was left with little more than its name and a demolished factory in Munich. Rebuilding was slow and painful, and it was not until 1952 that the first postwar vehicle was introduced. Throughout the 1950s, BMW's most

successful car was an egg-shaped three-wheeler powered by a motorcycle engine, a far cry from the performance-oriented luxury cars the company is known for today.

The Beginnings of Fine Cars

The ancestry of today's models can be traced to 1961, when the BMW 1500 was introduced. The car exemplified the combination of high performance and driver comfort in a functional body design that remains the hallmark of BMW cars more than two decades later.

The first BMWs came into this country in 1957, but it was not until 1966 that an independent distributor began to import them on a large scale. In 1975, the German company established a wholly owned American subsidiary, BMW of North America, to import and market the cars in the United States.

Today, the United States is BMW's second largest market and is two-fifths the size of the German market. The company expects to sell 65,000 cars here this year, ranging from its low-end 318i—if a car that sells for $16,400 can be called low end—to its status-conferring 633csi, which begins at $40,700.

While BMW of North America takes its cues from Munich, the American subsidiary is far ahead of the German parent when it comes to personal computers.

PCs made their first appearance at BMW of North America in 1982 when Tom Prisciantelli, a social worker turned computer expert who was then working as the MIS liaison in the service department, suggested supplying field service managers with portable computers.

In this plan, the field people would record information about their visits to dealerships on the micros, and then transmit the data back to the district and head offices.

To test the plan, Prisciantelli got evaluation machines from each of the manufacturers of portable personal computers. His intention was simply to identify the most suitable model for the field managers, but the scope of the project soon expanded. With 10 samples in house, a number of ambitious employees from various departments began using them for actual work. Inevitably, they got hooked.

"When we made our choice on a model and had to send the other loaners back, we found out that some of our test users had become dependent on them for actual business functions," Prisciantelli said.

At the same time, a parallel current toward PCs was flowing in the MIS department. For some time, MIS workers had planned to install an information center along the lines of the IBM model. Initially, it was envisioned as a minicomputer that would provide productivity tools for users.

This plan had been stalled for several years, but when new MIS Manager Bob Davidson joined the company last year, he steered the concept in a different direction.

"It was obvious that microcomputers were here to stay," Davidson said. "Unlike some MIS people in other companies who were defensive about micros, we decided to get out in front of the wave and lead it."

Davidson, Prisciantelli and Ken Barile, manager of systems programming and development, led the wave slowly and deliberately. By taking their time, they were assured that the microcomputer industry had matured sufficiently that certain products had become reliable standards.

They also bought some time before providing broad user access to corporate data on the mainframe. While they fully expect to provide such access, the MIS managers want to make sure that they have sufficient mainframe capacity and adequate security before opening the floodgates.

"We got involved at the right time and in the right way," Barile said.

In October 1983, a full-fledged Information Center was inaugurated with Prisciantelli as manager. Its first move was to reconsider the need for 30 Displaywriters the company had ordered. Of those, all but three were replaced with orders for IBM PCs.

"We saved thousands of dollars on each unit while giving people the ability to do much more than word processing," Prisciantelli said.

A year later, about 40 IBM PCs and Compaq Portables were installed at the headquarters in Montvale, and two more were connected at each of the six regional offices. "That total is going to expand considerably in this budget year," he said.

Besides Prisciantelli, the information center has two consultants. It maintains a room to provide training and evaluate products, puts out a newsletter and conducts user meetings.

No Roadblock

The information center also plays an active role in approving requests for new PCs. The justification procedure requires a review by the information center to determine whether the application is appropriate for PCs or if it should be handled another way. If the review suggests a PC, a test application is set up in the information center to verify the benefits. If that hurdle is met, Prisciantelli recommends a configuration and the user fills out a capital expenditure request to justify the cost.

The form must specify the benefits and possible alternative approaches to automation. In fact, though, no requests for machines have been denied by the budget department. "It is so easy to justify a micro because the opportunities for productivity savings are so great," Ken Barile said.

So far, Barile knows of no instances in which a worker circumvented the procedures in order to acquire nonstandard hardware or software.

"People only circumvent procedures when they inhibit them from getting their work done. But our information center is set up to be a service, not a roadblock," Barile said.

In carrying out that mandate, Prisciantelli embraces a populist philosophy. He sees micros as an instrument for creative thinking, and he urges all users to be experimental. By putting the tool in as many hands as possible, with a minimum of restrictions, the company will benefit from important, unforeseen applications, he said.

Another important rule he stresses is that the person in charge of a particular function design the application. Problems result when the responsibility to develop a system is delegated to someone who does not have an investment in it, he said.

Developing Applications

A corollary to that rule is that the information center should not develop any applications for users. Prisciantelli, however, has twice broken this rule himself.

"There were two applications that we took on when we started out because we wanted to show people the capabilities of the packages," he explained. "It was a way of gaining support for the info center."

The first was a system written in *dBASE II* to track and analyze all calls to BMW customer-relations offices in the six districts. By tracking the calls, the company can ensure that complaints are handled expeditiously and that problems are noticed and corrected quickly.

Before the advent of PCs, monthly reports were prepared in each district using dedicated word processors. These would be sent by facsimile machine to headquarters, where Frederick Peterson, national customer relations manager, would prepare a monthly summary. The whole process took as much as three days.

"There was a recognition that as the company grew, a more

sophisticated solution was needed," Peterson said.

"Giving our customers service helps assure that they will buy another BMW. Someone who invests $40,000 in a car expects perfection. We can't give perfection, but maybe we can make up for any problems he does have with efficient service."

The program runs on a PC at each regional office, logging information about every customer call. Statistics are compiled daily, and trends are identified that may suggest problems at a dealership.

At the end of the month, all the data is sent over modems to Peterson's office at company headquarters. Then he runs monthly reports on the consolidated data. Or he can pose ad hoc questions if he wants to pursue a hunch. "We can see the trends developing before they become crises," Peterson said.

For example, Peterson may note that several complaints concerning air conditioners have been received. From his PC, he can do a global search to isolate the part of the country from which the calls are originating. If so, he may be able to find out that the problem occurs under certain climatic conditions.

He then can go into the database a little deeper to find which dealers are getting the complaints. Then he can look at the training records from the particular dealers to find out if the mechanics from that shop had attended the air-conditioning course offered at the BMW technical school.

Under the old system, Peterson might have concluded that BMW has an air-conditioning problem, when, in fact, the company has a training problem.

"The system lets us pinpoint problems instead of taking wild guesses," Peterson said. "It is exciting for an auto company to be able to do that. It's not hit or miss anymore."

As pleased as Peterson and Prisciantelli are with the customer-contact system, it is only an interim solution. Since the customer data is used by different departments in the company, Peterson and Prisciantelli agree that the system should be on the mainframe.

When it was installed, the need for the system was urgent enough that the MIS managers consented to put the system on the PC. Barile and Davidson said the backlog in MIS would have delayed the project for more than two years.

In addition to customer service, Prisciantelli also wrote an applicant-tracking system for the personnel department.

Employment manager Debra DelGuidice said the company receives an average of 250 applications each week for positions ranging from entry level to senior management. Sometimes the total goes as high as 400.

The Dark Ages

Previously, the department kept a card file of the applicants. Each applicant's name and address had to be typed on the card and then again on the letter and envelope that would be sent in response.

"We were typing the same information over and over," DelGuidice said. "With the volume, we just couldn't handle it anymore and had fallen seriously behind in processing applications."

To reduce the backlog, the department ordered an IBM Displaywriter, but Prisciantelli recommended an IBM XT instead. Then he wrote a comprehensive tracking program in *dBASE II* to maintain a database of applicants. It also works in connection with form letters stored as *WordStar* files.

These letters are generated automatically after a decision has been reached about how to respond to a particular applicant. As a result of the program, it now takes half the time to get initial letters back to applicants. Also, the letters appear to be originals, DelGuidice said.

As with the customer-contact system, the personnel system has continued to evolve since Prisciantelli's first version. DelGuidice has added additional functions and revised other aspects of the database to match her needs more closely.

"The original design was based on what Debbie said she wanted to track," Prisciantelli said. "But the more you fool with any system, the more you see other issues."

For example, DelGuidice added a method of tracking personnel requisitions from the time a position opens until it is filled. "By tracking time to fill a position versus job description and location, we can determine what we need in terms of notice periods," she said.

"We do a lot of recruitment advertising in local newspapers around the country," DelGuidice said. "Before the applicant system was installed, we had no method to track the response to these ads so that we could determine how well a particular newspaper produced for us. The *dBASE* system has fields for the name of the newspaper and the

ad that ran. Now, every Friday, I produce a report from that data that I send to our recruitment advertising agency. As a result, we are staying away from certain newspapers, and have saved some money."

While the two departmental applications that Prisciantelli developed are database systems, the most common uses of PCs at BMW are for spreadsheet and graphic analysis of data.

Tom van Wort is considered the master of the spreadsheet in the finance department, where he serves as systems manager. "We have used Lotus 1-2-3 for everything we could think of and probably some stuff we shouldn't have," van Wort said. "We've put 85 percent of what used to be paper, manual spreadsheets up on Lotus at this point."

Van Wort said that Lotus models have cut the monthly closing time for the company books by as much as 2½ days. PCs also help in the way auto parts are carried on the books.

"When we receive parts from our parent company, they are activity in our general ledger, but we have to report them back to Germany according to when they were invoiced. We can enter the information once, and in a matter of minutes get two reports."

The Missing Link

One of the reports is the actual journal entry, from which the data is rekeyed on a mainframe terminal to be entered on the general ledger. Van Wort looks forward to the coming mainframe link to eliminate possible keying errors.

The major benefit, he says, is that he and his colleagues now can answer questions they would not

even have asked before. "It doesn't faze people anymore to take on large repetitive tasks, and that lets us get so much further down into the details in our analysis," he said.

As good as the spreadsheet is for analyzing data, it is not an ideal format for communicating information. For that purpose, graphic representation of spreadsheet data can have a tremendous impact, as was demonstrated when company executives presented their budget proposal to the German parent company this year. Partly as a result of graphs van Wort prepared using *Chart-Master,* the proposal sailed through without a hitch, Assistant Controller John Celenza said. Usually, cuts and other adjustments are made, he said.

"The visuals helped pull the presentation together. Charts promote group consensus in a way that raw data cannot," van Wort said.

Another user to take advantage of the analytic and graphic abilities of *1-2-3* is Corporate Treasurer Michael Solly. He used the program to analyze the details of a new venture, The BMW Credit Corp., which the company and General Electric Credit Corp. launched jointly at the end of last month.

The Credit Corp. is a captive finance company that provides financing for the sale and lease of BMWs. Using *1-2-3,* Solly analyzed the assumptions underlying the figures presented by GE. "Since we are such a lean organization, we don't have a big analytical group that we could put on the problem," Solly said.

Solly did the analysis himself. "It told us where we were going and was a tremendous aid in negotiating," he said.

Solly also has used *1-2-3* to develop an analytical routine to evaluate foreign-exchange investments. The model assists in the decision of whether to use forward contracts or options depending on changing exchange rates.

Praise the Strong Dollar

Exchange-rate options are a new type of instrument that allow a company to hedge its risk in the event of a dramatic shift in the exchange rate.

To judge the advantage of having an option to purchase foreign currency, as opposed to a contract to buy it, is difficult, Solly said.

"You can look at the numbers all day—I did for a lot of days—and not see the relationships," he said.

Solly's program works by laying out the differing financial impact of an option and a forward contract exercised at various strike prices.

"The advantage of this is that it is practically real-time decision making. To sift through all this information manually would take hours, and with these types of decisions, time is of the essence."

While PCs have made important inroads into many departments at BMW, most of the employees that Prisciantelli first sought to automate—the field service managers—still produce their dealership reports manually. Some in the eastern region, however, have gotten computers as part of a pilot project.

Meanwhile, Prisciantelli's original idea has expanded into a full-blown MIS plan to link hundreds of portable micros in the field to the corporate mainframe. All sales, parts and service field managers, the company representatives who serve as liasons with the BMW dealerships, would carry the portables to track information about the dealers' performance.

For example, when a service manager visited a dealer, he would enter information about the number of lifts, work stalls, technicians, hours of training and other factors into a *dBASE II* database. He also could make free-form comments. Then he would transmit this information to the region, where the data would be compiled and analyzed on a PC. In turn, the regional data would be uploaded to the corporate mainframe.

But the field communication system, still under development, recently suffered a blow when the maker of the portable computer that had been selected suddenly went out of business.

Of all the portables on the market, the Otrona 2001 had been tabbed because of its low weight, full-size cathode-ray display and synchronous data-link control communications compatibility. BMW had planned to lease about 70 machines, and possibly as many again for a second phase of the project.

"Now," Prisciantelli said, "we're shopping again."

Joseph Augello, the MIS project manager for the system, is hoping that a new "true portable" with a legible screen will arrive by the time the project is fully operational at the end of 1986.

Augello also is developing a related system for dealer communications. He plans to use this PC-based system to replace an existing arrangement that allows dealers to access BMW's mainframe from dumb terminals.

The system has two functions: to handle warranty transactions and to find vehicles according to specifications.

Captured Data

If a repair is made under warranty, the dealer keys the warranty information into the terminal.

At night, the mainframe captures the data and processes it. If the claim is accepted, the computer transmits a claim confirmation to the dealer the next day, and the amount is reimbursed by offsetting the dealer's parts account each month.

The vehicle-locator function lets the dealer search a mainframe database to locate a particular vehicle for a customer. If the desired model is available at another dealership in the district, the dealers make arrangements with each other for the car.

Of the more than 400 BMW dealers in the country, about 90 percent participate in the present system. A few do not participate, either because they say it is too expensive or because it is not compatible with other computer systems the dealer may have.

Since most BMW dealers also have one or more franchises from other car makers, they may have other computer systems. Many of them also have their own in-house systems for finance, accounting, parts ordering and inventory.

BMW's communications system is expensive because the dealer pays the on-line charges, which can be considerable. The total communications charge, which is billed back to the individual dealers, amounts to more than $40,000 a month. Also, the dealers depend completely on the performance of BMW's mainframe. If the system goes down or has slow response time, it inhibits the dealer or increases his communications cost.

A Money Saver

The new PC version of the system will be much less costly because the dealers will do the data entry and other work off-line, then use communications lines only when transmitting.

Augello said the system will be based on a new IBM communications environment called the Batch Communications Program, which permits remote data transmission at 9600 baud.

While a final decision has not been reached, Augello thinks that the program will use IBM PCs in each of the participating dealerships. Thus, the dealers will have access to the industry standard microcomputer for general uses when not using it for BMW business.

The menu-driven system will include many more functions than the present system, Augello said. In addition to warranty entry and vehicle locator, it will offer sales entry, back-order inquiry and electronic mail. Later, parts ordering and other functions will be added.

It will be developed in *dBASE II* because Augello's limited staff is more familiar with it than they are with C.

"We are looking to use *dB Compiler* [from WordTech Systems]," said Paul Marahrens, the systems analyst on the project. "Compiled *dBASE* programs run faster, and you don't have to have *dBASE* or the runtime version running on the PC for them to run."

"We will make *dBASE* available, however, for those dealers who have hacker potential," Prisciantelli said. "We would be happy if some of them designed add-on applications that we could share with other dealers."

"We expect to have a pilot going by the middle of January," Augello said.

When the full system is up and running, BMW will have completed one more big step toward incorporating personal computers into all levels of its operations.

Unlike its cars, BMW's PCs may not be the ultimate. But almost everybody can have one. And that, BMW is discovering, is a liberating factor that is paying substantial dividends.

Reprinted from *PC Week*, December 11, 1984 p. 57, copyright ©: 1984 Ziff-Davis Publishing Company.

DISCUSSION QUESTIONS

1. What is an information center?

2. Why should the person in charge of a particular function design the PC application?

3. The application case states that BMW's MIS backlog is two years. Is this typical of most firms?

4. Tom Prisciantelli stated "But the more you fool with any system, the more you see other issues." Do the requirements for information systems change often? If so, do changing requirements affect the methods and approaches we use in developing information systems?

5. How could the spreadsheet capability of Lotus 1-2-3 be useful to Corporate Treasurer Michael Solly in analyzing the details of a new venture, The BMW Credit Corp.?

6. How can a PC accept data entry offline and then later transmit data to the mainframe computer? How does this save communication costs?

PART TWO

Developing User Applications

Chapter 5

System Analysis

CHAPTER OUTLINE

PROLOGUE

About six months ago Tony, who owns and manages Tony's Pizza, purchased a microcomputer and software to provide information he needs to manage his three pizza restaurants. Shortly after contacting a computer salesperson, he purchased the hardware and software. He did not yet have a clear understanding of his information needs and how a computer would assist in meeting those needs. The computer salesperson reassured him by stating that "these microcomputers are so user-friendly and flexible that you will have no difficulty using it. Hundreds of thousands of small-business persons just like you are using them to greatly increase their profits. In today's competitive world you just can't afford to not own one." Tony has become very disillusioned with computers. He has even hired a part-time computer consultant to help him use the computer. Thus far, his computer has been of little practical use to him. How could Tony have avoided this waste of his time and money?

Introduction

Acquiring *application software,* whether you purchase it or develop your own, has become the most expensive aspect of information systems. The price of hardware has continued to decline because of technological advances. Unfortunately, software technology has not kept up with hardware advances. In fact, the cost of software continues to increase, primarily because software development is a labor-intensive process.

There have been, however, significant advances in the approaches to the development of application software. Chapters 5 through 7 will introduce you to them. These approaches have resulted in significant time and cost savings for many firms. Such businesses have avoided some of the perennial problems of application-software development, such as it being over-budget, and months and sometimes years late. There have been some real disasters in application development. Some systems do not produce the output that users want, some systems do not work at all, and some are out of date by the time they are operational.

If you, as a user, are to avoid these pitfalls, you need to be thoroughly familiar with the latest approaches to application-software development or purchase. You must be able to communicate with the system analyst who is responsible for designing and implementing the system. If a system fails, you as a user will lose, because it is your system that is being developed and you are ultimately responsible. This chapter explores the first major step in system development, systems analysis. First, we briefly discuss partitioning of systems upon which good system development is based. This is followed by a more detailed discussion of structured system analysis, an approach that has become quite popular in recent years.

Partitioning of Systems

As discussed in chapter 4, **system analysis** is a method for modeling and understanding complex systems. It is aimed at determining precisely what a new system must accomplish and how to accomplish it. If Tony or the computer salesperson had taken the time to determine Tony's information needs and how to accomplish them, his computer venture would have had a much better chance of success.

Perhaps the most important concept in systems theory that is used in the development of computer applications is the idea that any system can be *partitioned* into subsystems (or modules). Figure 5–1 illustrates a **hierarchical partitioning** of a management information system into leveled sets of subsystems. Notice that we have partitioned the accounting information system into its various subsystems and then the payroll system into three subsystems. If our system-development project is to modify the reports produced by the payroll system, then we have drawn a boundary around a module. The module that produces output will be our primary interest in the development process. This hierarchical partitioning is the key to structured analysis, design, and programming of computer applications.

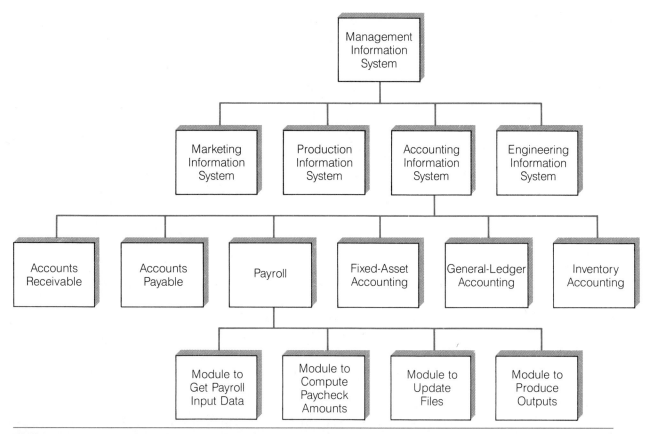

FIGURE 5–1 Partitioning of a System

In chapter 6 you will see that we call this chart a structure chart. It shows the hierarchical structure of a system.

We will use this concept in one form or another throughout the system-development process.

In fact, the term *structured* is closely related to hierarchical partitioning. The American Heritage Dictionary defines *structure* as the interrelation of parts, or the principal organization in a complex entity. In effect, we structure a system by hierarchically partitioning it. A system is **structured** if it is hierarchically partitioned into subsystems, and the subsystems' interfaces with one another are defined.

Structured System-Development Life Cycle

The essence of **structured system development** is threefold: (1) we partition complex systems into simple subsystems, (2) we analyze, design, and implement the **interfaces** that exist between subsystems, (3) we analyze, design, and implement the processes that go on within the subsystems. Think about these three

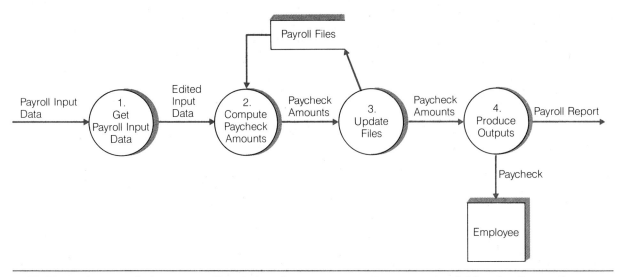

FIGURE 5–2   The Subsystems (Modules, Programs, or Processes) within the Payroll System

Shown here are the lowest-level modules of Figure 5–1 and the data flows or interfaces between those modules. We have also shown any files the modules use and external entities that interact with this system, in this case an employee who receives a paycheck.

steps; they are most important to your understanding how information systems are built. Refer to Figure 5–2. The arrows represent the interfaces or data flows between the subsystems, which are illustrated by circles. We analyze, design, and build both the subsystems and the interfaces between them. Then we combine them to produce a complete payroll system. By first dividing a complex system into understandable and manageable subsystems; then by designing, building, and testing each subsystem; and finally by combining them, we can produce very complex computer information systems.

Thinking About Information Systems 5–1

Sam Jones is vice president of marketing for Giles Development Corporation, a large developer of condominiums, apartments, and single-family homes. Sam has requested that system development commence work on a new marketing analysis system. This system will have the capability of tracking historical sales, following demographic trends, and projecting sales trends. The primary objective of the system is to provide Giles Development with information that will help it decide what type of housing unit to develop in the future and where are the best locations for the various types of units. System development has estimated that 40 percent of the effort in developing the system will be spent in the analysis phase. Sam is upset with this estimate. He feels that much less time should be spent on analysis and that system development should quickly get into the design and inplementation of the system. Do you agree or disagree with Sam's position?

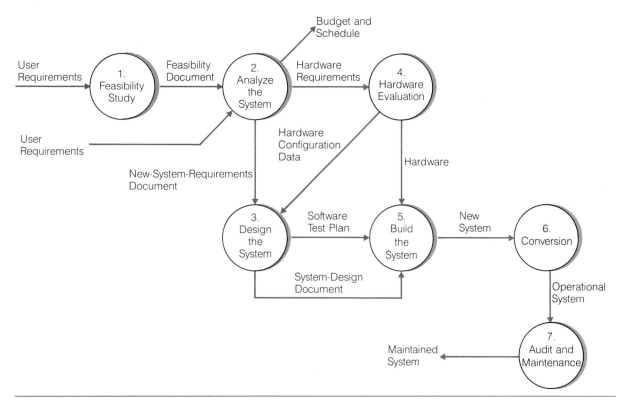

FIGURE 5–3 Structured System-Development Life Cycle

These steps should occur in any system development, whether it is a large complex system or one simple program.

Figure 5–3 illustrates the structured system-development life cycle. The **system-development life cycle** (**SDLC**) contains the steps we go through in building a computer information system. In this chapter we discuss the feasibility study and system analysis. Hardware evaluation is covered in Module D, and the remainder of the structured system-development life cycle is presented in chapter 6.

Angelo's Pizza

The structured system-development life cycle is much easier to understand than the older techniques that rely heavily on system and program flowcharts. However, concepts are always easier to learn if you can relate them to real-world cases. We will use the Angelo's Pizza case to illustrate the concepts presented in chapters 5 and 6.

Angelo Patti is the owner and manager of a large restaurant named Angelo's Pizza. Angelo is a very ambitious young man and he would like to have a chain

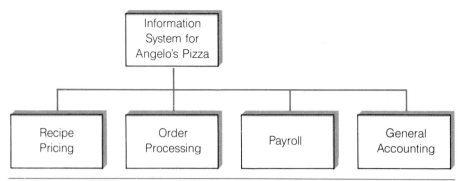

FIGURE 5–4 Information System for Angelo's Pizza

of Angelo's Pizza restaurants. He feels that computers could be useful in managing both his current restaurant and a chain of restaurants. Angelo has an old college buddy, Jose Wong, who established a computer consulting business after majoring in management information systems. Angelo hired Jose to help develop the computer information system. After a brief feasibility study, Jose recommended that Angelo start with an information system containing the four subsystems shown in Figure 5–4. To keep the illustrations simple, we will use only recipe pricing and order processing.

Feasibility Study

The **feasibility study** is an abbreviated version of the system-analysis phase. In fact, in this study the system analyst performs many of the same steps that will be performed in the system-analysis phase, but much less thoroughly. The primary purpose of the study is to identify the objectives of the user's proposed system, and to estimate whether or not the potential benefits of a new system justify the expense of a development project. The major inputs to the feasibility study are interviews and working documents from the users. The study produces a feasibility document which should contain the following:

1. project name
2. description of the problem
3. statement of the critical assumptions on which the feasibility document is based
4. statement of the performance requirements of the system
5. general description of the proposed system solution (this can be a new, modified, or existing system)
6. evaluation of the feasibility of the proposed system
7. possible alternative solutions

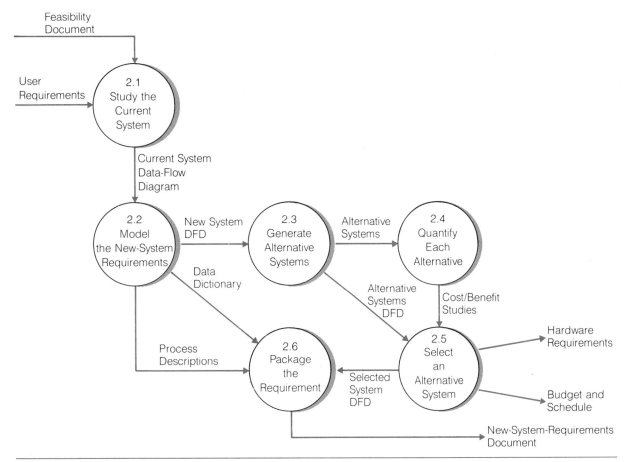

FIGURE 5–5 Structured System Analysis

System analysis has as its input the user requirements and feasibility documents. Its outputs include the hardware requirements, budget, and schedule for building the system and the new-system-requirements document.

Structured System Analysis

Figure 5–5 illustrates the phases within **structured system analysis.** You will note that this figure is a partitioning of process 2 in Figure 5–3. In fact, Figures 5–2, 5–3, and 5–5 are all **data-flow diagrams (DFDs).** Data-flow diagrams are the primary tool used in structured system development to graphically depict systems. You probably found that you could understand these figures without an explanation of data-flow diagrams. This is one of their advantages; they are easy to understand because they are not cluttered with a lot of technical symbols. Figure

Compute
Paycheck
Amounts

A process or data transformation:
A process that adds to, modifies,
or deletes data.

Employee

An external entity: A person,
organization, or system that is
outside the boundary of the system
being studied. An external entity
is an originator or receiver of
data processed by the system.

Payroll
Input
Data

A data flow: Data that flow into
or out of processes on a data-flow
diagram. Data flows are
sometimes called interfaces.

Payroll File

A data store: Any permanent
or temporary file of data.

FIGURE 5–6   Symbols Used in Data-Flow Diagrams

*Any information system, no matter how complex and large or how small and simple, can
be graphically represented by these symbols. They are beginning to be widely used by
systems analysts. Several programs use these symbols to draw data-flow diagrams with
computers. One program, DFD Draw from McDonald Douglas Automation Company, runs
on the IBM PC.*

5–6 illustrates the four symbols used in data-flow diagrams. Contrast the simplicity
of these DFD symbols with the **system flowchart** symbols shown in Figure 5–7.
Although system flowcharting with this large variety of symbols is still done, many
system professionals are using data-flow diagrams. You do not need the complex
symbols shown in Figure 5–7! Any information system, no matter how complex,
can be graphically depicted using the four symbols of data-flow diagrams. Only
three things happen within an information system:

1. data processing
2. data flows (input and output from processes)
3. data stores

In addition, we need the external-entity symbol to depict entities outside the
system that interact with it.

Note the numbering system used in data-flow diagrams. The fact that the first
digit of the numbers of the processes in Figure 5–5 is a *2* indicates that Figure
5–5 is a partitioning of the second process in Figure 5–3. We can carry this
partitioning to as many levels a necessary, creating **leveled data-flow diagrams.**
In practice it is rarely necessary to exceed five or six levels; they provide enough

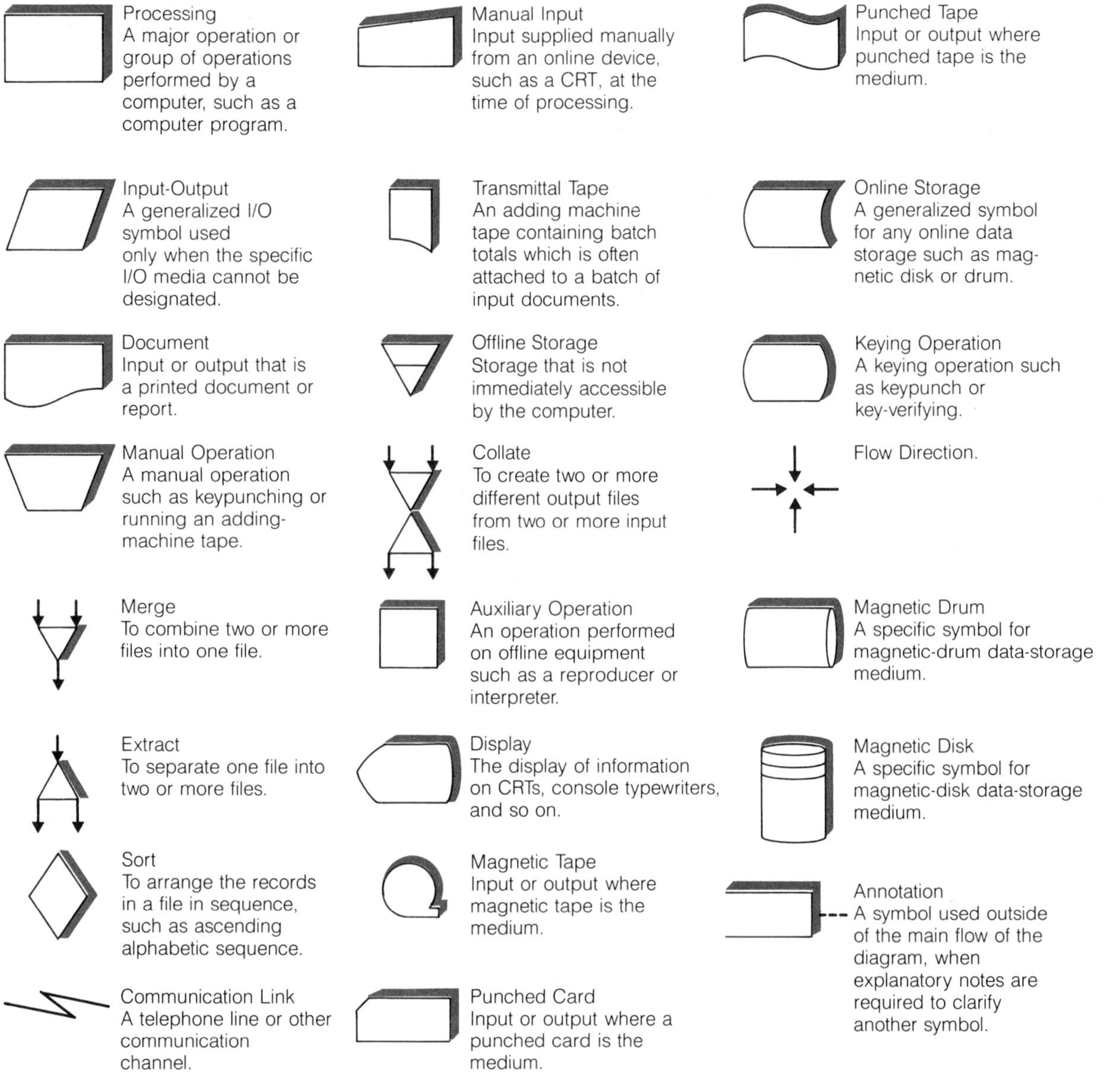

Processing
A major operation or group of operations performed by a computer, such as a computer program.

Manual Input
Input supplied manually from an online device, such as a CRT, at the time of processing.

Punched Tape
Input or output where punched tape is the medium.

Input-Output
A generalized I/O symbol used only when the specific I/O media cannot be designated.

Transmittal Tape
An adding machine tape containing batch totals which is often attached to a batch of input documents.

Online Storage
A generalized symbol for any online data storage such as magnetic disk or drum.

Document
Input or output that is a printed document or report.

Offline Storage
Storage that is not immediately accessible by the computer.

Keying Operation
A keying operation such as keypunch or key-verifying.

Manual Operation
A manual operation such as keypunching or running an adding-machine tape.

Collate
To create two or more different output files from two or more input files.

Flow Direction.

Merge
To combine two or more files into one file.

Auxiliary Operation
An operation performed on offline equipment such as a reproducer or interpreter.

Magnetic Drum
A specific symbol for magnetic-drum data-storage medium.

Extract
To separate one file into two or more files.

Display
The display of information on CRTs, console typewriters, and so on.

Magnetic Disk
A specific symbol for magnetic-disk data-storage medium.

Sort
To arrange the records in a file in sequence, such as ascending alphabetic sequence.

Magnetic Tape
Input or output where magnetic tape is the medium.

Annotation
A symbol used outside of the main flow of the diagram, when explanatory notes are required to clarify another symbol.

Communication Link
A telephone line or other communication channel.

Punched Card
Input or output where a punched card is the medium.

FIGURE 5–7 System-Flowchart Symbols

System flowcharts provide more information about how a system is physically implemented than do data-flow diagrams. For example, we could use the magnetic-disk symbol to indicate that a file is stored on magnetic disk, but this added complexity is totally unnecessary for good system analysis. Good system analysis focuses on what is done in an information system rather than how it is done.

detail to show what occurs within the most complex of systems. We will discuss data-flow diagrams in greater depth in the next section.

Study the Current System

The purpose of the first phase of systems analysis is to understand and document the user's current system. Usually, the user has a manual or a computer information system. Studying the system helps the analyst understand the user's information needs. Many of the processes performed by the current system will have to be performed by the new one also. The study relies on extensive interviews with user personnel, and frequent reviews with users regarding the documentation that the analyst is creating. These reviews are called *walkthroughs*. The primary documentation tool used is a leveled set of data-flow diagrams.

walkthrough
A step-by-step review of the documentation or other work produced by a system analyst or programmer.

Figure 5–8 and 5–9 are the DFDs that Jose drew for the current order-processing and recipe-pricing systems of Angelo's Pizza. Note that the emphasis of the data-flow diagrams is the flow of data.

Jose also decided to partition process 3 in Figure 5–8 in order to gain a better understanding of that process. This lower-level DFD is shown in Figure 5–10.

Model the New-System Requirements

By now the analyst should be thoroughly familiar with the current system. Our goal in defining the new-system requirements is to describe what has to be done, not how it will be done. Of course, the analyst will keep in mind some of the computer technology that could be used in the new system. For example, Jose may feel that an electronic spreadsheet could do Angelo's recipe pricing. But Jose is experienced enough in computer information systems to know that all the computer technology in the world will not help Angelo if he cannot define his information requirements.

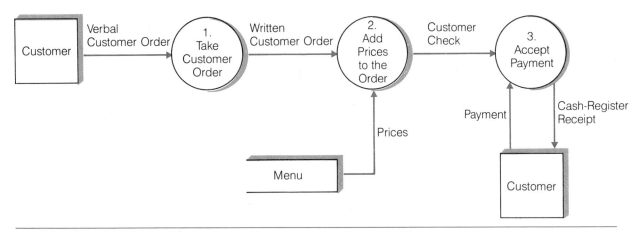

FIGURE 5–8   Current Order-Processing System, Angelo's Pizza

Notice that this data-flow diagram focuses on what is done rather than how it is done.

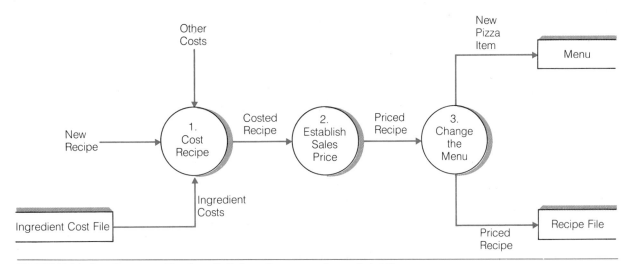

FIGURE 5–9   Current Recipe-Pricing System, Angelo's Pizza

Would you have to know anything about computer hardware to draw this data-flow diagram? Certainly not.

As the first step in defining the information requirements for Angelo's new system, Jose talked at length with Angelo about his needs, particularly about his business expansion plans. In summary, Angelo feels that quick, efficient customer service is important. Most pizza is cooked to the customer's order. Therefore, customers must wait for their orders. Angelo is sure that decreasing the wait time for an order would increase his competitive position. This is particularly true for lunchtime customers. Also, he would like to keep a name and address file on his customers, which would be used for mailing promotional material to them. He may even want to extend credit to selected customers.

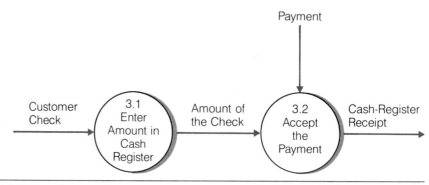

FIGURE 5–10   A Partitioning of Process 3 in Figure 5–8

Notice that the inputs and outputs here—customer check, payment, and cash-register receipt—are the same as those for process 3 in Figure 5–8.

After his discussions with Angelo, Jose believes that he can define a system that not only would provide better information, but would also improve Angelo's operations in processing customers' orders. In fact, he feels that the system will be so great a competitive tool that Angelo may want to rename the restaurant Angelo's Hi-Tech Pizza!

In defining the system requirements Jose will use data-flow diagrams, a data dictionary, and process descriptions to further define Angelo's information requirements. The **data dictionary** documents files and data flows. **Process** or **transform descriptions** document the internal workings of data processes.

physical implementation
The way a system is actually performed in the real world. Manual systems and automated systems, using computers, are different types of physical implementation.

Data-Flow Diagrams   Figures 5–11 and 5–12 are Jose's data-flow diagrams for Angelo's order-processing and recipe-pricing systems. Note that these DFDs do not differ substantially from those of the current systems shown in Figures 5–8 and 5–9. This is typical. Many of the basic information and operational needs are the same regardless of how a system is *physically implemented*.

Another most important point to understand about these two DFDs is that neither indicates how the system is to be physically implemented. Either system could be implemented many different ways on a computer. Or, they could even be performed manually! In fact, at this point it is not even important to think about how the systems will be physically implemented. Decisions about computer hardware are an unnecessary complication here. Angelo's information and operational requirements are the only important considerations. The points made in this paragraph are some of the most crucial to your future success in applying computer information systems. Most failures in computer information systems occur because users buy computer hardware before they have a clear understanding of their information needs. Never buy computer hardware without first knowing how it will help you in meeting your professional, business, or personal objectives.

Data Dictionary   A data dictionary contains information about and definitions of data used in a system. It gives you a single place to look up data definitions you do not understand. In addition, it may contain many other types of information and definitions, depending on the wishes of the analyst. For example, when con-

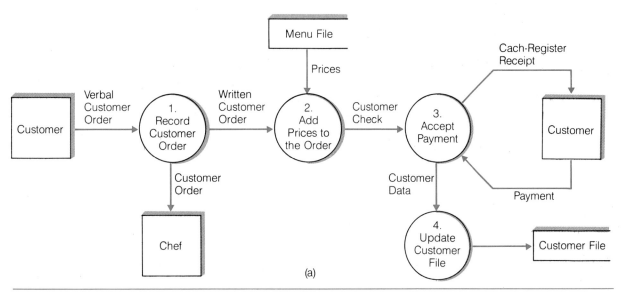

FIGURE 5–11 **New Order-Processing System, Angelo's Pizza**

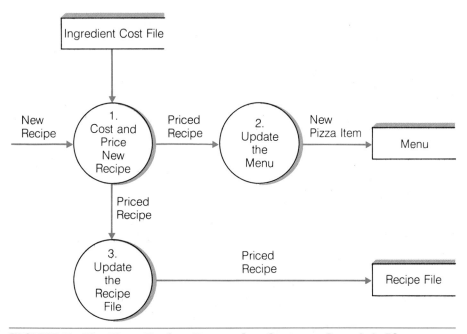

FIGURE 5–12 **New Recipe-Processing System, Angelo's Pizza**

sidering a particular data flow, the analyst may include information such as frequency, volume, affected users, security considerations, and implementation schedule.

For instance, Jose made an entry in his data dictionary that looked like this:

```
Customer_Check = Date + Table_Number + [Item_Ordered +
                      Item_Price]
          + Sales_Tax + Total_Amount
```

In other words, the data flow called "customer_check" consists of: date, table number, one or more items ordered with their item_price, as well as sales tax, and the total amount. The brackets indicate that there can be multiple items ordered and item prices.

Just as we have partitioned data-flow diagrams, we can also partition data flows. For example, Jose defined *date* in the data dictionary as

```
Date = Month + Day + Year
```

For our analysis to be complete, every data flow indicated on a leveled set of data-flow diagrams must have a definition entry in the data dictionary. Data dictionaries are also used to define files by specifying the data contained within each individual record.

Many firms use computer-automated data dictionaries. Such dictionaries are a very important part of large and complex information systems.

Process Descriptions   Even though we partition processes in leveled DFDs, at some point we cease to partition. At this most detailed level of the data-flow diagrams the processes are called **functional primitives.** But to be complete we still have to specify the data transformations that go on within these functional primitives. These specifications are called *process* (or *transform*) *descriptions*.

We will examine three ways to describe the data transformations that occur within functional primitives on data-flow diagrams. These are **structured English, decision tables,** and **decision trees.**

Structured English is plain English with a few restrictions. It is often also called pseudocode, because of its similarity to computer *program code.* In fact, the *syntax* of structured English is restricted to the same basic patterns as *structured programming.* Figure 5–13 illustrates the allowable structured-English patterns. When we discuss structured programming in the next chapter, we will use these same control patterns. Structured-English process descriptions are easy to convert to structured computer programs.

On one of the lower-level DFDs, not shown in the text, Jose had a process called "approve customer credit." The structured English that describes the internal workings of that process is shown in Figure 5–14.

Decision tables allow large numbers of conditions to be concisely documented. Figure 5–15 illustrates a decision table for the same customer credit approval that Jose defined with structured English in Figure 5–14. Decision tables are read from top to bottom. In the example, there are four sets of conditions that can occur. Looking at rule 1, we see that if the check is greater than fifty dollars and a bill is overdue by sixty-plus days, then Angelo refuses credit. The primary advantage

process descriptions
A description of the data transformations that occur within the most detailed processes on a data-flow diagram.

program code
The instructions used in a computer program.

syntax
The structure of expressions in a language.

structured programming
An approach to computer programming that restricts the sequence in which the statements are executed to four basic patterns: simple sequence, selection, loop, and case.

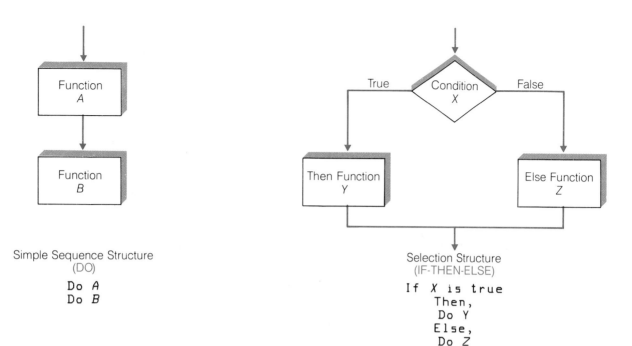

Simple Sequence Structure
(DO)

```
Do A
Do B
```

Selection Structure
(IF-THEN-ELSE)

```
If X is true
   Then,
      Do Y
   Else,
      Do Z
```

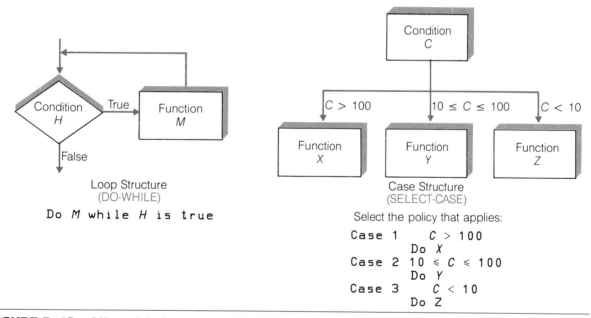

Loop Structure
(DO-WHILE)

```
Do M while H is true
```

Case Structure
(SELECT-CASE)

Select the policy that applies:

```
Case 1    C > 100
          Do X
Case 2 10 ≤ C ≤ 100
          Do Y
Case 3    C < 10
          Do Z
```

FIGURE 5–13 Allowable Structured-English Control Patterns

These control patterns are useful for describing processes on data-flow diagrams, but as we will see in chapter 6, they are also useful in writing computer programs.

```
IF the amount of the check exceeds $50,
    IF the customer has any bill more than 60 days overdue,
    THEN
        do not extend credit.
    ELSE (the customer has good credit),
        extend credit.
    ENDIF
ELSE (check is $50 or less),
    IF the customer has any bill more than 60 days overdue,
    THEN
        get manager's approval before extending credit.
    ELSE (the customer has good credit),
        extend credit.
    ENDIF
ENDIF
```

FIGURE 5–14   Structured English for Approval of Customer Credit, Angelo's Pizza

When structured-English process descriptions are put on a word processor, they can be modified and updated quickly for changes.

		Rules		
Conditions	*1*	*2*	*3*	*4*
1. Check > $50	Y	N	Y	N
2. Bill Overdue by 60+ days	Y	Y	N	N
Actions				
1. Extend Credit			Y	Y
2. Refuse Credit	Y			
3. Get Manager's Approval		Y		

FIGURE 5–15   Decision Table for Approval of Customer Credit, Angelo's Pizza

Although this decision table shows only one action for each rule, decision tables can easily document multiple actions for each rule.

of a decision table is that many different combinations of conditions and their appropriate actions can be documented in a compact form.

The credit-approval policy can also be documented with a decision-tree, as shown in Figure 5–16. The decision tree is read from left to right, starting at credit-approval policy. Each branch illustrates a condition that can occur. Combinations of conditions lead to the actions on the right. For example, if the check is greater than fifty dollars and the customer is in good standing, Angelo extends credit (action 2). As you can see, the decision tree is not as compact as a decision table, but most people find a decision tree easier to understand.

Generally, system analysts use structured English for transform descriptions because it is much easier to write program code based on it. Decision tables and decision trees are used in the few situations where there are large numbers of conditions and therefore several different actions that could occur based on the combinations of conditions.

In this phase of the analysis (modeling the new-system requirements), the analyst must have a good understanding of the information needs of the user. He or she develops a model of a system that will take data inputs and transform them into the information that the user needs. In doing this the analyst relies heavily on the original feasibility study and user interviews. The output of this phase is a leveled set of data-flow diagrams, process descriptions of functional primitives on the data-flow diagrams, and a data dictionary. These all serve to document the proposed new system.

Generate Alternative Systems

In this stage of structured system analysis, the analyst develops a number of configurations that will produce the required information. In fact, most managements expect analysts to propose several options.

Action

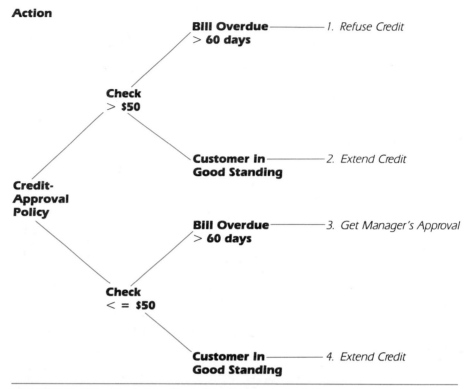

Check
> $50

Bill Overdue
> 60 days ———— *1. Refuse Credit*

Customer in
Good Standing ———— *2. Extend Credit*

Credit-
Approval
Policy

Bill Overdue
> 60 days ———— *3. Get Manager's Approval*

Check
< = $50

Customer in
Good Standing ———— *4. Extend Credit*

FIGURE 5–16   Decision Tree for Approval of Customer Credit, Angelo's Pizza

This figure shows two conditions at each node, but decision trees can have more than two conditions at each node.

In developing alternative systems, we are dealing with the how and what of the system, that is, its physical aspects. For each option, some parts of the system may be manual and others automated. In terms of automated parts, there may be several ways to apply the computer. The output of this phase will be several possible physical data-flow diagrams. One method for indicating the alternatives is to simply mark on copies of the new-system DFDs a proposed physical implementation of the system, as shown in Figure 5–17. For example, Jose is proposing that Angelo use Lotus 1-2-3 to cost and price new recipes.

Quantify Each Alternative

Each of the tentative new systems developed in the previous subphase have costs and benefits associated with it. To determine these costs and benefits, we must make a tentative selection of hardware and software, if it is to be purchased. This is only a very general selection. For example, we might decide that the automated system would be executed on a personal computer or minicomputer, or it might be an online system rather than a batch system. We do not want to lock ourselves into a certain set of hardware or software at this point.

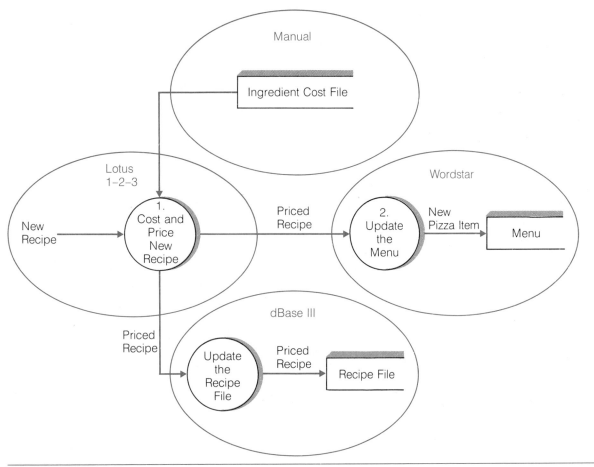

FIGURE 5–17 One Alternative for Implementing the New Recipe-Pricing System for Angelo's Pizza

Circles have been drawn around the various processes and files to show how they will be physically implemented.

Both costs and benefits can be classified as tangible or intangible.
Tangible costs include:

1. Maintenance and operating costs
2. Personnel costs
3. Training and orientation
4. Lease or purchase of new hardware and software
5. Site preparation
6. Design costs

Intangible costs include:

1. Negative effects on employee morale, resulting in decreased productivity
2. Negative effects on customers, resulting in decreased business
3. Decrease in control of the information system by operating management

4. Increased centralized control of the information system
5. Increased specialization in information processing
6. Increased potential cost for breakdowns or disaster when the information system becomes more centralized

Tangible benefits include:

1. Reduced maintenance and operating costs
2. Reduced personnel costs
3. Reduced investment in hardware and software
4. Reduced rental costs
5. Reduced space requirements
6. Reduced age of accounts receivable
7. Increased inventory turnover
8. Reduced investment in inventory

Intangible benefits include:

1. Freeing operating management from information-processing activities
2. Improved control over information-processing activities
3. Improved decision making
4. Increased emphasis on long-range planning
5. Improved employee morale

It is not always possible or necessary to quantify all these costs and benefits. But we should at least identify them if they exist.

Select an Alternative System

Based on the alternative systems the analyst has developed, and costs and benefits associated with each, management will make a decision on which option to implement. The data-flow diagrams of the new system are very important tools in this phase. Since they are easy to understand, the analyst can readily employ them in presenting the proposed systems to management.

Package the Requirements

The final output of the structured-analysis phase is integrated into a new-system-requirements document, consisting of:

1. an introduction containing the system's goals, objectives, and any background information that might be useful.
2. data-flow diagrams depicting the major partitioning of functions, and all the interfaces among the parts.
3. data dictionary documenting each of the interface data flows and data stores (that is, files).
4. tranform descriptions documenting the transformations that occur within each of the most detailed DFD processes through the use of structured English, decision tables, and/or decision trees.
5. input and output documents.
6. security, control, and performance requirements.

Advantages of Structured System Development

Most system analysts and users are beginning to see that the structured approach has significant advantages over other approaches to system development. Among these are:

1. Structured analysis requires a complete study of the user area, a study frequently omitted in other approaches.
2. Structured analysis requires that the analyst partition what he or she has specified. The tools of other approaches, system and program flowcharts, are not well suited for partitioning. As we have emphasized, this partitioning is the key to many of the advantages of the structured approach.
3. The structured system specification is very graphic and therefore easy to understand.
4. The other approaches tend to focus on the physical aspects of the system hardware, vendor, operating procedures, et cetera. By focusing on the logical aspects of data flows and data processes, the analyst can readily see the essential information flows and processes that are required in the new system.
5. The structured approach produces highly maintainable systems not only from the standpoint of the analysis phase, but, as we will see in the next chapter, also for design and programming purposes.
6. Structured development documentation is cumulative. The documentation developed in any phase builds on the preceding documentation, and serves as the basis for work in subsequent phases. For example, as we will see in the next chapter, the DFDs, process descriptions, and so on developed in the analysis phase will be used heavily in program design and coding.

A system's **maintainability** is the ease with which it can be changed when there is a change in requirements. In the real world, requirements change often. Maintainability problems are often responsible for the demise of most systems and thus are very important to consider. The structured approach produces maintainable systems primarily because of its partitioned or modular approach to systems design.

System Analysis and Application Development Without Programming

In chapter 1 we saw that many computer applications can be developed without programming. We will examine the methods for accomplishing this in chapter 7. However, at this point you may be wondering whether the system-analysis approaches discussed in this chapter are useful for application development without programming. The answer to this question is not clear-cut; it depends on the situation. But we can certainly give you some guidelines to use in deciding whether a structured system analysis is appropriate in a given situation:

1. Above all you must understand the inputs, data processes, and information outputs required of the system you are attempting to develop. If you are having difficulty understanding these, structured-system analysis will help you.
2. As systems become larger and more complex, the partitioning capabilities of structured system analysis become most useful.
3. If you plan to implement the system by writing program code in a language such as BASIC or COBOL, structured system analysis is more important. Changing program code is expensive. Structured system analysis helps to insure that you will not have to change your program code because you did not have a clear understanding of your information needs before writing the programs.
4. If you plan to implement the system with a flexible *fourth-generation language,* structured system analysis is less important and often not necessary. These fourth-generation languages, such as electronic spreadsheets and application generators, usually allow you to change a system much more quickly and with less expense that if it were programmed in a *third-generation language* such as BASIC or COBOL. Fourth-generation languages are tools to develop systems without programming. They often allow you to quickly develop an initial version of your system on a computer even when you have little understanding of your requirements. In effect, you can define your requirements and develop your system simultaneously in a trial-and-error fashion! This approach to developing systems is becoming so important that we will devote all of chapter 7 to it.

fourth-generation language
A flexible application development tool such as electronic spreadsheets, query languages, and application generators that allow you to develop applications by describing to the computer what you want rather than programming it in a how-to, step-by-step fashion.

third-generation language
A programming language such as FORTRAN, COBOL, PASCAL, or BASIC which requires you to instruct the computer in a procedural, step-by-step fashion.

Before we leave this topic, we should remember that the system-development life cycle is still a most useful tool, even with application development without programming. In one form or another the following steps must be performed in developing a complex system or a simple program:

1. Do a feasibility study
2. Analyze your information requirements
3. Design the system
4. Evaluate hardware (if new hardware is required)
5. Build and test the system
6. Convert to the new system
7. Maintain the system

It is a question of the degree to which these steps are done and how they are performed, not whether they are done. For example, if you are developing a simple electronic spreadsheet you should perform each of these steps. They may overlap and some, such as the feasibility study, can be done in your head. In this case, the analysis, design, building, and testing will occur simultaneously.

Most of the difficulties that users are now having in applying personal computers occur because they omit some or most of the steps in the SDLC. These steps have been developed and used over the years by computer-systems professionals. They are also useful when people want to develop their own applications.

Summing Up

□ Software development is the most expensive part of implementing a computerized system. A rational approach to system analysis can help to minimize this expense.

□ System analysis enables us to partition a complex system, and focus on the interactions between its parts.

□ The study of a large system is made possible through partitioning it into smaller, manageable parts.

□ Structured analysis begins with a detailed analysis of the current system. Data-flow diagrams are developed which depict the existing system.

□ A new system is designed, based on the review of the current system and new user requirements. The major tools used in this process are data-flow diagrams, data dictionaries, structured English, decision tables, and decision trees.

□ Several alternative ways to implement the system are generated. Since many different combinations may exist, it is necessary to compare the costs and benefits of the various options.

□ Once an alternative is selected, various system specifications are integrated into a complete package called the new-system-requirements document.

□ Structured analysis is superior to other approaches in many respects. Its primary advantage is that it leads to the creation of systems that are easier to understand and maintain.

☐ The system-development life cycle is useful even when applications are developed without programming. It is a question of the degree to which the steps in the SDLC are applied and how they are applied, rather than whether or not they will be applied.

Key Terms

system analysis
hierarchical partitioning
structured
structured system development
interface
system-development life cycle (SDLC)
feasibility study
structured system analysis
data-flow diagrams (DFDs)

system flowchart
leveled data-flow diagrams
data dictionary
process or transform descriptions
functional primitives
structured English
decision tables
decision trees
maintainability

Self-Quiz

Completion Questions

1. _____ is a method for modeling and understanding complex systems.
2. _____ partitioning is the key to structured analysis, design, and programming of computer applications.
3. The product of the feasibility study is a _____ document.
4. A _____ is the primary tool used in structured system development to graphically depict systems.
5. Reviews with users of the system-analysis documentation are often called _____ .
6. In data-flow diagrams, the _____ portrays a data flow.
7. A _____ contains information about and definitions of data used in a system.
8. Structured English is often called _____ , because of its similarity to program code.
9. Decision tables and decision trees are alternative tools for defining data processes, but _____ are easier for most people to understand.

10. A system's _____ is the ease with which it can be changed when there has been a change in requirements.

Multiple-Choice Questions

1. Which of the following is *not* a characteristic of structured system development?
   a. partitioning of systems into manageable levels of detail
   b. specification of the interfaces between modules
   c. the use of graphical tools, such as data-flow diagrams, to model systems
   d. specification of the data transformations within processes
   e. all of the above are characteristics
2. A feasibility document should contain all of the following except:
   a. project name
   b. problem descriptions
   c. feasible alternative solutions

d. data-flow diagrams

e. all of the above should be contained

3. In data-flow diagrams, an originator or receiver of data is usually designated by:

a. a square box

b. a circle

c. a rectangle

d. an arrow

e. none of the above

4. In system analysis we are most concerned with:

a. the computer hardware on which the system will be implemented

b. the information and operational requirements of the user

c. how the current system is implemented

d. the interfaces between subsystems

e. none of the above

5. Which of the following tools is not used in modeling the new system?

a. decision tables

b. data dictionary

c. data-flow diagrams

d. process descriptions

e. all of the above are used

6. The processes at the most detailed level of the data-flow diagrams are called:

a. functional primitives

b. transform descriptions

c. data flows

d. interfaces

e. none of the above

7. All of the following tools are used for process descriptions except:

a. data dictionaries

b. structured English

c. decision tables

d. pseudocode

e. all of the above are used

8. A: Decision trees are easier for most people to understand than decision tables.

B: Structured English is easier to convert to program code than regular narrative English.

a. Both A and B are true

b. Both A and B are false

c. Only A is true

d. Only B is true

9. In application development *without* programming, structured system analysis is:

a. not useful at all

b. of less use than in application development with programming

c. usually done after system design

d. not useful in helping you understand your information and operational needs

e. heavily used

10. Which of the following is not an advantage of the structured approach to system development?

a. The system specification is very graphic

b. The documentation is cumulative

c. The user area is studied thoroughly

d. It focuses on the physical aspects of the system

e. All of the above advantages

Answers

Completion	Multiple Choice
1. System analysis	1. e
2. Hierarchical	2. d
3. feasibility	3. a
4. data-flow diagram (DFD)	4. b
5. walkthroughs	5. e
6. arrow	6. a
7. data dictionary	7. a
8. pseudocode	8. a
9. decision trees	9. b
10. maintainability	10. d

Chapter 6

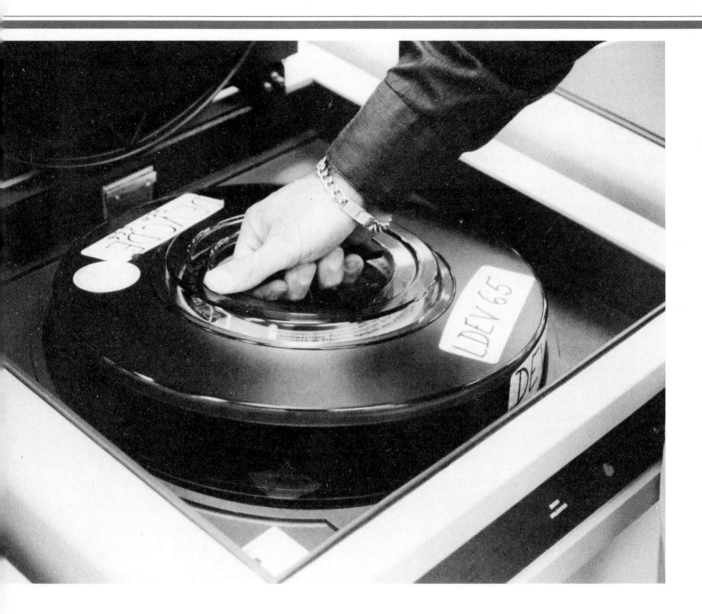

System Design and Implementation

CHAPTER OUTLINE

PROLOGUE

You have just been assigned to write your first computer program. Your professor has given you the program's requirements so you do not have to perform a system analysis to determine them. Where do you start? How do you structure your program? What tools can you use to design the program? What is the best way to test it to be sure it works? Read on.

Introduction

In the previous chapter we learned the techniques for structured-system analysis of a proposed system. The specifications (data-flow diagrams, process descriptions, and data dictionary) that were developed will be the primary inputs for the structured-design phase. In fact, we will find that designing a new system with these structured specifications is a relatively easy process. However, for simple programs or programs where the requirements are already known we will omit the analysis phase and begin with system design. In Figure 6–1 we have repeated the overview of the system-development life cycle so that you can readily see where design (process 3 in Figure 6–1) fits into the picture. This chapter will cover design and building of the new system, as well as conversion to the new system, and its audit and maintenance.

Design the System

Figure 6–2 is an overview of the structured-design phase. **Structured design** is the process of designing the computer programs that will be used in the system. The system design document produced by the structured-design phase is, in effect, a blueprint that the programmer follows in coding the programs. Also a plan for testing the programs is produced. There are only three activities within structured design. When we use structured analysis, there is relatively less work to be done in the design phase. In fact, a characteristic of structured analysis is that more work is done in planning the system and in the analysis phase than in the later stages of the system development cycle.

As we shall see, the primary advantages of structured design are that it produces computer programs (1) that are more easily maintained, (2) that can be tested *module* by module in a top-down fashion, and (3) that can be more easily understood. All of these advantages occur primarily because the program is broken down into logical modules during the structured-design phase. Usually the system analyst works on the design phase, although in some cases a system designer does it. Sometimes system designers are called programmer analysts since the process of designing the system requires both analyst and programmer skills.

module
A part of a computer program that is separate and identifiable. In a computer program one module can call (cause) another module to be executed. Synonym to *subroutine.*

Derive Structure Chart

The primary tool used in structured design is the structure chart. A **structure chart** is a graphic representation of the hierarchical relationships between modules within a program or system. To create a structure chart, we hierarchically partition into modules the tasks that a program must perform. Figure 6–3 shows a structure

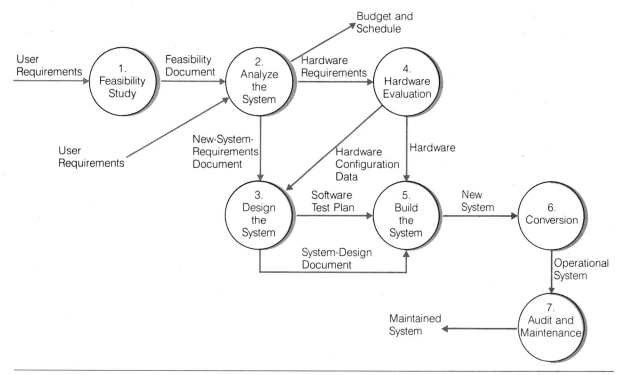

FIGURE 6–1   System-Development Life Cycle

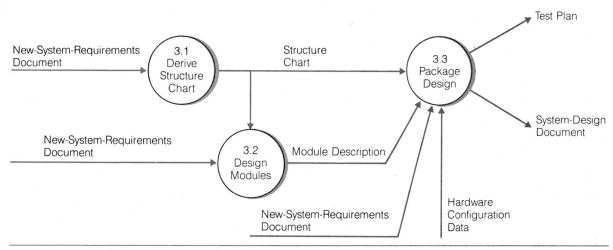

FIGURE 6–2   Overview of the Structured-Design Phase

The objective of this phase is to produce a blueprint (the system-design document) that will guide the building of the system.

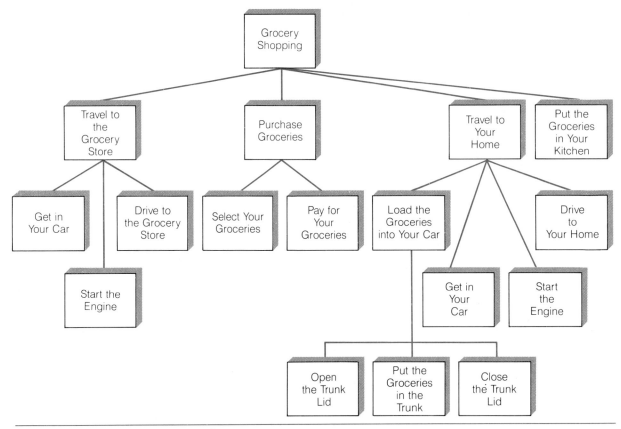

FIGURE 6–3 Structure Chart for Grocery Shopping

This is a hierarchical partitioning of the tasks that must be performed in shopping for groceries. Tasks performed by computers can be partitioned in similar ways.

chart that hierarchically partitions the tasks that must be done when you go grocery shopping.

An example of a structure chart used for an information system is shown in Figure 6–4. When a program is designed in a structured way, the approach is often called **top-down design.** The figure shows that the program is broken down into independent modules or *subroutines* from the top down. The module at the top is called a control module which, in Figure 6–4, is the accounts-receivable system. At the appropriate times, this module will call the three modules underneath to get the inputs from files, perform the processing, and write the outputs. We can continue subdividing modules into smaller parts, to simplify the program structure. Ideally, each module should perform a single function.

By now you probably have noticed that this structure chart resembles a data-flow diagram (DFD) in concept. Although the two do not look similar, a structure chart is an exercise in hierarchical partitioning just as a data-flow diagram is. In

subroutine
A separate, sequenced set of statements in a computer program. Synonym to *module.*

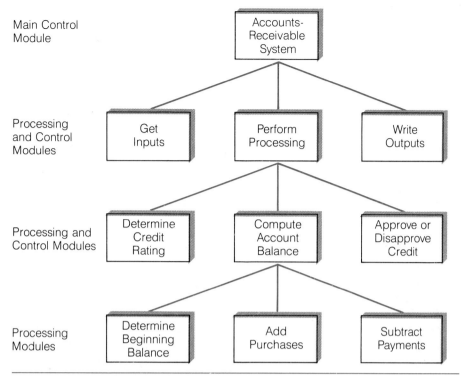

FIGURE 6–4 Structure Chart of an Accounts-Receivable System

We can make an analogy between a structure chart and the organization chart of a business. Top managers are at the top and those who do the detailed processing are at the bottom.

fact, all the advantages we talked about in relation to data-flow diagrams also apply to structure charts. There is a very strong correlation between structure charts and data-flow diagrams.

A data-flow diagram documents what has to be accomplished; it is a statement of information-processing requirements. A structure chart, on the other hand, documents how the requirements will be met in a computer program. The structure chart is the hierarchical partitioning of the programs we will write for the system.

Since there is a close relationship between DFDs and structure charts, we should be able to derive the structure chart directly from the DFD. In the next few paragraphs we will show how this is done. First, let's refine our knowledge of structured design.

As we have stated, a design is structured if it is made up of a hierarchy of modules. However, another requirement of structured design is that each of these modules or subroutines must have a single entry and a single exit back to its parent module. Each module should be as independent as possible of all other modules, except its parent. For example, in Figure 6–4 there should be no direct exit from the Determine Beginning Balance module to the Add Purchases module. Once the Determine Beginning Balance module has completed its processing, control of execution is passed back to the parent Compute Account Balance module.

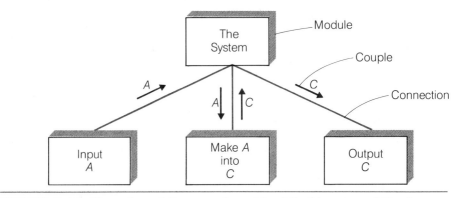

FIGURE 6–5 Notational Conventions Used in Structured Design

From there, control of execution can go back up to Perform Processing, or back down to any of the fourth-level modules. Control of execution passes along the connecting lines.

A third requirement of structured design is that within each module the code should be executed in a top-to-bottom fashion. There must not be any GO TO statements that cause the program statements to be executed in other than a top-to-bottom manner. Often called **go-to-less programming;** this requirement makes programs much easier to read. For example, how would you like to read a book that had a GO TO statement every few paragraphs, which caused you to go and reread previous paragraphs; then to go forward three pages and read something on that page; then to go back and finally transfer again to another page. You can see the problem with reading and understanding a program module that has GO TO statements. Program code with many GO TO statements is often referred to as **spaghetti code.**

There are also certain notational conventions used in structured design, as shown in Figure 6–5. By now you probably already recognize that the rectangular box is a module. A **module** is a bounded, named, and contiguous set of program statements often referred to as a **subroutine.** The line joining two modules is called a **connection.** This connection means that the upper module has the capability of *calling* the lower module. Finally, a couple is represented by a short arrow. A **couple** is a data item that moves from one module to another. For example, in the illustration the system sends the data item *A* to the module labeled Make *A* Into *C,* and then this module sends *C* back to the system.

Notice the general form of a structure chart. The input modules are on the left, processing modules in the middle, and output modules on the right.

Deriving structure charts from data-flow diagrams is straightforward. We will use Jose's DFD of the new order-processing system for Angelo's Pizza to illustrate how it is done (see Figure 6–6). First, we identify the central process in the DFD in Figure 6–6 (a). The **central process** is in the center of the DFD, therefore it is not involved with getting input or generating output. It is not important which process we choose; in fact, the choice can be arbitrary. In this case we can use number 2 as the central process. We make this process the top of the structure

call
To cause a module to begin execution.

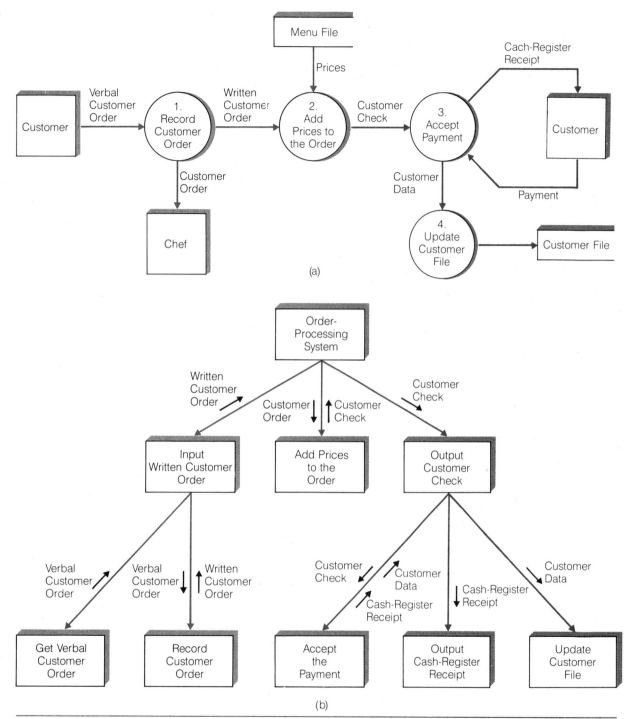

(a)

(b)

FIGURE 6-6   Deriving a Structure Chart for the New Order-Processing System for Ange-lo's Pizza

Each module on this chart will be a separate subroutine in a computer program.

chart, the system. Note that the top module in Figure 6–6 (b) has the same inputs and outputs as process number 2 in Figure 6–6 (a).

At the second level of the structure chart, we design one module for each input stream, one module for the central process, and one for each output stream. We use a similar approach for each of the succeeding lower levels. For example, in terms of the second-level module, Input Written Customer Order, there is one input stream which is Get Verbal Customer Order, and the transform of Recording the Customer Order. A **transform** is a process (or module) that changes data into another form or into new data. For example, the module Record Customer Order transforms a verbal customer order into a written customer order. Note that the couples represent the flow of data to and from the various modules.

Another pattern that you should notice in Figure 6–6 is that for each input process on the DFD, there is one two-part substructure (an input or get module and a transform module) on the structure chart. For each output process on the data-flow diagram, there is one two-or-more-part substructure (a transform module and one or more output modules) on the structure chart.

Let's look at one of the major advantages of deriving structure charts from DFDs. Refer back to Figure 6–6. Note that we have isolated the central part of the system, adding prices to the order, from the physical aspects of the input of the verbal customer order, the output of the cash-register receipt, and the update of the customer file. When changes occur in systems, the changes are very likely to affect inputs and outputs. We have hierarchically partitioned the system in such a way that these inputs and outputs are isolated. Therefore, it is very possible that we could make a change in this system by just changing one of these three isolated input or output modules. Remember that one of the primary advantages of the structured approach is the ease with which maintenance can be performed on the system. Many companies are now finding that they spend more money in maintaining existing systems than in designing and implementing new ones. Therefore, ease of maintenance is an extremely important consideration when a new system is being designed.

Our examination of structure charts in this chapter assumes that they are to be applied when we are designing computer programs. But they are also useful in application development without programming. When electronic spreadsheets or other fourth-generation languages are applied to complex problems, a structure chart can be used to organize and document the application. Unorganized and undocumented applications that are developed without programming are just as serious a problem as unorganized and undocumented programs.

In addition, we can implement some of the modules in a system by acquiring application software and others by coding programs. Recall Jose's plan (in Figure 5–17 of Chapter 5) to implement Angelo's recipe-pricing system by using an electronic spreadsheet for one process (module) within the system.

Design Modules

In this subphase of the structured-design phase, we design the internal processing within each module. If we did a good job with our structured-English transform description back in the analysis phase, and if the structure chart closely resembles the data-flow diagrams, then this subphase will be simple to accomplish. We can convert structured English to **pseudocode** by adding input and output statements as well as control-type statements, such as those which control processing when

pseudocode
English statements that look similar to computer program code. Since the statements are in English they are easier to read than program code.

PC USER TIP   Project-Management Software

There is an old management adage that says that any time you have more than five people working on a project you need at least one person to manage the project. In a similar vein, it has been suggested that any time you have more than twenty-five tasks you need the assistance of project-management software. For a complete list of conditions that indicate when project-management software would be useful, see *PC Magazine,* volume 3, number 21, pp. 109–117. Also see *PC World,* volume 2, number 10, pp. 240–50 for another discussion regarding this software. Many project-management packages are available for the PC. A few of the capabilities include:

1. Gannt chart. Gannt charts use a time line to display all the activities and tasks that must be accomplished in order to complete a project. However, there is no attempt to display the interrelationships between the tasks and activities.

2. CPM. CPM stands for the critical-path method. This project-scheduling method considers all the tasks and activities that must be accomplished in order to complete the project. The interrelationships between these tasks and activities are used to determine a critical path. Once the critical path is identified, those activities on the critical path are the focus of management, since those are the tasks which must be completed on a certain schedule in order for the project to be completed on time.

3. PERT. PERT stands for project evaluation and review technique. PERT is a project-scheduling method similar to CPM which produces not one estimate of project completion, but a pessimistic, best guess, and optimistic estimate.

If you become involved in a project consider project-management software as an aid in planning and controlling the project.

errors occur. The decision tables and decision trees developed in the analysis phase will also be useful in documenting the internal design of the modules.

Some designers prefer to use program flowcharts to document the internal design of modules (see Figure 6–7). If flowcharts are used they should be of a structured nature. In the previous chapter the allowable control patterns of structured English were introduced. The same control patterns are allowed when we do pseudocode or structured program flowcharts. These control patterns have been reproduced in Figure 6–8 to refresh your memory. When drawing a structured flowchart, we should use only these patterns. Note again that there is no reason to ever use a GO TO type of control pattern in structured programming.

Long and complex program flowcharts are often difficult to follow even when drawn in a structured manner. Therefore many designers are adopting the structured-English or pseudocode approach to documenting the processing that goes on within a module. Figure 6–9 shows a structured program flowchart, and the same procedure documented in pseudocode.

Package the Design

In packaging the design, we modify the design to fit the physical characteristics of the hardware and software configurations on which the system will be implemented. This physical environment can include such things as the program coding language, limitations of disk drives, and time restrictions. Thus far in the structured-design process we have attempted to produce an ideal design, independent of the physical environment in which it will be implemented. In packaging the design, we will modify it to fit the physical environment in such a way as to minimize deviation from the ideal design. We may have to do things like combine modules to produce a system which is efficient in terms of the machine resources (such as execution time and primary-storage usage) that it uses. However, in our pursuit of efficiency, we do not want to produce a system that compromises the modularity, and therefore produce a system that is difficult to modify.

Some analysts even go as far as to say that regardless of the physical environment, we should first implement the system based on the ideal design, developed back in the design-modules phase. Then, after the system is working, we can worry about modifying the system to improve efficiency. As Ed Yourdon states, "It is easier to make a working system efficient than to make an efficient system work."

This approach of implementing the ideal structured system is likely to become more widespread in the future. As hardware prices continue to decline, the efficiency at which a system executes is becoming less important. The human labor required to maintain and modify complex, nonstructured systems is a much more important consideration than how efficiently the system executes in a particular hardware environment.

The package-design phase produces two primary outputs: the **test plan,** which documents a plan for testing the system prior to implementation; and the packaged design itself. The **packaged design** includes the structured specifications of data-flow diagrams, data dictionary, structure charts, and module descriptions including pseudocode, structured English, decision tables, decision trees, and sometimes program flowcharts. In addition, the packaged design would include layout sketches that show how inputs and outputs are to appear on the CRT or on paper.

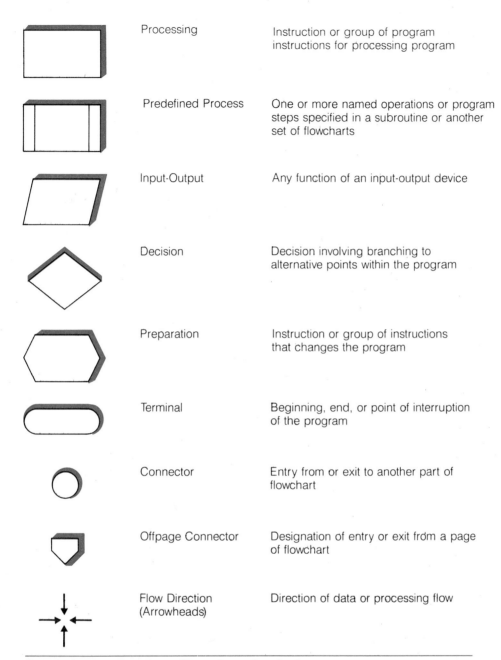

	Processing	Instruction or group of program instructions for processing program
	Predefined Process	One or more named operations or program steps specified in a subroutine or another set of flowcharts
	Input-Output	Any function of an input-output device
	Decision	Decision involving branching to alternative points within the program
	Preparation	Instruction or group of instructions that changes the program
	Terminal	Beginning, end, or point of interruption of the program
	Connector	Entry from or exit to another part of flowchart
	Offpage Connector	Designation of entry or exit from a page of flowchart
	Flow Direction (Arrowheads)	Direction of data or processing flow

FIGURE 6–7 Program Flowchart Symbols

Program flowchart symbols are much simpler than those used in system flowcharting, which we covered in chapter 5.

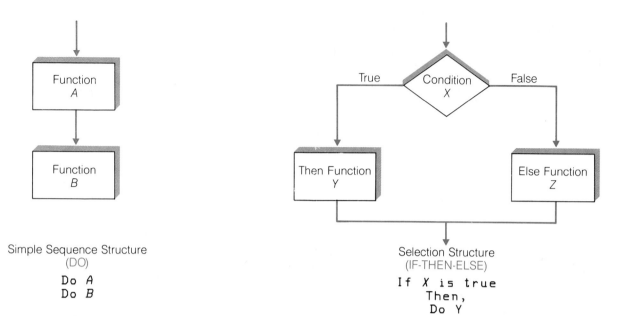

Simple Sequence Structure
(DO)
```
Do A
Do B
```

Selection Structure
(IF-THEN-ELSE)
```
If X is true
   Then,
   Do Y
   Else,
   Do Z
```

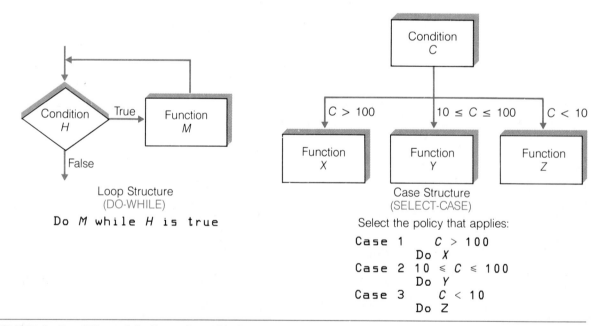

Loop Structure
(DO-WHILE)
```
Do M while H is true
```

Case Structure
(SELECT-CASE)

Select the policy that applies:
```
Case 1    C > 100
          Do X
Case 2 10 ≤ C ≤ 100
          Do Y
Case 3    C < 10
          Do Z
```

FIGURE 6–8 Allowable Pseudocode Control Patterns

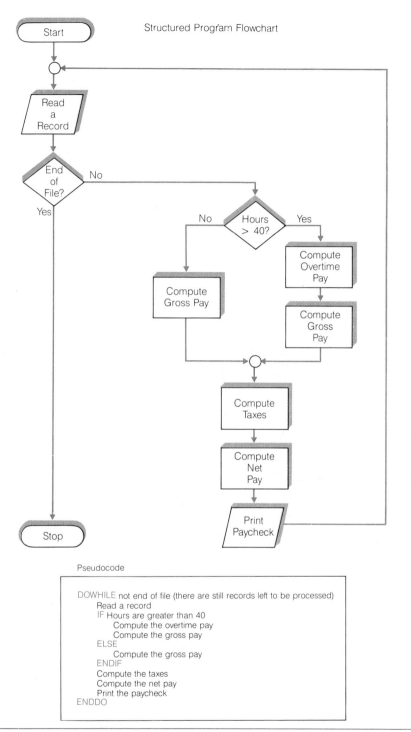

Structured Program Flowchart

Pseudocode

```
DOWHILE not end of file (there are still records left to be processed)
      Read a record
      IF Hours are greater than 40
           Compute the overtime pay
           Compute the gross pay
      ELSE
           Compute the gross pay
      ENDIF
      Compute the taxes
      Compute the net pay
      Print the paycheck
ENDDO
```

FIGURE 6–9   A Structured Program Flowchart and Pseudocode

A program flowchart is a graphical way of representing the logic steps within a computer program. Some people find program flowcharts easier to follow than pseudocode.

Build the System

The primary activities that occur within this phase are coding, testing, and developing manual procedures. **Coding** is the process of writing a program (or module) in a computer language, based on the packaged design generated in the structured-design phase. The task of coding the modules is often divided among several programmers in order to decrease the elapsed time necessary for coding. A well-structured and well-specified system will help ensure that each module is compatible with other modules even though they are written by different programmers.

Structured Walkthroughs

Prior to coding, many companies are now performing a **structured walkthrough** of the design. In a formal structured walkthrough the design documentation is made available to a review team of two to four people. These individuals review the design, and in a formal meeting the designer presents the system design to the review team. As the designer "walks" the review team through the design, questions are clarified. Quite often significant improvements are made in the system design.

Structured walkthroughs are often also used to review the program code after a module has been coded. This process is called a **code inspection.** Here, the programmer walks members of a review team through the module's program code. During this process, the program code is checked for compliance with the module specifications and for other types of errors in coding.

Top-Down Coding

Many firms that use structured programming advocate top-down coding. In **top-down coding** the modules on the structure chart are coded, starting with the top module and going down through the lower levels. The top module is coded and tested, then successively lower levels of modules are coded and tested, going from the top to the bottom of the chart. Many modules will be coded concurrently.

PC USER TIP   Word Processors Can Create Program Files

Almost all PC programming languages (especially interpretive languages, such as BASIC) come with a program editor to allow you to do very basic word processing. If you are going to write more than a few lines of code it will be more productive to use your word-processing software to write the program. You will be able to copy lines or sections of code and do other advanced word-processing functions that may not be available on your program editor. Using a word processor can also help to overcome other significant shortcomings of program editors, such as slow speed and small capacity.

The dBASE II and dBASE III program files, for example, can be created using WordStar or Ability. Simply give the file you are working with a file extension of .PRG so that dBASE can properly identify it as a program file.

In fact, sometimes the coding phase overlaps with the system-design phase. However, the emphasis is on starting and completing the coding of the top modules first. Certainly, coding of the higher-level modules can begin before the design of the lower-level modules is complete.

Top-Down Testing

After a module is coded, the first test to be performed is a **desk check**, which is a manual review of a module's logic. Both the programmer and the supervisor review the module. Desk checking also includes manual tracing of hypothetical data (both valid and invalid) through the module's logic in order to verify that it will process the data correctly. For example, a payroll check for one million dollars or a requisition from inventory in excess of ten thousand dollars can be evaluated in terms of the logic and controls incorporated in the system.

A structured walkthrough of the program module code can be very useful at this point. Either formal or informal inspections of the code by other programmers will often identify improvements that can be made in the program code.

After desk checking occurs, modules are *compiled* without execution. The compilation step almost always detects several deviations (*compiler diagnostics*) from the rules and syntax of the particular computer language being used. After these errors are corrected, the module is compiled and executed with test input.

When programs are structured, this testing can be done in a top-down fashion (see Figure 6–10). Top-down testing is performed when enough modules have

compile
To translate a computer program expressed in a problem-oriented language (such as COBOL or FORTRAN) into machine language.

compiler diagnostics
Errors detected in a computer program during its compilation.

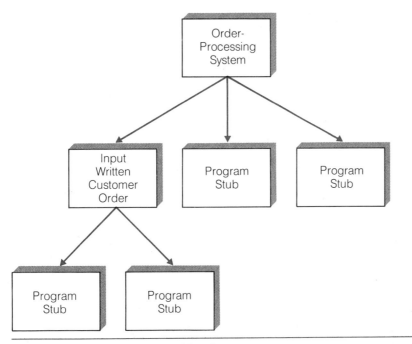

FIGURE 6–10   Top-Down Testing

Top-down testing allows a programmer to test a new system, using a module-by-module approach.

been coded (usually the top-level module and some of the second-level ones) to make the testing significant.

Program stubs are used to test these modules. **Program stubs** are dummy modules that are called by the parent module. They have input/output behavior which is sufficiently similar to the yet-to-be-coded real module that the parent module can be executed. Figure 6–10 illustrates testing with program stubs of a system depicted in Figure 6–6. The top module as well as one second-level one, the Input Written Customer Order module, have been coded. All the program-stub modules perform input and output functions simulating the modules that are yet to be coded.

In addition, the program stubs write out a message, such as "output customer check has been called," each time the particular dummy module is called. This provides a trace so that the programmer can identify when each program stub is called by the parent module. This makes the debugging task easier. As modules are coded they can be substituted for the program stubs. Then, in turn, if these modules call other modules that are yet to be coded, new program stubs can be inserted.

Top-down testing has very significant advantages. The testing of the system can proceed in a top-down fashion as each module is coded. This spreads the testing over a longer period of time, and avoids "crash" testing in a restricted time period after all the modules have been coded. In addition, errors are likely to be related to the most recently inserted module since all the other modules would have been previously tested and corrected. Therefore, errors are much easier to isolate.

Preparation of **test data** is a very important step. Inadequate test data can be very costly later on because of undetected errors (***bugs***). Test data should be comprehensive, covering every possible type of valid and invalid input that could exist when the module is operational. Development of adequate test data usually requires that users participate, since they are most familiar with the various combinations of inputs that may occur. When the test data are used, every statement in the module should be executed, including logic that is seldom used; otherwise the test will not be thorough. Software tools are available to identify the executed and unexecuted module statements. Given a set of test data, the expected output from the module's execution using these test data should be determined manually.

program bug
An error in a computer program.

Thinking About Information Systems 6–2

The system-development department for Gatt's Manufacturing Company has a policy whereby computer programs for new systems are written and tested by programmers. These programs are then put together into various subsystems. Once the subsystems have been written and tested, the whole system is integrated and tested by the user department. In the development of the last system, an integrated accounts-payable/purchasing system, a programmer did not properly code and test an error checking module that is used for month-end processing. At the end of the month, the program malfunctioned and brought the whole purchasing system to a halt. It took three weeks to correct the system because several programs had to be changed. A committee was formed to review the company's policies for designing and testing new systems. What design and testing strategy would have prevented this problem?

In this way the programmer can ascertain whether the module's processing is valid.

After each coded module has been tested in a top-down fashion and then corrected, the modules are tested collectively as a system, using similarly comprehensive test data. Once the system has been tested with hypothetical data, the final test prior to implementation should be the processing of real data at the volume levels expected when the system is installed.

Procedure Development

System analysis and user personnel usually develop procedures concurrently with module coding and testing. A complete written set of manual procedures must be developed that documents all manual processes to be performed by both user and data-processing personnel in the actual operation of the system. The procedures should cover such items as input preparation, control and balancing, error correction, and computer-operator instructions. Collectively, these procedures form a critical part of the system's documentation.

Documentation is sometimes the most neglected aspect of the system-development life cycle. Firms frequently depend on a key individual or group of individuals to design and operate an information system. If these people rely on their memories for programming, systems, and operating information, and then they find other employment, the firm has to study and document the existing system before work can begin on modifying it or designing a new one. Rarely can anyone remember all the detailed design information of a complex computer information system.

Adequate documentation includes:

1. all the specifications in the system-development life cycle,
2. data-flow diagrams and structure charts,
3. data dictionaries,
4. hardware specifications,
5. performance specifications,
6. job descriptions, and
7. procedure manuals.

Chief-Programmer Teams

Many firms organize their programing efforts into chief-programmer teams. This team consists of a chief programmer (who in effect supervises the team), one or more programmers, a librarian, and a back-up programmer. The back-up programmer acts as an assistant to the chief programmer. The chief programmer and the back-up programmer code the more important modules of a system while the other programmers in the team code the other modules.

The librarian is one of the key people on the team. The primary responsibility of the librarian is to maintain up-to-date documentation for the system the team is working on. Often, programmers do not enjoy doing the clerical and filing tasks that are necessary to maintain this up-to-date documentation. The documentation is centralized, rather than being under the control of individual programmers, and is available to anyone on the team. The librarian's functions include maintaining copies of program listings, updating test data, picking up computer output, and maintaining up-to-date documentation in a secure file.

Conversion

In the conversion phase of the system-development life cycle, the user and systems personnel must work closely together. Selling the new system to user personnel is a very important factor in its future success. Any new system, especially one involving a computer, can be viewed as a threat to the security of the user personnel. Some resistance to change can be overcome if user personnel are meaningfully involved in the SDLC, and this is possible for most phases of development.

A substantial training program may be required if the change in the system is significant. Often employees view training programs as a threat because they believe that evaluations made at the end of the program will be used against them. These people sometimes lack the self-confidence they need to return to school after many years of absence. The analyst must take these reservations into account when planning a training program. An orientation program should be prepared for all personnel that will, in any way, have contact with the system.

Two potentially difficult personnel problems are the relocation of displaced personnel and adjustments to the organizational structure. If relocation is necessary, the personnel department should be involved in the process as soon as possible, since relocation may require a large adjustment on the part of the employee. Also, the employees should be kept fully informed of the changes so that rumors are reduced to a minimum.

Adjustments to the organizational structure will present human-relations problems also. Changes in supervisory positions or in relationships should be handled in a professional manner. New positions should be meaningful and not created simply to postpone the retirement of an older employee. Job enrichment and other personnel programs are appropriate in these circumstances.

The major physical changes involved in the conversion phase are site preparation and file conversion. Changes in hardware or work flow will require changes in the physical location of the system or the personnel, or both. These must be well planned and coordinated. Inadequate preparation of the site will impair the performance of the system when it begins to operate.

Prior to conversion, files and data bases must be created for the system either through manual inputs (if the old system was manual), or a combination of manual inputs and conversion of data from the old files. Conversion of files and data bases is often time consuming and costly, and it requires special programs. A critical point in this phase is the control of file conversion. File-conversion programs must be thoroughly tested: new file listings must be manually reviewed for errors, and control totals must be balanced. Until file conversion has taken place, it is not possible to operate the new system.

After the personnel and physical changes have been taken care of in the implementation stage, steps must be taken to phase out the old system. Although this may seem obvious, there are numerous instances where new systems have been brought online and the old systems (especially manual ones) have not been terminated.

Post-Implementation Audit and Maintenance

A frequently overlooked but necessary step in the system-development life cycle is the **post-implementation audit.** Two general areas are reviewed at this point. The performance of the new system is evaluated in terms of the objectives that were stated in the feasibility and analysis phases, and the system-development cycle is reviewed. The budgets and schedules that were developed in the feasibility and analysis phases can be used to evaluate the performance of the system-development team.

For example, error rates and processing times can be compared with the rates in the design specifications of the system. User complaints can also be considered. Failure of the system to achieve the design specifications might mean that the expected benefits from the new system will never be realized. It also may mean that the system is not being operated according to the specifications.

Another aspect of evaluating the performance of the new system involves comparing the actual operating costs of the new system with the estimated costs. Significant deviations from the estimated costs have a negative impact on the cost-benefit ratios of the new system.

An important question is who should conduct the audit. For small projects, the supervisor of the system analysts is generally an appropriate choice. When a large project is reviewed, a team of systems personnel and managers who were not part of the project is appropriate. Internal auditors are frequently involved in the post-implementation audit of a large system. Sometimes outside people are brought in to conduct the audits. Their lack of personal connections, their broader experience, and their different view of the organization all contribute to a more objective

In the past year, the internal-audit department of Flextix Corporation, a watch manufacturer, hired an EDP auditor. The auditor recently completed a review of the administrative accounting systems and a review of the system-development methodology that had been used to implement the systems. He noted that once the systems had been implemented, no post-implementation audit had been performed. He discussed his concern with the system-development director and the corporate controller. The director argued that the post-audit was a waste of time because he and the controller maintained close contact with all user problems. He said that it was the internal-audit department's job to perform all auditing work in order to have an objective opinion on the status of a new system. The auditor argued that it was system development's responsibility to perform the audit. Are post-implementation audits needed, and if so, who should perform them?

Thinking About Information Systems 6–3

review. Many companies also have periodic audits of systems in addition to the post-implementation audit.

The life span of an application system can be significantly extended through proper maintenance. Maintenance consists of promptly correcting any additional errors discovered in modules, updating the program modules to meet modified requirements, and maintaining the documentation to reflect system and module program changes.

Summing Up

☐ The documents produced during structured analysis are extensively used during system design and implementation.

☐ A structure chart is a hierarchical diagram showing the relationship between various program modules. It is derived from data-flow diagrams.

☐ Using the structure chart as a guideline, we now design the individual modules. The structured-English statements written earlier may be used for documentation at this stage.

☐ The design is packaged and then modified to suit the hardware and software environment. In addition to the packaged design, a test plan is produced at this time.

☐ Structured walkthroughs are often used to review the packaged design as well as the program code.

☐ Coding and testing are done in a top-down manner. This means that the upper-level control modules are coded and tested before the detailed, lower-level modules are even written.

☐ Procedure manuals are generally written concurrently with coding and testing. These form a critical part of the final system.

☐ Programming personnel are often organized into a chief-programmer team. Many firms have found this to be an efficient structure.

☐ The conversion phase may involve many problems, such as user resistance, personnel relocation, and changes in the organizational structure. Careful planning is a must at this stage.

☐ After the system has been converted, an audit is done to judge its performance against the original system objectives.

☐ Maintenance of a system consists of removing any additional program errors and changing the system to meet new information-processing requirements.

Key Terms

structured design	module	transform
structure chart	subroutine	pseudocode
top-down design	connection	test plan
go-to-less programming	couple	packaged design
spaghetti code	central process	coding

structured walkthrough **desk check** **program bug**
code inspection **program stubs** **documentation**
top-down coding **test data** **post-implementation audit**

Self-Quiz

Completion Questions

1. _____ is the process of designing the computer programs that will be used in the system.
2. A _____ is a hierarchical diagram showing the relationship between various program modules.
3. A _____ is a bounded, named, and contiguous set of program statements.
4. _____ can be used to help organize and document a system that will be implemented without programming.
5. A _____ is an error in a computer program.
6. Prior to coding, the designer presents the system design to a review team and then answers any questions the reviewers may have. This process is called a _____ .
7. _____ is the process of writing a program in a computer language, based on the packaged design generated in the structured-design phase.
8. The _____ phase may involve many problems, such as user resistance, personnel relocation, and changes in the organizational structure.
9. _____ are dummy modules that are called by the parent routine.
10. Procedure manuals are generally written concurrently with coding and _____ .

Multiple-Choice Questions

1. Structured design produces computer programs that are:
   a. easily maintained
   b. easily understood
   c. tested in a bottom-up fashion
   d. a and b only
   e. a, b, and c

2. The primary tool used in structured design is a:
   a. data-flow diagram
   b. module
   c. structure chart
   d. program flowchart
   e. none of the above

3. Which of the following is not a requirement of structured design?
   a. It should use many GO TO statements.
   b. The code should be executed in a top-to-bottom fashion within each module.
   c. It should be made up of a hierarchy of modules.
   d. Each module should be as independent as possible of all other modules, except its parent.
   e. All of the above are requirements.

4. The structure chart is:
   a. a document of what has to be accomplished
   b. a hierarchical partitioning of the program
   c. a statement of information-processing requirements
   d. all of the above

5. A couple:
   a. is a data item that moves from one module to another.
   b. is represented by a line joining two modules.
   c. means that the upper module has the capability of calling the lower module.
   d. two of the above
   e. all of the above

6. Which of the following is NOT a characteristic of good test data?
   a. should be comprehensive
   b. users do not participate at this preliminary stage

c. every statement should be executed

d. expected output from the module's execution should be determined manually.

7. Coding and testing are done in a _____ manner.
   a. ad hoc
   b. cross-sectional
   c. bottom-up
   d. top-down

8. The packaged design includes all of the following except:
   a. system configuration
   b. module descriptions
   c. report layouts
   d. program flowcharts
   e. all of the above are included

9. Procedure development occurs within the _____ phase.
   a. structured-design
   b. system building
   c. conversion
   d. maintenance
   e. none of the above

10. Which of the following is *not* true of the conversion phase of the development life cycle?
    a. The user and systems personnel must work closely together.
    b. Steps must be taken to phase out the old system.
    c. Documentation should be emphasized.
    d. The nonmachine components of the system should be considered.
    e. All of the above are true.

Answers

Completion	Multiple Choice
1. Structured design	1. d
2. structure chart	2. c
3. module or subroutine	3. a
4. Structure charts	4. b
5. bug	5. a
6. structured walkthrough	6. b
7. Coding	7. d
8. conversion	8. e
9. Program stubs	9. b
10. testing	10. c

Chapter 7

Application Development by Users

CHAPTER OUTLINE

PROLOGUE

Application development by users will be the dominant means of providing computer information systems to users before the end of this decade. By 1990, information processing done by MIS professionals is likely to be only about 25 percent of the total processing performed. This is a major revolution in computer information systems, and it is already well under way. You should be prepared for it. How is this revolution being accomplished? What tactics and strategies are being used by those supporting this revolution?

Introduction

application development by users
This approach to application development is also often called end-user computing or application development without programmers.

end users
Persons who ultimately use application software.

fourth-generation language
User-friendly computer software that enables end users to create application software in one-tenth the time required by typical third-generation languages such as BASIC, FORTRAN, and COBOL. Examples of fourth-generation languages are Lotus 1–2–3, dBase III, and Focus.

Many information-systems experts believe that a large percentage of business applications can be developed by users. ***Application development by users*** means that the ***end users*** develop software without the assistance of programmers, and quite often without system analysts. This approach is often called application development without programming.

There are essentially three ways that users can create or obtain application software without programming. First, users can be given powerful but easy-to-use computer tools to create their own application software without assistance from systems analysts or programmers. These tools are often called *fourth-generation languages*. An example is an electronic spreadsheet. Second, consultants or system analysts can work directly with users to generate application software through the use of fourth-generation languages that are too technical for users to employ without assistance. Third, preprogrammed application software packages can be purchased from outside vendors. We will cover purchase of application software in Module D. Here, we will examine some of the problems associated with the conventional application-development approach. Next we will discuss a variety of methods users can employ to develop application software, and then cover the blending of user development with conventional development. Finally, the impact of user-developed software on the conventional information-systems organization will be examined. In this area we will cover the concept of an information center and the changing role of system analysts and programmers.

While reading this chapter keep in mind that application development by users does not make obsolete the basic steps used in the system-development life cycle we studied in chapters 5 and 6. As we stated at the end of chapter 5, application development by users only changes the degree to which these steps are performed and how they are performed, not whether they are done.

Problems with Conventional Application Development

Conventional application-systems development is the process studied in the last two chapters. Figure 7–1 illustrates the conventional system-development life cycle using the structured approach.

Increasing Labor Cost

The conventional development cycle is a labor-intensive, time-consuming process. Creating data-flow diagrams (for the old and new systems), drawing structure charts, and writing the programs are essentially manual processes, although recently the computer has been applied to assist in some of these tasks. The labor costs

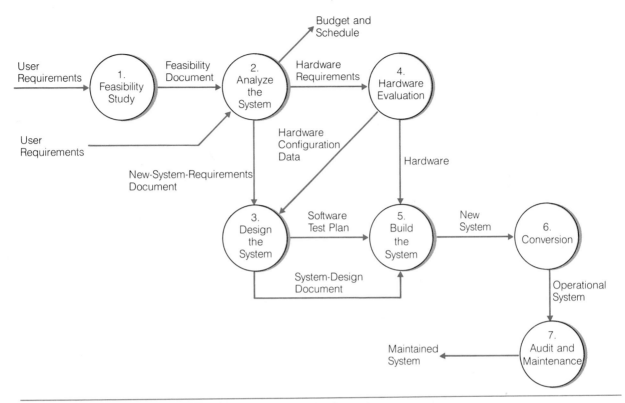

FIGURE 7–1 Structured Development Life Cycle

associated with system analysis and programming continue to increase, while the price of computer hardware continues to decline. This relationship is shown in Figure 7–2. In the late 1970s the cost of hardware was lower than labor cost for information-systems organizations. This relationship between labor and hardware costs makes it economical to substitute hardware for labor.

With application development by users, software is developed directly through the use of computers and fourth-generation languages, thereby eliminating the labor cost of programming, and to some extent system analysis. Obviously, this increases hardware costs because computers have to be used to execute fourth-generation languages. Also, these languages usually do not produce program code that executes as efficiently as program code written by programmers. However, this is of little concern because of the dramatic decline in hardware costs.

Long Time Span Required for Application Development

A major disadvantage of the conventional approach is the usually very long time span (months and sometimes years) required for the development of application

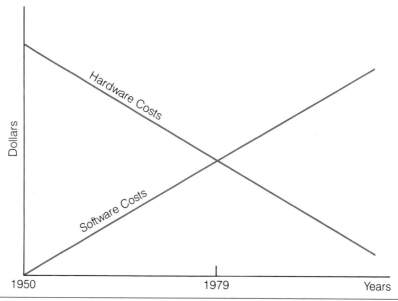

FIGURE 7–2 Software Costs versus Hardware Costs

As fourth-generation languages become more widely used, software costs should begin to decline.

software. Because of the dynamic nature of most businesses, the needs for the software (which were originally defined in the feasibility stage) may have changed substantially by the time the system is operational. Therefore, the system is sometimes obsolete by the time it is implemented.

Slow Implementation of Changes

James Martin
James Martin is a widely known author and lecturer who specializes in data-base management systems and fourth-generation languages. He is recognized as one of the premier authorities in these areas.

Closely related to the long time span for application development is the typically slow implementation of changes to the system. *James Martin* has stated that the mere act of implementing a system changes the requirements for that system. In other words, after a system is implemented it will affect the user organization in unforeseen ways. Martin maintains that it is impossible to foresee all the effects of a new system on an organization's information needs. There will be requests for changes to the system immediately, as it is implemented, since the user really cannot experience the new system until it is implemented. If systems are going to be successful, we must be able to implement changes rapidly. This is often difficult to do with the conventional development cycle.

Work Overload

Maintenance of application software is a major concern. In fact, most mature information-systems organizations find that over half and up to 75 percent of their programming effort is in the maintenance of existing systems as opposed to the programming of new systems. If this trend continues, we may find situations where almost all the programming effort within a firm is spent on maintenance of existing systems!

Owing to the declining price of hardware, many new users have purchased computers. If we depend on programmers to write the software for these computers, there will not be enough programmers to go around. In fact, for several years now there has been an acute shortage of application programmers. If all of the new computer users are to get even minimal use of their hardware, we simply must find new ways of creating application software.

Frank Shields, the system-development manager of the Carmel Corporation, has been inundated with requests to develop applications. In reviewing the file of unfulfilled requests, Frank began to wonder how many more requests users might have for systems-development services that have not even been made known to him. Frank has been reading about this invisible or shadow backlog of requests, and he does not know what to do. As much as Frank would like to maintain control over system development, he knows that he will one day have to let users begin developing some applications. What are some alternatives that Frank should consider in allowing users to create their own computer application systems?

Thinking About Information Systems 7–1

Prespecified versus User-Driven Computing

Martin has classified computing into two categories: prespecified and user-driven computing. In **prespecified computing,** processing requirements can be pretty well determined ahead of time. Therefore, formal requirement specifications can be created and the conventional development cycle can be used. In contrast, in **user-driven computing** users do not know in detail what they want until they use a version of it. They may modify the system frequently and quickly. Figure 7–3 summarizes the differences between prespecified and user-driven computing.

Today it is not entirely clear what percentage of business computing should be developed with the prespecified approach and what percentage with user-driven techniques. However, as users gain experience with the new tools that allow them to develop their own applications, user-driven techniques are certain to become the predominant approach. Martin states: "The requirements for management information systems cannot be specified beforehand and almost every attempt to do so has failed. The requirements change as soon as an executive starts to use his terminal. The point . . . is *not* that conventional application development . . . should be abandoned, but rather *it only works for certain types of systems.*"[1]

---

[1]James Martin, *Application Development without Programmers* (Englewood Cliffs, NJ: Prentice-Hall, 1982), 52.

Prespecified Computing
- Formal requirement specifications are created
- A development cycle such as that in Fig. 7–1 is employed.
- Programs are formally documented.
- The application development time is many months or years.
- Maintenance is formal, slow, and expensive.

Examples: Compiler writing, airline reservations, air-traffic control, and missile-guidance software development.

User-Driven Computing
- Users do not know in detail what they want until they use a version of it, and then they modify it quickly and often frequently. Consequently, formal requirement specification linked to slow application programming is doomed to failure.
- Users may create their own applications, but more often with an analyst who does this in cooperation with them. A separate programming department is not used.
- Applications are created with a fourth-generation language more quickly than the time to write specifications.
- The application development time is days or at most weeks.
- Maintenance is continuous. Incremental changes are made constantly to the applications by the users or the analyst who assists them.
- The system is self-documenting, or interactive documentation is created when the application is created.
- A centrally administered data-base facility is often employed. Data administration is generally needed to prevent chaos of incompatible data spreading.

Examples: Administrative procedures, shop-floor control, information systems, decision support, and paperwork-avoidance systems.

FIGURE 7–3   Prespecified versus User-Driven Computing

James Martin. *Application Development without Programmers,* © 1982, p. 55. Reprinted by permission of Prentice-Hall Inc., Englewood Cliffs, NJ.

Methods for User Development of Application Software

Application development by users became practical in the late 1970s and early 1980s owing to the availability of very powerful software. There are many of these fourth-generation tools. To be called fourth generation, a language should:

1. Enable users to develop software in one-tenth the time required by third-generation languages such as BASIC, COBOL, and FORTRAN.
2. Be user-friendly, user-seductive, and easy to learn and remember.
3. Be appropriate for use by both end users and information-systems professionals.

This kind of software can be classified into the six categories illustrated in Figure 7–4.

Personal-Computer Tools

There are a wide variety of **personal-computer tools** for end users. Electronic

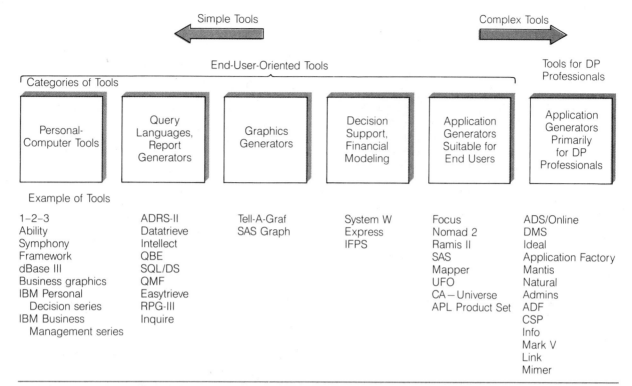

Simple Tools ←   Complex Tools →

End-User-Oriented Tools   Tools for DP Professionals

Categories of Tools

Personal-Computer Tools	Query Languages, Report Generators	Graphics Generators	Decision Support, Financial Modeling	Application Generators Suitable for End Users	Application Generators Primarily for DP Professionals

Example of Tools

1–2–3	ADRS-II	Tell-A-Graf	System W	Focus	ADS/Online
Ability	Datatrieve	SAS Graph	Express	Nomad 2	DMS
Symphony	Intellect		IFPS	Ramis II	Ideal
Framework	QBE			SAS	Application Factory
dBase III	SQL/DS			Mapper	Mantis
Business graphics	QMF			UFO	Natural
IBM Personal	Easytrieve			CA — Universe	Admins
Decision series	RPG-III			APL Product Set	ADF
IBM Business	Inquire				CSP
Management series					Info
					Mark V
					Link
					Mimer

FIGURE 7–4 Categories and Examples of Development Tools

Generally the easier-to-use tools run on personal computers. But some of the mainframe application generators such as Focus and Nomad 2 are also very user-friendly.

Reprinted with permission of *The James Martin Report on High-Productivity Languages,* published by Technology Insight, Inc., Marblehead, MA.

spreadsheets (Lotus 1–2–3 and Supercalc), data-base management systems (dBase III), and *integrated tools* (Enable, Symphony, and Ability) are all easily mastered by users. The ideal first step for those who are new to computers is to learn one of these tools, preferably one of the integrated tools.

Query Languages and Report Generators

Query languages are usually associated with data-base management systems. They allow a user to search a data base or file, using simple or complex selection criteria. The results of the search can be displayed in detail or in summary format. For example, the query might state "List all customer accounts that are thirty to sixty days overdue and have a balance in excess of a thousand dollars." This type of software is widely available today. Many of the packages also allow update of the data base as well as data retrieval.

Report generators are similar to query languages except that they can perform more complex data-processing tasks and produce reports in almost any format. Generally, query languages are designed to be used without assistance from infor-

integrated tool
A PC package which typically includes the functions of electronic spreadsheet, word processing, data-base management, and communications.

mation-systems professionals, whereas report generators sometimes require help from MIS professionals, such as system analysts. One popular report generator, RPG, is discussed in Module B.

Graphics Generators

Graphic output is becoming increasingly important to today's business management. **Graphics generators** allow users to retrieve data from files or data bases and display these data graphically. Users can specify the data they wish to graph and the basic format of the graph, such as pie, line, or bar. Figure 7–5 illustrates a graph made by a generator.

Decision Support/Financial Modeling Tools

two-dimensional
Allowing only rows and columns.

The most simple **decision-support/financial-modeling tools** are the *two-dimensional* electronic spreadsheets such as Lotus 1–2–3. More capable decision-support tools are available for large computers. Examples are System W, Express, and Integrated Financial Planning System (IFPS). These tools allow the construction of complex business models that have more than two dimensions.

Application Generators

validation
To check input for errors.

report generation
To produce information output.

Application generators can create an entire information-system application including input, input *validation,* file update, processing, and *report generation.* The user usually specifies what needs to be done and the application generator decides how it will be done. In other words, the application generator generates program code based on the user's requirements.

Many data-processing operations are routine and they tend to be performed in the same manner regardless of the application. For example, most applications have to communicate with terminals, update files, produce reports, et cetera. These

FIGURE 7–5 A Graph Produced by a Graphics Generator

Graphics generators have substantially decreased the costs of producing professional-quality graphics.

types of operations are preprogrammed in **generalized modules** included in the application generator. When these operations are required, the application generator retrieves the preprogrammed modules and modifies them slightly for the particular application's needs.

It is unlikely that everything that a particular application requires can be generated by an application generator. Each application is likely to have certain unique requirements. Therefore, most application generators contain what are known as user exits. **User exits** allow a user or programmer to insert program code that takes care of these unique requirements of the application. User-exit routines can be programmed in a variety of languages, such as BASIC, COBOL, and PL/I.

Most application generators are interactive. Sitting at a terminal, a user and/or a system analyst respond to questions from the application generator. Their responses define the application inputs, files, processes, and reports. Based on these responses the application generator generates code to execute the application. In a matter of hours, a ***prototype*** of the application may be up and running. This allows the user to experiment with the new application and make modifications if necessary. As you will notice in Figure 7–4, some application generators are suitable primarily for data processing professionals.

Table 7–1 provides examples of the tools just discussed. The packages are classified into those suitable for end users and those which require professional help. A package is classified as suitable for end users if a typical end user can, in a two-day course, learn how it works and can return to use the package after

prototype
An experimental version of a user-developed application.

TABLE 7–1 Leading Fourth-Generation Language Products

Notice that some of the application generators will also run on the IBM Personal Computer. Most application-generator vendors plan to have versions of their products running on the IBM PC. This will allow users to employ the same language on both mainframes and PCs.

Category/Product	Vendor	Environment	Suitable for	
			End User	Analyst
Integrated personal computer tools				
Dbase III	Ashton-Tate	IBM Personal Computer, Various	√	√
Framework	Ashton-Tate	IBM Personal Computer, Various	√	√
Symphony	Lotus Development	IBM Personal Computer, Various	√	√
1-2-3	Lotus Development	IBM Personal Computer, Various	√	√
Ability	Xanaro Technologies Inc.	IBM Personal Computer, Various	√	√
Query languages and report generators				
ADRS-II	IBM	IBM	√	√
Datatrieve	DEC	DEC	√	√
Easytrieve	Pansophic Systems	IBM, Siemons	√	√
Inquire	Infodata Systems	IBM	√	√
Intellect	Artificial Intelligence	IBM, Honeywell	√	√
RPG-III	IBM	System 38	√	√
QBE	IBM	IBM	√	√
QMF	IBM	IBM	√	√
SQL/DS	IBM	IBM	√	√
Graphics				
Business Graphics	Business Professional Software	IBM Personal Computer, Various	√	√
Tell-A-Graf	Issco	IBM, DEC	√	√
Decision support and financial modeling				
Express	Management Decision Systems	IBM, Prime	√	√
System W	Comshare, Inc.	IBM, IBM Personal Computer	√	√

several weeks of not working with it. The package should be easy to start so the user can gain confidence in his or her ability to use the package quickly. The user will learn more sophisticated applications as more experience is gained.

Figure 7–6 shows how Nomad 2, an application generator, generates the report in Figure 7–7. Note that only a minimum amount of information must be included in the commands to produce a report. Nomad 2 can easily produce much more complex reports than the one shown in Figure 7–7. Individuals experienced in writing programs in COBOL, BASIC, or FORTRAN are pleasantly surprised at how simple it is to produce meaningful reports with a language such as Nomad 2.

TABLE 7—1 (continued)

Category/Product	Vendor	Environment	Suitable for	
			End User	Analyst
Application generators suitable for end users				
CA—Universe	Computer Associates	IBM, DEC, Data General Corp.	√	√
Focus	Information Builders	IBM, IBM Personal Computer, DEC	√	√
Mapper	Sperry Corp.	Univac 1100	√	√
Nomad 2	D & B Computing	IBM, IBM Personal Computer	√	√
Ramis II	Mathematica	IBM, IBM Personal Computer	√	√
SAS	SAS Institute	IBM, DEC, DG	√	√
UFO	Oxford Software	IBM	√	√
Application generators for DP professionals				
ADS/Online	Cullinet Software	IBM	*	√
CSP	IBM	IBM		√
DMS	IBM	IBM		√
Application Factory	Cortex Corp.	DEC	*	√
Ideal	Applied Data Research	IBM	*	√
Info	Henco, Inc.	IBM, DEC, Prime	*	√
Linc	Burroughs Corp.	Burroughs	*	√
Mantis	Cincom Systems	IBM	*	√
Mark V	Informatics General	IBM	*	√
Mimer	Savant Institute	IBM, Various	*	√
Natural	Software AG	IBM, DEC	*	√
Provable specification language				
Use.It	Higher Order Software	DEC VAX		√

*Subset may be suitable for end users.

Reprinted with permission of *The James Martin Report on High-Productivity Languages*, published by Technology Insight, Inc., Marblehead, MA.

Blending User Development with Conventional Development

Types of Application Development

When a firm attempts application development by users, three types of development usually evolve:

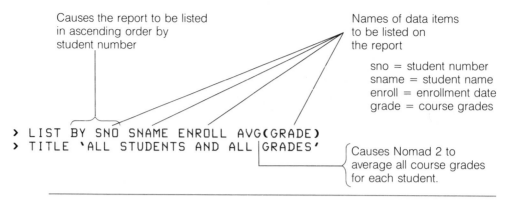

Causes the report to be listed in ascending order by student number

Names of data items to be listed on the report

sno = student number
sname = student name
enroll = enrollment date
grade = course grades

```
> LIST BY SNO SNAME ENROLL AVG(GRADE)
> TITLE 'ALL STUDENTS AND ALL GRADES'
```

Causes Nomad 2 to average all course grades for each student.

FIGURE 7–6   A Nomad 2 Report Request

1. The traditional development cycle, as illustrated in Figure 7–1. This is often used for those applications whose requirements can be prespecified and are likely to remain stable over a reasonable period of time.

2. A fourth-generation language used as a prototyping tool. The system analyst and the user quickly generate a **skeleton application program** which serves as a model for the application. The end user can interact and experiment with this prototype and thereby refine the system's requirements. After the final requirements have been defined, the application can be programmed in a conventional fashion. Quite often parts of the prototype code can be used directly in the conventional programming process.

3. A fourth-generation language used to develop the entire application. No programmers are used with this approach. The prototype itself becomes the application software.

The second approach is more likely to be successful in applications that process very high volumes of data because of efficiency considerations. The basic model of the application can be developed by using an application generator, but the final application program is written in a traditional programming language to produce code that is more efficient in terms of processing time and storage space. However, there are many business data-processing applications where the processing volume is not very high, and the number of times the program is run is very low. For example, some programs are of a one-time nature. Such applications are likely to use the third type of application development. Also, the third type of application development is more likely to be used whenever the application must be operational in a very short period of time and when the requirements are likely to change frequently.

We should also point out that the efficiency at which a particular program runs, that is, machine efficiency, is becoming less and less important because of the declining cost of hardware. Therefore, one of the primary reasons for using application development types 1 and 2 is declining in significance. Some would even argue that for most business data-processing applications, machine efficiency is not a significant consideration. By 1990 most application development will be done using the third approach.

PAGE 1

```
                    ALL STUDENTS AND ALL GRADES

STUDENT     STUDENT                    ENROLLMENT    AVG
NUMBER      NAME                          DATE      GRADE
-------     ----------------           ----------   -----

     76     PAUL BRAXTON               SEP 78        2.0
     92     ANITA MACDONALD            SEP 78        3.5
    167     BRAD WHITLOCK              SEP 79        2.3
    198     ANN DISCALA               SEP 79        3.1
    436     JOSEPH PANE               SEP 78        3.1
    466     MARTHA LEVIN              SEP 79        3.3
    468     GARY ZANDER               SEP 78              no grade
```

FIGURE 7–7   The Report Produced by the Nomad 2 Report Request in Figure 7–6.

The sequence of this report could be changed by simply saying "by sname" instead of "by sno" in Figure 7–6.

Table 7–2 illustrates the effects of these three types of application development on the various steps of the application-development cycle. Note that when application development is done without professional programmers, the cycle is radically modified and compressed in time. The development process becomes a quick, informal, and interactive process. The user directly or with the aid of a systems analyst creates and modifies his or her own applications.

Data-Base Administration

By now you may be thinking that application development by users will result in isolated users creating their own redundant data files, which could result in chaos.

Thinking About Information Systems 7–2

About two years ago, the JDF Corporation established an information center. Since then the company has strongly supported application development by users. Consequently, many users are actively engaged in developing their own applications, both for personal computers and for the mainframe. Recently the internal-audit department performed an audit of JDF's application-development-by-users approach. The audit report contains some rather disturbing findings. The auditors found numerous instances of the same data being stored several different times, both on the mainframe and on personal computers. In addition, they found that essentially the same application software had been created several times. For example, the home-appliances division and the home-electronics division had both created marketing-analysis systems using a mainframe program generator. Although these two systems are not identical, they are very similar. Based on their findings, the auditors have recommended that the corporation reassess its commitment to application development by users. Do you agree with the auditors that their findings are a serious problem? What recommendations would you have for the JDF Corporation?

TABLE 7–2 Effects of Types of Application Development on the Application Development Cycle*

	Type 1 Conventional Application Development	Type 2 Application Generator Used as a Prototyping Aid Followed by Programming	Type 3 Application Development Without Professional Programmers
Requirements Analysis	A time-consuming formal operation, often delayed by long application backlog.	The user's imagination is stimulated. He may work at a screen with an analyst to develop requirements.	The user's imagination is stimulated. He may develop his own requirements, or work with an analyst.
System Specification Document	Lengthy document. Boring. Often inadequate.	Produced by prototyping aid. Precise and tested.	Disappears.
User Sign-off	User is often not sure what he is signing off on. He cannot perceive all subtleties.	User sees the results and may modify them many times before signing off.	No formal sign-off. Adjustment and modification is an ongoing process.
Coding and Testing	Slow. Expensive. Often delayed because of backlog.	The prototype is converted to more efficient code. Relatively quick and error-free.	Quick. Inexpensive. Disappears to a large extent.
Documentation	Tedious. Time consuming.	May be partly automated. Interactive training and HELP response may be created on-line.	Largely automatic. Interactive training and HELP responses are created on-line.
Maintenance	Slow. Expensive. Often late.	Often slow. Often expensive. Often late.	A continuing process with user and analyst making adjustments. Most of these adjustments can be made very quickly—in hours rather than months.

*James Martin, *Application Development Without Programmers*, © 1982 pp. 66–67. Reprinted by permission of Prentice-Hall, Inc., Englewood Cliffs, NJ.

How can we have users from various departments going off and creating their own files containing redundant and uncoordinated data which cannot be accessed by other legitimate users? For example, data in a payroll system are often used by both the payroll department and the personnel department.

The solution to this potential problem is effective **data-base administration.** Data bases are essential to the effective use of application development by users; thus the role of the *data-base administrator* becomes very important. He or she must assure that the data contained in the data base are sufficient to meet the needs of various users and that one or more users cannot modify the data in such a way as to destroy their usefulness to other people. Does this mean that each user is constrained in the ways that the data can be used because of the needs of other people in the firm? Certainly not. A user can extract portions of the data

data-base administrator
The person responsible for coordinating the data base, including provisions for data security and for prevention of data redundancy.

base and set these data up in his or her own files. The data can then be modified and massaged in any way that the user sees fit, without harming the data in the data base.

Information Centers

If application development by users is to succeed, it must be coordinated and managed. The purpose of an **information center** is to manage the support for application development by users. Its primary objective is to encourage and accelerate the use of new software tools. The reasons that application development by users should be managed are as follows:

1. To encourage the rapid adoption of application development by users
2. To assist users in their development efforts
3. To prevent redundancy in application creation
4. To ensure that the data used in the various applications are coordinated and not redundant
5. To ensure that data are not simply created and stored in isolated personal files
6. To ensure that the systems created are controlled and auditable

Figure 7–8 illustrates a typical organization for an information-systems department that has an information center. The **technical specialists** at the information center are experts on the various software tools and can assist in training end users to utilize the tools. In a smaller organization, the information center usually relies on technical specialists from the software vendor. For example, if a firm was using Focus and a technical problem occurred, the company would get in touch with a specialist at Information Builders, the Focus vendor. Since application development by users is often done on PCs, there are **personal-computer consultants** at the information center. The **user consultants** work directly with users in creating applications.

The user consultants also work closely with the data-base administrator. This is necessary to ensure that data used in both conventionally developed applications and user-generated applications are coordinated and not redundant. Figure 7–9 lists the functions typically performed by an information center.

Changing Roles of System Analysts and Programmers

The advent of software that enables application development by users causes the roles of system analysts and programmers to change. If fourth-generation software is to be used effectively, system analysts must recognize that there are many ways to create a new application. In the requirements-analysis or feasibility-study phase,

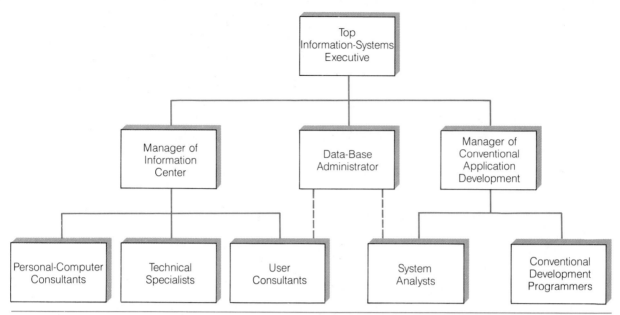

FIGURE 7–8 Organization of an Information-System Department that has an Information Center

Information centers began to be implemented in the early 1980s.

the system analyst must realize that there are many tools, any one of which may be appropriate for solving the user's problem. The tools for obtaining new applications are:

1. Conventional system-development cycle
2. Purchase of an application software package
3. End users generating their own applications without outside help
4. End users working with system analysts or information-center consultants, to generate the application
5. System analysts and end users generating a prototype, experimenting with the prototype, and then coding the application in a conventional manner

Many system analysts trained in conventional application development find it difficult to change their roles. Perhaps the best way for a systems analyst to encourage the use of these new software tools is to:

1. Search constantly for more effective and efficient ways of creating applications;
2. Avoid the use of programmers whenever possible; and
3. Take on a consultant role and encourage the users to employ the software themselves, rather than doing it for them.

Those of you who have planned a career in programming may be quite disturbed by the material we have covered in this chapter. It would be easy to imply that

Gallery 3
The Making of a Chip

This tiny computer chip has more calculating and storage power than an entire computer had just a few years ago. How are these little processors made and what are they made of? These questions are answered in the next few pages with color photos showing the many processes in the making of a chip.

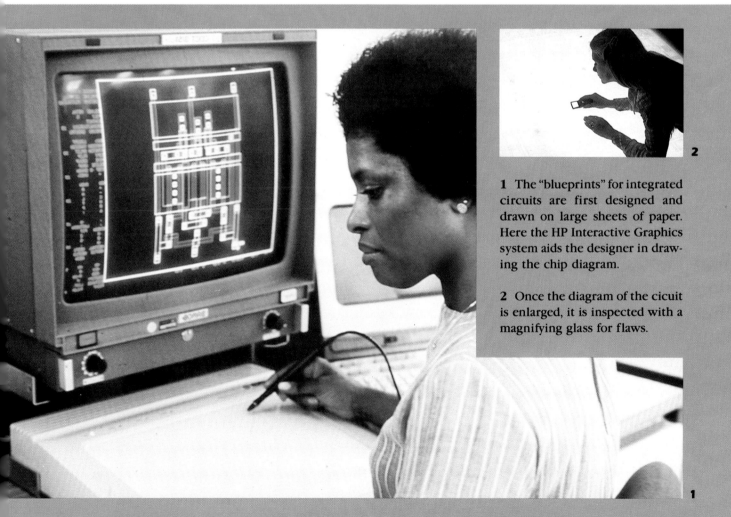

1 The "blueprints" for integrated circuits are first designed and drawn on large sheets of paper. Here the HP Interactive Graphics system aids the designer in drawing the chip diagram.

2 Once the diagram of the cicuit is enlarged, it is inspected with a magnifying glass for flaws.

2

1

3

4

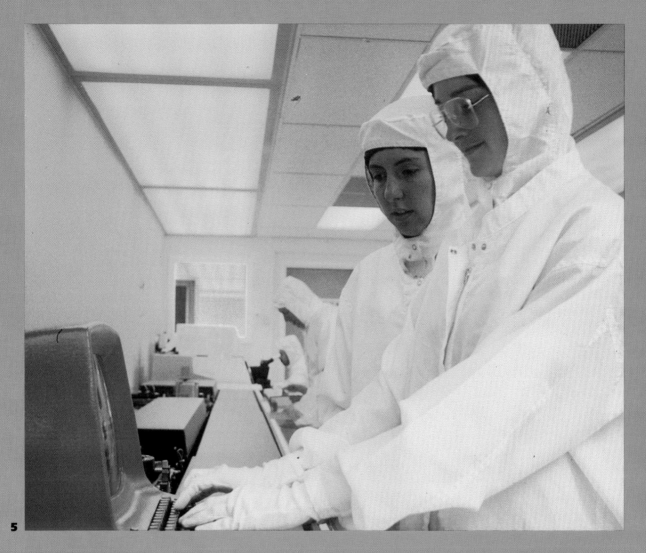

5

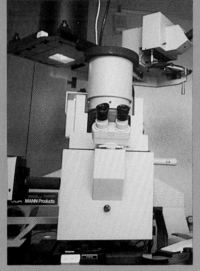

6

3 Then the diagram is photographically reduced as many as five hundred times and reproduced on a template called a mask.

4 Silicon wafers three to five inches in diameter are fabricated in "clean rooms," where any particle, no matter how small, could disrupt the circuitry of the chip to be produced on the wafer.

5 In the clean room a technician wearing a "bunny suit" enters a computer program to run a special costing process where a thin layer of photoresist is spun onto the silicon wafer. Photoresist is a light-sensitive plastic that hardens when exposed to ultraviolet light. Special yellow lights are used in the clean room because they do not interfere with the ultraviolet light processes.

6 The mask is placed over the coated silicon wafer and the wafer is exposed to ultraviolet light to harden. The areas of the wafer covered by the mask remain unhardened after the exposure. This "stepper" exposes each individual chip to light in a step-and-repeat process.

7

7 The unhardened residue is rinsed away in an acid bath, thereby etching the intricate patterns of the circuitry into the wafer.

8 The wafers are loaded into oxygen furnaces where they are baked at temperatures of fourteen hundred degrees Celsius.

9 The wafers are then inspected under a microscope for possible flaws. The processes of photoresist, masked ultraviolet-light exposure, acid bath, oxygen furnace diffusion, and inspection are repeated as many as fifteen times, creating one thin layer at a time on the silicon wafer. This photo shows the tiny microscopic layers on the silicon base that form the intricate patterns that make up integrated circuits.

10 A diamond saw, positioned by video displays, cuts the wafer into individual chips.

11 The extremely small size of a chip is emphasized when placed on this telephone pad. This tiny Digital Signal Processor chip contains about 45,000 transistors and can make over a million calculations per second.

12,13,14 Chips are then soldered and mounted into protective packages of metal or plastic, preparing the finished chips for use as primary storage or as a microprocessor.

8

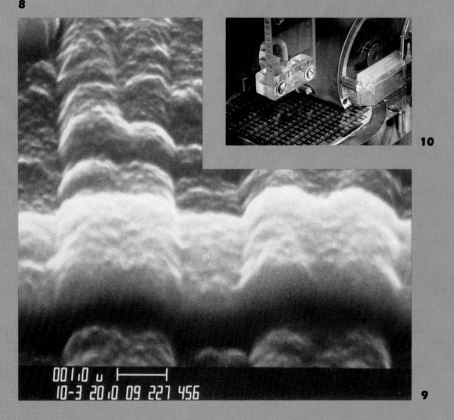

10

001.0 u ├──────┤
10-3 20.0 09 227 456

9

11

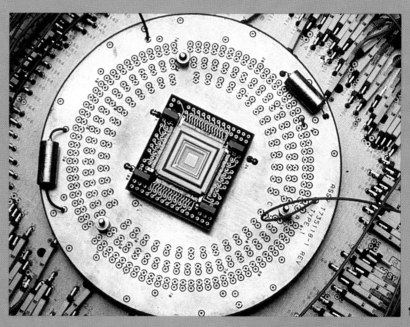

13

12

14

15 The finished chips are often plugged into or attached to a circuit board's specific processing areas.

16 This recently developed AT&T megabit memory chip stores over one million digital bits of information—that's more than entire rooms of vacuum tubes could store just a few decades ago.

17 New techniques, including those used in making chips for the Honeywell DPS 88, help to decrease the size of microprocessing chips. These CML (current mode logic) chips are mounted on a multilayer substrate and sealed with a metal-lid (not shown) and can be used to replace the two standard twelve-inch DIP boards shown behind it.

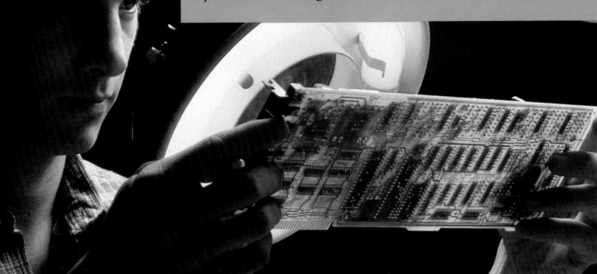

15

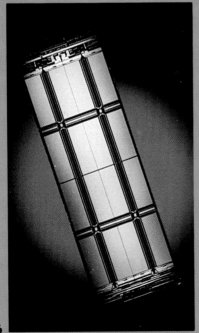

16

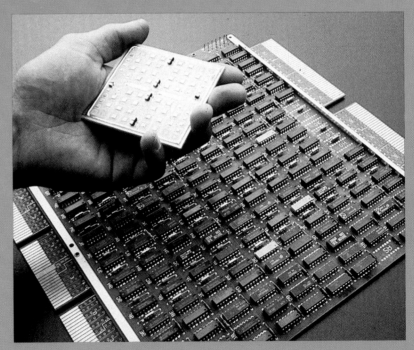

17

Gallery 4
A Tour of a Large Computer Center

The Norfolk Southern Corporation operates one of the largest rail systems in the United States. It was formed in 1982 with the merger of the Norfolk and Western Railway and the Southern Railway. Norfolk Southern serves a territory covering most of the eastern United States and the Midwest. Railroads have been major innovators in the application of computers to business problems. Norfolk Southern uses computers in many applications, from payroll to the makeup of trains and the tracking of shipments. For example, the physical makeup of an individual train is controlled by computers after the terminal trainmaster enters this makeup into the computer. After the train leaves the terminal, computers track the movement of the train to the next terminal. Recognizing the importance of computers to their operations, Norfolk Southern recently constructed a separate building for its computer facility. This facility represents state-of-the-art technology not only in large computer hardware but also in the security and backup arrangements for the facility. Let's begin our tour of this computer center.

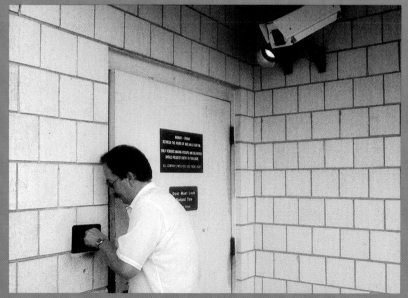

1 There are only two entrances to the building. The front entrance is monitored by a receptionist. The rear entrance is monitored by a TV camera, and employees must insert an identification card into a reader to gain entrance to the building. The identification number of the employee and the time of entry is recorded by a computer.

2

5

4

3

6

2 Visitors to the facility must sign in and obtain a visitor's badge. All employees wear a badge within the building. This receptionist has controls at her desk that will lock the front door and she also has a TV screen that monitors the rear entrance.

3 We will begin our tour by looking at data entry. Here a data entry operator is keying input to a minicomputer. This batch data entry to a minicomputer dedicated to the data entry process is shrinking in importance at Norfolk Southern. Most data today is entered through online terminals located in the field.

4 This is the minicomputer into which the data is entered. Actually there are two minicomputers here, one backing up the other. The data is entered to a magnetic disk and then it is copied to tape for transport to the mainframe computer, located in a separate secure room within the building.

5 Once inputs have been balanced, the reel of magnetic tape is carried to the computer room. Employees who do not work in the computer room pass inputs and other items through this window into the computer room. This area is also monitored by a TV camera.

6 The computer room is like a building within the building. It is constructed to withstand a fire in the main building for four hours without damage to the inside of the computer room. Access to the computer room is restricted to those whose jobs require it, such as the computer operators and service technicians. The door is unlocked by an identification card, and, as with the main building entrances, the identification of the person and time of entry is recorded by a computer.

7

8

7 The office of the shift manager for computer operations is immediately inside the computer room. Three computer terminals at the rear of the office enable the manager to monitor the operations of the computers in the facility. At the right rear of the office is equipment that monitors access to the main building and the computer room, and fire security for the building. We will take a closer look at this in the next photo.

8 This equipment monitors the access and fire security systems for the building, and to the computer room. In the top right corner of the equipment is a TV screen monitoring the back door access to the building.

9

9 This is a partial view of the 13,000 sq. ft. computer room, containing a large amount of computer hardware. Norfolk Southern runs two IBM mainframes, an IBM 3033 and an IBM 3084. The 3084 is in effect two mainframes itself containing two separate processors. The two separate processors within the IBM 3084 allows one to backup the other in case of failure.

10 This is the monitor used by computer operators to track the progress of jobs running on the computer systems. Significant job events are displayed in green on this monitor as they occur. Any job event that requires immediate operator attention is displayed in red. Norfolk Southern has such a smooth computer operation that on the day of our visit no red messages occurred.

11 Most input to Norfolk Southern's computers comes from terminals in the field. The network control systems shown in this photo process and control the messages from a large number of remote terminals and data acquisition stations.

10

11

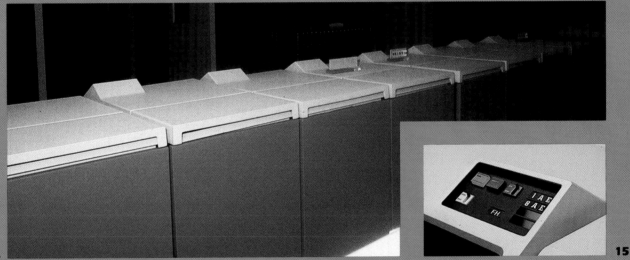

12 These are the local in-house communication lines which are in addition to those coming in from the terminals in the field. Norfolk Southern has over 1600 terminals that may access the computers in this facility. In addition, other terminals and many freight customers have dial-up access to these computers.

13 This is the network-control facility, which monitors the network of remote terminals and data acquisition stations on a twenty-four-hour basis. They help solve the problems that occur in the network. Most of the communication lines the network uses are Norfolk Southern's own microwave transmission facilities.

14 Large online computer networks must have large amounts of online disk storage. In the foreground we see two rows of IBM 3350 disk storage units. Each 3350 unit, about the size of a washing machine, can hold 635 megabytes of data or programs. In the background are several IBM 3380 disk storage units. Each of these can hold 2,520 megabytes of data or programs.

15 This is a photo of the buttons and switches on an IBM 3350 disk storage unit. This black switch just to the right of the blue attention button can be positioned at either a read/write position or a read only position. When the switch is positioned at the read only position, the data or programs stored in the unit can only be read and used. They cannot be modified. This capability may be used to protect production programs from unauthorized modifications.

17

18

16 Another form of data storage used by Norfolk Southern is magnetic tape. This photo of a small portion of the tape library illustrates the immense amount of data and programs that are stored on magnetic tape. This library contains over 30,000 reels of tape.

17 The tape drives are located just outside the tape library room. Here an operator is removing a reel of tape from a tape drive. In the background of this photo there is a computer monitor that displays messages telling the operators which tapes to mount and dismount.

18 The computer room sits on a floor raised eighteen inches above a concrete floor. Utilities such as electricity, water to cool the CPUs, communication lines, and cables between the hardware units pass through this space. As this photo

shows, removable panels provide easy access to these utility lines.

19 Adjacent to the computer room is a room that provides the electricity, air conditioning, and fire suppression halon gas for the facility. Here we see rows of batteries. All of the electrical power used to run the computers comes from these batteries. The batteries in turn are charged by electricity from regular electrical lines. Running the power through these batteries has two advantages. It conditions the power and smooths it out, preventing power spikes, such as those that result from lightning, from damaging the computer hardware. The batteries also provide a short duration backup of power in case the electricity fails.

20 Longer duration backup for electrical failures is provided by

two large diesel motor generators. These generators turn on automatically about twenty seconds after an electrical failure.

21 What happens if some of the backup motor generators fail and they cannot provide enough power to operate all three CPUs: the 3084A, 3084B, and the 3033? In such a case this computer-priority trip system will direct the remaining power to the computer or computers that have the highest priority.

22 These are the cylinders of halon gas that are used for fire suppression in the computer room. In case of fire this gas would be released into the computer room, suppressing the fire quickly, but not harming personnel. Halon gas is expensive. To replace the gas in these cylinders would cost approximately $50,000.

19

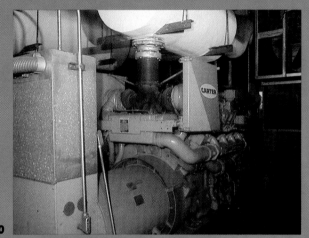

20

COMPUTER PRIORITY TRIP SYSTEM

21

22

23

24

25

23 Much of the output at Norfolk Southern is being produced on Xerox Corporation laser printers. Here we see a laser printer which is being repaired. The inner workings of a laser printer are rather complex.

24 An onput method that is rapidly becoming obsolete is high-speed line printers. In this photo, the cover of the printer has been raised and the printing mecha-nism is open, showing the paper. Norfolk Southern expects all paper printing to be done by laser printers.

25 Norfolk Southern's computer applications are developed and maintained by a systems and pro-gramming staff. This staff is located in the computer building on the second floor. Here we see a system analyst working at the terminal on an application.

26 One application that was being tested on the day of our visit was a system that will be used to mon-itor and record data about the fueling of locomotives. Data such as the time of fueling and the amount of fuel placed in the loco-motive will be recorded. The left side of the screen depicts the pumps from the alcohol and die-sel fuel storage tanks. Alcohol is placed with the diesel fuel during the winter to prevent freezing. The

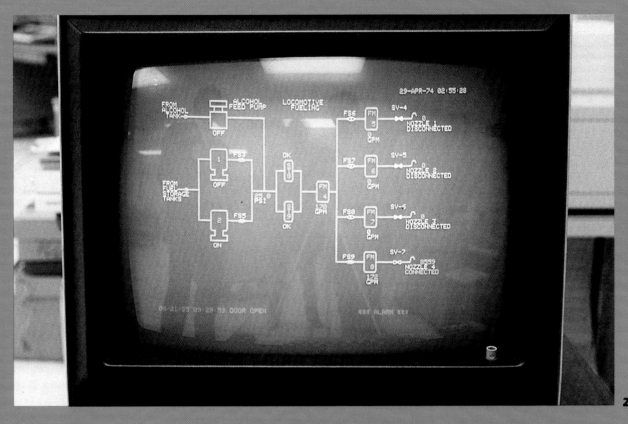

29-APR-74 02:55:26

FROM
ALCOHOL
TANK

ALCOHOL
FEED PUMP

LOCOMOTIVE
FUELING

OFF

FS3

FROM
FUEL
STORAGE
TANKS

1

OFF

FS4

OK

FS5

2

ON

PS 0
PS1

OK

FM
4
120
GPM

FS6

FM
5

SV-4

0
GPM

NOZZLE 1
DISCONNECTED

FS7

FM
6

SV-5

0
GPM

NOZZLE 2
DISCONNECTED

FS8

FM
7

SV-6

0
GPM

NOZZLE 3
DISCONNECTED

FS9

FM
8

SV-7

8559

120
GPM

NOZZLE 4
CONNECTED

06/21/93 05:29:59 DOOR OPEN   *** ALARM ***

26

right side of the screen depicts the four fuel nozzles that the locomotives can connect to. In this photo, nozzles one through three are disconnected and nozzle four is connected to a locomotive. Sensors detect the identifying number of the locomotive and it is displayed on the screen, in this case, number 8559. This system is expected to help Norfolk Southern manage and control its fuel consumption.

27 Documentation of computer applications is very important. Norfolk Southern stores its documentation in a central location. These cabinets have sliding doors that can be locked, controlling access to the documentation.

27

28

28 Norfolk Southern has established an office automation group that provides training and support for word processing and personal computer applications.

29 Railroads change as do computers. This old hand-powered railway car is displayed in the lobby of Norfolk Southern's computer facility. The equipment used on today's railroads has changed a great deal from this. But computer hardware has changed even more. Norfolk Southern has found that railroad equipment can be operated in a much more effective and efficient manner through the application of state-of-the-art computer technology. These computer applications ultimately benefit society through the availability of more efficient railway transportation.

29

By the Consultants:
- Training the users to employ the tools and create applications
- User encouragement, education, and selling
- Generation of applications (without programmers) in conjunction with users
- Generation and modification of prototypes
- Specification of changes to prototypes that may be needed to make them into working systems
- Consulting on user problems
- Determining whether a proposed application is suitable for Information Center development, and selecting the software and methods
- Demonstrations of Information Center capabilities to users, including senior management
- General communication with senior management
- Communication with traditional DP development
- Linking to the data administrator(s) in defining and representing data
- Maintaining a catalog of available applications and data bases
- Coordination to prevent duplicate or redundant application development

By the Technical Specialists:
- System set-up and support
- Dealing with technical and software problems
- Selection of languages and software and the versions of those which are used
- Assistance in choosing techniques or software for a given application (the job of the Techniques Analyst)
- Communication with vendors
- Monitoring system usage and planning future resources
- Charge-back to users
- Tuning or reorganizing an application for better machine performance
- Auditing system usage and application quality

FIGURE 7–9 Functions of an Information Center

James Martin, *Application Development without Programmers*, © 1982, p. 306. Reprinted by permission of Prentice-Hall Inc., Englewood Cliffs, NJ.

PC USER TIP   Information About Software Selection

There is a host of software available for personal computers and the variation in quality is enormous, ranging from state-of-the-art right down to worthless. How does the personal-computer user tell the good from the bad? What can you base your decisions on?

There are several sources at your disposal. The best are:

1. Review articles in periodicals
2. Vendor literature (including reader-inquiry cards)
3. Dealer (retailer) literature and advice
4. Demonstration software
5. Feedback from current users (see user tip 16-2)

Some periodicals with excellent reviews are:

1. *PC Magazine*
   P.O. Box 2445
   Boulder, CO 80322

2. *PC Week*
   One Park Avenue, Fourth Floor
   New York, NY 10016

3. *InfoWorld*
   375 Cochituate Road
   Framingham, MA 01701

the demand for programmers would decrease drastically and perhaps even disappear as application development by users continues to increase, which it will most certainly do. However, there will continue to be a large demand for programmers, for the following reasons:

1. The explosion in the use of computers has created a very large demand for application software developed both through conventional programming and through user development.
2. There will continue to be a significant proportion of all applications that are of a prespecified nature, and therefore are well suited to the conventional development cycle.
3. Systems software such as operating systems and data-base management systems, as well as application software created for sale by vendors, are likely to continue to be developed using conventional programming because of efficiency considerations. There is a large demand for programmers in this area. In fact, the most highly skilled programmers work for software vendors.

Summing Up

☐ The conventional process of developing applications has several disadvantages:

1. The high cost of programming expertise makes it very expensive
2. The time span for program development is usually very long
3. Program maintenance absorbs much programmer time, to the detriment of new-system development

☐ Computing can be classified into two categories:

1. Prespecified
2. User-driven

☐ User-driven systems can be created through the use of five techniques:

1. Personal-computer tools
2. Query languages/report generators
3. Graphics generators
4. Decision-support/financial-modeling tools
5. Application generators

☐ Where application development by users is employed, three types of application development usually evolve:

1. Conventional application development cycle
2. Prototyping with a fourth-generation language and subsequent coding with a conventional language
3. Total system development with a fourth-generation language

☐ Data-base administration is very important when users develop their own applications. It has to ensure that data redundancy is minimized, and shared data resources are properly used by all.

- ☐ The application development efforts of users can be coordinated by an information center. This center assists users in developing their own applications.
- ☐ With more and more users creating their own applications, the roles of systems analysts and programmers are changing.

Key Terms

application development by users
end user
prespecified computing
user-driven computing
personal-computer tools
query languages
report generators
graphics generators
decision-support/financial-modeling tools
application generators

generalized modules
user exits
prototype
skeleton application program
data-base administration
information center
technical specialists
personal-computer consultants
user consultants

Self-Quiz

Completion Questions

1. _____ means that the users develop software without the assistance of programmers, and quite often without system analysts.
2. Computer softwares such as Lotus 1–2–3 and dBase, which end users employ to create application software, are called _____ .
3. According to Martin, computing is classified into two categories: prespecified and _____ .
4. In _____ computing, processing requirements can largely be determined prior to developing the application.
5. _____ allow a user to search a data base or file, using simple or complex selection criteria.
6. The purpose of a(n) _____ is to manage the support for application development by users.
7. _____ allow a user or programmer to insert procedural program code in the generated application.
8. _____ are similar to query languages except that they can perform more complex data-processing tasks and can produce reports in almost any format.

9. _____ can create an entire information-system application, including input validation, file update, processing, and report generation.
10. The person responsible for coordinating the data base, including providing for data security and to prevent data redundancy is the

_____ .

Multiple-Choice Questions

1. Which of the following is not a characteristic of the conventional process of developing application systems?
   a. Increasing labor costs for programming and system analysis
   b. Slow implementation of system changes
   c. Minimized maintenance of application software
   d. Very long time span of development.
   e. All of the above are true.
2. When users do not know in detail what they want until they use a version of it, the type of computing is:

a. prospective
b. user-driven
c. prespecified
d. structured
e. none of the above

3. Prespecified computing is most appropriate for which of the following applications?
   a. administrative procedures
   b. decision-support systems
   c. information systems
   d. operating-system software
   e. paperwork-avoidance systems

4. Which of the following is not one of the three types of application development typically used by a firm where application development is done by users?
   a. conventional application-development cycle
   b. prototyping with a fourth-generation language
   c. total system development with a fourth-generation language
   d. all of the above are typically used by such a firm

5. Which of the following is not true of report generators?
   a. They are similar to query languages.
   b. They are generally used without assistance from information-systems professionals.
   c. RPG is a popular report generator.
   d. They can perform more complex data-processing tasks than most query languages.
   e. All of the above are true.

6. For a package to be considered suitable for end users, a typical end user must be able to learn to use it in a _____ course.
   a. two-day
   b. one-week
   c. two-week
   d. one-month
   e. six-month

7. Which of the following is not true of fourth-generation languages?
   a. They should enable users to develop software in one-tenth of the time required by third-generation languages.
   b. They should be user-friendly.

c. They should be appropriate for use by both end users and information-system professionals.
   d. Lotus 1–2–3 is an example of a fourth-generation language.
   e. All of the above are true.

8. Over the last thirty years, software labor costs have _____ and hardware costs have _____ .
   a. increased/decreased
   b. decreased/decreased
   c. increased/stayed approximately the same
   d. decreased/stayed approximately the same

9. Which approach is more likely to be successful in applications that process very high volumes of data?
   a. traditional development
   b. structured development
   c. prototyping with a fourth-generation language
   d. total system development with a fourth-generation language

10. Which of the following is not a role of system analysts when application development is being done by users?
   a. They should search constantly for more effective and efficient ways of creating applications.
   b. They should encourage the use of programmers.
   c. They should take on a consultant role.
   d. They should encourage rapid adoption of application development by users.
   e. All of the above are roles of system analysts.

Answers

Completion	Multiple Choice
1. Application development by users	1. c
2. fourth-generation languages	2. b
3. user-driven	3. d
4. prespecified	4. d
5. Query languages	5. b
6. information center	6. a
7. User exits	7. e
8. Report generators	8. a
9. Application generators	9. c
10. data-base administrator	10. b

How American Express Saves with PC XTs

By Arielle Emmett

Do you remember what he looks like? The tough cop, kind-eyed and fedora-clad, lurks behind curtains at operas and airports. "Don't leave home without them!" he exhorts, meaning the traveler's checks backed by the pillar of the financial community, American Express. Can the company that promotes the tough but kind image itself maintain a similar stance toward its own internal operations, cutting costs while providing high-quality services to both employees and customers?

At Amex's Human Resource Systems Department in the New York corporate headquarters, managers are cutting costs and maintaining a lean and security-conscious profile by using PCs to decentralize record keeping and report writing. The strategy is reducing the unit's reliance on the corporate mainframe for generating reports.

"Our general philosophy is that we're decentralizing many functions," says Walter Whitt, vice president of headquarter personnel and employee relations. "A major reason for going to the personal computer is cost. Within our department, on

an annual basis we'll reduce our operating costs by about $120,000 to $150,000. With a personal computer-based information retrieval package, we move from a complicated search-writing language on a mainframe to a simpler language. That move enables our personnel generalists to access data on the PC, which gives us our second major benefit."

Human Resource's central strategy involves linking an already existing personnel information system on severalk IBM and DEC mainframes to three IBM PC XTs equipped with PC/Focus, a database manager and application development tool. The Focus package by Information Builders, Inc. (New York, N.Y.) offers a screen manager and report writer, enabling personnel managers to develop selected employee data bases on hard disk or to write queries that extract personnel files from the mainframe. This package lets you manipulate and execute large

chunks of data, as well as reports, on the XT. Focus files are encrypted to ensure limited and secure access.

Corporate Human Resource Systems, Whitt's department, shares responsibility for keeping track of 25,000 American Express employee files with 10 personnal offices around the country. Amex's subsidiaries maintain separate personnel records. Whitt's department has had the additional task of developing microcomputing applications: among them, a master file on about 1000 corporate headquarter employees. This strategy, Whitt says, "reduces operating costs because we're no longer running those searches on our central processing unit."

Indeed, all current data on corporate headquarter employees is compiled on the XT's hard disk, which authorized personnel management can access. Details of salary, job classification, eligibility for bonuses, benefits, selected medical information, and demographics are sorted and extracted using PC/Focus's database management capabilities.

Personnel management can then print out any number of customized reports on benefits, compensation, recruitment, EEO (Equal Employment Opportunity), training, and management development. Amex uses such reports to track employee talent, determine salary and benefits structures, and forecast the effects of proposed policy changes on employee populations.

"We're doing almost all our master file searches with PC/Focus," says Claire Lichack, manager of human resource systems operations in the corporate division. She is responsible for researching and implementing new PC applications in the personnel area.

The corporate historical files will be converted to the XT next year. "We have an XT in the medical department now and one in employee relations," she says. "All these applications are being created with PC/Focus. It seems to be the answer for us."

The answer, though, grew out of a series of frustrations and uncontained costs. Amex's personnel divisions, Lichack says, had been tasked in the early 1980s with producing literally hundreds of reports each month. They used the company's IBM mainframe and a batch report generator package that had been installed in 1978.

"At one point in time, we weren't being charged for the reports, and then we were charged a flat rate," Lichack reports. The flat rate for each report was satisfactory at first because personnel did not produce that many computerized reports.

But needs changed. "Management wanted new ways to look at the data," Lichack observes. The numbers and statistical complexities of the reports increased dramatically. So did the cost: Some reports were $100 apiece.

"In 1982 we were experiencing very large costs to create these reports," Lichack says. "Part of the problem was that people in personnel weren't that familiar with the report generator on the mainframe. They were using inefficient coding techniques, and we didn't have the most efficient methods in place for doing batch searches. So we started to look into the possibility of getting

another report generator. That was like chasing the Holy Grail."

Lichack looked at many mainframe report generators and rejected most of them because of their inflexible reporting structure or lack of statistical measures. "I was particularly impressed with mainframe Focus because it was fairly easy to learn," Lichack says. However, a decision was made to stick with the current report generator.

"At the time we were making decisions about mainframe alternatives, we were also deciding to look into personal computers to see if they would be used for information retrieval. And that was the only thing we were looking at," Lichack notes. "If PCs could do information retrieval, we could really cut costs."

Her search for the right PC and software proved less quixotic than the mainframe software search. "We were basing the choice of personal computers on the software—software and communications," she says. "I wasn't about to buy a machine and then go looking around for software to run on it. I wanted to find the software first, then base the hardware decision on that."

Her strategy very quickly narrowed the search to IBM PCs and Apples, both of which run a variety of database management software. Lichack believes she was lucky that there were so few significant players in the market—and in Amex corporate headquarters.

"In house we had Apples and IBM PCs," Lichack recalls. "I didn't have to look at TRS-80s or Ataris or anything else. And I knew we wanted to get to the mainframe data." That

immediately imposed constraints on her choices.

"There were a lot of claims at the time by various vendors that they had an Apple link to the IBM mainframe," Lichack says. "I checked into a few of these claims, but nothing proved out." She decided to recommend the IBM PC at a time, "when it wasn't clear that IBM would be the winner." Amaex did not form a company-wide policy on personal computers until late 1983, when it chose IBM PCs.

Lichack's decision was a fortuitous one. Soon after the decision, Information Builders announced PC/Focus for the IBM XT. "PC/Focus seemed to be the answer to our problem because it was very similar to mainframe Focus. It offered similar coding and most of the features of the mainframe package." To Lichack, PC/Focus was a bargain at $1595 per package. It was capable of writing report queries and executing them on the XT or using Amex's existing personnel file on the mainframe.

Walter Whitt saw an immediate benefit. "We had problems in terms of people asking the [mainframe] system for one thing and getting something else," he says. With the IBM XT, we were looking at how we could separate our files and get each subsidiary's files separate for them."

The prospect of separate files, and easier access to files on the XT, meant more direct and responsible reporting. "Now someone such as myself, my secretary, or one of my managers in personnel can ask the computer for data when normally we'd have to go to Claire [Lichack] and her folks. About five people [out of an 11-person human resource department] use it now as compared to one person in the past."

The startup cost was about $10,000 for each XT. They are configured to act as either stand-alone computers or as links to Amex's IBM network of computers. The XTs that run the PC/Focus software package are equipped with 256 kilobytes of memory on the mother board. An expansion board from AST Research brings total memory up to 512 kilobytes.

The 10 megabytes of hard disk memory are enhanced with 20 megabytes of storage using an Iomega Bernoulli Box, a cartridge backup system. In addition, the XTs are equipped with an IRMA decision support interface board and software from Digital Communications Associates, Inc., which allows the XT to emulate an IBM 3278 terminal.

According to Lichack, tests of the XT-based personnel system were in full swing in the summer of 1983, and implemented on line this past January. Physically connected to an IBM 3274 control unit, which is linked to a traffic controller unit accessing Amex's communication network, the XTs can access files from three computers: two IBM MVS and VM system mainframes, as well as a DEC mainframe. In Lichack's office, managers write queries that extract selected files from the mainframes; these files are downloaded using the IRMA terminal emulator capability. They are stored on the XT's hard disk and then loaded into the PC/Focus program.

"We are downloading from the three computers," she says. "Before, it wasn't easy to take bonus data from the DEC and add it to the other files because they were on separate computers." Now the bonus data can be shuttled along the network from the DEC to the VM, and then downloaded directly to the XT. Selected extracts from main personnel files, known as timesharing option files, are downloaded as well. "We can utilize the data now since they're both in the same system," Lichack says. "It's a new way to use the data."

"I've done demos with executives who've never touched a computer before and they can produce simple reports [using PC/Focus] right away," Lichack reports. The software provides a relational data base; a single, straight-path data base is also available.

You can transfer Focus files to other software such as Lotus. "If I have Lotus, I can take the data and put it in a Lotus 1-2-3 or Symphony format," Lichack says. "If you have software that has DIF [data interchange format] files, then you can take the data from your PC/Focus report, format it in DIF and feed it into those files. There are a lot of options."

When Lichack wants to sort data, she enters a request on Focus. "A window appears with field names. The request can tell the system, for example, how you want it to sort a report—alphabetically or by some other measure. Once the sorting strategies are designated, Focus will extract the data requested and produce a report.

Lichack and Whitt say that applications are being developed on PCs to track employee assistance programs and a special employee "express-line"—a PC-based communication system for employees and managers. Lichack will further consolidate corporate employee records by incorporating historical files on the XT next year.

Amex as a whole is still tied to networked systems—nine major information processing centers and six worldwide data and timesharing networks. The number of PCs is small when compared with the 17,000 terminals Amex uses internally.

"But in our own department," says Whitt, "we've begun to revolutionize our process. By operating on our own PC system, we've reduced costs."

DISCUSSION QUESTIONS

1. What is your opinion of Claire Lichack's decision to look for software to meet Amex's needs prior to choosing a computer?

2. What advantages are there to choosing a software package that runs both on a personal computer and mainframes such as FOCUS?

3. Claire Lichack is now developing systems that meet Amex's information needs on personal computers. Do you think that any of the basic concepts of systems analysis, design and implementation that are used to develop systems for mainframes also apply to the development of systems for personal computers?

PART THREE

Computer
Resources

Chapter 8

The Central Processing Unit and Storage Devices

CHAPTER OUTLINE

PROLOGUE

Ann Martin is thinking about buying a personal computer. The choices she has to make concerning primary memory and secondary storage confuse her. Terminology such as RAM and ROM is unfamiliar to her. And there are floppy-disk drives, hard-disk drives, and laser-optical disk drives to consider. She would like to know what these devices are and to have a good understanding of the advantages and disadvantages of each. These and other topics will be examined in this chapter.

Introduction

The usefulness of a computer system for business purposes is largely determined by the characteristics of the **central processing unit (CPU)** and the storage devices. The CPU is the centerpiece of a computer system; strictly speaking, it is the computer (see Figure 8–1). Of course software and input/output devices are also important, but it is the traits of the CPU and storage devices, such as primary-storage size, that determine whether certain business applications are feasible on a given computer system. Therefore, understanding these basic characteristics is crucial to business users of computers.

In this chapter, we will distinguish between digital and analog computers, cover the primary components of a CPU, and explore the differences between mainframe, mini, and microcomputers. We will cover primary and secondary storage, including the current media used in these two types of storage and the technology likely to be used in future computer systems.

The Central Processing Unit

Digital versus Analog Computers

In a fundamental sense, all computers are symbol manipulators. They manipulate symbols such as numbers, alphabetic characters, names, amounts, and addresses. They can add two symbols together, move a symbol from one location to another, and compare symbols. Digital and analog computers differ in the way they represent symbols internally. Table 8–1 illustrates the representation of the decimal numbers zero through nine in a digital computer versus an analog computer. The **digital computer** represents the decimal numbers through a string of eight bits.

Table 8–1   Digital versus Analog Number Representation

Decimal Number Representation	Digital Computer Bits On (1) and Bits Off (0)	Analog Computer Voltage Level
0	1111 0000	10
1	1111 0001	12
2	1111 0010	14
3	1111 0011	16
4	1111 0100	18
5	1111 0101	20
6	1111 0110	22
7	1111 0111	24
8	1111 1000	26
9	1111 1001	28

Analog computers are primarily of historical interest since digital computers are rapidly replacing them.

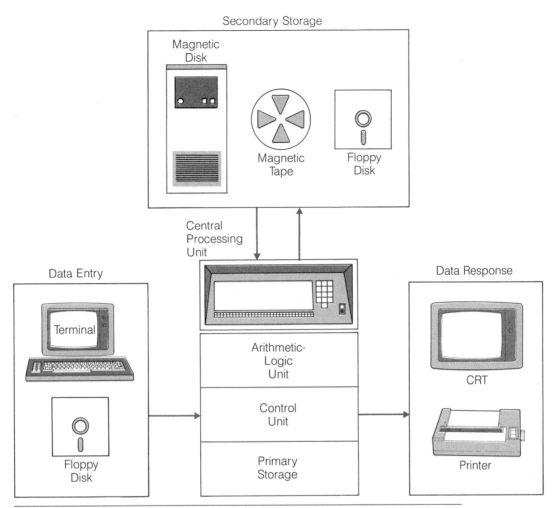

Figure 8–1   A Computer System

This chapter we will concentrate on the central processing unit and secondary storage. Chapter 9 will cover data entry and data response.

When the bit is on, it represents a one; when it is off, it represents a zero. The complete string of eight bits, called a byte, is used to code a character or represent a decimal number. In the computer, an "on" bit is represented by a positively charged magnetic domain such as a small spot on a tape or disk, or by the fact that a circuit is conducting an electrical flow. An "off" bit is represented by a negatively charged magnetic domain, or by the fact that a circuit is not conducting electrical flow. Thus digital computers operate directly with digits either at the bit level, which is short for *binary* digit, or at the byte level where a nonbinary digit such as a *decimal number* or alphabetic character is represented.

On the other hand, an **analog computer** does not operate directly with digits but rather represents digits through a continuous physical magnitude such as voltage level or the amount of rotation of a shaft. Table 8–1 illustrates the rep-

binary
(1) A condition that has two possible values or states. (2) A number system whose base is two.

decimal number system
A number system whose base is ten; that is, it represents numbers in terms of the powers of ten (for example, units, tens, hundreds, et cetera). This is the number system we use in our everyday lives.

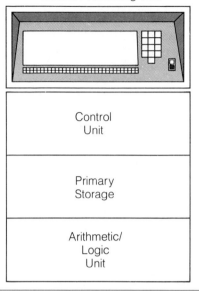

Central Processing Unit

Figure 8–2 Components of a CPU

The microprocessor on a semiconductor chip, used in personal computers, contains only the control unit and arithmetic/logic unit. Primary storage is contained on memory chips that plug into the system board.

resentation of the decimal numbers zero through nine through measurements of voltage levels.

Analog computers are used almost exclusively in process control and scientific applications. For example, they can monitor the thickness of steel coming out of a rolling mill and automatically adjust the mill to maintain the desired steel thickness. Digital computers are also used for process control. Digital computers are more accurate than analog computers and are more widely used in business information systems. For this reason we will discuss only digital computers. Figure 8–2 illustrates the components of a CPU—primary storage, the arithmetic-logic unit, and the control unit.

Primary Storage

Primary storage has three functions:

1. It stores operating-system programs which assist in managing the operation of the computer.
2. It stores the complete program that is being executed. (Except for virtual-storage systems, which are discussed in chapter 10, primary storage must store the complete program while it is being executed.)
3. It stores data while they are being processed by the CPU.

The bulk of data used by a computer application is stored in secondary-storage devices, but data must be stored in primary storage whenever the CPU is using

primary storage
The storage within a central processing unit which holds the program while it is being executed, the data which the program is using, and all or part of the operating system. Primary storage is often also called memory, internal storage, core storage, and RAM (random-access memory).

them in processing. Therefore, data are continually being moved into and out of primary storage during the execution of a program (see Figure 8-3). For example, a complete customer record—that is, all the data associated with a particular customer—would most likely be stored in primary storage while the CPU was processing that customer.

Compared with secondary storage, primary storage allows fast access. Fast-access primary storage is necessary because the other components of the CPU, the control unit and the arithmetic-logic unit, operate at electronic speeds. If the CPU had to depend on mechanical movement to retrieve specific pieces of data, as in the case of disk- or magnetic-tape storage, the primary-storage access speed would become a major bottleneck for the CPU, decreasing drastically the amount of work that could be performed in a given amount of time by the CPU. Ideally, the CPU should have a lot of very fast access primary storage; however, fast-access memory is more expensive than slower-access memory.

Early computer systems had modest amounts of primary storage. For example, a CPU with 64,000 bytes (characters) of primary storage was a large computer in the 1950s and 1960s. Many computers had 16,000 or less bytes of primary storage. Today large computer systems may contain 5 to 500 megabytes of primary storage. Even microcomputers have from 128 kilobytes to 1 megabyte of primary storage. In the 1950s and 1960s, primary storage was magnetic-core storage, as shown in Figure 8-4.

Magnetic cores are ferrite (iron) doughnut-shaped rings that can be *polarized* in either of two directions in order to represent a bit of data. Wires are strung through these cores so that data can be written on the cores and can be read from them. Core memory was widely used in the 1960s and early 1970s for primary storage; it is much more expensive to manufacture than the semiconductor memory widely used today for primary storage. Also, core memory is much slower than semiconductor memory. For these reasons magnetic-core storage is obsolete. However, the term *core* is often used to refer to primary storage, even though the storage is semiconductor.

Semiconductor chips contain electronic circuits that can be reproduced photographically in a miniaturized form on silicon chips. These chips are often referred to as large-scale integrated (LSI) circuits or, in the case of advanced semiconductor technology, very large scale integrated (VLSI) circuits. The development of semiconductor chips has revolutionized the computer industry as well as other industries. For example, the calculator that you can now buy at the grocery store for seven dollars would have cost more than a thousand dollars in the late 1960s.

The control unit and arithmetic/logic unit of a central processor can be placed on a single semiconductor chip. The processors on a chip are called microprocessors and are the basis for the microcomputer industry (see Figure 8-5). In fact, a CPU with much more computing power than the ENIAC computer of the 1940s can be placed on a chip approximately a quarter-inch square, whereas the ENIAC required a large room. Figure 8-5 shows a chip greatly magnified; the actual size is about a quarter-inch square. Figures 8-6 and 8-7 illustrate two of the tasks performed in manufacturing semiconductor chips.

There are two advantages of using the semiconductor chip in computer hardware. First, it can be reproduced in great quantities by automated means and is therefore inexpensive. A microprocessor (CPU) on a chip may cost less than ten

polarize
To cause a magnetic substance to contain a positive or negative charge.

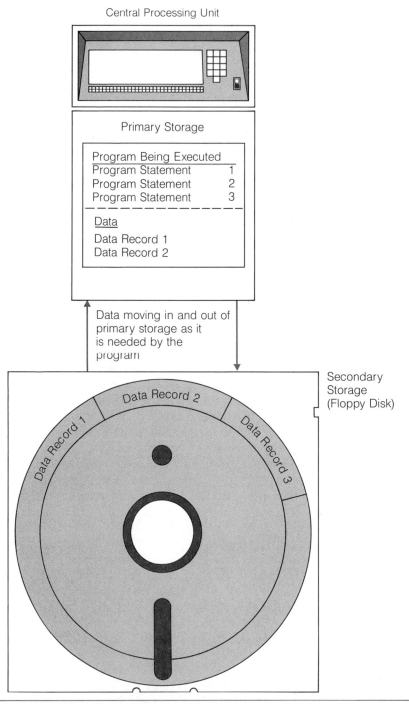

Central Processing Unit

Primary Storage

Program Being Executed	
Program Statement	1
Program Statement	2
Program Statement	3

Data

Data Record 1
Data Record 2

Data moving in and out of
primary storage as it
is needed by the
program

Secondary
Storage
(Floppy Disk)

Data Record 1
Data Record 2
Data Record 3

Figure 8–3 The Movement of Data Between Primary and Second-ary Storage

Some programs, such as electronic spreadsheets, move a complete file into primary storage rather than part of it at a time. Others, such as data-base management systems, move only a few records from a file into primary storage at a time.

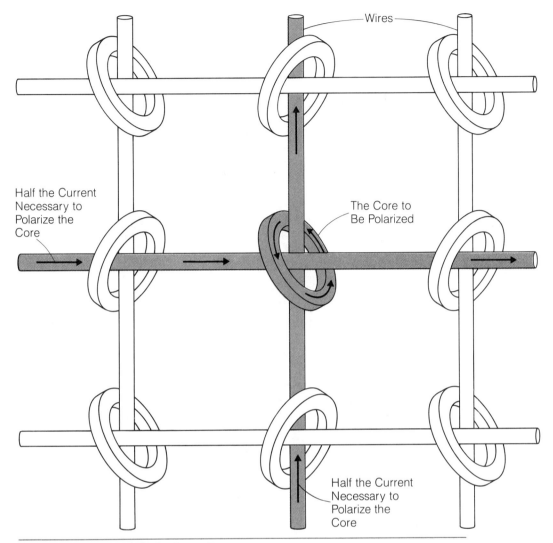

Wires

Half the Current
Necessary to
Polarize the
Core

The Core to
Be Polarized

Half the Current
Necessary to
Polarize the
Core

Figure 8–4 Magnetic-Core Storage

One-half the current necessary to polarize the core either positively or negatively is passed through two wires. The core at the intersection of these two wires is polarized. Passing current through the wires in the opposite direction polarizes the core in the opposite direction.

dollars per copy. Second, the miniaturization of circuits has greatly enhanced the speed of the computer. The speed at which a CPU operates is bounded by two factors—the speed at which electrical currents flow (about one-half the speed of light) and the distance over which they must flow. Computer designers have been able, through miniaturization, to greatly decrease this distance and thus greatly increase the speed of CPUs. Improvements in semiconductor technology are the primary driving force behind improvements in computer hardware. It appears that

nonvolatile storage
Primary or secondary storage that does not lose the data stored in it when the electrical power is interrupted.

random
Having no specific order or pattern. In the case of RAM, random access means that the computer can access any memory position directly and in any order, and the time necessary to access data is independent of the data's location in memory.

semiconductor technology has not yet reached its theoretical limits. Therefore we can expect substantial additional improvements in hardware performance.

Semiconductors used in primary storage represent a bit of data by means of an individual circuit that either conducts or does not conduct electricity. From this fact arises the primary disadvantage of using semiconductors for primary storage. When the electrical supply to a CPU using semiconductor storage is interrupted, none of the circuits conducts electricity. Therefore, the CPU loses the data contained in primary storage, including any programs located there. Semiconductor storage is **volatile,** that is, the storage loses its data representation when electrical power is interrupted. This can be overcome with an uninterruptible power source (provided by back-up batteries and generators). It can also be overcome by using **checkpoints.** At certain points (checkpoints) in the execution of a program, the data and status of the program can be written onto ***nonvolatile storage*** such as magnetic disks, so that if a power interruption does occur, the complete program will not have to be reexecuted. Instead, the computer system will go back to the nearest checkpoint and begin execution at that point. The volatility of semiconductor storage is a relatively minor disadvantage compared with the advantages of this type of storage.

Both 64K-bit chips and 256K-bit chips are widely used as primary memory for computers. In addition, 1-megabit chips have been announced by AT&T and will be used in future microcomputers. Table 8–2 illustrates the storage capacities of these chips.

There are two basic types of semiconductor memory: **random-access memory (RAM)** and **read-only memory (ROM).** Actually, magnetic core is also RAM memory since access to a particular area of the memory can be performed on a *random* basis. However, the term *RAM* is usually used to refer to random-access semiconductor memory. RAM and the term *primary storage* as we have been using it are synonymous. This kind of memory stores the user's program while it is being executed and the data while they are being processed by the CPU. The CPU can perform read or write operations at any memory position of random-access memory at any point in time. RAM is volatile memory.

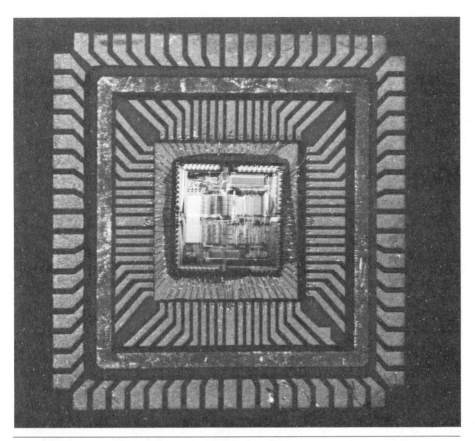

Figure 8–5   A VLSI Microprocessor

This is a 32-bit microprocessor, meaning that when it performs operations on data it moves 32 bits at a time (the equivalent of four characters).

Read-only memory can be read from but not written to. Therefore, ROM comes from the manufacturer with programs already stored in it which the user of the computer cannot modify. Because the storage is permanent, ROM is nonvolatile memory. ROM is used to store those programs which are frequently used by many computer applications. For example, the IBM Personal Computer stores a BASIC *interpreter* in ROM. It also stores part of the PC-DOS operating system, the basic input/output system (BIOS) in ROM.

This technique of placing software or programs in hardware (the ROM semi-conductor chip) is often called **microcoding** (also called **microprogramming** or **firmware**). The current trend is to replace more of the electronic logic circuitry with firmware. Microcoded programs in a computer can be changed simply by removing the ROM and replacing it with another ROM. Thus computers can be tailored to meet the needs of specific users.

There are two subclasses of ROM: **programmable read-only memory (PROM)** and **erasable programmable read-only memory (EPROM).** PROM can be programmed (a program can be read into the PROM) one time by either the

interpreter
A program that translates a high-level language like BASIC into machine language.

Figure 8-6 Seventy Thousand Parts per Quarter Inch

Tamara Bish inspects a reticle at NCR Corporation's microelectronics facility in Colorado Springs, Colorado. Comparable to a photographic negative, this reticle and others similar to it are used to pack more than 70,000 active microelectronic elements onto the NCR/32, a ¼-inch-square microcomputer chip. The reticle is inserted into a "wafer stepper" as part of the process of creating more than 100 microchips on a 5-inch silicon wafer.

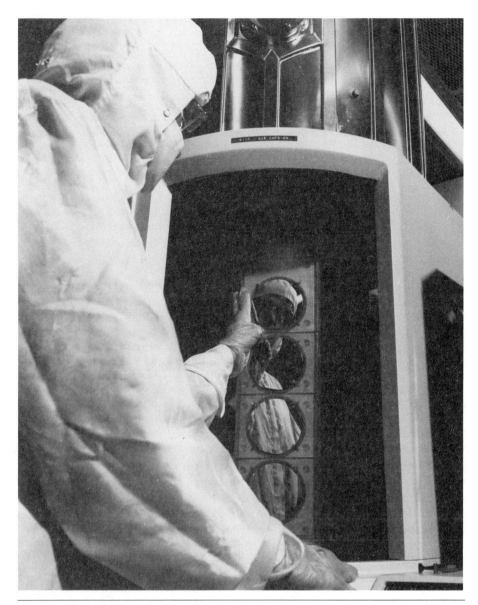

Figure 8–7 Mirror, Mirror

Technician Rosa Burch reflects on four silicon wafers she is loading into a "plasma etcher" at NCR Corporation's microelectronics facility in Colorado Springs, Colorado. More than a hundred computer microprocessor chips can be etched on each wafer. Snow White's nemesis probably would have received a much more complex response had she been talking to this device rather than to a standard wall mirror.

Table 8–2 Storage Capacities of Semiconductor-Memory Chips

Chip Size	Capacity in Bits	Capacity in Bytes (Characters)
64K-bit chip	65,536	8,192 or 8K bytes
256K-bit chip	262,144	82,768 or 32K bytes
1 megabit chip	1,048,576	131,072 or 128K bytes

Many personal computers contain 64K-bit memory chips. Each chip holds 8K bytes. To add 64K bytes of memory to such a PC you must buy nine memory chips: eight to hold the 64K bytes of data, and one in order to do parity checking.

manufacturer or the computer user. Once PROM is programmed, it is essentially the same as ROM since it cannot be modified. On the other hand, EPROM can be programmed and then erased through a special process. Once erased, EPROM can be reprogrammed. Semiconductor memory is illustrated in Figure 8–8.

Arithmetic-Logic Unit

The **arithmetic-logic unit** performs arithmetic operations such as multiplication, division, subtraction, and addition. It also performs logical operations such as comparing the relative magnitude of two pieces of information. Arithmetic-logic operations are performed serially, that is, one at a time, based on instructions from the control unit.

Control Unit

The **control unit** decodes program instructions and directs the other parts of the computer system to perform the tasks specified. The program instructions are in machine language. They consist of an **operation code** to be performed, such as add, subtract, move, or compare, and the **operands,** which are the entities to which the operation is applied, such as data and input/output units.

Two cycles are performed for each program instruction—the instruction cycle and the execution cycle. The process of executing an individual program instruction begins with the control unit moving the instruction from primary memory into the control unit for decoding. The operation code and the operands are examined and decoded. This process of decoding the instruction is called the **instruction**

Thinking About Information Systems 8–1

Mary Delafore is a freshman in an introductory information-systems class. She is an aspiring accounting major and hopes to become an auditor with a Big Eight accounting firm. One of the first topics in the course is the internal design of the computer and the differences in various sizes of computers including mainframes, minicomputers, and microcomputers. She feels that this study of hardware is a waste of time because it does not have anything to do with accounting and auditing. Can you think of any situations where Mary will need to know about computer hardware and processing in her career as an auditor?

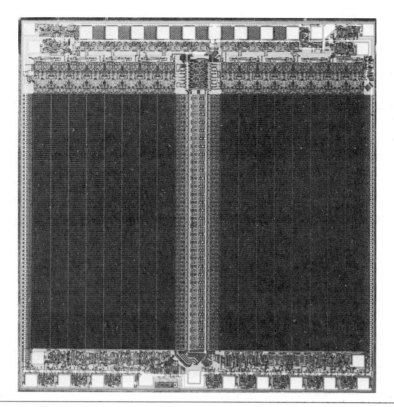

Figure 8–8   Semiconductor Memory Chip
The electronic circuitry shown here is reproduced onto semiconductor material, then contacts are added and the chip is coated in plastic.

cycle. The **execution cycle** begins when the control unit causes the appropriate unit to perform the operation called for in the instruction. This unit may be the arithmetic-logic unit, or it may be an input/output unit. Input/output to or from the primary storage of the CPU is handled by **channels,** which are, in effect, small specialized CPUs. Thus the main CPU does not have to perform the relatively mundane, standardized, and time-consuming task of handling input/output operations.

Micros, Minis, Mainframes, and Supercomputers

Microcomputers

The smallest and least expensive of the computer systems are called micros or **microcomputers** (see Figure 8–9). Since they are often used by one person, the term *personal computer* has become popular. Microcomputer systems typically have between 64K and 1 megabyte of primary storage. They can handle peripheral

Figure 8–9   Microcomputer System

Apple Computer has been one of the innovators in the personal-computer industry. It entered the PC field in 1977 (IBM entered it in 1981). For example, Apple's Macintosh computer had many features and capabilities not available in other personal computers when it was introduced.

devices like terminals, relatively slow-speed printers, cassette tapes, floppy disks, and Winchester hard disks. Because of their low cost, microcomputer systems are used by even the smallest of businesses.

Minicomputers

Minis or **minicomputers** are medium-sized systems that typically have from 128K to several megabytes of primary storage (see Figure 8–10). Their processing power is more than micros but less than mainframes. Minicomputers were first developed for use in process-control, scientific, and engineering applications. They were used, for example, to monitor automated manufacturing processes such as steel rolling and to adjust the equipment automatically in order to keep the output within specified tolerances. However, it was soon discovered that these computers had tremendous potential in data processing, especially for smaller companies. Mini-computer systems can be equipped with most of the input/output devices and secondary-storage devices that the large mainframe systems can handle, such as terminals and rigid disks. They are also used in **distributed data-processing** systems. Instead of a company having one large mainframe computer, it can dis-

Figure 8–10   Minicomputer System

Prime Computer, Inc. has been a leader in the production of minicomputer systems. Prime equipment is known for its advanced features and ease of use.

tribute its data processing with a minicomputer at each of its remote locations, and connect them to each other through telecommunication links.

Mainframe Computers

Mainframes are large systems having 5 to 200 megabytes of primary storage and the input/output units associated with a large computer system (see Figure 8–11). They can support several hundred online terminals. For online secondary storage they use high-capacity magnetic-disk drives capable of storing several *gigabytes* of data. Mainframe computers typically use high-capacity magnetic tape for *offline* storage of data. Most medium to large companies will have one or more mainframe computers which perform the bulk of their information processing. Applications that run on mainframes tend to be large and complex, where the data and information must be shared by many users throughout the organization.

Minis overlap mainframes, and micros overlap minis. As minis become more powerful, they tend to perform with equal efficiency the jobs that were done by mainframes. The boundary lines of the three types of computer systems are constantly changing.

gigabyte
one billion bytes.

offline
Data or a device that is not under direct control of the computer. Usually a person must place an off-line reel of tape on a tape drive before the computer can access data stored on it.

Figure 8–11   Mainframe Computer

The IBM 3084, shown here, is one of IBM's largest mainframes. It is widely used by large businesses.

Supercomputers

Supercomputers are even larger, in terms of processing power, than mainframes (see Figure 8–12). They are rarely used for business information systems. Their primary use is in scientific applications, especially where large simulation models are needed. In **simulation,** mathematical models of real-world physical systems are coded into software which is executed on a computer. The execution of the computer software then models the real-world system. For example, the National Oceanic and Atmospheric Administration uses supercomputers to model the world's weather system; such models improve weather predictions. Simulation models are often large and complex. Certainly a model of the world's weather system would be! For these models to execute in a reasonable length of time a supercomputer is necessary. This fact points to the primary difference between a supercomputer and a mainframe. Most supercomputers have a processing speed that is about four to ten times faster than mainframe computers.

Secondary Storage

Primary versus Secondary Storage

Earlier in this chapter, we covered primary storage and its characteristics. As illustrated in Figure 8–1, primary storage is a part of the CPU and it must allow very

Figure 8–12 A Supercomputer

This computer is capable of performing one billion combined arithmetic/logic operations per second! Its central processing unit is cooled with a liquid refrigerant to increase its speed.

fast access in order to increase the speed at which the CPU can operate. **Secondary storage,** on the other hand, is physically separate from the CPU. Why do we have this distinction in types of storage? Why isn't the CPU designed with large amounts of primary storage so that all of the data can be randomly accessible at electronic speeds, with no mechanical movement? The answer is cost. Primary storage is more expensive than secondary storage. Furthermore, the most widely used primary storage, semiconductor chips, is volatile. Secondary storage must be non-volatile, that is, it must be able to retain the data stored in it even when the electrical current is off. All widely used secondary-storage media require mechanical movement for access to the data. Therefore, it is relatively slow, but, in contrast to primary storage, it has the capability of storing large amounts of data at lower costs. Is it likely that computer systems in the future will use only one type of storage? Probably not, since the technologically most advanced, fastest, and therefore most expensive storage will be used in the CPU. Secondary storage will continue to use less expensive media.

Magnetic Tape

Magnetic tape has long been an important medium for secondary storage. Today it is used almost exclusively for backup purposes. For mainframes it is supplied on reels up to 2,400 feet long; the tape is usually one-half-inch wide and is similar in appearance to that used with tape recorders. Figure 8–13 illustrates data encoded on magnetic reel tape. Nine-track magnetic tape is by far the most common, although

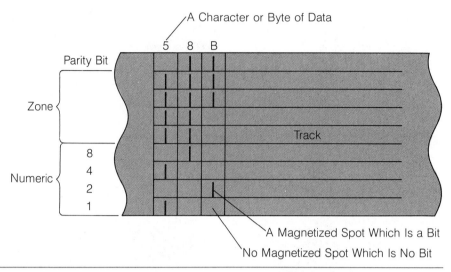

Figure 8–13   EBCDIC Coded Data on a Magnetic Tape

A character is recorded across the tape. The parity bit is used for checking purposes. Zone bits are needed only for encoding alphabetic and special characters, since only the four lower numeric bits are necessary to encode numeric data. In fact, when all the data to be stored are numeric, two numeric characters can be stored in one eight-bit byte. One of them is stored in the four zone bits. This type of storage is known as packed decimal.

seven-, eight-, and ten-track tapes are available. They use different coding schemes for each character. Figure 8–14 illustrates a typical magnetic-tape drive.

The **recording density** of magnetic tape refers to the number of bits per inch (BPI) or characters per linear inch that are recorded on a specific reel of tape.[1] The most common recording densities are 1,600 and 6,250 BPI.

Another form of magnetic tape used in microcomputer systems is cassette tape. These cassettes are physically identical to those used in stereo hi-fi systems. They are written to and read from by a standard audio tape recorder connected to the microcomputer.

Magnetic-tape cartridges with a storage capacity of 10 to 300 million characters are now being widely used to ***back up*** data stored on microcomputer hard disks (see Figure 8–15). As with all storage media, hard disks are subject to failure. Periodic copying of the data onto tape cartridges insures against loss of the data and programs stored on hard disks.

The advantages of magnetic tape are as follows:

1. The cost of tape is low compared with other forms of secondary storage.
2. Computer systems can use several tape drives simultaneously.
3. The rate at which data may be transferred to and from tape is very high for sequentially organized files.
4. As a storage media, magnetic tape is very compact and portable.

back up
To make an extra copy of current data and/or programs for use in case the original copy is partially or totally destroyed.

---

[1]BPI is also equivalent to bytes or characters per inch of magnetic tape, since a byte is recorded across the tape (see Figure 8–13).

Figure 8–14 A Magnetic-Tape Drive Used with Mainframes

The reel of magnetic tape usually is mounted and removed from the drive by a person. However, there are automated magnetic-tape libraries that retrieve, mount, and dismount tapes automatically. Magnetic tape is used primarily for backup. Optical-laser disks are likely to make magnetic tape obsolete.

5. Magnetic tape is ideal as backup storage for data.
6. Magnetic-tape devices have several self-checking features; therefore, the recording and reading of data on magnetic tape is highly reliable.
7. Record lengths on magnetic tape can be very large, as long as they are within the limits of the individual computer system.
8. We can use magnetic tape over and over for storage of different data simply by writing the new data over the old. We can also correct mistakes by writing over the old data.

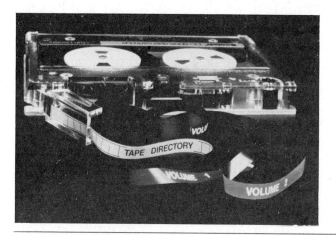
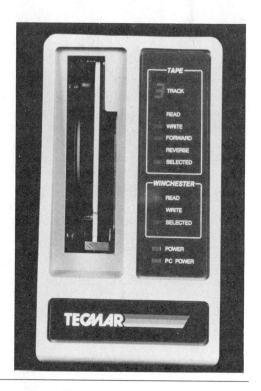

Figure 8–15   A Cartridge Tape and Drive

Cartridge tapes are widely used to back up data stored on fixed hard disks in personal computers. Copying data onto tape is much faster than copying it onto floppy disks. To use floppy disks to back up data stored on a ten-megabyte hard disk would require copying the data onto thirty individual floppy disks, a time-consuming process. One cartridge tape can store the complete ten or even twenty megabytes of data contained on a hard disk.

Disadvantages of magnetic tape include the following:

1. Magnetic tape is a sequential storage medium. Therefore, if a user wants to find an individual record stored on magnetic tape, the tape must be read up to the location of the desired record.
2. Damage to magnetic tape can result in the complete loss of data stored on the section of the tape that is near the damage: therefore, critical data should be stored on a backup tape or on another storage medium.
3. Magnetic tape is sensitive to dust, humidity, and temperature changes; consequently, the environment in which it is stored must be controlled.

Hard Disk

Magnetic disks are the most popular form of secondary storage. There are two basic types of disks: hard and floppy. Hard disks are widely used with all sizes of computers. They range in capacity from the 5-megabyte disk drives used with microcomputers to very high capacity disk drives such as IBM's 3380, which will store 5.04 gigabytes of data.

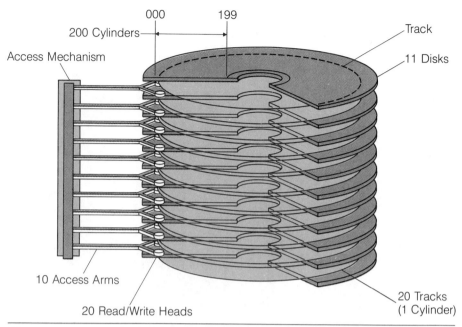

Figure 8–16   A Disk Pack

The access mechanism can position itself to access data from each of the two hundred cylinders. A cylinder is a set of all tracks with the same distance from the axis about which the disk pack rotates. In this example, there are twenty tracks in each cylinder.

Hard disks are aluminum or magnesium rigid platters with an iron-oxide (rust) coating. Data are stored as magnetic patterns in the coating. Figure 8–16 illustrates one type of disk pack used with mainframes. It has eleven individual platters, each with two surfaces, top and bottom. Since this is a *removable disk* pack, data are not stored on the top surface of the top platter or the bottom surface of the bottom platter because of the potential for damage to those surfaces. Therefore, there are twenty surfaces in the disk pack on which data can be stored. Within each surface, data are stored on **concentric tracks.** The same amount of data is stored on the outside tracks as is stored on the tracks in the center of the platter, even though the circumferences of these tracks differ substantially. The same amount of data is written on each track because the time that it takes for the disk to complete one revolution is the same for any track on the disk.

If the disk in Figure 8–16 has two hundred tracks on each surface, then the access arms can position themselves in two hundred track positions. When the access arm is positioned over one of these tracks, data can be read or written onto one track on each recording surface without the access arm being moved. The twenty tracks that are located at one position of the read/write access arms make up a **cylinder.** When data are stored sequentially on a disk, they are stored by cylinder; that is, all the tracks in one cylinder are filled before any tracks in the adjacent cylinder are filled. The cylinder approach improves read and write access speeds to the disk. The speed of access to data on a disk is a function of both the rotational speed of the disk and the speed with which the access arms move. Using

removable disk
A hard disk pack that can be removed from the disk drive.

concentric tracks
Circular tracks that have a common center.

Figure 8–17 A Disk Drive with Fixed Disk

Fixed disks can hold more data than the same size removable disks. They are sealed within the unit and are much more stable than removable disk packs.

the cylinder approach minimizes or eliminates the need for moving the access arms. Fixed and removable disk drives that are used with mainframes are illustrated in Figures 8–17 and 8–18.

Microcomputers use a type of hard disk known as **Winchester disks** (see Figure 8–19). Winchester disk units contain a small (five-and-a-quarter inch) hard disk with multiple platters, and they typically store from ten to twenty megabytes of data. They can be in the form of removable cartridge or *fixed disk*. Removable cartridges usually store from five to ten megabytes (see Figure 8–20); whereas fixed disks can store several hundred megabytes.

fixed disk
A hard disk pack that is permanently mounted in a disk drive and, therefore, cannot be removed.

Floppy Disk

Floppy disks (often called cassette disks, diskettes, or minidiskettes) are flat 3¼-, 3½-, 5¼-, or 8-inch disks of polyester film with an iron-oxide magnetic coating. As shown in Figure 8–21 the disk is covered with a protective jacket, and reading/writing from or to the disk is performed through the head access slot. Floppy disks have a capacity of 150K to more than 1 megabyte. Figures 8–22 and 8–23 illustrate floppy disk terminology and causes for data loss on floppy disks.

Floppy disks were originally developed by IBM in the early 1970s for use as secondary storage on minicomputers. However, they have become a widely used

Figure 8–18 Removing a Disk Pack from a Disk Drive

Removable disk packs allow one disk drive to access many disks. However, they are being used less, owing to the labor required in mounting and dismounting them.

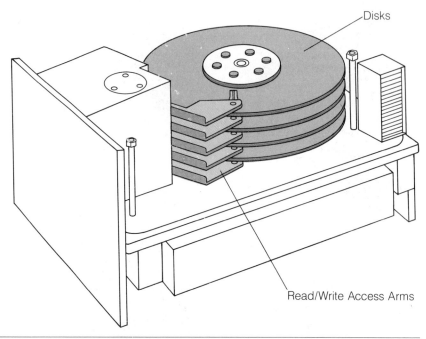

Disks

Read/Write Access Arms

Figure 8–19 Inside a Winchester-Disk Drive

Note the access arms in the center. Since the disk pack is not removable, data are stored on the top of the top platter and on the bottom of the bottom platter.

medium for secondary storage on microcomputers. Also, they are an important medium for *batch* data input to mainframe computers.

The primary advantages of floppy disks are their relatively low cost, large capacity, and small size. The equivalent of 180 double-spaced typewritten pages can be stored on a 360K floppy disk.

The advantages of magnetic disks (both hard and floppy) include the following:

1. The magnetic disk is a **direct-access storage** medium; therefore, the user can retrieve individual records without searching through the entire file.
2. Although disks are more expensive than magnetic tape, their cost has steadily declined over the years.
3. For online systems where direct access is required, disks are currently the only practical means of file storage.
4. Users can easily update records by writing the new information over the area where the old information was stored.
5. With removable disk packs or cartridges, a single disk drive can access a large number of disk packs. This method is especially economical with batch-processing applications which do not require frequent switching between disk packs. Because the same disk drive can be used to access more than one disk pack, the cost of the disk drive can be spread out over a larger volume of stored data.
6. Interrelated files stored on magnetic disk allow a single transaction to be processed against all of these files simultaneously. In addition, data can be

Figure 8–20 A Hard Disk Cartridge and Drive

Hard disk cartridges have essentially the same advantages and disadvantages as removable disks on large mainframe disk drives. One disk drive can access data on many different cartridges, but each cartridge must be inserted and removed.

Lowes Incorporated is a medium-sized regional department store. The company has a medium-sized IBM mainframe at its central headquarters. Accounts receivables is run on this mainframe and there are terminals in the various stores so that inquiries can be made concerning customer accounts. Some of the store managers feel that accounts receivable should be kept locally at each store. They argue that a microcomputer such as the IBM PC could be used to keep up with the accounts receivable at each store. Individuals in the central data-processing department argue that the volume of customers is too great for micros to handle accounts receivable. The managers counter this with the argument that two or more micros can be networked together to provide the necessary capacity, and that the micros in the various stores can be networked together. Which direction do you think Lowes should go? Should it maintain accounts receivable on the mainframe as it is doing now or convert the system to microcomputers?

Thinking About Information Systems 8–2

retrieved from interrelated files simultaneously. This capability makes possible relational data-base systems, as we will see in chapter 12.

The disadvantages of magnetic disks are as follows:

1. Compared with magnetic tape, hard disks are expensive.
2. Updating a master file stored on disk often destroys the old information. Therefore, disks may not provide an automatic **audit trail** and backup the

audit trail
The capability to reconstruct processing steps and trace information back to its origins.

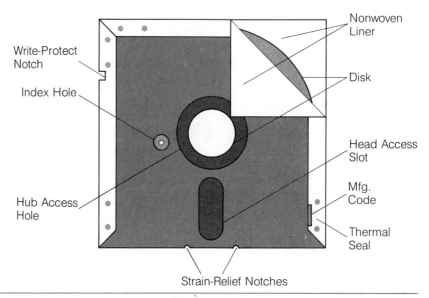

Figure 8–21 and labels:
- Write-Protect Notch
- Index Hole
- Hub Access Hole
- Nonwoven Liner
- Disk
- Head Access Slot
- Mfg. Code
- Thermal Seal
- Strain-Relief Notches

Figure 8–21   A 5¼-Inch Floppy Disk

The 5¼-inch diskette is often called a minidiskette because the first floppy disk produced was an eight-inch diskette. It was introduced in the 1970s for use with minicomputers.

way magnetic tape does. Subsequent to updating a master file stored on magnetic tape, there exists the old master file, the new master file, and the transaction file, on three separate reels of tape. When a disk is used, equivalent backup and audit trail require that each old master-file record be copied to another storage area prior to update.

3. For periodic batch-type systems where there is no need for between-run data retrieval from the files, magnetic tape serves just as well as disks for file-storage purposes—at substantially less cost.

Laser-Optical Disks

A type of secondary storage that is becoming very important is **laser-optical disks** (see Figure 8–24). These disks have the same technology as the digital compact disk players used with stereo systems. Currently, data can be written on them only one time; however, companies are planning erasable versions. The primary advantage of laser disks is large storage capacity at low cost; some of them cost less than ten dollars, and hold from 500 to 1,000 megabytes of data. Five hundred megabytes is the equivalent of 250,000 double-spaced typewritten pages, or the entire *Encyclopedia Brittanica* several times over! For mainframes, jukebox-like devices are being designed that will store and automatically retrieve large numbers of laser-optical disks. These devices will store hundreds of gigabytes of data or text. Optical disk drives for microcomputers cost 500 dollars or less.

The primary disadvantages of these disks include the write-only-once limitation and their slow access times compared with hard disks. Accessing data on laser disks is approximately ten times slower than on hard magnetic disks.

Disk or Diskette?

Definitions
- A disk is the circular-shaped media, inside the jacket, on which the magnetic data are stored.
- A diskette is a combination of the disk and its flexible jacket.

Flexible-Disk Construction Features

Index Hole	Physical hole in diskette which, when detected, notifies drive that beginning of track is under read-write head.
Hub Access Hole	Hole in center of jacket into which drive hub of transport fits.
Hub Reinforcement or Hub Ring	Ring added to hub hole area. Provides increased strength and support for diskettes during clamping.
Jacket	Protective vinyl covering which encloses disk but allows access to disk by head and drive hub.
Liner	Soft, nonwoven synthetic material bonded to inner side of jacket. Primary purpose is to wipe surface of disk as it rotates in jacket.
Strain-Relief Notch	Notches cut into jacket near head access slot to reduce creasing when jacket is flexed.
Write-Protect Notch	Notch in jacket which prevents inadvertent recording on an 8-inch diskette and allows recording on a 5¼-inch diskette.
Write Enable/ Protect Tab	Metalized, adhesive label which, when used to cover write protect notch, prevents recording on a 5¼-inch diskette or allows recording on an 8-inch diskette.
Head Access Slot	Slotted area of jacket which allows drive recording head physical access to media. All recording and data retrieval occur in this area.
Envelope	Outer protective covering which fits around diskette assembly to prevent damage and contamination during handling.

General Recording Terms

Bit	Smallest unit of information stored magnetically; usually it is the abbreviation for binary digit.
Byte	Eight bits equal one byte; usually equal to one alphanumeric character.

Media Terms

Oxide	Needle-shaped particles of iron oxide (rust). Used in manufacture of magnetic media.

Diskette Recording Terms

Sector	Division of magnetic surface of disk into separate, but contiguous, pie-shaped information zones by either magnetic or physical coding of disk.
Soft Sector	Sectors defined magnetically via software.
Hard Sector	Sectors defined physically by punching holes around inner or outer disk diameter.
Initialization/ Formatting	Magnetically coded pattern recorded on disk to identify each track and sector.
Single Sided	Diskette made for use on disk drives with one recording head. Only one side of diskette is certified 100% error-free.
Dual Sided	Diskette made for use on disk drives with two recording heads. Both sides of diskette are certified 100% error-free.
Single Density	Machine-controlled method of recording data on diskette.
Double Density	Machine-controlled method of recording twice the amount on diskette as is possible with single-density method.
Downward Compatibility	Using double-density diskette in single-density application.

Figure 8—22   Floppy Disk Terminology

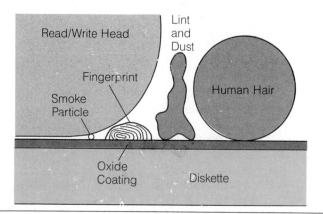

Figure 8–23 Some Causes of Data Loss on Floppy Disks

As you can see, some very small particles look huge in comparison to the distance between the surface of a diskette and the ceramic read/write head. If these particles become lodged between the head and the surface of the diskette, the surface may be scratched, resulting in data loss. So be sure to keep your dust covers on your diskettes.

Figure 8–24 Laser-Optical Disks

This one-sided optical storage disk can hold as much data as can be stored on 50 or more reels of magnetic tape.

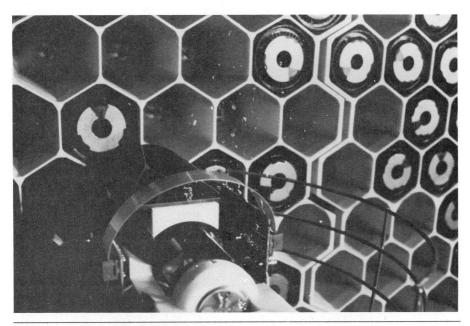

Figure 8–25   Mass-Storage Device

This device is used whenever very large amounts of data must be stored. For example, the Internal Revenue Service uses these devices to store income-tax data.

Laser disks are used for storing large volumes of data that are not accessed or changed often. They are likely to replace magnetic tape for backup purposes. They will also provide microcomputer users with large data banks such as historical stock-market prices. One of the most promising uses for these disks is in libraries; card catalogs, microfilm holdings, and Library of Congress collections are being put on laser disks.

Other Forms of Secondary Storage

Another type of direct-access storage is the **mass-storage** device. These devices (such as the IBM 3850) can store very large amounts of data and access these data without human intervention (see Figure 8–25). The 3850 mass-storage subsystem can store up to 472 billion bytes of data. This is approximately the amount of data that can be stored on 47,200 reels of magnetic tape! Data in this system are stored on small, fist-sized cartridges which are in turn stored in honeycomblike cells. Mechanical-cartridge access arms can remove the cartridges from the cell and place them on a read/write unit. The data are stored within the cartridge on a 3×770 inch strip of magnetic tape.

Because of the relatively large amount of physical movement, even though it is machine movement, mass-storage data systems provide much slower access to data than a magnetic disk unit. In fact, some users have found that data can be accessed just as fast using 6,250 BPI magnetic tape.

As technology continues to advance, new forms of storage are being developed. In the late 1970s, bubble storage was expected to make magnetic-disk storage

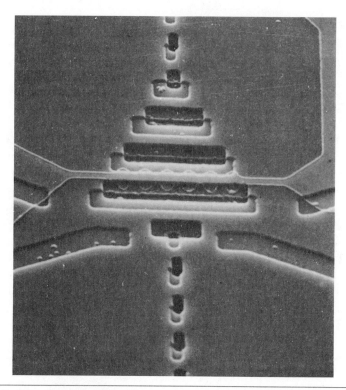

Figure 8–26 Bubble Storage

Bubble storage is a type of semiconductor storage. Here it is magnified 3,000 times. Each of the magnetic bubbles can be polarized, and the storage is nonvolatile.

obsolete (see Figure 8–26). In a **bubble storage** system, data are stored through the polarization of microscopic bubbles that exist in certain crystalline substances. Bubble storage has potentially faster access time and vastly greater miniaturization than disk storage. Honeywell ran advertisements claiming that it was developing a bubble-storage device with the capacity of storing all the data in the New York Public Library in an area the size of an average closet. Bubble storage appears to be an almost ideal form of secondary storage. However, it has not yet been widely used because its production cost has failed to decline, while significant advances have been made in both magnetic and laser disk storage technology. It is, however, being used today in limited applications such as internal storage for portable microcomputers. For this use, bubble storage has the advantage that it is nonvolatile (the data are retained when the electricity is turned off).

The same volatile semiconductor memory that is used for primary storage is also being used for secondary storage in microcomputers. For example, if you owned an IBM PC or compatible system you could buy a multifunction **memory board** for about six hundred dollars that would provide an additional 384K bytes of semiconductor memory (see Figure 8–27). This memory could be used as extra primary memory or the computer could use it as an additional disk drive. This use of memory is called a **RAM disk.** The advantage of a RAM disk is that access time to semiconductor memory is ten to fifteen times faster than to floppy disks.

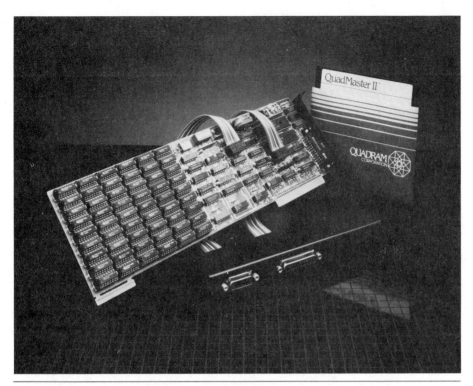

Figure 8–27   Multifunction Memory Board
These boards come with a floppy disk that contains programs to execute the clock/calendar, RAM disk, and other functions of the board.

Therefore, applications that read/write data to disks often would execute faster. At the end of an application the data stored in the semiconductor "disk drive" would be written to a hard or floppy disk, since semiconductor memory is volatile.

Certainly new forms of primary and secondary storage will be developed. However, magnetic disks and semiconductors will probably continue to be the major types in the 1990s and perhaps even longer, simply because improvements in these two technologies continue to significantly reduce their cost.

Summing Up

☐ The central processing unit of a computer is its single most important component.
☐ Digital computers represent information internally as strings of binary digits; that is, zeros and ones. These computers are used extensively in business applications.
☐ Analog computers represent quantities in terms of physical attributes, such as voltage level. These computers are used primarily for scientific and engineering purposes.

☐ The primary-storage unit stores the program that is currently being executed, along with the data records being processed.

☐ Primary storage must be a fast-access device in order for the CPU to be able to function at electronic speeds.

☐ Magnetic core used to be a common storage device for primary memory. Today, however, semiconductors provide a cheaper and much faster medium for storage. Advances in semiconductor technology promise even better performance in the future.

☐ Random-access memory (RAM) allows the CPU to read any particular data or program statement on a random basis.

☐ Read-only memory (ROM) can be read from but not written to. It is used to store programs which are frequently used by many computer applications, and which do not need to be modified.

☐ The arithmetic-logic unit performs arithmetic operations and logical comparisons on data.

☐ The control unit interprets program instructions and arranges for their execution. It typically calls on other units to actually execute the instructions.

☐ Computers are classified into four groups: microcomputers, minicomputers, mainframes, and supercomputers.

☐ Secondary storage is an essential part of a computer system. It is used for storing the bulk of data and the programs that are not in use. Secondary-storage devices usually use some mechanical movement to access data, thereby making it a relatively slow process.

☐ Magnetic reel tape, cassette, and cartridge tape are widely used secondary-storage media.

☐ Magnetic tapes offer the advantages of being inexpensive, compact, fast, accurate, portable, and reusable. However, it is necessary to handle them carefully and protect them from dirt and humidity.

☐ Magnetic disk is the most popular form of secondary storage. Its major advantage is its random-access capability. Any piece of information on the disk can be accessed quickly, with very little mechanical movement.

☐ The cost of disk storage is steadily declining. It is a very useful direct-access media for online systems. Its major disadvantage is that it does not provide an automatic audit trail or backup facility.

☐ Laser-optical disks with large storage capacities (one gigabyte per disk) are becoming a very important form of secondary storage. They are used for storing large volumes of data that are not accessed or updated often.

☐ Magnetic bubble storage and laser-optical disk storage will eventually increase in use. However, magnetic disk and semiconductor devices are expected to retain their importance for a long time.

Key Terms

central processing unit (CPU)
digital computer
analog computer
primary storage

magnetic cores
semiconductor chips
volatile
checkpoints

nonvolatile storage
random-access memory (RAM)
read-only memory (ROM)
microcoding or microprogramming or firmware
programmable read-only memory (PROM)
erasable programmable read only memory (EPROM)
arithmetic-logic unit
control unit
operation code
operands
instruction cycle
execution cycle
channels
microcomputers
minicomputers
distributed data processing
mainframes
gigabytes
supercomputers

simulation
secondary storage
magnetic tape
recording density
back up
magnetic disks
hard disks
tracks
cylinder
Winchester disks
floppy disks
direct-access storage
audit trail
laser-optical disk
mass storage
bubble storage
memory board
RAM disk

Self-Quiz

Completion Questions

1. Analog computers are used primarily in _____ control and _____ applications.
2. The components of a CPU are _____ , the arithmetic-logic unit, and the control unit.
3. Semiconductor chips contain _____ that can be reproduced photographically in a miniaturized form on silicon chips.
4. A central processor placed on a semiconductor chip is called a _____ .
5. Semiconductor storage is _____ , which means that the storage loses its data representation when electrical power is interrupted.
6. Two basic types of semiconductor memory are random-access memory and _____ .
7. Computers are classified into four groups: microcomputers, minicomputers, _____ , and supercomputers.
8. There are two basic types of disks: _____ disk and floppy disk.
9. The control unit performs two cycles for each program instruction. They are the instruction cycle and the _____ cycle.

10 _____ are small, specialized CPUs that handle input and output of data so that the main CPU does not have to handle these operations.

Multiple-Choice Questions

1. Which of the following is true of the digital computer?
   a. It represents the decimal numbers through a string of binary digits.
   b. It is used primarily in scientific applications.
   c. It is less accurate than the analog computer.
   d. All of the above.
   e. None of the above.
2. Which of the following is *not* true of primary storage?
   a. It stores the complete program that is being executed.
   b. It stores operating-system programs.
   c. It stores data while they are being processed by the CPU.
   d. It stores the bulk of data used by a computer application.
   e. All of the above are true.

3. Compared with secondary storage, primary storage is:
   a. slow and inexpensive
   b. fast and inexpensive
   c. fast and expensive
   d. slow and expensive
4. The CPU can perform read or write operations at any point in time in:
   a. ROM
   b. PROM
   c. EPROM
   d. RAM
   e. All of the above
   f. None of the above
5. The technique of placing software or programs in a ROM semiconductor chip is called:
   a. PROM
   b. EPROM
   c. firmware
   d. microprocessor
   e. none of the above
6. The advantages of magnetic tape include all of the following *except:*
   a. low cost
   b. direct-access storage medium
   c. compact and portable
   d. highly reliable
   e. all of the above are advantages
7. Currently the most popular form of secondary storage is:
   a. magnetic tape
   b. semiconductor
   c. magnetic core
   d. mass storage
   e. disk
8. Which of the following is an example of nonvolatile memory?
   a. ROM
   b. RAM
   c. LSI
   d. VLSI
   e. none of the above
9. _____ can be programmed one time by either the manufacturer or the computer user. Once programmed, it cannot be modified:
   a. RAM
   b. ROM
   c. PROM
   d. EPROM
   e. none of the above
10. Which of the following is *not* true of a magnetic disk?
    a. Users can easily update records by writing over the old data.
    b. It provides only sequential access to stored data.
    c. It is expensive relative to magnetic tape.
    d. It does not provide an automatic audit trail.
    e. All of the above are true.

Answers

Completion	Multiple Choice
1. process; scientific	1. a
2. primary storage	2. d
3. electronic circuits	3. c
4. microprocessor	4. d
5. volatile	5. c
6. read-only memory	6. b
7. mainframes	7. e
8. hard	8. a
9. execution	9. c
10. Channels	10. b

Chapter 9

Data Entry and Information Response

CHAPTER OUTLINE

PROLOGUE

Communication between computers and people has been an area of great innovation. As we saw in chapter 2, exotic devices (such as a mouse) are used to communicate with a computer. But the human/computer interface is still a very important problem in the application of computers. Ideally we should be able to communicate with computers many different ways. Most people would like to use a spoken language, such as English. Computers can talk to us, but can they understand spoken English? The various ways to communicate with computers are discussed in this chapter.

Introduction

Data-entry and **information-response** devices provide a link between the central processing unit (CPU) and the people who use it. Data-entry devices are used to provide input to the CPU. Information-response devices provide output from the CPU. Advances are continually being made in the human/computer interface. These advances make it easier and more natural for us to communicate with the computer. The term peripheral device is often used to refer to any hardware device that is not the CPU. Thus data-entry, storage, and output devices can also be called **peripheral devices.** As we examine data-entry devices you will note that quite often the same media (such as magnetic disks) are used for data entry and secondary storage.

A distinction is usually made between the media and devices used for data entry, storage, and output. The **medium** (such as a magnetic disk) is the material on which the data are actually recorded, whereas the **device** (such as a disk drive) is the complete unit that reads or writes on the medium. Similarly, a printer is an output device, and paper is an output medium.

Many different types of data-entry and information-response devices are available. This chapter will cover the most common ones as well as those which are expected to be in widespread use in the next three years.

Data Entry

Punched Cards

The eighty-column **punched card** illustrated in Figure 9–1 is the original input, secondary storage, and output medium for computers. It was developed by Herman Hollerith for use in the 1890 census, and was used in electronic accounting machine (EAM) equipment and in computer systems until about 1980.

Punched cards have rapidly become obsolete because of the use of CRT terminals and floppy disks for data entry. They are still sometimes used as ***turn-around documents,*** such as when a bill is mailed out in punched-card form and the card is returned (turned-around) with the payment.

turn-around document
An output document that is also computer readable and can be used later as an input media.

Key-to-Tape Data Entry

A **key-to-tape** device records data on magnetic tape in the form of reels or cassettes (see Figure 9–2). The key-to-tape system usually has a small memory which stores each record until the record is completely keyed in and then it is copied to the tape. A small CRT screen allows the operator to view the data that have been keyed in. Key-to-tape systems are either stand alone or clustered. In a **stand-alone system,** each keying device is separate and is not interconnected with other keying devices. The data recorded on individual tapes from each of the devices are combined into a single magnetic tape for computer processing. Under a **clustered**

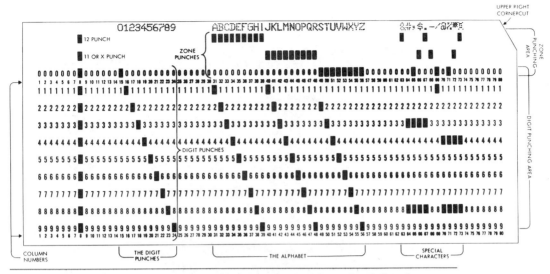

FIGURE 9–1 Eighty-Column Hollerith Coded Punched Card

The electronic accounting machines (EAMs) that used punched cards were mechanical and did not have stored-program capabilities. Data were stored in the cards, and the EAM machines read them and produced reports.

system, several keyboards are connected to one or two tape drives, thus individual tapes do not have to be combined. Clustered systems tend to be less expensive on a per-keyboard basis than stand-alone systems.

The primary advantages of key-to-tape are that the tape is reusable and that the keying operation is faster and much quieter than with punched cards. Furthermore, the magnetic tape is a compact data-entry medium. Use of key-to-tape data entry is quickly declining owing to the advantages of other methods of data entry.

Key-to-Diskette Data Entry

Both 5¼- and 8-inch diskettes (floppy disks) are used for data entry. **Key-to-diskette** systems can be either stand alone or clustered. The primary advantages of diskettes are their relatively low cost (since they can be reused over and over) and their large capacity and small size compared to punched cards. The equivalent of 6,400 fully punched cards can be stored on a single 512-kilobyte diskette.

Key-to-Disk Data Entry

Many medium- and large-sized companies are now using **key-to-disk** data input, as shown in Figure 9–3. With this approach, a minicomputer performs the data-entry function. This minicomputer supports a number of CRT terminals that are on-line to it. Thus, these are clustered data-entry systems. Also on-line to the minicomputer is a hard-disk unit that is used to store the data that have been keyed into the system. The typical procedure for using a key-to-disk input system is to key the data initially from the **source document** onto the disk from a keyboard. As the data are keyed in, the minicomputer can execute programs to screen the

source document
The form containing information that is being keyed into a computer system.

FIGURE 9–2 Key-to-Tape System

For off-line data entry, a key-to-diskette or key-to-disk system would be better than key-to-tape because of the random-access capabilities of disks.

data for errors. Errors, such as alphabetic data in numeric fields, can be detected without reference to the master files to which the transaction data pertain.

Once the data have been stored on the disk, **key verification** can be performed through the use of a program executed by the minicomputer. Essentially, the data are keyed in a second time, and the key-verification program compares the data that exist on the storage disk to the data that are keyed in the second time. After the data have been verified, the minicomputer can produce *control totals* for balancing purposes. When the balancing step has been completed and any necessary corrections to the data have been made, the data are transferred to the mainframe CPU for processing. This transmission is usually performed through communication lines between the minicomputer and the mainframe CPU; however, it can be done by other means, such as magnetic tape.

We should emphasize that key-to-diskette systems (as discussed in the previous section) can operate like hard-disk systems if the input device is a microcomputer

control total
A sum, resulting from the addition of a specified field from each record in a group of records; it is used for checking machine, program, human, and data reliability.

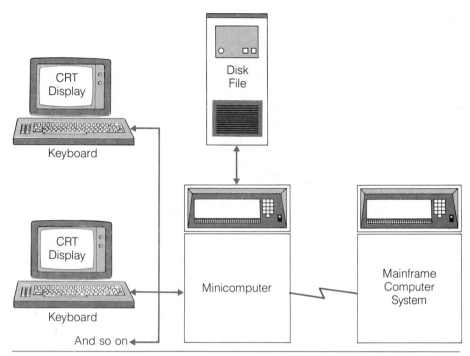

FIGURE 9–3 Key-to-Disk Data Entry

These types of systems are generally used by large companies that have large volumes of data to input from source documents.

and can therefore execute input programs. The primary difference between the two systems is that the floppy-disk system is for smaller-scale operations. Data-entry stations that can be used for either floppy-disk or key-to-hard-disk systems are shown in Figures 9–4 and 9–5.

The advantages of a key-to-disk input system are as follows:

1. A large percentage of the editing and control-total balancing can be performed at the time of data entry. Keying errors are often detected as they occur; therefore, the operator has a much better chance of correcting them.
2. Key verification is easily performed on a key-to-disk system where a mini or microcomputer is dedicated to the data-entry system.
3. The minicomputer can execute various programs that provide instructions, prompts, or **input masks** to assist the operator in entering data.
4. The minicomputer can compile and report various statistics concerning the data-input operation, including operator-productivity statistics and error rates. These statistics can be very valuable in helping a company determine which operators need additional instruction.
5. Input and verification with a key-to-disk system are considerably faster than with cards, since the mechanical movement of cards is not necessary.
6. It relieves the mainframe of much input processing and allows the mainframe to do the jobs to which it is best suited.

input mask
A form displayed on a CRT to guide the keying of input.

FIGURE 9–4   Data-Entry Stations

A minicomputer can service large numbers of data-entry stations.

FIGURE 9–5   A Data-Entry Terminal

Notice that the keyboard is connected to the monitor with a cord. This allows the user to move the keyboard around. Most people find this type of terminal easier to use than one in which the keyboard is physically attached to the monitor.

The primary disadvantages of key-to-disk data entry are as follows:

1. The initial cost of a separate computer system dedicated to data input may be prohibitive to small firms. However, the cost of computer hardware continues to decline.
2. A separate computer data-entry system may not be necessary when a company's computer system has excess capacity and *multiprogramming* capability. In this case, the data can be entered directly to the mainframe system and processed immediately, or stored in batches for later processing in a batch system.

multiprogramming
The capability of a computer CPU to execute two or more programs concurrently and, therefore, serve two or more users at the same time.

Interactive Data Entry

Under **interactive data entry,** data are input directly to the production CPU through a data-entry terminal (see Figure 9–6), with either immediate processing against the master file or storage in batches on magnetic disks for later processing. A **production CPU** is the CPU that processes the application to which the input data pertain. If the system is a batch-processing application, this type of data input is very similar to key-to-disk, except that the production CPU handles the task that the minicomputer would handle. This, however, is an inefficient application of mainframe power. For a realtime application, interactive data entry is the only practical type of input since the master file must be updated when an event occurs in order for it to reflect real-world activities.

Essentially, interactive input has all the advantages of a key-to-disk system, since the production computer can perform the same functions as a minicomputer. Other advantages are as follows:

1. Additional **data editing,** which is not possible with a minicomputer data-entry system, can be performed if the master files to which the transaction data pertain are on-line. Many edit checks depend on data stored in the mas-

---

PC USER TIP   **Voice Control**

An area that holds much promise for computers is voice control. The necessary hardware and software are already available for both speech synthesis (output) and speech recognition (input). When perfected, voice control and responses will have a place in a great deal of software, giving the user the ability to issue commands or receive messages when his or her hands or eyes are already busy. Imagine, for instance, the possibilities for cursor movement—you could move quickly around a spreadsheet entering or editing data without ever having to move your hands off the "home" typing keys.

Voice control has some other uses as well. It is a way for the sensory-impaired individual to have access to computing power. You can give your computer a command over the phone lines without needing a keyboard. Your computer can give spoken English messages back to you or to someone you have directed it to call.

This area of personal computing is new. The number of words that can be understood is limited, and slight variations in voice patterns can keep the computer from recognizing a command. The March 5, 1985 issue of *PC Magazine* (Volume 4, Number 5) focused on voice recognition and synthesis and is a good source of articles on specific products and audio technology in general.

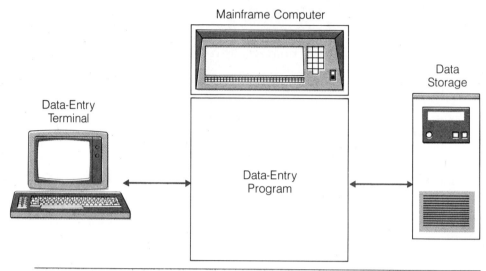

FIGURE 9–6   Interactive Data Entry

Interactive data entry is necessary for systems that maintain realtime files. Some companies may use interactive data entry also for batch systems when they have excess capacity on the mainframe computer.

ter file. For example, if all valid employees have a master-file record, the input of weekly time data for an employee can be checked against the master file so that the user can see whether the social-security number being input exists on the master file.

2. If excess capacity exists, the data-entry function can use production-CPU time that would otherwise not be used.

Disadvantages of interactive input are as follows:

1. The production CPU may not have enough excess capacity to perform the data-entry operation without increasing turn-around time on other jobs.
2. Unless master files are online and can be used for editing input data, a mini-computer can perform data-entry operations for batch-type systems as efficiently and often more efficiently than the mainframe CPU.
3. The production CPU may be located far away from the point where data are being entered, requiring use of expensive communication lines.

Source-Data Automation

Source-data automation is the capture of data, in computer-readable form, at the location and time of an event. Often the capture of data is a by-product of some other, unrelated operation. A good example is the capture of data by a computer-connected cash register upon the sale of merchandise.

Figure 9–7 illustrates traditional keypunch data entry from source documents. As you can see, data-entry editing and update of the computer files involve many steps. Errors always occur in data entry, whether keypunch or source-data automation is used. However, keypunching has disadvantages in terms of correcting

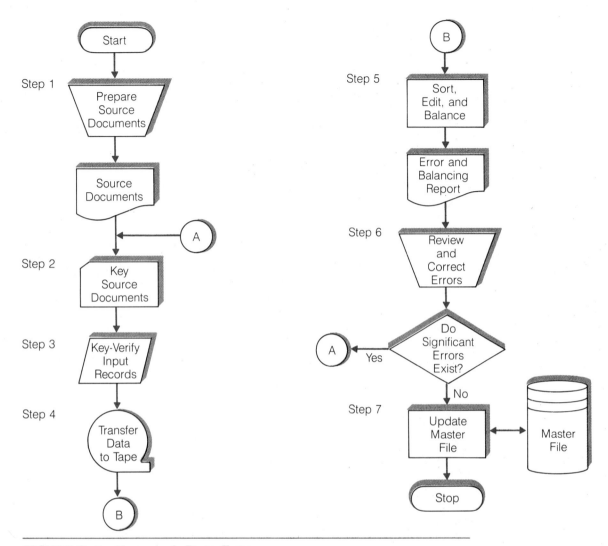

FIGURE 9–7 Keypunch Data Entry

Notice that steps 2, 3, and 4 indicate that data are being keyed from source documents onto cards which are then key verified and transferred to tape. Today when batch data are keyed, they are usually keyed to a disk, then key verified. Steps 1, 5, 6, and 7 would be the same under key-to-disk or diskette data entry.

errors. First, if in step 6 significant errors are found, the corrections must be keyed and key verified as in step 2 and 3 and then be combined with the original data-entry records, and steps 4 through 6 must be repeated. This process must be continued until no significant errors exist. Then the file update can be done.

Second, correcting errors is more difficult than with source-data automation. Since the process depicted in Figure 9–7 is usually separated both in time and distance from the original event, we often must go back to the people involved in the event in order to correct the data input. For example, if the event were customer payments on an account, the payment and the completion of the source document may have occurred several days ago and in another office, perhaps in a distant state. The individuals who completed the source document at the time of the event have the information needed to correct errors. It is preferable to detect and correct errors at the place and time of the event, since the particulars are at hand. Most of the disadvantages concerning keypunch data entry also apply to key-to-tape, key-to-disk, and key-to-diskette data entry.

Figure 9–8 depicts source-data automation. When data are entered through a terminal that is located at the site of the event, the data can be immediately edited by the computer and any errors sent back to the terminal screen for correction. Source-data automation that allows immediate entry of data and correction of errors has very significant advantages. However, not all source-data automation involves immediate error correction. For example, the **optical scan (opscan)** process depicted in Figure 9–8 is often a batch-processing operation performed separately, both in time and distance, from the event. Therefore, it has many of the same disadvantages as keypunch data entry.

Regardless of the type of source-data automation, it reduces the number of times the data have to be transcribed from one media to another, and therefore significantly reduces chances for error. Furthermore, all source-data automation reduces the amount of human labor needed for data entry.

Source-data automation is also often called distributed data entry. Essentially what we are doing is changing from a centralized data-entry function to a situation where data entry is distributed out to the locations where significant business events occur. This way we can capture data about those events directly and immediately with on-the-spot error correction.

POS Data Entry Source-data automation has given rise to **point-of-sale (POS)** equipment. In a typical POS configuration, as shown in Figure 9–9, cash registers are on-line to a minicomputer, that is in turn on-line to disk storage files containing such data as product description, selling price, and collected sales statistics. A **universal product code (UPC)** appears on each item sold (see Figure 9–10). It is read by the cash register with either a light wand or a reader embedded in the checkout counter (see Figure 9–11). The UPC is transmitted to the minicomputer, which retrieves a description and selling price for the item and transmits them back to the cash register. Simultaneously, sales statistics are collected and used to update cash receipts and to inventory master files.

POS equipment is used most extensively by the grocery industry, although it can be applied to any merchandising operation. There are also other applications for POS equipment. For example, some libraries place a UPC sticker on each book and on each patron's library card. When books are checked out, the patron's identification number on the card and the code of each book are read by a light wand. Similarly, when books are returned, their code is also read with a light wand. Master files maintained by minicomputers contain book codes and the corresponding Library of Congress identification, titles, authors, and other information. Other files contain patron identification numbers, names, addresses, and information on checked out books.

Magnetic-Ink Character Recognition **Magnetic-ink character recognition (MICR)** was developed by the banking industry for use on checks. MICR

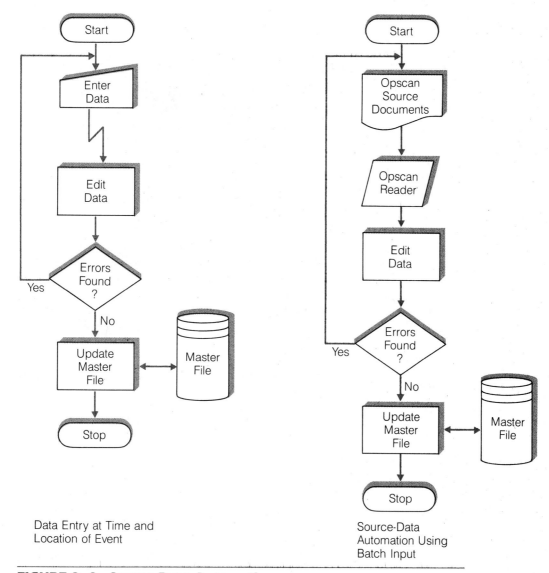

Data Entry at Time and
Location of Event

Source-Data
Automation Using
Batch Input

FIGURE 9–8   Source-Data Automation

If possible, the input of data to a system should be done through source-data automation.
Its advantages of reducing errors in data and reducing the human labor in data input are
very significant.

equipment reads data according to the shape of each individual character printed
with magnetic ink. Preprinted checks contain the bank's identification number and
the depositor's checking account number in MICR code at the bottom of the check,
as shown in Figure 9–12. When a check is processed, the amount is printed in
MICR code in the lower right corner. The MICR codes are used for sorting and
routing checks to banks and for updating the depositor's account. The use of MICR
is limited mostly to the processing of checks and credit-card transactions.

FIGURE 9–9   Point-of-Sale Data Entry

Have you ever examined your grocery receipt after checkout to see whether the computer made a mistake? It is extremely rare to find such errors because of the error-checking capabilities built into the POS equipment. However, you may discover that the price stored in the computer is different from that marked on the shelf.

Optical-Character Recognition and Optical-Mark Recognition   **Optical-character recognition(OCR)** devices read printed characters optically. Usually these must be in a special *font* because most OCR equipment can read only certain fonts. Figure 9–13 illustrates an OCR document. OCR devices are now available that will read a relatively wide range of fonts. This equipment is very useful in word-processing applications. Essentially, it provides automated input of text that has been previously typed in a wide variety of fonts, including standard typewriter fonts.

Optical-mark recognition (OMR) equipment can detect marks on a specially prepared form. Figure 9–14 illustrates an OMR form. OMR is widely used in academic testing and is sometimes used on turn-around documents where the recipient marks data to be read subsequently by OMR equipment.

Other Input Media and Devices   Voice-recognition systems have some limited applications. In **voice recognition,** a computer recognizes the patterns of an individual's (or several individuals') speech. Essentially, a person speaks into a microphone that converts the speech into analog electrical forms. These forms are recognized by the computer and converted to the digital signals of a digital computer system to represent individual word patterns. Several companies are working on a widely applicable voice-recognition system. The potential market for such a

font
A particular size and shape of printed or typed characters.

FIGURE 9–10   Universal Product Code (UPC)

Some railroad companies use a larger bar code (similar to this) on the side of railroad cars. Reading stations identify the cars as they pass by. This way the railroad company can keep track of the progress of its rail shipments.

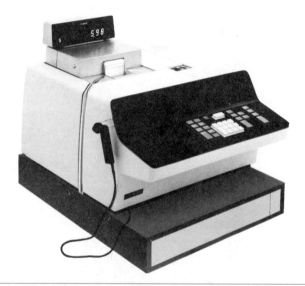

FIGURE 9–11   Light-Wand Reader Attached to a Cash Register

Although less expensive than cash registers having readers in the counter, this type of register is also less convenient. It takes two hands—one for the product and one for the wand. To use the register, the checker must put down either the product or the wand. When readers are embedded in the counter, the checker can use one hand to pass the product over the reader and the other to work the register.

system is enormous in the word-processing area. Textual material could be dictated to a voice-recognition system, and the computer could produce typed copy directly. There are voice-recognition systems with very high accuracy (98 percent) over a very limited vocabulary. These are usually employed in a "hands busy" environment, such as when production-line workers are busy with their hands and therefore cannot enter data through a keyboard.

Telephone touch-tone devices, as illustrated in Figure 9–15, can be used to enter data directly over telephone lines into computer systems. Many variations of these devices exist.

Other data-entry devices that are becoming increasingly popular are **portable terminals** and portable personal computers, as illustrated in Figure 9–16. These

MARY A. MORRISON
1765 SHERIDAN DRIVE
YOUR CITY, STATE 12345

101

_____ 19 _____ 00-6789/0000

PAY TO THE
ORDER OF_____ $

SAMPLE

_____ DOLLARS

DELUXE CHECK PRINTERS, INC.
YOUR CITY, U.S.A. 12345

"Safety Paper" checks
SPECIMEN
All checks the same

MEMO_____

⊕⑈:000067894⑈: 12345678⑈⁰
DELUXE CHECK PRINTERS LH

FIGURE 9–12   MICR Coded Check

Banks process huge numbers of checks. Without the automated processing made possible by MICR, banking would be considerably more expensive for customers.

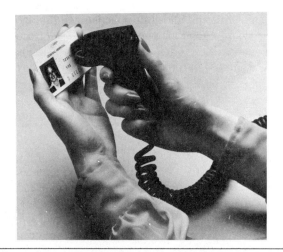

FIGURE 9–13   OCR Document and Input Device

OCR can be used to read identification cards. It is also often used on bills that are turnaround documents, where the bill is sent back by the customer and OCR equipment is used to read the bill.

terminals often have secondary-storage capability such as bubble storage (or floppy disk, in the case of portable PCs) so that data can be entered when the terminal is off-line from the computer, and can be stored and subsequently transmitted at high speed to the central computer. One application for these portable computers has been designed for traveling salespeople. In a customer's office the salesperson can connect the terminal over regular telephone lines (perhaps using a toll-free number) to the company's computer. The salesperson can inquire about the avail-

The Smith Company is a manufacturer of envelopes and paper products. Currently, when supplies or equipment need to be purchased, a form is filled out and is sent to the purchasing department for processing. Several managers have been complaining that the paper handling slows down the purchasing process by as much as two to three days. They have recommended that a purchase request be initiated through on-line computer terminals. Under this proposal, the purchasing department would retrieve the purchase requisition on its own computer terminal, verify the information, and assign the purchase to a vendor. Some people at Smith, including the internal auditors, argue that with paper forms, an individual authorized to make the purchase can write his or her signature on the purchase requisition. Thus the purchasing department has assurance that each purchase is authorized. They further argue that this vital control would be lost if an on-line terminal were used, since there would be no way the purchasing department could be assured that the individual inputting the purchase requisition is actually authorized to do so. Those advocating on-line terminals say that the person entering the purchase requisition would first have to enter a password that only he or she knows. The other group argues that passwords are easily misplaced and often are discovered by those who are not authorized to make a purchase. They argue that a signature is unique to an individual and cannot be easily copied by someone else. Which side of this argument would you support? State your reasons.

Thinking About Information Systems 9–1

ability of goods that the customer wishes to order and can immediately enter the customer's order into the computer. This can reduce the delivery time of the goods by several days.

Information Response

Visual Display Terminals

The most widely used output device is the **visual** (or video) **display terminal (VDT).** This terminal consists of a monitor with a cathode ray tube (CRT) and an attached keyboard (see Figure 9–17). Visual display terminals are also often called CRTs. The CRT is very similar to the picture tube in a television. VDTs have several advantages: they are inexpensive (less than a thousand dollars) and they produce output without making noise as most printers do. But perhaps their most important advantage is the speed with which they produce output. This speed is determined largely by the speed of the communication line between the VDT and the computer. Typical speeds are from 240 to 1,920 characters per second. The primary disadvantage of VDTs is that data must be read from a screen; many people prefer reading data from printed copy. Some people develop eyestrain from reading data on CRTs. Manufacturers are taking these complaints into consideration and are improving the readability of CRT screens.

Many companies are replacing VDTs with personal computers. The personal computer can act as a terminal connected to a host minicomputer or mainframe.

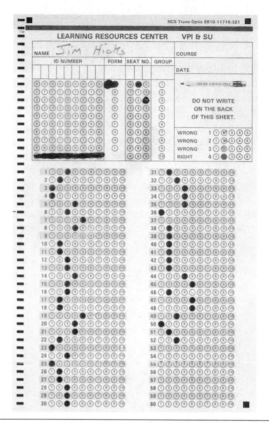

FIGURE 9–14 Optical-Mark Recognition Form

OMR is most often used in academic testing. Also, many universities use it for student registration.

For a few hundred dollars more than what a VDT costs, the firm can have the equivalent of both a VDT and a personal computer in one device called a **personal work station.** It can act as a display terminal as well as a data-entry terminal, it can upload and download information from the host computer, and it can act as a stand-alone personal computer. This is the approach that most companies will take in the future.

A disadvantage of the CRT display is the bulkiness of the CRT itself. The tubes are long, therefore causing the monitor of a VDT to have a substantial depth. In some applications, such as lap-top portable computers, it would be advantageous to have a very thin display of less than an inch.

An increasingly important type of VDT is the **flat-panel display** (see Figure 9–18). There are several types of flat-panel displays, the most common being **liquid crystal display (LCD).** The LCD technology is the same as that used in digital watch displays. The primary disadvantage of LCDs is that the characters are difficult to read when viewed from an angle. Another important type of VDT is the graphics terminal, which will be discussed later in the chapter.

FIGURE 9–15 Telephone Touch-Tone Device

Any telephone can be used as a low-volume data-input device. If the computer has voice-output capabilities, the phone can also be used as an output device.

Printers

Printers produce printed copy of information output. Printed copy is often called **hard copy.** A wide variety of printers are available; they may be categorized as character, line, and page printers.

Character printers print one character at a time, similar to typewriters. The technology used for producing the print is usually a **thimble, daisy wheel,** or **dot matrix** (see Figures 9–19, 20, and 21). Dot-matrix printers usually give lower-quality output. Therefore, when high-quality output is needed such as in word processing, thimble or daisy-wheel printers are often used.

Line printers print a complete line in one operation (see Figure 9–22). Their speeds can be as high as 2,000 lines per minute and they generally are used for high-volume printed output. Line printers use print drums, print bands, or print chains to do the actual printing (see Figure 9–23).

Page printers print a complete page at a time. An example is a **laser printer,** which is a nonimpact printer. Thus far we have described **impact printers,** which print characters and lines by having the type font strike the paper through an inked ribbon. **Nonimpact printers** do not use physical impact to transfer characters to paper. Examples are laser, xerographic, ink-jet, electrostatic, and electrothermal printers. Some of them (such as ink-jet and laser) can produce very high quality, letter-perfect printing. For example, laser printers are capable of

FIGURE 9–16 Portable Data Terminal

Newspaper reporters use this type of terminal for entering news stories. However, there is a trend toward replacing these data terminals with lap-top portable computers.

producing a wide range of type fonts and print quality equal to the best typewriters as illustrated in Figure 9–24. Laser printers are also very fast, producing output at up to 21,000 lines per minute. Laser printer technology is very similar to that of copying machines.

Electrostatic and electrothermal printer output is of a lower quality since they depend on dot-matrix technology to produce an image. Other advantages of non-impact printers are that they are usually much faster and require less physical movement for printing; therefore, they are more reliable and quieter than impact printers. A very significant advantage of laser, xerographic, and ink jet printers is the ability to produce graphic output interspersed with text on the same page. Some can also produce color output which is especially important for graphics applications.

Over the long run, nonimpact technologies such as lasers and ink jets will to a great extent replace impact printers. Laser printers have declined in price and can

If you do much printing with a dot-matrix printer, sooner or later you will get bored with the appearance of the output. Several programs that can help relieve this boredom are available. The basic concept of these programs is to use the printer in its graphics mode to print text with some pizzazz. For example, the program Select-A-Font* was used to create the following output on an EPSON MX-80 printer.

Fancy Fontwork!

Fancy Fontwork!

Fancy Fontwork!

𝕱ancy 𝕱ontwork!

This output was done using a text editor to create a file containing the following information.

```
.ce .fn3 Fancy Fontwork !
.ce .fn5 Fancy Fontwork !
.ce .fn7 Fancy Fontwork !
.ce .fn9 Fancy Fontwork !
```

The .ce commands center the text; the .fnX commands request the particular font to be used. This type of program could be used to create overheads or signs, or to print out reports in a different font. So the next time you get tired of the same old font on your printer, consider a font program to jazz things up.

*Select-A-Font is one example of this type of program. For a review of another font program, LePrint, see *PC Magazine*, vol. 4, no. 13, pp. 303–304.

FIGURE 9–17   Visual Display Terminal

Most VDTs can display only 80 columns across the screen, although there are some that can display 132 columns.

FIGURE 9–18   Flat-Panel Display on a Portable PC

In the near future, flat-panel displays will be available for television screens. Imagine hanging your TV screen on a wall!

FIGURE 9–19   A Thimble

To change the type font on a printer equipped with a thimble, you simply change the thimble. This is also true for a daisy-wheel printer.

FIGURE 9–20 Daisy Wheel

You can see why this is called a daisy wheel. Each character is contained on a daisylike spoke of the wheel. Both thimble and daisy-wheel printers produce letter-quality copy.

be purchased for personal computers for under $2,500. Copying machines that print output from computers, can be scattered throughout various offices and connected to a central computer so that high-quality output can be directed from the central computer to local offices. Such a configuration could be an important part of an electronic mail system. If a high-quality hard copy of mail is needed, it can simply be routed to the office copier/nonimpact printer for printing. Table 9–1 provides a comparison of the speed and quality characteristics of various printing devices.

Computer-Output Microfiche

Computer-output microfiche (COM) is used by many companies that need large amounts of computer-based data printed in a form readable by humans. Figure 9–25 illustrates a COM card. This 4 x 6-inch card can hold up to 270 page images of data with 99 lines per page. Some COM machines, like the one shown in Figure 9–26, read a reel of magnetic tape that holds the data to be produced. Others are connected directly to the CPU. Both types use a laser beam to image the data onto microfiche film. COM equipment can produce output at speeds of

Thinking About Information Systems 9–2

Lincoln Incorporated is in the process of developing a new budgetary control system. This system will produce information on a weekly and monthly basis and will keep the managers informed of their spending in relation to their budgeted amounts for expenditures. Preliminary plans are to produce output only on CRT terminals. Many managers already have terminals in their offices. When the new system is implemented, each manager will have a terminal and therefore will be able to call up budgetary information at any time. John Decker is manager of the manufacturing operations. John likes to play the role of a good ole' country boy, but underneath he is a very sharp and astute manager and very valuable to the company. In a recent meeting, system development presented the preliminary design of the system to the company's managers. When the plan to produce output only on terminals was discussed, John made this comment: "It seems that today the only thing anyone ever mentions as far as computer output is concerned is CRT terminals." He held up a piece of paper and in his drawl said: "One of these days somebody is going to discover paper and say, 'isn't this the best thing that has come down the pike; I can read it, I can write on it, I can put it in my briefcase, I can even take it to the bathroom with me.' " After the laughter died down, several managers joined with John in insisting that output be available in traditional paper form. System development countered with the arguments that many companies have in the past almost been choked to death by paper; that the trend is toward a paperless business environment through the use of sophisticated computer technology; and that the sooner the company gets used to this environment the more competitive it will be. Which side of the argument would you support?

Draft Quality

A B C D E F G H I J K L M N O P Q R S T U V W X Y Z
a b c d e f g h i j k l m n o p q r s t u v w x y z
0 1 2 3 4 5 6 7 8 9 ' - = \ [ ] ; ' , . / ~ ! @ # $
% ^ & * ( ) _ + | { } : " < > ?

Near-Letter Quality

A B C D E F G H I J K L M N O P Q R S T U V W X Y Z
a b c d e f g h i j k l m n o p q r s t u v w x y z
0 1 2 3 4 5 6 7 8 9 ' - = \ [ ] ; ' , . / ~ ! @ # $
% ^ & * ( ) _ + | { } : " < > ?

FIGURE 9–21 Character Set for a Dot-Matrix Printer

As you can see, each character is made up of small dots. The near letter quality dot-matrix printers print at high speeds (up to 200 characters per second), producing draft-quality copy similar to what is shown here. When switched to the near-letter-quality mode, the printer produces about 70 characters per second by restriking the characters in each line. The dot pins are slightly offset when the character is struck again, so spaces between the dots of the first strike are filled in, and the copy looks better.

FIGURE 9–22   A Line Printer

These printers are used with mainframes that have high-volume printed output. High-volume laser printers are making this type of impact line printer obsolete.

10,000 to 20,000 characters per second and up to 10,000 pages per hour. The advantages of COM are the compact size of its output and the speed with which output can be produced. However, COM equipment is expensive, and microfiche is not directly readable by humans, although microfiche readers are inexpensive and easy to operate.

Laser Disks

Laser disks are expected to become very important output media in the future (see Figure 9–27). Their primary advantage is that they can store very large amounts of data—up to one billion bytes. In fact, predictions are that laser disks will make computer-output microfiche obsolete. Currently they can be written onto only one time, but development of an erasable laser disk is under way. Their other disadvantage is that a computer is necessary for users to view the output stored on them.

Graphics

The ability to display computer-based data directly in graphic form is becoming an important business tool. Generally, the significance of data can be grasped much more easily by studying bar charts and line graphs than by examining the numerical data directly. Two types of graphics-output equipment are available: the **plotter,** which draws graphs directly on paper (see Figure 9–28); and the **graphics terminal** (see Figure 9–29). There are black-and-white and color models of both plotters and graphics terminals. Depending on the computer that supports the

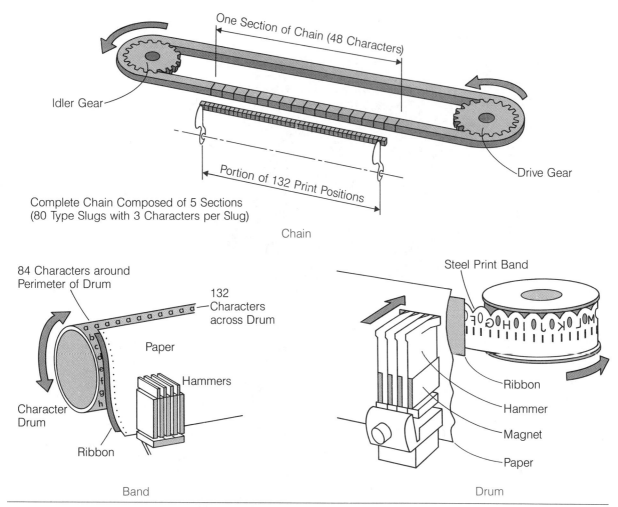

One Section of Chain (48 Characters)

Idler Gear

Drive Gear

Portion of 132 Print Positions

Complete Chain Composed of 5 Sections
(80 Type Slugs with 3 Characters per Slug)

Chain

84 Characters around
Perimeter of Drum

132
Characters
across Drum

Paper

Hammers

Character
Drum

Ribbon

Band

Steel Print Band

Ribbon

Hammer

Magnet

Paper

Drum

FIGURE 9–23   Chain, Band, and Drum Printer Mechanisms

These printing mechanisms operate in various high-speed impact printers.

terminals and the communication lines available, graphics terminals can almost instantaneously display a complete graph on their screens. Thus management can quickly examine sales trends, profit trends, and other information.

Other Output Media

Many of the input and secondary-storage media, such as magnetic tape and disk, can also serve as output media. In addition, **audio-response output** devices are being used in some applications. For example, certain railroads use audio-response devices for customer inquiries. Through a touch-tone telephone, customers can access the railroad's computer system, key in a shipment code, and then receive an audio response that indicates where their shipment is now and when it is likely to arrive at the customer's door.

TABLE 9–1   Comparative Characteristics of Printing Devices

Device	Category	Speed	Quality of Printout
High-Speed Line Printer	Impact Line Printer	High	Low/Medium
Dot-Matrix Printer	Impact Character Printer	Low/Medium	Low/Medium
Daisy-Wheel Printer	Impact Character Printer	Low	High
Laser Printer	Nonimpact Page Printer	Medium/High	Very High
Ink-Jet Printer	Nonimpact Character Printer	Medium	Very High

Most ink-jet printers have the capability of printing in color. They can even print color onto transparencies for use in overhead presentations.

```
                                               Page 1
                                               Run Date 1-5-86

                        GROSS PROFIT BY ITEM
                              REPORT
                        MONTH ENDING 12/31/85

                                                          QTY
        ITEM  ITEM                       QTY    GROSS     SOLD
        NO    DESCRIPTION       SALES     SOLD   PROFIT    YTD
        ============================================================
        ============================================================

        1003  PAPER, 3H, LOOSE LEAF   187.50    250     40.00    3520
        1004  PAPER, TYPING, BOND    7187.50   1250   1000.00    7500
        1005  PAPER, MIMEO, 8.5x11   2835.00    750    885.00    6000
        7085  PEN, BALLPOINT         3185.00   3500    385.00   24500
        4106  PENCIL, DRAWING 3H     1425.00    475    209.00    1900
        8165  STAPLER REMOVER         675.00   1500     90.00   16500
```

FIGURE 9–24   Laser Printer Output

Laser printers are revolutionizing the printing of computer output. They are even available for microcomputers for less than $2,500, and the price is expected to decline further.

Summing Up

☐ Data-entry and information-response devices provide a link between the central processing unit and the people who use it.

☐ The punched card is the oldest medium used to input and store data in a computer. The data punched on a card can also be typed on it, which means users can read it. For this reason, cards are sometimes used as turn-around documents to accompany bill payments.

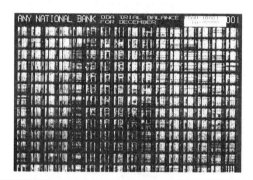

FIGURE 9–25   Computer Output Microfiche

Optical-laser disks will largely replace the use of COM in the future. They are less expensive to produce and can hold much more data.

FIGURE 9–26   COM Equipment

Microfiche is a photographic film. Therefore, after exposure the microfiche must be developed. COM equipment automatically develops the film.

FIGURE 9–27 Optical Laser Disk

Because of their large capacity (up to one billion bytes) and low cost (less than ten dollars each), these disks will have a revolutionary impact on computer output and secondary storage. Books and perhaps complete libraries can be stored on laser disks. Applications have just begun to be discovered.

☐ Key-to-tape data-entry systems have one or more keyboards connected to one or two tape drives. This type of data entry is fast and quiet. Moreover, magnetic tape is an economical, reusable input medium.

☐ In a key-to-diskette data-entry system, data are transferred from the keyboard to a floppy disk. Floppy disks are low-cost, reusable storage devices.

☐ A key-to-disk data-entry system allows some editing and verification of data upon entry. A mini or microcomputer is used to perform the editing and verification functions. It may also provide other data-input assistance, such as instructions, prompts, control totals, and error rates.

☐ Interactive data entry allows the input of data directly to the production CPU. This kind of data entry is essential for realtime systems where the master file must be updated immediately. Since data are entered directly to the master file, it is possible to execute a large variety of edit checks, including comparisons with existing data.

☐ Source-data automation permits the capture of data as a by-product of a business event. Some source-data-automation techniques in use are point-of-sale data entry, magnetic-ink character recognition, optical-character recognition, optical-mark recognition, voice recognition, and portable terminals.

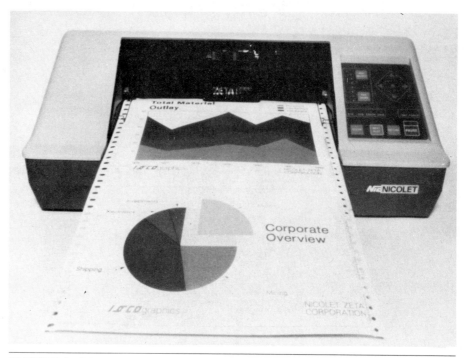

FIGURE 9–28   A Plotter

Plotters usually have several different color pens which draw the graph. These plotters are likely to be replaced by laser printers as laser printers gain the capability of producing color output.

☐ Visual display terminals are the most widely used method of displaying output for reading by humans.

☐ Printers are output devices that provide information response in the form of hard copy. Printers may be categorized as line versus character printers, or as impact versus nonimpact printers.

☐ A line printer prints a complete line at one time, whereas a character printer prints a character at a time, just like a typewriter.

☐ The type font of an impact printer actually strikes the paper to create character images. Nonimpact printers use techniques like laser beams, xerography, ink jets, and electrostatic printing to transfer information to paper.

☐ Computer output microfiche can store large amounts of computer-generated data in human-readable form. Although it requires some expensive output devices, computer output microfiche can be produced at a high speed and it requires very little storage space.

☐ Plotters and graphics terminals are becoming popular information-response devices. They help summarize business data by presenting them in an easy-to-understand pictorial format.

FIGURE 9–29   A Graphics Terminal

Graphics CRTs are available in both high and low resolution. Resolution is a measure of how many dots the CRT is capable of displaying on a screen. High-resolution screens will display a smoother graphics line. Diagonal lines displayed on a low-resolution screen often appear jagged and stair-stepped.

Key Terms

data entry
information response
peripheral devices
medium
device
punched card
turn-around documents
key-to-tape
stand-alone system
clustered system
key-to-diskette
key-to-disk
source document
key verification
control totals
input masks

interactive data entry
production CPU
data editing
source-data automation
optical scan (opscan)
point-of-sale (POS)
universal product code (UPC)
magnetic-ink character recognition (MICR)
optical-character recognition (OCR)
font
optical-mark recognition (OMR)
voice recognition
portable terminals
visual display terminal (VDT)
personal work station
flat-panel display

liquid crystal display (LCD)
hard copy
character printers
thimble
daisy wheel
dot matrix
line printers
page printers

laser printer
impact printers
nonimpact printers
computer-output microfiche (COM)
laser disks
plotter
graphics terminal
audio-response output

Self-Quiz

Completion Questions

1. Any hardware device that is not the CPU is often referred to as a _____ .
2. _____ is the capture of data, in computer-readable form, at the location and time of an event.
3. Printed copy is often called _____ .
4. The _____ is the material on which the data are actually recorded, whereas the _____ is the complete unit that reads or writes on it.
5. Data-entry systems may be either stand-alone or _____ systems.
6. Under _____ data entry, data are input directly to the production CPU through a data-entry terminal.
7. _____ can store large amounts of computer-generated data in a form readable by humans.
8. The currently available types of graphics-output equipment are the _____ and the graphics CRT terminal.
9. _____ printers do not use physical impact to transfer characters to paper.
10. _____ devices are used to read printed characters optically, whereas _____ equipment can detect marks on a specially prepared form.

Multiple-Choice Questions

1. Which of the following is not true of punched cards as data-entry media?
   a. They can be used as turn-around documents.
   b. They are inexpensive.
   c. Input is slow compared with other media.
   d. They are easily damaged.
   e. All of the above are true.
2. The primary advantage of key-to-tape data-entry systems is:
   a. A large percentage of editing can be performed at the time of data entry.
   b. Key verification is easily performed.
   c. The tape is reusable.
   d. Keying errors can be detected as they occur.
   e. All of the above.
3. Linkage between the CPU and the users is provided by:
   a. peripheral devices
   b. storage
   c. control unit
   d. software
   e. all of the above
4. Which of the following is widely used in academic testing?
   a. MICR
   b. POS
   c. OCR
   d. OMR
   e. CRT
5. The _____ is a nonimpact printer that can produce very high quality, letter-perfect printing.
   a. dot-matrix printer
   b. daisy-wheel printer
   c. electrostatic printer
   d. laser printer
   e. none of the above
6. The POS data-entry system is used most extensively by the:
   a. banking industry

b. grocery industry
c. railroad industry
d. word-processing industry
e. none of the above

7. A disadvantage of the laser printer is:
   a. it is quieter than an impact printer
   b. it is very slow
   c. the output is of a lower quality
   d. it cannot produce a wide range of type fonts
   e. none of the above

8. Data entry can be performed with all of the following except:
   a. OCR
   b. OMR
   c. COM
   d. Voice-recognition systems
   e. MICR

9. Magnetic tape can serve as:
   a. input media
   b. output media
   c. secondary-storage media
   d. a and b only
   e. b and c only
   f. all of the above

10. The advantages of COM are its _____ and _____ .
    a. compact size; readability
    b. compact size; speed

c. readability; speed
d. low-cost; readability
e. compact size; low cost

Answers

Completion

1. peripheral device
2. Source-data automation
3. hard copy
4. medium; device
5. clustered
6. interactive
7. Computer output microfiche (COM)
8. plotter
9. Nonimpact
10. Optical-character recognition (OCR); optical-mark recognition (OMR)

Multiple Choice

1. b
2. c
3. a
4. d
5. d
6. b
7. e
8. c
9. f
10. b

Chapter 10

System Software

CHAPTER OUTLINE

PROLOGUE

Kevin Oliver is a venture-capital broker. He is considering buying a personal computer to help in recordkeeping and typing. He thinks that an electronic spreadsheet could help him make profit/loss projections. He has been told that there are personal-computer operating systems that allow several employees to use the same computer concurrently. He has also heard that he should buy an electronic spreadsheet that has virtual-storage capabilities. Some of Kevin's profit/loss projections are very large and complex. Thus, they may require a large amount of primary memory. Are concurrent operating systems and virtual storage available in personal computers? What are they? Read on.

Introduction

In most organizations the computer is a very valuable resource. Among the resources that a computer has are processing time, storage space, printers, and terminals. The management of these resources is performed largely by a type of system software called an operating system. When users interact with the computer, much of this interaction is with the system software. System software directly affects the ease with which users interact with a computer. Furthermore, system software is a very significant determinant of whether or not a particular computer's resources are used optimally. For these reasons it is important that users of computer systems have a basic knowledge of system software.

In this chapter we will first distinguish between system software and application software, then we will explore the functions, components, and types of operating systems. Finally we will see how operating systems make possible multiprogramming, virtual storage, timesharing, and multiprocessing computer systems.

System Software versus Application Software

There are two broad categories of software: system software and application software. **System software** is a set of programs that manage the resources of a computer system (processing time, storage space, and so on) so that they are used in an optimal fashion, provide routine services such as copying data from one file to another, and assist in the development of application programs. System software consists of general programs that assist the computer in the efficient execution of application programs. **Application software,** on the other hand, performs specific tasks for the computer user. Figure 10–1 illustrates the different types of system and application software.

System Software

operating system
A set of integrated programs that controls the execution of computer programs and manages the storage and processing resources of a computer system.

job queue
A line of programs awaiting their turn for execution.

System software began to be used extensively with the second-generation computers in the early 1960s. Prior to this, the operation of a computer was controlled primarily by human operators. These operators monitored the processing of each job. Typically, when a job ended, a bell rang or a light flashed to indicate that another job should be input to the computer and started by the operator. If a job ended while the operator was having a coffee break, the computer might have sat idle for five or ten minutes or longer. In addition, the operator had to activate each peripheral device when that device was needed by the computer. This type of human intervention wasted large amounts of computer time and human resources. To automate these functions, companies developed programs called *operating systems.* These programs are stored partially in primary storage and partially in direct-access secondary storage so the computer can access them immediately when they are needed. With operating systems, a *queue* of jobs that are awaiting

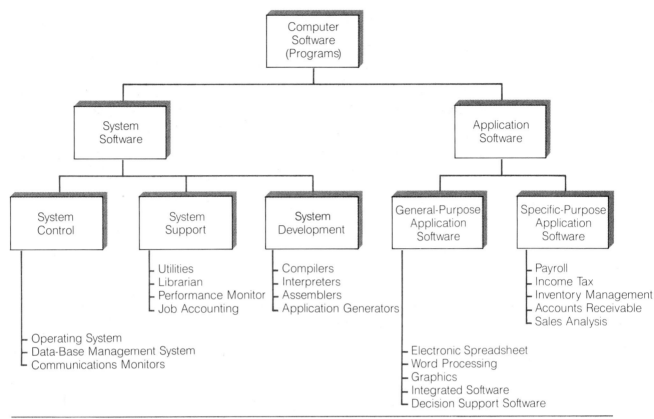

FIGURE 10–1 Types of System and Application Software

Application software performs tasks for the computer user. System software assists in the control, support, and development of application software.

execution can be read onto a disk. The operating system will start each job when system resources are available for its execution. Since human intervention is eliminated, computer idle time is significantly reduced.

There are three types of system software:

1. **System control programs** control the execution of programs, manage the storage and processing resources of the computer, and perform other management and monitoring functions. The most important of these programs is the operating system. Other examples are data-base management systems and communication monitors.
2. **System support programs** provide routine service functions to other computer programs and computer users. Examples are utilities, librarians, performance monitors, and job accounting.
3. **System development programs** assist in the creation of application programs. Examples are language translators such as a BASIC interpreter, and application generators such as IBM's Application Development Facility.

System programs are developed and sold by both computer companies and specialized software firms. **System programmers** write system software. Most

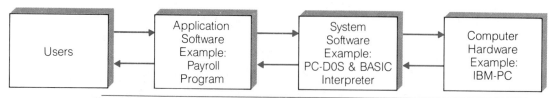

FIGURE 10–2 The Interaction Between Users, Application Software, System Software, and Computer Hardware

Application and system software act as interfaces between users and computer hardware. If this software did not exist, very few people would be using computer hardware. As application and system software become more capable, people find computers easier to use.

large firms have their own staff of system programmers who are capable of modifying an operating system to meet the unique requirements of the firm.

Application Software

An **application program** is a program written for or by a user to perform a particular job. **General-purpose application software,** such as an electronic spreadsheet, has a wide variety of applications. **Specific-purpose application software,** such as payroll and sales analysis, is used only for the application for which it is designed. **Application programmers** write these programs.

Generally, computer users interact with application software as shown in Figure 10–2. The system software controls the execution of the application software and provides other support functions, such as data storage. For example, when you use an electronic spreadsheet on an IBM-PC, the storage of the worksheet files on disk is handled by PC-DOS, the computer's operating system.

Types of System Software

System Control Software

initial program load
The initialization procedure that causes an operating system to commence operation.

bootstrap
When referring to personal computers, people often use this term instead of initial program load.

A very important part of the system control software is the operating system, which performs many functions. Two of its more critical tasks are starting the computer (*initial program load* or *bootstrap*) and initiating the processing of each job. To understand these functions, let's examine the Personal Computer Disk Operating System (PC-DOS) used in the IBM-PC. The components of PC-DOS are illustrated in Figure 10–3. Figure 10–4 shows the steps that PC-DOS goes through in bootstrapping the computer and loading an application program written in BASIC.

Operating systems on minis and mainframes also perform **job scheduling** functions by examining the priority of each job awaiting execution. Jobs with higher priorities are executed first. **Access security** is also a very important function of the operating system. This function is carried out through various password schemes that identify valid users and determine which data files they may access.

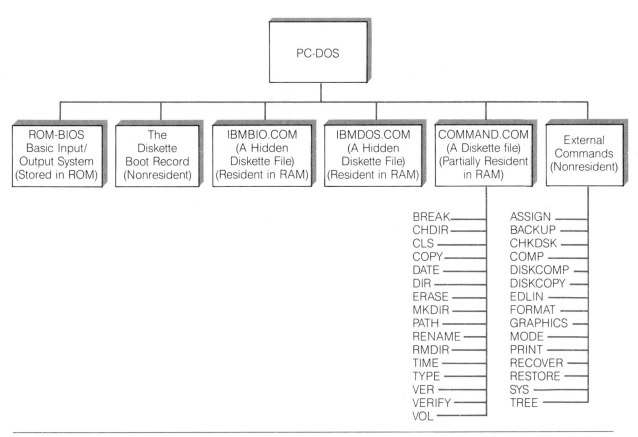

FIGURE 10–3 Personal Computer Disk-Operating System (PC-DOS) on the IBM-PC

ROM-BIOS provides very fundamental services needed by the computer, such as a self-test of memory, starting up (booting) the computer, and input/output services between the central processing unit and peripheral devices such as printers and disks. It is stored permanently in ROM. The diskette boot record is a very short and simple program stored at the beginning of the DOS diskette. Its purpose is to begin the process of loading the operating system when the PC is first turned on. Nonresident means that it is not stored in RAM while the PC is operating. Both IBMBIO.COM and IBMDOS.COM are extensions of ROM-BIOS. They provide additional input/output interfaces with peripheral devices. They are stored on the DOS diskette, but they are hidden files. A hidden file is not displayed when a DIR (directory) of the diskette is produced. They are resident in RAM while the PC is operating. The primary job of COMMAND.COM is to process and interpret the commands that you type into DOS. It also contains the programs that execute several DOS commands. These programs are resident in RAM. The final part of DOS, the external commands, are not resident in RAM; these are moved from the DOS diskette to RAM whenever they are needed.

Figure 10–5 illustrates the storage of a mainframe operating system. The **system residence device** stores the complete operating system. Today this is usually a disk unit. As portions of the operating system are needed for execution, they can be readily loaded into primary storage.

There are generally four types of operating-system programs: the **initial program loader (IPL)**, the **supervisor**, the **job-control program**, and the **input/output (I/O) control program.** In mainframe computers the bootstrap program is known as the initial program loader. Its purpose is to start up operations. It performs this function by reading the resident portion of the supervisor from

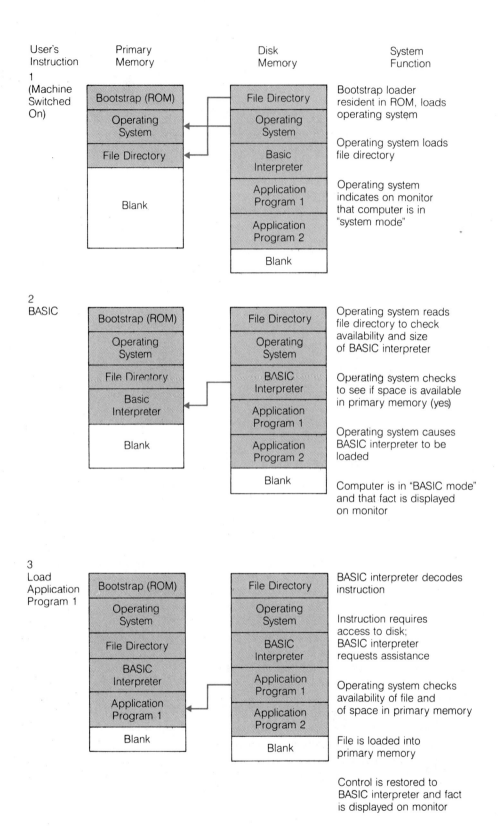

User's Instruction	Primary Memory	Disk Memory	System Function
1 (Machine Switched On)	Bootstrap (ROM) / Operating System / File Directory / Blank	File Directory / Operating System / Basic Interpreter / Application Program 1 / Application Program 2 / Blank	Bootstrap loader resident in ROM, loads operating system. Operating system loads file directory. Operating system indicates on monitor that computer is in "system mode"
2 BASIC	Bootstrap (ROM) / Operating System / File Directory / Basic Interpreter / Blank	File Directory / Operating System / BASIC Interpreter / Application Program 1 / Application Program 2 / Blank	Operating system reads file directory to check availability and size of BASIC interpreter. Operating system checks to see if space is available in primary memory (yes). Operating system causes BASIC interpreter to be loaded. Computer is in "BASIC mode" and that fact is displayed on monitor
3 Load Application Program 1	Bootstrap (ROM) / Operating System / File Directory / BASIC Interpreter / Application Program 1 / Blank	File Directory / Operating System / BASIC Interpreter / Application Program 1 / Application Program 2 / Blank	BASIC interpreter decodes instruction. Instruction requires access to disk; BASIC interpreter requests assistance. Operating system checks availability of file and of space in primary memory. File is loaded into primary memory. Control is restored to BASIC interpreter and fact is displayed on monitor

FIGURE 10–4 Loading an Application Program on a Personal Computer

Functions of the operating system are illustrated by the successive events required to load an application program. (1) Switching the computer on actuates a bootstrap program that loads the operating system into primary memory. The operating system transfers a file directory from disk memory to primary memory; in the file directory is listed the address, or position, of every program and data file recorded on the disk. In response to the next instruction, (2), the operating system finds the BASIC interpreter on the disk and, after making certain there is enough space for it, loads it into primary memory; the user is notified that the interpreter is ready. (Some personal computers perform step 2 automatically as part of the switching-on sequence.) The operating system is called on to load the application program itself. (3) Now, with the interpreter again in control, the application program can be run. Output will be a new data file in primary memory, which can be transferred to disk storage.

secondary storage and loading it into primary storage. Since the operating system is constantly supervising and monitoring the computer, a frequently used portion of the operating system, called the **resident supervisor,** is stored in primary storage while the computer is operating. Other parts of the supervisor are used less frequently. They are stored only temporarily in the supervisor transient area of primary storage when they are in use (refer to Figure 10–5).

Once the resident portion of the supervisor is loaded into primary storage, control is passed to the supervisor and the operation of the computer begins. The supervisor programs (often called **monitor** or **executive programs)** are the principal managers in an operating system. They organize and control the flow of work by initiating and controlling the execution of other computer programs.

As operating-system software replaced human operators in the control of mainframe computers, new languages were developed to enable users and programmers to communicate with the operating system. A **job-control language (JCL)** requires that the user include several job-control statements along with a program. The statements identify the job and its steps, and specify the system resources to be used (for example, expected run time, input/output device to be used, and memory space required). Job-control language also describes the data sets or files that are to be used in the various job steps. Figure 10–6 shows how JCL works. Job-control languages are used primarily with the large multiuser computer systems. JCL is not used with personal computers since they are usually single-user systems. The information provided through JCL can be furnished to a personal computer interactively or by defaulting to standard assumptions for the information.

Figure 10–7 illustrates how the supervisor and the job-control program interact to stop the execution of one program and begin the execution of another. Let's take a closer look at this program-to-program transition. After the job-control program has identified the system resources required for the next program, the supervisor makes several decisions prior to beginning the execution of program 2. For example:

1. Does program 2 have the highest priority among the programs awaiting execution?

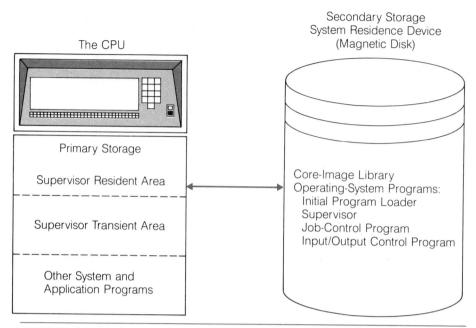

FIGURE 10–5 Storage of a Mainframe Operating System

A core-image library means that the programs stored on the disks can be moved directly into primary storage without modification. This improves the speed with which parts of the operating system can be moved into the supervisor transient area as needed.

2. Are all the system's resources that program 2 will need during execution available (such as disk units, tape drives, et cetera)?
3. Does program 2 have a valid password?

If the answer to these and other questions is yes, then program 2 is allowed to run.

The supervisor and job-control programs acting together issue many instructions to the human operator. Examples of these include instructions to mount or dismount a tape or to load or unload a disk pack. If special forms are needed for printing the output, the programmer specifies these forms through the JCL statements. When the job is ready to be printed, the computer sends a message to the operator to mount the special forms on the printer. A large percentage of the work a computer operator performs is in response to instructions from the operating system. These instructions originate from the JCL that the programmer includes with his or her program.

Input/output control programs manage the movement of data between primary storage and peripheral devices such as disk and tape drives. These programs also can check for errors. For example, if an error is detected while a program is reading from a disk the I/O control program rereads the data several times in an attempt to obtain error-free data. If the error continues to occur, then an appropriate

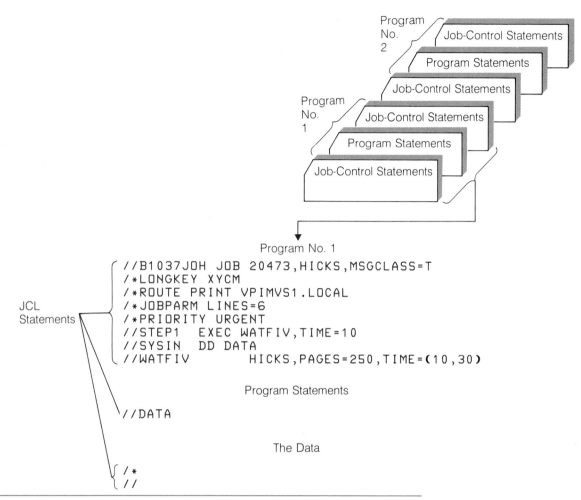

FIGURE 10–6 Relationship of Programs and Job-Control Language (JCL)

JCL is used with batch processing on mainframes to communicate information (about programs and their requirements for system resources) to the operating system. JCL statements must occur before and after each program.

error message is displayed or printed. Data-base management systems and communication monitors are discussed in chapters 12 and 13 respectively, therefore we will not discuss them here.

System Support Software

Most computer systems have support software, called **utility programs,** which perform routine tasks. These programs sort data, copy data from one storage medium to another, output data from a storage medium to the printer and perform

	Primary Storage

Program 1 in Control and
Executing

Supervisor
Program 1

Control Passed to
Supervisor

Supervisor
Program 1

Job-Control Program
Entered

Supervisor
Job-Control Program

Control Passed to Job-Control
Program

Supervisor
Job-Control Program

Job-Control Program Reads JCL and
Identifies Systems Resources Required for Next Job

Supervisor
Job-Control Program

Control Returned to
Supervisor

Supervisor
Job-Control Program

Program 2 Entered

Supervisor
Program 2

Control Passed to
Program 2

Supervisor
Program 2

Program 2 in Control
and Executing

Supervisor
Program 2

FIGURE 10–7 Program-to-Program Transition in Primary Memory

Because of the information conveyed to the operating system through JCL, a mainframe computer can execute many batch jobs contained in a job queue, without human intervention.

other tasks. Utility programs are usually supplied by the computer manufacturer as part of the operating system. They may be called by any application program and used by that program.

Another common type of support software is a librarian. The primary function of the **librarian** is to maintain a catalog of the locations and usage of all program and data files. Librarians often execute password controls.

Performance monitors such as IBM's system management facilities (SMF) are a part of most system software. **Performance monitors** collect and record selected activities that occur within a computer system. For example, they collect data about CPU idle time, which operations are using the system (and how long they use it and what hardware they employ), whether each job is successfully executed, and

276 10 SYSTEM SOFTWARE

the amount of primary storage each job employs. This information can be used in charging departments within the firm for use of the computer facility. Most firms feel that charging users for computer services is an important part of the control over computer resources.

Monitors also collect information about which files are used in performing a job. This provides an excellent audit trail concerning data and file usage. It is possible to determine, for example, which files were used when a particular program was run. It will also identify who the user was when the file access was made, plus the date and time of the access.

System Development Software

System development programs assist a programmer or user in developing and using an application program. Examples of these programs are language translators, linkage editors, and application generators.

A **language translator** is a computer program that converts a program written in a procedural language, such as BASIC, into machine language that can be directly executed by the computer (see Figure 10–8). Many different language translators

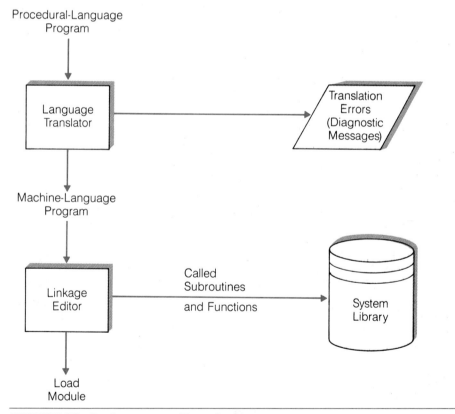

FIGURE 10–8 Language Translation

Computers can execute only machine-language programs. Programs written in any other language must be translated into a machine-language load module which is suitable for loading directly into primary storage.

exist, in fact, there is one for each programming language. They are categorized as compilers, interpreters or assemblers. Programming languages and language translators are discussed in more detail in Module B.

Quite often in writing a program, a programmer will call prewritten subroutines (or subprograms) which are stored on the system residence device, to perform a specific standard function. For example, if a program required the calculation of a square root, the programmer would not write a special program. He or she would simply call a square-root subroutine to be used in the program. The function of the **linkage editor** is to gather all of these called subroutines and place them into the application program. The output from the linkage editor is called a load module. (The term *module* is often used synonymously with *program*.) A **load module** is a program that is suitable for loading directly into primary storage for execution.

Application generators are programming productivity tools that partially automate the programming process. For example, one type of application generator, the report generator, allows a programmer or user to simply describe the contents of a report rather than write the report in a procedural language such as COBOL. Some report generators (or query languages) even allow report requests to be made in conversational English. For example, a query language called Intellect will process the following query:

```
REPORT THE BASE SALARY, COMMISSIONS AND YEARS OF SER-
VICE BROKEN DOWN BY STATE AND CITY FOR SALES CLERKS
IN NEW JERSEY AND VIRGINIA.
```

Types of Operating Systems

There are basically two types of operating systems: batch and interactive.

Batch Systems

A **batch operating system** accepts jobs and places them in a queue to await execution. This process is often called **spooling.** (Spooling is short for **simultaneous peripheral operations on line.**) Essentially what happens is the jobs are placed in a queue on a disk unit. As execution time becomes available, the operating system selects jobs based on priorities from this job queue. Batch jobs may be executed on a serial basis, where one job is executed at a time; or a multiprogramming basis, where multiple jobs are executed concurrently. Most operating systems in personal computers work on a batch-serial basis without using spooling. Serial versus multiprogramming execution will be discussed in more detail later in this chapter.

Interactive Systems

An **interactive operating system** allows users to interact directly with a computer from a terminal. In effect, the user can interrupt a low-priority batch job and cause the computer to perform his or her high-priority work. Interactive operating systems must be multiprogramming systems. Also, realtime systems must be interactive since realtime files must be updated immediately after real-world events occur. An **interrupt** is required, which is the suspension of the execution of a computer program, caused by an event external to the program, and performed in such a way that the execution can later be resumed. Examples of such external events would be a request for data, or input of data, from an interactive terminal.

The remainder of this chapter will explore in more depth batch versus interactive operating systems and their relationships to multiprogramming, virtual storage, timesharing, interactive computing, and multiprocessing. These systems are the predominant mainframe operating systems today. Personal computer operating systems are moving toward many of these capabilities, such as multiprogramming and virtual storage.

Multiprogramming

Multiprogramming (sometimes called multi-tasking) is the capability of a CPU to execute two or more programs concurrently. In fact, multiprogramming operating systems designed for personal computers are called concurrent-processing operating systems. Multiprogramming capability is accomplished through the operating system. Essentially, two or more programs are stored concurrently in primary storage, and the CPU moves from one program to another, partially executing each program in turn. Early computer systems and many personal computers execute programs on a batch-serial basis; that is, each program is executed in the order in which it is read into the system, and only one program is executed at a time.

Advantages of Multiprogramming

Increased Throughput   Several disadvantages are associated with the batch-serial approach to program execution. First, throughput is not maximized under a batch-serial approach. **Throughput** is a measure of the total amount of processing that a computer system can complete over a fixed period of time. The disadvantage is due to the relative speeds of computer system components. The CPU operates without mechanical movement, depending only on the flow of electronic pulses which travel at about half the speed of light. Therefore, it is very fast compared to the speed of input/output devices, which depend on mechanical movements or humans to operate them. Figure 10–9 depicts the elapsed time necessary to execute one job under batch-serial and three jobs under multiprogramming. Total throughput is significantly increased in multiprogramming, because the CPU is not waiting for input/output for the program it is executing. It simply rotates to another program and begins executing.

Shorter Response Time   A second disadvantage of the batch-serial approach is its longer turnaround or response time. **Turnaround time** refers to the elapsed

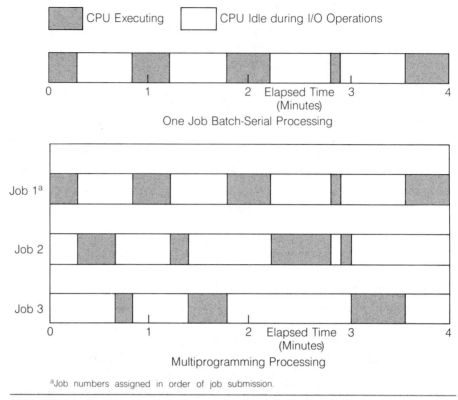

CPU Executing CPU Idle during I/O Operations

0   1   2 Elapsed Time 3   4
(Minutes)

One Job Batch-Serial Processing

Job 1[a]

Job 2

Job 3

0   1   2 Elapsed Time 3   4
(Minutes)

Multiprogramming Processing

[a]Job numbers assigned in order of job submission.

FIGURE 10–9 Elapsed Time under Batch-Serial and Multiprogramming Systems

In this illustration, three jobs are executed in four minutes under multiprogramming, whereas only one job is executed in four minutes with a batch-serial operating system. The reason for the difference is that the multiprogramming operating system allows the CPU to execute other jobs while it is waiting for input/output to occur.

time between the submission of a batch job and the availability of the output. **Response time** refers to the elapsed time between submission of a command to an on-line system and the completion of that command as evidenced by a message on the terminal screen or printer. Turnaround on small jobs usually takes longer in a batch-serial environment, than it does in a multiprogramming environment. Refer to Figure 10–9, and assume that jobs 1 and 2 are long, requiring 1.5 and 0.75 hours of CPU time respectively. Under the batch-serial approach, the turnaround time for job 3 would be 2¼ hours, plus execution time of about 1 minute. Under multiprogramming, the turnaround time for job 3 would be approximately 3 to 4 minutes, plus output printing time. Essentially, job 3 will execute completely in a short elapsed time by utilizing the CPU, which would otherwise be waiting for I/O for jobs 1 and 2. Therefore, turnaround time for short jobs can be greatly improved under multiprogramming. The turnaround time for long jobs is usually lengthened since the CPU is devoting part of its time to short jobs. This is not a disadvantage, however, because long batch jobs usually have a lower priority.

Multiprogramming systems usually have priority schemes whereby any job, including a long one, can be executed under a higher priority, if necessary.

Ability to Assign Priorities to Jobs   Most multiprogramming systems have schemes for setting priorities for rotating programs. They specify when the CPU will rotate to another program, and which program it will rotate to. The user, through JCL or other specification of execution priorities for each job, can influence the priority under which a job will execute.

Multiprogramming with priority schemes improves **system availability;** that is, it increases the speed with which the system can respond to high-priority, unanticipated requests on its resources. System availability under batch-serial mode can be very poor when long jobs are executing. Under multiprogramming, high-priority jobs can be executed almost immediately.

On-line, realtime, and timesharing systems would not be practical without multiprogramming. The response time at the terminals would be intolerable if all instructions from the terminals and the batch jobs were executed on a batch-serial basis. Instructions from terminals must be executed under high priority.

Improved Primary-Storage Allocation   In early multiprogramming systems, the programs being executed had to all reside in primary storage until their execution was complete. A constraining factor on the throughput of a multiprogramming system is the number of jobs that can reside in primary storage at a given point in time. If only two large programs will fit in main memory, the CPU may be idle a large percentage of the time while waiting for I/O. The greater the number of programs that primary storage can hold, the greater the probability that the CPU will be able to execute at least one program while waiting for I/O for the others. This line of reasoning led to the approach of writing out to secondary storage the programs that were waiting for I/O. They were written back into primary storage when the I/O operation was completed and they were ready for additional execution. In the vacated primary storage space, a program that was ready and waiting for execution was written in. This approach cleared main storage of all programs waiting for I/O. Therefore, in principle, all the programs residing in primary storage were either running or awaiting execution. This technique led to the concept of virtual storage, which will be discussed later in the chapter.

Disadvantages of Multiprogramming

Multiprogramming does have its disadvantages, but they are minor. First, multiprogramming is implemented through an operating system, which is a program that requires space in primary storage since it must be executed by the CPU. The operating system overhead (its primary-storage requirements and CPU execution time requirements) is greater with multiprogramming than with batch-serial.

Another potential problem with multiprogramming systems is **interprogram interference,** either intentional or accidental. While executing, a program can theoretically write to any area of primary storage. Under multiprogramming, other areas of primary storage contain other programs or their data. Therefore, a program could accidentally or intentionally modify another program while both are concurrently executing. So that this is prevented, operating systems assign each program its own unique password while it is executing. In order to write to or read from, let's say, program A's assigned area of primary storage, the writing or reading program must present the proper password. This password is known only to program A. Therefore, only program A has access to its area of primary storage.

Thinking About Information Systems 10–1

Tieko, Incorporated is trying to decide which of two personal computers to choose as the company's standard. The computer selected will be used throughout the company. One of the machines has available a multiprogramming operating system which allows the personal computer to execute two or more programs concurrently. The alternative machine does not have a multiprogramming operating system, but otherwise it is somewhat superior to the first machine. Those in the organization who favor the machine without the multiprogramming operating system argue that a personal computer can have only one user at a time, therefore there is no need for a multiprogramming operating system. How would you respond to this position?

Virtual Storage

Virtual storage is primary storage that does not actually exist. It gives the programmer the illusion of a primary storage that is, for all practical purposes, unlimited. The computer system itself maintains this illusion through a combination of hardware and software techniques.

Before a program can be executed, each of its instructions must be resident in the real primary storage, but not all instructions of a program have to be resident at the same time. Essentially, virtual storage involves storing in primary storage only those instructions of the program that are currently executing, and storing the remainder on less expensive secondary storage, such as disks. Figure 10–10 illustrates virtual storage.

A virtual-storage system divides every program into pages, each of which has a size of, let's say, 4K. The operating system rolls pages of programs into primary

Gallery 5
Human/Computer Interaction

In the past few decades technology has introduced many ways for people to interact and communicate with computers. Computer punch cards of yesterday have been replaced by touch-sensitive display screens, light pens, optical devices, and even the human voice as means of inputting information into computers. Likewise, new high-resolution color monitors and high-speed printers and plotters have significantly improved the quality of computer output.

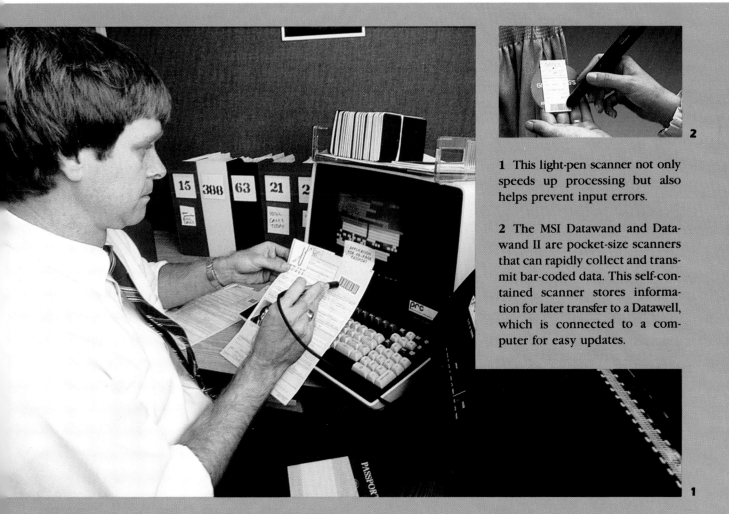

1 This light-pen scanner not only speeds up processing but also helps prevent input errors.

2 The MSI Datawand and Datawand II are pocket-size scanners that can rapidly collect and transmit bar-coded data. This self-contained scanner stores information for later transfer to a Datawell, which is connected to a computer for easy updates.

1

3

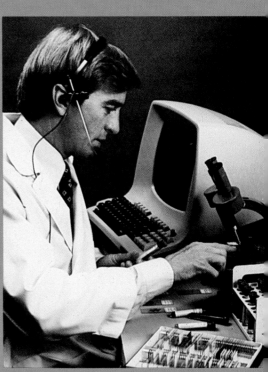

4

5

6

3,4 Touch-screen personal computers are becoming more popular for routine procedures. This user simply touches his choice of the commands displayed on the monitor.

5,6 Voice-input computers can recognize several hundred words and are amazingly accurate. These new devices free the user's hands for other tasks during inputting. Voice-recognition units are being used in a variety of work settings.

7 The Keyport 300 from Polytel is a keypad with three hundred programmable keys for easy use with most major word processing and spreadsheet packages. Instead of having to learn commands, the user simply chooses from the choices available on the keypad. Keyware is also available for advanced users to design their own customized application for end users.

8 Templates fit over standard keyboards and are available for many software packages. Commands and an explanation of each function key are written on the template for easy reference. This template aids the user with commands for the word processing package WordPerfect.

9 This Macintosh computer from Apple is equipped with a mouse, which allows the user to move the cursor anywhere on the monitor by rolling the mouse in the desired direction. A menu item is selected by moving the cursor to the item and pressing a button on the mouse.

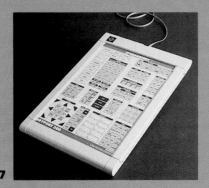

7

8

9

10 Supermarkets use laser scanners to read the Uniform Product Code bar codes, which speeds customer checkout and aids in inventory control.

11 This waitress is using a nationwide credit verification system called CATNET to verify a customer's credit card number. CATNET identifies the customer through a magnetic strip on the back of the credit card.

12 This self-service banking machine can dispense exact change and bills in five denominations and authorize or cash checks, allowing supermarkets and other stores a cost-effective way to offer these banking services to their customers.

13 Children use computers in a variety of games and toys that are designed to both teach and entertain.

14 This digitizer (right) is used to input large diagrams that can be professionally printed on a plotter (left). Digitizers are also available for use with personal computers in business.

15 This print head contains thirty-two tiny electrodes that form letters or other images by removing an aluminum coating from a special paper to create camera-ready masters for printing.

16 An optional feature of the Xerox 4050 Laser CP (copier/printer) allows users to make quick copies of originals at the speed of ten pages per minute. The printer can print text, data, and a wide variety of graphics.

17 Newer plotters have the ability to draw in a variety of colors, which helps give depth and separation to diagrams.

11

10

12

13

15

16

14

17

18

19

20

18,19 Computer aided design (CAD) systems graphically display three-dimensional structures on computer monitors to help in the design and testing of many items, including buildings, cars, spaceships, and maps.

20 The IBM 5080 Graphics system uses its advanced technology to design complex computer chips that further expand information handling.

Gallery 6
Telecommunications

Communication has been an important research focus over the past few decades. Remarkable advances in computer communication techniques are appearing in our everyday lives, helping to give rise to the information age. This gallery shows some of these advances.

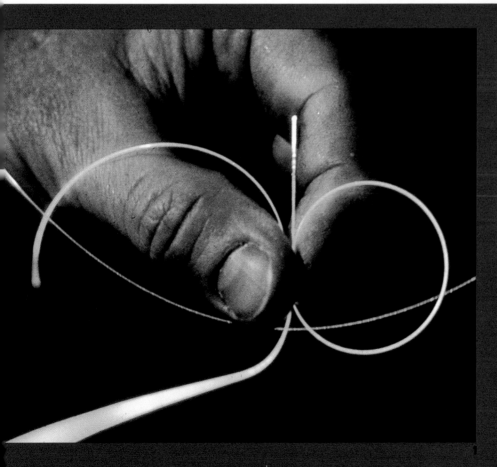

1

2

1 Today fiber optic cables are replacing coaxial cable. Fiber optic cables use light waves traveling in glass strands thinner than hair. Signals can travel at the speed of light in the cable.

2 These ultra-thin fiber optic strands are often sheltered in "ribbons" that become part of a lightguide cable.

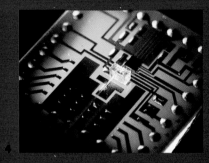

4

6

7

8

3 Fiber optic links have the potential to replace wire in countless commercial and industrial applications, reducing weight and increasing reliability.

4 This experimental amplifier chip can transmit data at a rate equivalent to seventeen thousand typewritten pages per second when used in conjunction with fiber optics.

5 Home networks allow large numbers of users to obtain information from a centralized data base. These networks provide a means for news updates and for paying bills and shopping.

6 Modems allow dumb terminals and personal computers to connect with computers all over the world using telephone lines.

7 Videotelephones allow both written and verbal communication.

8 Automobile phones are becoming an important convenience to many executives who spend time traveling. Portable computers can use these mobile communication lines to connect with other computers.

9 This electronic blackboard called GEMINI (developed by Bell Laboratories) reproduces any mark made on the board on remote monitors located anywhere there are communication lines.

10 IBM provides concurrent technical training via satellite from New York City to customers across the United States.

11 This EADAS/NM (Engineering and Administrative Data Acquisition System/Network Management) system is organized by a hierarchy of switching offices to help managers at AT & T localize communication network problems.

12 This advanced control center at Motorola Inc. features distributed multiprocessor control systems and digital audio switching to expand their ability to control radio telephone resource management, closed circuit TV monitor, alarm, and control systems from one centralized modular workstation.

13 This digital transmission system is being developed for the international market by Telectron, Ltd and AT & T International. Digital transmission allows both voice and data to be transmitted in digital rather than analog form.

14 The seismic vessel *Edward O. Vetter* is the first ship to transmit data via satellite at fifty-six kilobits per second.

15 Signals from the *Edward O. Vetter* are received at a data processing center where data is transformed into various displays.

16

16 This earth station in Roaring Creek, Pennsylvania, is one of the newest and largest international earth stations. It operates with satellites over the Atlantic Ocean to transmit and receive signals worldwide.

17 INTELSAT satellites are used to transmit and receive telephone, teletypewriter, data, facsimile, and television communications to and from the United States. INTELSAT provides two thirds of the world's overseas television. Each satellite has the average capacity of twelve thousand telephone circuits and two television channels.

18 Advanced technology in computers, telecommunications, and space exploration is closely related. Many of the advances in the miniaturization of computer circuitry came as a result of space exploration's demand for light weight, reliable computers. Here we see a Delta rocket launch of a communication satellite.

18

17

Gallery 7
Computer Security

As more vital and confidential information is stored on the computer, protection of this information is a challenge. Passwords can be stolen, lost, or calculated through the use of random character generators, and the information becomes vulnerable to anyone who is able to get to it. Fraud, sabotage, and embezzlement have meant multibillion dollar losses for corporations and financial institutions. How can it be stopped? This gallery illustrates a number of devices used to protect computer facilities and information.

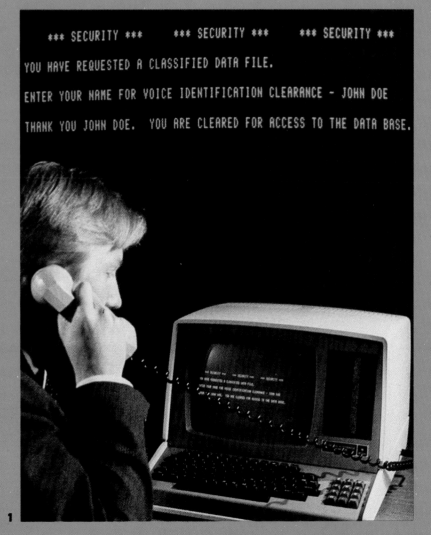

1 This computer security system, using a voice-recognition device, gives access only to specific individuals. The computer can identify an individual from the patterns of his or her voice.

2 The OMNIGUARD system (formally GUARDIAN) protects user access by causing passwords to automatically expire on a periodic basis. Users must then establish new passwords. Complete audit records are kept for extra-tight security.

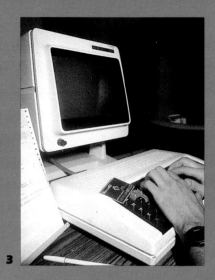

3

4

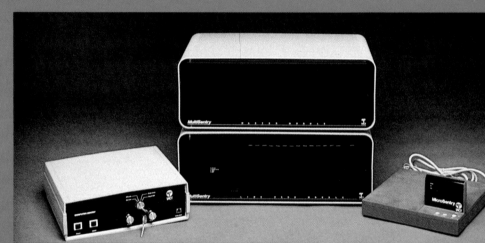

5

3 Security Dynamics has created passwords that change every sixty seconds with its SecurID card. Each SecurID card is about the size of a credit card and contains an integral microprocessor, power source, and liquid crystal display that changes unpredictably once a minute. When the full series of digits on the card is keyed in, the computer can tell which digits should be appearing on the card in the liquid crystal display at that given moment. The card which self-destructs at a predetermined time, can be disabled by a supervisor if it is lost or stolen. A complete and detailed audit trail is recorded and can be summarized on a number of different reports showing all log on attempts, enabling of new cards, disabling of old cards, and denied requests. Although the security system is costly, it can be modified to suit individual needs and appears to be one of the best computer security systems available today.

4 This computerized locker system called Compu-Lock requires both a special code number and a key to open lockers containing printouts of a company's infor-

mation. This locker system prevents printed information from entering the wrong hands and contains an audit trail record to keep track of each entry into the locker. The documents are loaded through the rear from inside the computer area.

5 These modem security devices require callers to provide a series of codes before allowing them access to the computer. The devices can be programmed to offer either direct access or assigned call-back access modes where a caller can only use predetermined phone numbers for access.

Assigned call-back is a very important security system for dial-up computers.

6 Paradyne's Info-Lock provides an effective solution to the problem of protecting classified information through the use of encryption. This process uses an algorithm, under the control of a specific key, to transform plain text into an unreadable form. The data must be decrypted through the same key before it can be read.

7 The IBM PC AT computer requires a key specific to the machine to be in place before use.

6

7

8

9

10

11

8 Identimat from Stellar Systems is one of the most sophisticated access-control devices on the market. Utilizing hand geometry, Identimat quickly verifies the identity of the person attempting to gain access to a sensitive area or device. Verification is accomplished when an individual's hand geometry characteristics are compared against data previously encoded into the system. Upon verification, the hand reader provides an "access" signal that can unlock a door, activate a turnstile, or provide access to a data terminal. Hand geometry data can be encoded on a magnetic-strip card for a stand alone system or can be stored in the memory of any general purpose computer.

9 Portable hard disks, like the Maynard Electronics TRANS-PORT, are used to physically transfer computer files. The portable drives can be easily removed from the computer and either stored in a safe place at the end of a work day or taken to a different location for use in a compatible computer.

10 Some automatic teller machines are equipped with cameras that photograph users during a bank transaction. This provides added security in case of improper procedures.

11 Many companies require employees to carry cards with magnetic strips allowing access to secured areas. The access systems can be tailored to employee schedules, business operation hours, or employee rank.

12A

13

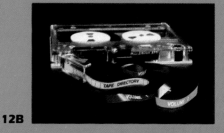

12B

15

14

12a/b Backup of data and files is a great concern in computer security. Tecmar's QIC-60 is an enhanced backup system that allows backup of selected files to tape or removable hard disk. A power sensor alerts and freezes the write head if the power is reduced, eliminating the chance of disk damage. A data management tool is included to sense bad disk sectors and automatically reroutes data to safe locations for improved data reliability.

13 Many companies store copies of crucial programs and data off-site in bank vaults.

14 Access to tape libraries should be restricted to the tape librarians.

15 Devices that allow access through keys, magnetic cards, or keyed-in passwords are also available for personal computers.

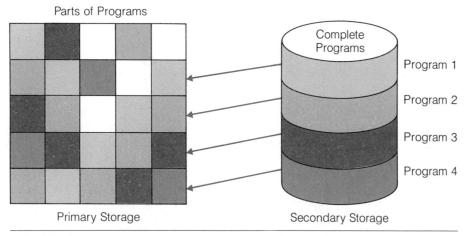

Parts of Programs

Complete Programs

Program 1

Program 2

Program 3

Program 4

Primary Storage

Secondary Storage

FIGURE 10–10 Overview of Virtual Storage

Virtual storage allows the computer to execute a program even though only a part of the program is in primary storage. The parts of a program are called pages, and they are swapped in and out of primary storage as they are needed for execution.

memory as they are needed for execution. Under virtual storage, only the page of the program that is currently executing must be stored in primary storage. All other program pages can be stored on a peripheral disk unit until each is required for execution. The operating system also maintains tables that tell the CPU where in primary storage each page of a program is located. Figure 10–11 illustrates **paging**.

Advantages of Virtual Storage

Virtual storage has two major advantages. First, the CPU is utilized more fully. Pages of many different programs can reside in main storage simultaneously since only one page of each program is resident in primary storage at any time. Thus primary storage can contain pages of many different programs before encountering size constraints.

The second advantage of virtual storage is that programmers no longer need to concern themselves about primary-storage size constraints when writing programs. When the complete program has to reside in primary storage, an individual program's primary-storage requirements can not exceed the primary storage remaining after the operating system's requirements have been met. This is the case with most PC operating systems. Under virtual storage, there is no practical limit on a program's primary-storage requirements.

As mentioned before, personal computer operating systems are moving toward virtual-storage capabilities. This allows them to execute larger programs. For example, the size of most electronic spreadsheets is constrained by primary-memory size. Virtual-storage capabilities accommodate much larger spreadsheets.

Current developments in the virtual-storage concept are tending toward a single-level storage concept. Single-level storage treats all storage, primary and secondary, as a single unit or level. Therefore, the real difference between primary and

transparent
An element of a computer system that a user or programmer can ignore when using the system.

secondary storage is *transparent* to the programmer. An example of such a system is IBM's System/38.

Disadvantages of Virtual Storage

As one might expect, there are disadvantages to virtual storage. Overhead costs increase. CPU time is required to page (read/write) all those pages in and out of main storage. Additional primary storage is required to hold the tables that keep track of the pages, and to hold a virtual-storage operating system.

Another potential problem is **thrashing,** which occurs when one or more pages of a program have to be paged in and paged out of primary storage frequently during execution of the program. Thrashing could reach a point where the CPU is spending too much time on paging in and out as compared to time spent on program execution.

Program structure can have a significant positive or negative impact on the problem of thrashing. Consider the segment of a FORTRAN program illustrated in Figure 10–12. If, as illustrated, page 2 of the program ends at statement number 40 and page 3 begins at statement number 50, significant thrashing is going to occur when this program is executed. Pages 2 and 3 will have to be paged in and out as many as 100 times each, as the program branches from statement 50 to statement 30. Therefore, when writing a program that is to be executed many times on a virtual-storage system, the programmer should minimize the branching within the program. Structured programming (which is sometimes called GOTO-less programming) is a technique that can minimize program branching.

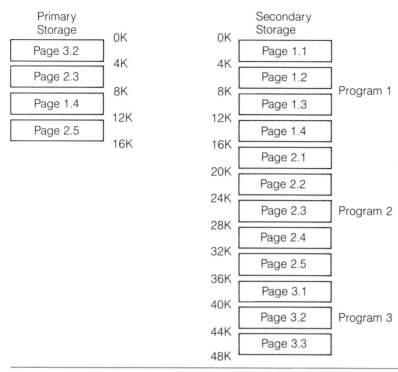

FIGURE 10–11 Paging in a Virtual-Storage System

Notice that to store all of the three illustrated programs would require 48K. However, because of the virtual-storage capability, the CPU can execute all three of these programs concurrently even though there is only 16K of primary storage available. For execution of a program to occur, only one page of the program must be in primary storage.

Timesharing and Interactive Computing

A **timesharing** system allows access to a CPU and data files through many remote terminals. The central computer system is often owned by the company whose employees use it, but there are also public timesharing systems owned by a time-sharing vendor where the users pay for the service. The cost is based on a fixed charge plus a usage charge. The services that you can access with your personal computer to retrieve data or order products (such as The Source and Dow Jones News Retrieval) execute on public timesharing systems.

From the viewpoint of the user, the computer system appears to be dedicated exclusively to the user's terminal because of the fast response of the CPU to commands from the terminal. In reality, the CPU is servicing many terminals and perhaps several batch jobs. Multiprogramming is the method of implementing timeshared operations, since fast response to terminal commands is necessary.

Many businesses have used timesharing as a means of automating information processing. Before timesharing, a decision to automate involved a choice between

service bureau
A company that provides
batch-processing service
on an as-needed basis,
and charges an hourly
rate.

investing in an in-house system or using a batch *service bureau.* Timesharing used to be suitable only in situations where a minimum of input or output was involved. It was not suitable for high-volume, batch-type operations because of the high cost and time required. Changes have occurred in the technology, however. Much data preparation can be done off-line, which does not involve a usage charge. Timesharing now has the capability of sending or receiving large amounts of data through remote job entry.

Unnecessary costs are incurred if an interactive timesharing mode is used when a batch mode could carry out some of the processing. A relatively new service, called remote computing services, involves the use of timesharing and batch processing. It is also referred to as **interactive batch.** The system permits the user to have an application program, originally developed for interactive processing, to be run in a batch mode. The computer accepts data commands from a file in the program as if it were the user at the terminal. Programs most likely to be entered for interactive batch are long ones that come up at a busy time of day or at the end of the day.

Thinking About Information Systems 10–2

The First Federal Savings and Loan Association is a local and relatively small firm. Currently the recordkeeping is done through timesharing with a computer service bureau. The association is satisfied with the timesharing service. However, several software firms have recently presented the firm with a complete package (including software and personal computers) that could perform the association's information-processing needs locally. The software companies claim that their systems are flexible and can produce a wide variety of information for management needs. They also maintain that processing customer records locally would improve the confidentiality of the association's records. They argue that there have been instances of customer data being divulged to unauthorized persons at service bureaus. Which direction do you think the savings and loan association should take?

Multiprocessing

As explained earlier in the chapter, a multiprogramming system executes two or more programs concurrently on a single CPU. In contrast, under **multiprocessing,** a single program is processed by two or more CPUs. The most typical type of multiprocessing occurs in systems that support both a batch mode and many remote terminals (see Figure 10–13). When a system has only a few remote terminals to support, the main CPU can handle all the terminal interrupts and trivial jobs, such as editing. However, the processing requirements of a large number of remote terminals can overload the main CPU. In this case, terminal

```
             │ 15 K = 0
             │ 25 N = 100
    Page 2   │ 30 K = K + 1
             │ 40 SUMY2 = SUMY2 + Y(K)**2
─────────────┼──────────────────────────────
             │ 50 IF (K.LT.N) GO TO 30
    Page 3   │ 60 K = 0
             │
```

FIGURE 10–12   A Program That Can Cause Thrashing

The IF statement (Statement 50) in this FORTRAN program branches back to Statement 30. Each time this branch occurs during execution, page 2 will have to be swapped with page 3.

interrupts and trivial jobs can be handled by a mini-computer, which, in the configuration shown in Figure 10–13, is called a **front-end processor.** The main CPU processes batch jobs and executes interactive programs that the front-end processor cannot handle.

Multiprocessing systems can take many forms. For example, a third CPU, equivalent in processing power to the existing main CPU, could be added. The new CPU would handle all the timesharing processing that is not handled by the front-end processor. The existing CPU would be used for batch processing and would be able to accept and execute batch jobs from the timesharing CPU that were originated by a terminal. Usually these jobs have long run times, and the output can be directed to the high-speed batch printer rather than back to the originating terminal.

Personal computers often use multiprocessing. For example, the IBM-PC has a math co-processor that handles mathematical processing at speeds up to 80 times faster than the PC's microprocessor.

Multiprocessing systems substantially increase the throughput capabilities of a system with an overloaded CPU. Another advantage of multiprocessing is the backup CPU capability provided by two or more CPUs, which are, in some configurations, identical.

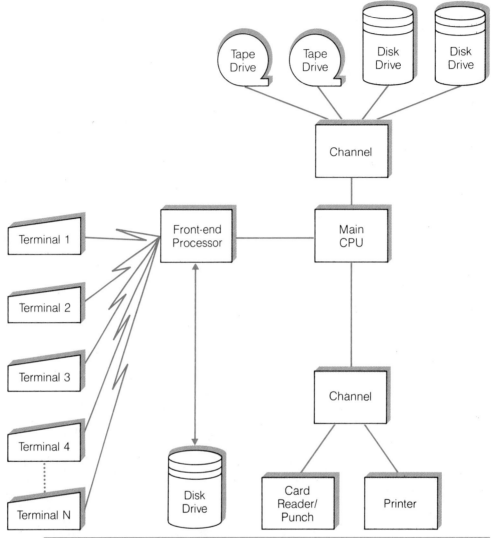

FIGURE 10-13 A Multiprocessing System

Multiprocessing is widely used with large computers. Some mainframe systems may have several communications processors attached to them.

Summing Up

☐ System software is a set of programs that manage the resources of a computer system, provide routine services such as copying data from one file to another, and assist in the development of application programs.

☐ Application programs are written to perform specific jobs for computer users.

☐ System control programs control the execution of programs, manage the storage and processing resources of the computer, and perform other management and monitoring functions. The most important of these programs is the operating system. Other examples are data-base management systems and communication monitors.

☐ System support programs provide routine service functions to other computer programs and computer users. Examples are utilities, librarians, performance monitors, and job accounting.

☐ System development programs assist in the creation of application programs. Examples are language translators such as a BASIC interpreter, and application generators such as IBM's Application Development Facility.

☐ The major functions of an operating system are to control the execution of computer programs and manage the storage and processing resources of a computer system.

☐ The programs in an operating system start up the computer, schedule the execution of various user programs, supervise the allocation of resources to these programs, and facilitate interaction between the CPU and I/O devices like terminals and printers.

☐ Batch-type operating systems line up jobs as they are received and then process them when time is available. In contrast, interactive systems start executing a job as soon as it is received, so that the user does not have to wait at the terminal.

☐ The major advantages of multiprogramming are improved throughput, better turnaround, and less response time. These advantages are achieved primarily through the use of job rotation and priority schemes.

☐ The concept of virtual memory refers to storing only the active segments or pages of a program in primary storage. The rest of the program is stored in secondary storage, and parts of it are called in when required.

☐ A timesharing system allows many interactive users to use the CPU concurrently. This is made possible through the use of multiprogramming operating systems. CPU processing time is distributed among users by a sophisticated job-rotation and priority-allocation system.

☐ Multiprocessing systems allow the same job to be run on two or more CPUs. This improves system throughput by letting the different CPUs specialize in those functions which they perform best.

Key Terms

system software	application program
application software	general-purpose application software
operating systems	specific-purpose application software
job queue	application programmers
system control programs	initial program load or bootstrap
system support programs	job scheduling
system development programs	access security
system programmers	system residence device

initial program loader (IPL)
supervisor
job-control program
input/output (I/O) control program
resident supervisor
monitor or executive programs
job-control language (JCL)
utility programs
librarian
performance monitors
language translator
linkage editor
load module
application generators
batch operating system
spooling (simultaneous peripheral operations on line)

interactive operating system
interrupt
multiprogramming
throughput
turnaround time
response time
system availability
interprogram interference
virtual storage
paging
thrashing
timesharing
interactive batch
multiprocessing
front-end processor

Self-Quiz

Completion Questions

1. _____ is a set of programs that manage the resources of a computer system, whereas _____ perform specific tasks for the computer user.

2. _____ are a set of integrated programs that control the execution of computer programs and manage the storage and processing resources of a computer system.

3. A frequently used portion of the operating system, which is stored in primary storage when the computer is operating, is called the _____ .

4. Programs that perform routine tasks such as sorting and copying are called _____ .

5. A program that is suitable for loading directly into primary storage for execution is called a _____ .

6. In a batch mode, an operating system accepts jobs and places them in a queue to wait for execution. This process is called _____ .

7. _____ refers to the elapsed time between the submission of a batch job and the availability of the output.

8. _____ is the capability of a CPU to execute two or more programs concurrently.

9. _____ is a measure of the total amount of processing that a computer system can complete over a fixed period of time.

10. Under _____ , a single program is processed by two or more CPUs.

Multiple-Choice Questions

1. An example of system development programs is:
   a. operating systems
   b. performance monitors
   c. data-base management systems
   d. language translators
   e. None of the above

2. Which of the following is *not* a part of the operating system?
   a. supervisor
   b. performance monitor
   c. job-control program
   d. input/output control program
   e. initial program loader

3. If special forms are needed for printing the output, the programmer specifies these forms through:
   a. JCL
   b. IPL

c. utility progams
d. load modules
e. none of the above

4. Which of the following is not an advantage of multiprogramming?
   a. increased throughput
   b. shorter response time
   c. decreased operating-system overhead
   d. ability to assign priorities to jobs
   e. all of the above are advantages

5. The problem of thrashing is affected significantly by:
   a. program structure
   b. program size
   c. primary-storage size
   d. none of the above
   e. all of the above

6. Two basic types of operating systems are:
   a. sequential and direct
   b. batch and timesharing
   c. sequential and realtime
   d. direct and interactive
   e. batch and interactive

7. Under multiprogramming, turnaround time for short jobs is usually _____ and that for long jobs is slightly _____ .
   a. lengthened; shortened
   b. shortened; lengthened
   c. shortened; shortened
   d. shortened; unchanged
   e. none of the above

8. Remote computing services involve the use of timesharing and _____ .
   a. multiprocessing
   b. interactive processing
   c. batch processing
   d. realtime processing
   e. none of the above

9. Under virtual storage,
   a. a single program is processed by two or more CPUs.
   b. two or more programs are stored concurrently in primary storage.
   c. only the active pages of a program are stored in primary storage.
   d. interprogram interference may occur.

10. A front-end processor is usually used in:
    a. multiprogramming
    b. virtual storage
    c. timesharing
    d. multiprocessing
    e. none of the above

Answers

Completion

1. System software; application programs
2. Operating systems
3. resident supervisor
4. utility programs
5. load module
6. spooling
7. Turnaround time
8. Multiprogramming
9. Throughput
10. multiprocessing

Multiple Choice

1. d
2. b
3. a
4. c
5. a
6. e
7. b
8. c
9. c
10. c

Chapter 11

Data Storage and Processing

CHAPTER OUTLINE

PROLOGUE

Dianna Davis is in the rare-plant business, with mail-order customers from all parts of the United States. She has a mailing list of about 10,000 customers on her personal computer. When she makes a computer run that must access each record in the customer list, it takes the computer about thirty minutes to make the run. Yet when she accesses a single record, the computer retrieves the record in a fraction of a second. Doesn't the computer have to search through all the records in a file to find a single record? How does it retrieve the record so fast? Read on.

Introduction

In chapter 1, we covered basic data storage and processing. Here we will discuss these concepts in more detail. Recall the components of the data hierarchy, which are listed again here in ascending order of complexity:

1. Bit
2. Byte
3. Field or item
4. Record
5. File or data set
6. Data base

By now you should feel fairly comfortable with these terms. (If you don't, go back and review data storage in chapter 1.) In this chapter, we will first look at how bits are used to represent data. We will also explore file organization. And finally, information-processing modes and their relationships to on-line direct-access and realtime systems will be examined.

Data Representation

True Binary Representation

As you will recall from chapter 1, all data in digital computers are represented by a **bit** being either on or off. Bit is short for binary digit. Since bits can store only two states, on or off, they are binary in nature. To store a large number of different alphabetic, numeric, and special characters, computers combine several bits into one byte. A **byte** is a combination of bits that represent one character of data. We will examine several ways that bits are combined to represent data.

True binary representation uses the **binary number system.** To illustrate this system, we need to first look at the **decimal number system** with which we are all familiar. The decimal number system uses the number ten as a base.

Each place within a decimal number has a certain value. Refer to Figure 11–1. At the bottom of the figure is a table that indicates the **place value** of each place within a decimal number. Starting with the right-most digit in the number, we see that the first place has a value of 1 (10^0), the second a value of 10 (10^1), the third a value of 100 (10^2), and so on.

Any number from any number system can be converted to a decimal number by multiplying each digit in the number by its respective place value. To illustrate, let's convert the decimal number 14,635 (as shown at the top of Figure 11–1) to a decimal number. (Of course, the conversion of a decimal number to a decimal number will produce the original number; but this will at least prove that our system works.) First we multiply the digit 5 X its place value of 10^0 (or 1). Then

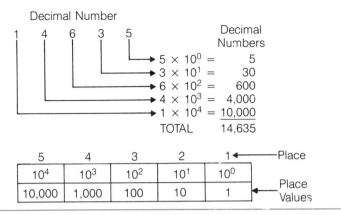

FIGURE 11–1 Conversion of a Decimal Number to a Decimal Number

The decimal number system is based on 10. Therefore, each place in the number system has a value that is a power of 10.

we multiply 3×10^1, and so on. When we add up all of these products we find that the total is 14,635—the original number.

Let's now look at the binary number system, a system with the number two as a base. At the bottom of Figure 11–2, we see the place values of a binary number system. The first place from the right has a value of 1 (2^0), the second place a value of 2 (2^1), the third place a value of 4 (2^2), et cetera. Note that these place values exactly double each time since we're raising two to a power to derive the place values.

Conversion of a binary number to a decimal number proceeds in exactly the same manner as calculating the decimal number. We multiply the digit in each

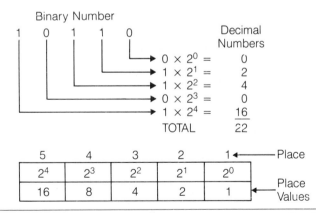

FIGURE 11–2 Conversion of a Binary Number to a Decimal Number

The binary number system is based on 2. Therefore, each place in the binary number system has a value that is a power of 2.

place by its respective place value, as illustrated at the top of Figure 11–2. $0 \ X \ 2^0$ is equal to 0; $1 \ X \ 2^1$ is equal to 2; et cetera. We sum these products and obtain a total of 22, so the binary number 10110 is equivalent to the decimal number 22.

True binary representation is used only to store numeric data. The primary advantage of true binary representation is that it requires fewer bits to store a given number. For example, the number 3985 can be stored in twelve bits if true binary representation is used. With twelve bits we can store any number from 0 through 4095, since in twelve bits there are 4096 (2^{12}) possible combinations of binary digits. If another binary coding scheme is used, EBCDIC—which we mentioned in Chapter 1 and will discuss in more detail later—the computer needs a minimum of sixteen bits to represent the number 3985.

EBCDIC Representation

The **Extended Binary Coded Decimal Interchange Code** or **EBCDIC** (pronounced *ib-si-dick*) is an IBM-developed binary code used on mainframe computers which represents each numeric, alphabetic, or special character with eight bits per byte (character). For example, the decimal digit 9 is represented by the code 11111001. Table 11–1 illustrates the EBCDIC code for uppercase alphabetic characters and the numeric characters zero through nine.

As shown in Figure 11–3, the eight bits in EBCDIC are divided into four numeric bits and four zone bits. You will notice in Table 11–1 that only the four right-most bits, the numeric bits, are necessary to code the numeric digits 0 through 9, since the four zone bits are always turned on and do not vary. The zone bits are used to code uppercase and lowercase alphabetic characters as well as special characters, such as commas and question marks. EBCDIC can code up to 256 different characters ($2^8 = 256$). This ability to code a wide range of characters is one of the primary advantages of EBCDIC.

Another advantage of EBCDIC is that we can represent two numeric digits within the eight bits of the EBCDIC code. If the data we are representing are all numeric, the computer divides the eight-bit code into two separate four-bit codes; in other words, the zone bits are used just like they were numeric bits. This form of data representation is called **packed decimal.** Since the maximum number of combinations we can represent with four bits is 16 (2^4), it is possible to represent all ten numeric digits with just four bits.

ASCII-8 Representation

Another commonly used code for encoding bytes of data is the **American Standard Code for Information Interchange** or **ASCII** (pronounced *As'-key*). This code was developed by the American National Standards Institute (ANSI), with the objective of providing a standard code that could be used on many different manufacturers' computer hardware. Like EBCDIC, ASCII-8 is an eight-bit code, but there is also a 7-bit version of ASCII (see Table 11–2). The advantages of ASCII-8 are the same as those of EBCDIC. ASCII-7 is used primarily on microcomputers and in data communication.

TABLE 11–1   EBCDIC Coding Scheme

Character	EBCDIC Bit Pattern
A	1100 0001
B	1100 0010
C	1100 0011
D	1100 0100
E	1100 0101
F	1100 0110
G	1100 0111
H	1100 1000
I	1100 1001
J	1101 0001
K	1101 0010
L	1101 0011
M	1101 0100
N	1101 0101
O	1101 0110
P	1101 0111
Q	1101 1000
R	1101 1001
S	1101 0010
T	1110 0011
U	1110 0100
V	1110 0101
W	1110 0110
X	1110 0111
Y	1110 1000
Z	1110 1001
0	1111 0000
1	1111 0001
2	1111 0010
3	1111 0011
4	1111 0100
5	1111 0101
6	1111 0110
7	1111 0111
8	1111 1000
9	1111 1001

With 8 positions in a byte, EBCDIC can encode up to 256 alphabetic characters, numbers, special characters, and symbols. This table only shows a portion of the characters that can be coded in EBCDIC.

Place Values in EBCDIC							
Zone Bits				Numeric Bits			
8	4	2	1	8	4	2	1

FIGURE 11–3   EBCDIC Place Values

Since EBCDIC is encoded in a binary number system, its place values are also powers of 2.

TABLE 11–2 ASCII-7 Coding Scheme

ASCII Character	ASCII Bit Pattern	ASCII Character	ASCII Bit Pattern
NUL	0000000	@	1000000
SOH	0000001	A	1000001
STX	0000010	B	1000010
ETX	0000011	C	1000011
EOT	0000100	D	1000100
ENQ	0000101	E	1000101
ACK	0000110	F	1000110
BEL	0000111	G	1000111
BS	0001000	H	1001000
HT	0001001	I	1001001
LF	0001010	J	1001010
VT	0001011	K	1001011
FF	0001100	L	1001100
CR	0001101	M	1001101
SO	0001110	N	1001110
SI	0001111	O	1001111
DLE	0010000	P	1010000
DC1	0010001	Q	1010001
DC2	0010010	R	1010010
DC3	0010011	S	1010011
DC4	0010100	T	1010100
NAK	0010101	U	1010101
SYN	0010110	V	1010110
ETB	0010111	W	1010111
CAN	0011000	X	1011000
EM	0011001	Y	1011001
SUB	0011010	Z	1011010
ESC	0011011	[	1011011
FS	0011100	\	1011100
GS	0011101	]	1011101
RS	0011110	^	1011110
US	0011111	_	1011111

With 7 bits, ASCII-7 can encode up to 128 alphabetic characters, numbers, special characters, and symbols. They are all shown in this table.

Hexadecimal Representation

Often programmers must examine the content of a storage location within the computer in order to debug a program. The internal storage is in binary form. To print out (or dump) the contents of memory in binary form would be of little use since the programmer would see only a string of ones and zeros on the printout. Conversion to decimal equivalents would be laborious and time consuming. Thus, some computer systems perform *memory dumps* in hexadecimal representation.

Hexadecimal has a base of 16; that is, there are 16 symbols in hexadecimal, 0 through 9 and A through F. Table 11–3 illustrates binary, hexadecimal, and decimal equivalent values. When hexadecimal is used, the contents of each four bits are converted to the corresponding hexadecimal symbol and printed out on the memory dump. For example, if the four bits are 1110, the hexadecimal symbol E would

memory dump
To print the contents of primary storage.

TABLE 11–2 continued

ASCII Character	ASCII Bit Pattern	ASCII Character	ASCII Bit Pattern
SP	0100000		1100000
!	0100001	a	1100001
''	0100010	b	1100010
#	0100011	c	1100011
$	0100100	d	1100100
%	0100101	e	1100101
&	0100110	f	1100110
'	0100111	g	1100111
(	0101000	h	1101000
)	0101001	i	1101001
*	0101010	j	1101010
+	0101011	k	1101011
,	0101100	l	1101100
-	0101101	m	1101101
.	0101110	n	1101110
/	0101111	o	1101111
0	0110000	p	1110000
1	0110001	q	1110001
2	0110010	r	1110010
3	0110011	s	1110011
4	0110100	t	1110100
5	0110101	u	1110101
6	0110110	v	1110110
7	0110111	w	1110111
8	0111000	x	1111000
9	0111001	y	1111001
:	0111010	z	1111010
;	0111011	{	1111011
<	0111100			1111100
=	0111101	}	1111101
>	0111110	~	1111110
?	0111111	DEL	1111111

be printed out. Sixteen symbols are used since the maximum number of bit combinations of four bits is 16 (2^4).

The decimal equivalent of a hexadecimal number can be determined by multiplying each digit by its appropriate power of the base 16 and summing the products just like we did with decimal and binary number conversion to the decimal system. The primary advantages of a hexadecimal system are that conversion from hexadecimal to decimal is much easier than from binary to decimal, and the volume of printout when we use hexadecimal is much smaller than when we use binary to print out a memory dump.

Parity Bits

The actual encoding of data using EBCDIC, or any other coding scheme, also contains an extra (or check) bit. A **parity bit** is included to detect errors. For

TABLE 11–3   Binary, Hexadecimal, and Decimal Equivalents

Binary System (Place Values)				Hexadecimal System	Decimal System
8	4	2	1		
0	0	0	0	0	0
0	0	0	1	1	1
0	0	1	0	2	2
0	0	1	1	3	3
0	1	0	0	4	4
0	1	0	1	5	5
0	1	1	0	6	6
0	1	1	1	7	7
1	0	0	0	8	8
1	0	0	1	9	9
1	0	1	0	A	10
1	0	1	1	B	11
1	1	0	0	C	12
1	1	0	1	D	13
1	1	1	0	E	14
1	1	1	1	F	15

Notice that you can add up the place values of the binary system for the bits that are on, and the sum will be equal to the number in the decimal system.

example, with an even parity machine, the computer expects the number of bits turned on in a byte always to be even (if the machine was designed as an odd parity machine, the number of bits turned on should always be odd). Refer to Table 11–4, which illustrates the use of parity bits. Notice that when the number of on bits in the regular eight bits of the code is even, the parity bit is off; whereas if the number of on bits in the regular eight bits is odd, the parity bit is turned on to make the total number of on bits even. Bits can be erroneously changed from on to off, or off to on, when data are moved from one storage location or medium to another. If such an erroneous bit change occurs, the number of bits

TABLE 11–4   EBCDIC with Even Parity

Decimal Equivalent	P*	8	4	2	1	8	4	2	1 ← Place Values	
0	0	1	1	1	1	0	0	0	0	EBCDIC
1	1	1	1	1	1	0	0	0	1	Code with
2	1	1	1	1	1	0	0	1	0	Parity Bit
3	0	1	1	1	1	0	0	1	1	
4	1	1	1	1	1	0	1	0	0	

*Parity Bit

Each row of bits represents a byte. Count the number of on bits in each row and see whether it adds up to an even number.

on would not be even, thus signaling an error. Various environmental factors (such as dust) can cause these errors to happen. It is very important that computer hardware contains automatic parity checking to detect errors in bit patterns.

Record-Access Methods

Primary and Secondary Keys

As discussed in Chapter 1, the storage of data in an information system can be considered a data hierarchy. Data bases contain files, files contain records, records contain fields, fields contain bytes (or characters), and bytes are represented by bits. A most important concern of business information systems is the methods by which we can access individual records within files. Records contain data on subjects. For example, a subject in a student registration system would be an individual student; in a payroll system, an individual employee. For this information to be of use we must be able to access it. To access an individual record, we must be able to uniquely identify that record. We do this through a **primary key** which is a field that uniquely identifies the record and thus separates it from all other records in the file. A student record is illustrated in Figure 11–4. The primary key of the record is social security number, since an individual's social security number is different from all other social security numbers in the file. Normally, users or programs access individual records by supplying the primary key. Primary keys are also used when we change data within a record or delete a record. In performing these operations we must uniquely identify the record on which the delete or change is being made.

Records may also be accessed through **secondary keys.** Any field within a record can be a secondary key. Secondary keys do not have to be unique. For example, in the student records file, as illustrated in Figure 11–4, there would certainly be many freshmen. In this example, we might make class a secondary key

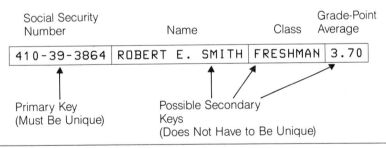

FIGURE 11–4   Primary and Secondary Keys

Since the primary key must be unique, there can be only one record with a social security number of 410-39-3864. Since name, class, and grade-point average are used only as secondary keys, there could be multiple Robert E. Smiths, multiple freshmen, and multiple 3.70 grade-point averages.

since we may often want to retrieve all the records of students in the freshman class. Since secondary keys allow us to retrieve information based on any field within the record, they are very valuable.

Sequential Access

In **sequential access** we process every record in the file. Starting at the front of the file, we process the records in a record-by-record order. Sequential access is only efficient in terms of time, when the file activity ratio is high. The file activity ratio is a percentage of file records actually used in a given processing run. For example, most payroll systems would use sequential access when producing paychecks since most if not all employees of a company receive a paycheck in each payroll period. A very large percentage of the payroll file records would be used during such a run. In much of the routine, high-volume business information processing, there is a high file activity ratio; thus, sequential access is an efficient approach.

Random Access

random
Something that occurs in no particular order.

Quite often we want to retrieve only one record from a file. Thus the percentage of records we use in the file is extremely low. The need for these individual records usually occurs *randomly*. For example, when a grocery checkout clerk uses a uniform-product-code scanner, the grocery items are passed over the scanner in a random order. The computer must be able to immediately retrieve individual records from the pricing file in order to price each item. It obviously could not access these price records sequentially, since there would be thousands of individual records—one for each item in the grocery store. File organization methods must be used that will allow quick direct access to these randomly occurring requests for pricing data. Keep in mind there may be fifteen to twenty checkout lanes going simultaneously, all serviced by the same computer. Just as there is a need to process records sequentially, there is also a very large need in business information systems today to access individual records randomly. Many applications, like airline reservations, must have **random access** because information needs to be processed immediately. In the next section we will discuss the various ways files are organized to meet the requirements of both sequential and random access.

File Organization

Terminology Used with Files

There are a few terms we should define before discussing **file organization.** First, the term *address* identifies the location in which the record is stored. Note the difference between address and primary key. Primary key uniquely identifies

Relative Address					
1	Data Record
2	Data Record
3	Data Record
4	Data Record
5	Data Record

Physical Address

Cylinder	Track	Sector	
9	3	1	Data Record
9	3	1	Data Record
9	3	2	Data Record
9	3	2	Data Record
9	3	2	Data Record

FIGURE 11–5   Relative and Physical Addresses

A physical address is equivalent to your street address. A relative address is equivalent to your saying, "I live in the fourth house on the left from the street intersection."

a record, but address identifies where it is stored on the storage medium, which is usually magnetic disk. For example, your name uniquely identifies you but it does not identify where you live—your address does. There are two types of addresses: physical and relative (see Figure 11–5). A **physical address** deals with the physical characteristics of the storage medium. For example, on magnetic disk the physical address is composed of a **cylinder,** a **track,** and a **sector** (see Figure 11–6). To find an individual record on a magnetic disk, a computer ultimately must know its physical address. Some file organizations such as index-sequential access produce physical addresses for records. However, the more widely used file organizations today use the concept of **relative address** (refer again to Figure 11–5). In relative addressing an individual record's address depends on its relative position in the file. If it is the third record in the file, then it has a relative address of 3. Thus, what we are doing is assigning an address based on the record's relative position from the beginning of the file. As mentioned earlier, a relative address must ultimately be converted to a physical address in order for us to find a record. However, the methods by which this is done are not important here.

Individual data records may contain the relative address of other data records. They are used to link together similar records. A file containing pointers of this type is called a **linked list.** In the linked list in Figure 11–7 we have linked the records that contain the same class. As you can see, all the freshman records are linked together. The first freshman record has a pointer to the relative address of the second freshman record, and it has a pointer to the third freshman record which is in relative address 5, and so on. We will have another example of a linked list when we discuss direct file organization.

The last term we should define before discussing file organization is directory. A **directory** is a list of the file names contained on a particular storage medium such as a magnetic disk pack. Figure 11–8 illustrates a PC file directory. It lists all the files stored on one floppy disk.

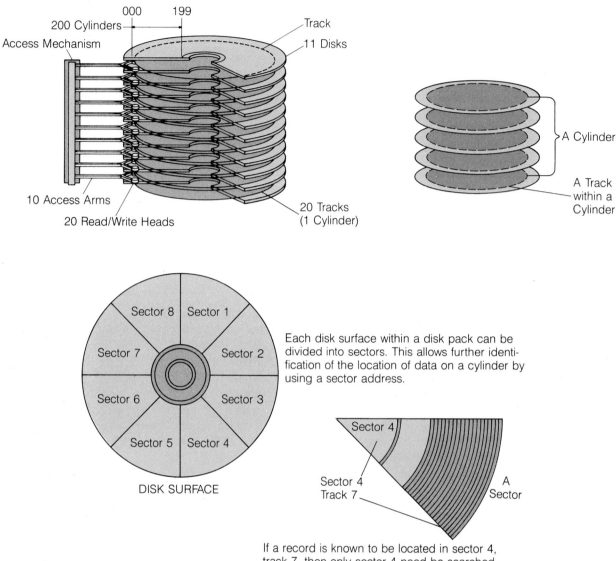

000   199

200 Cylinders

Access Mechanism

Track

11 Disks

10 Access Arms

20 Read/Write Heads

20 Tracks
(1 Cylinder)

A Cylinder

A Track
within a
Cylinder

Sector 8 | Sector 1

Sector 7

Sector 2

Sector 6

Sector 3

Sector 5 | Sector 4

DISK SURFACE

Each disk surface within a disk pack can be divided into sectors. This allows further identification of the location of data on a cylinder by using a sector address.

Sector 4

Sector 4
Track 7

A
Sector

If a record is known to be located in sector 4, track 7, then only sector 4 need be searched.

FIGURE 11–6   Cylinder, Track and Sector Addresses

The set of all tracks with the same distance from the center of the disk form a cylinder. The number of cylinders on a disk pack is equal to the number of tracks across a disk surface. The number of tracks within a cylinder is equal to the number of disk surfaces on which data are stored.

index
A list used to indicate the address of records stored in a file. It is similar to a book index.

Figure 11–9 is an overview of the file organizations covered in this section. There are three basic types: sequential, direct, and *indexed*. We will discuss fully indexed files as well as a class of indexes called tree indexes. The most widely used of these file organizations are sequential, direct, and the tree indexes. The balanced tree (B-Tree) index is becoming a very popular method for indexing files.

Relative Address		Class	Pointer (to a Relative Address)
1	Other Data	Freshman	4
2	Other Data	Sophomore	3
3	Other Data	Sophomore	6
4	Other Data	Freshman	5
5	Other Data	Freshman	7
6	Other Data	Sophomore	8
7	Other Data	Freshman	0
8	Other Data	Sophomore	0
9	Other Data	Junior	0

FIGURE 11-7 A Linked List

After reading the first freshman record we can directly read each additional freshman record without reading nonfreshman records. Record 1 points to record 4, record 4 points to record 5, record 5 points to record 7, and record 7 indicates (with a zero in the pointer field) the end of that linked list.

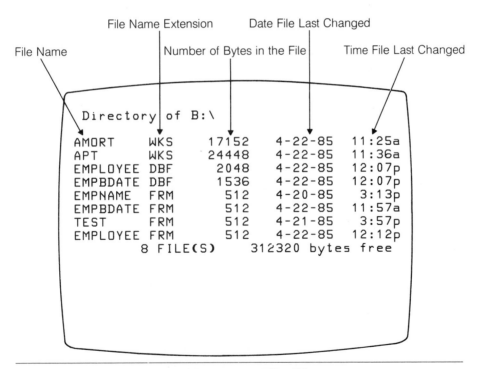

File Name

File Name Extension

Number of Bytes in the File

Date File Last Changed

Time File Last Changed

```
 Directory of B:\

AMORT    WKS    17152    4-22-85    11:25a
APT      WKS    24448    4-22-85    11:36a
EMPLOYEE DBF     2048    4-22-85    12:07p
EMPBDATE DBF     1536    4-22-85    12:07p
EMPNAME  FRM      512    4-20-85     3:13p
EMPBDATE FRM      512    4-22-85    11:57a
TEST     FRM      512    4-21-85     3:57p
EMPLOYEE FRM      512    4-22-85    12:12p
         8 FILE(S)     312320 bytes free
```

FIGURE 11-8 A Personal-Computer File Directory

This floppy disk has very little stored on it. There are 312, 320 bytes of space that are unused.

If you are running DOS version 2.0 or higher, you have the capability to organize your files in different levels. This is particularly important if you are working with a fixed disk since it can hold hundreds of files. A system of subdirectories can be set up so that you can group your files. A typical file directory tree structure is shown here.

When you first boot your computer and request a directory, only the files in the highest directory (called the root directory) are listed. Additionally, the names of any directories the next level down (called subdirectories) are shown. Once you have set up a directory tree you can move from one directory on the disk to another as needed. Also, you can, using the wildcard

specifier (*), copy, erase, and otherwise manipulate files in any directory. Any wild-card references will affect files in the current directory or other specified directory only. For more information on how to set up and use multilevel directories, look in your DOS reference manual under the following commands.

MKDIR—make a directory

RMDIR—remove a directory

CD—change directory

TREE—display all directory names and the directory structure

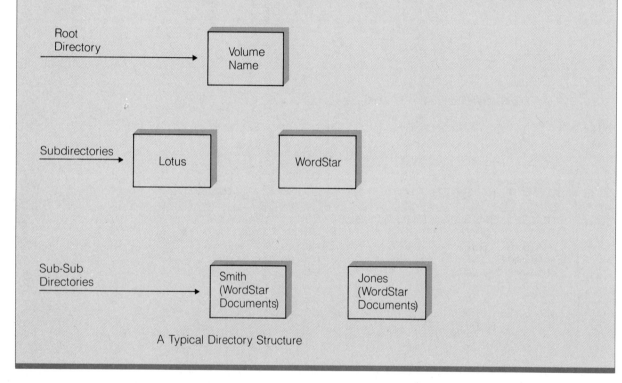

A Typical Directory Structure

Sequential File Organization

With **sequential file organization,** records are stored either in the order they are entered into the file or in ascending order by primary key. For example, in a sequential student-records file, the records would be in ascending order by the students' social security numbers. For an individual record to be found, a sequential search, beginning at the first record on the file, must be performed. Each record

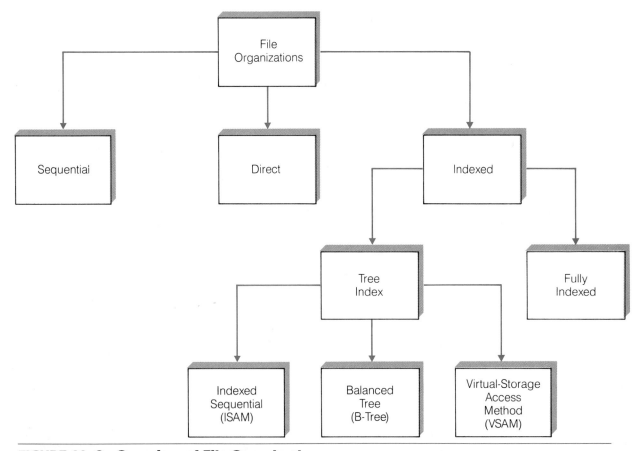

FIGURE 11–9   Overview of File Organizations

must be examined until the required one is located. There is no index to the file.

Such a search can be time consuming when the file is large. Therefore, sequential organization is impractical for an application that requires immediate access to individual records. On the other hand, sequential organization is good for a payroll system that produces paychecks every week, since almost every record on the file must be accessed.

Certain storage media, like magnetic tape, allow only sequential file organization. In order for a record on a reel of magnetic tape to be located, the tape must be read sequentially, beginning with the first record. It is physically impossible for a tape drive to locate individual records directly because of the amount of winding and rewinding that must be performed. However, a direct-access storage device (DASD), such as a disk, allows sequential, direct, and indexed file organization.

Direct File Organization

A **direct file organization** allows immediate, direct access to individual records on the file. The organization scheme must allow retrieval of the individual record with little, if any, searching among the records on file. A direct file organization is usually used when there is a high volume of random requests for individual

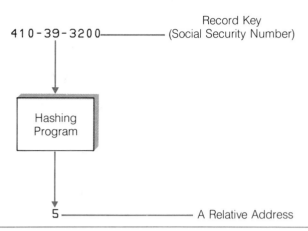

410-39-3200 ——————— Record Key
(Social Security Number)

Hashing
Program

5 ——————— A Relative Address

FIGURE 11–10 Overview of Direct Addressing

One method by which a hashing program can derive a relative address is illustrated in Figure 11–11.

records and there is relatively little need to print out the complete file in sequential order by record key. An example of such an application is a grocery-store checkout. Grocery items are processed at several checkout lanes in a random order. The price file has to be accessed very quickly so the checkout process is not slowed.

The essence of direct addressing is being able to quickly produce a relative address from a record's primary key. Figure 11–10 shows how this is done. The record key for social security number is input to a hashing program which computes a relative address from the social security number. This relative address in effect is a random number. In fact, the word **hash** is a synonym for randomize. The records in the file are stored in order by relative address. However, they are stored randomly in reference to the record key.

One of several hashing methods for computation of direct addresses is the **division/remainder method,** shown in Figure 11–11. At the bottom of the figure there is a file with student information stored. Assume we want to store approximately 950 students in this file. We set aside space for 999 records on a magnetic disk. There are 999 record-storage locations, each with a relative address that shows the record's position within the file. The division/remainder method divides the record key, in this case the social security number, by a number very near the number of storage locations set aside in the file. In our example we will divide by the number 999. The remainder of this division process is added to the number 1 and the result is used as the relative address. In our example the remainder will always be between 0 and 998. When 1 is added to the remainder, a social security number is very quickly converted into a random number between 1 and 999, which we use as a record's relative address. After placing the record in its relative-address location, we can retrieve it by simply supplying the social security number (which is the primary key); our hashing program will quickly compute the relative address.

The primary advantage of direct file organization is that we can access an individual record in a very small fraction of a second, even if the file has millions of records. Imagine how long it would take to find an individual record in a sequential file if the file contained ten million records.

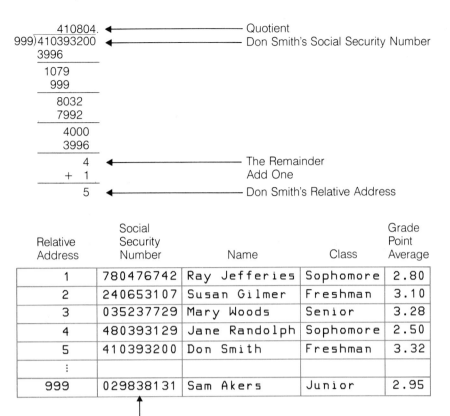

Notice that the social security number
is in random order

**FIGURE 11–11 Computation of Direct Addresses by the Division/
Remainder Method**

Try dividing some of the social security numbers in the file by 999 to see whether your
result matches the relative address shown. Divide your own social security number by 999
to see at what address your record would be placed.

The primary disadvantage of a direct file organization is that the records are actually stored in a random order. As you can see in Figure 11–11, the records are not in sequential order by social security number. What if we had a need to produce a report of these records in sequential order by social security number? If the need for this report was only occasional and the file wasn't too large, we could simply sort a copy of the file in order by social security number. We could also maintain a linked list similar to the one shown in Figure 11–7, except in this case we would be linking the records in order by social security number. Each pointer would point to the relative address of the next social security number, in ascending sequence. However, it takes computer time to maintain linked lists, since they must be changed when records are added or deleted. Also, space must be set aside in the record to store the pointer. Generally, when records in a file must be produced in some sequence on a frequent basis and accessed directly, an indexed file organization is used.

Indexed File Organization

An **indexed file organization** has another file associated with it which is used to indicate the address of the records stored in the primary file. The file that stores these addresses is called an index file, and it is similar to a card catalog in a library. When you look for a book in the library, you first go to the card catalog which is an index to the actual books stored in the library. Similarly, an index file is an index to the records stored in the primary file. We will discuss two basic types of index files: fully indexed and tree indexed.

Fully Indexed Files   A full index is illustrated in Figure 11–12. For a **fully indexed file** there is an entry in the index for each record in the primary file. Figure 11–12 shows a full index on the social-security-number primary key of the same file we used in Figure 11–11. A full index may be constructed on any field within a file.

As files get large, a lot of time could be spent searching for the relative address of an individual record in the index. However, a full index can be searched rapidly if it is stored in RAM and if it is searched with a binary search. A **binary search** splits the index file in half and then determines in which half the desired key is stored. That half is then split in half again to determine in which quarter the key is stored, and so on until the required key is found. A binary search is considerably more efficient than a sequential search of the index file.

Tree Indexed Files

Indexed Sequential File Organization. The **indexed sequential file organization,** or indexed sequential-access method (ISAM; pronounced *i-sam*), is a cross between sequential and indexed file organizations. The records within the file are stored sequentially, but random access to individual records is possible through an index. Thus, records may be accessed either sequentially or randomly.

Primary Key

Social Security Number	Relative Address
029838131	999
035237729	3
240653107	2
410393200	5
480393129	4
780476742	1
⋮	
998396732	128

FIGURE 11–12   A Full Index

In a full index, the relative address of each record in a file is stored. Although this may seem to be the best way to derive relative addresses, the process is time consuming because the full index itself must be both maintained and searched.

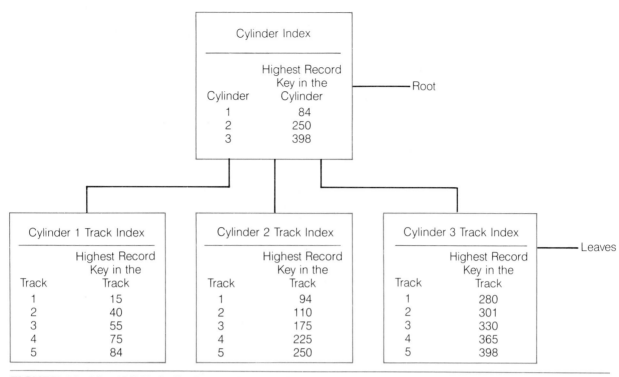

Cylinder Index	
Cylinder	Highest Record Key in the Cylinder
1	84
2	250
3	398

— Root

Cylinder 1 Track Index	
Track	Highest Record Key in the Track
1	15
2	40
3	55
4	75
5	84

Cylinder 2 Track Index	
Track	Highest Record Key in the Track
1	94
2	110
3	175
4	225
5	250

Cylinder 3 Track Index	
Track	Highest Record Key in the Track
1	280
2	301
3	330
4	365
5	398

— Leaves

FIGURE 11–13   ISAM Cylinder and Track Index

Notice the tree nature of an ISAM index.

Figure 11–13 illustrates a cylinder and track index for an ISAM file. Notice that this index has a treelike structure. (Actually, it resembles an upside-down tree.) For a record to be found, the cylinder index is searched to locate the cylinder address, and then the track index for the cylinder is searched to locate the track address of the record. Using Figure 11–13 to illustrate, let's say the required record has a primary-key value of 225. The cylinder address is 2, since 225 is greater than 84 but less than 250. Then we search the track index for cylinder 2 and find that 225 is greater than 175 and equal to 225; therefore, the track address is 4. With the cylinder address and the track address known, the disk control unit can then search through the records on track 4 within cylinder 2 to retrieve the record. As you may have noticed, the ISAM technique provides a physical address (cylinder and track) rather than a relative address.

The ISAM approach is useful when records must be retrieved randomly and when they must also be processed in sequential order by the primary key. An example is checking accounts where customers randomly access their accounts through automated teller machines. Also, the bank is processing checks on a batch basis once per day. The check-processing run would have a high file-activity ratio, and thus would access the file sequentially.

B-Tree Index.   An indexing technique that is very widely used is the **B-Tree index** (balanced tree index). Such an index is illustrated in Figure 11–14. This index is

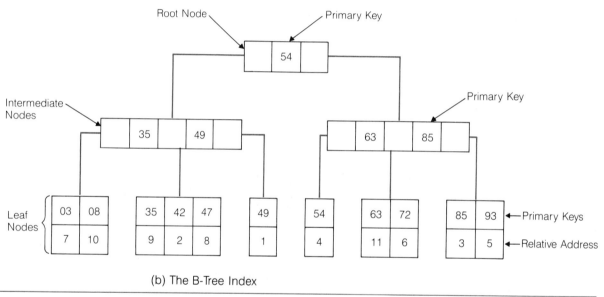

Relative Address	Primary Key	Other Data
1	49	
2	42	
3	85	
4	54	
5	93	
6	72	
7	03	
8	47	
9	35	
10	08	
11	63	

(a) The file to be indexed

(b) The B-Tree Index

FIGURE 11–14 A B-Tree Index

Most indexes used on personal computers are B-Tree.

called a balanced tree index because all of the leaves are on the same level of the tree. The B-Tree index in Figure 11–14b is an index to the primary file shown in Figure 11–14a. A search of the B-Tree index begins at the root. Let's assume that we need to know the address of a record whose primary-key value is 72. We would look at 54 in the root and decide that 72 is greater than 54, and then branch to the right. If the primary key we were looking for was less than 54, we would branch to the left. We would then examine the primary keys in the next lowest level index. Seventy-two is greater than 63 but less than 85; therefore we would go to the primary keys that branch between 63 and 85. At this point we are at the leaves of the tree which contain the relative address of each record. We find that 72 is in relative address 6. With three accesses (at the root, at the intermediate level, and at the leaves), we have found one address out of eleven records.

B-Tree indexes are very efficient in search time. This is true because we can put a large number of primary keys in each of the nodes. For example, what if we put a hundred primary keys in each of the nodes in Figure 11–14? We would have a hundred primary keys in the root node, ten thousand primary keys in the intermediate nodes, and one million primary keys in the leaf nodes. With such a B-Tree index, we could find the address of one in one million records with just three disk accesses! Of course, we would have to do some searching within the hundred primary keys in each root node, but this would be done in primary memory at very fast speeds. The slow part of searching for records is in reading data or indexes from magnetic disks. The B-Tree index of one million records would require only three disk accesses to find the address of an individual record. Most data-base management systems that run on all sizes of computers use B-Tree indexes. They can be used whether the file is physically in sequential order by a primary key or is physically in random order. B-Tree indexes can be created on any field within a file. They are very good at servicing ad hoc queries such as the following: "provide a list of all students who are seniors and have a grade-point average greater than 3.2 and who have taken a Spanish course." If the file from which this information is to be retrieved has a B-Tree index on class, grade-point average, and courses taken, the request can be met without having to search the complete file. The primary disadvantage of a B-Tree index is that it must be kept up-to-date.

Virtual Storage Access Method. The **virtual storage access method (VSAM)** is used on IBM mainframes. VSAM uses a B-Tree type index to retrieve records from a file. The word *virtual* is used in the VSAM method because VSAM is independent of hardware; that is, it does not store and retrieve data by cylinders and tracks.

Selecting a File Organization

Several factors must be considered in determining the best file organization for a particular application: file activity, file volatility, file size, and file query requirements. We defined **file activity** earlier as the percentage of file records that are actually used or accessed in a given processing run. At one extreme (with a low file activity) is an airline-reservation application, where each transaction is processed immediately and only one file record is accessed. If the file is rarely processed sequentially, the direct-access method would be used. In between is the bank-checking application, where the records must be accessed both randomly and sequentially. This file would be best organized with one of the indexing approaches. At the other extreme is the payroll master file, where almost every record is accessed when the weekly payroll is processed. In this case, a sequential file organization would be more efficient.

File volatility refers to the number of additions and deletions to a file in a given period of time. The payroll file for a construction company where the employee roster is constantly changing is a highly volatile file. An indexed file would not be a good choice in this situation, since many additions and deletions would necessitate frequent changes in the indexes. A sequential file organization would be appropriate if there were no query requirements.

File query refers to the retrieval of information from a file. Figure 11–15 provides a summary of file-access methods. If the access to individual records must be fast to support a realtime operation such as airline reservations, then some kind of direct organization is required. If, on the other hand, requirements for data can be delayed, then all the individual requests for information can be batched and run in a single processing run with a sequential file organization.

Large files that require many individual references to records with immediate response must be organized under some type of random-access method. On the other hand, with small files, it may be more efficient to search the entire file

File Organization	Record-Access Method Sequential	Random
Sequential	Yes	No
Direct	Usually No	Yes
Indexed Sequential	Yes	Yes
Balanced Tree	Yes	Yes
Virtual Storage	Yes	Yes
Fully Indexed	Yes	Yes

FIGURE 11–15   Summary of File-Access Methods

A direct file organization allows sequential record access if the records are chained together in sequential order with a linked list.

sequentially to find an individual record, than to maintain complex indexes or direct-access schemes.

We have discussed only the primary factors in determining the best file organization. "Best" is certainly a relative term, and the final answer depends on the individual application. Other factors that most companies would consider are ease of implementing and maintaining a particular file organization, its cost, and whether software is readily available to implement the file organization.

The Lowery Engineering Consulting Company employs about seventy-five engineers who work with clients in product design for farm equipment. Leroy Jones, a computer consultant, was recently hired to design a new computerized timekeeping system in order for the firm to keep track of consultant hours charged to various projects. The new design requires that each engineer complete a time sheet every week for the number of hours charged to specific projects. The time sheets would be batched and would update the system on weekends. Leroy envisions three computer files: an employee master file, a project file, and a file of hours charged to projects per employee. Leroy still needs to determine what the best file organization should be. Can you help him?

Thinking About Information Systems 11–1

Information-Processing Modes

In the preceding sections we have discussed two basic types of file organization and record access methods: those which allow sequential access to records and those which allow direct access to individual records on a random basis. There are also two ways to process data—batch and immediate. In this section we will first examine batch and immediate processing. Then we will further refine our knowledge of information-processing modes by examining how the two types of record-access methods are combined with the two ways to process data to form three information-processing modes: batch-sequential, batch-direct, and immediate-direct. Immediate-sequential is impractical since records cannot be retrieved randomly from sequential files that are not indexed.

Batch Processing

Under **batch processing,** changes to and queries of the file are stored for a period of time, and then a processing run is made periodically to update the file and to obtain the information required by the queries and scheduled reports. The batch runs may be made on a scheduled periodic basis, such as daily, weekly, or monthly, or they may be made on an as-required basis.

Figure 11–16 illustrates batch processing with a sequential file stored on magnetic tape. As shown in the figure, a new master file on a separate volume of tape is produced whenever the file-storage medium is magnetic tape. If the storage medium is direct access, then the updating is in-place updating, and the new master-

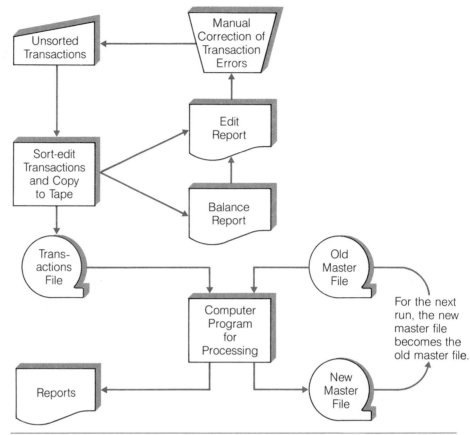

FIGURE 11–16   Batch-Sequential Processing with Tape Files

If the files were stored on disks, the only difference in this figure would be that there would be no old and new master files since each record in the master file would be updated and then written back to its original location on the disk.

file records reside physically in the same area of the direct-access storage device (DASD) as the old records. In-place updating, sometimes also referred to as destructive updating, simply writes the new data over the physical area that the old data occupied on the DASD.

Immediate Processing

Under **immediate processing,** transactions are processed to update the file immediately or shortly after a real-world event occurs. Usually these real-world events occur in a random order. Immediate processing is illustrated in Figure 11–17.

Batch-Sequential

The **batch-sequential mode** was illustrated in Figure 11–16. With this type of processing, changes and queries to the file are batched and processed periodically

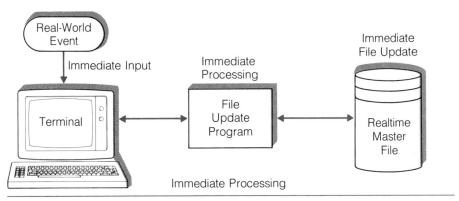

FIGURE 11–17 Immediate Processing

Immediate processing is likely to be the predominant method of processing business transactions in the future.

on a sequential-access basis. In a practical sense, the only way to process a sequential-access file is on a batch basis since there is no random direct access to individual records. Earlier data-processing applications were always batch-sequential, but the mode is declining in popularity because of the decreasing costs of direct-access storage devices.

Batch-Direct

The **batch-direct mode** is used when random direct-access files are updated on a batch basis. For example, weekly payroll data are usually batched and processed on a batch basis even if the file is stored according to a random-access file organization. Batch-direct processing is sometimes done even though it is inefficient in a payroll run because the file-activity ratio is high. The batch-direct mode is most efficient when the activity ratio is less than 50 percent. Batch-direct processing is illustrated in Figure 11–18.

Immediate-Direct

Immediate processing of random direct-access files is the approach that information processing is moving toward. The **immediate-direct mode** is essential for real-time files, which are required in many information systems. For example, an airline-reservations system could not function without realtime files. Other examples of information systems that require realtime files are finished-goods inventory files where order entry is computerized, and student-record files for course-registration systems.

Many other applications use immediate-direct processing because if transactions are captured near the point of the event, errors can usually be corrected with relative ease. A properly designed, immediate-direct processing system can potentially control input much better than a batch-processing system. All of the edit checks that are performed on batch input can also be performed on immediate input. In addition, under an immediate-direct system, errors are communicated

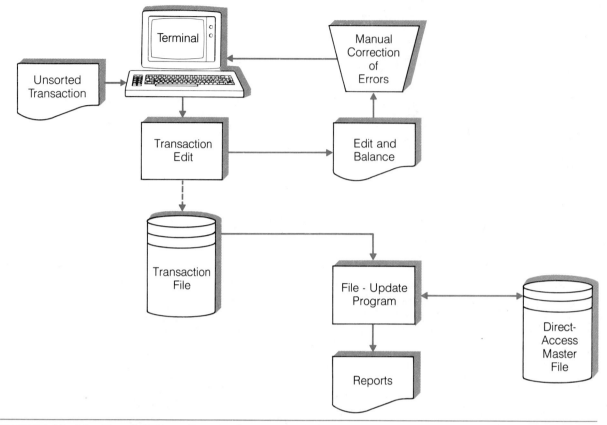

FIGURE 11–18 Batch-Direct Processing

Contrast this illustration with Figure 11–16. Here, the files are stored on a direct-access storage device, allowing random updating.

immediately to the data-entry operator, who is thus better able to correct them. Also, the computer can provide the operator with instructions and aids through the terminal. Figure 11–19 illustrates immediate-direct processing.

On-Line Direct-Access Systems

In the term *on-line direct-access systems,* **on-line** refers to any computer system, peripheral device, or file, such as a terminal or disk pack, that the CPU can control without direct human intervention. For example, a reel of magnetic tape in the library cannot be processed by the CPU without human intervention and therefore is not on-line. In contrast, a disk pack mounted on a disk drive that is accessible to the CPU is on-line. Peripheral devices or files not in direct communication with the CPU are **off-line. Direct-access** refers to a file organization where records

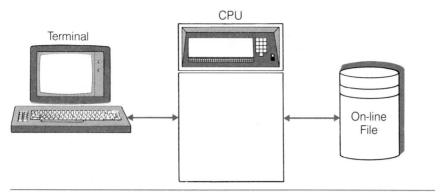

FIGURE 11–19   **Immediate-Direct Processing**

can be retrieved by the CPU without much searching. Direct and indexed file organizations allow direct access.

An **on-line direct-access system** is one with several terminals in direct communication with the CPU, which in turn can retrieve data from one or more files directly for immediate processing without human intervention. Figure 11–20 shows a typical on-line direct-access system.

On-line terminals without on-line direct-access capability would be impractical. The turnaround time and processing costs would be intolerable if an operator had to mount each file asked for and the record search were performed sequentially.

Random direct-access files are usually associated with on-line terminals. One of the primary reasons for random direct-access files is to allow for immediate processing of inquiries and updates to the file from on-line terminals scattered throughout the user organization. Therefore, the terms *on-line* and *direct-access* are usually used together when referring to a complete computer system.

On-line direct-access systems serve three primary functions—inquiry, update, and programming. Inquiry terminals retrieve information from files in response to inquiries. Update terminals access files, modify data, and provide information in response to inquiries. Programmers use on-line direct-access systems widely when they write or change program code. Copies of production or new programs are stored in a programmer area on an on-line disk pack, and coding is done through a CRT terminal on the programmer's desk.

A final observation is that on-line direct-access systems are not necessarily real-time systems. These two terms are often erroneously used interchangeably. The distinction between them will be discussed in the next section.

Realtime Systems

A **realtime information system** can immediately capture data about ongoing events or processes and provide the information necessary to manage them. Examples of realtime systems are manufacturing-process control and airline-reservation

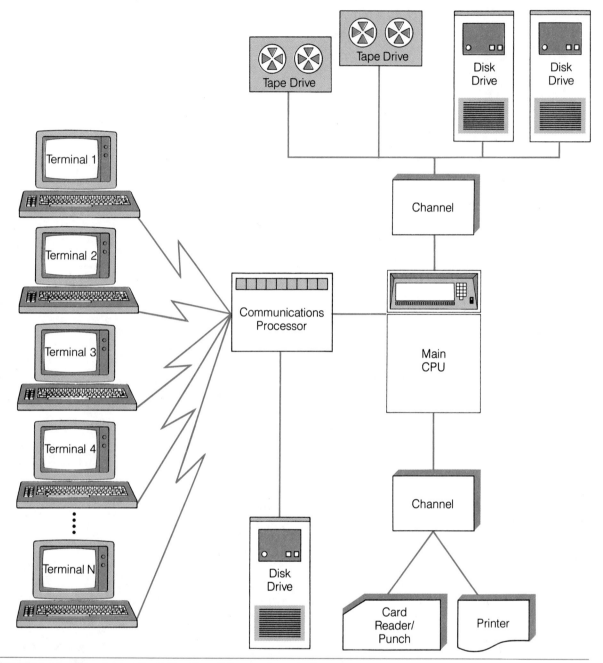

FIGURE 11–20 A Typical On-line Direct-Access System

The terminals at the left may access the communication processor through a direct line, through a local area network, or through regular telephone dial-up lines.

systems. An essential component of a realtime system is realtime master files, which are updated immediately after a real-world event occurs. Consequently, at any point in time, the data in realtime master files should accurately reflect the status of the real-world properties they represent. For example, when a customer reserves a seat on an airline flight, the reservations agent keys in the customer's reservation, and the inventory of nonreserved seats on that flight is immediately updated to reflect one less available seat. Obviously, an immediate processing system is necessary to respond to customer inquiries about available seats. A batch system would be inadequate because the data on the master file would not be up-to-date.

Many colleges and universities use realtime systems to register students for classes. The students request classes through a computer terminal. They can be notified immediately about whether their schedules are confirmed because the inventory of unfilled class seats is on a realtime file. Figure 11–21 illustrates a realtime system.

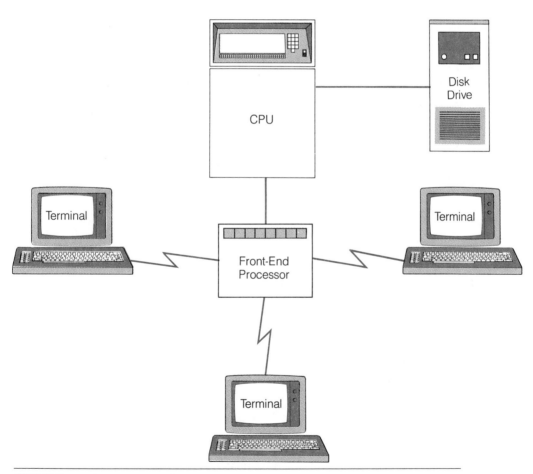

FIGURE 11–21 A Realtime System

In a realtime system the terminals as well as files must be on-line to the CPU.

Realtime systems are most useful at the transaction-processing and operational decision levels, for example in order-processing systems that depend on realtime inventory master files. Management decisions at the tactical and strategic levels generally do not require realtime information. Information that is a day, a week, or even a month old, such as profit and loss statements, can be just as valuable as realtime data for tactical or strategic decision making. However, as the cost of storage and processing declines, more realtime systems are being implemented for transaction processing. More of the data used in tactical and strategic decisions are becoming available on a realtime basis. For example, tactical sales-analysis data can be retrieved from realtime point-of-sale systems, even though in some cases it is not necessary for such data to be realtime.

Certain transaction-processing applications do not require realtime updating. For example, updating the payroll master file on a realtime basis for hours worked by each employee is unnecessary. If payroll checks are produced weekly, the information can be updated every week via the batch-processing method.

The computer configuration to support a realtime system must allow on-line direct access to data. The files must be structured to allow random access, since fast response to inquiries is required, and update transactions are processed as they occur, rather than on a delayed, batch basis.

Realtime systems have the primary advantage of providing timely information. Certain computer applications can function only on a realtime basis. Others are most cost-effective using a batch mode. The primary disadvantage of realtime systems is that hardware and communication costs are greater and the operating system and applications software necessary to support them are more complex.

<table>
<tr><td>Thinking About Information Systems 11–2</td><td>Basic Hardware is a medium-sized chain of hardware stores located primarily in the southeastern states. The company is considering some type of point-of-sale capture of sales data through cash registers for input to sales analysis and inventory reordering systems. The choices are a true realtime system and a batch system that is updated daily. With a realtime system, each cash register would be on-line to the central computer through regular telephone lines during business hours. Under the batch system, each cash register would have the capability of storing one day's worth of sales data. At the end of the day the data would be transmitted to the central computer. Although the realtime option has the advantage of providing realtime information, it also is more expensive primarily because it would tie up long-distance telephone lines during business hours. With the batch approach, a line would be in use for approximately fifteen minutes at the end of each day. Do you think realtime information in this situation would justify the additional communication costs?</td></tr>
</table>

Summing Up

☐ Data are internally represented in the computer in the form of binary digits. Any number can be converted to binary representation by expressing it in terms of the powers of two.

- The Extended Binary Coded Decimal Interchange Code (EBCDIC) represents a character or a digit as a combination of eight bits, called a byte. This code is used extensively on IBM hardware.
- The eight-bit American Standard Code for Information Interchange (ASCII-8) is another popular coding scheme used by many hardware manufacturers.
- If it is necessary to examine the contents of the computer's memory, the hexadecimal system may be used. Since this system represents numbers in powers of 16, it is much more compact and readable than binary representation.
- Usually a byte of data has an extra bit, called a parity bit. The machine sets the value of the parity bit such that the total number of on bits in every byte is either always even or always odd. If a byte has an odd number of on bits in an even parity machine, it means the data have been damaged and must be corrected.
- There are two types of access to records stored in files: sequential and random.
- Data records stored in a sequential file are ordered by the order in which they were entered or by record key. Sequential files are usually used for batch-type processes where most of the records have to be accessed every time the program is run.
- Direct file organization allows rapid access to any individual record by converting its primary key directly to an address. This is usually done through the division/remainder approach.
- Indexed files are associated with another file called an index, which is used to locate information records in the indexed file on a random-access basis.
- The indexed sequential-access method (ISAM) uses an index to determine the cylinder and track location of a record, and then that track is searched sequentially for the desired record.
- B-Tree indexes are widely used because they allow fast access to very large files and they can be used on any field in the file.
- To select the best file organization for an application, it is necessary to consider many factors, including file volatility, file activity, file size, and file query requirements.
- In a batch-processing system, queries and updates to the system are accumulated for some time and are then executed all in one run. With immediate processing, on the other hand, transactions are individually entered into the files soon after the real-world event occurs.
- Three modes of information processing are used: batch-sequential, batch-direct, and immediate-direct. Most applications are now being designed for the immediate-direct mode.
- An on-line direct-access system consists of several terminals connected to the CPU, which in turn are connected to several random-access files.
- A realtime information system is a special kind of on-line direct-access system. It captures data immediately after the occurrence of an event, processes it right away, and returns information that is used to manage ongoing events.

Key Terms

bit
byte
binary number system
decimal number system
place value
EBCDIC (Extended Binary
  Coded Decimal Interchange Code)
packed decimal
ASCII (American Standard
  Code for Information Interchange)
memory dump
hexadecimal
parity bit
primary key
secondary keys
sequential access
random access
file organization
physical address
cylinder
track
sector
relative address
linked list

directory
sequential file organization
direct file organization
hash
division/remainder method
indexed file organization
fully indexed file
binary search
indexed sequential file organization
B-Tree index
virtual-storage access method (VSAM)
file activity
file volatility
file query
batch processing
immediate processing
batch-sequential mode
batch-direct mode
immediate-direct mode
on-line
off-line
direct access
on-line direct-access system
realtime information system

Self-Quiz

Completion Questions

1. Data representation in a computer uses the _____ number system.
2. A percentage of file records actually used in a given processing run is the file _____ ratio.
3. The _____ uniquely identifies a record, whereas the _____ identifies where it is stored on the storage medium.
4. There are two types of addresses: physical and _____ .
5. A _____ is a list of the file names contained on a particular storage medium.
6. There are two basic types of indexed files: fully indexed and _____ indexed.
7. File _____ refers to the number of additions and deletions to the file in a given period of time.

8. _____ refers to any computer system, peripheral device, or file that the CPU can control without direct human intervention.
9. A _____ computer system can immediately capture data about ongoing events or processes and provide the information necessary to manage them.
10. File _____ refers to the retrieval of information from a file.

Multiple Choice Questions

1. EBCDIC can code up to how many different characters?
   a. 8
   b. 16
   c. 32

d. 64

e. 256

2. The hexadecimal number system has a base of:
   a. 2
   b. 4
   c. 8
   d. 10
   e. 16

3. The parity bit is added for _____ purposes.
   a. coding
   b. indexing
   c. error-detection
   d. controlling
   e. updating

4. Which of the following fields in a student file can be used as a primary key?
   a. class
   b. social security number
   c. GPA
   d. major
   e. all of the above

5. The two basic types of record-access methods are:
   a. sequential and random
   b. direct and immediate
   c. sequential and indexed
   d. on-line and realtime
   e. none of the above

6. Which file organization is allowed by a direct-access storage device?
   a. direct only
   b. sequential and direct only
   c. indexed and direct only
   d. sequential, indexed, and direct

7. Sequential file organization is most appropriate for which of the following applications?
   a. grocery-store checkout
   b. bank checking accounts
   c. payroll
   d. airline reservations
   e. none of the above

8. Which of the following is not a practical data-processing approach?
   a. batch-sequential

b. batch-direct

c. immediate-sequential

d. immediate-direct

e. all of the above are proper approaches

9. Which of the following file organizations is most efficient for a file with a high degree of file activity?
   a. sequential
   b. ISAM
   c. VSAM
   d. B-Tree index
   e. all of the above

10. Which of the following is not one of the three primary functions that on-line direct-access systems can serve?
    a. inquiry
    b. backup
    c. update
    d. programming

Answers

Completion
  1. binary
  2. activity
  3. primary key; address
  4. relative
  5. directory
  6. tree
  7. volatility
  8. On-line
  9. realtime
  10. query

Multiple Choice
  1. e
  2. e
  3. c
  4. b
  5. a
  6. d
  7. c
  8. c
  9. a
  10. b

Chapter 12

RELATIONAL FILE JOINING

...iles can be "JOINED" at runtime,
...onsolidating data from separate files...

PARTS FILE
- PART NUMBER
- DESCRIPTION

ORDER FILE
- ORDER NUMBER
- DATE
- CUSTOMER
- PART NUMBER

JOIN →

PART   DESCRIPTION   CUSTOMER

Data-Base Management Systems

CHAPTER OUTLINE

PROLOGUE

The Atlantic Life and Casualty Insurance Company is a large firm located in an eastern city. It has millions of customers on which it keeps data. Many applications, such as customer service, accounts receivable, accounts payable, and salesperson-commission reports, use the data about customers and their insurance coverage. How do all these applications use the same data? What keeps track of where these data are stored and who may use it or change it? Does a user have to know where the information is physically stored before using it? Read on.

Introduction

Perhaps the most important challenge facing information systems is to provide users with timely and versatile access to data stored in computer files. In a dynamic business environment there are many unanticipated needs for information. Often the basic underlying data to satisfy these information needs are contained in computer files but cannot be accessed and output in a suitable format on a timely basis. Data-base management systems have the potential to meet this challenge. In this chapter we will first contrast the traditional and the data-base approach to information processing. Then we will look at some of the logical ways users view data stored in a data-base. And finally, we will explore the advantages and disadvantages of data-base management systems.

The Traditional Approach to Information Processing

The traditional approach to information processing is file-oriented. Prior to the advent of data-base management systems, (DBMS), each application maintained its own master file and generally had its own set of transaction files. Figure 12–1 illustrates this traditional approach. Files are custom-designed for each application, and generally there is little sharing of data among the various applications. Programs are dependent on the files and vice-versa; that is, when the physical format of the file is changed, the program also has to be changed. The traditional approach is file-oriented because the primary purpose of many applications is to maintain on the master file the data required to produce management information. Therefore, the master file is the centerpiece of each application. Although the traditional, file-oriented approach to information processing is still widely used, it does have some very important disadvantages. Among them are the following.

Data Redundancy

Often identical data are stored in two or more files. Notice that in Figure 12–2 each employee's social security number, name, and department are stored in both the payroll and personnel files. Obviously such **data redundancy** increases data editing, maintenance, and storage costs. In addition, data stored on two master files (which should in theory be identical) are often different for good reason; but such differences inevitably create confusion.

Lack of Data Integration

Data on different master files may be related, as in the case of payroll and personnel master files. For example, in Figure 12–2, management may want a report displaying employee name, department, pay rate, and occupation. However, the application approach does not have the mechanisms for associating these data in a logical way to make them useful for management's needs.

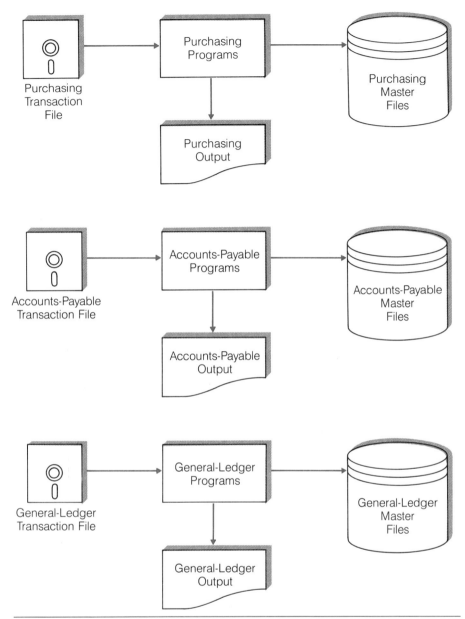

FIGURE 12–1   Traditional Approach to Information Processing

Notice that each application has its own master file.

Program/Data Dependence

Under the traditional, file-oriented approach, programs are tied to master files and vice versa. Changes in the physical format of the master file, such as the addition of a data field, require changes in all programs that access the master file. Consequently, for each of the application programs that a programmer writes or main-

Payroll File

Social Security Number	Employee Name	Pay Rate	Year-to-Date Earnings	Department
385686293	Joseph Hawkins	$12.50	4005.50	380
390328453	Samuel Smith	$13.25	5100.60	390
410686392	Theodore Thatcher	$ 5.50	2495.60	312
425786495	Robert Benson	$25.80	8135.50	312
510933492	Thomas Benson	$12.50	4005.50	095
511945893	Jane Benson	$30.50	9617.55	100

Personnel File

Social Security Number	Employee Name	Department	Age	Date Hired	Occupation
385686293	Joe Hawkins	380	25	03 JAN 83	Wife's Brother
390328453	Sam Smith	390	55	05 SEP 65	Goof Off
410686392	Ted Thatcher	312	28	15 JUN 81	Golfer
425786495	Bob Benson	312	45	20 JUL 64	Super Star
510933492	Tom Benson	095	38	31 DEC 68	My Brother
511945893	Jane Benson	100	43	20 JUL 64	The Boss

FIGURE 12–2 Data Redundancy and Lack of Integration among Files

A payroll file stores data concerning employees' wages and salaries. A personnel file contains data about employees' work and education histories as well as occupational skills. Many large firms have separate payroll and personnel departments. A data-base management system would allow the two departments to share data.

tains he or she must be concerned with data management. There is no centralized execution of the data-management function; data management is scattered among all the application programs. Think of the thousands of computer programs that had to be altered when the U.S. Postal Service changed from a five-digit to a nine-digit zipcode. A centralized DBMS could have minimized the number of places this change had to be made.

Lack of Flexibility

The information-retrieval capabilities of most traditional systems are limited to predetermined requests for data. Therefore, the system produces information in the form of scheduled reports and queries which it has been previously programmed to handle. If management needs unanticipated data, the information can perhaps be provided if it is in the files of the system. Extensive programming is often involved. Thus, by the time the programming is completed, the information may no longer be required or useful. This problem has long plagued information systems. Management knows that a particular piece of information can be produced on a one-time basis, but the expense and time involved are generally prohibitive. Ideally, information processing should be able to mix related data elements from several different files and produce information with a fast turnaround to service unanticipated requests for information.

The Data-Base Approach to Information Processing

A **data-base management system (DBMS)** is a set of programs that serve as an interface between application programs and a set of coordinated and integrated *physical files* called a data base. A DBMS provides the capabilities for creating, maintaining, and changing a data base. A **data base** is a collection of data. The physical files of the data base are analogous to the master files of the application programs. However, with DBMS, the data among the physical files are related with various **pointers** and keys, which not only reduce data redundancy but also enable the unanticipated retrieval of related information. Figure 12–3 illustrates the DBMS approach.

physical file
The actual storage of data on storage media.

Logical versus Physical Views of Data Storage

With most traditional data-storage techniques, the programmer needs to be aware of the physical layout of data records on storage devices and thus needs to understand the technical characteristics of many kinds of hardware. The problem gets even more complex in a multi-user environment where one programmer may have to use data files designed by another programmer. Often a lot of time is wasted just trying to figure out what a particular data field is supposed to represent.

A DBMS overcomes this problem by providing two views of data: physical and logical. The **physical view** of data is similar to traditional file systems. It deals with the actual location of bits and bytes on memory devices. Some MIS personnel need this information to be able to make efficient use of storage and processing resources. However, knowledge of all these details would serve no useful purpose for the application programmer who is interested only in using the information, no matter how it is stored.

The **logical view** represents data in a format that is meaningful to the user and the application programmer. The emphasis here is on interrelating data fields and records such that they represent the underlying business reality. For instance, a marketing executive's logical view of sales data may resemble Table 12–1. In this format the data can easily be used to generate reports needed in decision making. The data-base approach allows the user to maintain this kind of conceptual (logical) view of data.

The data might be physically disaggregated and stored on magnetic disk according to some complex addressing mechanism; but the DBMS assumes the responsibility of aggregating the data into a neat, logical format whenever the application program needs it. This frees application programmers from having to worry about tracks and cylinders, and lets them concentrate on the business aspects of the problem to be solved.

Figure 12–4 shows how the DBMS insulates the user from physical-storage details. The user or application programmer can refer to data items by using meaningful names, such as CUSTOMER-NAME and TOTAL-PURCHASE. He or she no longer has to worry about specifying things like the number of bytes in a field.

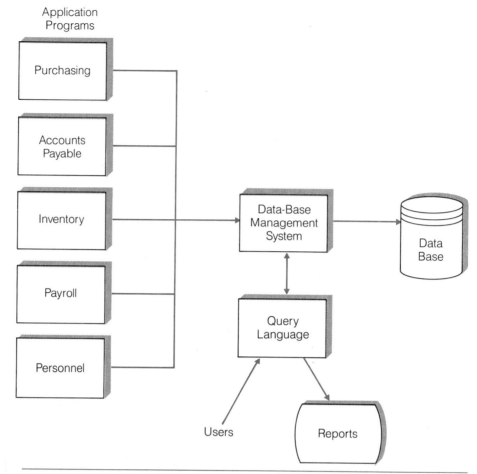

Application
Programs

Purchasing

Accounts
Payable

Inventory

Payroll

Personnel

Data-Base
Management
System

Data
Base

Query
Language

Users

Reports

FIGURE 12–3   The DBMS Approach

The data-base management system stores, updates, and retrieves data for all application programs. Data can be readily shared among these programs to prevent data redundancy. Easy-to-use query languages allow users to produce ad-hoc reports.

The data-base environment has four components: the users, the DBMS software, the data base, and the data-base administrator. Figure 12–5 illustrates the interaction of these components.

The Users

Users consist of both the traditional users (such as management) and application programmers, who are not typically considered to be users. Users interact with the DBMS indirectly via application programs or directly via a simple **query language.** The user's interactions with the DBMS also include the definition of the logical relationships in the data base (the logical view), and the input, alteration, deletion, and manipulation of data.

query language
A high-level and easy-to-use computer language used to retrieve specific information from a data base.

TABLE 12–1 Logical View of Sales Data

Salesperson			Year-to-date Sales		
I.D. #	Name	Region	Product A	Product B	Product C
223	Smith	S.W.	6,395	4,328	5,875
227	O'Neill	S.W.	4,326	898	1,587
241	Maxwell	S.W.	12,331	8,976	7,215
256	Ware	East	8,232	6,554	7,321
257	Charles	East	2,111	4,573	5,321
258	Scholar	Midwest	5,221	6,632	6,331
276	Williams	Midwest	11,213	10,709	9,318
283	Mufti	Midwest	2,124	5,335	6,326
285	Cadd	Midwest	7,224	5,019	2,020
300	Harris	N.E.	3,423	3,302	8,824
307	Bentley	N.E.	8,635	5,661	3,624
310	Curtis	N.E.	10,728	7,187	8,721
322	May	N.E.	7,853	5,354	6,332

This is only one logical view of sales data. Manufacturing managers might be interested in sales data by product, instead of data on salespersons and regions as shown here.

The Data-Base Management System

The data-base management system is a complex software package that enables the user to communicate with the data-base. The DBMS interprets user commands so that the computer system can perform the task required. For example, it might translate a command such as GET CUSTNO, AMOUNT, INVNO into "retrieve record 458 from disk 09."

Conceptually, a data-base management system uses two languages—a **data-definition language (DDL)** and a **data-manipulation language (DML).** The DDL is essentially the link between the logical and physical views of the data base. As discussed earlier, logical refers to the way the user views data; physical refers to the way the data are physically stored. The logical structure of a data base is sometimes called a **schema.** A **subschema** is the way a particular application views the data from the data base. There may be many users and application programs utilizing the same data base, therefore many different subschemas can exist. Each user or application program uses a set of DDL statements to construct a subschema which includes only those data elements which are of interest. Figure 12–6 shows statements from a data-definition language.

The DDL is used to define the physical characteristics of each record: the fields within the record, and each field's logical name, data type, and length. The logical name (such as SNAME for the student name field), is used by both application programs and users to refer to a field for the purpose of retrieving or updating the data in it. The DDL is also used to specify relationships among the records. The primary functions of the DDL are to:

1. Describe the schema and subschemas.
2. Describe the fields in each record and the record's logical name.
3. Describe the data type and name of each field.
4. Indicate the keys of the record.
5. Provide for data security restrictions.

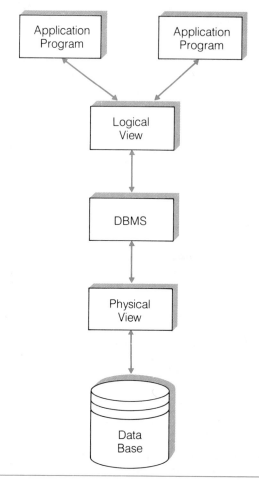

FIGURE 12–4　Logical versus Physical Views of Data

The ability to establish different logical views of the same data while insulating the user from concerns about how the data are physically stored has been a major contribution to the user-friendliness of information systems.

6. Provide for logical and physical data independence.
7. Provide means of associating related data.

The data-manipulation language (DML) provides the techniques for processing the data base, such as retrieval, sorting, display, and deletion of data or records. The DML should include a variety of manipulation verbs and operands for each verb. Table 12–2 contains some of these verbs and corresponding *operands*.

Most data-manipulation languages interface with high-level programming languages such as COBOL or PL/I. These languages enable a programmer to perform unique data processing that the DBMS's data-manipulation language cannot perform.

A key feature of a DML is that it uses logical names (such as CUSTNO for customer number) instead of physical storage locations when referring to data. This capability

operand
An entity to which an operation is applied; that which is operated upon.

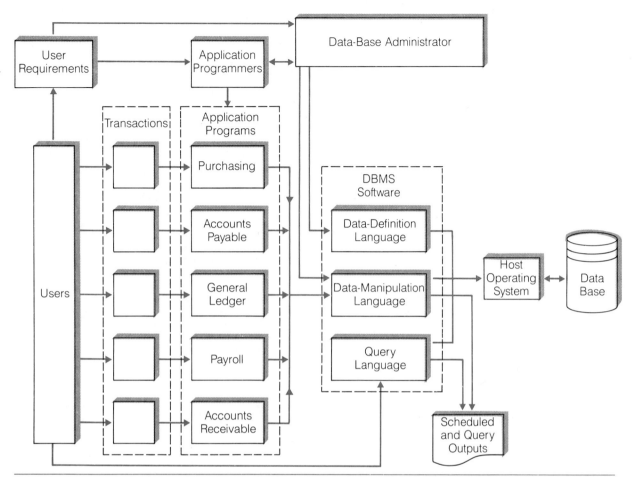

FIGURE 12–5 Interaction among DBMS Components

TABLE 12–2 Data Manipulation Language Verbs

Verbs	Operands
Delete	Record Key, Field Name, Record Name, or File Name
Sort	Field Name
Insert	Record Key, Field Name, Record Name, or File Name
Display	Record Key, Field Name, Record Name, or File Name
Add	Field Name

The verbs in this table are combined with operands to manipulate data. For example, a command might be

```
DELETE CUSTNO 5.
```

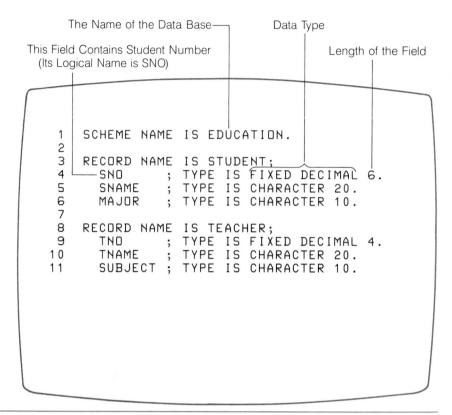

The Name of the Data Base

This Field Contains Student Number
(Its Logical Name is SNO)

Data Type

Length of the Field

```
 1 │ SCHEME NAME IS EDUCATION.
 2 │
 3 │ RECORD NAME IS STUDENT;
 4 │   SNO     ; TYPE IS FIXED DECIMAL 6.
 5 │   SNAME   ; TYPE IS CHARACTER 20.
 6 │   MAJOR   ; TYPE IS CHARACTER 10.
 7 │
 8 │ RECORD NAME IS TEACHER;
 9 │   TNO     ; TYPE IS FIXED DECIMAL 4.
10 │   TNAME   ; TYPE IS CHARACTER 20.
11 │   SUBJECT ; TYPE IS CHARACTER 10.
```

FIGURE 12–6   Statements from a Data-Definition Language

Notice that this DDL is describing the physical characteristics of the data, such as the data type and length of each field.

is possible since the data-definition language provides the linkage between the logical view of data and their physical storage. The functions of a DML are to:

1. Provide the techniques for data manipulation such as deletion, replacement, retrieval, sorting, or insertion of data or records.
2. Enable the user and application programs to process data by using logically meaningful data names rather than physical storage locations.
3. Provide interfaces with programming languages. A DML should support several high-level languages such as COBOL, PL/I, and FORTRAN.
4. Allow the user and application programs to be independent of physical data storage and data-base maintenance.
5. Provide for the use of logical relationships among data items.

The Data-Base Administrator

The **data-base administrator (DBA)** and staff perform the following functions:

1. Maintain a data dictionary. The data dictionary defines the meaning of each data item stored in the data base, and describes interrelations between data items. Since the data base is shared by many users, it is necessary to have

---

1. Data-Base Task Group (DBTG) DML defined for COBOL

```
PERFORM UNTIL FLAG = 'RED'
    FIND NEXT OVERDUE WITHIN ACCOUNTS
    IF EOF NOT = 'YES'
        IF OVERDUE = 'YES'
            MOVE 'RED' TO FLAG
        END-IF
    END-IF
END-PERFORM
```

2. Information Management System (IMS) DML (DL/1)

```
      GU ACCOUNTS (OVERDUE = 'YES'
VA GN ACCOUNTS (OVERDUE = 'RED'
      go to VA
```

3. Stuctured-English Query Language (SEQUEL)

```
SELECT ACCTNO FROM ACCOUNTS
    WHERE OVERDUE = 'YES'
```

FIGURE 12–7   Statements from Three Data-Manipulation Languages

The verbs in data-manipulation languages differ widely. For example, the verbs (such as find, move, and select) used in these three languages all differ from the verbs shown in Table 12–2.

clear and commonly agreed upon meanings for the stored items. A part of a data dictionary is shown in Figure 12–8. The trend in DBMS is to combine the functions of the data-definition language and data dictionary into an **active data dictionary.** It is called "active" because the DBMS continuously refers to it for all the physical data definitions (field lengths, data types, and so on) that a DDL would provide.

2. Determines and maintains the physical structure of the data base.
3. Provides for updating and changing the data base, including the deletion of inactive records.
4. Creates and maintains edit controls regarding changes and additions to the data base.
5. Develops retrieval methods to meet the needs of the users.
6. Implements security and disaster-recovery procedures.
7. Maintains configuration control of the data base. **Configuration control** means that changes requested by one user must be approved by the other users of the data base. One person cannot indiscriminately change the data base to the detriment of other users.
8. Assigns user access codes in order to prevent unauthorized use of data.

A data-base administrator is extremely important, working very closely with users in order to create, maintain, and safeguard the data base. In effect, the DBA is the liaison between the data base and its users and therefore must be familiar with their information requirements. The administrator must also be technically competent in the areas of DBMS and data storage and processing. Data-base administration is becoming an attractive career option to individuals with programming, systems, and business backgrounds. Figure 12–9 indicates the position of the DBA in a business organization.

The Data Base

The data base is the physical collection of data. The data must be stored on direct-access devices like magnetic disks. However, well-managed installations create backup copies of the data base on off-line storage media such as magnetic tape. These security measures are extremely important in a data-base environment, since many departments and application programs may be dependent on a single, centralized data base.

Data-base management systems are designed with a view toward optimizing the use of physical storage and CPU processing time. The logical view may contain redundant data items in order to make them more understandable to users. But the physical implementation of the DBMS attempts to make the physical storage nonredundant. This not only saves space, but also precludes the possibility of different values existing for the same data item at one time. The DBMS also uses other techniques to optimize resource utilization. Data records that are seldom

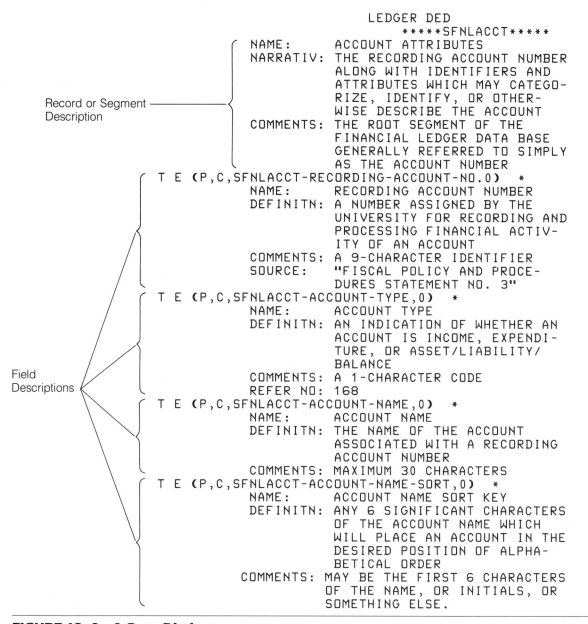

```
                                      LEDGER DED
                                   *****SFNLACCT*****
                    ┌  NAME:      ACCOUNT ATTRIBUTES
                    │  NARRATIV:  THE RECORDING ACCOUNT NUMBER
                    │             ALONG WITH IDENTIFIERS AND
                    │             ATTRIBUTES WHICH MAY CATEGO-
Record or Segment ──┤             RIZE, IDENTIFY, OR OTHER-
Description         │             WISE DESCRIBE THE ACCOUNT
                    │  COMMENTS:  THE ROOT SEGMENT OF THE
                    │             FINANCIAL LEDGER DATA BASE
                    │             GENERALLY REFERRED TO SIMPLY
                    └             AS THE ACCOUNT NUMBER
                  ┌ T E (P,C,SFNLACCT-RECORDING-ACCOUNT-NO.0)  *
                  │    NAME:      RECORDING ACCOUNT NUMBER
                  │    DEFINITN:  A NUMBER ASSIGNED BY THE
                  │               UNIVERSITY FOR RECORDING AND
                  │               PROCESSING FINANCIAL ACTIV-
                  │               ITY OF AN ACCOUNT
                  │    COMMENTS:  A 9-CHARACTER IDENTIFIER
                  └    SOURCE:    "FISCAL POLICY AND PROCE-
                                  DURES STATEMENT NO. 3"
                  ┌ T E (P,C,SFNLACCT-ACCOUNT-TYPE,0)  *
                  │    NAME:      ACCOUNT TYPE
                  │    DEFINITN:  AN INDICATION OF WHETHER AN
                  │               ACCOUNT IS INCOME, EXPENDI-
                  │               TURE, OR ASSET/LIABILITY/
                  │               BALANCE
Field             │    COMMENTS:  A 1-CHARACTER CODE
Descriptions ─────┤    REFER NO:  168
                  ┌ T E (P,C,SFNLACCT-ACCOUNT-NAME,0)  *
                  │    NAME:      ACCOUNT NAME
                  │    DEFINITN:  THE NAME OF THE ACCOUNT
                  │               ASSOCIATED WITH A RECORDING
                  │               ACCOUNT NUMBER
                  └    COMMENTS:  MAXIMUM 30 CHARACTERS
                  ┌ T E (P,C,SFNLACCT-ACCOUNT-NAME-SORT,0)  *
                  │    NAME:      ACCOUNT NAME SORT KEY
                  │    DEFINITN:  ANY 6 SIGNIFICANT CHARACTERS
                  │               OF THE ACCOUNT NAME WHICH
                  │               WILL PLACE AN ACCOUNT IN THE
                  │               DESIRED POSITION OF ALPHA-
                  │               BETICAL ORDER
                  │    COMMENTS:  MAY BE THE FIRST 6 CHARACTERS
                  │               OF THE NAME, OR INITIALS, OR
                  └               SOMETHING ELSE.
```

FIGURE 12–8   A Data Dictionary

This is a portion of the data-dictionary entry that describes data concerning an account in a general-ledger accounting system.

used may be placed on inexpensive, slow-memory devices; whereas frequently used data may be put on the faster, but more expensive media.

Data-base systems are rapidly gaining popularity among business users. Since data-base operations tend to be high-volume processes, they often consume a large portion of the time and memory resources of the computer. Some vendors have

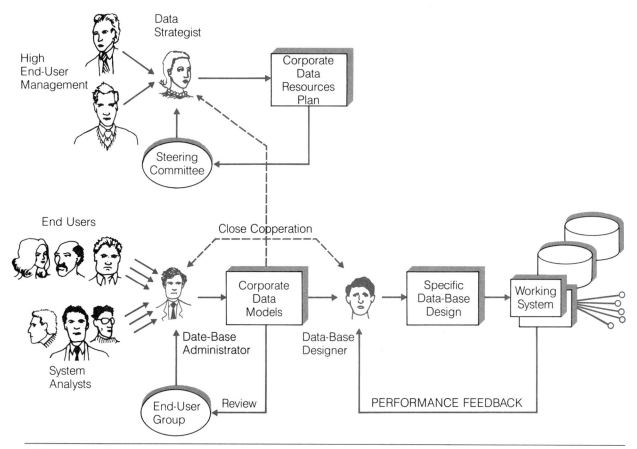

FIGURE 12–9 The Data-Base Administrator

Some companies have three people involved in the data-base administrator's job: a data strategist, a data-base administrator, and a data-base designer. The data strategist helps the end-user management define its logical data needs. The data-base designer handles the physical aspects of data storage.

Thinking About Information Systems 12–1

During the last five years, Bohlin Incorporated has been converting its existing applications to IBM's Information Management System (IMS). The company has also developed most new applications on the IMS. The initial expectation was that the IMS data-base management system software would assist in producing highly integrated application systems. This would allow managers to easily associate related data within the data-base management system. Currently, it is evident that this expectation has not been fulfilled. Personnel manager Chuck Bloss is very disappointed that the system does not integrate the personnel and payroll systems. When he retrieves data from the personnel system and attempts to retrieve related data from the payroll system, there is no link between the two systems. In fact, there are numerous examples where integration of the systems is lacking on the DBMS. How do you think this situation occurred? After all, aren't data-base management systems designed to produce integrated systems that can associate related data automatically?

FIGURE 12–10   A Data-Base Computer

developed computers that are dedicated entirely to data-base operations. These computers, frequently referred to as data-base machines, are special-purpose units (see Figure 12–10). Certain capabilities are built into the hardware which make retrieval, sorting, updating, and other operations more efficient than with software programs.

Logical Data-Base Structures

Two key features of a DBMS are the ability to reduce data redundancy and the ability to associate related data elements such as related fields and records. These functions are accomplished through the use of keys, embedded pointers, and linked lists. An **embedded pointer** is a field within a record containing the physical or relative address of a related record in another part of the data base. The record referred to may also contain an embedded pointer that points to a third record, and so on. The series of records tied together by embedded pointers is a **linked list.** (Linked lists were covered in Chapter 11.) Three basic types of logical structures are used by a DBMS: tree, network, and relational structures. These structures are, in effect, models on which the user can build logical views of data. Some real-world data-base management systems allow users to model and implement data on a tree, network, or relational basis; others allow only one model, such as relational. Tree and network structured DBMSs usually tie related data together through linked lists. Relational DBMSs relate data through information contained in the data, as we will see later in the chapter.

Tree Structures

Figure 12–11 illustrates student data in a tree (hierarchical) structure. The lower part of Figure 12–11 shows the data fields in each record. A **tree structure** consists of records (often called *segments*) that are linked to related records in a one-to-many relationship., The distinguishing feature of a tree structure is that records have a one-to-many relationship. Each record may have only one parent but an unlimited number of children. The top record is called the root. As shown in Figure 12–11, each student can attend many semesters and take many courses in each semester. However, each course is tied to a single semester, and the data in each semester record are in turn tied to a single student.

An important point to understand concerning tree structures (as well as network structures) is that the structure is a logical representation of the data. The physical storage of the data in Figure 12–11 might be quite different from that shown in the figure. Physically, the records could be stored one after another (sequentially) on a disk. The related records would be linked together by addresses or embedded pointers within each record. With a tree structure, each record must have a minimum of two embedded pointer fields. One field contains the address of the first child of the record; the other holds the address of the record's twin. In Figure 12–11, for example, the fall-semester record contains the address of course CIS 1010 (the first child) as well as the address of the spring semester (the twin of the fall semester). Tree structures can represent many different types of data and are widely used in data-base management systems. For example, IBM's Information Management System (IMS), a mainframe DBMS, uses tree structures for modeling data.

Network Structures

A **network structure** allows a many-to-many relationship among the **nodes** in the structure. Figure 12–12 illustrates a network structure between courses and students. Each student can enroll in several classes; each class has many students.

The physical storage as well as data linkage in a network structure involve embedded pointers in each record as in a tree structure. There are several schemes for using pointers with network structures. One is similar to the scheme discussed under tree structures, where each course record (for example, course 1) contains the address of the first student in the course, and then the first student record, in

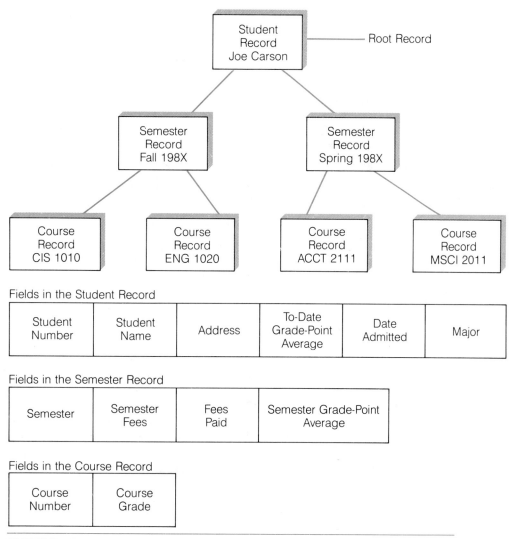

Fields in the Student Record

Student Number	Student Name	Address	To-Date Grade-Point Average	Date Admitted	Major

Fields in the Semester Record

Semester	Semester Fees	Fees Paid	Semester Grade-Point Average

Fields in the Course Record

Course Number	Course Grade

FIGURE 12–11   A Tree Structure

In this data structure, each student can attend many semesters and take many courses in each semester.

turn, contains the address of the second student in the course, and so on, thereby forming a linked list.

Data represented by a network structure can also be represented by a tree structure through the introduction of redundancy, as illustrated in Figure 12–13. As can be seen, the tree structure requires that the student information be stored two or more times, depending on the number of classes in which a student is enrolled. Tree structures are inefficient if there is substantial redundancy. The avoidance of redundancy is an advantage of network structures when many-to-many relationships exist in the data.

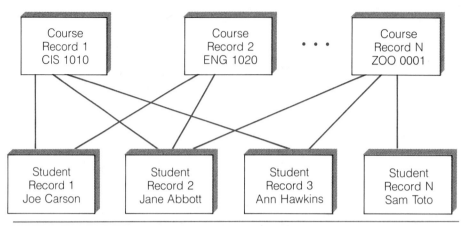

FIGURE 12–12   A Network Data Structure

Notice that with a network data structure, the course records are stored only once. Contrast this with the tree structure shown in Figure 12–11, where the course record must be stored for each student who takes a particular course.

Relational Structures

Most business data have traditionally been organized in the form of simple tables with only columns and rows. In a relational DBMS, these tables are called relations (see Table 12–3). This data structure is known as the **relational model,** since it is based on the mathematical theory of relations. One of the greatest advantages of the relational model is its conceptual simplicity. The relational or tabular model of data is used in a large variety of applications, ranging from your weekly shopping list to the annual report of the world's largest corporation. Most people are familiar with the relational model as a table. But the relational model does use some unfamiliar terminology. What we have come to know as a file is called either a **table** or relation. Each row in the table is called a **tuple** (rhymes with *couple*). A

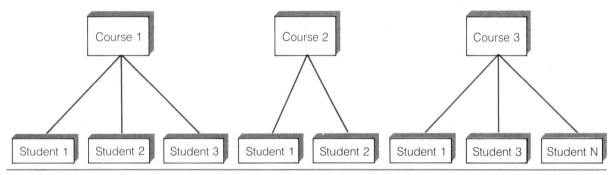

FIGURE 12–13   Tree Representation of the Network Data Shown in Figure 12–12

Some data-base management systems do not allow data to be stored in a network structure. As shown here, however, if the DBMS does allow a tree structure, network data can be stored by introducing redundancy.

Student Relation (Table or File)

Student Number	Student Name	Grade-Point Average GPA	Major
124693298	Joe Smith	2.58	ACCT
138942824	Chris Todd	3.62	CIS
362982353	Ray Gilmer	3.23	MSCI
468329312	Ann Sneed	2.95	MGT
560782392	Angela Brown	3.01	ECON

Tuples (Rows or Records)

Attributes (Columns or Fields)

TABLE 12–3 Terminology of a Relational DBMS

The correct (formal) terms for a relational DBMS are relation, tuples, and attributes. However, the terminology shown in parentheses in this table is often used.

tuple is the same as a record in regular file terminology. The columns of the table are known as **attributes** and they are equivalent to fields within records. Instead of using the formal relational terminology of relations, tuples, and attributes we will use the more familiar files, records, and fields as do most real-world relational data-base systems.

Table 12–4 shows how a college registrar may perceive some of the data to be stored when using a relational DBMS. A relational DBMS allows a conceptually simple view of data, but also provides a set of powerful data-manipulation capabilities. For example, if the registrar wants a report listing student number, student name, course number, and grade of all students enrolled in CIS 1010, it could easily be derived from the files shown in Table 12–4. But how will the information needed for the report be related? It's in two different files and there are no linked

TABLE 12–4 Student Data Base Relations

Student File

Student Number	Student Name	Grade-Point Average GPA	Major
124693298	Joe Smith	2.58	ACCT
138942824	Chris Todd	3.62	CIS
362982353	Ray Gilmer	3.23	MSCI
468329312	Ann Sneed	2.95	MGT
560782392	Angela Brown	3.01	ECON

Registration File

Student Number	Course Number	Grade
124693298	CIS 1010	B
124693298	ACCT 2111	B
138942824	CIS 1010	A
362982353	MSCI 3840	A
468329312	CIS 1010	C
468329312	MGT 3010	A
560782392	ECON 2111	C

Course File

Course Number	Course Title	Instructor
ACCT 2111	PRINCIPLES OF ACCOUNTING	PATON
CIS 1010	INFORMATION SYSTEMS	HICKS
ECON 2111	PRINCIPLES OF ECONOMICS	SAMUELSON
MGT 3010	MANAGEMENT PRINCIPLES	TAYLOR
MSCI 3840	APPLIED SIMULATION	FORRESTOR

Notice that these tables are subject-oriented. The student file contains information about students, the registration file contains information about student registration for particular courses, and the course file contains information about courses. The subjects of these three files are students, registration, and courses. One of the approaches to designing files for a relational DBMS is to concentrate on the subjects.

lists or pointers! This leads to the second major advantage of a relational DBMS: the relationships among data are carried in the data themselves. As long as two or more files contain the same field, a relational DBMS can relate the files. In Table 12–4 both the student file and the registration file contain student number, therefore the relational DBMS can relate (technically, the word is *join*) the two files. In addition, both the registration file and the course file contain the course number. Thus we can join together all three of these files, producing any imaginable combination of information. The join is an extremely powerful and important capability!

Now let's see how we would produce the registrar's report. Using a simple DML statement such as the one shown in Figure 12–14a, we get the report shown in

Figure 12–14b. With a traditional, file-oriented system it would have been necessary to write a complex computer program to perform this kind of data manipulation. A tree- or network-structured data base would have allowed this manipulation, but only if it had been anticipated at design time and the necessary pointers had been embedded in the records. Since the relational approach does not suffer from either of these restrictions, it is a very effective tool for quickly generating unanticipated reports for management. Relational data bases are being implemented at a rapid pace and they will be the dominant data base of the future.

The Lord Delaware High School recently purchased IBM personal computers for both students and teachers. Cheryl Haymes, a math teacher, was put in charge of acquiring software. She has been trying to decide whether to buy a data-base management system, but she is confused by many of the software ads for data-base packages. Cheryl knows that relational data-base structures are the latest in technology, and many software vendors claim that their package is a true relational data base for a personal computer. What uses would a high school have for a PC data-base management system? What are the most important capabilities of a relational DBMS which Cheryl should look for in choosing a package?

Thinking About Information Systems 12–2

Advantages and Disadvantages of the Data-Base Approach

Advantages

Eliminates Data Redundancy   Under a DBMS, data that are normally stored at two or more places are stored in one spot. This reduces both storage costs and the confusion that may occur when data are stored at two or more locations.

Ability to Associate Related Data   The ability to associate related data not only allows data redundancy to be reduced but also provides the ability to process unanticipated requests for data. This capability is best met by a relational DBMS.

Program/Data Independence   With a DBMS, programs can be changed without the data storage being changed, and data storage can be changed without the programs being changed. The DBMS serves as an interface between the programs and the data so that the programs are concerned only with the logical symbolic names of the data, not physical storage. This advantage frees the programmer from the detailed and complex task of keeping up with the physical structure of the data.

Improvement of the Interface Between the User and the System
A DBMS provides simple query languages through which the user, or the user

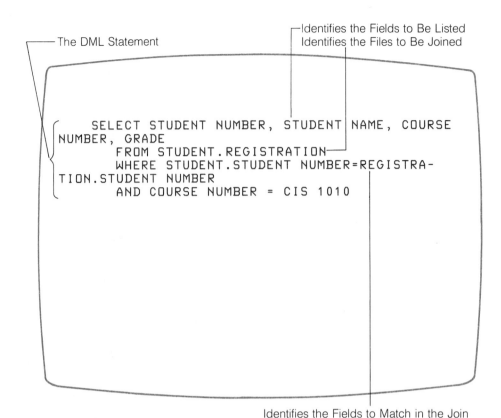

The DML Statement

Identifies the Fields to Be Listed
Identifies the Files to Be Joined

```
     SELECT STUDENT NUMBER, STUDENT NAME, COURSE
NUMBER, GRADE
        FROM STUDENT.REGISTRATION
        WHERE STUDENT.STUDENT NUMBER=REGISTRA-
TION.STUDENT NUMBER
        AND COURSE NUMBER = CIS 1010
```

Identifies the Fields to Match in the Join

```
The Report                                    Date 02 MAY 8X
STUDENT NUMBER      STUDENT NAME      COURSE NUMBER      GRADE

   124693298        JOE SMITH         CIS 1010             B
   138942824        CHRIS TODD        CIS 1010             A
   468329312        ANN SNEED         CIS 1010             C
```

FIGURE 12–14   A Relational Data-Base Query

If the registrar wants the report in an ascending order by grade, a line reading ORDER BY GRADE is added to the DML statement.

assisted by an application programmer, can retrieve information quickly to fill unanticipated needs for information. In addition, these languages enable users to write their own programs to retrieve information on an ad-hoc basis.

Increased Security and Integration of Data   Data contained in a data base are likely to be more secure and better integrated than data in traditional files because the data-base administrator's primary function is to provide for the integration, physical storage, and security of the data. Under the traditional approach, several individuals handle this job.

Considering these advantages of a DBMS, you can see how important a DBMS is to management. The ability to associate related data in processing unanticipated requests for data and the improvement of the interface between user and system are indispensable tools in a MIS. You will learn in Module C that a DBMS is also central to many decision support systems.

Disadvantages

The disadvantages of data-base management systems are relatively few, and in the long-run are outweighed by the advantages. One disadvantage is that DBMS software is complex; the concepts used are often new to users. Therefore, a DBMS requires sophisticated data-processing personnel and sometimes a reeducation of users. The current trend is to produce data-base management systems that are easier for users to understand.

Another disadvantage is that DBMS software creates additional overhead because it requires computer time to execute, disk space for software storage, and so on. However, as we discussed in chapter 10, this is a disadvantage of all systems software. It is also not likely to be a major problem in the future as the cost of computer hardware declines.

Summing Up

☐ Traditional information processing is file-oriented, where each application has its own separate data storage. This approach has several disadvantages:

1. Redundant data may be stored
2. It is difficult to integrate data from various sources
3. Data storage is tied up with specific application programs
4. It is difficult to respond to unanticipated information requests

☐ The data-base approach integrates the data into one large storage structure which may be used by many different users and application programs.
☐ The physical view of data defines the layout of data records on actual physical devices such as disk packs.
☐ The logical view represents the data in a way that is meaningful to users and application programmers.
☐ The data base may be accessed by users either directly or through an application program.
☐ A data-base management system is a complex program that manages a firm's data resources. It uses a data-definition language to link the logical view with actual physical storage.
☐ A data-manipulation language allows the user to input, access, modify, and retrieve data in a data base. It is often used in conjunction with a regular programming language to process data in ways the DBMS by itself cannot.
☐ The data-base administrator (DBA) is a key person in a data-base environment.
☐ The DBA is responsible for:

1. Maintaining a data dictionary
2. Ensuring physical security of the data
3. Controlling changes in the logical and physical structures of the data base

□ The data base is usually stored on direct-access devices. The DBMS tries to arrange data storage in a way that minimizes storage and processing costs.

□ A nonrelational DBMS uses embedded pointers and linked lists to reduce data redundancy and to establish logical relationships among data elements.

□ A tree structure is a logical data model that arranges data according to some natural hierarchy on a one-to-many basis.

□ A network structure allows logical relationships among entities on a many-to-many basis.

□ A relational structure organizes data in the form of two-dimensional tables. The data in these tables may be manipulated in many ways. Because of its conceptual simplicity and ability to relate data, this data model is rapidly becoming more popular.

□ The data-base system has these major advantages:

1. It eliminates data redundancy
2. It integrates related data
3. It provides data independence
4. It provides an interface between users and the data through query languages

□ The disadvantages of a DBMS are that it can be complex and can require substantial computer resources to execute.

Key Terms

data redundancy
data integration
program/data dependence
data-base management system (DBMS)
data base
pointers
physical view
logical view
users
query language
data-definition language (DDL)
data-manipulation language (DML)
schema

subschema
data-base administrator (DBA)
active data dictionary
configuration control
embedded pointer
linked list
tree structure
network structure
nodes
relational model
table
tuple
attributes

Self-Quiz

Completion Questions

1. A _____ is a program that serves as an interface between application programs and a set of coordinated and integrated physical files.

2. In the _____ view of data, the emphasis is on interrelating data fields and records such that they represent the underlying business reality.

3. A data-base management system (DBMS) uses two languages—a data-definition language (DDL) and a _____ .

4. The logical structure of a data base is sometimes called a _____ .

5. A(n) _____ is a field within a record containing the physical or relative address of a related record in another part of the data base.

6. In the relational model, the columns of the table are known as _____ .

7. The _____ view of data defines the layout of data records on actual devices such as a magnetic disk.

8. A key person in a data-base environment is the _____ .

9. A _____ structure is a logical data model that arranges data according to some natural hierarchy on a one-to-many basis.

10. The _____ is the physical repository for data.

Multiple-Choice Questions

1. Which of the following is *not* true of the traditional approach to information processing?
   a. There is common sharing of data among the various applications.
   b. It is file-oriented.
   c. Programs are dependent on the files.
   d. It is inflexible.
   e. All of the above are true.

2. The data-base environment has all of the following components except:
   a. users
   b. separate files
   c. data base
   d. data-base administrator
   e. query languages

3. The way a particular application views the data from the data base that the application uses is a:
   a. module
   b. relational model
   c. schema
   d. subschema
   e. none of the above

4. Which of the following is true of the data-manipulation language (DML)?
   a. It refers to data using physical addresses.
   b. It cannot interface with high-level programming languages.
   c. It is used to define the physical characteristics of each record.
   d. It is essentially the link between the logical and physical views of the data base.
   e. None of the above.

5. Which of the following is not a logical data-base structure?
   a. tree
   b. relational
   c. network
   d. chain
   e. all of the above are logical structures

6. The relational model uses some unfamiliar terminology. A tuple is equivalent to a:
   a. record
   b. field
   c. file
   d. data base
   e. data item

7. The logical data structure with a one-to-many relationship is a:
   a. network
   b. tree
   c. chain
   d. relational

8. The data-base administrator is, in effect, the coordinator between the _____ and the _____ .
   a. DBMS; data base
   b. application program; data base
   c. data base; users
   d. application programs; users

9. Which of the following is true of a network structure?
   a. It is a physical representation of the data.
   b. It allows a many-to-many relationship.
   c. It is conceptually simple.
   d. It will be the dominant data base of the future.
   e. None of the above.

10. Which of the following is not an advantage of the data-base approach?

a. elimination of data redundancy
b. ability to associate related data
c. increased security
d. program/data independence
e. all of the above are advantages

Answers

Completion

1. data-base management system (DBMS)
2. logical
3. data-manipulation language (DML)
4. schema
5. embedded pointer
6. attributes
7. physical
8. data-base administrator
9. tree
10. data base

Multiple Choice

1. a
2. b
3. d
4. e
5. d
6. a
7. b
8. c
9. b
10. e

Chapter 13

Distributed Data Processing and Office Automation

CHAPTER OUTLINE

PROLOGUE

Huge quantities of information are moved between computers daily over telecommunications channels. This information varies from detailed numerical data to written correspondence. Much of the high-volume data communication is between large mainframes, but personal computers communicate with each other also. PC users can readily access mainframes and capture information as diverse as stock-market quotes, shopping information, and sports results. How does this communication work? What should you consider when selecting a data-communication system? Read on.

Introduction

In the early days of electronic data processing (EDP), the computer was a highly centralized company resource. High equipment costs and difficult-to-operate software systems prevented the spread of EDP resources to user departments. During the last decade, however, this situation has changed dramatically. The cost of hardware has decreased sharply, and software is becoming easier to use. As a result, many people can now use the computer without the help of EDP specialists. By carefully dispersing computer resources throughout the organization, a business can significantly reduce paperwork costs and improve turnaround time on applications. The management of dispersed EDP facilities is generally known as **distributed data processing (DDP).** In this chapter we will discuss the major concerns in designing and operating a DDP system.

The entry of computer equipment into user departments has far-reaching effects on office procedure. While managers are delighted to see the productivity of their offices grow rapidly, they have to ensure that office personnel willingly adopt the new procedures. Nothing could be more disastrous for a distributed data-processing system than a hostile attitude among users. In the last section of this chapter we will discuss the automation of some major office procedures, and issues arising from the man-machine interface.

Distributed data-processing facilities depend heavily on the communication of data between computers. Designing a communication system is a complex engineering task, generally beyond the competence of the business manager. It is, nevertheless, important for the manager to understand the fundamentals of data communications. This can help him or her recognize communication problems, and formulate policies regarding the efficient use of alternative communication methods. We will, therefore, start this chapter with a discussion of the basic concepts of data communications.

Data Communication

The communication of data from one point to another is a crucial business function. Methods of **data communication** vary from the use of existing telephone lines to satellite transmission. In a DDP environment the communication function can become very complex as a result of growth, and integration of previously independent systems. Every DDP system has a unique communication system to link its devices together. This typically evolves as a response to the company's growth, and the information-processing strategy employed by management.

Types of Data Communication

There are three basic configurations in data communications: computer/peripheral device, computer-to-computer, and communication through a data switch.

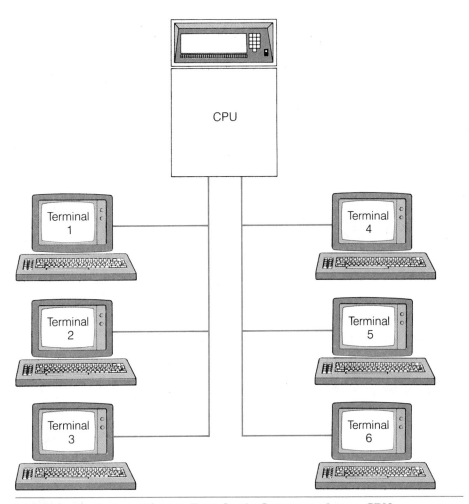

FIGURE 13–1   Intelligent Terminals Connected to a CPU

Intelligent terminals contain a microprocessor that allows them to detect which signals are meant for them.

Computer/Peripheral-Device Communication   This involves the transfer of data between a CPU and a peripheral device, such as a terminal or a storage medium. The storage or terminal device is completely under the control of the CPU. It is customary to call this kind of setup a **master-slave relationship.** The master (the CPU) determines when and how data are to be transferred to and from the slave (the peripheral device).

As illustrated in Figure 13–1, it is possible to place a number of terminals on a single line from the computer. The computer addresses each terminal in turn for input or output (I/O). Such terminals are considered intelligent since they know when the computer is talking to them. There are also dumb terminals. These need to be connected to the computer through separate lines, since they are not able

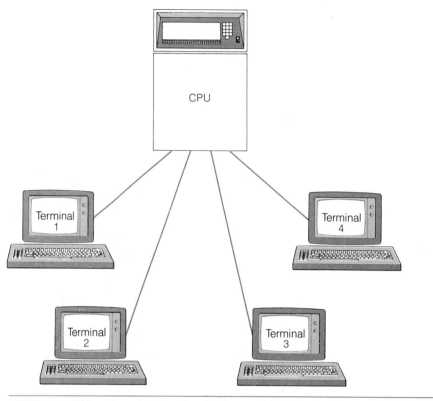

FIGURE 13–2   Dumb Terminals Connected to a CPU

Under this configuration, the CPU addresses each terminal separately on a different communciation line.

to tell when they are being addressed. They just assume that any signal coming down the line is meant for them. Figure 13–2 shows a number of dumb terminals linked to a CPU.

Computer-to-Computer Communication   Often it is necessary to transfer data from one computer to another. For instance, some grocery-store chains have linked their computers to the computers of their major suppliers through communication lines (refer to Figure 13–3). When an item needs to be reordered, the computer automatically places the order over the communication line. The supplier's computer can then process the order immediately. This procedure not only eliminates the possibility of human error, but also permits better inventory management by speeding up the reordering process.

Communication between two computers may be a master-slave connection. An example is the relationship between a mainframe computer and a special-purpose minicomputer (see Figure 13–4). The minicomputer typically performs an auxiliary function for the mainframe, such as editing input data. However, since the minicomputer is in the position of a slave, it cannot initiate any communication with the mainframe unless the mainframe allows it to do so.

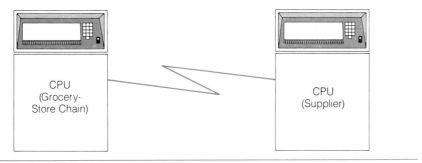

FIGURE 13–3   CPU-to-CPU Communication

This type of data communication is increasing with the widespread use of personal computers.

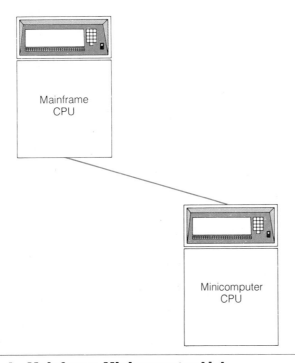

FIGURE 13–4   Mainframe-Minicomputer Link

The master-slave relationship depicted here indicates that the minicomputer is subservient to the mainframe. The mainframe controls all communication between the two computers.

On the other hand, a communication link may be a connection between equals. As in the grocery-store example, two mainframe CPUs may interact. In this kind of situation, each computer has to have the consent of the other machine's operating system before it can initiate a data transfer.

Communication through a Data Switch   A **data switch** is a device similar to a telephone exchange. A number of CPUs and peripheral devices are linked to

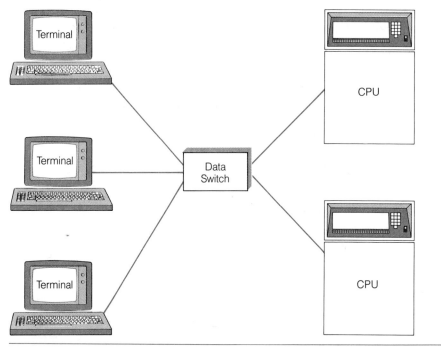

FIGURE 13–5 A Data Switch

Data switches are used quite often in companies that have multiple CPUs. The data switch allows a terminal to communicate with any of the CPUs.

---

network

In data communication, a configuration in which two or more terminals or CPUs are connected.

it, and it can connect any two of them together, on demand. This kind of arrangement has several advantages. A user can access many different computers from the same terminal. A CPU can exchange data with any one of the other CPUs on the *network*.

A data switch can be used not only to link communication lines, but also to provide various translation services. As we will see in the next section, hardware devices differ in the way they organize the flow of data. The data switch, which is actually a minicomputer, can change the format of data in transit so that it conforms with the hardware requirements of the receiving device. Figure 13–5 illustrates a data switch.

The Data Transmission Process

Protocols The flow of data between devices is basically a stream of bits, represented by "on" or "off" line conditions. Unfortunately, it is not enough merely to send raw data from place to place. It is necessary to package the data into blocks or "messages." The intervening communication hardware can then check for transmission errors, and route the message to its correct destination.

A **communication protocol** is a set of rules governing information flow in a communication system. These rules define the **block format,** or **message enve-**

One strong justification for the purchase of personal computers, especially for students, is that PCs can be used as a smart terminal to a mainframe computer. Computing tasks, such as word processing, that do not require mainframe power, can be done on the personal computer's CPU. When more power is needed, the user can connect the personal computer to the mainframe through telephone lines. Even editing of mainframe program files can be done on the personal computer and then "uploaded" to the mainframe for execution. This can save a significant amount of mainframe CPU time.

The attractiveness of using personal computers in this way has encouraged hardware and software manufacturers to develop low-cost, easy-to-use tools for establishing links between personal computers and mainframes. Some of the more popular packages used today are:

Cross Talk XVI   Microstuf, Inc.
1000 Halcomb Woods Parkway
Roswell, GA 30076

Smartcom   Hayes Microcomputer Products
5923 Peachtree Industrial Blvd.
Norcross, GA 30092

Kermit   Kermit Distribution
612 W. 115th Street
New York, NY 10025

When deciding on communication software, make sure you understand the difference between a package capable of file transfer and a package capable of terminal emulation. File-transfer packages can send and receive files and sometimes do basic line editing but you cannot perform full-screen terminal-emulation functions. Packages that provide these functions tend to be a little more expensive but they provide much more power. For more information on micro-mainframe communications, see the January 22, 1985 issue of *PC Magazine* (Volume 4, Number 2) which contains a series of articles and reviews on this topic.

lope, which packages each message to be transmitted. This envelope usually contains control characters to mark the message's beginning and end, as well as an address, so that data can be directed to particular terminals. It might also contain some characters that are used for error detection. Figure 13–6 shows a typical message envelope. A terminal that conforms to an error-checking protocol operates error-free, since it automatically retransmits any erroneous data. Communication protocols enable terminals to be bunched together on a single line because these terminals can be selectively addressed or **polled** by the CPU. The computer polls the terminals by addressing each one in turn. If a terminal does not respond, the computer goes on to the next one.

Unfortunately, there are many incompatible and competing communication protocols. Two of the more widely used protocols are the RS232C standard which is often used for communication between microcomputers, and IBM's BISYNC protocol which is used with mainframes.

Transmission Mode   Data are usually sent along a single line, defining successive intervals of time as consecutive bits in a byte. The bit coding scheme used to represent a byte (a character of data) is typically the seven-bit American Standard Code for Information Interchange (ASCII). We discussed ASCII in chapter 11.

Two possible conditions, "on" and "off," representing binary digits one and zero, respectively, are imposed on the line by the transmitter. The receiver monitors

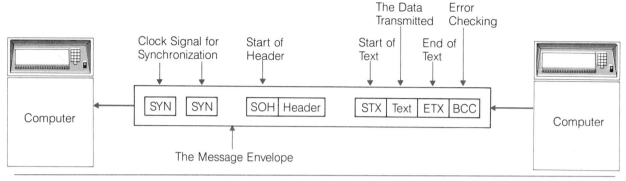

FIGURE 13–6 A Message Envelope

This protocol is IBM's widely used BISYNC (Binary Synchronous Communication Protocol).

this train of signals and reconstructs the incoming byte. This can be done in two ways.

The simpler method, typically employed by microcomputers, is **asynchronous transmission** (see Figure 13–7). In this type of transmission the condition always goes off for one interval before a byte is sent, and always reverts to on for at least one interval at the end of each byte. This allows the receiver to synchronize with the transmitter at the beginning each byte and start reading at the correct time. The two extra bits per byte increase the number of transmitted bits from eight to ten, but the real information content of the package, including the necessary parity bit, is only eight bits. Since 20 percent of the data transmitted is merely control information, this method is considered inefficient in terms of line usage. It is, however, easy to implement.

A more economical method, used by complex, high-speed terminals, is **synchronous transmission** (refer to Figure 13–7). With this method, the receiver's clock is not synchronized with the sender for each individual byte. It is synchronized at the beginning of the transmission session and is allowed to run continuously. Therefore, it is not necessary to send signals at the beginning and end of each byte. However, if there are gaps in the data stream, they must be filled with "idle" bytes to maintain synchronization. At the beginning of the data stream there is a predetermined pattern of bits which causes the receiver to synchronize its clock and start receiving the data.

Transmission Speed **Data transmission speed** is measured in **bits per second (bps).** Sometimes the term *baud* is used interchangeably with bits per second. This is not strictly correct, since a baud rate is a telegraphic concept that is not necessarily applicable to computer data communications.

Some devices employ a technique called **serial transmission.** Figure 13–7 is an example. A byte is transmitted one bit at a time, in a serial fashion, over a single communication channel. Other devices use **parallel transmission.** This involves the simultaneous transmission of eight bits across an eight-channel line (see Figure 13–8). Since these eight bits constitute a byte or character, the speed of such systems is quoted in characters per second. You can see that parallel transmission

Asynchronous Bit Stream

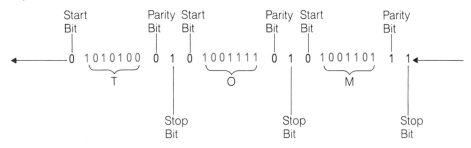

Synchronous Bit Stream

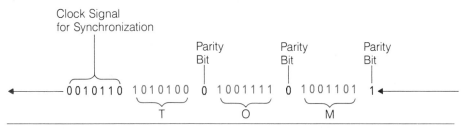

FIGURE 13–7 Asynchronous and Synchronous Bit Streams to Transmit the Name TOM

The difference between these two data transmission modes is that with asynchronous transmission a start bit is transmitted before each byte. With synchronous transmission a clock signal synchronizes the sender and receiver so that several bytes can be transmitted without sending a start bit prior to each byte.

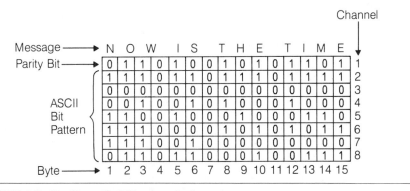

FIGURE 13–8 Parallel Transmission

Since there are eight channels in this parallel transmission, a complete byte of eight bits can be transmitted in the time that it would take to transmit one bit with serial transmission.

DATA COMMUNICATION **363**

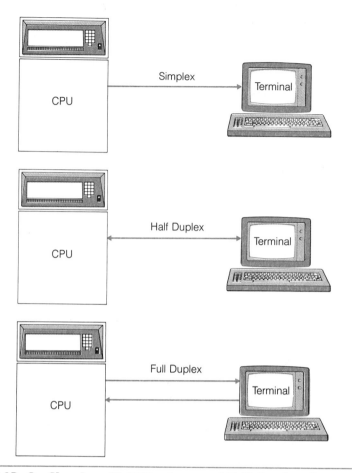

FIGURE 13–9 Simplex, Half-Duplex, and Full-Duplex Channels

Data communication over regular telephone lines is normally done in half duplex. When large-volume transmissions are required between CPUs, a full-duplex channel is usually established.

is faster than serial. Most microcomputers communicate with their printers in parallel model. Communication between microcomputers, over regular telephone lines, is done in serial mode since these lines can transmit only one bit at a time over the single channel that is available.

Transmission Direction   Data transmission can also be characterized by the direction that the communication channel allows. There are three combinations of transmission directions, as shown in Figure 13–9. A **half-duplex channel** can send and receive data, but only in one direction at a time. With a **full-duplex channel,** data can be sent and received at the same time. Full-duplex channels are usually used in computer-to-computer communications. A **simplex channel** allows data to be transmitted only in one direction. This channel is rarely used, since usually data must flow in both directions between a terminal and a CPU or between two CPUs.

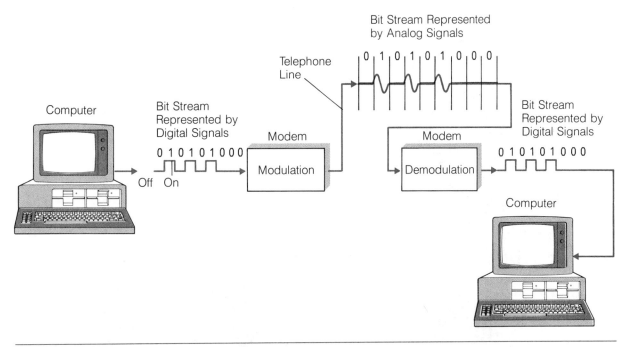

FIGURE 13–10 Conversion of Digital Signals to and from Analog Form

Modems are designed to either send or receive data over analog telephone lines. Thus the same modem can perform both modulation and demodulation depending on the direction in which the data are flowing.

Communication Hardware

Modems Many different media are used to convey data. Satellite communication is being used more and more for long-distance transmission. Short- and medium-distance communication is done primarily through telephone lines. Although telephone systems are now being designed to carry digital signals, most of the lines used for data transmission are traditional telephone lines that were meant to carry voice messages. These lines operate only in analog waveform. Before transmission, the digital data signals must be converted into analog form (see Figure 13–10). This conversion process is called **modulation.** At the receiving end, the sound signals are converted back to digital form through a **demodulation** process. A device called a **modem** (short for modulator-demodulator) is used for this purpose. PC modems operate from 300 to 2,400 bits per second and transmit data in an asynchronous mode. Figure 13–11 shows a typical modem.

Data communication is moving away from analog transmission with modems. Many of the networks discussed later in this chapter use digital transmission. Furthermore, most voice messages will likely be transmitted and stored by digital means in the future.

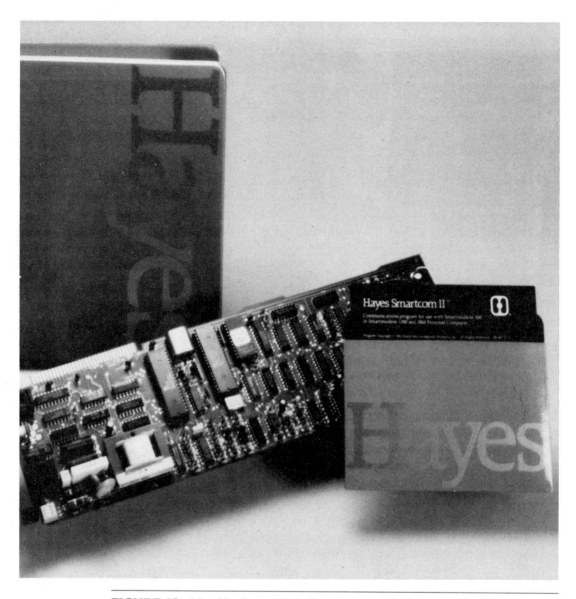

FIGURE 13–11 Modems and Communication Software

When using a modem with a personal computer you must have communication software. This software executes on the PC and performs such tasks as dialing the other computer and handling the data communication itself.

buffer
A storage device used to compensate for a difference in rate of data flow, or time of occurrence of events, when transferring data from one device to another.

Multiplexors While information is being keyed into a *buffer* at a terminal, or is being processed by the CPU, the communication line remains idle. If a number of terminals are installed at one location, line idle time can be reduced by sharing the line among them. A sophisticated modem known as a **multiplexor** is used. Some multiplexors divide the telephone line into different frequency bands. Each frequency band is then allocated to a separate terminal. Other multiplexors divide

Frequency-Division Multiplexing:

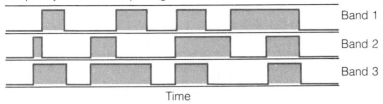

Band 1

Band 2

Band 3

Time

Time-Division Multiplexing:

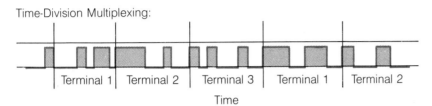

| Terminal 1 | Terminal 2 | Terminal 3 | Terminal 1 | Terminal 2 |

Time

FIGURE 13–12 Multiplexing

The multiplexors here are dividing a communication line among several computer terminals. However, multiplexors are available that divide one communication line, such as your home telephone line, between your personal computer and normal voice use of that communication line. With this voice/data multiplexor you can talk on your telephone at the same time that your PC is using the line for data communication.

the transmission into small time slices. Each terminal is allowed one time slice in turn (see Figure 13–12). A **statistical multiplexor** is similar to a time-division multiplexor but is a more intelligent device that allocates more transmission time to terminals that are sending and receiving a larger volume of data (see Figure 13–13).

Data-Switching Networks One of the most complex hardware configurations is a **data-switching network.** As discussed earlier, this kind of setup allows communication among many terminals and CPUs. Using statistical multiplexors, the network converts many low-speed data streams into a few high-speed streams. These are then transmitted in digital form over long-distance lines. Some of these networks transmit data at over 50 million bits per second.

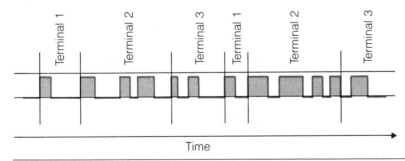

Time

FIGURE 13–13 Statistical Multiplexing

Terminal 1 is using the communication line less than terminal 2, therefore the multiplexor allocates more time to terminal 2.

Front-End Processors With most hardware, a CPU has to communicate with several terminals at the same time. Routine tasks such as polling, synchronization, and error checking can absorb a large proportion of the CPU's processing time. This often leads to degraded performance on more important jobs. In order not to waste this precious mainframe CPU time, many systems have a small computer that is dedicated solely to the communication function. Known as a **front-end processor,** this computer manages all routine communications with peripheral devices. Figure 13–14 depicts a network that uses front-end processors to manage communications.

Network Systems

The rapid growth of the data communications industry has given birth to literally hundreds of types of networks. Many of these systems are designed to work primarily with one vendor's products. Others try to establish communication between different vendors' equipment. We will briefly discuss two major systems and then look at local area networks.

System Network Architecture (SNA) Developed and promoted by IBM, this system fulfills all the communication needs for a distributed data-processing system built with IBM equipment. The basic structure of **system network architecture (SNA)** consists of a large CPU that controls a number of terminals through a front-end processor (see Figure 13–15). An enhanced version of SNA allows several CPUs to access a population of terminals or personal computers through a network of front-end processors. If one of the CPUs breaks down, its work can be transferred to another processor.

Advanced Information System/Net 1 A project of the large telecommunications company, AT&T, this system is still in the development stage. When it is fully operational, the **advanced information system/net 1 (AIS)** is expected to provide comprehensive data-switching facilities. Working similar to a telephone exchange, this network can put through "calls" between terminals and computers that are connected to it. Each terminal or CPU is referred to as a node. Unlike the hierarchical structure of SNA, AIS treats all nodes as equals. It is expected that the AIS will ultimately be able to link up with the equipment of most computer vendors, and thereby provide a truly public wide-area data-switching network. Many larger firms have established their own wide-area private networks.

Local Area Networks An even more widespread phenomenon is the establishment of the **local area network (LAN).** Firms are installing these networks to provide for local communication needs. For example, an individual plant might have its own LAN. LANs are often PBX (Private Board Exchange) based so that they handle both voice and data communications. They transmit information between all sizes of computers in a digital format on a single-channel cable system, with very high speeds—from 56 thousand to 50 million bits per second.

Local area networks are also being widely used to network personal computers. These networks usually consist of three components: a networking expansion board to be installed in one of the five expansion slots of the system unit of each PC,

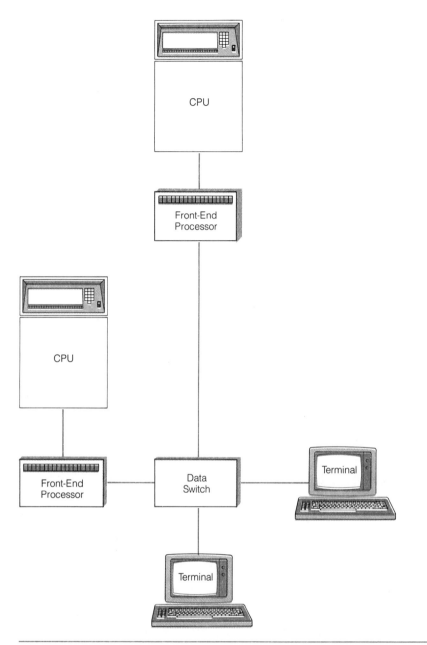

FIGURE 13–14   Front-End Processors in a Communication Network

The front-end processor performs the routine tasks associated with communications, thereby freeing the CPU to do more important work.

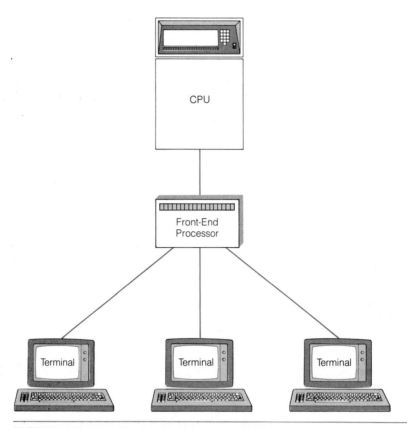

FIGURE 13–15   Basic Structure of SNA

the necessary cable for connections between computers, and software to control the network. Typically, they cost about $1,000 for every PC that is connected. These networks not only allow data communication between PCs, but they also allow PCs to share expensive peripherals such as Winchester disks and laser printers.

Distributed Data Processing

Spreading the data-processing function throughout an organization entails more than merely dispersing physical equipment and providing for data communication. It requires creative programming and system design, so that maximum benefits can be derived from the distributed data-processing system. The following section considers some of the major reasons for adopting DDP, and the types of problems to be expected when implementing it. This will be followed by a discussion of how to distribute hardware, software, and data resources. While you read this section it is useful to remember that the computers that are distributed can be either mainframe, mini, or micro.

The Need for Decentralized Processing

DDP offers several advantages over centralized processing. First, it is often cheaper to dedicate a micro or minicomputer to performing certain tasks instead of a mainframe. This may also reduce data communication costs because more processing is done at branch locations. Second, system reliability may be improved because if one CPU crashes, its workload can be distributed to others. Third, and probably most important, DDP allows the end users to interact directly with the computer. Although this creates some control problems, it has a very favorable effect on employee productivity.

DDP also offers many advantages to the system designer. Since system components may be added as demand grows, DDP is extremely modular. This is in contrast to a traditional system where a large computer has to be installed in anticipation of future workload additions, even though current needs do not justify it. Moreover, the system designer can tailor the DDP system to the firm's organization structure. A centralized firm may want the central computer to closely supervise branch-office computers. A decentralized firm might require only a loose connection between home-office and branch-office processors.

Distributed data processing also has a number of disadvantages.

1. Communication costs can easily run over the budget, unless line usage is carefully controlled.
2. It may be difficult to link together incompatible hardware existing at various locations.
3. Software written at different locations may be incompatible.
4. Locally developed systems may not be able to aggregate data to meet central management's need for information.

Some of the most difficult problems arise in selling the DDP system to employees. Data-processing managers often resent their loss of control. User employees sometimes resist working directly with a computer. Some opposition to change is expected; however, a distributed data-processing system requires widespread acceptance and support from users. The list of DDP systems that have failed because of user indifferences is long.

Hardware Distribution

To be considered a DDP system, a computer should have more than one CPU on the network. The CPUs may be arranged in many different configurations. Here we explore some of the more common ones.

Star Configuration   Under a **star configuration,** remote computers are connected radially to a central processor, as depicted in Figure 13–16. The remote computers perform I/O operations as well as data processing. For example, minicomputers at the branch offices of a bank may process deposits and withdrawals, and then transmit summary data to the head office.

Ring Configuration   A **ring configuration** is another popular setup which joins a number of CPUs in a circular pattern. As can be seen in Figure 13–17, each

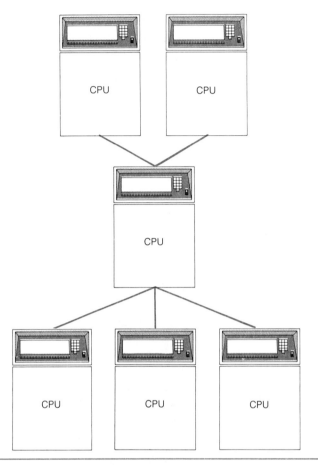

FIGURE 13–16   A Star Configuration

computer can communicate with its neighbors. Actually, a CPU can communicate with any other CPU on the ring. It just has to ask the intervening computers to relay the message on toward its destination.

Hybrid Configuration   A **hybrid configuration** is a ring-structured network where every node is the center of a star network. Such an arrangement is often used in a data-switching environment. The nodes on the ring (see Figure 13–18) perform only data-communication functions. The actual processing is done by the computers that are on the tips of the stars.

Broadcast Configuration   A **broadcast configuration** is an extension of the ring configuration. All computers can directly communicate with each other (see Figure 13–19). Although this speeds up communication between CPUs, the additional hardware and communication costs may be substantial.

Tree Configuration   As Figure 13–20 shows, a **tree configuration** links a number of computers in a hierarchy. This arrangement might be suitable for a

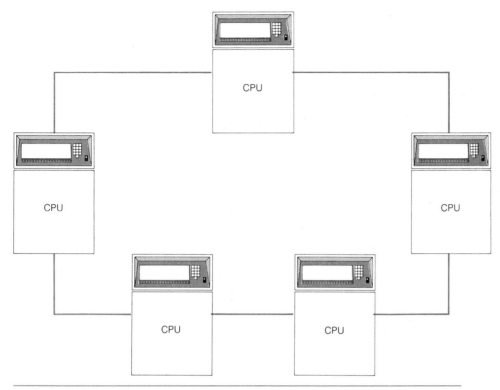

FIGURE 13–17   A Ring Configuration

large, centralized firm. A central mainframe would control the operations of several computers in regional offices. Each regional-office computer would, in turn, be responsible for supervising a number of minicomputers at branch locations.

Bus Configuration   A network often used in personal computers is a **bus configuration** (see Figure 13–21). Each PC is connected to a single cable, called a bus. Data transmission can occur between any two PCs over the bus. One of the PCs executes the software that controls the network.

Software Distribution

A distributed system provides communication among several CPUs. However, it is not necessary that these CPUs spend most of their time communicating with each other. In most cases, a CPU uses the bulk of its time to process locally, and only a small fraction of it to communicate with other computers.

Many application programs executed by a computer are specific to that location. For example, the different divisions in a large firm may run their own specialized applications on their computers (see Figure 13–22). This makes it possible to decentralize the tasks of application development and maintenance. Each functional area (manufacturing or marketing, for example) develops its own application software and assumes the responsibility of maintaining it.

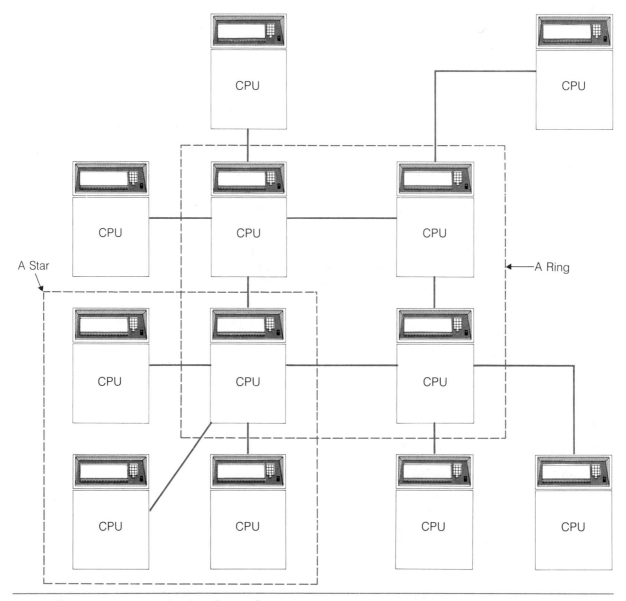

FIGURE 13–18   A Hybrid Configuration

This, in effect, requires that application development know-how be dispersed throughout the organization. This notion is sometimes unappealing to system development managers, who feel that it would undermine their authority. But with the demand for application software increasing rapidly, it is necessary to decentralize application development. User departments should be able to create their own application programs, either by training non-data-processing staff or by setting up their own specialized application development departments.

Although some application programming may be distributed, some of it has to be done centrally. For instance, a large holding company may allow its subsidiaries

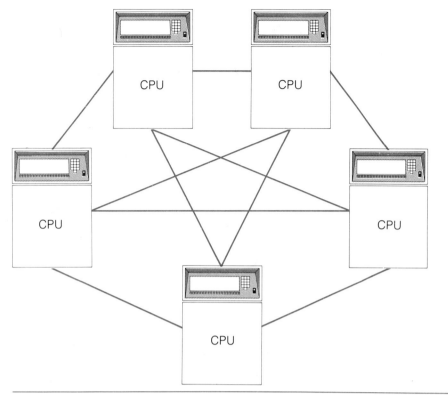

FIGURE 13–19 A Broadcast Configuration

PC USER TIP

Modems

A modem is a MOdulator-DEModulator. It takes signals from your computer's serial port and puts them into a form that can be sent over phone or other communication lines. A modem can also convert incoming signals to a form your computer can understand. By using a modem, you can access a number of national data systems and retrieve information on stock prices, the weather, commodity prices, and countless other subjects. A modem can be used as a medium for sending electronic mail, making airline reservations, or doing personal banking. A modem can also connect two computers together so that you can access the resources of a distant computer. Modems are capable of transmitting at various speeds. Modems that operate at 300 bps (bits per second) are

very slow and today are almost unavailable. Most modems that use regular phone lines operate at 1,200 or 2,400 bps, a more reasonable speed. Local-area networks that use dedicated lines can run at higher speeds. Shown below are different modem speeds and the associated amount of time it would take to fill up a PC display screen.

Bits per Second	Time to Fill a Full Screen
300	64 seconds
1,200	16 seconds
2,400	8 seconds
9,600	2 seconds

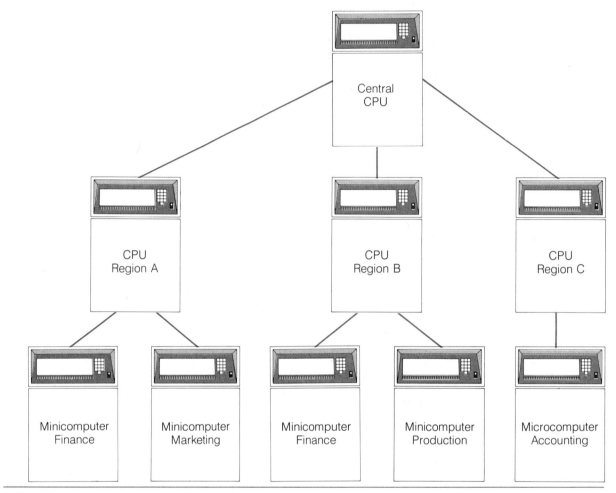

FIGURE 13–20   A Tree Configuration

to develop their own manufacturing and marketing software but may want to develop most of the financial software at headquarters. In general, most of the application software that is used across the communication network must be developed centrally. Moreover, the central information systems department should ensure that uniform documentation standards and security controls are used by local departments.

A major concern in DDP systems is the system software. The complexity of the hardware configuration places a great burden on the operating system. In a DDP environment, a computer also has access to the storage and I/O devices of other computers. Its operating system must have the capability of recognizing and addressing these foreign devices, in addition to its own peripheral equipment.

As we will discuss in the following section, a DDP system might involve the maintenance of a **distributed data base.** In this case, the DBMS must be capable of accessing storage devices on different machines. Again, this involves interaction

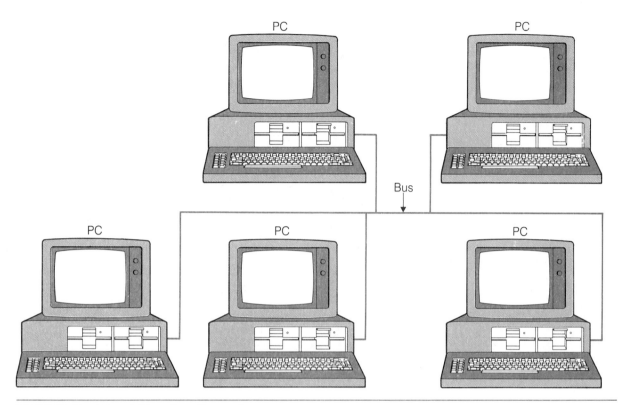

FIGURE 13–21   A Bus Configuration

among the operating systems of various computers. Centralized programming is required in this situation.

Data Decentralization

When data processing is distributed, the problem of data storage tends to get very complex. A decision has to be made as to where the data should be stored. Some of these data are shared among various nodes, and these **shared data** must be made accessible to them all. However, a lot of data are used only locally, and thus are referred to as **local data.** It would serve no useful purpose to make these data available to the whole network.

Whether data are stored in files or in a data base, it is necessary to keep track of what is stored, and where. The data-base administrator must maintain an up-to-date data dictionary for all shared data.

DDP is often used for realtime applications, such as inventory control, hotel reservations, and law enforcement. Since realtime applications are best supported by a data-base management system, it is not surprising that distributed data bases have become a major concern in the DDP field. Each DDP system develops its own unique distributed data base depending on its hardware configuration and user demands. The local data presents no special problems. The DBMS treats it in

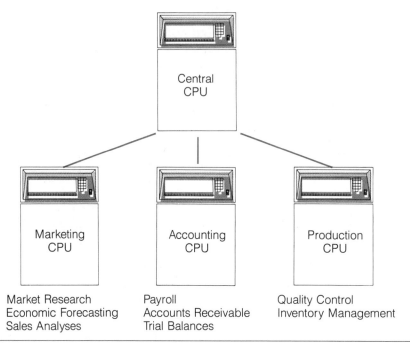

Central
CPU

Marketing
CPU

Accounting
CPU

Production
CPU

Market Research
Economic Forecasting
Sales Analyses

Payroll
Accounts Receivable
Trial Balances

Quality Control
Inventory Management

FIGURE 13–22 Applications Specific to Each Division Within a Firm

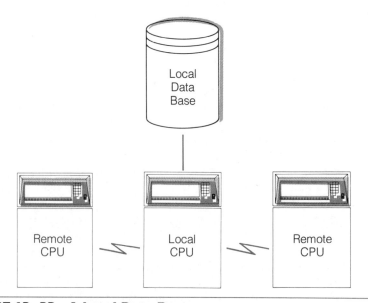

Local
Data
Base

Remote
CPU

Local
CPU

Remote
CPU

FIGURE 13–23 A Local Data Base

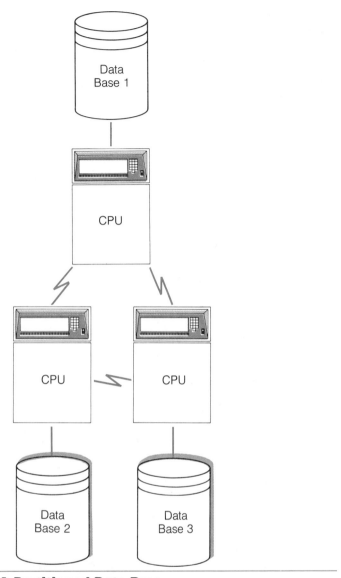

FIGURE 13–24   A Partitioned Data Base

Any of the CPUs in this network can access any of the three data bases. However, data are stored at the CPU that uses them most often.

the regular manner, as discussed in chapter 12 (see Figure 13–23). However, there are two approaches to maintaining shared data: partitioning and replication.

Partitioning   With **partitioning,** a particular kind of record is stored at the location that uses it the most (see Figure 13–24). When another node requests that record, the DBMS consults the data dictionary to determine the record's location, and retrieves it from there. For instance, a bank may store a customer's account balance at the branch where the customer usually does business. On rare occasions the customer might execute a transaction at another branch. At such times the DBMS would have to retrieve the data via communication lines. Since most data retrievals are done locally, communication costs are minimized.

Replication With **replication,** duplicate copies of the data base are stored at all locations. Changes to the data base are periodically copied to all locations. This approach is useful with small data bases, where it is cheaper to store multiple copies of the data than to use communication lines to retrieve individual records from distant locations. A large East Coast textile manufacturer uses replication in its distributed data base. The data base, containing orders, customer data, production data, and warehouse information, is periodically updated at all locations. Another example of replication is a local decision-support system on a micro. The user may periodically replicate from the central data base those portions of the data which supports his or her decision-support system.

Thinking About Information Systems 13–1

Dublin Furniture is a medium-sized furniture manufacturing operation in Virgina with five plants scattered over five counties in the southwest part of the state. Currently the company has one central computer, an IBM 4341. Each of the plants have access to the central computer through a variety of on-line terminals. For the last few months, manufacturing managers at the various plants have been building a case for distributed data processing. They argue that manufacturing resources planning (MRP) systems are becoming essential to effective manufacturing management. Their plan calls for a minicomputer to be purchased for each of the plants. Each plant would run its own MRP system. In addition, they argue other applications could be distributed from the central computer to these minicomputers. For example, each plant could maintain its own personnel system. If you were chief executive officer of Dublin Furniture, would you approve the distributed data-processing proposal?

Word Processing and Office Automation

As data-processing equipment continues to move out of the EDP department and into users' offices, office workers depend more and more on the computer to do their daily jobs. Some of the most significant effects of this distribution of computer processing have been in the area of **word processing** and office automation. The remainder of this chapter describes the changes that are occurring in today's computerized office, and how they affect the lives of office personnel.

Word Processing

Just as computers can process numerical data, they can also process words. Textual material such as letters, reports, and books, can be stored on the same storage media as numerical data. A **dedicated word-processing system** is essentially a

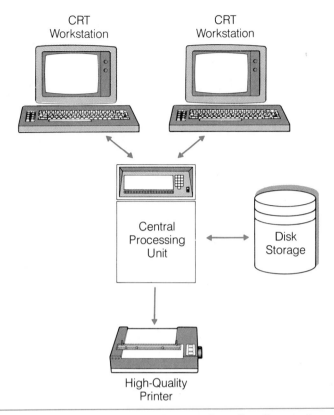

CRT
Workstation

CRT
Workstation

Central
Processing
Unit

Disk
Storage

High-Quality
Printer

FIGURE 13–25   A Typical Word-Processing Configuration

One or more CRT workstations can be connected to a word-processing CPU.

small computer with one or more CRT input stations, a high-quality printer, and disk storage that is used solely for word processing (see Figure 13–25). Word processors basically are small computer systems that cost from $5,000 to $25,000.

From a hardware standpoint, one of the most expensive parts of a typical word-processing system is the high-quality printer. These printers are usually based on ink jet, daisy-wheel, or laser technology. The workstation is a standard CRT that enables the operator to see the words being processed. The CPUs in word processors are relatively low-powered and are usually microprocessors. The processing of words requires comparatively little processing capacity. Storage may be either floppy or hard disk. Some word-processing systems have only one CRT workstation, others have many—sometimes a hundred or more.

Much word processing is being done on personal computers that are used for other tasks as well. Inexpensive software, such as WordStar, Word, and Word Perfect, makes the PC a very efficient word processor. PC-based word processing is covered in depth in Appendix B of this text.

The advantages of word processing are based on the fact that the system will store textual data on a disk, and retrieve, modify, or print it on command. A report, for example, can be initially typed through a CRT workstation, stored on disk, and printed. Corrections to the report can be made directly through the workstation. Words, sentences, paragraphs or even whole pages can be inserted, deleted, or moved. The report can be corrected and polished before a final copy is printed. Among the capabilities of word processing are the following:

1. Detection and correction of spelling errors.
2. Automatic changing of margin width. This is done without retyping the material. The operator simply tells the system the new margins and the CPU automatically sets them.
3. Deletion, insertion, or modification of any text material.
4. Automatic centering.
5. Automatic underlining.
6. Automatic hyphenation of words.
7. Automatic page numbering.

The advantages of word processing are many; they include:

1. Reduction of typing time (some say up to 50 percent of the typing and retyping time is saved with a word processor).
2. Reduction of proofreading time.
3. Cleaner, more professional-looking final copies.

Most individuals who are not skilled typists find that typing on a word processor is easier than on a typewriter since corrections can be made so readily. The fear of making an error and having to correct it with an eraser or correction fluid is totally eliminated. If the material is dictated, the typist enters the material on a word processor. Then the originator of the text calls it up on his or her workstation, reviews it, makes final corrections, and prints the final copy.

Electronic Mail

Many companies with networked information-processing systems are now expanding them into an **electronic mail** network (see Figure 13–26). Since the textual material is stored in electronic form in the word-processing system, it can be easily transmitted over long distances through regular commercial channels such as

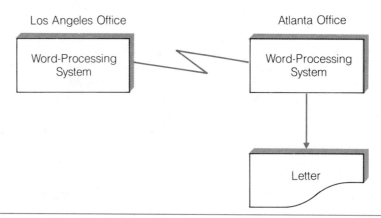

FIGURE 13–26 Electronic Mail
Electronic mail is becoming widespread within large firms. It is used much less between firms.

microwave and telephone lines. Some companies, such as Amoco Oil and Citicorp, have extensive electronic-mail capabilities.

When an executive receives electronic mail on his or her local workstation, the message can be read from the screen. A printed copy is readily available if needed. These systems have several advantages, which include the following:

1. The time between creation of information and its receipt by interested parties is minimized.
2. By relying on typed messages rather than voice communications, managers waste less time in dialing the telephone, only to hear a busy signal.
3. Messages and documents do not need to be physically copied in order to be routed to many people.
4. Electronic mail may be filed by the recipient, or dispatched to an "electronic wastebasket." The wastebasket retains messages for a period of time before destroying them.

Automated Office

A step further in the word-processing evolution is office automation. In an **automated office,** most if not all printed documents are stored electronically rather than in printed form. These can be retrieved, used, or printed whenever necessary. Advanced systems even provide the capability of storing text data and *digitized* voice communications. Using the system's data-manipulation language, managers can easily retrieve required information without physically searching through thick volumes of reports. Lawyers often use this technique. By specifying a few keywords, a lawyer can get the computer to search through a large data base of court cases and print out relevant citations. Another use of text searching is in strategic planning. Top managers frequently need descriptive data on various subjects, but don't know where to look. Using a DBMS, they can search different data bases and quickly pinpoint the required information sources.

digitize
To convert voice or other patterns to digital signals so they can be processed and stored by a digital computer.

The management of the Real-Time Orange Juice Company is concerned about the growing amount of paperwork inundating the corporate headquarters. The computer is being considered as a way of eliminating some of the paperwork. One of the computer managers suggested using the value-added concept of transaction processing for the purchasing department. A manager in a department would complete a purchase requisition on a computer terminal and would authorize it with a password and user identification number. The requisition would be sent electronically to purchasing for approval. Each purchasing agent would have an electronic "in basket" or computer file where requisitions would be stored until approved. The purchasing agent would "add value" to each item in his or her computer file by attaching the purchasing agent's identification number to the item. This "electronic signature" would serve as the approval to purchase the item. The document would then be sent through the proper channels until the items had been ordered and the invoice paid. The computerized document would finally be stored on a magnetic-tape history file. What would be some considerations in implementing this type of paperless purchasing system?

Thinking About Information Systems 13–2

This approach is often called the paperless office. Although parts of an automated office are being used in many companies, no company has a completely paperless office. Considerable advances will have to be made in the ease with which people can use office automation systems before paperless offices are feasible. Most people still prefer to work with a paper copy in hand.

Integrated Word Processing/Data Processing

Very often, businesses need to combine the output of their data-processing system with textual material to create a final document. If data processing and word processing are performed on separate systems, it is necessary to retype some of the information in order to obtain the final printout. **Integrated word processing/data processing (WP/DP)** systems can save this extra labor by processing the data and then using the results as input to a word-processing operation.

Customer Mailing Lists Data from accounting or marketing records can be combined with text to create high-quality correspondence material. For instance, a hospital computer can search patient records to find people who have not been in for a checkup in over a year. After checking the current appointments file, the system can automatically produce letters to remind patients to come in for their annual visit. Figure 13–27 shows how the system would print a high-quality letter by merging data files with precomposed text.

Report Generation Managers frequently prepare reports that include both data and descriptive text. For example, a report from a regional sales manager may include detailed sales data as well as a subjective evaluation of the future market. Figure 13–28 illustrates how an integrated WP/DP system would produce a tabular report combined with the manager's remarks. In addition, systems are now available that can insert graphics output on a report along with the data and text.

Integrated Personal-Computer Software The equivalent of integrated mainframe WP/DP on a personal computer is the software that combines spreadsheet, word processing, graphics, data-base management, and communication. Examples are Ability, Symphony, Framework, and Jazz software packages.

Office Decentralization and Productivity

A major incentive for office automation is improved productivity. Information-processing technology serves the cause of productivity in two ways. First, computers perform many of the routine tasks that people used to perform manually. This not only speeds up the work, but also reduces errors in the results. Second, information-processing equipment lets people produce output in greater quantities and of better quality.

Using distributed data processing, many firms are now decentralizing their office operations. Marketing professionals use portable terminals to enter data from remote places. Executives save on travel time by employing "teleconferencing." Technical experts improve their productivity by staying at home and working through remote terminals. This not only saves commuting time, but also helps

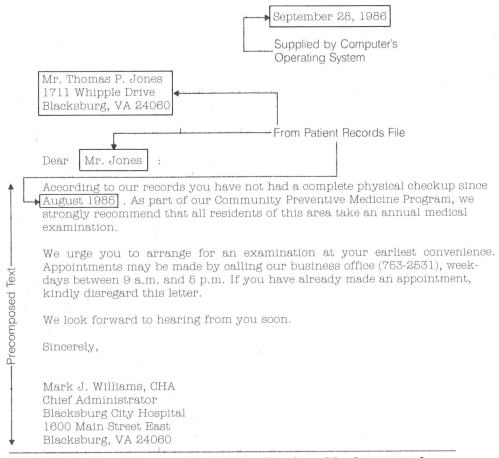

September 28, 1986

Supplied by Computer's Operating System

Mr. Thomas P. Jones
1711 Whipple Drive
Blacksburg, VA 24060

From Patient Records File

Dear Mr. Jones :

According to our records you have not had a complete physical checkup since August 1985 . As part of our Community Preventive Medicine Program, we strongly recommend that all residents of this area take an annual medical examination.

We urge you to arrange for an examination at your earliest convenience. Appointments may be made by calling our business office (753-2531), weekdays between 9 a.m. and 5 p.m. If you have already made an appointment, kindly disregard this letter.

We look forward to hearing from you soon.

Sincerely,

Mark J. Williams, CHA
Chief Administrator
Blacksburg City Hospital
1600 Main Street East
Blacksburg, VA 24060

Precomposed Text

FIGURE 13–27   A Personalized Letter Produced by Integrated Word Processing/Data Processing

The word-processing capabilities of integrated personal-computer packages such as Ability and Symphony can integrate data into a report or letter from a spreadsheet, a data base, or a graph.

them avoid the distractions of the office. In short, office automation reduces the need for direct person-to-person contact, and accelerates the throughput of work.

Unfortunately, this increased productivity is not an unmixed blessing. Many workers do not like to work in isolation. The opportunity to socialize in the work environment is of significant value to them. To take it away would have a negative impact on their morale. The business itself may suffer if employees do not interact on a personal basis. Many new ideas and strategies develop during informal communications between employees. Excessive decentralization of the office would be detrimental to such brainstorming.

Human Factors

Just as the "scientific management" techniques of the early twentieth century caused concern among factory workers, "office automation" is a disturbing phenomenon

Green Forest Products, Inc.
Quarterly Sales Summary ($'000)
Southwest Region
2nd Quarter 1986

Product	% Change	April	% Change	May	% Change	June
White Paper	+1.4%	162	+ 0.62%	163	− 7.89%	150
Hardboard	+0.85%	85	+ 2.35%	87	+ 5.75%	92
Plywood	+1.43%	123	+ 4.88%	129	+ 6.20%	137
Wallpaper	+3.15%	55	−23.64%	42	+21.43%	51

Comments

1) White paper sales dropped in June, mainly owing to school and office vacations.
2) Hardboard and plywood sales were up sharply because of a seasonal rise in construction activity.
3) Wallpaper sales fell drastically during May. The major reason was the low introductory prices of a new competitor, Frisco Paper Company. However, we were able to regain our market share in June, because of aggressive marketing and an increase in Frisco's prices.

FIGURE 13–28 Sales Report Including Both Data and Text

This capability is very useful to most businesses. Executives like to have data reports analyzed and explained through text comments, as shown here.

for many office personnel today. Since the technology is still evolving, there is great uncertainty about its ultimate impact on office life.

Many white-collar workers fear losing their jobs to a machine. These fears are not justified. Although computers do automate many manual functions, they also tend to create new jobs that are more interesting and challenging. What is really needed is a retraining of existing personnel to take over the newly created jobs. Most data-processing installations arrange seminars and hands-on training courses for user department personnel. Many private firms and software vendors provide similar services on a commercial basis.

As more experience is being gained with office machines, the design of computer equipment is being more closely tailored to human needs and comfort. Design engineers are making keyboards and CRT screens to fit the human physique better. These improvements favorably affect the work environment of clerical personnel, who have to use computer terminals for long periods of time.

Some executives are reluctant to use computer terminals because they don't like to type. Light pens, mice, and touch-sensitive screens can help them overcome this "terminal phobia." Letter-quality printing and graphic output are other means of winning over skeptical top managers.

One major obstacle to users' acceptance of a system is poorly designed software. Sometimes a program is written without much regard for whether users can easily interact with it. A good system designer must always keep in mind the technical competence and knowledge level of the end user. Although actual system design depends on the unique requirements of the business, the following guidelines should be considered in order to make the software "user-friendly" or ideally, "user-seductive."

1. Screen messages should be clear and concise, so that a nonprogrammer can understand them. Unnecessary abbreviations must be avoided.
2. Whenever possible, provide complete error messages on-line instead of listing error numbers. The user probably has more important things to do than to search through heavy manuals to find out what error number "X953-E22$G" stands for.
3. Provide on-line help facilities. If a user does not know what to do at any point in the program, the system should display the available options.
4. Use menu-driven systems that allow the user to choose among several options as a way of providing instructions to a computer. Menus are easier to use than a system where users must type in commands.
5. Design input and output formats to coincide with the user's conceptual view of documents.
6. Supply easy-to-use but comprehensive user manuals. These should be written in plain language, not programmer jargon. For instance, a record may simply be called a line or a row, and an attribute, a column. The purpose is to aid the user in operating the system, not to write a formal technical document. A friendly, easy-to-use system is much more likely to be accepted by office personnel than an exacting and intolerant program that does not allow any human error.

Summing Up

☐ In recent years there has been a tendency to disperse data-processing facilities throughout the user organization. As a result, office procedures and work habits are rapidly changing.

☐ A DDP system is crucially dependent on the data communication system used to connect various devices.

☐ Three basic configurations are used in a data communication network:
   1. Computer/peripheral-device communication
   2. Computer-to-computer communication
   3. Communication through a data switch

☐ The flow of information is governed by a set of rules known as the communication protocol. The protocol also determines whether transmission will be asynchronous or synchronous.

☐ Depending on the characteristics of the communication channel, data may be transmitted either one bit at a time or a character at a time. The mode of the terminal and the type of communication channel determines whether data flows in only one direction or in both.

☐ A large number of devices exist to facilitate data communication, using either telephone lines or special digital cables. The most important devices are modems, multiplexors, statistical multiplexors, and front-end processors.

☐ Two of the most important data communication systems are IBM's SNA and AT&T's AIS/Net 1.

☐ Distributed data processing (DDP) offers several advantages, including more efficient CPU time utilization, sometimes lower data communication costs, and direct interaction between users and the computer. Further, the system designer is better able to tailor the system to the company's need.

☐ The disadvantages of DDP include sometimes higher communication costs and equipment incompatibility problems. The most difficult part of implementing a DDP system is obtaining the active support of user personnel.

☐ There are many ways of arranging computers in a distributed system. The most important configurations are star, ring, hybrid, broadcast, tree, and bus.

☐ In a DDP system, software development and maintenance are often distributed among user departments. It is, however, necessary to centralize system software and those application programs which are shared among nodes.

☐ In a distributed data-base environment some of the data are shared among the nodes, whereas some are used only locally. Local data are stored at the appropriate node. Shared data are stored at the node that uses them most, or are replicated and stored at all locations.

☐ Word-processing facilities can enhance office productivity in many ways.

1. Electronic filing systems speed up document storage and retrieval.
2. Text searches can be executed using DBMS.
3. Interoffice communications are improved through the use of electronic mail.

☐ Word processing can be combined with the company's data-processing facilities. This leads to the efficient generation of high-quality output for mailing lists, management reports, and so on.

☐ Distributing the data-processing function allows the decentralization of office facilities in some cases. This may improve productivity because users reduce their travel time and avoid the distractions of a large office.

☐ The reactions of personnel to office automation critically affect the success of a DDP system. The automation of the office can raise questions about job security and the quality of the work environment.

☐ The design of friendly software systems is an important element in selling DDP to user departments. Programs must be written with the user's convenience in mind.

Key Terms

distributed data processing (DDP)
data communication
master-slave relationship
data switch

communication protocol
block format
message envelope
polled

asynchronous transmission
synchronous transmission
data transmission speed
bits per second (bps)
serial transmission
parallel transmission
half-duplex channel
full-duplex channel
simplex channel
modulation
demodulation
modem
multiplexor
statistical multiplexor
data-switching network
front-end processor
system network architecture (SNA)
advanced information system/net 1 (AIS)

local area network (LAN)
star configuration
ring configuration
hybrid configuration
broadcast configuration
tree configuration
bus configuration
distributed data base
shared data
local data
partitioning
replication
word processing
dedicated word processing system
electronic mail
automated office
integrated word processing/data processing (WP/DP)

Self-Quiz

Completion Questions

1. Some terminals know when the computer is talking to them. These are called _____ terminals.
2. When the storage or terminal device is completely under the control of the CPU, this kind of setup is customarily called a _____ relationship.
3. A set of rules governing information flow in a communication system is a _____ .
4. Data transmission speed is measured in _____ .
5. In data transmission, the sound signals are converted to digital form through a _____ process.
6. The computer that manages all routine communications with peripheral devices is known as a _____ .
7. In a _____ configuration, remote computers are connected radially to a central processor.
8. There are two approaches to maintaining that part of the data base which is shared among nodes: _____ and replication.
9. Under the _____ concept, most, if not all, printed documents would be stored electronically rather than in printed form.
10. Under a network configuration often used in personal computer networks, each PC is connected to a single cable, which is called a _____ .

Multiple-Choice Questions

1. Which of the following is not a basic configuration used in a data communication network?
   a. computer/peripheral-device configuration
   b. computer-to-computer communication
   c. computer to front-end processors communication
   d. commmunication through a data switch
2. In data transmission, the bit coding scheme used to represent a byte is typically:
   a. EBCDIC
   b. ASCII
   c. SNA
   d. Hexadecimal
   e. None of the above

3. Which of the following is true of parallel transmission?
   a. It involves the simultaneous transmission of eight bits.
   b. The speed is quoted in bits per second.
   c. It is slower than serial transmission.
   d. Most microcomputers communicate with other computers in this mode.
   e. All of the above are true.

4. Which of the following is not a device used in data communication?
   a. modem
   b. multiplexor
   c. statistical multiplexor
   d. front-end processor
   e. all of the above are used in data communication

5. Data are allowed to be transmitted in only one direction in a:
   a. simplex channel.
   b. dumb channel.
   c. half-duplex channel.
   d. full-duplex channel.

6. Which of the following is not a common configuration used in a DDP system?
   a. star
   b. ring
   c. tree
   d. realtime
   e. bus

7. Duplicate copies of the data base are stored at all locations under:
   a. partitioning
   b. polling
   c. replication
   d. data sharing
   e. none of the above

8. Which of the following is not an advantage of decentralized processing over centralized processing?
   a. reduced data communication costs
   b. improved system reliability
   c. increased employee productivity
   d. increased computer system control
   e. all of the above are advantages

9. The front-end processor is dedicated to perform which of the following function(s)?
   a. polling
   b. synchronization
   c. error checking
   d. two of the above
   e. all of the above

10. Which of the following is not true of office automation?
   a. It enhances office productivity.
   b. Human factors should be considered in implementing office automation.
   c. It will increase informal communications between employees.
   d. Software should be designed to be user-friendly.
   e. All of the above are true.

Answers

Completion
1. intelligent
2. master-slave
3. communication protocol
4. bits per second
5. demodulation
6. front-end processor
7. star
8. partitioning
9. office automation (automated office)
10. bus

Multiple Choice
1. c
2. b
3. a
4. e
5. a
6. d
7. c
8. d
9. e
10. c

A Well-Oiled Machine: PCs Are Helping Tampa's Government Keep Up with Its Booming Growth

By Carolyn J. Mullins and Nicholas C. Mullins

Tampa, Fla., is a Sunbelt boom town. In a state whose population has been growing steadily, Tampa has changed in one generation from a lazy backwater hamlet to the 53rd largest city in the United States.

As Tampa has grown, so has its government. Today it employs 4,000 people, 800 of them professionals. To keep a handle on such massive growth, Tampa Mayor Bob Martinez is turning to IBM PCs as a central part of the city's information-management strategy.

Tampa has used computers—mostly mainframes—for 25 years, for everything from police dispatch to traffic-light control. The city bought its first microcomputer, an Apple, in 1978 for use in traffic engineering. This began a trickle of PCs that soon became a flood.

"[PCs] were popping up like mushrooms after a spring rain," said Curtis Kellogg, who leads Tampa's pilot program in PC integration. "We were smart enough to catch it early."

"The city had many kinds of machines, and they couldn't talk to each other," said MIS Director John McGrath. "We had no central control of acquisition or use."

"The mayor wanted to use new technology but in a controlled way," he added. "He charged me to get control, so in 1982 we began to require departments to identify their needs for automation.

"Between 1982 and 1983, we cut the number of word processing and other equipment vendors so we could provide better support. In 1984, demand for PCs began to grow, and the mayor asked us to study the problem," McGrath explained.

"The mayor didn't want to approve wholesale buying of PCs without positive cost/benefit analysis: Will PCs get sewers built faster? Build roads more cheaply? We wanted either improved productivity without wasted staff time or improved work quality," he explained.

One of the reasons for the influx of PCs was crowding on the IBM 4341 mainframe used for most administrative computing chores.

"Planning uses huge data files and does lots of data manipulation," observed Roger Wehling, director of planning. "But the 4341 and DP staff are so heavily tied up with personnel and other administrative records that work like ours is hard to find time for.

"We'd like to be able to download and work with just the data we need," he explained.

At about the time these problems were being discussed, the budget office asked for authorization to replace its word processor and also to bring in some microcomputers.

"Budget is a fairly small unit, and it's on the same floor as the planning offices and the mayor's staff," McGrath said, "so it would give us a controlled setting to try out PCs.

"We proposed [to use it as] a pilot project to get a comprehensive look at automation."

Pilot Takes Off

The six-month pilot program, which emphasizes learning and development of standards, began this January. Responsibility for planning the project lies mainly with MIS, under the direction of PC Project Leader Curtis Kellogg. The budget for project hardware and software is $105,000.

It is known as the Eighth Floor Project because most pilot PCs are located on the eighth floor of the municipal office building, City Hall Plaza. The pilot program comprises the Revenue and Finance Department (budget and planning areas) as well as executive and senior staff.

Although Mayor Martinez approved the pilot, he will not have a PC on his desk nor will many of his immediate staff. This is because governments, unlike corporations, are political entities with built-in turnover at the top levels and longevity among professional, technical and support personnel. It is these mid- and lower-level employees who

are most intensely involved in the project.

Mike Salmon, senior administrator in Water Resources and Public Works, is typical of these PC boosters. "If I don't stay involved with PCs," he said, "I won't stay current as a manager.

"Right now," he continued, "I have to depend on professional contacts for product data, but that's not systematic, and sometimes the informant is biased.

"Tampa's facilities are very advanced technologically, but we're still making many decisions in a vacuum. There's a lot of public investment out there. All cities could do better work if we could just get pertinent data."

Dedicated word processors were rejected for use in the pilot as expensive, cumbersome or incompetent to combine text with data produced on PCs, and stagnant technologically. IBM PCs were chosen because they offer speed and flexibility without sacrificing communication, integration and access.

Game Plan

PCs let users do a variety of tasks on the same machine. Also many PC word processors outperform dedicated systems and would foster standardization. "With any equipment you have questions," Kellogg said, "but at least with IBM you have the same questions."

The project calls for 27 IBM PCs or compatibles to be linked in a network. (By March 1, 25 had been installed and two ATs were still on order.) Compatibles to be used in the network had to have a keyboard similar to the IBM PCs. They also

had to be able to accept IBM-compatible plug-in boards, run all or most IBM PC programs, read and write directly to IBM floppy disks and run PC-DOS or MS-DOS. (All the PCs in place so far are IBM.)

Most of the PCs have two drives, 256K bytes of random-access memory, color monitors and adapter boards as required for networking and printing.

Users will have 70M bytes of central fixed-disk space available, with ATs and XTs acting as file servers. Telephone communication will link the PC network with the mainframe. This is badly needed, because City Hall Plaza and the Library Annex (where MIS has its offices) are nearly a mile apart. The other eight municipal buildings are at similar or greater distances. All PCs will be able to provide terminal emulation (up to eight at a time).

Network plans call for a broadband configuration because, in the future, the city plans to link not only computers but institutional cable TV channels and telephone lines as well. The IBM Network has been chosen because it supports broadband and will "probably become standard," according to Kellogg. If it isn't released soon, however, he said he will go with either Novell or the 3M LAN/PC.

Since the budget and planning departments need to use huge (7M byte and up) files that could take as much as seven hours per week to download from the mainframe via telephone lines, the city is seeking ways to download in the computing center directly to floppies or a removable hard disk, then carry the medium to the network. Products suitable for this task, including mainframe tape readers and Bernoulli boxes, are still being evaluated.

Dot-matrix and inkjet printers were chosen for draft printing, but two of the word-processing stations have laser printers. This exception was made because laser printers are quieter and their greater speed offsets their greater price.

Physical security of PCs will be handled mainly by keeping equipment behind locked doors after work. Confidentiality of data isn't a concern because Florida's "sunshine law" requires that all except police databases be open for public scrutiny.

Integrity of data is also important. Kellogg is looking at software to protect data and procedures to prevent catastrophes such as a reformatted hard disk. Steps also have been taken to prevent damage from power fluctuation in what McGrath refers to as "the lightning capital of the world." Maintenance contracts won't be used. "For the amount of failure experienced, the cost is prohibitive," he explained.

Who Needs Software?

To discover specific software needs for the pilot project, Janett Martin, management improvement officer, coordinated the collection of work samples (letters, documents, slides and so on), administered a questionnaire and interviewed 47 executive, professional and support staff about the amount of time they spent on 22 activities, ranging from preparing presentations and writing reports to telephoning and keeping their calendars.

She discovered that the budget and planning staff needed spreadsheet and time-management software, including an easy-to-learn calendar system that could schedule group meetings for at least 20 people. Planning also needed project-management programs for scheduling and tracking tasks such as budget preparation, and it needed mapping software to monitor and display demographic characteristics graphically.

Most staff needed word-processing and communications software that could transfer data between workstations and send documents to the publications department for typesetting. For reports, they needed graphics and slide production software.

The pilot project's initial strategy for meeting software needs was to supply a list of basic tools, such as *1-2-3*, and let users move to more sophisticated programs as they need them. To ensure easy access to programs by all users, McGrath and Kellogg have emphasized the use of packaged applications software and have discouraged programming languages. Standardization is also important because the city has a limited training and support staff.

1-2-3 was chosen for spreadsheets only. "Integrated programs are dinosaurs," Kellogg said. "One function may be excellent, but the rest can nearly always be done better with dedicated software." *Symphony*, for instance, was rejected as having inadequate word processing and requiring too much memory.

Samna III was chosen for its ease of learning and range of functions. Kellogg is still waiting for a network version, however, and he remains

concerned about its extremely slow reformatting.

Three calendar programs still being tested are *Calendar Management, Shoebox* and *Calendar Plus*. Two project managers being evaluated are Microsoft *Project* and *Visi-Schedule. EasyTrieve* will enable staff to manipulate mainframe data. Statistics will continue to be done on the mainframe.

The project planners confronted the potential problem of software piracy from the beginning. "We're very conscious of needing to protect software vendors' rights," McGrath said. Software copying will be partly prevented at purchase time. The MIS Information Center staff will check to ensure that adequate software is purchased to perform the tasks specified in the needs statement. In addition, a library of software will be available for users to test and use for occasional tasks.

Getting Involved

The city's strategy has been to involve users at every step and let them use technology as a learning tool. One purchasing requirement is that users take time to test a program before they order so they know they're getting what they need.

Users have undertaken to evaluate programs related to their work. As a result of such involvement, testing time has been largely absorbed by departments, not left to MIS. Another result has been an enthusiastic response to PCs. People "really went for them," Kellogg said.

As a result of the pilot's initial software needs survey, Martin, the management improvement officer, and Kellogg have recommended general instruction for executives and more detailed instruction for professional, technical and support staff.

For the long run, Kellogg is thinking seriously about purchasing all or most training from outside vendors and combining that with support for self-training. In the meantime, the MIS Information Center is providing some training, with the cost being charged against departmental operating expenses. Patrick Miller has been hired to handle training and support, and is currently teaching *1-2-3*.

In addition to software, training will cover good computer practices such as proper backup and retrieval and disk handling.

"Basically, we're decentralizing responsibility for backup and routine maintenance of equipment," Kellogg said.

For training and walk-in use, the MIS center will install four PCs. Several more on rolling workstations may be installed at City Hall.

For novices especially, McGrath hopes to require commitment to a week of training as one purchasing requirement. "If you don't already know how to use the equipment, you probably won't take the time once it arrives," he said. "I'd like buyers committed to a full week of training when their PCs arrive so they get up to productive speed fast. This should pay off in fewer questions later on."

Reaching a Verdict

PCs are expected to increase productivity and improve work quality. On budget preparation, the anticipated savings relate to report production (currently done mainly with pencil, paper and calculator), presentations and publications. (In-house graphics will save the cost and time of sending work out.)

Faster revision of reports, better and faster graphics and better access to mainframe data will improve planning. Senior staff expect to benefit from better graphics.

Other anticipated benefits are improved intra- and interoffice communication, better use of time and greater job satisfaction as PCs reduce tedious rote chores.

Assessing the actual impact of the pilot program presents a challenge. Martin, who collected the initial work samples to establish needs, plans to "use the pilot project to establish standards."

Although her follow-up plans aren't yet firm, toward the end of the six-month project she will probably collect work samples again to compare with earlier samples and to assess work quality from both the initiator's and the recipient's viewpoints. She plans to measure machine use by observing users and asking them to keep logs.

Martin expects her final report to cover cost/benefit analysis, before-and-after work patterns, minimum standards for future workstations,

such as desk size and structure, and employees' attitudes.

She is looking particularly for changes in work patterns: Which tasks are no longer done? Which are done differently? What new activities have been made possible by PCs? McGrath hopes also to learn which employees really need PCs on their desks and which might share workstations.

The second phase of PC integration, which will build on the pilot project, will continue to emphasize learning and expand office automation via networked PCs to 10 buildings throughout the city. Estimates of the total number of PCs at the end of the second phase range from 400 on up, depending on their price.

"Eventually," said McGrath, "we'd like to replace terminals with PCs and make them available to anyone in city government who could benefit from one."

One fact is clear: The beginning of Phase Two won't wait for the end of Phase One. The stream of enthusiasm is rising as pilot project users attract attention from other departments. And even though the project is officially experimental, the users' attitudes say you would have a tough time taking their PCs away.

DISCUSSION QUESTIONS

1. How can PCs build roads more cheaply?

2. Why would Tampa want a network that uses broadband communication channels?

3. Tampa appears to be standardizing on IBM hardware. What are the advantages and disadvantages of such a move?

4. Kellogg believes that "integrated programs are dinosaurs." Why would he hold such an opinion? Is the acceptance of integrated programs by users likely to increase in the future? What are the advantages of integrated programs?

5. What do you think the strong and weak points of Tampa's personal computer implementation strategy are?

PART FOUR

Information Systems, Management, Society, and You

Chapter 14

Managing the Information-System Resource

PROLOGUE

Computer information systems are often large and complex. With the advent of the mini and personal computers, computer systems are being dispersed to even far-flung locations. Computer technologies such as electronic mail, decision-support systems, personal computers, application development by users, computer networks, computer-assisted design, and computer-assisted manufacturing are causing monumental changes in the conduct of business activities. Those managers who successfully manage this technology will be winners in the competitive business arena. In this chapter we will see how information systems are managed.

Introduction

Management of information systems has seen significant changes in recent years. In the 1960s and 1970s, information-system managers gradually increased their power and influence within most organizations. Typically, they moved from managerial positions within a department, such as accounting, to full-fledged vice presidents of information systems. These managers were looked upon as experts in information processing and, in effect, they held the keys to the computer resource. In recent years, however, the role of the information-system manager has been changing. With users directly purchasing hardware and either purchasing or creating software, many people see the role of the information-system manager changing to that of a consultant, advisor, and coordinator. Of course we will continue to have centralized computer facilities, especially for large batch runs and large data bases that support many users concurrently. Certainly, the challenge of administering centralized data bases and communication networks with distributed computing means that information-system managers will continue to play a crucial role in the management of business organizations. In this chapter, we will discuss the structure of the management information system (MIS) function and then we will look at managing system development, system maintenance, and data-processing operations. Finally, we will cover physical security of computer operations.

Structure of a MIS Function

The Organizational Location of MIS

Typically the MIS function is located in one of two areas in an organization. The chief MIS executive may be reporting to the vice president and controller, as shown in Figure 14–1, or he or she may be vice president of management information systems and be reporting directly to the president, as depicted in Figure 14–2. There are advantages and disadvantages of both cases. The **controller,** being the chief accounting officer in a corporation, is looked upon as the primary provider of financial management information. In addition, functions in the controller's area such as payroll, accounts payable, and accounts receivable were often the first computerized applications. Therefore, the information systems function often originated and matured within the controller's organization. The primary disadvantage of the chief MIS executive reporting to the controller is that the computer resource may be dominated and used primarily to solve problems within the controller's area, and therefore other functions are neglected. Marketing, engineering, and production applications of the computer are of equal or more importance than many of the applications in the accounting area. The primary advantage of the chief MIS executive reporting to the controller is that accounting is an information-oriented discipline and accountants are well trained in the area of control. These

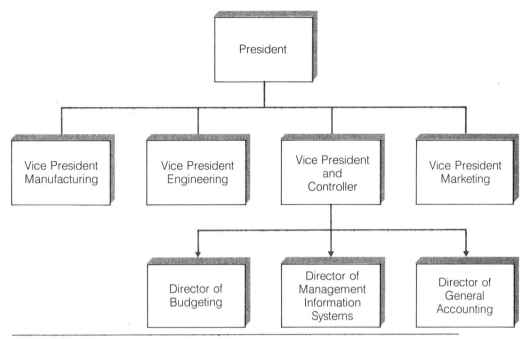

FIGURE 14-1   Chief MIS Executive Reporting to the VP/Controller

This organizational location for the chief MIS executive often occurs in smaller and medium-sized companies or in firms that are just beginning to install computer information systems.

skills of accountants may produce a computer system that is much more controlled and auditable.

Many of the larger, more mature MIS organizations are separate and have a chief MIS executive who is a vice president and reports directly to the president, as illustrated in Figure 14-2. This location for the MIS function helps to ensure that each of the areas receives unbiased attention from the MIS department. Today, with computers penetrating many areas, it is particularly important that the chief MIS executive be a member of the unbiased vice-presidential level of management.

The Internal Structure of MIS

The organization of the MIS function itself varies from firm to firm. Figure 14-3 depicts a typical MIS organization in a large firm. In smaller firms, many of these functions would be consolidated or would not exist. For example, in a small firm all software may be purchased, so there would be no need for the systems and programming department and the systems software function.

At the manager level shown in Figure 14-3, there are six distinct functions that should be carried out within the MIS or arranged to be done through outside sources. A specific MIS organization chart may look quite different. However, the major functions that an MIS organization is concerned with are shown in the figure.

The **information center** is responsible for coordinating and supporting application development by users. The staff are technical experts on software such as

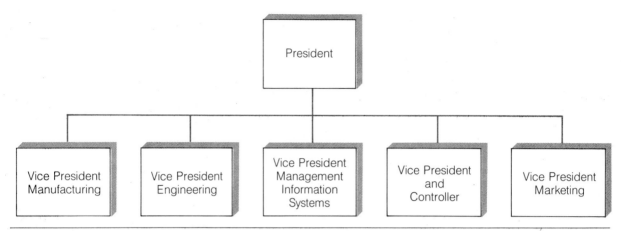

FIGURE 14–2 Chief MIS Executive Reporting to the President

In the larger firms and where a MIS has been developed to its full potential, the vice president of the MIS usually reports to the president.

PERT and CPM
These two scheduling methods use graphic networks to depict the activities and time that are necessary to complete a project. The minimum amount of time in which a project can be completed is computed by these methods. They also highlight those activities whose completion are most critical to the successful completion of the project.

Lotus 1-2-3 and Focus. They act as consultants and assist the user in application development without programming. Since the personal computer is an important tool in this effort, the coordination of personal computing is often carried out by the information center. As discussed in chapter 2, the personal computer has brought several challenges. As you will recall, one of them is managing the personal computer. The responsibilities of the personal-computer coordination group are listed in Figure 14–4.

The **systems software department** installs and maintains system software such as operating systems and data-base management systems. The staff are technical and very highly skilled programmers who rarely deal directly with users.

Application software is developed by (or selected and purchased with the help of) the **systems and programming department.** The personnel in this department interact heavily with users as they develop user applications.

The **technical support staff** is in charge of maintaining hardware and establishing data-processing standards. **Standards** are very much like procedures for the data-processing function. They include such things as program, data, and application naming conventions; procedures for maintaining the integrity of communication systems; and standards that govern the content of user procedure manuals.

The **data-processing operations department** manages the day-to-day operations of the computer hardware. It also monitors the processing of computer jobs and assists where human intervention, such as mounting tapes, is required.

A function that is relatively new in most larger MIS organizations is that of **database administration (DBA).** The DBA department is responsible for coordinating the data base, which includes providing for data security.

The MIS steering committee is a most important part of the MIS function. A **steering committee** is made up of high-level managers from each department within the business, including marketing, accounting, MIS, manufacturing, and so on. Its purpose is to guide the overall direction of the MIS. For example, the steering committee decides the priorities for implementing specific application systems. Much of the high-level planning for the MIS is either performed or approved by the steering committee. Ideally, the steering committee provides the broad perspectives and guidance necessary to assure that the MIS supports the objectives of the business as a whole.

Managing System Development

Perhaps the most important aspect of managing the system development effort is the **system development methodology** used. In previous chapters we discussed the structured approach to system development, system prototyping, and application development by users. It is important that a structured methodology, blended with system prototyping and application development by users, be used to develop new systems.

The Cancun Corporation recently acquired a fourth-generation software package that allows end users to quickly write their own programs to produce ad-hoc management reports from the corporation's data base. The package was so successful that users began implementing their own systems without the aid of the system development department. The head of that department began to worry that users might be unaware of the ramifications of not specifying new systems according to an established system development methodology. She also thought that information stored in the various systems might be redundant. What might be a solution for controlling the applications developed by users, or should they even be controlled?

Thinking About Information Systems 14–1

Another aspect of managing system development is the process by which development efforts are actually controlled. Most system development organizations use a project management approach. Under the **project management approach** each application development of significant size is assigned to a project development team. This team is usually headed by a senior system analyst or sometimes a user department manager who has system development experience. Sufficient resources in the form of programmers, system analysts, hardware, and software, are assigned to the team to complete the project.

Each project is assigned its own financial budget and time schedule. The financial budget performance is tracked by periodic reports that compare actual expenditures to budgets. Schedule performance is managed and controlled through one of several tools, such as **program evaluation and review technique (*PERT*), critical path management (*CPM*),** and ***Gantt charts.*** There are several good project-manager software packages available for personal computers, such as the Harvard Total Project Manager and the Primavera Project Planner. The Primavera package can schedule up to 10,000 tasks, assign resources to tasks, track costs and produce reports, Gantt charts, and PERT charts. It is important that computer-based

Gantt chart
A graph where output activities are plotted as bars on a time scale. This chart was developed by Henry L. Gantt in 1917. Gantt charts indicate who is assigned responsibility for completing certain tasks, the estimated or planned dates on which tasks are to be started and completed, and the actual dates on which particular tasks have been started and completed.

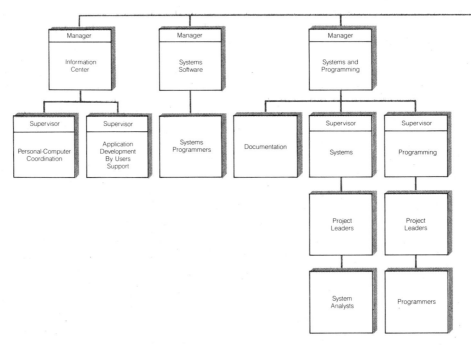

FIGURE 14–3 Large MIS Organization

As computer information systems have become more important to organizations, the MIS organization itself has grown in size and influence. The area that is growing most rapidly is the information center, with its personal-computer coordination and support of application development by users.

tools such as these be used in project management. They allow the project manager to quickly see the impact of schedule and resource changes.

Gantt charts are the most conceptually simple of the scheduling techniques. Figure 14–5 illustrates a typical Gantt chart. Planned times for the various tasks are represented by solid bars; the actual times are shown by cross-hatched bars. The chart shows that for project A, task A–1 was started on time and completed

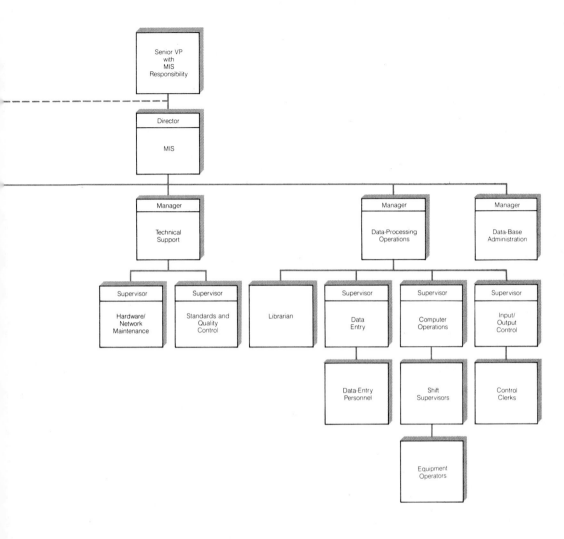

FIGURE 14–3 (continued)

before schedule. Task A–2 was started before it was scheduled and has not yet been completed, although more than the planned time has elapsed. A Gantt chart can be a valuable measurement tool in a complex project. It aids in scheduling and coordinating and provides a visual means of evaluating progress. Since preparing a Gantt chart does not require extensive effort or data, the potential benefits generally exceed the cost.

- Standardizing hardware purchases
- Standardizing software purchases
- Providing PC access to mainframe data bases
- Preventing the redundant development of software
- Preventing the redundant creation and storage of data
- Assuring that data stored on personal computers are secure
- Providing personal-computer training
- Maintaining the firm's in-house "personal computer store" where users can try out a wide variety of PC hardware and software

FIGURE 14–4 Responsibilities of the Personal-Computer Coordination Group

Personal-computer coordination groups originated in the early 1980s. Information processing by PCs and application development by users are expected to represent 75 percent of the total information processing of firms by the end of this decade.

Managing System Operation

System Maintenance

system maintenance
The correction of errors discovered in programs and the changing of the programs to satisfy modified user requirements or conditions. Changes in programs are often also necessary when new hardware is introduced.

System maintenance has become a challenge for many MIS organizations. In many cases it is consuming 70 to 80 percent of the systems and programming resources. Such situations leave little resources for developing new systems. Methods for decreasing the cost of system maintenance are of paramount concern to MIS managers.

As with managing system development, the adoption of a structured methodology will greatly enhance the ability to manage system maintenance. Efficient and effective system maintenance requires that personnel understand the program to be modified. Structured methodologies produce programs that are easier to understand. Programming personnel must be able to effect the change by changing the program statements in a confined and isolated area of the program. If a change

---

PC USER TIP   **Should You Buy a Maintenance Contract?**

There are two main options for maintaining your personal computer in operating condition. First, you could choose a maintenance contract. For an annual fee you can get your computer repaired whenever it malfunctions. The cost of the contract varies, but generally it is about 10 percent of the purchase price of the computer. This type of service is basically an insurance contract.

The other option is to "fix it when it breaks." The owner waits until the computer malfunctions and then pays for the necessary repairs at that time. The IBM PC and many of its compatible counterparts have proven so durable that the cost of maintenance contracts has steadily fallen. A maintenance contract is particularly hard to justify in an organization that has a lot of personal computers. Such organizations could practice self-insurance at a very minimal risk.

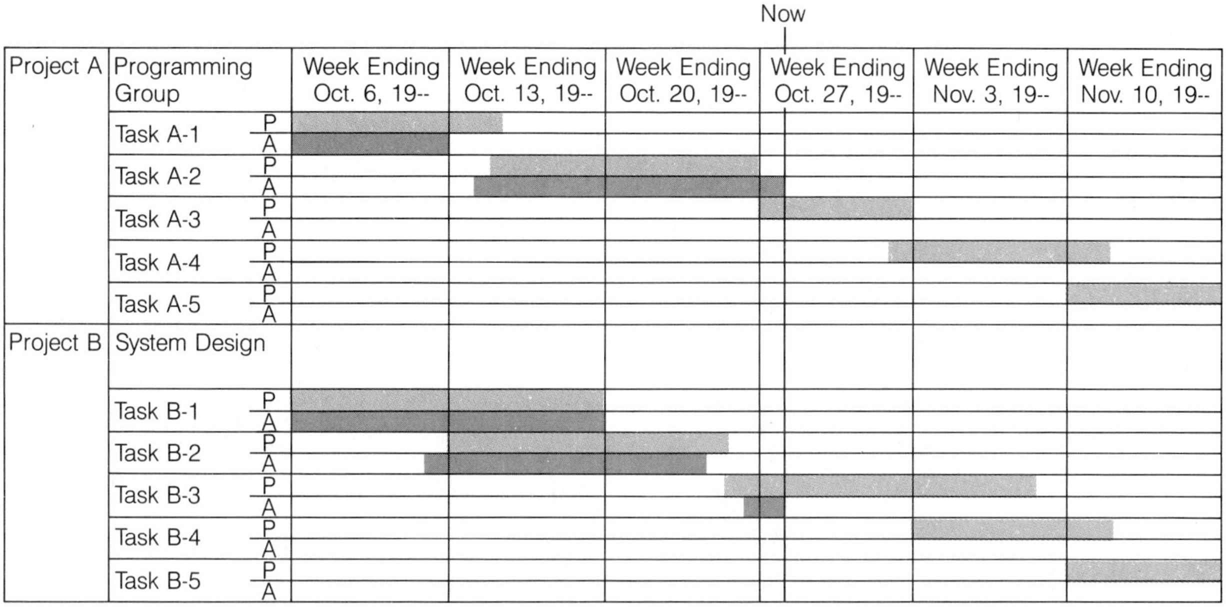
Now
Project A
Programming Group
Week Ending Oct. 6, 19--
Week Ending Oct. 13, 19--
Week Ending Oct. 20, 19--
Week Ending Oct. 27, 19--
Week Ending Nov. 3, 19--
Week Ending Nov. 10, 19--
Task A-1
Task A-2
Task A-3
Task A-4
Task A-5
Project B
System Design
Task B-1
Task B-2
Task B-3
Task B-4
Task B-5
P
A

FIGURE 14–5 Gantt Chart

Gantt charts are easily understood tools that allow managers to visualize the schedule for a project. Inexpensive personal-computer plotters produce these charts quickly.

requires modification in many different areas of the program or system, then system maintenance becomes an almost impossible task. As we learned in previous chapters, structured methodologies produce programs that are modular. Each of these modules is as independent and self-contained as practical. Therefore, changes are likely to affect only a restricted area of one module.

Active data dictionaries also simplify system maintenance by restricting both the number and locations of program changes. An **active data dictionary** allows data to be defined in one location and this definition is used by all programs that process those data. The programs use the data simply by referring to data names like ZIP CODE for an address zip code. The physical format of the information such as its type (character or numeric) and its length must be known to each program that uses it. So instead of the physical-format definition of the same data item being buried in many different programs, it is stored in one place, the active data dictionary. The term *active* is used since each program "actively" uses the data dictionary for definitions.

To understand how an active data dictionary aids in system maintenance, consider the recent U.S. Postal System change from a five-digit to a nine-digit zip code. Many firms have literally hundreds of programs that use zip codes. To search through all these programs, locate where the format of zip code is defined, and make the change from five to nine digits would be a monumental task. With an active data dictionary, only one change in the dictionary is needed. None of the programs that use the data dictionary has to be manually changed. Each of them may have to be recompiled, but this is an automated process.

Jim Brown was a cost accountant for the Southern Pines paper-processing plant and made extensive use of a popular spreadsheet program. He had created several programs for analyzing overhead accounts and everyone in the cost-accounting department of the firm used the programs. The policy of the firm was for the cost-accounting manager to review the logic of all spreadsheet programs before the spreadsheets were used for everyday reporting. One day a vice president of the company approached Jim and asked him to make a change in a spreadsheet program format. Jim made the change without approval, and accidentally changed a cost-calculation formula. The vice president used the erroneous information in a company bid, and the bid was lost because the cost estimate was too high. The following week, the cost-accounting manager noticed the faulty spreadsheet calculation and subsequently both Jim and the vice president were fired. What controls should have been in place that would possibly have prevented this fiasco?

Requests for changes in programs originate with the users. A formalized **change authorization form** should be used. On this form the user identifies the program and/or system to be changed and outlines the changes desired. An important part of this form is the authorization signatures, which must be obtained prior to changing the programs. Authorizing signatures typically include user management, the systems and programming manager, and sometimes the data-processing steering committee. Figure 14–6 shows a change authorization form.

The actual changes to the programs must be well managed and controlled. Control of program changes is discussed in depth in Module E. After the changes have been made, the system must be thoroughly tested prior to implementation. The same set of tests that were used when the system was developed should be run before implementing the changed system.

Data-Processing Operations

Managing data-processing operations is much like managing any production shop within an organization. Management must be concerned with maintaining sufficient capacity to process the computer jobs. Users of the resource should be charged for the resources they use. Personnel must be hired, managed, and sometimes dismissed and the machines must be maintained in operable condition.

bottleneck
The component of a computer system that is limiting the amount of work it can perform.

software monitor
A program that monitors the usage and performance of various computer system devices.

Processing capacity may be limited by any number of factors, including primary-storage size, secondary-storage size, CPU power, number of terminals, and so on. Any of these can become the **bottleneck** that limits the capacity of the computer system. Data-processing management must monitor these resources and determine whether one is likely to become a bottleneck in the future. Additional resources can usually be obtained at a reasonable price if the potential bottleneck is identified promptly. **Software monitors** such as IBM's systems management facility (SMF) are very valuable in determining the levels of use of various system resources. For example, we could determine the percentage of time various terminals are being used and the time of day they are being used. We could also determine whether the CPU is running close to its maximum capacity at any given point during the day. Trends of system resource utilization enable us to project when various resources will be used at their capacity, and therefore when expansion should be planned.

```
REQUEST FOR SYSTEM MODIFICATION
_____

User Name:

Department:

Telephone No.:
_____

System Name:

Module(s) to be changed (if known):


Please describe the change(s) desired and explain the reasons thereof:
```

```
          Signature          Approved        Rejected        Comments


_____
      Requestor
                            [        ]      [        ]

_____
     Dept. Manager          _____
                            [        ]      [        ]

_____
   MIS Liaison Officer      _____
                            [        ]      [        ]

_____
   Manager, Systems         _____
   and Programming
```

FIGURE 14–6   Change Requests in an Authorization Form

The authorization and documentation of changes made to systems are crucial to well-maintained systems. Without such documentation, fraudulent changes could easily occur or the system could be changed to the point where no one really knows what the system does.

Hardware monitors are sometimes used to detect bottlenecks and determine utilization levels for various devices. Figure 14–7 shows the output of a hardware monitor used to control resource usage.

One of the best ways to ensure that the computer is used efficiently is to charge users for their use of the various computer resources, including CPU time, disk space, tapes, and printing. Under a **user-billing system,** the data-processing operations department is set up as a service center for the rest of the firm. Its services are available to anyone in the firm who is wiling to pay for them. Rates should be similar to outside rates, such as what a service bureau would charge.

hardware monitor
A device that monitors usage and performance of various computer system devices.

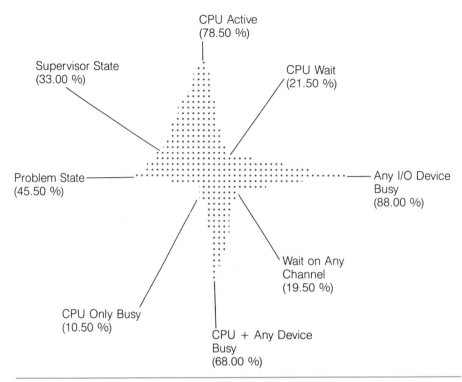

FIGURE 14–7 Sample Hardware-Monitoring Report

This graph displays eight variables being monitored. Each variable has a value of 0 to 100 percent. The length of the asterisks away from the center of the graph illustrates the magnitude of each variable. For example, the CPU is active 78.5 percent of the time, whereas the CPU only is busy 10.5 percent of the time. Notice that the "CPU active" and "CPU wait" add up to 100 percent. The "CPU only busy" and the "CPU plus any device busy" add up to the 78.5 percent time that the CPU is active. When the CPU is active it is either executing the operating system (which is called the supervisor) or it is executing a particular application program called a problem. Therefore, the total of the supervisor state and the problem state is 78.5 percent, the same as the "CPU active" percent.

Physical Security

In many computer systems today, the MIS resource is a crucial asset. Even a temporary loss of this resource through fire, sabotage, or other disaster can be very costly. You may learn the importance of contingency planning with backup of files firsthand someday. After you have worked for several days on an electronic spreadsheet, program, or word-processing file you may accidentally lose or erase it. One such experience usually teaches the importance of planning for disasters. Imagine the cost to a large business of failure to plan for disasters. Imagine if it lost all its files in a fire and no backups had been made!

File backup is a technique for recovering from a disaster after it occurs. In this chapter we examine physical security that helps prevent disasters from occurring.

Gallery 8
The "Blue-Collar" Computer
Robots and Industrial
Automation

When some people hear the word *robot,* the first thing that comes to mind is either R2-D2 from the movie *Star Wars* or the big metal creature waving his arms and yelling "Warning! Warning!" on "Lost in Space" reruns. But, the computer-based robots of today are quite different. They are used to automate tasks that are dangerous, difficult, or tedious for humans.

1 Robots have proved to be useful to the automobile manufacturing industry. This assembly line of robots welds automotive bodies. Robots also paint the finished body parts before the actual assembly of the auto. The robotic machines are more efficient and consistent than humans and less costly than human labor.

1

2

3

4

2 In an automobile factory, this robot moves the passenger-side doors to a conveyer belt leading to the assembly division.

3 Robots can lift objects that humans would not be able to move efficiently. This robot moves cast blades and vanes for jet aircraft turbine engines.

4 This robot is programmed to move heavy plates used in making personal computer boards.

5 This robot loads paper from a conveyor belt to a skid in a paper plant.

6 A light trace illustrates the path that a robot arm is programmed to follow. Robots can be programmed to perform many different tasks.

7

8

7 This robot is used by Whirlpool Corporation to scan microwave ovens for defective parts and radiation. This would be difficult and dangerous for humans.

8 Computer-automated systems are often used in the production of silicon chips, which requires precision and cleanliness. This system produces masks used in the making of computer chips.

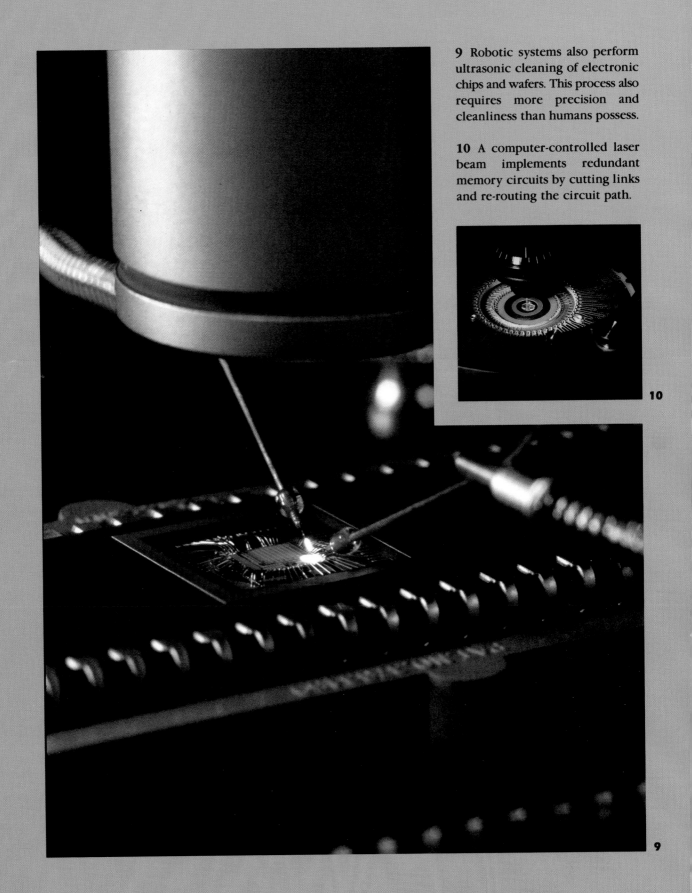

9 Robotic systems also perform ultrasonic cleaning of electronic chips and wafers. This process also requires more precision and cleanliness than humans possess.

10 A computer-controlled laser beam implements redundant memory circuits by cutting links and re-routing the circuit path.

10

9

11 An engineer completes the installation of a robotic system on an automated assembly line for a new computer display.

12 Robotic micropositioners capable of precision to twenty millionths of an inch are used to manufacture circuit boards.

11

12

13

16

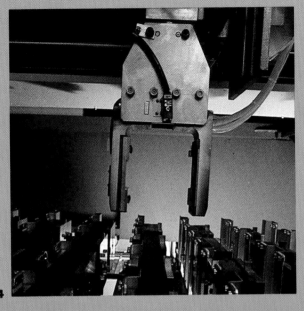

14

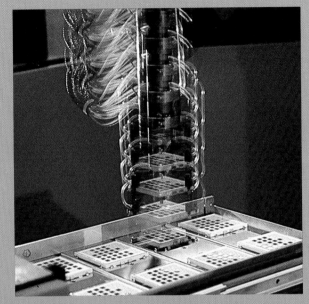

15

17

13 This robotic system installs chips into circuit boards used in computers.

14 Motor assemblies used in disk storage units are tested automatically with this robotic system.

15 The quality of logic circuitry is tested by this computer-operated system.

16 A keyboard is put through its paces by a robotic tester in this production plant.

17 Odetics is working to develop a robot that can walk efficiently. Getting machines to walk has been a problem for automated developers for many years. This time-exposed shot shows their Functionoid model in walking action.

18 The Functionoid, like almost all robots, is computer operated. This photo illustrates the complex mechanical parts within the robot.

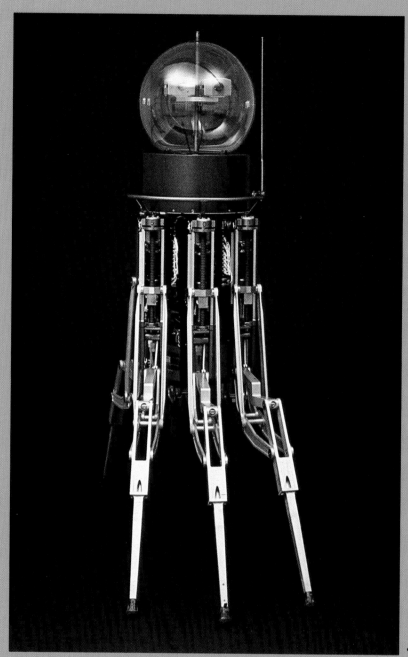

18

There are many different disk-operating systems available for the personal computer. Some of these systems are very similar, and in that respect, some personal computers can run a number of operating systems. Some operating systems, however, are very different, and even those which are similar have subtle differences. Some of the more popular disk-operating systems are IBM DOS, MS-DOS, COMPAQ DOS, TRS-DOS, APPLE DOS, and CP/M.

IBM DOS, MS-DOS, and COMPAQ DOS are similar operating systems used for IBM and IBM-compatible computers. Almost all of the commands in these three operating systems are identical. The largest difference among them is in the read-only memory of the computers. Programs such as the BASIC interpreter that make calls to the ROM BIOS, are not directly compatible from machine to machine even though programs written in BASIC are identical. BASIC programs written to run on one of these computers will run on the others. IBM DOS, MS-DOS, and COMPAQ DOS all use the same types of diskettes and format them in the same way. This allows you to use the same software (on the same diskette) in any of the machines.

TRS-DOS, APPLE DOS, and CP/M, on the other hand, are not compatible with the three just mentioned, nor are they compatible with each other. They do not use the same type of diskettes, and the formatting scheme is very different. In these cases, software cannot be easily moved from one computer to another. The vendors can code the same software to run on a number of machines, but this software will be offered on different diskettes for each machine.

We will cover five areas: entry controls, sabotage controls, fire controls, natural and environmental disaster controls, and power controls.

Entry Control   A well-designed **entry control** system will control entry to the computer facility. Only operations personnel are allowed to enter the computer facility itself. Manually delivered programs and data are passed through a window of the computer room. Of course, most programs and data today are transmitted electronically to and from the computer. Entry control is usually done through a locked door to the computer room. The doors are opened through various means, such as plastic cards with magnetic strips (similar to credit cards) or a combination of both the plastic card and the entering of a memorized entry code.

Plastic cards and keys can be lost or misplaced, though. Providing 100 percent positive identification has been difficult. There have been a wide variety of techniques and machines tested to provide positive identification of personnel entering computer facilities. One machine examines the pattern of the person's fingerprints. You cannot misplace your fingerprints! But it has been found that a photocopy of a person's fingerprints will trick the machine into unlocking the door. Another technique works in a similar way, except you have to kiss the machine! Lip prints uniquely identify a person. But aside from its obvious drawbacks, a photocopy of one's lip prints would also mislead this machine. A third device shines light into a person's eyes and makes an identification based on the patterns within his or her eyeballs! Although the technique is harmless, I doubt that employees would accept it. Eventually we will have machines that are highly reliable in identifying a particular person.

Sabotage Control   Physical sabotage of the hardware, programs, and data is prevented to a large extent through passwords and by physical-entry controls of the computer facility itself. Firms that have specifically designed a secure computer facility usually construct the computer room to bomb-proof specifications. It is interesting to note that when computers were first used in the 1950s and 1960s, it was common to have large glass windows in the walls of the computer center so that a firm could show off its computer facilities. A saboteur could have easily tossed a bomb through these windows.

Fire Control   The most likely physical threat to a computer facility is fire. The best security procedure is to store backup copies of data and programs at another location and to arrange for emergency use of alternative computer hardware. In addition, many computer centers use a fire-suppression gas known as halon. The halon is released by fire and smoke detection systems and is effective in extinguishing fires. The primary disadvantage of halon is its cost. If the gas is accidentally released, a firm may have to pay several thousand dollars just to replace it. Less expensive gases exist, but are impractical because they are poisonous. Halon is nonpoisonous.

Natural and Environmental Disaster Control   Firms need to consider natural and environmental hazards when choosing the site for a computer room. These include floods, hurricanes, and bursting pipes. Water can destroy the sensitive electronic equipment of a computer. Fire-control water sprinklers on floors above the computer room are an environmental hazard that is sometimes overlooked. Water leaking down through pipe holes and other crevices onto computer equipment, tapes, and disks can be very damaging. For this reason, the floor above the computer room should be thoroughly sealed to prevent water leakage.

Power Control   Large computer systems should have uninterruptible and controlled power supplies. Plugging such computer systems directly into electrical lines is not a good idea. Remember that if the power goes off, even momentarily, the data and programs stored in semiconductor primary storage are lost because semiconductor storage is volatile. Furthermore, power spikes (increases in the current voltage) can heavily damage a computer system. Such power spikes are quite often caused by electrical thunderstorms. Some computer centers guard against this type of power spike by shutting down computer operations during such storms. Often, however, this is not a viable alternative.

Many organizations use power-supply systems. These systems consist of batteries and backup generators. The batteries are continuously being charged by the incoming electrical service, and the computer draws its power from the batteries. Thereby the computer is insulated by the batteries from the electrical service lines, and power spikes are prevented. If there is a power outage, the batteries will be sufficient for a short duration. Longer-lasting power outages are covered by the backup generator system.

As organizations become more dependent on computer systems, managing information-system resources becomes more critical. Many of you will in varying degrees be involved in this management. In the next two chapters we will see how computers impact society and you.

Summing Up

☐ In recent years the role of the information-system manager has changed as users have become more actively involved in data processing.

☐ The MIS function may be located within the controller's organization, where the controller is considered to be the primary provider of information. On the other hand, many organizations treat information systems as a separate function with a vice president who reports directly to the president.

☐ It is important that a structured methodology is used for system development. Usually system development is carried out using the project management approach for project control.

☐ With a structured methodology, program maintenance becomes a much easier task. All changes must be authorized and properly documented in order to prevent confusion and chaos.

☐ Active data dictionaries substantially reduce the program changes that must be made when the format of data changes.

☐ Operations should be constantly monitored in order to detect bottlenecks and inefficiencies. Users should be billed to ensure efficient use of resources.

☐ Physical security of the EDP system is a major responsibility of system management. Procedures should be implemented for both the prevention of disasters and recovery from disasters such as fires and floods.

Key Terms

controller
information center
systems software department
systems and programming department
technical support staff
standards
data-processing operations department
data-base administration (DBA)
steering committee
system development methodology
project management approach
program evaluation and review techniques (PERT)
critical path management (CPM)

Gantt charts
system maintenance
active data dictionary
change authorization form
bottleneck
software monitors
hardware monitors
user-billing system
entry control
sabotage control
fire control
disaster control
power control

Self-Quiz

Completion Questions

1. _____ is responsible for coordinating the data base, including providing for data security.
2. Schedule performance is managed through project schedule-performance tools such as PERT, CPM, or _____ .
3. The _____ is responsible for coordinating and supporting application development by users.

4. System _____ involves correcting errors discovered in programs and changing the programs to satisfy modified user requirements or conditions.
5. The _____ simplifies system maintenance by restricting both the number and location of program changes.
6. _____ are very valuable in determining the levels of use of various system resources.
7. _____ and encoding are used as safeguards to prevent unauthorized access to data and programs.
8. One of the best ways to assure that the computer resource is used efficiently is to employ a _____ system.
9. _____ are used to detect bottlenecks and to determine utilization levels for various devices.
10. Large computer systems should have uninterruptible and controlled power supplies mainly because semi-conductor storage is _____ .

Multiple-Choice Questions

1. Typically the chief MIS executive does *not* report to the:
   a. controller
   b. treasurer
   c. vice president
   d. president
2. The function of the systems and programming department is:
   a. maintenance of system software
   b. coordination of the data base
   c. supporting application development by users
   d. development or purchase of application software
   e. none of the above
3. The coordination of personal computing is often carried out by the:
   a. information center
   b. data-base administrator
   c. data-processing operations department
   d. technical support staff
   e. systems and programming department
4. Which of the following is *not* true of the Gantt chart?

a. It is the most conceptually simple of the scheduling techniques.
b. It provides a visual means for evaluating progress.
c. Its usefulness is limited to a simple project.
d. It does not require extensive efforts or data to prepare.
e. All of the above are true.
5. The authorization signatures for the change authorization form typically include the following except:
   a. user management
   b. systems and programming manager
   c. DP steering committee
   d. chief executive officer
6. In most cases, the first applications computerized would be:
   a. engineering
   b. accounting
   c. production
   d. marketing
7. Processing capacity may be limited by the following factors except:
   a. primary-storage size
   b. secondary-storage size
   c. CPU power
   d. number of terminals
   e. all of the above can limit processing capacity
8. Which of the following is the best procedure to protect against fire?
   a. To install fire-control water sprinklers in the computer room
   b. To use a power-supply system.
   c. To use a fire-suppression gas known as halon.
   d. To store backup copies of data and programs offsite.
   e. None of the above.
9. Which of the following is true concerning physical security of computer systems?
   a. The only way to prevent power spikes during electrical thunderstorms is to shut down computer operations.
   b. Power spikes cannot cause loss of data stored in semiconductor primary storage.
   c. If the power goes off momentarily, the data

stored on magnetic-tape secondary storage are lost.

d. The most likely physical threat to a computer facility is fire.

e. None of the above.

10. Which of the following is not a tool used to manage and control schedule performance?

a. CAD

b. PERT

c. CPM

d. Gantt Chart

e. All of the above are used.

Answers

Completion	Multiple Choice
1. Data-base administration (DBA)	1. b
2. Gantt charts	2. d
3. information center	3. a
4. maintenance	4. c
5. active data dictionary	5. d
6. Software monitors	6. b
7. Passwords	7. e
8. user-billing	8. d
9. Hardware monitors	9. d
10. volatile	10. a

Chapter 15

Information Systems and Society

CHAPTER OUTLINE

PROLOGUE

What has produced the most change in our society during this century? The automobile? The airplane? No, not the computer. In fact, the answer is certainly none of these. People produce change. Humans, like you and I, are behind the major developments in new hardware and software. The founders of Apple Computing were two college students in their early twenties. They revolutionized the computer industry. People also apply computers. If necessary, they can change the impact of computers on society. But first we must know what those impacts are likely to be.

Introduction

Our assumption throughout this book has been that the application of computers will enhance both our work and our personal lives. Most would agree with this assessment, although some would say that these enhancements have been slow in coming and that the computer has not yet produced the revolution that it promised. Quite certainly though, any revolution, even one that enhances our lives, produces changes. Changes have both positive and negative consequences. Dislocations occur and the change must be adjusted for. In this chapter, we will look at what impacts computer information systems may have on society and some of the challenges that these systems pose for society. We will first examine the potential impact of computer information systems, then we will explore the areas of automation and artificial intelligence. Next, we will consider the privacy questions associated with computerized information and the very significant effects that personal computers are having on our lives. Finally, we will explore the problems of international data transfers and the very serious problem of computer crime.

The Potential Impact of Computer Information Systems

The Information Revolution

Information is wealth. Although some would say that the computer has caused information to be wealth, information has always been wealth. For example, if you have information about where an interstate highway is to be built before others know the location, purchasing land in that area is almost certain to increase your wealth. The computer is simply a new source of significant amounts of information. Those who can afford to buy a computer and have the skills to use it will be better able to acquire information than those who cannot use the technology. Will the computer revolution produce two new classes in our society, the information-rich and the information-poor?

There are proposals to produce electronic newspapers. You would simply connect your personal computer through regular telephone lines to the newspaper's large computer. You would have the ability to retrieve any news item. In addition, you could retrieve articles from past newspapers—perhaps up to several years old—through key words. You could even select only those news articles which are of interest. In effect, you would be making your own newspaper! For example, you could simply enter the name of your favorite sports team and retrieve all articles about the team, if that's all you wanted to read. But in reading newspapers we acquire a broad spectrum of information. Would the ability to select our reading material tend to make our knowledge base more narrow?

Already there are **information services** such as *The Source* and *Dow Jones News Retrieval* which allow you to retrieve a wide variety of information. Figure

FIGURE 15–1 Using the Dialog Data Base

Dialog subscribers pay from $45 to $130 per connect hour while using the data base.

15–1 shows the Dialog data base which may be accessed with a remote terminal. It contains information on a large number of subjects, ranging from accounting to zoology. These types of services allow you to retrieve stock-market quotes, order airline tickets, and order various merchandise. With such a service, you could save money (and thereby increase your wealth) by having the computer search for the least expensive airline fare when you plan to travel.

Some people suggest that we establish an information-assistance program, similar to current fuel-assistance programs for the disadvantaged in our society. Otherwise, those people will become further disadvantaged because they can't access the information that personal and business computers provide. Should we have an information-assistance program? To provide such a plan, of course, is a political decision. However, this illustrates the degree of impact that some feel the computer revolution may have on society.

If we reach the point where we do a significant amount of our shopping through electronic means, we work at home on a personal computer connected to an office computer, and we receive most of our entertainment as well as our religious and educational instruction through cable TV, some very significant questions arise. Can we all retreat into our electronic cottages and still function as a society? Possibly not. Many would argue that a democratic society requires frequent **face-to-face contact** among its citizens. Further, an electronic society provides very great threats to privacy, as we will discuss later in the chapter. These threats decrease our personal freedom and increase the ability of others to manipulate and monitor our personal lives. The potential is there, as we will see.

Working at Home

Would you really want to work for a company where you did all of your work at home through electronic means? Off the top of your head, you might answer with an enthusiastic yes. No doubt there would be many advantages to such an arrangement. You could live almost anywhere you wanted to and spend more time with your family. But working where you have direct contact with other people also has significant advantages. The social interaction and exchange of ideas, triumphs, and so on among co-workers is a significant contributor to the mental well-being of most individuals. Consider the fact that most surveys show that the most common way to meet a marriage partner is at work.

In any case, you may in the very near future have a chance to decide whether to work at home or at a traditional workplace. If a significant number of people decide to work at home, there will be noticeable impacts on society. However, it is a good guess that most individuals will quickly become bored with working at home and will prefer at least a portion of their work to be in a workplace.

Control Problems

To illustrate another potential problem that computers and the emerging communication technology can cause, let's consider the **electronic shopping** systems such as QUBE. The **QUBE system** has been tested in Columbus, Ohio. It is essentially a combination of a cable TV system and computer technology that allows viewers of any TV program to respond electronically to such things as surveys and orders for merchandise. Some have said such a system could produce instant responses to surveys, allow shopping by electronic mail, and even allow instant electronic democracy where voters could respond to an issue through their QUBE terminal systems. Such proposals are questionable, however. For example, how do we know who is pushing those buttons out there in a survey? Is it an adult or a three-year-old child who just happens to be watching the program and likes to push buttons?

Picture our presidential candidates stating their positions in a TV debate. After the debate is over, we push our buttons and elect the president! This, of course, is absurd. The control problems would be horrendous. Consider the case of a straight-as-an-arrow married couple who subscribe to the QUBE system. They began receiving sexually explicit materials through the mail. To their amazement they found that their four-year-old child had actually ordered the materials by pushing the appropriate button while watching a cable TV program. Since the parents were the cable TV subscriber, the materials were shipped in their name, and they, of course, ended up on the mailing lists of places dealing with such materials. What if your five-year-old turned on your personal computer and started transferring your bank-account funds? Certainly, many of these problems have solutions, but as yet the problems still exist.

Displacement of Human Beings

In the early days of computers, in the 1950s, many people were concerned that computers were going to displace large numbers of people from their jobs, particularly those in clerical occupations. They worried that as clerical functions became automated, there would be no need for people with clerical skills. This did not occur to the extent predicted. In general, more jobs were created than were lost, although the new jobs often call for different skills, such as programming and system analysis.

The Fairfax Company is in the process of developing a new computer-based accounting system. This new system will result in the loss of ten clerical positions in the accounting department. Overall, though, the company will not experience a reduction in personnel owing to the new system. New positions will be created both in system development and accounting. However, these new positions require different and a higher level of skills than the current clerical personnel have. With three of the employees, retraining for the new positions is feasible. The other seven are long-time employees of the company and most will reach retirement age in approximately ten years. Management has decided that retraining these employees would not be feasible. Furthermore, even if it were feasible it is doubtful that any of them would want to go through the retraining. If you were the manager making the decision about the future of these seven employees, what would you do?

Thinking About Information Systems 15–1

Automation

In general, managements use computers to generate more information. They do not use them to generate the same amount of information as before and thereby reduce the labor force. However, this is beginning to change. Computers are being used to control robots that are quickly replacing human workers on assembly lines in industry (see Figure 15–2). There are now factories in Japan where the whole

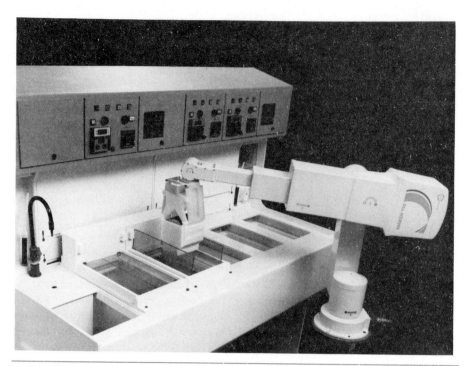

FIGURE 15–2   A Robot

production line is automated on certain shifts. The only human beings at the factory are security guards. The robots even have the capability of repairing themselves whenever they break down. For example, when a drill bit breaks, the machine simply replaces it from a bin of replacement bits. These factories do require maintenance personnel during the day shift.

Office automation is likely to reduce the need for typists, clerks, and other office personnel. Prior to personal computers, computers were primarily used for high-volume tasks. Many of the day-to-day tasks were still done manually. Personal computers are rapidly changing this.

If automation, through computers, does displace significant numbers of workers from their jobs, will society support the retraining of these workers? Will there be enough alternative jobs? It seems there will. There is always something to be done, regardless of how many tasks are performed by computers and machines. And usually these remaining jobs and new jobs are more interesting. The computer often does the dull and routine jobs such as assembly-line and clerical work. The bottom line, though, is that anytime we can replace a human being with a machine at a cheaper cost, society as a whole benefits because the standard of living rises.

Artificial Intelligence

Artificial intelligence is a computer application where the computer makes decisions or judgments that appear to require human intuition, reasoning, and intelligence. One type of artificial intelligence that is beginning to see practical use is the expert system. **Expert systems** attempt to provide the same judgmental advice that human experts such as doctors provide. In the areas where they have been successful, these systems can equal and often surpass the best judgments made by humans. For example, they have been applied to the diagnosis of illnesses. Given the symptoms of the patient, the expert system may ask more questions, request additional laboratory tests, and eventually arrive at a diagnosis that is as good as or better than the best doctors in very limited areas of medicine. One approach to developing these expert systems is to model the thought processes that a physician goes through when he or she makes a diagnosis. This not only results in an artificial intelligence system, but also provides very interesting insights into how humans reason and make judgments.

Will these systems ever replace experts such as doctors, lawyers, engineers, accountants, and information-systems consultants? Certainly some of these expert systems may make better judgments than the least competent people in these areas, but most professionals will use the systems as tools. A medical diagnosis expert system could assist doctors greatly in narrowing down the possibilities of the diagnosis for a particular patient.

Will the professionals accept these systems, which may seem to diminish the experts' importance to society? I think they will. Most true professionals are always looking for ways to improve their productivity and the quality of the service they provide to their clients.

One final danger of these expert systems is that people may think that the systems are infallible since they are computer-based. Nothing can be further from the truth. These systems are models of the human judgment process, and many human judgment imperfections will also be a part of expert systems. Professionals, such as doctors, must continue to know enough about their field to recognize when the computer-based expert system is providing answers or diagnoses that are unreasonable.

Computers and Individual Privacy

Potential Problems

If I were asked by a totalitarian regime what would be the best way to provide almost total surveillance over the country's population, I would suggest establishing a pervasive **electronic funds transfer system (EFTS)** and eliminating paper, coin, and check money as much as possible. I would also recommend installing two-way cable TV systems with centrally located computers as a part of the cable system, and perhaps a computer in each home. You may be wondering what this has to do with surveillance. In fact, it appears to be the direction we are headed in our society. Think for a minute—what actions can you perform in our society, or in any modern society, without spending money? You cannot travel, you cannot buy food, and you cannot rent a motel room. You can do very little without spending money. If every time you spent money, you gave the merchant, the airline, or the gas station a plastic card, your transaction could be recorded through a communication system to a central data base. Your funds would be electronically transferred from your account to the merchant's account. The computer could very easily also record the time of the transaction, the day, where you are, and other surveillance information. In fact, we could keep a record of all of your movements and all your purchases, and through the cable TV system we could know what programs you are watching on TV and when you watch them. You can see that we could very easily obtain a great deal of information about almost all your actions and know approximately where you are at any point in time.

Now you may be thinking that such a situation could never occur in this country. Certainly the technology is here for this system and we are moving rapidly toward these capabilities as electronic funds transfer, two-way cable systems, home electronic shopping, and other systems are implemented. Consider one actual case. In Columbus, Ohio where the QUBE system was installed, a local movie-theater owner was taken to court over an allegedly pornographic movie that was shown at his theater. Currently, the test that the Supreme Court applies as to whether a movie is pornographic or not is whether or not it goes beyond the moral values and standards of the community in which it is being shown. In this case, by coincidence the same movie had recently been shown on the local QUBE system. So the theater owner's defense lawyer summoned the records from QUBE to determine who in the community watched the allegedly pornographic movie on the cable network. This was a brilliant move by the lawyer. If a significant number of people watched the movie, including supposedly outstanding citizens, then the movie did not go beyond the community's moral values. But do you want judges, lawyers, and jurors reviewing the records of what you have watched on cable TV? Is this an invasion of your privacy? Fortunately, the judge in this case had the good judgment to keep all names confidential. The case against the theater owner was dismissed.

Privacy Legislation

From the examples just given, you can probably see some of the problems related to privacy. Through two-way cable systems, computers could constantly monitor our financial transactions and the entertainment and goods we purchase. In addition, governmental agencies and private businesses maintain large data bases with information that concerns private individuals. In the 1970s there was substantial legislation passed that addresses the privacy issues of these data bases.

In the nongovernmental or private area, the major legislation was the **Fair Credit Reporting Act** of 1970. Many lending agencies and credit bureaus maintain records concerning your credit worthiness and your financial transactions. The act helps you ensure that this information is correct. First, you have a right to access the data stored about you, and second, you have a right to challenge the data in order to correct any inaccuracies. You should know, however, that the institutions still have the right to maintain the information concerning you—it just has to be correct, and they must allow you access to it.

Perhaps the greatest effect of privacy legislation has been on the operations of the federal government. There are four acts in this area. The first, the **Freedom**

of Information Act of 1970, allows individuals to access any information about them that is stored in a federal government data base or file.

The **Educational Privacy Act** applies to educational institutions that are funded by the federal government. This applies to almost all educational institutions because almost all receive at least some federal funds. The act states that a student's educational records may be accessed by both the student and his or her parents, and that information can be collected only by certain authorized individuals and distributed to only certain authorized individuals and agencies. The rights provided for under this act may be waived by the student.

The **Privacy Act of 1974** applies only to federal government agencies and provides that:

1. Information collected for one purpose cannot be used for other purposes unless the individual gives consent.
2. There must be no secret collections of data.
3. Individuals must have a right to access and correct erroneous data.

Agencies collecting information are responsible for assuring its accuracy and protecting against its misuse.

The **Right to Financial Privacy Act** of 1978 addresses a threat to privacy that exists within financial institutions. Currently every check and credit-card transaction that you make is recorded on microfilm by your bank and stored for five years. Prior to the Right to Financial Privacy Act, governmental investigative bodies such as the IRS and FBI could access these microfilm records and examine them without your knowledge. As we have seen, a great deal of information can be collected from these financial transaction records. The act provides that if an investigative body wishes to access your personal financial data stored at a financial institution, you must be notified. This notification provides you with an opportunity to challenge the access in court.

The federal privacy legislation does not apply to most state institutions, with the exception of state educational systems. So, many states have passed their own privacy legislation. The provisions of the state laws are usually similar to the provisions of the federal Privacy Act of 1974.

Carolyn Short is a programmer for the Appalachian Tire Company. The main language used in the computer information system is COBOL. To help reduce the application backlog, the computer center management recently began purchasing personal computers for some user departments. It also started thinking about buying some application productivity tools for prototyping and managing system development. Management assured Carolyn that COBOL would still be used as the main language, and that she would have plenty of work to do. Carolyn did become worried, though, that her current skills in COBOL would no longer be needed because in the future, COBOL might be replaced by a high-level language that nonprogrammers could easily use. Is Carolyn justified in her worries that she could be replaced?

Thinking About Information Systems 15–2

Personal Computers

We have explored personal computers in other sections of this book. However, it would be useful to examine here some of the impacts they are likely to have on society. Earlier in this chapter we indicated that access to personal-computer technology may differentiate between those who can use information to produce wealth and those who cannot.

One of the more significant questions is, will we lose many of our current mental skills as the computer performs these tasks for us? For example, most of the math that engineers learn in college and use in their day-to-day work and certainly all basic mathematical functions can be performed by the computer. Children are using the computer to complete their mathematics homework in elementary and secondary schools. Will this dependence on the computer cause us to lose our math skills?

Perhaps a more significant question is, does it make any difference if we lose a skill that we can purchase for a few hundred dollars or less? Certainly as we have advanced over the centuries, we have lost many skills that were absolutely necessary to our survival in earlier times. There are very few people, if any, today who have the necessary skills to survive through hunting and food gathering in a stone-age fashion, without the use of modern firearms. This question of loss of skills is certainly an important controversy. Some say it won't make any difference; others are very concerned about the loss of mental skills.

On a more positive note, there is no question that personal computers are going to make our lives more productive and take away some of the more boring tasks that we have to currently perform. These electronic tools are going to become much more **user-friendly.** In fact, many people find them very easy to use.

International Data Transfers

Most countries now restrict the movement of secret, classified data outside of their country. But what about nonclassified data? Multinational firms have offices and factories in many different countries. On their large computer networks, data can

---

PC USER TIP   License Agreements

One way that software vendors are fighting back at illegal copying is through the use of license agreements. Most software sold today contains a license agreement which states that the software, manual and all, are the property of the software company and are only being leased to the purchaser. This method of distribution gives vendors more rights and control over the software's use. It is the license agreement that usually requires a software package be used on only one computer. When you purchase software, make sure that you read the license agreement and can live with the terms in it. Opening of the package that contains the diskettes is usually considered acceptance of the terms of the license agreement.

very quickly move all the way around the world. Some countries, particularly European ones, have been concerned about the movement of data out of their nations. This concern has brought about legislation that restricts the international flow of data from some countries.

On what basis can a country justify such legislation? Remember, earlier in the chapter we argued that information is wealth. Many countries currently restrict the transfer of wealth or funds outside their borders. There are, of course, several examples of valuable information such as engineering design data, or financial and economic data. Customer lists can be very valuable from a marketing standpoint, or a country may simply want to protect its citizens from unsolicited mail-order campaigns that originate outside its borders.

However, restrictions on **international data transfers** are a threat to the free movement of goods and ideas among countries. They would also hamper a multinational corporation's ability to function smoothly. Most international economists would agree that such consequences would diminish international economic growth, particularly the growth of a country that severely restricts international data transfers.

Computer Crime Cases

Another very important area of the computer's impact on society is **computer crime.** Several sensational computer crimes have been uncovered. Most experts, however, maintain that the computer crime discovered thus far is only the tip of the iceberg; most of it remains hidden. As we discuss in the module on control of computer information systems, a computer system that is not well controlled provides almost unlimited opportunities for a person wanting to steal funds or goods and conceal the theft. The amount of money taken in an average armed robbery is very small compared with the amounts taken through computer theft. Often those who perpetuate a computer crime are not prosecuted when they are

Midland Bank, a medium-sized bank in a Virginia city, has recently discovered that an employee has used the computer to embezzle $75,000 from the bank. The bank's management has decided to handle the case in the following manner. It will confront the employee with the evidence it has concerning embezzlement. If the employee will return to the bank a substantial portion of the $75,000, it will agree to dismiss the employee without calling in law enforcement officers and the case will be closed as far as the bank is concerned. It will also agree that the dismissal will be handled like a normal resignation and that the bank will give the employee favorable recommendations for any new job that he might pursue. The bank's primary rationale for this approach is that it cannot afford the adverse publicity that would ensue if the embezzlement were publicized in the newspaper. Public questions over the security of deposits might cause the bank to lose customers. Evaluate the bank's approach.

Thinking About Information Systems 15–3

caught. Managers sometimes feel that the organization would be embarrassed if the public learned of the crime. Perhaps the public would lose confidence in the firm's ability to function effectively.

One of the more interesting aspects of computer crime is the fact that almost none of the crimes have been uncovered by auditors. Certified public accountants maintain that it is not a part of their responsibility in an audit to uncover crime since to do so would require procedures that are prohibitively expensive. However, most of the public feels that the detection of fraud is a part of the auditor's responsibility. Somehow this inconsistency must be resolved. As auditors become more competent in computer technology and use that technology as an audit tool, we might see more computer crime uncovered by auditors. Let's look at three cases.

Equity Funding

The management of Equity Funding Life Insurance Company used the computer to perpetrate a major fraud against investors and creditors. The company generated bogus insurance policies with a total face value of over two billion dollars. These policies were then sold to reinsurers. Computer programs were rigged so that the auditors could not easily access the files of the nonexistent customers. The fraud was finally exposed when a former employee disclosed it, and the stockholders lost enormous amounts of money.

Pacific Bell

In this case, a teenager retrieved passwords, user manuals, and other confidential documents from the trash cans outside the phone company's office. He then proceeded to steal equipment from supply centers. Using his knowledge of the company's computer system and a remote terminal, he would alter accounting records to show the theft as a bona fide use of equipment. The fraud was not discovered until an accomplice turned himself in.

Wells Fargo

Two employees of the Wells Fargo Bank collaborated with an account-holder to make fraudulent deposits to his account. Using the computerized interbranch settlement system, the bank employees would make an offsetting entry to another branch's account. This entry would be rolled over every ten days so that no actual payment was demanded from the other branch. The criminals withdrew $21.3 million before the fraud was discovered, which happened when they made an improper entry.

Summing Up

☐ Information is wealth, and computers assist us in obtaining this wealth. Those who do not possess knowledge about the computer might end up being poor because they lack the information necessary to compete with others.

- Working at home with a remote terminal might seem like an interesting option. It could, however, lead to boredom and social isolation.
- Although automation does take away jobs temporarily, in the long run it creates more jobs. Moreover, it helps to raise the society's standard of living.
- Artificial intelligence aids experts in making better-informed decisions in areas such as medicine and engineering. These systems, however, do not replace human intelligence; rather they complement it with the computer's immense memory and fast speed.
- The computer can potentially be used to monitor most of our actions, thus robbing us of privacy. Recognizing this threat to our basic freedom, Congress has enacted several acts in recent years to protect the privacy of citizens.
- The advent of personal computers could cause us to lose some of our basic skills. On the other hand, the personal computer will make life much more interesting by performing many of our routine chores for us.
- Some countries are concerned about transborder flows of data, and have imposed certain restrictions on them. This could hamper world economic growth by restricting the free movement of information among countries.
- Computer crime is a growing threat to society. The average take in a computer fraud is many times greater than in a traditional robbery. Unfortunately, auditors have had little success in detecting computer fraud so far.

Key Terms

information services
face-to-face contact
electronic shopping
QUBE system
artificial intelligence
expert systems
electronic funds transfer system (EFTS)
Fair Credit Reporting Act

Freedom of Information Act
Educational Privacy Act
Privacy Act of 1974
Right to Financial Privacy Act
user-friendly
international data transfers
computer crime

Self-Quiz

Completion Questions

1. _____ is an application of the computer where the computer makes decisions or judgments that appear to require human intuition, reasoning, and intelligence.
2. _____ is and always has been wealth, and computers assist us in obtaining this wealth.
3. Working at home might seem like an interesting option. However, _____ contact with other co-workers does have advantages.
4. _____ attempt to provide the same judgmental advice that human experts such as doctors provide.

5. The computer can potentially be used to monitor most of our actions, thus robbing us of _____ .

6. In the nongovernmental or private area, the primary piece of privacy legislation was the _____ of 1970.

7. The _____ of 1978 addresses a threat to privacy that exists within financial institutions.

8. QUBE is an example of _____ systems.

9. The Privacy Act of 1974 applies only to _____ .

10. The _____ applies to educational institutions that receive funds from the federal government.

Multiple-Choice Questions

1. Under the Fair Credit Reporting Act, you have the right:
   a. to challenge the data about you in order to correct any inaccuracies.
   b. to stop institutions from maintaining the data concerning you.
   c. to access the data stored about you.
   d. two of the above.
   e. all three of the above.

2. Which of the following is (are) not available currently?
   a. electronic funds transfer system
   b. electronic newspaper
   c. home electronic shopping system
   d. two-way cable system
   e. all of the above are available

3. The advent of personal computers:
   a. could cause us to lose some of our basic skills.
   b. will make our lives more productive.
   c. will take away some of the boring tasks that we have to perform.
   d. two of the above.
   e. all three of the above.

4. If an investigative body such as the FBI plans to access your personal financial data stored by a financial institution, it:
   a. must notify you.
   b. must have your consent.
   c. must have consent from both you and the financial institution.

   d. can access the data without restrictions.
   e. none of the above.

5. Which of the following computer crime cases was (were) uncovered by auditors?
   a. Equity Funding
   b. Pacific Bell
   c. Wells Fargo
   d. all of the above
   e. none of the above

6. Which of the following is most responsible for the inability of auditors to uncover computer crimes?
   a. The auditor's lack of knowledge in computer technology.
   b. The prohibitively expensive audit procedures needed to detect computer frauds.
   c. The relatively small average take of computer frauds.
   d. The client's concern that the public will learn of the crime.

7. Which of the following is not a requirement of the Privacy Act of 1970?
   a. Information collected for one purpose cannot be used for other purposes unless the individual gives consent.
   b. Individuals must have a right to access data.
   c. Individuals must have a right to correct erroneous data.
   d. There must be no secret collections of data.
   e. All of the above are requirements of the act.

8. Which of the following could have prevented the Pacific Bell computer crime?
   a. The programmers should not have direct access to data files.
   b. Higher-level personnel should be required to take vacations.
   c. The access to system documentation should be controlled.
   d. None of the above.

9. Which of the following is (are) true of an artificial intelligence system?
   a. It is a computer application where the computer makes decisions or judgments.
   b. It is infallible since it is computer-based.
   c. Ultimately, it is expected to replace professionals such as doctors.

d. Two of the above.

e. All three of the above.

10. Which of the following is most likely to occur in the near future?

a. Most workers will choose working at home, so the traditional workplace will disappear.

b. The political issue of establishing an information-assistance program will be raised.

c. The presidential election will be done by pushing buttons at home.

d. Automation will reduce job opportunities, thus resulting in a lower standard of living.

e. all of the above

Answers

Completion

1. Artificial intelligence
2. Information
3. face-to-face
4. Expert systems
5. privacy
6. Fair Credit Reporting Act
7. Right to Financial Privacy Act
8. electronic shopping
9. federal government agencies
10. Educational Privacy Act

Multiple Choice

1. d
2. b
3. e
4. a
5. e
6. b
7. e
8. c
9. a
10. b

Chapter 16

Information Systems and You

CHAPTER OUTLINE

PROLOGUE

Susan has tentatively decided that she would like to pursue a career in computer information systems. She feels that computers are going to become increasingly important in the future. Being practical, she agrees with the advice that it is easier to ride a horse in the direction in which it is traveling than to make it go in a different direction. Thus, she plans to tie her career to the growing field of computer information systems. But she has a nagging doubt. You see, Susan is really a "people person." She likes dealing with people and she is afraid that computer careers are technology- and machine-oriented. Are there careers for people-oriented individuals, like Susan, in computer information systems?

Introduction

Most of us realize that computer information systems have had and will continue to have a significant impact on our lives. Many experts agree that this impact is just beginning. Computers will be even more pervasive and useful in the future. In this chapter we will first examine the effect of computers on professional careers, then we will explore the various information-system careers available. We will also look at the several professional associations and certification programs associated with information systems. Finally, we will discuss two suggested models for information-system education.

The Effect of Computers on Professional Careers

There are very few careers, if any, that will not be affected by computers. Business professionals are relying very heavily on computers for their record keeping and information needs. Certainly those who know how to use computer technology effectively will be at a competitive advantage. As we discussed in the previous chapter, artificial intelligence or expert systems will even affect the most prestigious of careers such as medicine, law, and accounting. These and other careers are based on information or expert knowledge. Computer systems may be able to provide much of this expert knowledge more effectively and at a lower cost.

Most business professionals will find that computers will relieve them of many of the boring, time-consuming, and repetitive details of their jobs. This will leave the more exciting, challenging, and interesting aspects of a professional career for people to master. You will probably be much more productive in your career than your predecessors. But regardless of how sophisticated computer systems become, there will always be areas of knowledge and action that require human discretion.

Many experts have said that we are entering the **information age** because of computer information systems. A greater percentage of the work force will be employed as **information workers.** Large amounts of information will be almost instantly available to decision makers. It is important that they not only understand the information technology but also the decision models, such as economic-order quantity, linear programming, and others on which computer information systems rely. A decision maker must be able to decide whether the information supplied by the computer or the action that the computer recommends is reasonable. As business professionals, we cannot simply turn the decision making over to the computer without understanding what is going on. So, in summary, the computer will provide us with a great deal of information, but we must still understand the underlying processes. Otherwise, the actual intelligence behind these systems, the human mind, will lose control. We must continue to exercise creative thinking and control. The computer is simply a very important tool that must be used effectively if professionals want to maintain their competitive advantage.

Information-System Careers

The largest impact of the computer revolution will be on information-system careers. The bureau of labor statistics has predicted that the number of jobs for all information-system professionals will increase by approximately 84 percent during the 1980s. The increases in specific fields are as follows:

system analysts—an increase of 119 percent

programmers—an increase of 102 percent

computer operators—an increase of 116 percent

computer service technicians—an increase of 154 percent

The number of information-system specialists recruited is expected to be greater than any other profession.

The primary reason for this increase is the declining cost of hardware and therefore the increase in the number of computers. Once businesses and other organizations acquire computers, they want them to perform specific jobs. This takes software which in turn usually requires programmers and system analysts. Someone must also operate the computer and service it.

This forecasted large increase in jobs in the information-system area does not mean these jobs are recession-proof. In the midst of the recession of 1982, the job market dried up for entry-level programmers without experience. There was an oversupply of these people. At the same time, the market was still very good for programmers who had three to four years of experience.

Figure 16–1 illustrates the relationships among the main careers in information systems. Let's look at some of these positions.

Campbell Manufacturing Company is a large, diversified manufacturer of industrial and consumer products located in the northeast. Campbell is considering a policy of encouraging personnel in user departments to transfer to the MIS department for a minimum period of two years, and encouraging employees in the MIS department to transfer to user-type jobs in marketing, finance, personnel, et cetera, also for a minimum of two years. Campbell's management feels that this cross-training will be very useful in the future, especially as users begin to develop applications themselves. Do you think this is a good policy? Would you be willing to make such a transfer if you were an employee?

Thinking About Information Systems 16–1

Programmer

As we have discussed in previous chapters, there are two types of **programmers:** application programmers and system programmers. System programmers write and maintain system software such as operating systems, compilers, utilities, and data-base management systems. These individuals usually have a degree in com-

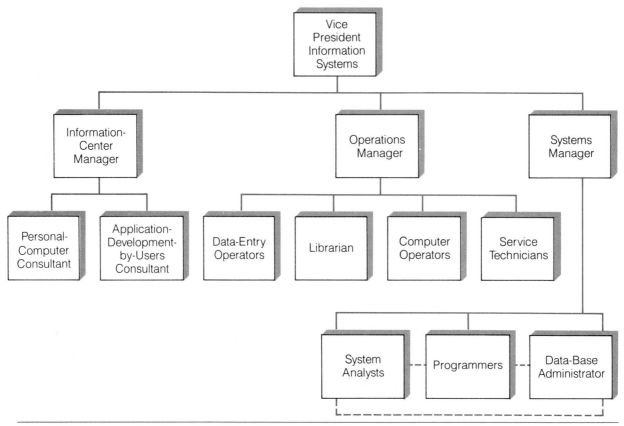

FIGURE 16–1   The Information-System Department

College graduates entering the information system field usually start in the information center or the system department. Both types of consultants within the information center are currently high-visibility positions with a lot of exposure to different user applications.

puter science. They quite often work for computer manufacturers and software development firms. Most large computer systems require a few system programmers, whereas most medium-sized and smaller ones do not employ a full-time system programmer.

Most jobs in programming are for application programmers. These people write computer programs that perform jobs specified by the user, such as inventory control, accounts receivable, accounts payable, airline reservations, marketing analysis, and personnel information systems.

It is possible to obtain a job as an application programmer without a four-year college degree. Individuals who obtain their programming education in technical schools and community colleges quite often become application programmers. Many of them, however, have college degrees in computer science, information systems, mathematics, or a host of other areas. Most employers prefer that application programmers not only have training in the computer area, but also have education or experience in their application area. For example, it is helpful to a programmer writing application programs in the accounting area to have accounting expertise; or in the marketing area, to have marketing expertise. Therefore, many employers are seeking application programmers who have a broad, business-oriented degree with a major in information systems, and who have taken all the other general business courses, including accounting, finance, economics, business law, marketing, management, and quantitative methods.

Although the demand for programmers is projected to remain large, there is certainly the possibility that new programming tools, such as application generators, will decrease the demand for programmers. In addition, application development by users without programmers is likely to become much more prevalent in the future.

System Analyst

A system analyst may be compared to an architect. The **system analyst** analyzes and designs application systems. In carrying out this responsibility, the analyst is heavily involved with the system-development life cycle from analysis through implementation. Often the analyst is looked upon as an intermediary between the users and programmers. Most analysts do not perform programming, and they do not have to be highly skilled programmers. However, the analyst should be familiar with several different business-oriented languages. Some firms have positions known as **programmer/analysts.** In this case the system analyst performs both programming and analysis functions and therefore must be competent in programming as well.

It is more important that system analysts have competence in the application area in which they are working than in programming. The analyst must deal directly with users and must understand their applications in order to design a new system. For these reasons, an analyst sometimes has a formal education in areas such as marketing, economics, accounting, or management. But the best combination is to have an education in one of these application areas plus an information-system education. In fact, system analysts are often employed by and report to the user organization rather than the information-system function. They analyze and design

---

PC USER TIP   Protect Your Investment

A personal-computer system with software and a printer will typically cost about $3,000. The range of performance and therefore prices that are available run from less than a hundred dollars to over twenty-five thousand dollars. Given the size of the investment in a PC system, it is a good idea to take the necessary steps to protect it. Two things that many people consider necessary for the protection of their investment are insurance and surge protectors. Surge protectors guard the circuitry of your personal computer as well as open data files from voltage spikes and other electrical fluctuations.

An insurance policy will protect you from loss owing to natural disaster or theft. You should be aware that most home owners' policies do not cover a personal computer. They will most times allow for the addition of a rider to your home owners' or renters' insurance to cover a personal computer. If this is not possible, you can get a policy specifically for your machine. The small cost of these two items is well justified when you consider the value of the assets you are protecting—the computer system, and more important for many individuals and companies, the data.

new systems and then turn the specifications over to the information-system organization for programming.

Whereas programmers often work with machines and program code, system analysts work directly with people (user personnel and programmers) most of the time. A good system analyst must have highly developed communication skills. Listening, persuasion, teaching, and consulting skills will help ensure success for a system analyst.

The job outlook for system analysts is indeed bright. They can initially pursue a career in system analysis, and then decide whether to remain in the information-system organization or to move into management in the application area in which they are trained, such as finance, accounting, or marketing. They are usually actively recruited by user organizations because of their computer expertise. Even if users develop many of their own applications in the future, they will need individuals with the expertise of system analysts to guide them in the use of new software such as application generators and data-base management systems.

EDP Auditor

A subspecialty of the auditing field is EDP auditing. An **EDP auditor** has computer expertise and thus can assist traditional auditors both in the review of computer controls and in the production of audit information through the use of computers. Currently there is a high demand for EDP auditors. Some people think that in the long run traditional auditors will acquire the necessary computer expertise and EDP auditors will no longer be needed. This probably will not happen. It is very difficult for one individual, an auditor, to maintain a high level of expertise in computer technology, auditing, and accounting at the same time. Furthermore, computer technology will continue to advance. In the foreseeable future there will be a need for specialist EDP auditors who keep abreast of the latest computer technology and the methods for controlling application systems based on that technology.

Data-Processing Operations

Data-entry operators, librarians, and computer operators work in the field of data-processing operations. A **data-entry operator** keys data from source documents into computer-readable form, usually disk storage. Job openings in this area are expected to decline in the future. This is owing primarily to source-data automation where terminals, cash registers, and other devices capture data at the point of an event or transaction. Data-entry operators generally have only a high-school diploma. There is no need for advanced education at the college level. The primary skill required is good typing.

A **librarian** is responsible for storage of computer program and data files. These files are stored on tape or disk. The job entails keeping records of the use and storage of these files and operating equipment that tests the storage media (such as tape and disk) to assure that data are stored without error. A high-school diploma is sufficient for this job.

Computer operators run the computer equipment. Most have only a high-school diploma. However, the operator must be familiar with the equipment and be able to operate various types of equipment, such as printers, card readers, tape drives, disk drives, plotters, CPUs, and data switches. This requires some technical training. In addition, the operator must be able to convey to programmers and sometimes system analysts and users the nature of problems that occur in the execution of computer jobs.

Data-Base Administrator

A **data-base administrator (DBA)** is responsible for the design and control of a company's data base. This is a management position. In medium-sized and larger firms there are several individuals in the DBA's department. Data-base administrators must have a high level of technical data-base expertise. They also must be able to communicate effectively with various user groups since their primary responsibility is meeting the often conflicting needs of users. The major duties of the DBA are: designing data bases; developing data dictionaries; designing and implementing procedures that will ensure the accuracy, completeness, and timeliness of data stored in the data base; mediating and resolving conflicts among users' needs for data; and advising programmers, analysts, and users about the efficient use of the data base.

Information-System Consultant

An **information-system consultant** is very much like a system analyst. This individual may be employed within an organization's information department or by outside management consulting firms or CPA firms. The consultant's role ranges from helping a user develop an application to performing a complete analysis, design, and implementation of a system.

Consultants that are employed by a firm in its information center may hold specialized positions either as a personal-computer consultant or as an information-center consultant. Personal-computer consultants coordinate usage and assist users in applying personal computers. Information-center consultants may also assist PC users, but generally their efforts are directed toward helping users retrieve and manipulate data stored on mainframe data bases. As personal-computer hardware

---

A personnel officer of the Computer Consulting Company was interviewing and looking at the resume of a prospective employee. He noticed that the interviewee held a bachelor's in accounting and a master's in information systems, was a CPA, and had five jobs working with computers over the last eight years. The personnel officer stated to the interviewee, "Your resume looks impressive with your education and certifications. You have also worked with some major companies and have had many duties that indicate that you perform well. But I still have one question: why do you change jobs so often, if I may ask?" The prospective employee replied that he was always looking for a challenge, since new computer technology is always being developed. He commented, "Your firm seems to be on the leading edge of this technology in the system development field." The personnel officer was not quite satisfied with the answer and really considered whether he should hire someone who switches jobs almost every two years. Should he hire this person?

Thinking About Information Systems 16–2

and software become more powerful, the jobs that these two types of consultants do are likely to merge. They both are currently aimed at assisting the user in developing applications without programming.

Consultants who work for outside consulting firms are more likely to be involved in the complete development of a system. Often they are employed as an alternative to developing a system in-house.

Many information-system consultants, particularly those employed by outside consulting firms, hold advanced degrees such as a master's in business, information systems, or accountancy. To be a successful consultant requires a special set of skills and experience, including maturity, an ability to communicate effectively, a high level of technical knowledge both in computer systems and in computer applications, and the ability to recognize problems and come up with solutions quickly without getting bogged down in the details.

Information-System Manager

In all the information-system careers discussed, there are management positions. Usually a person starts out in one of the careers and then moves up to a management position in that area. In addition to needing technical expertise, **information-system managers** need the management skills that are universal to all management positions. These include the ability to communicate both orally and in written form; ability to plan, organize, and implement; and human-relations skills, which are so necessary in the supervisory function of management. Almost all information-system managers have a college education.

Professional Associations

There are several professional associations in the field of computer information systems. Most have as their primary purpose the continuing education of computer professionals and the exchange of ideas. Some also offer professional certification programs. Many of these associations welcome student members. In fact, some, such as the Association for Computing Machinery, have local student chapters on many campuses.

AFIPS

The **American Federation of Information Processing Societies (AFIPS),** 1815 North Lynn Street, Arlington, Virginia 22209, (703) 558–3600, is a federation of information-processing societies. Among the societies represented by AFIPS are the Data Processing Management Association (DPMA). The Association for Computing Machinery (ACM), the Institute of Electrical and Electronic Engineers (IEEE), the American Statistical Association (ASA), and the American Institute of Certified Public Accountants (AICPA). The primary activities of AFIPS are to sponsor the yearly national computer conference and exposition, and to represent its constituent professional societies in a similar international group called **International Federation of Information Processing Societies (IFIPS).**

DPMA

The **Data Processing Management Association (DPMA),** 505 Busse Highway, Park Ridge, Illinois 60068, (312) 825–8124, was founded as the National Machine Accountants Association. Its name was changed to DPMA in 1962. The association holds monthly meetings at its local chapters, holds an annual data-processing conference, sponsors an annual information-system education conference, publishes a monthly journal called *Data Management,* and sponsors various educational programs. This is a business-oriented data-processing association. Its membership is made up largely of practicing business data-processing professionals. However, there are also more than four hundred student chapters of DPMA.

ACM

The **Association for Computing Machinery (ACM),** 11 West 42nd Street, New York, NY 10036, (212) 869–7440, has as its primary objective the advancement of the science and art of information processing. It is the largest technical, scientific, and educational computing organization. Many of its members are computer science faculty members at universities. The ACM has many **special-interest groups (SIGs).** For example, ACM members who have a special interest in small computers are members of SIGSMALL. Other special-interest groups are Data Base, Computer Science Education, and Programming Languages. Active ACM chapters are located on many college campuses and in most cities.

ASM

The **Association of Systems Management (ASM),** 24578 Eardley Drive, Cleveland, Ohio 44118, (216) 243–6900, was founded in 1947 and is a national organization. ASM publishes a monthly journal called *Journal of Systems Management* and has local chapters in most cities. It holds an annual conference and its membership is made up largely of system analysts and information-system managers.

SIM

The **Society for Information Management (SIM),** 111 East Wacker Drive, Suite 600, Chicago, Illinois 60601, (312) 644–6610, was founded in 1968. Its members include information-system managers, business system analysts, and educators. The SIM holds an annual conference and also sponsors an annual International Conference for Information Systems Education. The latter has in recent years become an important event, where papers and ideas are exchanged among business information-system educators.

EDP Auditors Foundation

The **EDP Auditors Foundation,** 373 South Schmale Road, Carol Stream, Illinois 60187, (312) 653–0950, is a professional association of those auditors who specialize in EDP auditing. It has local chapters in all major cities and holds an annual conference. In addition, it publishes a journal called *The EDP Auditor.* One of the more important activities of this foundation is sponsorship of the Certified Information Systems Auditor (CISA) exam. This will be discussed in the next section.

The millions of PC users in the world face the same questions over and over again. What software should I buy? Will this software interface with my hardware? One successful way for users to share in their experiences, problems, and knowledge is through user groups. Here, people can gain useful information from each other to help them make decisions and overcome difficulties.

Another advantage of user groups is that the sheer number and therefore power of the group can justify attention from software and hardware manufacturers and distributors. Vendors often arrange software and hardware demonstrations which can be extremely helpful to a person deciding what hardware and software to purchase. User groups often provide newsletters and other forms of communication at a relatively low cost.

One special user group that has come into existence is the manager's user group. Here, the specific problems associated with corporate PC decisions can be brought to light. One such group, Microcomputer Managers' Association, has grown to a national level and can be reached at 80 Boylston St., Suite 359, Boston, MA 02116. To look for a user group in your area, check with a local computer store such as Entre or Computerland or check the Club News Section of *PC Magazine*. It lists dozens of user groups around the country.

Professional Certification Programs

There are several professional certification programs in the information-system area. Students who plan careers in information systems should take the exams relating to their career interests. The best time to sit for these exams is during the senior year or shortly after graduation, since the tests are based on material learned in an undergraduate program.

The CDP and CCP

The **Certificate in Data Processing (CDP)** examination and the **Certificate in Computer Programming (CCP)** examination are administered by the **Institute for Certification of Computer Professionals (ICCP),** 35 East Wacker Drive, Chicago, Illinois 60601, (312) 782–9437. This organization is nonprofit and was established in 1973 with the purpose of testing and certifying computer professionals. As with AFIPS, the ICCP is made up of several constituent societies. The CDP examination originated with DPMA but was turned over to the ICCP in 1974. Candidates for the CDP exam must have at least five years of professional experience in information systems. The exam consists of five sections: data-processing equipment, computer programming and software, principles of management, quantitative methods, and system analysis and design. The CCP is also a five-part exam and is designed to test the knowledge and skills required of a senior-level programmer.

CISA

The **Certified Information Systems Auditor (CISA)** exam is administered by the EDP Auditors Foundation, 373 South Schmale Road, Carol Stream, Illinois 60187,

(312) 653–0950. This is a multiple-choice exam that covers the following general areas:

application-system controls
data integrity
system-development life cycle
application development
system maintenance
operational-procedures controls
security procedures
system software
resource acquisition
resource management
information-system audit management

In addition to passing the exam, the applicant must have a minimum of five years of practical experience in EDP auditing in order to become certified.

The Abbett Company is considering a policy which would require that all of its computer professionals, including EDP auditors, have an appropriate professional certification. Individuals within the system development department could hold either the Certificate in Computer Programming or the Certificate in Data Processing. EDP auditors would need to be Certified Information Systems Auditors. Abbett management believes that this policy would build a spirit of professionalism in the computer-oriented staff. Managers feel that this is now lacking and to some extent, accounts for the high staff turnover the company has experienced in these areas in the past. Do you think this is a good policy?

Thinking About Information Systems 16–3

Information-System Education

Two professional organizations have been active in designing **model curriculums** for information-system education. Both the ACM and the DPMA published model curriculums in the early 1980s. Outlines of these curriculums are shown in Figures 16–2 and 16–3. As you can see, the course titles of these two curriculums differ substantially. The primary difference between the two models is that the ACM curriculum has a more theoretical and conceptual basis, whereas the DPMA model curriculum is more practical and applied in nature. Another difference is that the DPMA model curriculum emphasizes that information-system education should be housed within colleges of business.

It is rare that an information-system curriculum at a specific university or college exactly matches either of these two curriculums. Model curriculums are designed to be just that—models that are modified to fit the particular needs of a particular university or college. You do not have to follow these model curriculums exactly to receive a good information-system education.

FIGURE 16–2 DPMA Model Curriculum for Computer Information Systems

This curriculum is oriented toward undergraduate information-system programs in business colleges.

List of Courses
CORE COURSES

CIS/86-1	Introduction to Computer Information Systems
CIS/86-2	Microcomputer Applications in Business
CIS/86-3	Introduction to Business Application Programming
CIS/86-4	Intermediate Business Application Programming
CIS/86-5	Systems Development Methodologies: A Survey
CIS/86-6	Data Files and Databases
CIS/86-7	Information Center Functions
CIS/86-8	Systems Development Project

ELECTIVE COURSES

CIS/86-9	Advanced Office Systems
CIS/86-10	Computer Graphics in Business
CIS/86-11	Decision Support and Expert Systems
CIS/86-12	Artificial Intelligence in Decision Making
CIS/86-13	Advanced Business Applications Programming
CIS/86-14	Computer Control and Audit
CIS/86-15	Distributed Intelligence and Communication Systems
CIS/86-16	Programming Languages: Procedural, Nonprocedural, and Fourth Generation
CIS/86-17	Computer Hardware, System Software, and Architecture
CIS/86-18	Information Resource Planning and Management
CIS/86-19	Systems Development Project With Information Center Techniques
CIS/86-20	CIS Communication, Reporting, and Documentation Techniques

BUSINESS SUPPORT COURSES

BUS-1	Financial Accounting Practices
BUS-2	Managerial Accounting Practices
BUS-3	Quantitative Methods in Business
BUS-4	Principles of Management
BUS-5	Principles of Marketing
BUS-6	Principles of Finance
BUS-7	Organizational Behavior
BUS-8	Production and Operations Management
BUS-9	Business Policy

(From *The DPMA Model Curriculum for Undergraduate Computer Information Systems,* copyright 1985, Data Processing Management Association Education Foundation. All rights reserved. Reprint permission granted.)

Summing Up

☐ Most business professionals will now have to rely on computer-generated information to perform effectively in their jobs. However, in order to make informed and responsible decisions they must also understand the processes used by the computer in generating the information.

☐ The bureau of labor statistics has predicted a large increase in information-system jobs during the 1980s. Careers in information systems may be categorized as follows:

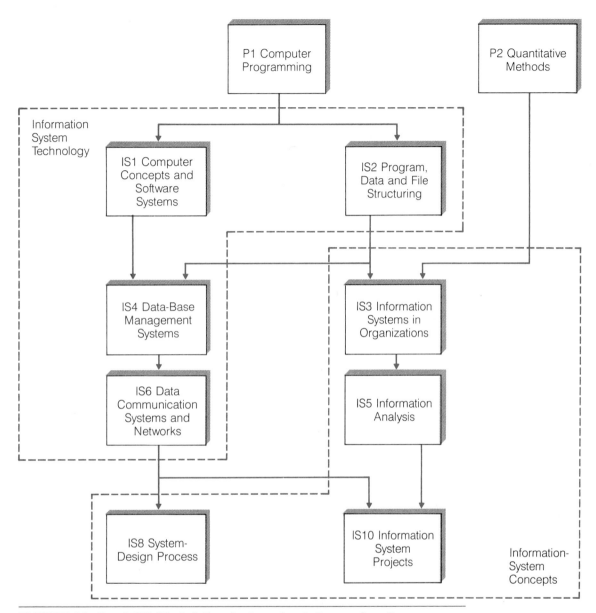

FIGURE 16–3   ACM Model Curriculum for Information Systems

The ACM model curriculum has been implemented at both the undergraduate and graduate levels.

- programmer
- system analyst
- EDP auditor
- data-processing operations
- data-base administrator
- information-system consultant
- information-system manager

□ There are many professional associations for information-system personnel. Some of the more prominent are:

American Federation of Information Processing Societies (AFIPS)
Data Processing Management Association (DPMA)
Association for Computing Machinery (ACM)
Association of Systems Management (ASM)
Society for Information Management (SIM)
EDP Auditors Foundation

□ Several professional certifications exist in the information-system area. The Certificate in Data Processing, Certificate in Computer Programming, and Certified Information Systems Auditor are widely recognized qualifications for EDP personnel.

Key Terms

information age
information workers
programmers
system analyst
programmer/analysts
EDP auditor
data-entry operator
librarian
computer operators
data-base administrator (DBA)
information-system consultant
information-system managers
American Federation of Information
  Processing Societies (AFIPS)

International Federation of Information
  Processing Societies (IFIPS)
Data-Processing Management Association (DPMA)
Association for Computing Machinery (ACM)
special-interest groups (SIGs)
Association of Systems Management (ASM)
Society for Information Management (SIM)
EDP Auditors Foundation
Certificate in Data Processing (CDP)
Certificate in Computer Programming (CCP)
Institute for Certification of Computer
  Professionals (ICCP)
Certified Information Systems Auditor (CISA)
model curriculums

Self-Quiz

Completion Questions

1. _____ write computer programs that perform jobs specified by the user.
2. The analysis and design of application systems are the responsibility of a _____ .
3. _____ assist traditional auditors both in the review of computer controls and in the production of audit information through the use of computers.
4. A _____ is responsible for the design and control of a company's data base.

5. The storage of computer programs and data files are the responsibility of a _____ .
6. The _____ is a business-oriented data-processing association which publishes a monthly journal, *Data Management*.
7. The EDP Auditors Foundation sponsors the _____ exam.
8. The Institute for Certification of Computer Professionals (ICCP) currently administers the

Certificate in Computer Programming (CCP) and the _____ examinations.

9. There are several careers within data-processing operations, including data-entry operator, librarian, and _____ .

10. The model curriculum for information-system education suggested by the _____ has a more theoretical and conceptual basis, whereas the model by the _____ is more practical and applied in nature.

Multiple-Choice Questions

1. Which of the following is (are) true concerning information-system careers?
   a. The number of information-system specialists recruited is expected to be greater than any other profession in the 1980s.
   b. The primary reason for this increase is the declining cost of hardware.
   c. An information-system career is one of the few areas that is recession-proof.
   d. Two of the above.
   e. All three of the above.

2. In which area are job openings expected to decline in the future?
   a. computer operator
   b. data-entry operator
   c. system programmer
   d. application programmer
   e. none of the above

3. Which of the following is (are) true of system analysts?
   a. They are heavily involved with the system-development life cycle.
   b. Their responsibility is to analyze and design system software.
   c. They may be looked upon as an inter-mediary between users and programmers.
   d. Two of the above.
   e. All three of the above.

4. A person who has a high-school diploma would be least likely to obtain which of the following jobs?
   a. librarian
   b. computer operator

   c. data-entry operator
   d. programmer

5. The major responsibilities of the data-base administrator are all of the following except:
   a. analyzing application systems
   b. designing data bases
   c. developing data dictionaries
   d. advising programmers
   e. all of the above are the responsibilities of the DBA

6. Which of the following abilities is required for both the system programmer and the EDP auditor?
   a. knowledge in computer science
   b. knowledge in accounting applications
   c. knowledge in information systems
   d. two of the above
   e. all three of the above

7. If you are an information-system manager, which organization is most appropriate for your interest?
   a. ACM
   b. SIM
   c. IEEE
   d. ASA
   e. all of the above

8. Individuals who intend to pursue a career as an information-system manager should have:
   a. technical expertise in information systems
   b. ability to communicate in written form
   c. human-relations skills
   d. two of the above
   e. all three of the above

9. Which of the following is not true of the EDP Auditors Foundation?
   a. It is a professional association of those auditors who specialize in EDP auditing.
   b. It publishes a journal, *The EDP Auditor.*
   c. It sponsors the CISA exam.
   d. It is a member of the AFIPS.
   e. All of the above are true.

10. Which of the following is (are) true of the EDP auditors?
    a. They should have computer expertise.
    b. They will be replaced by traditional auditors in the near future.
    c. Currently, there is a very high demand for

them, particularly from firms that use
personal computers.
d. two of the above
e. all three of the above
f. none of the above

Answers

Completion	Multiple Choice
1. Application programmers	1. d
2. system analyst	2. b
3. EDP auditors	3. d
4. data-base administrator	4. d
5. librarian	5. a
6. Data Processing Management Association (DPMA)	6. a
7. Certified Information Systems Auditor (CISA)	7. b
8. Certificate in Data Processing (CDP)	8. e
9. computer operator	9. d
10. ACM; DPMA	10. a

General Foods: Getting PCs And People Working Together

By Susan Jelcich

Yoav Levy

For a corporation that spends much of its time freeze-drying Sanka and vacuum-packing Birds-Eye vegetables, General Foods Corp. has a genuine and all too rare consideration for the human element, its employees.

General Foods knows that a respected and well informed work force is effective and efficient. So when the time came to investigate the personal computer's place within General Foods, the corporation used its employee philosophy.

Unlike companies that allow PCs to trickle into the operation before devising a coordinated plan, General Foods determined its PC strategy before the first PC was purchased. One result of this strategy was the six-person Personal Computer Center at the corporation's headquarters in White Plains, NY.

Headed by office-automation and microsystems Manager Gary Schnorr, the center consists of microsystems consultants Pat Kohler and Lee Rivers, office systems consultant Susan Pagano, administrative coordinator Jean Borsellino and microsystems assistant Paula A. Fields. The center handles all PC-related problems and inquiries for General Foods' domestic operations, everything from debugging software to finding power cords.

The center staff made General Foods' PC strategy an effective solution to the problem of adding PCs where once there had been none.

"We have been supporting PCs for about three years on an active basis," Schnorr said. "We have about 600 PCs in place right now within the headquarters area. Probably close to 90 percent of them are IBM-compatible, moving totally in that direction. But when we began the program, IBM wasn't even in the marketplace with their PCs, so we began by supporting PC applications on Apples and Radio Shacks, and there are still some of those in place."

An Invitation to Users

The idea of a Personal Computer Center might conjure images of a massive technological wonderland, a mix of conservative corporate decor and an army of straightfaced programmers manning complex state-of-the-art systems. In reality, the center is an unobtrusive room the size of some companies' reception areas. The center "is primarily an education and training center," Schnorr said.

It coordinates purchasing, computer research and development and introduces users to new technology, Schnorr said.

"We've got a variety of machines here that span the gamut from Wang Systems—which we support— Apples, Compaqs, PC*jr*s, some of which are in here on evaluation basis," Schnorr said. "Also, it's a central library/repository for software. The same group provides the direct R&D activity for new application software."

The atmosphere is personable and approachable; busy but not hysterical. Employees are encouraged to drop in and discuss new applications or new software, to ask questions and to resolve any problems they might have with hardware. Also, the center has a telephone hot line for employees, if, for example, they find a glitch in their programs or have trouble with a printer. The center receives an average of 60 to 100 phone calls daily from people seeking technical support, people who want to know what's new and people who ask, "Can you see what's wrong with my computer?" Rivers said.

The interest and enthusiasm among employees is not accidental. It is the result of careful consideration.

The center reflects General Foods' overall attitude toward the PC, which company officials saw as part of a system. They saw the PC as a way to increase productivity when the economy and the corporation's fiscal policy were changing, Schnorr said.

When first seeking ways to increase productivity through computers, the firm looked almost exclusively at word processing. Being a large corporation, General Foods had many tasks that could be automated, but converting to computers "tended always to be pushed down on the priority list," he said.

But, when officials "looked at those early applications for PC technology. . . we started to see the introduction of low-cost reliable hardware."

The Top-Down Approach

General Foods first introduced PC technology by using the top-down approach, meaning executives were trained first and other workers, later.

The program included a one-on-one meeting with each senior manager to explain the Information Systems Management Department's plan to introduce PCs.

"It was an opportunity for them to become involved in the process, to gain a greater understanding of how the technology was developing and how it would affect their organizations," Schnorr explained.

Also, each one was offered a personal computer to take home for four months and receive training,

support and consultation for themselves and their families.

"It was more an effort to simply raise their awareness," Schnorr said.

Once the executives were aware of the advantages of using PC technology, the department began selling the idea to all employees. "Everyone was in a reactive mode to PC technology" coming in, he said.

So, the second part of the three-pronged introduction was the bottom-up approach, in which PC technology was outlined to users "in a non-threatening, user-friendly kind of way," Schnorr said.

Microsystems consultant Rivers said, "The thing that was most important when I was hired, the thing that I was told the most was 'Take the fear away. That's all you have to do is take the fear away.'"

The company did not employ storm-trooper tactics, in which the information systems management department came in and said, "Good morning. Your department has been allotted five personal computers. See you around." Rather, employees were trained in the use of PCs, and training became the third prong of the PC introduction.

"When we began this program," Schnorr said, "we had end-user computing within General Foods, which [was] primarily people using CRTs, accessing time-sharing, probably [500] or 600 people on an active basis, domestically. Today, we've probably trained about 4,000 people through this facility in some personal-computing discipline. We probably were on the leading edge of this whole personal-computer-center program because there was a Harvard case study done in 1982

because of the uniqueness of our program.

"Ours was not a retrofit," he said. "That was before we had any PCs coming into the company. . . . At the same time, we were introducing the rest of the program, so that they had first-hand knowledge of the direction setting and the strategy."

No Programming, Please

Teaching the users to program was not one of General Foods' objectives, however. Instead, the company encourages workers to use certain programs so employees can "hit the ground running," Schnorr said.

The PC group serves as a consultant to explore potential applications and help users determine which software packages best fill their needs.

The PC group considered each "application from the context of General Foods' information-processing network and helped the user understand how to fit into that," Schnorr said. "If they were looking for information, we didn't want to have them reinvent the wheel, if that existed already in another system."

The other objectives were to provide an environment that supported and encouraged the use of personal computers.

General Foods' PC plan never included orphan PCs.

Instead, it intended that each PC "be an integrated part of a total information-systems network that would link the desktop into our department minicomputers and link the individual's desktop into our mainframe," Schnorr said.

The key to the strategy was the intelligent terminal, the ability of the PC to communicate and manage information on other systems and the emerging role of the multifunction workstation.

Information sharing from mainframes, from time-sharing systems and from minicomputers was extended to the desktop, providing the missing link so the individual could access and manage information from his desk. The only piece missing from General Foods' plan was the willingness and the ability of the employees to use PCs effectively and efficiently. No matter how well planned the approach, its success depended on the employees' cooperation.

The company wasn't interested in turning each employee into a myopic automaton who knew only a single step-by-step approach to operating a PC within one specific, job-related application. It wanted vibrant, knowledgeable users curious about new packages and applications, enthusiastic about the computer's potential and interested in the latest trends.

This was partially accomplished by getting each employee's family involved in computing through the Personal Computer Center. Since the company could hardly initiate a loaner program for all employees, as it had done for executives in the top-down approach, the center was opened to employees' families.

For example, families interested in buying a home computer could test a system in the center at their leisure, without having high-pressure salespeople looking over their shoulders.

Even for families not buying PCs for their homes, having access to a PC through the center was important, for example, for children being taught computing in school.

The center staff also conducts formal classes for employees within specific applications. Anyone is eligible to attend, but as Rivers said, "So we don't get people who just want to kill 3½ hours, you have to get approval from your boss to take it. But it is only a 3½-hour morning session." Once a class ends, the staff encourages the employees to return in their free time to practice what they learned in class, to strengthen their retention, so they will be ready for the material to be covered in the next class.

Combatting Computerphobia

In addition to the scheduled classes, the center staff offers personal, individual instruction in which staff members might indulge in a bit of computer psychology, helping confused or intimidated employees overcome PC phobia.

"We are trying to stay on the same level as they are," Rivers said. "So we talk to them on a level that's not very technical."

"[We] have them sit in front of a machine and explain to them that they can do things and not fear a terrible reaction to their computers. [We say,] it's a tool. That's all. It's nothing without you. You are in control. This is not replacing you. This is helping you."

Schnorr commented that "We probably see more people on an informal basis than the 4,000 we've seen in the classroom."

The open-facility approach combined with the staff's patience in allaying employees' fears have produced positive results. "People like to come in and talk all the time," Rivers said. "And people are always coming in and saying, 'What's new? Did you buy anything new this week?' and they always want to see what's going on."

Once employees learn the basics, they are not left to fend for themselves. "I think that technical support is very important to our user community," Rivers said. "[If you run into a problem] you don't have to pore over a manual. You can call [us] up.

"Even [with] some of the more complicated macro questions, you get a lot of the same type of questions," Rivers said. "You get very common things. And they're things that I think would take people another 20 minutes to work out, and I can tell them in two."

After training, counseling, technical support, research and development, purchasing and debugging software, the staff decided to build a library of all of the PC applications in the company.

"I think it might have been somewhat idealistic on our part to assume that we could maintain a current list of every application that was on the PC in some type of library," Schnorr said. A central library was one of his original objectives for the center, and initially he surveyed employees, asking that they describe each application.

"But that placed a burden on the user community that said, 'Not only are you expected to do your job more effectively and efficiently and take advantage of all of this and increase your workload, but every once in a while, take 20 minutes to fill out this form,' " Schnorr said.

A more effective method of tracking each application is through an informal network of users "because we have so much contact with the users," he said.

Having the center as a focal point for training, questions and research and development puts the staff in contact with most of the users each month, Schnorr said.

"We understand what the applications are, because it is centralized, and we have this focal-point activity. We can say, 'I don't know the answer to that, but talk to so and so in this division. I know that they're doing something very much like that.' "

By getting users to talk to each other, the center has established a broad network that reflects the General Foods philosophy, a rare consideration for the human element.

Reprinted from *PC Week*, February 26, 1985. Copyright © 1985, Ziff-Davis Publishing Company.

DISCUSSION QUESTIONS

1. What approaches has General Foods used to take away the fear of computers?

2. What are the advantages of encouraging employees not to program?

3. Why is technical support very important to the user community?

4. If you were in charge of implementing personal computers at General Foods what would you do different from the approaches they have used.?

5. Do you feel that a Personal Computer Center would be a good place to start your career? Why or why not?

Module A

History of the Computer Industry

MODULE OUTLINE

PROLOGUE

The computer industry is unique in many ways. How many products or services do you know that have steadily declined in price while their quality and performance have dramatically increased? Very few! The computing power that you can buy today for two thousand dollars in the form of a personal computer would have cost more than one million dollars in the early 1960s. The history of the computer industry is short, but it is most interesting. It is a classic case of human innovation!

Introduction

Advances in computer hardware and software are generally classified into generations. The first generation started in 1951 and the current (fourth) one in 1971. This module will cover the significant developments of each computer generation. We will also speculate about the characteristics of future computer systems. But first, we will discuss the early developments in data processing and see how they eventually led to punched-card equipment and the first electronic computers.

Early Developments in Data Processing

The Abacus

Movable beads on a wire frame constituted the first known calculating device, called an **abacus** (see Figure A–1). The abacus was used by the ancient Greeks and Romans, although most of the significant contributions to its design were made by the Chinese. The Chinese abacus is called *suan pan,* which means counting board. Beads are stored at one side of the frame, and calculations are performed

FIGURE A–1   The Abacus

Although the abacus is an ancient calculating instrument, it is still used in many parts of the Far East. (I recently saw one in use by an elderly Japanese man in a small restaurant in Hawaii. Using an abacus, he calculated all the meal checks faster than most people could on an electronic calculator.)

at the other side by moving beads against that side of the frame. The significant conceptual contribution of the abacus is the use of position to represent value, as shown in Figure A–1.

Mechanical Calculators

The **mechanical calculators** used until about 1970 resembled a calculating machine invented in 1642 by **Blaise Pascal**, a French mathematician and philosopher. Pascal developed a gear-driven machine capable of addition, subtraction, and multiplication. Manipulations were performed by rotating wheels, and a mechanism made possible an automatic carry. The automatic carry was the significant contribution from Pascal's machine.

In 1671 the German mathematician and philosopher **Gottfried von Leibnitz** improved Pascal's design and built a machine that multiplied, divided, and determined square roots (see Figure A–2). This calculator consisted of a cylindrical drum with nine teeth along its surface. The teeth varied in length, and when the drum rotated, some of them engaged a sliding gear on the axle. This gear principle was employed in many mechanical calculators until they were replaced by electronic calculators in the 1960s.

Jacquard's Loom

In 1801 a Frenchman named **Joseph Jacquard** perfected a **loom** that was controlled by holes in cardboard **punched cards** (see Figure A–3). The design for woven fabric was represented by a series of holes punched in the card. In the loom's control mechanism, mechanical fingers were activated by the presence or absence of a hole in the card. The movement of the fingers determined what threads were to appear in the fabric. By sequencing the cards, the loom could produce a large number of patterns and designs. When the cards for a particular pattern were repeated, the pattern would be repeated automatically. As we will see, punched cards were later used extensively in the processing of data. Also,

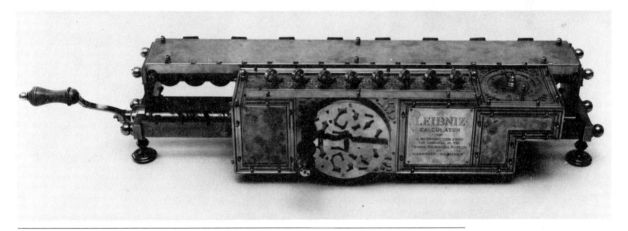

FIGURE A–2   Gottfried von Leibnitz's Calculator

Mechanical calculators which are descendants of Leibnitz's machine were used even in the 1960s.

FIGURE A–3 Jacquard's Loom

Notice the punched cards at the top of the diagram near the letter *C*. They were strung together and rotated to produce the fabric pattern.

Jacquard's punched cards were, in effect, a program for the loom. They stored the various fabric designs. There is a similarity between Jacquard's cards and stored programs in a computer.

Babbage's Engines and Ada, Countess of Lovelace

In 1812 **Charles Babbage**, an English mathematician and inventor, found that certain principles from Jacquard's loom could be used in numerical computation. He saw that if computing steps could be stored in advance of computation, it would be possible for a machine to process data unaided. Babbage thus developed the concept of the **stored program** for data processing—the capability that differentiates computers from calculators. He is generally recognized as the first person to propose the concept of the computer.

Babbage called his first machine a **difference engine** and designed it to calculate logarithm tables (see Figure A–4). A series of levers was to enter the data, and a device similar to a typewriter was to print the output. Unfortunately, the metallurgy technology of that time was not sufficiently advanced to allow a practical difference engine to be built.

Babbage did not give up easily. He went on to design an **analytical engine**. It was designed to add, subtract, multiply and divide through the use of a stored program. The program was to be entered on a series of punched cards similar to those used on the Jacquard loom.

The four major components of the analytical engine were input and output devices, an arithmetic unit to perform the calculations, and a memory to store the intermediate calculations. Modern computers are organized in a similar manner. Despite the advanced design features of this engine, Babbage never succeeded in building this machine either. However, after his death, his son built a working model of the analytical engine in 1871. Perhaps if someone had carried on Babbage's research we would have had computers sooner.

A significant contributor to Babbage's research was **Augusta Ada Byron,** Countess of Lovelace. Babbage met her when he was working on his analytical engine. She was the daughter of Lord Byron, the famous English poet. Ada Byron was an accomplished mathematician and she recorded and analyzed many of Babbage's ideas. Because of her work in developing (programming) the mathematical tables for the analytical engine, she is recognized as the first programmer. A new programming language, Ada, is named after her.

Punched-Card Equipment

Metcalfe's Cards

The next significant historical development took place in the 1870s at the Frankford Arsenal in Philadelphia. When Lieutenant **Henry Metcalfe** started to reorganize the arsenal's cost-accounting system, he found that he could not produce the

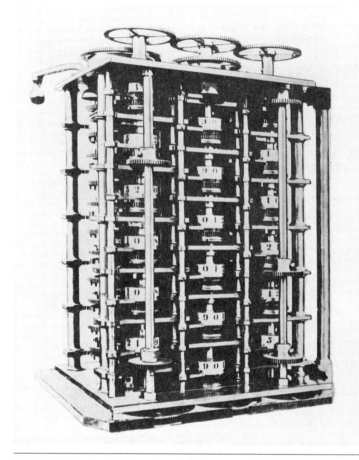

FIGURE A–4 Babbage's Difference Engine

The idea for a difference engine that would compute mathematical tables such as loga-
rithms was first conceived by Babbage in 1812. After twenty years of labor, he had to stop
because of financial difficulties, and the machine was never completed.

information that management needed because records were kept in leatherbound
ledgers by department. Retrieving information from these ledgers and sorting it
in the order required for reports was a laborious and often impractical task.
Extrapolating from the practice of librarians who index books on cards that are
not punched, Metcalfe transferred some of the arsenal's accounting records from
ledgers to cards. Then the decks of cards could be manually sorted, summarized,
and manipulated to better meet the information needs of management. This system
required a sophisticated **coding scheme**, a well-defined **unit record**, and a
system design that specified the flow of data.

Today, computer information systems electronically perform many of the functions of Metcalfe's system. The concept of a record and the use of codes in storing
information were developed by Metcalfe.

Hollerith's Punched Cards

At about the same time, the federal government began to encounter problems in data processing. It took seven years to compile the statistics from the 1880 census, and it became apparent that it would be time to begin a new census before the analysis of the previous one was completed. In 1880, a statistician employed by the United States Census Bureau began experimenting with punched cards for use in data processing. Although punched cards were used in process control, as with Jacquard's loom, they had not been successfully employed in data processing (Metcalfe's cards were not punched). **Herman Hollerith** designed a device called the **tabulating machine**, which used machine-readable punched cards (see Figure A–5). Initially, Hollerith's cards had round holes and forty-five columns. His machine reduced tabulating time on the 1890 census to one-eighth the time required by the old methods. Hollerith founded the Tabulating Machine Company in 1896 to manufacture and sell his new inventions. In 1911 the Tabulating Machine Company merged with the International Time Recording Company, the Dayton Seale Company, and the Bundy Manufacturing Corporation to form the Computing-Tabulating-Recording Company (CTR). CTR was renamed the International Business Machine Corporation (IBM) in 1924.

Powers's Punched Cards

James Powers, an engineer who worked for the Census Bureau, produced several refinements of Hollerith's machine and patented a punched-card machine in 1908. Powers developed the concept of **simultaneous punching**. The operator depressed

FIGURE A–5   Hollerith's Tabulating Machine

This machine not only helped in the 1890 census, but it was also a forerunner of the IBM Corporation. From the early 1900s to about 1950, the mainstay of IBM's business was tabulating equipment.

keys to cause punching, but holes were not actually punched until the release key was depressed. Thus, corrections could be made prior to punching. Powers also developed a sorting machine and tabulators that were employed in the 1910 census. He formed the Powers Accounting Machine Company, which in 1926 merged with Remington Rand Corporation. Later, Remington Rand Corporation merged with Sperry Gyroscope Company to form Sperry Rand Corporation, which produced UNIVAC computers.

Punched-card data processing was widely used until the early 1960s when electronic computers began to replace punched-card equipment in significant numbers. Several types of electromechanical devices were used to process punched cards, including **key-punches, key-verifiers, sorters, reproducers, collators** and **tabulating machines**. Two of these devices, the key-punch and key-verifier, were also used with electronic computer systems, since cards were an important type of input to these systems. However, card input has now been largely replaced by CRT terminal or floppy-disk input. Very few companies currently use cards in the data-processing function.

Until the beginning of World War II, only two companies in the United States were involved in the punched-card data-processing business. IBM Corporation produced machinery that used the **eighty-column Hollerith card**, and Remington Rand Corporation produced machinery that employed the **ninety-column Powers card**. The war created great demands for high-speed calculating equipment. Developments in long-range artillery, aircraft, and the atomic bomb required machines that could calculate at speeds never before dreamed possible.

Mark I Electromechanical Computer

In 1937 **Howard Aiken** of Harvard University started to build a machine that integrated punched-card and calculating technology. Aiken received help from graduate students and IBM engineers, and in 1944 the **Mark I** digital computer was completed (see Figure A–6). This machine had an automatic sequence-controlled calculator that was operated entirely by mechanical switches and electromagnetic relays. It was an **electromechanical computer**, not an electronic one. Ironically, Babbage's analytical engine was displayed at Harvard University; how-

FIGURE A–6 The Mark I Automatic Calculator

This machine used electromagnetic relays for switches. When the machine was running, the clicking of all the relays produced a very loud noise.

ever, Aiken had almost completed Mark I before he became aware of Babbage and his work. Mark I was the first machine to successfully perform a long series of arithmetic and logical operations. Several Mark I machines were built for the United States Navy, and they made a significant contribution to the war effort.

Commodore **Grace Murray Hopper** programmed the MARK I while at Harvard. Hopper became an important contributor to computer languages, especially COBOL, as we will discuss later in this chapter. Hopper is still active in the computer field today.

The First Electronic Computers

The ENIAC

In 1939 at the Moore School of Electrical Engineering at the University of Pennsylvania, **John W. Mauchly** and **J. Presper Eckert, Jr.** led a team that developed the first electronic digital computer (see Figure A–7). This machine, which was

FIGURE A–7   The ENIAC

Since the ENIAC was based on electronic parts (vacuum tubes) it could perform a multiplication in three-thousandths of a second. The Mark I, based on mechanical electromagnetic relays, took about three seconds to perform a multiplication. Thus the ENIAC was a thousand times faster.

completed in 1946, used **vacuum tubes** in place of electromagnetic relays. The substitution increased the calculation speed by a thousand times. The **ENIAC (Electronic Numerical Integrator and Calculator)** was built for the United States Army and was designed to calculate the mathematical tables for artillery trajectories.

The ENIAC was an enormous computer by today's standards. It weighed 30 tons and covered 1,500 square feet of floor space. The ENIAC used 150,000 watts of electricity, equal to about 200 horsepower. The ENIAC could solve in half a minute a problem usually requiring twenty hours with a desk calculator.

The original ENIAC design was partially controlled by a combination of switches and a telephone-switchboard-like arrangement of "patch cords." Several hours of manual disconnecting and replugging these patch cords into new locations were necessary to change a program. The ENIAC was a stored-program computer in the sense that once the machine was wired properly for a given task, the program was in effect stored. However, changing to a different task required "rewiring" for the new program. It is interesting to note that the electromechanical punched-card equipment of the 1940s also had the switchboard-like patch-cord technology, which enabled them to perform different tasks. Therefore, it was natural for Mauchly and Eckert to use this approach in their computer. A computer that stores programs electronically, the same way data are stored, has significant advantages over the ENIAC.

The Binary Number System

In 1945 **John von Neumann**, a Princeton mathematician, suggested that both data and programs be stored internally, in high-speed memory, using the **binary number system**. This number system uses the digits zero and one rather than the ten digits in the decimal system. On and off, magnetized and not magnetized, are states that generally describe the condition of electronic components. The use of the binary system greatly facilitated the design of electronic computers because zero and one are used to represent the condition of electronic components. Finally, von Neumann demonstrated how the instructions could be coded using the binary system. These concepts form the basis for today's electronic computer.

The EDVAC and EDSAC

In 1946 Mauchly, Eckert, and their colleagues began to construct a computer based on the concepts suggested by von Neumann, the **EDVAC (Electronic Discrete Variable Automatic Computer)**. However, Eckert and Mauchly left the Moore School over patent disagreements in 1946. This seriously impeded progress on the EDVAC. It was completed in 1952 and was used by the United States Army. Meanwhile, **Maurice Wilker** of Cambridge University in England attended a course taught by Eckert and Mauchly entitled "The Theory and Techniques for Design of Electronic Digital Computers." He returned home and began work on the **EDSAC (Electronic Delay Storage Automatic Computer)**. The EDSAC was completed in 1949, about two years before EDVAC was finished. Therefore, the EDSAC is credited as the first **stored-program electronic digital computer**.

In 1946 Mauchly and Eckert formed their own company. Their firm was acquired by Remington Rand in 1951. From this point on in the early 1950s, the development of computers has been classified in terms of **generations**. Major technological developments caused each new generation to supersede the last. These developments have increased capabilities and reduced costs.

Thinking About Information Systems A–1

Susan Wright is a freshman at a large state university. She is currently enrolled in a course entitled Introduction to Computer Information Systems primarily because it is required for her major. Susan has stated several times that "with the rapid advances expected in computer hardware and software, computers will become as easy to use as a telephone. I didn't have to take a course in how to use the telephone and study how a telephone works. The computer is just a tool, like a telephone. Why should I spend my time studying something that in a few years will be very simple to use? I'll even be able to converse with the computer in English!" Do you agree or disagree with Susan? Why?

First-Generation Computers: 1951–1958

Univac-I

In 1951 Remington Rand produced the first commercially available computer, called **UNIVAC-I (Universal Automatic Computer)**; see Figure A–8. The UNIVAC-I was first used by the U.S. Census Bureau in 1951. This machine was retired in 1963 after 73,500 hours of operation. It was the first commercial computer to use a compiler to translate program language into machine language. General Electric acquired one of these machines in 1954 and installed it in the GE Appliance Park in Louisville, Kentucky. This event marked the first business data-processing application of a computer.

First-generation computers used vacuum tubes for switching and controlling functions. **Magnetic drums** were used for primary storage and punched cards or punched paper tape were used for secondary storage. The tubes generated a great deal of heat, which meant that large air-conditioning units were needed to control the environmental temperature of the machine. First-generation machines were very large and required continuous maintenance because of the large number of vacuum tubes they contained (see Figure A–9).

First-Generation Software

The biggest advance in software was the use of **symbolic languages** for programming. All computers execute only **machine-language** programs, which are in the binary form of ones and zeros. Programming in machine language is very

FIGURE A–8   UNIVAC-I

Although this machine marked the first use of a computer for business data processing, most UNIVACs were used for scientific applications.

time consuming and difficult. A symbolic language expresses operation codes of instructions and data addresses in symbols understood by users, rather than in machine language. For example, a programmer could write the word "add" for an operation code instead of the binary numbers which the machine understands for the addition operation code. A **translator** program translated the symbolic language into the binary machine language that the computer executed. Symbolic-language programming increased programmer productivity by a large factor. First-generation computers were applied primarily to relatively simple business functions, such as processing payroll.

Second-Generation Computers: 1959–1964

Hardware Advances

In 1948 a small **semiconductor** device called a **transistor** was developed by Bell Laboratories. Unlike the vacuum tube, the transistor does not depend on a heat filament. It is much smaller, much more reliable, and when employed as a switching device, much faster than the vacuum tube. Besides making possible the pocket radio, the transistor made possible the second generation of computers.

   Second-generation computers were considerably smaller. The need for air con-

FIGURE A–9 Vacuum Tubes, Transistors, and Chips

You probably can't even see the chip on this photograph. The vacuum tube is on the left, the transistor is in the center, and the small speck on the right is a chip. By 1986 manufacturers will be packing more than a million transistors on a single chip, and by 1990 more than four million transistors will be placed on a quarter-inch-square chip.

ditioning was reduced, and a significant increase in speed was realized. Speeds were measured in microseconds (millionths of a second), and maintenance costs were significantly reduced because new and better components were used throughout the computer.

The most widely used business-oriented second-generation computer was the IBM 1401; the IBM 7090–7094 Series were the most widely used scientific computers. A new type of primary storage, **magnetic core**, was developed. This donut-shaped iron core could be magnetized either positively or negatively by sending electrical currents through the wires which run through the center of each core. Thus it is a binary storage device, capable of representing zero or one.

Magnetic tape was used extensively for secondary storage of data. Magnetic tape provided much faster input and output of data compared to punched cards. In fact, most large, second-generation computers were configured to accept only input or output on magnetic tape. Cards were transferred to magnetic tape and reports were printed from magnetic tapes by separate, smaller computers. This approach allowed the larger computers to operate at greater speeds; they did not have to wait on the relatively slow input of data from cards or output to printers. Processing was performed under the batch mode, with sequentially ordered files.

Later in this period, magnetic disks were developed for secondary storage (see

FIGURE A–10   Magnetic Disks

Magnetic disks were an extremely useful innovation for data storage. They made data randomly accessible, enabling computer systems to respond fast to information queries. They first appeared in the 1960s.

Figure A–10). Magnetic disks allowed for random file organization whereby a particular record could be retrieved immediately.

Software Advances

Operating systems were developed for use in second-generation computers. An **operating system** is software that controls execution of programs and manages computer resources. These operating systems were primitive batch serial systems that allowed execution of only one program at a time.

A major evolution in programming languages occurred during the second generation: the development of **high-level procedural languages**, such as **COBOL (Common Business-Oriented Language)** and **FORTRAN (Formula Translator)**. COBOL was developed by the **Committee on Data Systems Languages (CODASYL)** of which Hopper was a prominent member. CODASYL has been a major force in the continuing evolution of the COBOL language. COBOL and FORTRAN are much more like English than either machine or symbolic language. They are called procedural languages because they were developed to facilitate the programming of certain procedures. With FORTRAN the procedures are scientific, and with COBOL they are business-oriented. Updated versions of both of these languages are still widely used today.

Third-Generation Computers: 1965–1971

Hardware Advances

In the 1960s, the development of **integrated circuits** brought about the third generation of computers. Integrated circuits contain transistors that are deposited photochemically on a chip silicon material (see Figure A–11). The primary contributions of integrated-circuit technology were miniaturization and decreased costs. Miniaturization also increased speed because the distance that electronic pulses had to travel decreased. The nanosecond (one billionth of a second) became the new standard for measuring access and process time. This generation of computers began when IBM first delivered its System/360 computers.

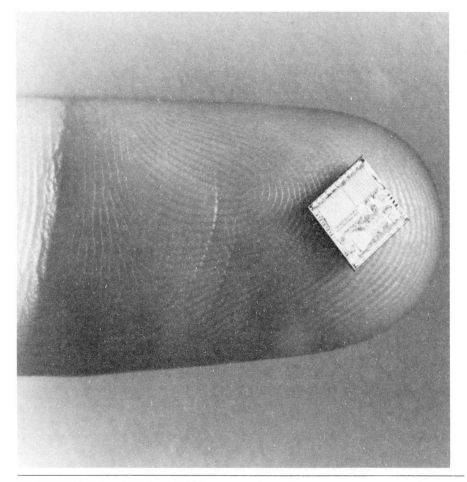

FIGURE A–11   A Silicon Chip

By the late 1980s and early 1990s we will be able to place the equivalent of today's mainframes and super computers in a computer the size of today's personal computers. This will be a direct result of decreasing chip sizes.

The first minicomputer was also developed in the mid-sixties by the Digital Equipment Corporation (DEC). Minicomputers are smaller versions of the larger mainframe computers which were originally developed for process control and military applications. However, as with earlier computers, business applications of these minicomputers quickly developed. Today minicomputers are very powerful machines, containing many more capabilities and features than the largest computers available in the 1960s.

On-line, realtime systems first became popular with third-generation computers. These systems were possible because of advances in disk-storage technology, enabling large amounts of data to be stored, with immediate random retrieval.

Software Advances

On-line, realtime systems are not possible without multiprogramming operating systems. These were developed for third-generation computers. **Multiprogramming operating systems** allow the concurrent execution of two or more programs. For example, while the computer is executing a batch payroll program, a sales person could query the inventory system through a terminal to determine quantity on hand of a particular item in the warehouse. This was a major advance in operating-system software. One computer could simultaneously handle high-priority on-line, realtime queries and time-consuming batch processing. Through a **remote terminal** over regular telephone lines or leased lines, data could be accessed from almost any location. In addition, these remote terminals could be used to initiate the execution of programs from remote locations and print the results out at the remote location. Many different users could be interacting with the computer at the same time. This approach is called **timesharing**. Multiprogramming operating systems make timesharing possible.

This generation of computers was the first to handle both business and scientific applications equally well. IBM Developed **PL/I**, a general-purpose language designed to replace FORTRAN and COBOL. However, it never succeeded in replacing them primarily because they had already become firmly established. Making the change to PL/I would have required tremendous retraining and reprogramming costs.

Along with vastly improved operating systems, the other major development in the software area during the third generation was the beginning of the software industry. Software firms write general-purpose application and system software and sell or lease its use to computer users. Examples of software that can be purchased are payroll, accounts-receivable, and general-ledger applications.

Fourth-Generation Computers: 1971–Present

Hardware Advances

The major technological development that distinguishes fourth-generation computers is the use of **large-scale integrated (LSI) circuits** for both logic and memory circuits. The primary computer to use this technology is the IBM 370 series, introduced in 1971. The more recent fourth-generation computers are employing **very large-scale integrated (VLSI) circuits**. With this technology, it is possible to place a complete CPU on one very small semiconductor chip. These circuits increase the speed of computers and drastically reduce the production cost. In fact, a primary distinguishing feature of the fourth generation is the decreased cost and increased performance of computer hardware. The processing power that could have been purchased for approximately one million dollars in the 1960s can be purchased now in the form of a personal computer for less than two thousand dollars.

In the fourth generation, LSI and VLSI circuits have replaced magnetic core as the dominant form of primary storage. Significant advances have also been made in the storage capacity, access speed, and costs of disk storage. It is common to see manufacturers announce new disk storage with double the capacity at no increase in cost or even a reduction in cost.

CRT terminals have become very widespread as processing moves from a batch mode to on-line. In the late 1970s **graphics terminals,** which can display charts and graphs in color, provided a new and exciting way of presenting information to management.

The dramatic decrease in the cost of computers has led to **distributed data processing (DDP)**. DDP is the installation of micro or mini computers at a company's remote locations. Local data processing is handled by a computer at the remote location.

The widespread use of CRT terminals and DDP has made **data communication** more important. This has led to new competitors (IBM and new companies such as MCI) for American Telephone and Telegraph Company (AT&T) in the data-communication business. In the early 1980s AT&T divested its local operating companies so that its Long Lines Division could better compete in the data-communication market and enter the computer field.

The fourth-generation development most likely to affect people is the micro computer or **personal computer** (see Figure A–12). As mentioned earlier, the ability to place a complete CPU on a single chip dramatically reduces the cost of computer hardware. For $99 to $1,000, an individual can purchase a basic micro computer that, when connected to a TV set, can assist in many household and personal-business tasks such as recipe filing, list keeping, checkbook balancing, and personal budgeting. In addition, this machine can entertain with computer games and provide security with fire and burglar alarm systems. These small computers are suitable for most elementary and secondary schools and are appearing in increasing numbers in their classrooms. In fact, one personal-computer company, Apple, proposed in 1982 to give an Apple personal computer to every elementary and secondary school in the United States. More sophisticated personal computers with disk drives and better-quality printing currently cost in the vicinity of $1,500 to $5,000.

Software Advances

There have also been very significant advances in computer software during the fourth generation. Data-base management systems, which assist in storing and retrieving large amounts of data, were introduced. The primary development in operating systems was the addition of **virtual-storage operating systems**. These

FIGURE A–12 Apple II-Plus Personal Computer

The Apple II along with Radio Shack's TRS–80 pioneered the personal-computer industry.

systems allow secondary storage to be used as if it were primary storage, hence the term **virtual storage** (the secondary storage is virtually primary storage).

Another trend in software was the development of **user-friendly systems**, especially electronic spreadsheets and word-processing packages. The idea was to develop software that would make computers easier to use. Some of this software, which is usually called fourth-generation languages, even allows users to develop applications without the assistance of programmers and system analysts. The trend toward user-friendly systems results partly from the increasing demands for computer software and the corresponding increase in costs to develop it. A summary of the characteristics of the computer generations is presented in Table A–1.

History of Personal Computers

PC Hardware

The personal computer has become so important that we should also examine its relatively short history. The first personal computer, the **Altair 8800**, appeared in 1975. A company called MITS sold it as a kit for $397. The Altair was bought by electronic hobbyists, who found it difficult to assemble. Even if the person was

Table A–1 Characteristics of Computer Generations

First Generation: 1951–1958

Drum primary storage
Punched-card and paper-tape secondary storage
Vacuum-tube circuits
Continuous maintenance required
Applications: payroll and other simple applications in large companies
Batch processing
Machine and symbolic language programming
Different computers for scientific and business applications

Second Generation: 1959–1964

Magnetic-core primary storage
Tape secondary storage
Transistor circuits
Greater reliability and speed
High-level procedural languages FORTRAN and COBOL
Applications: payroll, inventory, and accounts receivable in large and medium-sized
    companies
Batch processing

Third Generation: 1965–1971

Magnetic-disk secondary storage
On-line realtime processing
Multiprogramming operating systems
Integrated circuits
Increased miniaturization, speed, and reliability
Multipurpose computers capable of performing both scientific and business tasks
Development of minicomputers
Applications: order processing, airline-reservation systems, and realtime inventory control

Fourth Generation: 1971–Present

Large-scale and very large-scale integrated circuits
Semiconductor primary storage
Dramatic decrease in hardware cost
Increasing costs of software
Development of the micro/personal computer
Development of electronic spreadsheet
Point-of-origin data capture and entry
Widespread use of CRT terminals
Data-base management systems
Application development by users
User-friendly software
Virtual-storage operating systems
Distributed data processing
Increased use of data communication and computer networks
Graphics terminals
Applications: corporate modeling, decision-support systems, electronic funds transfer,
    electronic spreadsheet, word processing, and small business applications

Future Computers

Organic chips
Decreasing costs of software
Decreasing costs of hardware
Super and ultra personal computers
Increased miniaturization
Vast improvements in the price-performance ratio
Applications: artificial intelligence, robots, large-scale corporate modeling, oil exploration,
    weather-system modeling, star-wars systems, and personal robots

successful in assemblying the Altair, there was virtually nothing that could be done with it! The Altair 8800 had no keyboard or monitor. Both programs and data had to be painstakingly entered in binary form via 16 switches that could be turned on or off. Output was displayed, also in binary form, by 36 light-emitting diodes. Since there were no application programs available for the Altair, a user had to write them in binary machine language.

The Altair was a great machine for those who input, think, and see in binary form. I know of no human who does. Yet thousands of the Altair 8800s were sold. It was an instant success. Why? Prior to the Altair, only large corporations and organizations could afford this wondrous machine called a computer. At the time the only IBM computer that came close to being a personal computer was the 5100, which sold for $19,000. Few individuals bought it. But many people could afford an Altair. I suspect that many Altair owners saw their computer as a status symbol.

Let's think like entrepreneurs. If thousands of people will pay $397 for a box of electronic parts that are difficult to assemble into a computer that does nothing useful, there must be an incredible market for personal computers! Several entrepreneurs jumped at this opportunity. From 1975 through 1978 IMSAI sold a machine similar to the Altair. Both MITS and IMSAI were fertile breeding grounds for personal-computer entrepreneurs. Bill Millard, who started Computerland, was associated with IMSAI. Both Bill Gates, a founder of Microsoft Corp., and David Bunnell, a founder of *PC Magazine* and *PC World,* were employees of MITS. But most important, this opportunity spurred the second generation of personal computers. The most prominent were introduced in 1977: the **Apple II** and Radio Shack's **TRS–80**. These computers had features that the Altair lacked, such as monitors, keyboards and more primary memory. They were very successful. The TRS–80 sold in its first month three times the number projected for the entire year of 1977.

Even more remarkable was the success of the Apple II. Apple Computer was developed in a garage in 1977 and in less than seven years was one of the largest five hundred corporations. The company was started by Steve Wozniak, a young electronics engineer from Hewlett-Packard, and Steve Jobs, who in his early twenties, was new to the entrepreneurship game. They both were avid members of the Homebrew Computer Club which was a group of Altair 8800 enthusiasts. Wozniak sold his Hewlett-Packard calculators and Jobs sold his Volkswagen bus to raise money to start Apple. As they grew they had the good sense to hire professional business managers and a first-rate advertising agency. Today Apple Computer, with its MacIntosh, is in perhaps a life or death struggle with IBM for the business PC market.

IBM was a latecomer to the PC market when it introduced the **IBM PC** in September 1981. Prior to the PC, IBM had built computers around its own *proprietary* technology. This protected the market for its computers. Competitors had difficulty building similar computers without violating patent or copyright laws. However, IBM adapted to the open nature of the personal-computer market by encouraging others to build both hardware and software that would operate with the IBM PC. IBM even chose an outside vendor, Microsoft Corporation, for the **disk operating system (DOS)**. The IBM PC is literally an assembly of many components from several companies.

proprietary
That which is exclusively owned by an individual or corporation, such as a patent.

Since neither the operating system nor most of its hardware components are proprietary to IBM, many other companies have produced IBM PC compatible machines. The most successful is Compaq, another new company. The IBM PC has quickly given legitimacy to the personal computer in the business world and has become a standard for the industry.

PC Software

In personal-computer software the most significant development was **VisiCalc** (Visible Calculator), introduced in 1979. VisiCalc automated the very widespread business chore of calculating spreadsheets. It was indeed revolutionary! VisiCalc gave almost every business a reason to own one or more personal computers. Two Harvard MBA students originated the VisiCalc idea.

One of VisiCalc's former employees, Mitch Kapor, along with a single programmer, produced Lotus 1–2–3. An improved electronic spreadsheet, **Lotus 1–2–3** was designed for the IBM PC. Suddenly, it became the standard spreadsheet and produced another new, fast-growth company, Lotus Development Corporation.

Other software has contributed to the usefulness of personal computers, particularly word processing. The first word-processing program for PCs was **Electric Pencil**, developed by Michael Shrayer. It was developed for the Altair but was subsequently rewritten to run on many PCs. The most widely used word-processing software has been **WordStar**. It was produced by Micro Pro International, a company started by two people involved with IMSAC. Today a wide range of software, such as data-base managers, project managers, communication software, and integrated software are contributing to the widespread use of PCs. We will see much more useful software introduced in the future.

PC USER TIP   Market versus Personal Obsolescence

A common fear of people about to buy a PC is obsolescence. It is not uncommon to hear someone contemplating the purchase of a PC say, "I would buy one today but I am afraid that tomorrow they will come out with a new model and then mine will be obsolete." Certainly there is some reason to be concerned when you are entering a market where a five-year old product is considered an antique. However, there are several types of obsolescence and it is important to keep them straight in your mind. First there is market obsolescence. It is the type of obsolescence referred to by the person just quoted. Clearly if it is your goal to have the state-of-the-art computer on your desk at all times, market obsolescence is a major worry. But besides a retail PC store and perhaps a few individuals, this kind of obsolescence should not be of concern to most individuals. Most people should worry about something else—personal obsolescence. Individuals purchase personal computers for a variety of reasons, but in general they purchase them because the PC performs some task for them. They do word processing or keep track of a customer list, for example. Personal obsolescence occurs when a new product enters the market that does your tasks so much better than the existing machine that it becomes obsolete. Even then the computer you bought will continue to perform the tasks it always has performed. This type of obsolescense happens much less frequently than market obsolescence. The next time you hear yourself say you would like to buy a personal computer but you are concerned about obsolescence, ask yourself whether it is market or personal obsolescence. If it is market obsolescence, stop and think again.

Future Computers

By the end of 1982 there were more computers on earth than there were people—more than five billion computers were in use, from microchips to mainframes. They are literally everywhere; in automobiles, appliances, business information systems, and military hardware. With electronic technology advancing rapidly, the use of computers is expected to grow even faster in coming years. We will explore some areas of potential growth based on current trends.

One computer prediction is a sure bet. Computers will increase in performance and decrease in size and cost. As shown in Figure A–13, these trends began with the first generation of computers. Software costs have continued to increase. This is because software grows in complexity and its development is a labor-intensive process. However, new approaches to developing software, such as the structured system development life cycle, prototyping, and application development by users, are beginning to decrease the costs of producing software. In addition, the costs of personal computer software packages are expected to decline.

Some people wonder why we need computers to be any faster than they already are. The fact is that many problems cannot be adequately solved at the speed at

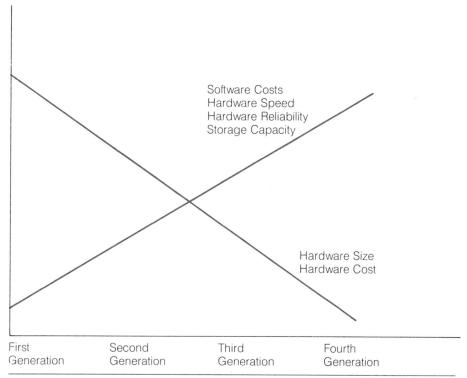

FIGURE A–13   Computer Hardware and Software Trends

Computer hardware has become so inexpensive that it is a relatively minor part of the information-processing costs of today's organizations.

simulate
To build a model or imitation of something that exists in the real world, such as a business, a weather system, or aircraft. Simulations that are built on computers are mathematical models.

which today's computers operate. An extremely important application of computer technology is modeling and simulation. Diverse users such as business strategic forecasters, government economists, design engineers, and geologist *simulate* real-world events on computers to aid in better decision making. Faster turnaround on these applications could lead to significant savings owing to more timely decisions.

Even with existing hardware technology there are many fields in which electronic data processing has not yet been applied to full advantage. In coming years industry is expected to increase the use of **computer-aided-design and computer-aided-manufacturing (CAD/CAM)** techniques. This will require, among other things, refinement of graphics techniques, improvement of production-control software, and developments in robot technology.

The revolutionary increase in computer hardware performance compared to cost is just beginning. Experimental silicon chips that contain more than a million transistors will be in production by 1986. This means that a mainframe computer could be packed onto a single chip! Imagine a mainframe or even a supercomputer (having the size and price of today's personal computers) sitting on your desk! This is not wild speculation. It is here-and-now engineering, planning, and investing by the world's semiconductor manufacturing companies. Figure A–14 illustrates the advances in semiconductor chips that are expected in the next ten years. If these expectations materialize they will literally revolutionize most human endeavors. Computers will be able to mimic human intelligence, such as the abilities to see, reason, and converse in a natural language such as English.

Behind these advances in semiconductor technology are researchers in both Japan and the United States who have embarked on the ambitious **fifth-gener-**

Year:	1980	1985	1987	1990	1995
Circuit Size:	4 Microns	2 Microns	1 Micron	0.5 Micron	0.25 Micron
Memory Capacity:	64K	256K	1,024K	4,096K	16,384K
Power Range:	Desktop Microcomputer	Minicomputer	Mainframe Computer	Supercomputer	Ultracomputer
Applications:	Digital Watches, Video Games, Personal Computers	Lap Computers, Engineering Work Stations, Programmable Appliances	Pocket Computers, Electronic Map-Navigators, High-Resolution TVs	Robots that can see, Freeze-frame TVs, Computers that Recognize and Use Natural Languages	Star Wars Systems, Personal Robots, Computers with Human-like Logic

FIGURE A–14   What Packing More Power on a Chip Will Bring

The memory capacity of chips increased four-fold from 1980 to 1985. From 1985 to 1990 it is expected to increase sixteen-fold, and another four-fold from 1990 to 1995. This averages out to a doubling of chip memory capacity about every two years!

ation project to produce major advances in hardware and software. In Japan this effort is subsidized by the Japanese government. The United States effort is being led by the Microelectronics Computer Corporation, a consortium of several U.S. computer companies. IBM has not joined this consortium and is pursuing fifth-generation research independently. The goal of the fifth-generation projects is to produce radically different computer systems whose primary characteristic is **artificial intelligence.**

Many experts now anticipate that computers will be used for very practical artificial intelligence systems within the next ten years. These computers will be able to reason, see, converse in English, make expert judgments, and perhaps even learn. If this occurs, the world may change dramatically. The major characteristic that distinguishes humans is our ability to reason. Are we on the brink of creating a machine that has greater reasoning powers than 99 percent of the human population? Will we need as many human experts, such as doctors, lawyers, and system analysts? Will expert computer systems produce a profound increase in the quality of human existence? Let's assume the experts' predictions come true. What impacts, both positive and negative, will artificial intelligence have on the career you plan to pursue?

Thinking About Information Systems A–2

Other researchers believe it will soon be possible to use the chemistry of living cells to produce computers. These organic computers may operate at the speeds well above today's supercomputers and could store much more data. The researchers feel that these computers would have significant advantages over silicon-based chips—they would not generate heat and could be much smaller. An organic chip may be able to store one billion times as much data as a similar-sized silicon chip. The direction of this research seems to confirm the fact that the human brain is the most remarkable of all computers. This fact is not likely to change in your lifetime.

Even with current technology the office of the future should be a more efficient and productive place to work. As office workers, from the receptionist to the president of the firm, learn more about the computer, it will become a much larger part of their daily routine.

Like any other technology, computer information systems are expected to give rise to some undesirable phenomena. When billions of dollars' worth of assets are controlled and processed by computers, the risk of fraud is extremely high. Businesses have a strong interest in ensuring that only authorized transactions are executed by their information systems. This should lead to the development of sophisticated computer security and computer audit techniques. The growth of distributed data processing and data-communication usage will further enhance the importance of such control mechanisms.

Office managers and **ergonomists** are voicing their concern over the harmful effects of computer usage in the office such as eye strain, exposure to radiation, and general fatigue from long hours of operating a video display terminal. As a result, design improvements are expected in both hardware and software products.

ergonomics
The science of designing computer hardware and software to make them easier for people to use.

Strong competition in the information-systems market will force vendors to make their products more suitable for human use, rather than requiring that people adapt themselves to the computer.

Summing Up

☐ The abacus, invented by the Chinese and used by the ancient Greeks and Romans, is the first known calculating device.

☐ Mechanically operated calculators were used from 1642 to about 1970. Blaise Pascal, a Frenchman, is credited with inventing these machines. Later, Gottfried von Leibnitz improved Pascal's design for a calculator.

☐ In the early nineteenth century Joseph Jacquard used punched cards to control textile-mill operations.

☐ Charles Babbage proposed the construction of an analytical engine, using punched cards. This machine, like today's computers, would have had input and output devices, a CPU, and memory space.

☐ Ada Byron, Countess of Lovelace, is recognized as the first programmer for her work in developing (programming) mathematical tables for Babbage's analytical engine.

☐ In the 1870s Henry Metcalfe developed the unit-record concept. By storing cost-accounting information on cards, he was able to manipulate it much more easily than was possible with the traditional leatherbound ledgers.

☐ Starting with the 1880 U.S. Census, punched-card equipment was increasingly used for data processing by government and industry. Herman Hollerith and James Powers developed this equipment. The need for computing equipment during World War II greatly stimulated the beginning of the computer industry.

☐ Howard Aiken of Harvard University built the first electromechanical computer in 1944, the Mark I.

☐ Commodore Grace Murray Hopper programmed the Mark I, and was a major contributor to the COBOL language.

☐ The first electronic computer, capable of running stored programs, was completed at the University of Pennsylvania in 1946 by John W. Mauchly, Jr. and J. Presper Eckert, Jr. This was soon followed by computers using the binary number system for internal storage.

☐ First-generation computers (1951–1958) used vacuum tubes for switching and controlling functions. A major breakthrough of this generation was the use of translators to convert symbolic-language programs into machine-language instructions.

☐ The second-generation machines (1959–1964) offered a number of improvements over the first generation. The vacuum tubes were replaced by transistors, which reduced size and increased speed. Faster memory devices such as magnetic core, tapes, and magnetic disks were extensively used. The major software developments in this period were the use of operating systems to control program execution, and the creation of high-level procedural languages such as COBOL and FORTRAN.

☐ Third-generation computers (1965–1971) were even smaller and faster, thanks to the development of integrated circuit technology. On-line, realtime applications could be run under multiprogramming operating systems. Through the use of remote terminals, these systems allowed a much larger number of users to access the computer from their own locations.

☐ Fourth-generation computers (1971–present) employed very sophisticated technology to improve processing speed and reduce production costs. The application of semiconductor technology has greatly reduced the cost of memory space. Lower costs have led to the widespread use of computers in applications ranging from simple household budgeting to extremely complex distributed data-base systems.

☐ The first personal computer, the Altair 8800, was produced by MITS. It was in kit form and had very limited capabilities.

☐ The TRS–80 and Apple II were second-generation personal computers that were purchased by many individuals.

☐ The IBM PC was introduced in September 1981. It legitimized the personal computer in the business market and established itself as the standard.

☐ VisiCalc, the first electronic spreadsheet, was a major factor in making personal computers useful to the business professional.

☐ In the future, computers are expected to be much faster and smaller. Personal computers will have today's super-computer capabilities. They will be able to solve many problems that today's computers cannot cope with owing to speed and memory limitations. Sophisticated systems will be developed to automate work in the factory as well as in the office. At the same time it will be necessary to improve control over computerized systems so that unauthorized operations cannot be performed.

Key Terms

abacus
mechanical calculators
Blaise Pascal
Gottfried von Leibnitz
Jacquard's loom
punched cards
Charles Babbage
stored program
difference engine
analytical engine
Augusta Ada Byron
Henry Metcalfe
coding scheme
unit record

Herman Hollerith
tabulating machine
James Powers
simultaneous punching
key-punches
key-verifiers
sorters
reproducers
collators
tabulating machines
eighty-column Hollerith card
ninety-column Powers card
Howard Aiken
Mark I

electromechanical computer
Grace Murray Hopper
John W. Mauchly
J. Presper Eckert, Jr.
vacuum tubes
ENIAC (Electronic Numerical Integrator and Calculator)
John von Neumann
binary number system
EDVAC (Electronic Discrete Variable Automatic Computer)
Maurice Wilker
EDSAC (Electronic Delay Storage Automatic Computer)

stored-program electronic digital computer
generations
UNIVAC-I (Universal Automatic Computer)
magnetic drums
symbolic languages
machine language
translator
semiconductor
transistor
magnetic core
magnetic tape
operating system
high-level procedural languages
COBOL (Common Business-Oriented
  Language)
FORTRAN (Formula Translator)
Committee on Data Systems
  Languages (CODASYL)
integrated circuits
on-line, realtime systems
multiprogramming operating systems
remote terminal
timesharing
PL/I

large-scale integrated (LSI) circuits
very large-scale integrated (VLSI) circuits
CRT terminals
graphics terminals
distributed data processing (DDP)
data communication
personal computer
virtual-storage operating systems
user-friendly systems
Altair 8800
Apple II
TRS–80
IBM PC
disk operating system (DOS)
VisiCalc
Lotus 1–2–3
Electric Pencil
WordStar
computer-aided-design and
  computer-aided-manufacturing (CAD/CAM)
fifth-generation project
artificial intelligence
ergonomists

Self-Quiz

Completion Questions

1. The capability that differentiates computers from calculators is the _____ .
2. The four major components used in Babbage's analytical engine were input and output devices, an arithmetic unit, and a _____ .
3. The first electronic digital computer is the _____ .
4. The biggest advance in software in first-generation computers was the use of _____ for programming.
5. The second generation of computers were possible largely owing to the development of the _____ .
6. On-line, realtime systems first became popular with _____-generation computers.
7. The development of _____ technology brought about the third generation of computers.

8. The primary advance in operating systems in fourth-generation computers was the addition of _____ operating systems which allow secondary storage to be used as if it were primary storage.
9. In the fourth generation, _____ replaced magnetic core as the dominant form of primary storage.
10. A trend in software for fourth-generation computers was the development of _____ systems, which make computers easier to use.

Multiple-Choice Questions

1. Advances in computer hardware and software are generally classified into generations. We are currently in which generation.
   a. second
   b. third

c. fourth
d. fifth

2. The first machine to successfully perform a long series of arithmetic and logical operations was:
   a. ENIAC
   b. Mark I
   c. Analytic engine
   d. UNIVAC-I
   e. EDSAC

3. Which of the following was (were) not used in first-generation computers?
   a. vacuum tubes
   b. cards
   c. magnetic core
   d. punched paper tape
   e. all of the above were used in first-generation computers

4. Which of the following was not associated with second-generation computers?
   a. high-level procedural language
   b. operating system
   c. magnetic core
   d. transistor
   e. all of the above were associated with second-generation computers

5. Which of the following is true of the ENIAC?
   a. It was developed by Charles Babbage.
   b. It was the first stored-program electronic digital computer.
   c. It was an electromechanical computer.
   d. It used vacuum tubes in place of electromagnetic relays.
   e. None of the above.

6. The third generation of computers covers the period:
   a. 1959–1964
   b. 1965–1971
   c. 1971–1981
   d. 1981–now

7. In the third generation of computers:
   a. high-level procedural languages were first used
   b. an operating system was first developed

c. distributed data processing first became popular
d. on-line, realtime systems first became popular
e. all of the above

8. All of the following became popular during the fourth generation of computers except:
   a. minicomputers
   b. semiconductors
   c. CRT terminals
   d. personal computers
   e. all of the above were popular

9. The decreased cost and increased performance of computer hardware were the distinguishing features of which generation of computers?
   a. first
   b. second
   c. third
   d. fourth
   e. all generations

10. Which of the following is not true of future computers?
    a. increased use of CAD/CAM techniques
    b. faster turnaround time
    c. developments in artificial intelligence systems
    d. development of products more suitable for human use
    e. all of the above are true

Answers

Completion	Multiple-Choice
1. stored program	1. c
2. memory	2. b
3. ENIAC	3. c
4. symbolic language	4. e
5. transistor	5. d
6. third	6. b
7. integrated-circuit	7. d
8. virtual-storage	8. a
9. semiconductors	9. e
10. user-friendly	10. e

Module B

Programming Languages

MODULE OUTLINE

PROLOGUE

All computers understand only binary machine language, a string of ones and zeros. However, we have developed complex programming languages that can instruct computers. Some are easy to learn, others are better for business applications. Some languages are even like English. What are the characteristics, advantages, and disadvantages of the major languages? Read on.

Introduction

Software for large, complex, and/or unique applications is usually written by an application programmer to fulfill a particular user or application requirement. The development of application software should be performed using structured methodology, as discussed in chapters 5 and 6. Before any coding (programming) is done, the application must be analyzed and a structured physical design developed, which is in effect the programmer's blueprint for coding the application. From this structured design specification, a suitable language is used to code the program(s). A **program** is a set of instructions executed by the computer. The instructions cause the computer to perform a desired task. The selection of a language depends primarily on the nature of the problem or application, as well as the individual programmer's choice, which language is standard within the company, and the capabilities of the hardware.

This module will introduce you to the most widely used programming languages. In addition, factors influencing the selection of a language will be discussed.

Types of Programming Languages

Machine Language

The evolution of software is characterized by various stages or generations, beginning with the tedious machine language, and evolving to the present-day **high-level languages. Machine language,** as the name implies, is a machine-oriented language. Programmers using such a language must be extremely familiar with the design, operation, and peripherals of a particular computer. This creates a **semantic gap** between the application and the programming language. In other words, a programmer cannot write a machine-language program directly from the structured design specifications developed for the application, and expect any similarities between the program and the specifications. In fact, the machine code would be unintelligible to most users. For example, a program that computes tax, written in machine code, is in no way similar to the English description of the computation.

object code
A machine-language program that has been produced from a higher-level language through the compilation process. It is called object code since its production is the *objective* of compilation or translation.

A machine-language program is a set of instructions that have a one-to-one correspondence to every operation that must be performed. It is the only language that a computer can understand. All programs written in other languages must be compiled or translated into machine language for execution. A machine-language program is also known as *object code.* Object code is machine-readable and requires no translation process before execution. This feature allows for extremely fast processing time, and more efficient use of primary storage.

However, programming in machine code is very tedious because the programmer is concerned not only with problem definition but also with the clerical tasks such as manually assigning primary-storage locations in which to store the data and program. The programmer must keep track of each memory location used throughout the program. This task makes writing and debugging a machine-language program extremely difficult. The probability that the programmer may inadvertently write data or instructions into primary-storage locations that contain other data or instructions, and thereby destroy them, is very high. Changes in instructions are extremely difficult to make because the programmer must reassign all references to storage locations manually, making the program inflexible. Because of the difficulties of programming in machine language, it is not used today. Instead, symbolic or high-level procedural languages are used.

Symbolic Languages

As the evolution of software continued, **symbolic languages** were developed. The IBM **assembly language,** which uses **mnemonics** or symbols for each machine-language instruction, is an example. Assembly language allows the programmer to specify constants and storage locations symbolically. This feature takes some of the tediousness out of programming in machine language, and gives the responsibility to a program called an assembler. Like machine language, an assembly language is designed for a specific machine. Therefore, the program makes efficient use of the time and resources of the CPU. In general, there is still a one-to-one correspondence between instructions and actual computer operations. Each symbol corresponds to one machine operation, and is descriptive of that particular operation. The ***assembler*** translates the assembly-language program into machine code, and then references and assigns all addresses and storage locations. An assembly, or higher-level language program, is known as ***source code.*** It is written by an application programmer, and must be translated or compiled into object code (machine-language code) before it is executed.

Since machine-language code and assembly languages are difficult to comprehend, a simple example will be used to illustrate the nature and complexity of programming in these languages. Figure B–1 illustrates a simple program that adds two variables, X and Y, and then places the result in a third variable, *SUM.* In **pseudocode,** the program would be expressed as follows:

```
program ADD;
    declare X            real initial (1),
            Y            real initial (2),
            SUM          real;
    SUM = X + Y;
end ADD;
```

To illustrate the complexity of the machine code, we will look at only the LOAD instruction. The LOAD instruction in Figure B-1 is broken down as follows:

```
58  2  0  F  010
```

where   58 is the hexadecimal representation for the LOAD operation code,
          2 is the hexadecimal representation for "register 2,"
          0 is the hexadecimal representation for the index register (not used in this example),

assembler
A computer program that translates an assembly-language program into machine language.

source code
A program written in a higher-level language than machine language. It is called source code because it is the starting point or *source* in the compilation process to produce object code.

F   is the hexadecimal representation for the base register,

010   is the hexadecimal representation for the relative location of contents to be loaded.

This example shows the clerical detail involved in coding the program. The programmer must determine which storage areas (or **registers**) will be used in the program. In statement 2 of the assembly-language program, register 15 is designated as the **base register** from which all storage locations associated with the program will be determined. The base register contains the relative address of the next instruction, which is the LOAD instruction (statement 3) at relative location 000000. Statements 3 through 5 use register 2 for temporary storage during the addition process. Statement 3 is the instruction that will "load register 2 with the contents of the memory location (000010), designated X." Statement 4 will "add to register 2 the contents of the memory location (000014), designated Y." Statement 5 "stores the contents of register 2, the sum of X and Y, in the memory location (000018), designated SUM."

Today, application programmers seldom write in assembly language, though some use it to write programs that are executed many times (such as arithmetic functions and specialized input/output programs). Assembler is also used to provide access to operating-system resources that may be unavailable in high-level languages, such as graphics and physical input and output. Because assembly-language programs are efficient in terms of processing time and primary-storage utilization, assembly language is generally used by system programmers who write operating-system programs. For these programs execution time is a primary consideration.

Thinking About Information Systems B–1

The Hercules Company recruits a large number of business graduates with majors such as management, marketing, finance, management science, and accounting. Ramon Noegel is director of personnel. Several operational managers in the company have suggested that he require all new hires to have taken at least one programming course in their college career. They argue that a person must understand programming in order to use computers effectively and to really understand what the computer is doing. Ramon maintains that programming is becoming an obsolete skill. He states that business personnel who are not programmers can certainly utilize the computer in many effective ways without knowing how to program. He cites the fact that there are many user-friendly packages available for microcomputers, such as electronic worksheets, report generators, data-base management systems, and graphics, that can be used without programming. Do you think that learning at least one programming language is useful to a business student?

High-Level Languages

The third stage of software evolution brought about the development of procedure-oriented high-level languages (FORTRAN, COBOL, and PL/I) and problem-oriented high-level languages (RPG). A **procedure-oriented language** is a language in which the programmer gives step-by-step instructions to the computer. Using a **problem-oriented language,** the programmer only needs to describe the functions the computer must perform. A **compiler** for the problem-oriented language generates the necessary machine-language instructions for the computer. These languages help bridge the semantic gap between problem definition and the language.

With these machine-independent languages, the programmer needs to know very little about the machine on which the program is executed. Programming is now simpler because there is a buffer, the compiler, which handles all cross-referencing and storage allocation. However, processing speed and efficient use of computer memory are sacrificed for the advantage of simplified programming. The high-level-language program must go through three processes before it is ready to be executed:

1. **Translation** (Compilation): The translator (compiler) program translates the source code into object code (machine-language code).
2. **Linking:** The linkage editor combines with the program any *called* instructions or *library routines.*
3. **Loading:** The loader program *loads* the object code and its appended library functions/instructions into main memory for execution.

Figure B–2 illustrates these processes. They are performed for most high-level programming languages.

Our discussion will include five procedure-oriented languages (FORTRAN, COBOL, PL/I, BASIC, PASCAL, and ADA), and one problem-oriented language (RPG). We will illustrate selected languages with an example that calculates and prints a payroll report called the Payroll Register. A description of the program is as follows:

1. Print the *header* for the payroll register.
2. For each employee, read in a record containing the job code which identifies the type of job the employee holds, the employee's social security number, the number of hours worked, and current hourly wage.
   a. If the job code is equal to 1111 then the employee works part-time and no deductions are taken except for federal and state income taxes.
   b. If the job code is equal to 1120 then the employee works full time and all deductions are taken except for credit-union dues.
   c. If the job code is equal to 1122 then the employee works full time and all deductions are taken.
3. Calculate the payroll for each employee with a valid job code, or print an error message.
4. Finally, when the end of the input file is reached, print the totals for the Payroll Register.

This program is designed to process any number of employees and print the total net earnings. A sample of the output, the Payroll Register, is illustrated in Figure B–3.

FORTRAN **FORTRAN** (FORmula TRANslator), created in 1954, is considered one of the oldest high-level languages. Prior to its development most programming

call
The action of bringing a computer program, a routine, or subroutine into effect; for example, to summon a library routine for use in a program.

library routines
Standard programs that are used quite often as part of another program, such as a program that sorts data in ascending sequence. Library routines are stored on disk and the linkage editor combines them with any program that calls them so that the program does not have to rewrite them each time they are used.

load
To bring a program into primary storage for execution.

header
The top part of a report, including the column headings.

FIGURE B–1 A Program Coded in Machine and Assembly Language

Machine Code

MEMORY LOCATION	OBJECT CODE	ADDR1	ADDR2
0000000			00000
000000	5820 F010	00010	
000004	5A20 F014	00014	
000008	5020 F018	00018	
00000C	07FE		
00000E	0000		
000010	00000001		
000014	00000002		
000018			

Assembly Language

STMT	SOURCE	STATEMENT		Explanation
1	ADD	CSECT		;IDENTIFIES BEGINNING/NAME OF PGM
2		USING	*,15	;IDENTIFIES R15 AS BASE REGISTER
3		L	2,X	;LOAD '1' INTO R2
4		A	2,Y	;ADD '2' TO CONTENTS OF R2
5		ST	2,SUM	;STORE CONTENTS OF R2 IN SUM
6		BR	14	;RETURN CONTROL TO CALLER PGM
7	X	DC	F'1'	;RESERVE MEMORY LOCATION FOR X, INIT TO '1'
8	Y	DC	F'2'	;RESERVE MEMORY LOCATION FOR Y, INIT TO '2'
9	SUM	DS	F	;RESERVE MEMORY LOCATION FOR SUM
10		END		

These two programs are merely adding X + Y and placing the result in SUM. What an incredible amount of detail to perform such a simple operation! It is no wonder that higher-level languages for computers were developed.

Job Code	Employee Number	Hours Worked	Hourly Wage	Gross Pay	Social Security Tax	Federal Income Tax	State Income Tax	Credit Union	Retirement	Net Pay
1111	400941648	33.00	4.51	148.83	0.00	1.04	1.19	0.00	0.00	146.60
1122	224949460	40.00	5.10	204.00	13.67	23.05	6.12	10.20	10.20	140.76
1120	900221792	44.00	4.51	207.46	13.90	23.44	6.22	0.00	10.37	153.52
1122	224885493	45.00	7.25	344.38	23.07	38.91	10.33	17.22	17.22	237.62
1111	900120001	25.00	3.25	81.25	0.00	0.57	0.65	0.00	0.00	80.03

Total Earnings: 758.53

FIGURE B–3 Payroll Register

The term *register* is often used for computer reports, especially those which are accounting oriented.

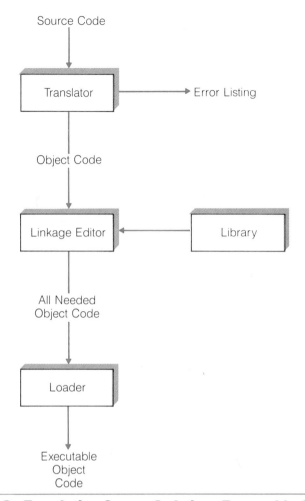

Source Code

Translator → Error Listing

Object Code

Linkage Editor ← Library

All Needed
Object Code

Loader

Executable
Object
Code

FIGURE B–2 Translating Source Code into Executable Object Code

The object code is machine code, as illustrated in Figure B–1. The translator or compiler is a program that converts the source code of a high-level language (such as COBOL) into the machine-language object code.

was done in machine or assembly language. FORTRAN was developed to code scientific and mathematical expressions. Therefore, *algorithms* dealing with processing of numbers or *arrays* of numbers can be coded in FORTRAN. Several versions have been released, beginning with the original version, FORTRAN I. In 1958 FORTRAN II was devised, and FORTRAN IV was developed in 1962. In 1966 the language was standardized, bringing about the *ANS* FORTRAN version. Finally, in 1978, a new version called FORTRAN 77 was developed, which provides for structured, modular programs enhancing readability and overall writing. An instructional version called **WATFIV** was developed at the University of Waterloo in Canada.

A FORTRAN program is a sequence of **statements.** All statements are composed of keywords, variable names, and symbols. **Keywords** are verbs that tell the computer which operations to perform, such as READ, WRITE, STOP, DO, and IF.

algorithm
A set of well-defined rules for solving a problem in a finite number of steps.

array
An arrangement of numbers or characters with one or more dimensions.

ANS
American National Standard. The American National Standards Institute is an organization whose purpose is to assist in the development of voluntary industry standards.

```
 1          REAL EXTRA,OTIME,TOTAL,FCRATE,FTRATE,STRATE,CURATE,RTRATE,
       1       HOURS,RATE,GROSS,FICA,FIT,SIT,RETIRE,CUNION,NET,WHRS
 2          INTEGER EMPNO,JOBCODE
 3          COMMON WHRS,OTIME,FCRATE,FTRATE,STRATE,RTRATE,CURATE,TOTAL,
       1       HOURS,RATE,GROSS,FICA,FIT,SIT,RETIRE,CUNION,NET
 4          COMMON JOBCODE,EMPNO
 5          DATA TOTAL/0.0/
 6          WRITE (6,300)
 7          WRITE (6,500)
 8          WRITE (6,400)
 9     10 CONTINUE
10          READ (5,200,END=100) JOBCODE,EMPNO,HOURS,RATE
11          OTIME=0.0
12          WHRS=HOURS
13          FCRATE=0.0
14          FTRATE=0.0
15          STRATE=0.0
16          RTRATE=0.0
17          CURATE=0.0
18          IF (JOBCODE.EQ.1111)THEN
19             FTRATE=0.007
20             STRATE=0.008
21             CALL CALC
22          ELSE
23             IF ((JOBCODE.EQ.1120).OR.(JOBCODE.EQ.1122))THEN
24                FCRATE=0.067
25                FTRATE=0.113
26                STRATE=0.03
27                RTRATE=0.05
28                IF (JOBCODE.EQ.1122)THEN
29                   CURATE=0.05
30                END IF
31                IF (HOURS.GT.40.0) THEN
32                   EXTRA=HOURS-40.0
33                   OTIME=EXTRA*RATE*1.5
34                   WHRS=40.0
35                END IF
36                CALL CALC
37             ELSE
38                WRITE (6,900)
39             END IF
40          END IF
41          GO TO 10
```

FIGURE B–4   Payroll Program Written in FORTRAN

Indenting nested statements within a program improves its readability. For example, statements 18, 22, and 40 are all part of a single IF-THEN-ELSE statement. Notice we have indented the nested IF-THEN-ELSE statements within the first level. For example, the second level is line 23, 37, and 39, another IF-THEN-ELSE statement.

Variable names are used to designate storage locations. Symbols, such as +, −, and ∗ are used primarily for arithmetic operations. Figure B–4 is an example of a FORTRAN 77 program.

There are two types of FORTRAN statements: executable and nonexecutable. **Nonexecutable statements** are used to declare various characteristics of the program such as data types and input/output formats. These statements are known

```
42       100 CONTINUE
43           WRITE (6,500)
44           WRITE (6,700) TOTAL
45           WRITE (6,800)
46           STOP
47       200 FORMAT (I4,I9,F5.2,F4.2)
48       300 FORMAT ('1',50X,'Payroll Register')
49       400 FORMAT (' ',56X,'Social',5X,'Federal',5X,'State'/
        1         ' ',4X,'Job',5X,'Employee',5X,'Hours',4X,'Hourly',5X,
        2         'Gross',5X,'Security',5X,'Income',4X,'Income',4X,'Credit',
        3         20X,'Net'/
        4         ' ',2X,'Code',7X,'Number',5X,'Worked',5X,'Wage',7X,'Pay',
        5         8X,'Tax',9X,'Tax',8X,'Tax',6X,'Union',4X,'Retirement',
        6         6X,'Pay'/)
50       500 FORMAT (' ',1X)
51       700 FORMAT (' ',95X,'Total Earnings: ',F8.2)
52       800 FORMAT ('1',1X)
53       900 FORMAT (' ',2X,'Invalid Job Code.')

54           END
55           SUBROUTINE CALC
56           REAL EXTRA,OTIME,TOTAL,FCRATE,FTRATE,STRATE,CURATE,RTRATE,
        1         HOURS,RATE,GROSS,FICA,FIT,SIT,RETIRE,CUNION,NET,WHRS
57           INTEGER EMPNO,JOBCODE
58           COMMON WHRS,OTIME,FCRATE,FTRATE,STRATE,RTRATE,CURATE,TOTAL,
        1         HOURS,RATE,GROSS,FICA,FIT,SIT,RETIRE,CUNION,NET
59           COMMON JOBCODE,EMPNO
60           GROSS=(WHRS*RATE)+OTIME
61           FICA=GROSS*FCRATE
62           FIT=GROSS*FTRATE
63           SIT=GROSS*STRATE
64           RETIRE=GROSS*RTRATE
65           CUNION=GROSS*CURATE
66           NET=GROSS-(FICA+FIT+SIT+SIT+RETIRE+CUNION)
67           TOTAL=TOTAL+NET
68           WRITE (6,600) JOBCODE,EMPNO,HOURS,RATE,GROSS,FICA,FIT,SIT,
        1                     CUNION,RETIRE,NET
69       600 FORMAT (' ',2X,I4,5X,I9,4X,F6.2,4X,F6.2,4X,F7.2,5X,F6.2,6X,F6.2,
        1         4X,F6.2,4X,F6.2,6X,F6.2,6X,F7.2)
70           RETURN
71           END
```

FIGURE B–4 (continued)

as **specification statements.** They tell the computer how information is to be arranged when it is transferred between the computer and an I/O device (see statements 47 through 53) in Figure B–4. A specification statement can also tell the computer the **data type** of a particular variable (see statements 1 and 2 in the figure). In FORTRAN, a *real variable* may have fractional values, whereas an *integer variable* can have only whole values.

real variable
A number that may have fractional values.

integer variable
A whole number without fractional parts.

Executable statements tell the computer which operation to perform, through the use of keywords and symbols. There are several types of executable statements:

1. **Assignment statements** perform a series of arithmetic operations, placing the results of the operation into a storage location designated by the variable name to the left of the equal sign. Examples are statements 60 through 67 in Figure B–4.
2. **Control statements** control the order of execution within the program. Figure B–4 illustrates the use of the IF-THEN-ELSE statement. Statement 18 determines whether the job code of the present time card is equal to 1111. If yes, deduct only 0.7 percent for federal withholding and 0.8 percent for state withholding. Else, if the job code does not equal 1111, then perform statements 23 through 39. The END IF, at line 40, signals the end of the IF-THEN-ELSE statement.
3. **Input/output statements** instruct the computer from which input device or to what output device data are to be transferred. In Figure B–4, statement 10 will read in the input values, using statement 47 to describe how the input data will be arranged. Statement 44 will transfer data to an output device, the printer, using statement 51 to describe the layout of the data.

FORTRAN has a large amount of experience behind its design, implementation, and standardization. It has a vast library of mathematical, statistical, and engineering subroutines. Even though FORTRAN was primarily designed for scientific applications and efficient mathematical manipulations, the language has been used for business data-processing and file-handling applications. However, before the advent of FORTRAN 77, which allows for **structured programming** techniques, logical problems were difficult to express in FORTRAN. The FORTRAN 77 version has made writing and debugging programs easier and faster. FORTRAN processes large volumes of mathematical calculations efficiently and has good input/output facilities. However, FORTRAN can be expensive in terms of primary-memory allocation for variables and constants. Another disadvantage of FORTRAN is that the language is "non-English-like" and requires extensive internal ***documentation.***

FORTRAN has been implemented on microcomputers. However, the standardization level of microcomputer FORTRAN varies, ranging from various additional nonstandard features to a lack of very basic features. The most common version on microcomputers is FORTRAN IV.

documentation
English statements that describe the steps in a program.

COBOL COBOL (Common Business-Oriented Language) is one of the leading and most widely used business-oriented programming languages today. This language is considered to be the industry standard for business-oriented languages. COBOL was first conceived in 1959 by a group of users, programmers, and manufacturers from the government and business sectors, referred to as the CODASYL Committee (Conference On DAta SYstems Languages). The goal of this committee was to design and implement an English-like common business language (COBOL). In December, 1959, the initial specifications for COBOL had been drafted with the basic objectives of being highly machine-independent and *self-documenting*.

self-documenting
A characteristic of a computer language whose statements are easy enough to understand so that English descriptions of the program steps are not necessary.

The first version of COBOL was published in 1960, known as COBOL–60. The second version was released in 1961 and it included many changes in the procedure division. An extended version of COBOL–61 became available in 1963, which

A BAT file is a group of DOS commands strung together into an executable file. When the BAT file is executed, each command within the file will be executed sequentially. This saves a person from having to key in a frequently used set of commands. Execution of a BAT file can be started by typing the name of the file while in the DOS environment. An AUTOEXEC.BAT file is a special type of BAT file that will automatically be executed when you boot up your computer. An AUTOEXEC.BAT file is often used as a convenient way to start application software. For example, you might want to set up an AUTOEXEC.BAT file on your LOTUS 1-2-3 system disk so that it picks up the date and time from a clock/calendar on a board and then loads LOTUS 1-2-3. Assuming that your computer has an AST Research clock/

calendar, you would need an AUTOEXEC.BAT file containing the following two commands:

```
ASTCLOCK
123
```

Your DOS manual explains how to create or modify AUTOEXEC.BAT files. The easiest way to enter a short AUTOEXEC.BAT file is to send the command lines straight from the console (keyboard) to a file. As an example, the file above would be entered by typing:

```
COPY CON:AUTOEXEC.BAT
ASTCLOCK
123
```

(at the end of the file press the [F6] key and then [enter])

---

included sorting and report-writing routines. In September 1962, ANSI (American National Standards Institute) formed a committee to standardize COBOL. Grace Hopper was a member of this committee (see Module A). Several versions of COBOL were developed since 1962, so this committee finally used COBOL–68 as a basis for COBOL standardization. The standardization process was a very strict one, thereby solving the portability problem of having too many dialects of the language. This makes COBOL a truly common language. The CODASYL committee, in an effort to update the language, meets on a regular basis every year.

COBOL is English-like, making the language easier to read and code. COBOL can be loosely compared to an English composition which consists of headings, sections, paragraphs, and sentences. Various aspects of the COBOL language are shown in Figure B–5.

The COBOL program is divided into four major parts called **divisions.** Each division and its function is listed in the order it must appear within a program:

1. The *identification division* identifies the name and various documentary entries of the program.
2. The *environment division* identifies the input/output hardware needed to support the program.
3. The *data division* identifies the storage-record layout for input, output, and the intermediate results (working-storage).
4. The *procedure division* contains the instructions that tell the computer what operations to perform. This division is most like programs written in other languages.

All divisions except the identification division are further divided into **sections.** The procedure division has a structure different from the other divisions. It consists only of **sentences** which are combinations of **statements.** For example, statement 64 in Figure B–5,

```
        IDENTIFICATION DIVISION.
        PROGRAM-ID.
            PAYROLL.

        ENVIRONMENT DIVISION.
        CONFIGURATION SECTION.
        SPECIAL-NAMES.
            C01 IS TOP-OF-PAGE.
        INPUT-OUTPUT SECTION.
        FILE-CONTROL.
            SELECT CARD-IN-FILE ASSIGN TO UT-S-SYSIN.
            SELECT LINE-OUT-FILE ASSIGN TO UT-S-SYSOUT.

        DATA DIVISION.
        FILE SECTION.
        FD  CARD-IN-FILE
            LABEL RECORDS ARE OMITTED.
        01  CARD-IN-RECORD.
            05  I-JOBCODE          PICTURE X(4).
            05  I-EMPNO            PICTURE X(9).
            05  I-HOURS            PICTURE 999V99.
            05  I-RATE             PICTURE 99V99.
            05  FILLER             PICTURE X(58).
        FD  LINE-OUT-FILE
            LABEL RECORDS ARE OMITTED.
        01  LINE-OUT-RECORD        PICTURE X(133).
        WORKING-STORAGE SECTION.
            77  WS-EXTRA           PICTURE 999V99.
            77  WS-OTIME           PICTURE 999V99.
  1         77  WS-TOTAL           PICTURE 999V99 VALUE ZEROES.
            77  WS-FCRATE          PICTURE 9V999.
            77  WS-FTRATE          PICTURE 9V999.
            77  WS-STRATE          PICTURE 9V999.
            77  WS-RTRATE          PICTURE 9V999.
            77  WS-CURATE          PICTURE 9V999.
            77  WS-WHRS            PICTURE 999V99.
            77  WS-GROSS           PICTURE 9999V99.
            77  WS-FICA            PICTURE 999V99.
            77  WS-FIT             PICTURE 999V99.
            77  WS-SIT             PICTURE 999V99.
            77  WS-CUNION          PICTURE 999V99.
            77  WS-RETIRE          PICTURE 999V99.
            77  WS-NET             PICTURE 9999V99.
  2     01  OUT-OF-CARDS-FLAG      PICTURE X VALUE 'N'.
            88  OUT-OF-CARDS                 VALUE 'Y'.
  3     01  FLAG                   PICTURE X VALUE 'N'.
```

FIGURE B–5 Payroll Program Written in COBOL

Notice how long this program is compared to the payroll-register programs of the other languages. No wonder COBOL is considered wordy! This wordiness supposedly improves COBOL's readability. Examine the procedure division starting at statement 33 and determine whether you think COBOL is more understandable than the other languages discussed in this module.

```
        01  WS-DETAIL-LINE.
4           05  FILLER              PICTURE XXX VALUE SPACES.
            05  JOBCODE             PICTURE X(4).
5           05  FILLER              PICTURE X(5) VALUE SPACES.
            05  EMPNO               PICTURE X(9).
6           05  FILLER              PICTURE X(4) VALUE SPACES.
            05  HOURS               PICTURE ZZ9V99.
7           05  FILLER              PICTURE X(4) VALUE SPACES.
            05  RATE                PICTURE ZZ9V99.
8           05  FILLER              PICTURE X(4) VALUE SPACES.
            05  GROSS               PICTURE ZZZ9V99.
9           05  FILLER              PICTURE X(5) VALUE SPACES.
            05  FICA                PICTURE ZZ9V99.
10          05  FILLER              PICTURE X(6) VALUE SPACES.
            05  FIT                 PICTURE ZZ9V99.
11          05  FILLER              PICTURE X(4) VALUE SPACES.
            05  SIT                 PICTURE ZZ9V99.
12          05  FILLER              PICTURE X(4) VALUE SPACES.
            05  CUNION              PICTURE ZZ9V99.
13          05  FILLER              PICTURE X(6) VALUE SPACES.
            05  RETIRE              PICTURE ZZ9V99.
14          05  FILLER              PICTURE X(6) VALUE SPACES.
            05  NET                 PICTURE ZZZ9V99.
15          05  FILLER              PICTURE X(14) VALUE SPACES.
        01  WS-HEADER-LINE.
16          05  FILLER              PICTURE X(51) VALUE SPACES.
            05  FILLER              PICTURE X(16)
17              VALUE 'Payroll Register'.
18          05  FILLER              PICTURE X(66) VALUE SPACES.
        01  WS-COL-LINE-1.
19          05  FILLER              PICTURE X(57) VALUE SPACES.
            05  FILLER              PICTURE X(28)
20              VALUE 'Social     Federal     State'.
21          05  FILLER              PICTURE X(58) VALUE SPACES.
        01  WS-COL-LINE-2.
22          05  FILLER              PICTURE XX VALUE SPACES.
            05  FILLER              PICTURE X(118)
23              VALUE 'Job       Employee     Hours     Hourly     Gross
        -           '     Security     Income     Income     Credit
        -           '            Net'.
24          05  FILLER              PICTURE X(16) VALUE SPACES.
        01  WS-COL-LINE-3.
25          05  FILLER              PICTURE XXX VALUE SPACES.
            05  FILLER              PICTURE X(117)
26              VALUE 'Code        Number     Worked     Wage      Pay
        -           '     Tax          Tax          Tax      Union    Reti
        -           'rement       Pay'.
```

FIGURE B-5 (continued)

```
                              `rement      Pay'.
27          05  FILLER                 PICTURE X(16) VALUE SPACES.
       01  WS-FOOTER-LINE.
28          05  FILLER                 PICTURE X(96) VALUE SPACES.
            05  FILLER                 PICTURE X(16)
29              VALUE `Total Earnings:  '.
            05  TOTAL-EARNINGS   PICTURE ZZZZ9.99
30          05  FILLER                 PICTURE X(14) VALUE SPACES.
31     01  EMPTY-LINE              PICTURE X(133) VALUE SPACES.
       01  ERROR-MSG              PICTURE X(21)
32          VALUE `Invalid job code'.

33     PROCEDURE DIVISION.
       MAIN-LINE-ROUTINE.
34         OPEN INPUT CARD-IN-FILE
               OUTPUT LINE-OUT-FILE.
35         PERFORM HEADER-PARAGRAPH.
36         READ CARD-IN-FILE
37             AT END MOVE `Y' TO OUT-OF-CARDS-FLAG.
38         PERFORM PROCESS-PAYROLL
               UNTIL OUT-OF-CARDS.
39         PERFORM FOOTER-PARAGRAPH.

40         CLOSE CARD-IN-FILE
               LINE-OUT-FILE.
       MAIN-LINE-ROUTINE-EXIT.
41         STOP RUN.

       HEADER-PARAGRAPH.
42         WRITE LINE-OUT-RECORD FROM WS-HEADER-LINE
               AFTER ADVANCING TOP-OF-PAGE.
43         WRITE LINE-OUT-RECORD FROM WS-COL-LINE-1
               AFTER ADVANCING 2 LINES.
44         WRITE LINE-OUT-RECORD FROM WS-COL-LINE-2
               AFTER ADVANCING 1 LINES.
45         WRITE LINE-OUT-RECORD FROM WS-COL-LINE-3
               AFTER ADVANCING 1 LINES.
46         WRITE LINE-OUT-RECORD FROM EMPTY-LINE
               AFTER ADVANCING 1 LINES.
       PROCESS-PAYROLL.
47         MOVE `Y' TO FLAG.
48         MOVE ZEROS TO WS-OTIME, WS-FCRATE, WS-FTRATE, WS-STRATE,
                         WS-RTRATE, WS-CURATE
49         MOVE I-HOURS TO WS-WHRS.
50         IF I-JOBCODE IS EQUAL 1111
               THEN
51                 PERFORM JOBCODE-1111-PARA
               ELSE
```

FIGURE B–5 (continued)

```
52          IF I-JOBCODE IS EQUAL 1120
                THEN
53                  PERFORM JOBCODE-1120-PARA
                ELSE
54          IF I-JOBCODE IS EQUAL 1122
                THEN
55                  PERFORM JOBCODE-1120-PARA
56                  PERFORM JOBCODE-1122-PARA.
57          PERFORM COMPUTE-PAYROLL-PARAGRAPH.
58          PERFORM WRITE-LINE-PARAGRAPH.
59          READ CARD-IN-FILE
60              AT END MOVE 'Y' TO OUT-OF-CARDS-FLAG.

        JOBCODE-1111-PARA.
61              MOVE 0.007 TO WS-FTRATE.
62              MOVE 0.008 TO WS-STRATE.
63              MOVE 'N' TO FLAG.

        JOBCODE-1120-PARA.
64          MOVE 0.067 TO WS-FCRATE.
65          MOVE 0.113 TO WS-FTRATE.
66          MOVE 0.03  TO WS-STRATE.
67          MOVE 0.05  TO WS-RTRATE.
68          IF I-HOURS IS GREATER THAN 40.0
                THEN
69                  SUBTRACT 40.0 FROM I-HOURS GIVING WS-EXTRA
70                  COMPUTE WS-OTIME ROUNDED =
                            WS-EXTRA * I-RATE * 1.5
71              MOVE 40.0 TO WS-WHRS.
72          MOVE 'N' TO FLAG.

        JOBCODE-1122-PARA.
73          MOVE 0.05 TO WS-CURATE.
74          MOVE 'N' TO FLAG.

        COMPUTE-PAYROLL-PARAGRAPH.
75          COMPUTE WS-GROSS ROUNDED = (WS-WHRS * I-RATE) + WS-OTIME.
76          MULTIPLY WS-GROSS BY WS-FCRATE GIVING WS-FICA ROUNDED.
77          MULTIPLY WS-GROSS BY WS-FTRATE GIVING WS-FIT   ROUNDED.
78          MULTIPLY WS-GROSS BY WS-STRATE GIVING WS-SIT   ROUNDED.
79          MULTIPLY WS-GROSS BY WS-RTRATE GIVING WS-RETIRE ROUNDED.
80          MULTIPLY WS-GROSS BY WS-CURATE GIVING WS-CUNION ROUNDED.
81          COMPUTE WS-NET = WS-GROSS -
                    (WS-FICA + WS-FIT + WS-SIT + WS-RETIRE + WS-CUNION)
82          ADD WS-NET TO WS-TOTAL.
```

FIGURE B–5 (continued)

```
        WRITE-LINE-PARAGRAPH.
83          IF FLAG = 'N'
                THEN
84                  MOVE I-JOBCODE TO JOBCODE
85                  MOVE I-EMPNO TO EMPNO
86                  MOVE I-HOURS TO HOURS
87                  MOVE I-RATE TO RATE
88                  MOVE WS-GROSS TO GROSS
89                  MOVE WS-FICA TO FICA
90                  MOVE WS-FIT TO FIT
91                  MOVE WS-SIT TO SIT
92                  MOVE WS-CUNION TO CUNION
93                  MOVE WS-RETIRE TO RETIRE
94                  MOVE WS-NET TO NET
95                  WRITE LINE-OUT-RECORD FROM WS-DETAIL-LINE
                        AFTER ADVANCING 1 LINES
                ELSE
96                  WRITE LINE-OUT-RECORD FROM ERROR-MSG
                        AFTER ADVANCING 1 LINES.

        FOOTER-PARAGRAPH.
97          MOVE WS-TOTAL TO TOTAL-EARNINGS.
98          WRITE LINE-OUT-RECORD FROM WS-FOOTER-LINE
                AFTER ADVANCING 2 LINES.
99          WRITE LINE-OUT-RECORD FROM EMPTY-LINE
                AFTER ADVANCING TOP-OF-PAGE.
```

FIGURE B–5 (continued)

```
MOVE 0.067 TO WS-FCRATE.
```

is an imperative sentence, which tells the computer to assign the value 0.067 to the variable WS-FCRATE, and statements 54 through 56,

```
IF I-JOBCODE IS EQUAL 1122
    THEN
        PERFORM JOBCODE-1120-PARA
        PERFORM JOBCODE-1122-PARA.
```

is a conditional sentence where

```
PERFORM JOBCODE-1120-PARA.
```

is a statement beginning with the verb PERFORM. A statement is a combination of **words,** symbols, and phrases beginning with a COBOL verb. COBOL words are of three types:

1. **Reserved words** have special meaning to the compiler. The COBOL verbs COMPUTE, ADD, and SUBTRACT are examples.

2. **User-defined words** are created by the programmer. Examples (in Figure B–5) are CARD-IN-FILE, LINE-OUT-FILE, and MAIN-LINE-ROUTINE.
3. **System names** are supplied by the manufacturer of the hardware to allow certain elements in the program to correspond with various hardware devices. Examples are UT-S-SYSIN specifying the card reader, and UT-S-SYSOUT specifying the line printer in the input-output section of the environment division in Figure B–5.

COBOL is a very standardized language and therefore can be used by different kinds of computers fairly easily. The advantage of COBOL is that it was conceived especially for data processing. It can manipulate many different types of data files, and it is much more readable and self-documenting than most languages. However, efficiency in terms of coding and actual execution is sacrificed because of its wordiness. Also, because of the nature of the syntax of COBOL, **semantic errors** can occur that are very difficult to detect. For report generation, COBOL can be an extremely useful tool because of its report-writer facility. COBOL has limited facilities for mathematical notation, but excellent capabilities for character and file processing. COBOL compilers are available for microcomputers.

PL/I   **PL/I** (Programming Language/I) is a comprehensive language that has a wide variety of applications. PL/I can be used for scientific, business data processing, text processing, and system applications. The language was conceived in the 1960s when programmers were divided into three distinct groups: scientific, business/commercial, and special-purpose.

IBM, along with SHARE and GUIDE (a scientific user group and a commercial user group, respectively) developed PL/I with the following objectives in mind:

1. machine independence
2. access to the machine's operating system
3. structured and modular programs
4. easy-to-learn language
5. readable and easy-to-write code
6. a bridging of the gap between commercial and scientific high-level languages

In 1964 the specifications for the language were presented to GUIDE and SHARE. The specifications incorporated features from FORTRAN, COBOL, and ALGOL (expressive algebraic language). Although PL/I was successful in meeting the objectives established, it is not as widely used as FORTRAN or COBOL. The language was standardized by ANSI in 1976 after further development.

A PL/I program consists of statements separated by semicolons. Being a **block-structured language,** PL/I programs are headed by labeled statements and terminated by an END statement. The header statement in Figure B–6 is statement 1:

```
payroll:PROCEDURE OPTIONS (MAIN);
```

where "payroll" is the program name. Another major block resides within the program and it must also be headed by a labeled statement (statement 42). This block of statements is called an **internal subroutine.**

```
1    payroll:PROCEDURE OPTIONS (MAIN);
2        DECLARE empno                                FIXED DECIMAL (9),
                 (fcrate,ftrate,strate,curate,
                  rtrate)                             FIXED DECIMAL (4,3),
                 (extra,otime,hours,whrs,fica,
                  fit,sit,cunion,retire)              FIXED DECIMAL (5,2),
                  rate                                FIXED DECIMAL (4,2),
                 (gross,net)                          FIXED DECIMAL (6,2),
                  total                               FIXED DECIMAL (6,2)
                                                        INITIAL (0),
                  jobcode                             FIXED DECIMAL (4);
3        DECLARE(eof,no)                              BIT(1) INITIAL ('0'B),
                 yes                                  BIT(1) INITIAL ('1'B);
4        DECLARE sysin                               FILE STREAM INPUT,
                 sysprint                            FILE STREAM OUTPUT;
5        ON ENDFILE (sysin) eof = yes;
6        PUT PAGE EDIT ('Payroll Register')(X(50),A);
7        PUT SKIP(2) EDIT ('Social       Federal       State')(X(56),A);
8        PUT SKIP EDIT ('Job','Employee','Hours','Hourly','Gross',
                        'Security','Income','Income','Credit','Net')
                       (X(1),A,X(5),A,X(5),A,X(4),A,X(5),A,X(5),A,X(5),A,
                        X(4),A,X(4),A,X(20),A);
9        PUT SKIP EDIT ('Code','Number','Worked','Wage','Pay','Tax','Tax',
                        'Tax','Union','Retirement','Pay')
                       (X(2),A,X(7),A,X(5),A,X(5),A,X(7),A,X(8),A,X(9),A,
                        X(8),A,X(6),A,X(4),A,X(6),A);
10       PUT SKIP;
11       GET SKIP EDIT (jobcode,empno,hours,rate)(f(4),f(9),f(5,2),f(4,2));
12       DO WHILE (eof = no);
13          otime = 0.0;
14          whrs = hours;
15          fcrate = 0.0;
16          ftrate = 0.0;
17          strate = 0.0;
18          rtrate = 0.0;
19          curate = 0.0;
20          IF jobcode = 1111
                 THEN DO;
21                   ftrate = 0.007;
22                   strate = 0.008;
23                   CALL calc_payroll;
24                   END;
```

FIGURE B–6 Payroll Program Written in PL/I

PL/I is a structured programming language. Statement 12, the DO-WHILE, is a structured loop that ends with statement 40. Statements 12 through 40 are executed over and over until an end-of-file (eof) is encountered on the input file.

```
25                    ELSE
            IF jobcode = 1120 | jobcode = 1122
                    THEN DO;
26                      fcrate=0.067;
27                      ftrate=0.113;
28                      strate=0.03;
29                      rtrate=0.05;
30                      IF jobcode=1122
                            THEN curate=0.05;
31                      IF hours > 40.0
                            THEN DO;
32                          extra = hours - 40.0;
33                          otime = extra * rate * 1.5;
34                          whrs = 40.0;
35                              END;
36                      CALL calc_payroll;
37                        END;
38                    ELSE
                        PUT SKIP EDIT ('Invalid Job Code.')(X(3),A);
39                    GET SKIP EDIT (jobcode,empno,hours,rate)
                                (f(4),f(9),f(5,2),f(4,2));
40      END;
41      PUT SKIP(2) EDIT ('Total Earnings: ',TOTAL)(X(96),A,F(7,2));
42  calc_payroll:PROCEDURE;
43      gross = (whrs * rate) + otime;
44      fica = gross * fcrate;
45      fit = gross * ftrate;
46      sit = gross * strate;
47      retire = gross * rtrate;
48      cunion = gross * curate;
49      net = gross - (fica + fit + sit + retire + cunion);
50      total = total + net;
51      PUT SKIP EDIT (jobcode,empno,hours,rate,gross,fica,fit,sit,cunion,
                    retire,net)(X(2),F(4),X(5),F(9),X(4),F(6,2),X(4),
                    F(6,2),X(4),F(7,2),X(5),F(6,2),X(6),F(6,2),X(4),
                    F(6,2),X(4),F(6,2),X(6),F(6,2),X(6),F(7,2));
52  RETURN;
53  END;

54  END;
```

FIGURE B–6 (continued)

The most widely used statements are discussed next by statement type.

Data Definition Data elements are introduced into a PL/I program through the use of the DECLARE statement. This statement specifies the data element, its data type, and its precision level. For example,

```
DECLARE total FIXED DECIMAL (6,2)    INITIAL (0)
```

tells the PL/I compiler that the variable "total" has a type of fixed decimal (for business applications) and a *precision* as follows:

```
XXXXVXX
```

where the "X"s are numeric digits and "V" is an implied decimal point. The initial value of zero is also placed in the variable at compilation time.

Control Statements Statements that control the flow of execution through the program in Figure B–6 are as follows:

1. the IF-THEN-ELSE statement
2. the DO-WHILE statement

These are illustrated in Figure B–6. The IF-THEN-ELSE was introduced in the FORTRAN section. Statement 12 is the beginning of a DO-WHILE which will perform the statements up to statement 40, the END statement, until the end of the input file is reached. In other words, the DO-WHILE is a repetitive loop in which statements are executed while the condition in statement 12 is met.

Input/Output Statements Examples of input/output statements in Figure B–6 are the GET EDIT and the PUT EDIT statements. Statement 11 is an **edit-directed** input statement which means the programmer must tell the computer how the data are arranged when they are read into the program. Statements 6 through 10 are edit-directed output statements. Again, the programmer specifies the layout of the data to be printed.

Assignment Statements The assignment statement is in the following form:

variable = expression;

where the expression specifies that a particular computation takes place, and the results of the computation are assigned to the variable to the left of the equal sign.

For the novice programmer, PL/I is easy to learn because of its *default* features. If the programmer is vague in specifying any features within the program, the compiler will assume (default to) the most frequently used specifications. Also, PL/I is well-suited for the experienced programmer because the language is designed so that the programmer can better utilize the resources of the computer.

PL/I has substantial character-handling facilities and is well-suited for business data processing. The language has very good file-handling characteristics, as with COBOL, without being limited to particular types of applications as COBOL is. PL/I is a powerful language; however, efficiency in terms of compilation time, execution, and storage is sacrificed for this power.

PL/I is not generally available on microprocessors owing to the size of the compiler, although variations of PL/I (PL/M and MPL) are available.

BASIC   **BASIC** (Basic All-Purpose Symbolic Instruction Code) is a programming language that has been implemented on virually every type of computer—from the smallest micro to the largest mainframe. BASIC was conceived in 1963 and implemented in 1964 at Dartmouth College. The language was designed as an easy-to-learn, easy-to-use, interactive language, with no particular application area targeted. BASIC was created because of the trend away from batch processing toward *interactive* systems.

There are many versions of BASIC available which have the essence of the Dartmouth version within their design. An effort to standardize BASIC began in 1970. An ANSI standard was established in 1978. However, there are many versions of BASIC, either on the market or by some hobbyist's own invention. A standard does exist, but the term BASIC refers to a classification of the language, not to the particular, standard version.

As previously stated, BASIC is an easy language to use, once the following core statements have been learned. These statements are used in almost every version of BASIC implemented.

Data-Definition Statements   The data-definition statement DIM is used to define arrays, and REF is used to define functions used within the program.

Control Statements   Control of the flow of execution is performed by the GO-TO, IF-THEN, FOR-NEXT, and GOSUB-RETURN statements. The GO TO statement causes an unconditional branching to a designated statement. The IF-THEN statement (see statement 230 in Figure B–7) causes a conditional two-way branching. The FOR-NEXT construct allows for repetitive looping. The statements will be executed at least once before the condition is tested. In other words, there is no pretest of the condition. The GOSUB, used in conjunction with a RETURN, allows modularity through the use of subroutines. The statements between the referenced statement in the GOSUB and the RETURN are executed and the flow of execution returns to the statement following the GOSUB.

Input/Output Statements   Input of data is performed either by the INPUT statement for interactive mode, or the READ statement (see statement 220) for batch mode. The READ statement reads in the data contained in the DATA statements (see statements 640 through 681). Output is performed by the PRINT statement which sends output back to the terminal.

Assignment/Arithmetic Statements   Assignment and arithmetic statements are similar to those in FORTRAN except that these statements are prefixed with the key word LET (see statement 460). The syntax is as follows:

```
LET variable = expression
```

Figure B–7 also includes REMARK statements (abbreviated REM). This statement is used when the programmer internally documents the program.

BASIC is used, with much innovation, on most microcomputers. Even though BASIC is standardized, many versions are available. Consequently, the **portability**

interactive
An application in which each entry calls forth a response from a system or program, as in an inquiry system or an airline-reservation system. An interactive system may also be conversational, implying a continuous dialogue between the user and the system.

```
100     PRINT TAB(51),'Payroll Register'
101     PRINT ' '
110     PRINT TAB(57),'Social',TAB(68),'Federal',TAB(80),'State'
120     PRINT ' '
130     PRINT TAB(2),'Job',TAB(13),'Employee',TAB(26),'Hours',TAB(35),
140     PRINT 'Hourly',TAB(46),'Gross',TAB(56),'Security',TAB(69),'Income',
150     PRINT TAB(79),'Income',TAB(89),'Credit',TAB(115),'Net'
160     PRINT TAB(3),'Code',TAB(14),'Number',TAB(25),'Worked',TAB(36),
170     PRINT 'Wage',TAB(47),'Pay',TAB(58),'Tax',TAB(70),'Tax',TAB(81),
180     PRINT 'Tax',TAB(90),'Union',TAB(99),'Retirement',TAB(115),'Pay'
190     PRINT ' '
200     LET T =   0.0
210     REM......read in job code, empno, hours, and hourly rate
220     READ O1,E1,H,R3
230     IF O1 = 0.0 THEN 580
240        LET W = H
250        LET O2 = 0.0
260        LET F1 = 0.0
270        LET F2 = 0.0
280        LET S1 = 0.0
290        LET R1 = 0.0
300        IF O1 = 1111 THEN 340
310        IF O1 = 1120 THEN 400
320        IF O1 = 1122 THEN 380
330        GO TO 610
340     REM....for job code 1111
350        LET F2 = 0.007
360        LET S1 = 0.008
370        GO TO 450
380     REM....for job code 1122
390        C1 = 0.05
```

FIGURE B–7 Payroll Program Written in BASIC

Notice this is the shortest program in the module. Because of this conciseness and the lack of structured programming statements, BASIC programs can be difficult to read. Readability can be improved by liberal use of REM statements within the BASIC program (for example, statements 340 and 380).

of the language (the transferability of programs from one machine to another) is low. In other words, one version of BASIC may not be compatible with one compiler or interpreter to another. BASIC enjoys a great deal of popularity with users of small computers even though it is an unstructured language and has very limited screen-handling facilities. A major reason for this popularity is that the language is very easy to learn and is applicable to many areas, from a very simple arithmetic program to a very complicated file-handling system. However, the availability of these capabilities depends on the BASIC version being used.

PASCAL The programming language **PASCAL** (named after Blaise Pascal, French mathematician) was developed as an educational tool to encourage the writing of well-structured, readable programs. It is adaptable to business and scientific applications and is considered a simple yet versatile language. PASCAL was first imple-

```
400     REM....for job code 1120 and 1122
410        F1 = 0.067
420        F2 = 0.113
430        S1 = 0.03
440        R1 = 0.05
450     REM....calculate payroll and print line
460        LET G = (W * R3) + 02
470        LET F3 = G * F1
480        LET F4 = G * F2
490        LET S2 = G * S1
500        LET C2 = G * C1
510        LET R2 = G * R1
520        LET N = G - (F3 + F4 + S2 + C2 + R2)
530        LET T = T + N
540        PRINT TAB(3),O1,TAB(12),E1,TAB(25),H,TAB(35),R3,TAB(45),G,
550        PRINT TAB(57),F3,TAB(69),F4,TAB(79),S2,TAB(89),R2,TAB(101),C2,
560        PRINT TAB(113),N
570     GO TO 210
580     REM....write total net earnings
590     PRINT TAB(96),'Total Earnings: ',TAB(117),T
600     GO TO 690
610     REM....write error message
620     PRINT TAB(3),'Invalid job code.'
630     REM....data cards
640     DATA 1111, 400941648, 33.00, 4.51,
650     DATA 1122, 224949460, 40.00, 5.10,
660     DATA 1120, 900221792, 44.00, 4.51,
670     DATA 1122, 224885493, 45.00, 7.25,
680     DATA 1111, 900120001, 25.00, 3.25,
681     DATA 0, 0, 0, 0
690     END
```

FIGURE B–7 (continued)

Jill Johnson is designing a personnel tracking system for King William County. She was at the local library designing some of the computer programs in BASIC language on the library's personal computer when she saw her friend Susan Cox, a consultant for a CPA firm. Susan asked Jill why she was programming in BASIC. Jill said that BASIC was the only language she knew and that it was an excellent choice for implementing the system. Susan replied that there were many relational DBMS packages such as dBASE III on the market and that dBASE would be more efficient; it would reduce programming time because of its data-base capabilities. Jill was adamant about not changing the language because she had already done quite a bit of programming. Do you think that Jill should continue writing in BASIC or should she try an alternative?

Thinking About Information Systems B–2

mented in 1970 in Zurich, Switzerland. The PASCAL design is very similar to ALGOL-60 (as is PL/I). PASCAL was intended to be a low-cost, student-oriented language. By low cost we are speaking in terms of storage and processing time.

PASCAL, like PL/I, is a block-structured language consisting of groups of statements enclosed within the BEGIN statement (statement 24), and the END statement (statement 76). Header statements are needed for a major block of code. In Figure B–8, the statement:

```
PROGRAM payroll (INPUT,OUTPUT);
```

is needed for the main program. As in PL/I, the internal procedure (located at the beginning of the PASCAL program) must also have a header statement (statement 9). Note that the procedure is also enclosed within BEGIN and END statements.

PASCAL is very similar to PL/I in statement structure, except for minor differences in the use of the BEGIN and END statements and the use of the semicolon as a statement separator.

Data-Definition Statements Data within a PASCAL program may be introduced through the use of the VAR statement (statements 2 through 7). The programmer can specify the **data type** of the variables used within the program as REAL, INTEGER, CHARACTER, and BOOLEAN. The language has strong data-structuring capabilities provided by the compiler, making less work for the programmer. In other words, the programmer does not include precision levels for the variables when declaring them, as is done in PL/I.

Control Statements Statements that control the flow of execution in a PASCAL program are as follows:

1. the IF-THEN-ELSE statement
2. the WHILE-DO statement
3. the REPEAT-UNTIL statement
4. the CASE statement

The IF-THEN-ELSE and WHILE-DO were illustrated in previous sections. The REPEAT-UNTIL is similar to the WHILE-DO in that it is a repetitive loop. However, the statements within the loop are executed before the condition is checked. Therefore, the statements are always executed at least once. The CASE statement is similar to a series of IF-THEN-ELSE statements. A certain path through the program will be taken, depending on which of the multiple conditions is true.

Input/Output Statements Input into a PASCAL program is done by utilizing the READ or READLN statements. The READ statement reads until a blank character appears within the input file, whereas the READLN reads the input until the end of the line or card image. Data types are checked by the system, so the programmer need not specify the format of the input file, as with PL/I.

Output is performed through the use of the WRITE or WRITELN statements. The WRITE statement writes the data out to the output device, one data element at a time, without moving to the next output line. Therefore, the next output statement places the data on the same line following the previous data element. The WRITELN

```
1  |    PROGRAM payroll (INPUT,OUTPUT);
2  |       VAR
3  |          empno,jobcode : INTEGER;
4  |          fcrate,ftrate,strate,curate,rtrate : REAL;
5  |          extra,otime,hours,whrs,rate : REAL;
6  |          fica,fit,sit,cunion,retire : REAL;
7  |          gross,net,total : REAL;
8  |
9  |    PROCEDURE calculate_payroll;
10 |       BEGIN
11 |          gross := (whrs * rate) + otime;
12 |          fica := gross * fcrate;
13 |          fit := gross * ftrate;
14 |          sit := gross * strate;
15 |          retire := gross * rtrate;
16 |          cunion := gross * curate;
17 |          net := gross - (fica + fit + sit + retire + cunion);
18 |          total := total + net;
19 |          WRITELN (jobcode:6,empno:14,hours:10:2,rate:10:2,gross:11:2,
20 |                   fica:11:2,fit:11:2,sit:11:2,cunion:10:2,retire:12:2,
21 |                   net:13:2)
22 |       END;
23 |
24 |    BEGIN
25 |       total :=0.0;
26 |       PAGE;
27 |       WRITELN ('Payroll Register':66);
28 |       WRITELN ('  ');
29 |       WRITELN ('Social     Federal     State':84);
30 |       WRITELN ('Job' :7,'Employee':13,'Hours':10,'Hourly':10,
31 |                'Gross':10,'Security':13,'Income':11,'Income':10,
32 |                'Credit':10,'Net':23);
33 |       WRITELN ('Code':6,'Number':13,'Worked':11,'Wage':9,'Pay':10,
34 |                'Tax':11,'Tax':12,'Tax':11,'Union':11,'Retirement':14,
35 |                'Pay':9);
36 |       WRITELN ('  ');
37 |       WHILE NOT EOF DO
38 |          BEGIN
39 |             READLN (jobcode,empno,hours,rate);
40 |             otime := 0.0;
41 |             whrs := hours
42 |             fcrate := 0.0;
43 |             ftrate := 0.0;
44 |             strate := 0.0;
45 |             rtrate := 0.0;
46 |             curate := 0.0;
47 |             IF jobcode = 1111
```

FIGURE B–8   Payroll Program Written in PASCAL

PASCAL is also a structured programming language. Notice the WHILE-NOT statement (no. 37) and the IF-THEN-ELSE starting with statement 47.

```
48 |                        THEN BEGIN
49 |                           ftrate := 0.007;
50 |                           strate := 0.008;
51 |                           calculate_payroll
52 |                              END
53 |                        ELSE
54 |                  IF (jobcode = 1120) OR (jobcode = 1122)
55 |                     THEN BEGIN
56 |                           fcrate := 0.067;
57 |                           ftrate := 0.113;
58 |                           strate := 0.03;
59 |                           rtrate := 0.05;
60 |                           IF jobcode = 1122
61 |                              THEN curate := 0.05;
62 |                           IF hours > 40.0
63 |                              THEN BEGIN
64 |                                 extra := hours - 40.0;
65 |                                 otime := extra * rate * 1.5;
66 |                                 whrs := 40.0
67 |                                    END;
68 |                           calculate_payroll
69 |                              END
70 |                     ELSE WRITELN ('Invalid Job Code.':24);
71 |                  END;
72 |            WRITELN (' ');
73 |            WRITELN ('Total Earnings: ':110.total:9:2);
74 |            PAGE;
75 |            WRITELN ('  ')
76 |         END.
```

FIGURE B–8 (continued)

writes the data out to the output device, then moves to a new line. Thus when the next output statement is encountered, the data will be written on the next line.

Assignment/Arithmetic Statements The syntax of the assignment statement in PAS-CAL is as follows:

```
variable := expression;
```

The assignment statement is essentially the same as that used in PL/I, except the assignment operator is ":=" as illustrated in Figure B–8, statements 11 through 18.

PASCAL is an excellent language for a microcomputer because its compiler is of a manageable size, and it is cost efficient in terms of memory allocation. Other factors are the language's simplicity, versatility, fast execution time, and its character-manipulation capabilities. PASCAL is fairly standardized (de facto), largely owing to the Jenkins and Wirth document "The PASCAL Report." The language is also extremely compact in that there are very few reserved words to learn. A disadvantage of PASCAL is its very poor character-handling facilities. The language only processes one character at a time, requiring the use of arrays which can be very cumbersome.

ADA   From 1975 to 1979, progressively comprehensive specifications were developed by the Department of Defense (DOD) for a new programming language. As a result of this effort, in 1979, **ADA** was designed (named for Augusta Ada Byron, the first programmer; see Module A). ADA, based on PASCAL, was created for the DOD as a portable, well-structured language, to be used primarily in a multiprocessor environment for scientific and system programming. The language was developed because the DOD needed a common language to meet its programming needs. Thus ADA is versatile enough to be used in a wide variety of applications.

ADA is a block-structured language that provides for a strict form of modular programming. All major blocks of code are headed by declarative statements and are set off by BEGIN-END statements. Subroutines are located at the beginning of the program, as shown in Figure B–9. Modularity is enhanced in the language through the use of modules that can be written and compiled separately from the main procedure. **Modules** are collections of variables, constants, statements, subroutines, or other modules. Modules are of two types:

1. **Packages**—logical collections of entities (declarations, statements, procedures, et cetera) that cover a certain logical aspect of the application.
2. **Tasks**—independent collections of statements that are executed in the order required by the system, without any dependency or order among the tasks. These tasks facilitate the multiprocessor environment.

ADA is very similar to PASCAL in syntax, except for minor variations. The language uses **terminating keywords** (END IF, END LOOP, END CASE, et cetera) in place of BEGIN-END statements, and semicolons are used as statement terminators as in PL/I, not as statement separators as in PASCAL.

Data-Definition Statements   In ADA, data types are declared in the data-definition statements. This feature was inherited from PASCAL. The declaration statements for variables are in the form:

```
variable : data type;
```

Examples in Figure B–9 are statements 4 through 8.

Control Statements   Statements that control the flow of execution through the ADA program are as follows:

1. the IF-THEN-ELSIF-ELSE statement
2. the LOOP statement
3. the WHILE-LOOP statement
4. the FOR-LOOP statement
5. the CASE-OF statement

The IF-THEN-ELSE statement (statements 61 through 81) is similar to other languages; however, a new keyword ELSIF is used. The ELSIF allows for nested conditional statements. The LOOP is an infinite repetitive loop only terminated by

```
 1  |    WITH TEXT_IO; USING TEXT_IO;
 2  |    PROCEDURE payroll IS
 3  |       PRAGMA MAIN;
 4  |          empno Jobcode : INTEGER;
 5  |          fcrate,ftrate,strate,curate,rtrate : FIXED;
 6  |          extra,otime,hours,whrs,rate : FIXED;
 7  |          fica,fit,sit,cunion,retire : FIXED;
 8  |          gross,net,total : FIXED;
 9  |
10  |    PROCEDURE calculate_payroll IS
11  |       BEGIN
12  |          gross := (whrs * rate) + otime;
13  |          fica := gross * fcrate;
14  |          fit := gross * ftrate;
15  |          sit := gross * strate;
16  |          retire := gross * rtrate;
17  |          cunion := gross * curate;
18  |          net := gross - (fica + fit + sit + retire + cunion);
19  |          total := total + net;
20  |          PUT (jobcode,6);
21  |          PUT (empno,14);
22  |          PUT (hours,10,2);
23  |          PUT (rate,10,2);
24  |          PUT (gross,11,2);
25  |          PUT (fica,11,2);
26  |          PUT (fit,11,2);
27  |          PUT (sit,11,2);
28  |          PUT (cunion,10,2);
29  |          PUT (retire,12,2);
30  |          PUT (net,13,2);
31  |          PUT (NEWLINE);
32  |       END;
33  |
34  |       BEGIN
35  |          total := 0.0;
36  |          PUT ('Payroll Register',66);
37  |          PUT (NEWLINE);
38  |          PUT ('   ');
39  |          PUT (NEWLINE);
40  |          PUT ('Social     Federal      State',84);
41  |          PUT (NEWLINE);
42  |          PUT ('Job      Employee     Hours      Hourly',40);
43  |          PUT ('      Gross      Security    Income     Income',44);
44  |          PUT ('    Credit                    Net',33);
45  |          PUT (NEWLINE);
```

FIGURE B–9 Payroll Program Written in ADA

Notice the similarity of this ADA program to the PASCAL program shown in Figure B–8.

```
46 |              PUT ('  Code       Number      Worked       Wage' ,39);
47 |              PUT ('       Pay       Tax        Tax         Tax',43);
48 |              PUT ('       Union    Retirement      Pay',34);
49 |           PUT (NEWLINE);
50 |           PUT ('  ');
51 |           PUT (NEWLINE);
52 |           WHILE NOT END_OF_FILE LOOP
53 |                 GETLN (jobcode,empno,hours,rate);
54 |                 otime := 0.0;
55 |                 whrs := hours;
56 |                 fcrate := 0.0;
57 |                 ftrate := 0.0;
58 |                 strate := 0.0;
59 |                 rtrate := 0.0;
60 |                 curate := 0.0;
61 |                 IF jobcode = 1111 THEN
62 |                     ftrate := 0.007;
63 |                     strate := 0.008;
64 |                     calculate_payroll;
65 |                 ELSIF jobcode = 1120 OR jobcode = 1122 THEN
66 |                     fcrate := 0.067;
67 |                     ftrate := 0.113;
68 |                     strate := 0.03;
69 |                     rtrate := 0.05;
70 |                     IF jobcode = 1122 THEN
71 |                         curate := 0.05;
72 |                     END_IF;
73 |                     IF hours > 40.0 THEN
74 |                         extra := hours - 40.0;
75 |                         otime := extra * rate * 1.5;
76 |                         whrs := 40.0;
77 |                     END_IF;
78 |                     calculate_payroll;
79 |                 ELSE
80 |                     PUT_ LINE ('Invalid Job Code.',24);
81 |                 END_IF;
82 |             END_LOOP;
83 |         PUT ('  ');
84 |         PUT (NEWLINE);
85 |         PUT ('Total Earnings: ',110);
86 |         PUT (total,9,2);
87 |         PUT (NEWLINE);
88 |         PUT ('  ');
89 |         PUT (NEWLINE);
90 |     END payroll;
```

FIGURE B–9   (continued)

the EXIT statement which flags an exception. This loop would be used in a program that constantly monitors an apparatus or device. The WHILE-LOOP statement (statement 52) performs a pretest before executing the repetition, and the FOR-LOOP statement is an iterative repetition that is controlled by counting. The CASE-OF statement is similar to the CASE statement used in PASCAL.

Input/Output Statements   ADA provides a package for input/output facilities. Subroutine calls are used for input/output functions. All text output in Figure B–9 is performed by the procedure PUT (statements 20 through 31), which is similar to the WRITE in PASCAL. This procedure uses parameters specifying variable types and the layout of these variables. Input of data is performed by the procedure GET, which is equivalent to the READ in PASCAL. In Figure B–9, input is performed by the GETLN procedure (statement 53), which is equivalent to the READLN in PASCAL. These input/output procedures can be written by the application programmer and contained within the package TEXT IO.

Assignment/Arithmetic Statements   The syntax of the assignment statement in the ADA language is as follows:

```
<<label>> variable := expression;
```

where the statement *label,* enclosed in double-angle brackets, is optional.

ADA is a very versatile language. An advantage of ADA is that it is an up-to-date language incorporating new technology and experiences of other languages. Therefore, it is an efficient, modular language that is vey flexible. A disadvantage of ADA is that it is a very complex language to learn and use. This disadvantage may possibly outweigh the advantages.

RPG   **RPG** (Report Program Generator) is a problem-oriented language. The programmer or user describes the report desired, and the RPG system creates it.

PC USER TIP   Keyboard Macros

No matter what software you frequently use, you will often find yourself repeating a series of keystrokes over and over. These keystrokes could represent a series of commands, a phrase in a word-processing document, et cetera. Most software contains a means for you to store a series of keystrokes and then execute those keystrokes all at once. For example, if you were working on a program file called LABELS in dBASE II, you would need to enter the command MODIFY COMMAND LABELS whenever you wanted to change something in the program file. You could store this series of keystrokes by typing SET F1 to MODIFY COMMAND LABELS. You would then be able to execute the modify command by pressing the [F1] key. If a software package does not allow for keyboard macros, you can use another software package first, such as PROKEY, that builds the keyboard macros before you enter the application software. For further details on keyboard macros, consult your application software manual. In dBASE II and III, look under the SET FUNCTION command. In LOTUS, look up Macros in the index or choose Macros from the online help index. In ABILITY, look under Keyboard Macros.

The basic objective of RPG is to simplify and facilitate the generation of reports from sequential files.

RPG was introduced in 1964 and improved versions, RPG II and RPG III, have followed. RPG is designed for only one application: to update and produce output from other files. RPG is a descriptive language. The input into the RPG system are specification forms on which the programmer describes the report to be generated.

A report is composed of three major parts: the header, detail lines, and the footer. The programmer uses the specification forms to describe the input record layout and field definitions; indicators used in the program; intermediate calculations performed; and the formats of the header, detailed lines, and footer. The forms are as follows:

1. The input specifications form describes the layout of an individual input record. The type of records and which input records are to be read within the file are also defined. The input record is eighty characters long.

   The input form identifies the input file for a particular record. A record is composed of **fields** (the basic unit of data in RPG). The input form also describes the format of each field within that record.

2. The calculation specifications form specifies what operation is to be performed. This form also describes the conditions that make it necessary to perform the operation as well as what tests should be performed on the results.

3. The output specifications form describes the layout of the header, detail lines, and footer of the output files. Any file used for output must have an output format description. The output form specifies the exact layout of each report in the output file. Also, the form specifies the conditions on which each record should be generated.

   As with the input form, the output form has two parts: a file identification, which identifies the output records and how they should be generated, and a file description, which identifies the format of each field within the output record.

4. The file-description specifications form identifies the I/O files and their attributes and characteristics. This form also designates the I/O device and medium to be used.

5. The file-extension specifications form provides descriptions for additional features such as table searching, merging multiple input files, and accessing nonsequential files.

6. The line-counter specifications form is used when reports are placed on an intermediate storage medium (tape or disk) from where they will ultimately be output. This form defines the printer carriage control used during the process of creating the report.

RPG is a very machine-dependent language, primarily supported by IBM. Other manufacturers have their own versions: therefore, there is no standard. RPG is very limited in its scope and is generally used for report generation in data-processing applications. The language is not suited for complex problems requiring extensive programming logic. An advantage of RPG is that it can be implemented at small computer installations because it has minimal storage requirements.

Language Selection

Here we will not attempt to make comparisons between the languages just discussed. Rather, we will explain the factors that influence language selection. Selecting a language for a particular programming application is a very important, and sometimes difficult, task. The first consideration should be the relevance of the language to the application for which it is to be used. Many languages are designed to be used for a particular application, and are subordinate choices in other applications. For example, COBOL was designed for the business data-processing application and does not have the facilities to support complex numerical computations characteristic of scientific applications.

A second consideration is: can the language be efficiently implemented on the existing system? Efficiency is measured in terms of compilation time, execution time, primary-storage requirements, and the labor efficiency in using the language. For example, PASCAL and BASIC are excellent languages for microcomputers, because these languages require very little primary storage for compilation and execution.

Organizational aspects must also be considered. Staff requirements should be determined, and the cost of training the staff should be weighed against the cost of acquiring new talent. The language can play a big role in determining the amount of time and cost required for orientation. The language should also be versatile and flexible enough to meet the changing needs of the organization. The selector must consider all the objectives and try to make an optimal decision. No language will satisfy all objectives, and the selector must allow for trade-offs among desired objectives.

Keeping in mind these factors, we will now discuss the various features of a programming language. The following is a brief outline of essential features determining a language's effectiveness:

1. Readability/overall writing features
   Modularity
   Structural clarity
   Compactness
   Simplicity
2. Application-oriented features
   Functional support
   Flexibility
   Versatility
3. Standardization and portability features
4. Software development features
   Editing/debugging facilities
5. Efficiency features
   Compilation
   Execution
   Primary-storage requirements
   Labor efficiency

These features should be viewed with varying degrees of importance depending on how and in what environment the language will be used. For example, in an interactive system, execution time is critical. That is not necessarily the case in a batch-processing environment where jobs can be run overnight.

Desirable qualities of a language are ease of overall writing and readability. These can directly affect personnel costs associated with the initial learning and acquiring proficiency of the language. Modularity and structural clarity is essential in enhancing readability and coding; it should be possible to break down the program into more visible logical units. These features also aid in the development and continual maintenance and modification of structured software throughout its life cycle. Examples of a modular language with structural clarity are PASCAL and PL/I.

Other features desirable for ease of overall writing are compactness and simplicity. Compactness refers to the ability to write a program with a minimum number of keywords and symbols. These features also aid in the maintenance of the language. Examples of a compact language are PASCAL and BASIC. COBOL is not a compact language because its goal of being English-like requires the use of words, instead of symbols, when coding.

Once again, relevance of a language to a given application is very important. When selecting a language, evaluate the language's functional support facilities. Does the language support facilities that enhance its performance within a given application, thereby making less work for the programmer? For example, FORTRAN has several built-in functions for evaluating complex numerical equations; and COBOL supports a built-in report-writer and sorting routine. Flexibility is essential in meeting the changing needs of the organization. Application software that can be quickly and accurately altered to specification is most important. Versatility is another feature that enhances a language's performance. PL/I is a versatile and flexible language because of its suitability to both business and scientific computing.

For most business information systems, an important consideration is the ability to run a program on different computers. This capability is known as portability, as discussed earlier. It is most important to be able to upgrade to new hardware without having to modify programs. The standardization of languages contributes greatly to portability. Standardization is a continuing challenge to the profession. The most prominent organization to produce standardization is ANSI (American National Standards Institute).

Software development aids are a feature that cannot be overlooked. The selector should evaluate the implementation's editing and debugging facilities—are the *compile-time* and *execution-time diagnostics* adequate? The WATFIV version of FORTRAN is an example of an implementation with superior debugging facilities (that is, descriptive diagnostics which aid in debugging).

Finally, efficiency of a programming language is measured by compilation time, execution time, and primary-storage requirements. Machine and assembly languages utilize these resources very efficiently at the expense of portability, flexibility, and programmer time. PL/I has a large compiler and therefore uses a lot of primary storage and takes a long time to compile, whereas PASCAL uses very little primary storage. The machine efficiency of programming languages is becoming less important as hardware costs decline. Much more important is the human labor required to use the language.

compile-time diagnostics Error diagnostics that are produced when a program is compiled.

execution-time diagnostics Error diagnostics that are produced when a program is executed.

Summing Up

☐ Software may be purchased, or developed in-house. If it is internally developed, a suitable programming language must be selected.

☐ Machine language, which is written in binary representation, is the only language the computer understands. Programs written in other languages must be translated into machine language, with the help of a compiler or translator.

☐ Assembly language is similar to machine language in that every machine operation must be individually described. But in assembly language, operations and variables are represented by mnemonics instead of by binary numbers. This makes assembly-language programs easier to read.

☐ A high-level language is much easier for people to write and understand. The compiler automatically generates most of the routine machine instructions, making life easier for the programmer. High-level languages may be either procedure oriented or problem oriented.

☐ FORTRAN is one of the oldest high-level languages. Although it was originally designed for scientific applications, it is sometimes used in business data processing.

☐ COBOL is an English-like language designed for business applications. A COBOL program contains paragraphs, sentences, and clauses. The major advantages of this language are high portability and self-documentation.

☐ PL/I is a comprehensive language suitable for both business and scientific programming. It is a powerful language because both the novice and the experienced programmer can use it. Versatility in handling character data and strong file-management capabilities make PL/I a good candidate for business applications.

☐ BASIC is an all-purpose language that is easy to learn. Although it is not well structured, it is extremely popular among users of microcomputers. Many vendors and users have developed their own versions of BASIC, thereby reducing its portability.

☐ Like PL/I, PASCAL is a well-structured language suited to both business and scientific applications. It can be used on microcomputers because the compiler does not require an excessive amount of storage space.

☐ One of the newest high-level languages, ADA, is intended to be portable, well-structured, and versatile. ADA has been developed by the Department of Defense, primarily for use in a technical environment.

☐ RPG is a popular problem-oriented language. Used widely on small computers, RPG operates only on sequential data files. Its basic function is to generate data files and reports, although some limited data-manipulation features are available.

☐ When evaluating a computer language, the selector should consider the following characteristics:

1. Readability/overall writing
2. Application-oriented features
3. Standardization and portability
4. Software development aids
5. Efficiency

Key Terms

program
high-level languages
machine language
semantic gap
object code
symbolic languages
assembly language
mnemonics
assembler
source code
pseudocode
register
base register
procedure-oriented language
problem-oriented language
compiler
translation
linking
loading
FORTRAN
WATFIV
statements
keywords
nonexecutable statements
specification statements
data type
executable statements
assignment statements
control statements

input/output statements
structured programming
documentation
COBOL
divisions
sections
sentences
statements
words
reserved words
user-defined words
system names
semantic errors
PL/I
block-structured language
internal subroutine
edit-directed
BASIC
portability
PASCAL
data type
ADA
modules
packages
tasks
terminating keywords
RPG
fields

Self-Quiz

Completion Questions

1. _____ was developed as an educational tool to encourage the writing of well-structured, readable programs.
2. _____ was developed to bridge the gap between scientific and commercial programming languages.
3. A _____ is a language in which the programmer gives step-by-step instructions to the computer.
4. The most business-oriented language is _____ .
5. A machine-language program is also known as _____ , whereas an assembly or higher-level-language program is known as _____ .
6. High-level languages are either procedure oriented or _____ oriented.
7. A FORTRAN program is a sequence of _____ .
8. A COBOL program is divided into four major parts called _____ .
9. A _____ is a set of instructions executed by the computer.

10. _____ was designed as an easy-to-learn, easy-to-use, interactive language.

Multiple-Choice Questions

1. All computers execute
   a. BASIC programs.
   b. COBOL programs.
   c. machine language programs.
   d. FORTRAN programs.
   e. PL/I programs.

2. Which of the following is most oriented to scientific programming?
   a. FORTRAN
   b. COBOL
   c. BASIC
   d. PL/I
   e. RPG

3. All of the following are disadvantages of RPG except:
   a. It is a very machine-dependent language.
   b. It is very limited in its scope.
   c. It is not suited for complex problems requiring extensive programming logic.
   d. It has large storage requirements.
   e. All of the above are disadvantages.

4. Which of the following is *not* one of the processes that a high-level language program must go through before it is ready to be executed?
   a. translation
   b. controlling
   c. loading
   d. linking
   e. All of the above are necessary processes

5. Which of the following is *not* true of FORTRAN?
   a. It was developed for scientific and mathematical applications.
   b. It is one of the oldest high-level languages.
   c. It is a problem-oriented language.
   d. It requires extensive internal documentation.
   e. All of the above are true.

6. All of the following are divisions of the COBOL program except:
   a. Input-output
   b. Identification

   c. Procedure
   d. Data
   e. All of the above are divisions

7. In a COBOL program, the input-output section is within the _____ division.
   a. identification
   b. procedure
   c. configuration
   d. environment
   e. none of the above

8. Which of the following is not a characteristic of COBOL?
   a. It is a very standardized language.
   b. It is very efficient in terms of coding and execution.
   c. It has limited facilities for mathematical notation.
   d. It is a very readable language.
   e. All of the above are characteristics.

9. Which of the following is an example of a problem-oriented language?
   a. BASIC
   b. PL/I
   c. FORTRAN
   d. All of the above
   e. None of the above

10. In the evaluation of a computer language, all of the following characteristics should be considered *except:*
    a. application-oriented features.
    b. efficiency.
    c. readability.
    d. software development aids.
    e. hardware maintenance costs

Answers

Completion	Multiple Choice
1. PASCAL	1. c
2. PL/I	2. a
3. procedure-oriented language	3. d
4. COBOL	4. b
5. object code; source code	5. c
6. problem	6. a
7. statements	7. d
8. divisions	8. b
9. program	9. e
10. BASIC	10. e

Module C

Decision-Support Systems

MODULE OUTLINE

PROLOGUE

Bob Lexington is the chief executive officer of Phillips Products Incorporated. In a recent meeting with his vice president, he expressed the opinion that computer information systems are very valuable for transaction processing and for support of operational-level decision making. He feels, however, that computer information systems are a long way from providing significant support for tactical and strategic level decision making, especially for unstructured and unanticipated decisions. He states, "for the type of decisions I make, most of the data and information comes from informal and often outside sources. Of course, our computer information systems can provide me with background information. But this is a relatively small percentage of the information I need to make most decisions. The idea of a decision-support system for tactical and strategic level decisions is just too new. I think we should wait several years before investing our resources in this untried concept." Do you agree with Mr. Lexington?

Introduction

Computer information systems follow a natural evolution in organizations. Most organizations start with data-processing systems that support transaction processing and evolve to management information systems to support tactical and strategic level decision making. In the past few years a new type of system called a decision-support system (DSS), has gained popularity in the information systems field. In this text we view decision-support systems as an evolutionary extension of a management information system.

In this module we will define a decision-support system, identify its functions, and explore the need for such a system. We will also examine some of the organizations where a decision support system is likely to be successful, and cover the steps in building a decision support system.

What Is a Decision-Support System?

Definition

structured decision
A decision where the methods and rules for making the decision are well defined and known. Examples are when to reorder inventory, and whether or not to grant credit to a customer.

In chapter 3 we explored the relationship between objectives, decisions, and information. We stressed that the purpose of management information systems is to provide information for decision making. If a management information system supports decision making with information, why is a decision-support system an extension of a MIS? Management information systems in the past have been most successful in providing information for routine, *structured,* and anticipated types of decisions. In addition, they have succeeded in acquiring and storing large quantities of detailed data concerning transaction processing. They have been less successful in providing information for semistructured or unstructured decisions, particularly those which were not anticipated when the computer information system was designed. The basic idea underlying decision-support systems is to provide a set of computer-based tools so that management information systems can produce information to support semistructured and unanticipated decisions.

We will define a **decision-support system** as an integrated set of computer tools that allow a decision maker to interact directly with computers to create information useful in making semistructured and unstructured decisions. Examples are decisions involving mergers and acquisitions, plant expansion, new products, stock-portfolio management, and marketing.

It is important that a distinction be made between a decision-support system and the software and hardware tools that make it possible. Electronic spreadsheets, such as Lotus 1–2–3 and Ability, are DSS tools. A particular decision support system is an application of DSS tools, not the tools themselves.

Decision-support systems and application development by users are closely related. A DSS must be inherently flexible to respond to unanticipated needs for information. This type of flexibility requires that decision makers be directly involved in designing a DSS. Building and using a DSS is a form of application development by users. In fact, many of the hardware and software tools (such as personal computers, electronic spreadsheets, and financial-modeling software) used for application development by users are also used in decision-support systems.

DSS Software

The software components for decision-support systems are illustrated in Figure C–1. The major components include a **language system** which enables the user to interact with the decision-support system, a **problem-processing system** which is made up of several components that perform various processing tasks, and a **knowledge system** which provides data and artificial-intelligence capabilities to the decision-support system.

The language system may have both procedural and nonprocedural language capabilities. A **procedural language** requires that the user provide the logical steps or procedures to be used in solving a particular problem. Examples of procedural languages are FORTRAN, COBOL, and BASIC. Most decision makers do not use procedural languages, these languages are generally used by professional programmers. However, in a DSS there may be specific problems that the nonprocedural language cannot address; therefore, a procedural language could be useful.

With a **nonprocedural language** the user simply specifies the characteristics of a problem or information query and lets the DSS determine the logical steps necessary to provide the information. An example of a nonprocedural command is: "Retrieve sales for last year for all stores in the state of New York." This nonprocedural query is very English-like. Nonprocedural languages can be English-like or be in many other forms that are user-friendly.

The problem-processing system is the heart of the decision-support system. It should contain several capabilities, including the ability to collect information from data bases through data-base management systems. It should make available a wide variety of management-science models, such as regression, time-series analysis, and goal programming. It also should have a graphics capability, and an electronic-spreadsheet feature similar to those offered by packages such as Lotus 1–2–3 and SuperCalc. In fact, many decision-support systems are being built with an electronic

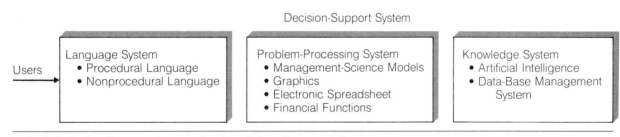

FIGURE C–1 Components of a Decision-Support System

A DSS typically has several tools. Each tool provides one or more of the components illustrated here.

spreadsheet as the main focus. Most decision-support systems include standard financial functions such as return on investment and net present value.

The knowledge system is made up of the data-base management system and the associated files stored and managed by the DBMS. These files contain detailed data that have been collected through transaction processing and from other sources. Another type of knowledge that is beginning to be useful in decision-support systems is **artificial intelligence** (sometimes called an expert system). It acts much in the same manner as a human expert consultant, providing advice and explaining the advice when necessary. Artificial intelligence is beginning to be applied successfully in several areas, including medicine and prospecting for minerals.

Thinking About Information Systems C–1

The Morton Manufacturing Company has recently installed a complete management information system on its mainframe. The next item in Morton's strategic plan for computing is to install a decision-support system. Several analysts have already been assigned to a project team to evaluate decision-support software. Their first task is to interview various user managers to determine what type of decisions the managers make from the data that are already in the new management information system. Next, the analysts must document their findings and evaluate vendor literature on decision-support software. In addition to being able to answer the questions posed by the user managers, what are some specific features that should be in a good decision-support package?

Functions of a Decision-Support System

Briggs has provided a summary of several functions and features that DSS applications should contain.[1]

Model Building

The building of a model of the decision-making problem is a central purpose of most decision-support systems. This model is often in the form of a two- (or more) dimensional table, such as the electronic spreadsheet. The first two dimensions of the table might contain an income statement, the third dimension could represent various products, and the fourth dimension could represent multiple retail outlets. In this case, model development involves specifying in mathematical terms the relationships among the various sales and expense variables. For example, in building this model, we may assume that sales is a function of advertising expense. In mathematical terms this function might be stated as sales $= 20\ X$ advertising expense. This function indicates that for each dollar spent on advertising, sales will increase by twenty dollars.

[1]Warren G. Briggs. "An Evaluation of DSS Packages." *Computer World,* Vol. XVI, No. 9, 1982, p. 31.

Procedural and/or Nonprocedural Language

As discussed earlier, these languages allow the user to communicate with the DSS. Most users find nonprocedural languages more convenient to use.

What-If Analysis

The ability to show the impact of changes in data and assumptions is perhaps the most useful feature of a DSS. For example, a DSS could show the impact on profit if sales grew at a rate of 7 to 10 percent instead of 5 percent. Most DSS applications can show instantaneously on the CRT the impact of such changes in assumptions. Electronic spreadsheets are especially good for **what-if analysis.**

Goal Seeking

A DSS should be able to show what value a particular *independent variable* such as advertising expense would have to be in order to produce a certain target value for the *dependent variable* such as sales. In effect, the user is asking: "if my goal is $20 million in sales, what must the advertising expense be?" Most electronic spreadsheets for personal computers do not have this capability. However, mainframe financial-modeling tools, such as the Integrated Financial Planning System, perform **goal seeking.**

independent variable
In a mathematical formula, a variable that can be varied.

dependent variable
In a mathematical formula, the variable that is determined by the value of the independent variable(s). For example, in the formula sales = 20 X advertising expense, sales is the dependent variable and advertising expense is the independent variable.

Risk Analysis

A very useful piece of information for a decision maker is a probability distribution, which is obtained through a **risk analysis.** This provides the probabilities that a particular critical measure, such as profit, will reach a certain level. For example, it would be useful to know the probability that the profit growth rate will be zero, the probability it will be 5 percent, and the probability it will be 10 percent. Such information can be generated using management-science techniques, provided that certain data are available. The necessary data are the probability distributions of the underlying independent variables, such as sales and expenses.

Statistical Analysis and Management-Science Models

A good DSS will be able to provide several useful **management-science models** such as regression and time-series analysis. These two models may be used to project historical data, such as sales, into the future.

Financial Functions

Preprogrammed **financial functions** for commonly used calculations are usually included in DSS packages. These may include corporate tax rates, depreciation methods, and return on investment.

Graphics

An extremely important feature in a decision-support system is a graphics generator. The system should be able to depict any of the data contained in the system in various graphic forms, such as line or pie graphs.

Hardware Capabilities

Decision-support systems in one form or another can be implemented on machines as small as personal computers and as large as mainframes. When a DSS is installed on a PC, the PC should have a large amount of data storage. Mainframes usually have large data storage and processing capacity, so more complex models can be implemented on them. A current trend (which is expected to continue) is the use of PCs in combination with mainframes for decision-support systems. The PC is linked to the mainframe to retrieve data for subsequent processing on the PC if the data volume and procesing volumes are relatively small. If, on the other hand, large amounts of data and processing are required, some parts of the DSS may be performed on the mainframe. Many of the DSS software tools, such as IFPS and FOCUS, can run on both PCs and mainframes.

Data Bases and External Files

It is crucial that a DSS be able to access data stored in the organization as files. Much of the knowledge-producing data that a DSS uses are stored in these files. This access can be done either through the data-base management system's capabilities or through the DSS's own capability to access external files. In addition, most DSS tools have the capability of maintaining their own internal files once the data are retrieved from other sources.

PC USER TIP   Spreadsheet Design and Documentation

Here is a list of tips for designing and documenting your spreadsheets:

1. Separate the areas in your spreadsheet where numbers are input and where calculations are performed.

2. When developing spreadsheets to be used by others or to be used many times, use the Protect or Lock features to guard against errors in data entry.

3. Use name ranges to make formulas more understandable.

4. If you have a complex formula, break it down into pieces in separate cells and then combine these cells to get the final result.

5. Use parentheses in formulas to indicate the order of calculation.

6. Avoid putting so much into a small area that revisions become difficult.

7. Be careful when inserting and deleting rows and columns. These can have disastrous effects on your existing formulas, named ranges, and macros.

8. Test a spreadsheet by using simple numbers as input, or numbers for which the results are known.

9. Document macros. Often documentation can be placed in the column beside the macro.

10. Document named ranges. List the name, location, purpose, and where used.

For more tips see *PC Magazine,* "Spreadsheet Clinic Column," and *Lotus* Magazine.

Why Do Managers Need Decision-Support Systems?

There has always been a need for the types of information that a DSS produces. Decision-support systems have become popular primarily because of the hardware and software tools that make them possible. The declining cost of computer hardware has made computer processing and computer storage relatively inexpensive. Second, the advent of data-base management systems in the 1970s provided means for storage and management of large amounts of detailed data. These data are now relatively easy to retrieve for use in a decision-support system. Third, there has been a large increase in the number of software packages that incorporate the functions of a DSS. These packages can be used directly to implement DSS applications. And finally, many college graduates trained in analytic techniques are now reaching the middle and upper levels of management where most semistructured and unstructured decisions are made. These individuals know how to use the tools that decision-support systems provide.

Organization Environment for a Successful DSS

There are several characteristics of organizations that have been successful in implementing decision-support systems. First, the company has well-controlled and well-structured data-processing systems. Second, the organization has the extra dollars and personnel to maintain a research-and-development focus. Establishing a DSS is a development effort. Therefore, the organization must be willing to commit dollars and personnel to a project where the benefits may be unknown. Third, the *line departments* of the organization have established open communication with the central computer groups. Fourth, the line departments have sufficient confidence to initiate and manage system projects. They are continually looking for new ways to use computer-based systems. Fifth, the computer groups act primarily as consultants to assist line departments in implementing systems. Sixth, the computer groups have several people on their staff who either came from line departments or have substantial background in disciplines such as manufacturing, finance, accounting, or marketing. And finally, education and training are used to build understanding between line departments and the computer group.

line departments
The departments of an organization that are responsible for producing and selling its products or services

Many of these characteristics are similar to those of organizations that have adopted application development by users. As mentioned earlier, the subject of application development by users is closely related to DSS. You should note the potential application of the techniques discussed in chapter 7 to decision-support systems.

Wythe Industries is a fast-growing clothing manufacturer located in the southeast. Most of Wythe's data-processing applications are computer-based. However, none of them are installed on a data-base management system. Each application stands alone, although there are some links among the applications. Traditionally, central data processing and its system-development staff have done all of the application development within the company. Most staff members have a computer background, with very little experience in user areas. The management at Wythe is considering a decision-support system. Would you advise Wythe to invest resources in a decision-suport system at this time? Support your answer.

Building a Decision-Support System

In chapter 5 we presented the structured system-development life cycle, which includes the major processes involved in developing either a data-processing or a management information system. Building a DSS is quite different from this life cycle. Design, implementation, and evaluation of decision-support systems tend to be done at the same time. These processes are evolutionary in that upon initial implementation, a decision-support system is likely to be incomplete. Owing to the semistructured and unstructured nature of problems addressed by a DSS, managers change their perceived needs for information, and therefore the DSS must also change. There may be no precise end to implementation. Since decision-support systems are likely to be in a constant state of change, it is most important that users be directly involved in initiating and managing this change.

Predesign

Keen and Morton have outlined the major processes involved in building a decision-support system.[2] Figure C–2 is a summary of these processes. The first step in the predesign process is to define the objectives for the decision-support effort, which involves laying out the overall goals of the project.

The second step is to identify the available resources that can be applied to the project. Quite often a firm will already have hardware and software, such as a data-base management system, that can be used in a DSS.

Perhaps the most crucial step in the project is to determine the **key decisions** in the problem area. For example, in a stock-portfolio management system the key decision might be to select the correct stocks for a particular customer's needs. Now, we might conclude that it would be difficult to provide information that would tell a portfolio manager which stock to select, because of the many factors involved, such as varying customer needs. Some customers might be very conservative and therefore would want their money invested in safe stocks. Others might prefer high-risk situations because of potential high gains. Two points should

[2]Peter G. W. Keen and Michael S. Scott Morton. *Decision Support Systems: An Organizational Perspective.* Addison Wesley Publishing Co., Reading, Massachusetts, 1978, pp. 167–225.

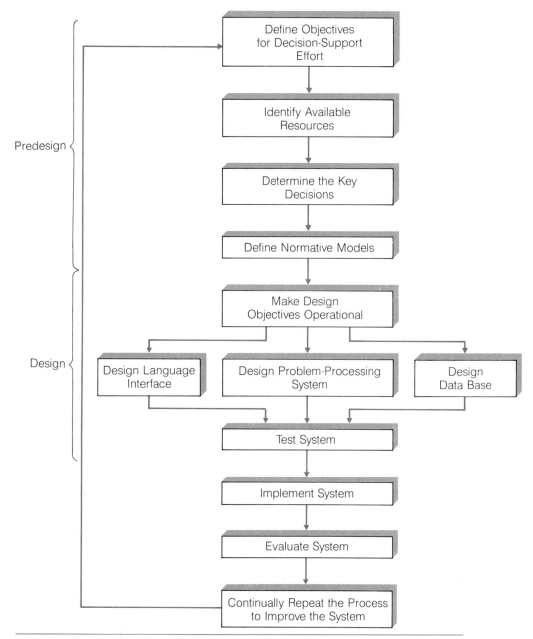

FIGURE C–2   Steps in Building a Decision-Support System

Building a DSS is a highly iterative process, with many of these steps going on simultaneously and being repeated. In essence, a DSS is continually being refined.

be made that relate to this concern. First, the decision-support system is only a tool that provides information to the portfolio manager. The portfolio manager makes the final decision as to what stock to select. Second, even though we may find it difficult to provide relevant information for a decision, it is still very crucial that we identify the key decision. Providing very relevant information for the wrong decision will get us nowhere. Providing marginally helpful information for the key decision is a useful contribution.

The next step is to define the normative models. A **normative model** is a highly rational approach to providing useful information to the manager making key decisions. The word *normative* means a standard, or what should be. Normative models are likely to be highly idealistic and theoretical. For example, in the stock-portfolio DSS, the ideal information would be the price of stocks at some future date, which is obviously impossible to obtain. It is unlikely that we will attain the level of the normative model in the actual implementation of the DSS. It is a goal that we attempt to implement in a real-world situation. Even though we would not be able to provide the actual future stock prices to the portfolio manager, we could furnish information to improve the manager's forecast of future stock prices. It may not be practicable or advisable to implement the normative model, but we must keep it in mind when designing the actual DSS. Normative models become a major part of our design objectives.

Design

The first step in the design process is to make the design objectives operational. In this step we decide what can be done in a real world implementation of the DSS. The next step is to design the language interface. Ideally, this language interface should be a nonprocedural language, since most users find that it is easier to communicate a problem to a DSS than to tell the DSS the procedural steps necessary to solve the problem. Designing the problem-solving system is largely a matter of selecting the management-science models (such as regression) and the computer software (such as graphics and electronic spreadsheet) that can be applied to the DSS application. These models and software must be combined in a way that allows the user to readily select and use them in operating the DSS.

Portions of the knowledge system may already be in place. Most companies that are implementing a DSS already have a great deal of basic data stored in data-base management systems. The final step in design is to thoroughly test the system prior to its implementation.

Implementation

Implementation is a crucial process in building a DSS. Essentially we are asking the user to change from something that he or she is doing now and accept a new system. The organization or individual must have a felt need for the new DSS. There are several ways in which this need can be created. Obviously, if our boss tells us that we will use the new DSS, this can create a need. However, in the long run this may be counterproductive. Developing user confidence in and need for a system really begins early in the building process. Perhaps one of the most effective ways is to involve the user as much as possible in the development process. As mentioned previously, the ideal situation would be to have the user initiate and manage this process with a computer system specialist acting as a consultant. If this occurs the user will see a system as his or her own and therefore will more likely support and use the DSS.

Evaluation

If we plan to evaluate the contributions of a DSS there must be some criteria for evaluation. This is particularly difficult with a DSS since the system is evolutionary in nature and therefore does not have a neatly defined completion date. It is unlikely that a DSS will be justified through reductions in clerical costs. Usually the justification is the provision of more timely and better information. This is a very general benefit and difficult to evaluate. However, it should be possible to measure the impact of this information on better decisions and therefore, better ultimate results. For example, in a portfolio management system used by an investment firm, the ultimate result should be more satisfied customers, and in turn, greater revenue for the firm.

There are three key components in the evaluation process. First, there should be prior definitions of "improvements." These definitions, or criteria for evaluation, should be established very early in the building process. Second, a means of monitoring the progress toward these improvements must be defined. And finally, a formal review process that periodically measures performance against the definition of improvement should be established.

Summing Up

☐ A decision-support system is an integrated set of computer tools that allow a decision maker to interact directly with computers to create information useful in making semistructured and unstructured decisions.

☐ The major components of a decision-support system include the language system, problem-processing system, and knowledge system.

☐ There are several characteristics of organizations that have been successful in implementing decision-support systems:

1. A well-controlled and well-structured data-processing system exists.
2. There is a willingness to commit dollars and personnel to the project.

3. There is good communication between line departments and central computer groups.
4. The line departments have sufficient confidence to initiate and manage system projects.
5. The central computer groups act primarily as consultants.
6. The central computer groups have several people on their staff with expertise in the user disciplines.
7. Education and training are used to build understanding between line departments and the computer groups.

☐ There is usually no precise end to the development and implementation of a decision-support system. The major steps in building a DSS are predesign, design, implementation, and evaluation.

Key Terms

decision-support system
language system
problem-processing system
knowledge system
procedural language

nonprocedural language
artificial intelligence
what-if analysis
goal seeking
risk analysis

management-science models
financial functions
key decisions
normative model

Self-Quiz

Completion Questions

1. A _____ is an integrated set of computer tools that allow a decision maker to interact directly with computers to create information useful in making semistructured and unstructured decisions.
2. The major components of a decision-support system include a language system, a problem-processing system, and a _____ system.
3. A _____ system enables the user to interact with the decision-support system.
4. A _____ language requires that the user provide the logical steps or procedures to be used in solving a particular problem.
5. The problem-processing system should provide management-science models, graphics capabilities, a(n) _____ , and standard financial functions.
6. One type of artificial intelligence is a(n) _____ .

7. A(n) _____ model is a highly rational approach to providing useful information to the manager making key decisions.
8. The major steps in building a decision-support system are predesign, design, _____ , and evaluation.
9. The heart of the decision-support system is the _____ system.
10. In a decision-support system, the language interface should ideally be a(n) _____ language.

Multiple-Choice Questions

1. Which of the following is not one of the major components of a decision-support system?
   a. language system
   b. knowledge system
   c. expert system
   d. problem-processing system

2. A decision-support system is intended to produce information to support which type of decisions?
   a. well-structured
   b. unstructured
   c. anticipated
   d. routine
   e. none of the above

3. The major function of the language system is:
   a. to perform various processing tasks
   b. to provide artificial-intelligence capabilities to the DSS
   c. to provide data to the DSS
   d. to enable the users to interact with the DSS
   e. none of the above

4. Which of the following is not true of nonprocedural languages?
   a. They can be English-like.
   b. They can take user-friendly forms.
   c. BASIC is an example of a nonprocedural language.
   d. They allow the user to simply specify the characteristics of a problem and to leave the determination of the logical steps to the DSS.
   e. All of the above are true.

5. A central purpose of most decision-support systems is
   a. to build a model of the decision-making problem
   b. to design a data-base management system
   c. to build an expert system
   d. to determine the key decisions in the problem area
   e. none of the above

6. Which of the following should be done in the design process of building a decision-support system?
   a. defining the objectives for the decision-support effort
   b. designing the language interface
   c. defining the normative models which can provide information for the key decisions
   d. two of the above
   e. all three of the above

7. Information concerning the probability distribution of a profit rate can be generated by using:
   a. electronic spreadsheet
   b. artificial intelligence
   c. time-series analysis
   d. management science techniques
   e. sensitivity analysis

8. Which of the following is not a primary reason for the popularity of decision-support systems?
   a. declining cost of computer hardware
   b. advent of data-base management systems
   c. increased number of programmers
   d. management trained in analytic techniques
   e. increased number of software packages

9. To be successful in implementing DSS, organizations should have the following characteristics except:
   a. a well-controlled data-processing system
   b. willingness to commit dollars and personnel to the project
   c. education and training by the organization
   d. powerful central computer groups to initiate and manage system projects
   e. all of the above are important

10. Which of the following is not a key component of the evaluation process in building a DSS?
    a. criteria for evaluation
    b. means of measuring system-development time spent on the project
    c. means of monitoring the progress of the DSS
    d. formal review process
    e. all of the above are key components

Answers

Completion	Multiple Choice
1. decision-support system	1. c
2. knowledge	2. b
3. language	3. d
4. procedural	4. c
5. electronic spreadsheet	5. a
6. expert system	6. b
7. normative	7. d
8. implementation	8. c
9. problem-processing	9. d
10. nonprocedural	10. b

Module D

Computer System Evaluation and Acquisition

MODULE OUTLINE

PROLOGUE

The Boston Insurance Company is a medium-sized property and casualty insurance company. All of its policy and claims processing is performed on large mainframe computers. The computer information systems it uses are the latest, state-of-the-art on-line systems. The company is heavily dependent on these systems, both for transaction processing and for management information. Yet it does not own a single computer! Neither does it employ system analysts or programmers! How could this be?

Introduction

Users have become increasingly involved with the evaluation and acquisition of computer hardware and software. Often managers serve on user committees that are responsible for selecting a computer system. Even when the information-systems function is not a routine responsibility of the manager, he or she will often become involved with selecting a computer system because of the computer's impact on his or her department.

Since we discussed personal-computer hardware and software in chapter 2 and in the photo essay on purchasing a PC system, we will not present that material here. However, many of the techniques covered in this module are useful in evaluating and acquiring any size computer, from mainframe to personal computer.

We will first discuss how various computer systems are evaluated, including the very important area of evaluating purchased software. Then we will examine the methods for financing computer systems. Finally, we will explore the various sources for EDP equipment and services.

Conducting an Evaluation of a Computer System

Approaches to acquiring computer hardware and software have changed over the years. Available hardware and software used to be much more limited. Purchasing a particular manufacturer's hardware usually locked the buyer into that company's software and utility programs since they were sold as a package. This practice was known as **bundling.** Hardware components of different manufacturers were usually incompatible. **Plug-compatible** hardware units (units produced by other manufacturers that directly replace hardware units produced by major manufacturers such as IBM) did not exist. Therefore, acquiring a computer tended to be very informal. Decisions were based on a review of the manufacturer's specifications, what competitors were doing, other computer users' recommendations, or the desire to buy from a favorite manufacturer. Today, sophisticated computer users employ a more structured approach. The range of systems and costs within the computer industry is simply too broad for an unstructured evaluation to be successful.

As illustrated in Figure D–1, the evaluation process has five primary steps:

1. system feasibility study,
2. system analysis,
3. development of a request for proposal,
4. proposal evaluation, and
5. *vendor* selection.

vendor
A supplier of computer hardware and/or software.

Although we will discuss the evaluation steps sequentially, the actual process can be highly iterative, and the steps can overlap. Steps 1 and 2 were discussed

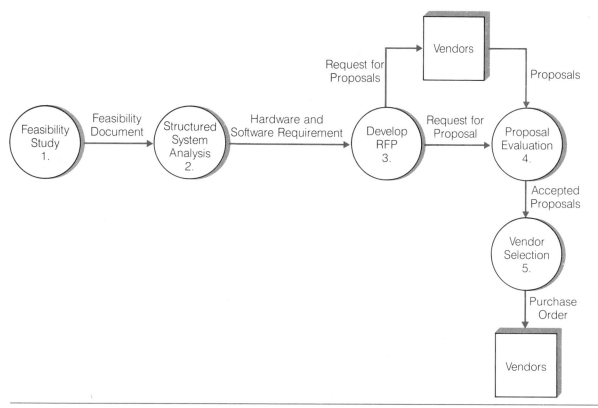

FIGURE D–1 Steps in Evaluation and Purchase of Computer Hardware and Software

Determining your hardware and software requirements through structured system analysis is an important step. Many firms have purchased inappropriate hardware and software because they did not first determine their requirements.

in chapter 5, System Analysis; therefore, this module will begin with step 3, which is the first task to be completed when purchasing hardware or software.

Development of a Request for Proposal

The **request for proposal (RFP) document** puts the requirements for the equipment and software in a form that vendors of hardware and software can respond to. It serves as a communication tool between the potential buyer and vendor. It is sent to each vendor that is asked to propose hardware and software for the system. Among the areas it should cover are:

1. A description of present and proposed applications, including for each application: processing mode (batch or iterative), input/output volumes, data-flow diagrams, file descriptions (including size), data-base characteristics, and how often the application will be run.
2. Reliability requirements.
3. Backup requirements.

4. Vendor service requirements.
5. Outline of any specific hardware or software features required, such as printer speed or disk capacity.
6. Criteria for evaluating proposals.
7. Plans for a vendor demonstration of hardware and software to the buyer.
8. Implementation schedule.
9. Price constraints.
10. List of any specific questions about the characteristics of the vendor's hardware and software.
11. Procedures for clarifying the RFP and submitting the proposal, including the person to contact for RFP clarification and the scheduled date for submitting the proposal.

The RFP is sent to each prospective vendor, along with an invitation to bid. The buyer should expect a notification from each vendor as to whether it will bid or not.

Proposal Evaluation

Hardware and Software Demonstration   In the first phase of proposal evaluation, vendors demonstrate their proposed systems to the potential users. Usually only a few vendors are invited to demonstrate. They generally present the major features of their proposals orally. The complete system may be demonstrated at the buyer's location, if the system is easily portable. If not, the buyer may visit the vendor's facility for the demonstration. The vendors' presentations enable several of the buyer's employees to gain an understanding of the features of the various proposals. However, most buyers use more substantial techniques to evaluate these proposals than merely listening to oral presentations, watching demonstrations, and reading proposals.

Evaluation Techniques   Performance evaluation of computer hardware and software is a major tool used in the selection of new equipment. For each proposal, the buyer would like to know the performance characteristics (job run time, throughput, idle time, response time, and so on) when executing current and planned applications. Obtaining such information is obviously impossible. Planned applications have not been developed, and current applications may not execute on the various equipment involved without program modification. However, there are techniques available to assist the buyer in obtaining approximate performance data. Performance evaluation techniques fall into two categories. Traditional techniques provide very gross measures of a system's performance characteristics. Current techniques provide the buyer with much more reliable and extensive measures of a system's performance.

Traditional Techniques   The traditional techniques of performance evaluation compare performance characteristics such as number of bits processed in each operation by the CPU, primary and secondary memory access time, millions of instructions per second (MIPS) executed by the CPU, and an average time for a mix of instructions. All are very gross measures of computer performance, with only limited usefulness—and then only when the various computers have similar internal organization. These techniques ignore the effects of software on system performance.

Another traditional technique is the **kernel program,** which is a small sample program executed on each proposed computer. In some cases the kernel program is not actually executed, but the run time is derived on the basis of instruction execution time. This approach may be helpful in standard mathematical applications, but it is not very useful for business systems since software and input/output effects are ignored.

Current Techniques   Several more reliable techniques are benchmark programs, workload models, simulation, and monitors. **Benchmark programs** are sample programs or test jobs that represent at least a part of the buyer's primary computer workload. They include software considerations and can be current application programs or new programs that have been designed to represent planned processing needs. The buyer can design these programs to test any characteristic of the system. For example, the benchmark might test the average response time for inquiries from terminals when the system is also executing a **compute-bound** batch job. Terminal inquiries during the test can be handled manually, or a tape or disk unit can be set up to simulate them. Figure D–2 illustrates benchmark tests that can be used to evaluate a data-base management system.

compute-bound job
A computer run that requires large amounts of CPU time and relatively little input and output.

Workload models are computer programs that accurately represent the buyer's planned computer workload. The model programs require the same mix of demand for computer resources that the buyer's application programs will require. For example, if the buyer's total workload is expected to contain 15 percent high CPU demand work, 10 percent compilation, 30 percent terminal input/output, and 45 percent batch input/output, the workload model programs should contain the same mix. Workload models differ from benchmark programs in that the latter usually do not accurately represent the buyer's complete planned workload.

Simulation techniques have been used extensively to evaluate complex alternative systems where it is not possible to analytically determine which alternative is preferable. For example, a computer simulation can be used to determine which aircraft would be the best purchase for an airline, given its present fleet, its expected route structures, and its passenger demand. Simulation is equally applicable to the evaluation of alternative computer systems.

| Time to Create the Structure of a File |
| Time to Enter a Sample of Standard Data |
| Time to Execute a Standard Task |
| Time to Perform a Sort |
| Time to Retrieve Records Randomly |
| Time to Create a Standard Report on the Screen |
| Time to Execute a Standard Report to the Screen |

FIGURE D–2   Benchmark Tests for a Data-Base Management System
Tests like these can produce valuable data on which to judge various software.

Simulation packages can simulate almost any computer system. Input to these packages includes descriptions of expected workloads, files, input/output volumes, and the vendor's equipment. The simulation program then simulates the running of the user's described workload on the described equipment. Simulating the equipment of different vendors is accomplished by changing the equipment-description input. Validity of the simulation greatly depends on how accurately the simulation models the equipment and the buyer's anticipated workload. Since a valid simulation can be difficult to achieve and perhaps more difficult to recognize by people inexperienced in simulation, it should be used by only the more sophisticated computer buyers.

Monitors are hardware or software devices that monitor the operation of a computer and provide operating statistics such as idle time of the CPU and average job-execution time. Software monitors are programs that periodically interrupt processing to collect operating statistics. They are part of the operating system and therefore have access to all operating-system data. Hardware monitors are devices attached to the hardware component being monitored and collect data on whatever characteristic is being measured.

Monitors are used primarily in the evaluation and **fine tuning** of existing computer systems, rather than in the selection of new systems. Employed as a fine-tuning tool, they can indicate where bottlenecks occur within the system. For example, the CPU may not be fully utilized while jobs are waiting in queue, because input-output channels are operating at capacity.

We have discussed several traditional and current techniques for evaluating computer systems. For most firms, a combination of benchmarking and workload models is the best technique for evaluating performance. Often vendors will already have the results of several benchmark runs, which the buyer can use. The extent to which benchmarking and workload models are used will depend on the size of the computer being purchased. Personal computers are usually purchased without the buyer using either technique.

Other Evaluation Criteria

Equipment Criteria Many technical criteria should be considered in selecting computer equipment. Some examples are:

1. Primary-memory size
2. Storage-device characteristics
   a. Disk drives (including *transfer rate,* capacity, and whether removable or fixed)
   b. Tape drives (including capacity, transfer rate, and recording density)

3. Data channels
   a. Transfer rate
   b. Number
   c. Effect on the CPU

Software Criteria In software, the primary areas of concern are operating systems, compilers, and application programs. Operating systems have a major impact on

transfer rate
The speed with which a peripheral device moves data to and from the CPU.

the efficiency of computer processing. Some of the features that should be evaluated are:

1. Multiprogramming capabilities
2. Job-management features
3. Availability of utility programs
4. CPU time and primary-storage-space overhead required by the operating system
5. Quality of the operating system's documentation

In terms of the program compiler, the user should determine whether the major compiler to be used is available and if it is well supported by the vendor. In mainframe business information systems, COBOL is the primary compiler; PL/I is used quite often on IBM equipment also. On minicomputers and microcomputers, the primary languages are Report Program Generator (RPG) and BASIC, respectively.

The main concern with application programs is the availability, capabilities, and reliability of necessary application programs. Users may want to purchase applications software and make minor modifications to adapt the programs to their particular needs. In such a case, the extent of the documentation and the ability of the programs to be modified are important considerations. The reliability and capabilities of application software can usually be best determined by consulting current users. The evaluation of purchased software is covered in more detail later in this module.

General Criteria   Other more general criteria to be evaluated when selecting computer systems include vendor support, compatibility, and modularity. **Vendor support** is crucial to the success of a computer system in a variety of areas, including:

1. Personnel training
2. Repair and maintenance
3. Installation
4. Preinstallation testing
5. Hardware backup arrangements

Vendor support is generally adequate among the larger, more established computer vendors. However, there are many new firms in the minicomputer and PC industry, and in some cases their support is minimal. In addition, even with larger computer vendors, repair and maintenance services may be slow and expensive when the user is located in rural or remote areas.

Compatibility can be divided into two parts: hardware and software compatibility. Users should know how compatible a potential vendor's hardware is with the hardware of other vendors. Compatibility enables a buyer to consider other vendors for certain components of the system. For example, since many companies sell remote terminals, the buyer could realize substantial savings by purchasing them from the smaller computer vendors. In addition, some computer manufacturers specialize in less expensive, plug-compatible units that will replace the major components (the CPU, for example) of the large vendors' systems. However, the use of mixed systems (plug-compatible units) can increase management problems because it is difficult to assign responsibility for hardware failures when there are two or more vendors' units.

The primary concern about software compatibility is whether the user's existing software will execute on the proposed system. In addition, the user should determine whether the new software is compatible with other computer systems, both from other vendors and from the proposed vendor. If the compatibility of proposed new software is limited, this can be a major restriction to a buyer who later wants to change systems. Vendors often offer families of computers (such as the IBM 370, 303X, and 308X series). Transition from one member to another of these families is very easy since peripheral equipment and operating systems are compatible throughout the line.

A final general criterion that a user should evaluate is **modularity.** The modularity of a computer system is its ability to add capacity or components to the system. It allows for growth without changing systems. For example, additional main memory or disk units can be added when processing requirements dictate such expansion. This capability is crucial if the user's information-processing requirements are expected to increase.

Evaluation of Purchased Software

in-house development
When a firm produces its own application software.

System software is almost always purchased from a vendor or supplied as a package along with the hardware. There is also a trend toward purchasing application software instead of developing it *in-house*. In this section we will discuss the evaluation of purchased software. In-house development was covered in chapters 5, 6, and 7.

Purchasing application software packages has several advantages:

1. Software development is basically labor intensive. Therefore, it is becoming increasingly expensive. Costs per user can be cut by spreading development and maintenance costs over many users.
2. Purchased software is often better documented.
3. Purchased packages are often very flexible. They can be adapted to fit specific user needs without modifying programs.
4. Applications can be implemented faster since the long lead time involved in software development is eliminated.

5. The risk of large cost and time overruns of in-house development is reduced.

Among the disadvantages of purchased software are:

1. Purchased software is not likely to meet the needs of the user as closely as software developed in-house.
2. Certain uncontrollable risks are assumed when software is purchased. For example, the vendor may go out of business, or fail to maintain and update the software.
3. The expertise in the application program is outside the user company, whereas with in-house development that expertise is also in-house.

There are many sources for application software. To find out what packages are on the market, the buyer should consult **software directories** such as those published by International Computer Programs, Auerbach, or Datapro.

The overall approach to evaluating software packages is very similar to evaluating hardware. The primary factors are:

1. Does the package meet the user's needs or can it be modified at a reasonable cost?
2. What are the initial and yearly costs of the package?
3. How efficient is the package? How much of each computer resource (run-time, primary storage, and secondary storage) does the package require?
4. Will additional hardware be required?
5. What are the operating-system requirements of the package?
6. How satisfied with the package are other similar users?
7. Is the package well documented?

American Chemical is a large chemical company headquartered on the West Coast. About two years ago American decided that it needed a new computer-based accounts-payable system. After doing a feasibility study and developing a requirements document, the company decided to purchase an accounts-payable package from a large and reputable software house. Based on demonstrations of the system and subsequent evaluations, it was decided that the package should be modified to fit American's specific needs. A contract was developed with the software house to make the necessary modifications. About eight months later, it became apparent that the software house was not going to be successful in making these modifications. By this time, American had invested several hundred thousand dollars in the package. The software house couldn't even get the package to execute after the modifications. In an attempt to salvage its investment, American hired another software development firm to try to straighten out the mess. This attempt was unsuccessful as well. Primarily because of this disastrous experience, the director of MIS for American Chemical instituted a policy which stated that before an outside software package is purchased, the package must meet American's needs close enough that no modification will be required, or alternatively, it must be a situation where American Chemical can change its way of doing business to fit the way the package operates, without modification. Evaluate this policy.

Thinking About Information Systems D–1

8. Does the vendor provide extensive training in the use of the package to the user's employees?
9. Is the vendor viable? What is the vendor's financial status? How long has it been in business?
10. Does the package appear to be viable over the long run? Can it accommodate changes in hardware and operating systems as well as changes in the user company's needs?
11. Are the performance claims of the vendor specifically guaranteed by the terms of the contract?
12. Does the vendor provide a free trial period? Is this period sufficiently long, given normal implementation time spans?
13. Does the package provide adequate data editing, audit trail, and other control features?

Vendor Selection

In most cases, more than one computer system or software package can meet a user's needs. A widely used method for ranking competing systems is to assign points based on the degree to which each system meets important criteria, and then to total the points to obtain a ranking (see Figure D–3). Of course, the difference among vendors on one or two factors can override the total score based on the ranking. For example, vendor support could be so poor that it precludes the purchase of an otherwise outstanding system. Communicating with the vendors about the point ranking system can be an effective tool for helping them respond more effectively to the RFP.

System Characteristics	Maximum Points	Points Assigned			
		System			
		A	B	C	D
Hardware					
Memory size	20	10	15	20	10
Data channels	10	10	8	5	10
Disk capacity	20	20	5	15	10
Modularity	30	30	20	25	15
Compatibility	30	30	10	15	20
Software					
Operating System	30	20	15	25	30
Compilers	20	15	10	15	20
Application programs	40	30	40	20	25
Compatibility	30	30	30	25	25
Vendor support	40	20	30	35	40
Cost	50	30	40	40	50
Benchmarking results	50	50	40	45	30
Total	370	295	263	285	285

FIGURE D–3 Outline of a Point Ranking System

The maximum points are assigned, based on the relative importance that the buyer feels each system characteristic should have. Usually a team of two to four people independently rank each system being considered.

Financing Alternatives

Essentially, there are three financing alternatives for computer systems: purchase, rental, and lease. Usually all of them are available from manufacturers or their representatives, and rental and lease arrangements can also be made through a *third party*. There are many companies that rent or lease computer hardware and software.

third party
A company other than the user or the computer-system manufacturer.

Purchase

The primary advantage of purchasing equipment is the potential cost savings if the equipment is kept for its useful life, normally three to six years. Furthermore, the purchaser can take the investment tax credit and depreciate the asset for tax purposes. The rental or lease payment is also tax deductible.

Although purchasing equipment generally results in lower overall costs, the buyer assumes the **risk of obsolescence,** and does not have the **flexibility** of canceling the arrangement. Furthermore, purchasing requires capital that may be better utilized elsewhere.

Another consideration when purchasing computer equipment is maintenance. If the equipment is rented, the manufacturer usually provides maintenance services. If the equipment is purchased, the company has several maintenance alternatives:

1. Purchase a maintenance agreement that provides for all maintenance, parts, and labor.
2. Pay for maintenance on a per-call basis, as required.
3. Use the company's own employees for maintenance.

Rental

Under the rental option, the company rents the equipment on a monthly basis directly from the manufacturer or a third party. Most agreements have a minimum rental period, such as ninety days. After the minimum period, the user can cancel

---

PC USER TIP   PC Cooperatives

A personal-computer cooperative, like any other co-op, uses group purchasing power to reduce the cost of commodities to group members. The most popular co-op for personal computers is PC Network. This national co-op provides software and hardware to its members at 8 percent over wholesale cost. The 8-percent margin provides the necessary operating funds to run the co-op and a profit to the co-op's founders. This margin is also used to cover the cost of a wholesale catalog and regular newsletter which are provided to each member.

Local co-ops, where members can participate in the operations of the group, may provide an even lower markup to members. Further information on PC Network can be obtained by writing to:

PC Network
320 West Ohio
Chicago, Illinois 60610
1-800-621-7283

the agreement with short notice—one to two months. This flexibility is perhaps the major advantage of renting. However, the value of this flexibility is often overestimated since the user may have a large investment in training, preparation, and implementation.

Rental agreements generally provide for 176 hours of use of the equipment per month (8 hours per day $\times$ 22 average workdays per month = 176 hours). Using the equipment for more than eight hours a day may require an additional rental payment, although at a reduced rate.

Renting is the most costly approach in terms of overall cash flow. However, the user does not need the large capital outlay required in purchasing equipment. In addition, the risk of obsolescence and the responsibility for maintenance are borne by the manufacturer. In some cases, renting the equipment may produce a greater continuing contact with, and support from, the manufacturer than purchasing it will.

Leasing

Leasing is a compromise between purchasing and renting. Typically, leasing costs less than renting but more than purchasing. Most risks of obsolescence can be transferred to the lessor through an option to purchase the equipment at the end of the lease. Moreover, leasing is not as flexible as renting because the lessee is locked in until the lease expires—typically after five years. However, sometimes the lease can be terminated early through the payment of a termination charge.

Lessors are often third-party, independent leasing companies. The lease agreement may provide a maintenance contract and does not usually charge for operation beyond 176 hours per month. Leasing offers substantial cost savings over renting for the user who is willing to forego the additional flexibility that renting offers.

The ultimate choice of financing involves a trade-off between risks of obsolescence, flexibility, and costs. These trade-offs are illustrated in Figures D–4 and D–5. The flexibility variable has become less important because computer systems themselves are now designed to be much more flexible. They can be upgraded through additional primary storage, secondary storage, or attached CPUs.

Sources of Information-System Equipment and Services

Information-system equipment and services are widely available. The computer industry is intensely competitive, and this has been a major factor in the rapid technological advancement of the industry. The suppliers are innovative and they continually look for unfilled customer needs. This competitive atmosphere can result in substantial cost savings for the buyer. In this section, we will discuss the major equipment and service options available.

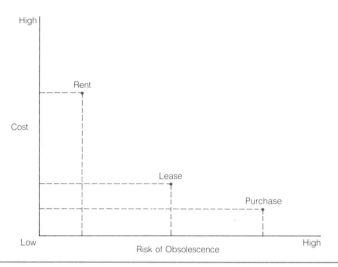

FIGURE D–4   Costs versus Risk-of-Obsolescence Trade-offs of Financing Alternatives

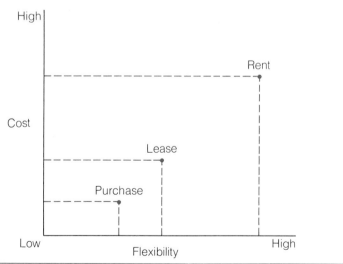

FIGURE D–5   Costs versus Flexibility Trade-offs of Financing Alternatives

Carolina Manufacturing is considering installing a manufacturing resources planning (MRP) system. Carolina has had extensive experience in the use of computers, having installed its first computer-based system in the late 1950s. In addition, Carolina has a great many manufacturing experts on its staff. However, no one working for the company has had experience with MRP systems. The director of manufacturing and the director of MIS currently disagree on how to gain the necessary MRP experience to implement this system. Angela Battle, the director of MIS, advocates hiring an outside consulting firm to guide the company in the implementation of the MRP system. Consulting rates in the area are $125 per hour, and it is expected that the total consulting fee would be approximately $100,000. Jim Johnson, the director of manufacturing, feels that it would be much better for Angela to hire someone with MRP experience to join the MIS staff. Such an individual could be hired for about $50,000 per year, which includes fringe benefits. Which approach do you think Carolina should take?

Computer Manufacturers

Many manufacturers produce complete lines of computer systems, including mainframes, minis, and personal computers. IBM dominates this market with more than 50 percent of the information-processing market. IBM was late to enter the computer market. When it introduced its IBM 650 computer in the mid-1950s, Sperry Univac was already established. However, IBM quickly became dominant and successfully defended its market against strong competitors such as RCA, General Electric, and Xerox, all of which have dropped out of the mainframe business.

Other producers of large computers include Burroughs, Sperry Univac, Amdahl, Cray Research, Honeywell, Hewlett-Packard (HP), National Cash Register (NCR), Digital Equipment Corporation (DEC), and Control Data Corporation (CDC). These manufacturers tend to specialize, often in areas that IBM historically has not covered well. Cray Research specializes in very large super computers that usually have scientific, military, or space applications. Control Data Corporation also tends to specialize in scientific computers. Burroughs deals in banking applications, although it does have small business computers. Hewlett-Packard, DEC, and Honeywell tend to specialize in engineering and scientific applications, with their minicomputers, microcomputers, and interactive computer systems. The primary manufacturers of small business computers are IBM, NCR, and Burroughs.

Personal computers are now used extensively in both large and small businesses. IBM also dominates this market with the IBM-PC. There are, however, a host of other PC manufacturers including Apple, Compaq, Radio Shack, and almost all the mainframe and minicomputer manufacturers. Medium-size and large companies usually purchase personal computers directly from the manufacturer. Small firms buy them from retail computer stores and local offices of computer manufacturers.

All these manufacturers sell software for their computers. Prior to 1969, computer hardware and software were sold as an inseparable package (bundle). When IBM unbundled in 1969, most other manufacturers followed suit. The most extensive business-oriented software is available from IBM, Burroughs, and NCR. Minicomputer manufacturers that specialize in scientific computers naturally offer less business software.

Retail Computer Stores

We discussed sources of personal computers in chapter 2. It is important to remember that **retail computer stores,** including mail-order firms, have become a very large supplier of personal computer hardware and software. These stores began appearing in the late 1970s. They have been a significant factor in making PC hardware and software accessible to individuals and small businesses.

Software Vendors

In the early 1970s, court decisions required hardware manufacturers to sell their hardware without also requiring the customer to purchase the manufacturer's software. This unbundling produced a new market for companies that do not manufacture computers but do produce computer software. Since hardware and software no longer come as one package, the user is free to purchase software separately.

In addition, the advent of personal computers has spawned a large number of software vendors for these machines. Purchasing software from software vendors often affords significant price and performance advantages. The complete range of software, including application programs, application generators, data-base management systems, utility programs, and operating systems, is available from these vendors. In the application programs area, a software vendor will often have specialized programs, such as a package for project scheduling, that are not available from the computer manufacturers.

Service Bureaus

Service bureaus are companies that provide computer processing services on an as-needed basis. They generally charge for the services at an hourly rate. Service bureaus are a primary source of computer services for small businesses and they routinely handle standard applications, such as payroll and accounts receivable. Either the service bureau or the customer provides the programs.

Using a service bureau can reduce costs. It also provides the opportunity to test programs prior to installing a new computer, and to arrange backup services for a company that owns its own computer. Service bureaus also handle data entry or temporary processing overloads.

The main disadvantage of service bureaus is that companies may lose control over data. This could result in serious security problems. Related to the question of data security is the problem of data-file ownership. Users of service bureaus or timesharing services (discussed in the next section) should be sure that they retain all rights of file ownership, including access and use. Another potential problem with service bureaus is lengthy processing turnaround, since the user does not have control over the processing schedule.

Timesharing Services

Timesharing services provide the user with access to a computer through a remote terminal, located at the user's place of business. The CPU and secondary storage are located at the site of the timesharing service. Execution of user programs is initiated through commands issued at the terminal. Turnaround is very fast because programs are executed under a multiprogramming operating system that rotates among programs, allowing each program a CPU time slice. Thus, many independent users can gain access to a computer system at the same time. The characteristics of a typical timesharing system include the following:

1. Each user has access to the computer system through one or more terminals, typically a hardcopy typewriter or a CRT device with hardcopy print capability.
2. Data and instructions arrive at the CPU simultaneously from many users, and all users are serviced concurrently by giving each some small time slices of CPU time on a rotating basis.
3. Each user feels that he is the sole user of the system.
4. Each user's data files are stored by on-line, direct-access storage devices at the central computer site, and are protected by password access systems. This allows the user immediate access to data.
5. Users can have their own private application programs, or they can use the public programs provided by the timesharing service.

Timesharing in commercial firms tends to be limited to jobs with small amounts of input and output, such as statistical programs and financial-planning models. However, timesharing is ideally suited for scientific jobs since they usually have small input/output and relatively more computation.

Timesharing has the following advantages:

1. The user has immediate and continuous access to the computer, and the response is immediate.
2. Small jobs, which could not be handled by service bureaus because of the time it takes to process and transport jobs to and from the service bureau, are often quite feasible as timesharing jobs since the access is immediate.
3. Timesharing for the casual user of computers is often less expensive than other modes of access to computer services.
4. The user has access to a wide variety of standard and utility programs stored on the timesharing computer system.

The disadvantages of timesharing include the following:

1. The potential for data loss or for unauthorized access to a user's data is increased since data are stored at the central computer site. A timesharing user should closely evaluate the installation's data-control procedures.
2. Timesharing is usually more expensive than service-bureau processing and may be more expensive than using personal computers.
3. Input-output capabilities of most timesharing services are limited; therefore, jobs requiring large I/O are impractical to process with timesharing.

Computer Lessors

As mentioned earlier, a potential computer user can lease hardware rather than purchase it. Many companies specialize in leasing computers. Generally the user can lease a computer for substantially less than it would cost to rent one. However, the lessee gives up flexibility since leasing is a long-term commitment.

Facilities-Management Vendor

A **facilities-management vendor** specializes in managing, staffing, and operating computer information systems for users. This may include all aspects of the system, including computer operations, programming, and system analysis. Usually users own or lease the hardware installed at their sites. The user establishes the guidelines under which the facilities-management vendor operates the computer.

This approach is advantageous primarily to the company that is installing its first computer. A facilities-management vendor can offer its expertise and its experienced personnel to the new user. An established, smoothly operating installation has its own expertise. The primary disadvantage of facilities management is that outsiders manage an extremely important segment of a company's operations.

Peripheral-Hardware Manufacturers

Much of the peripheral hardware in a computer system can be acquired from vendors other than the CPU manufacturers. Components such as tape drives, disk drives, and printers are plug-compatible with the hardware produced by the computer manufacturers. In fact, some companies produce CPUs that can replace widely used CPUs such as IBM computers. Such equipment can be significantly less expensive. However, the user may encounter service and maintenance problems when dealing with more than one vendor. When equipment fails, it may be difficult to pinpoint which vendor's equipment is responsible.

Information-System Consultants

Certified Public Accountant (CPA) firms and management consulting firms both provide information-system consulting services. Almost all of the management advisory service work that CPA firms provide is in the area of EDP consulting. Consultants can be invaluable to the new user and to experienced users who are making major changes in their systems. Equipment salespeople are not always accurate in their performance claims. **Information-system consultants** can help the user evaluate these claims and choose a satisfactory system.

Summing Up

☐ Generally, users are heavily involved with the evaluation and acquisition of computer hardware and software. A major portion of the business of most management consulting firms is in evaluation and installation of computer information systems.
☐ The primary topics in this chapter were system evaluation, financing alternatives, and sources of EDP equipment and services.
☐ A system evaluation consists of the following steps: feasibility study, structured system analysis, development of a request for proposal, proposal evaluation, and vendor selection.
☐ Essentially, three financing alternatives are available: purchasing, renting, and leasing. The trade-offs among the three options primarily involve

considerations of costs, capital availability, risks of obsolescence, and flexibility.

☐ The buyer or user of computer information systems has a wide choice of sources for EDP equipment and services. Among them are:

1. computer manufacturers
2. retail computer stores
3. software vendors
4. service bureaus
5. timesharing devices
6. computer lessors
7. facilities-management vendors
8. peripheral-hardware manufacturers
9. information-system consultants

Key Terms

bundling
plug compatible
request for proposal (RFP) document
kernel program
benchmark programs
compute-bound
workload models
simulation techniques
monitors
fine tuning
vendor support

compatibility
modularity
software directories
risk of obsolescence
flexibility
retail computer stores
service bureaus
timesharing services
facilities-management vendor
information-system consultants

Self-Quiz

Completion Questions

1. The computer-system evaluation process has five primary steps: (1) system feasibility study, (2) _____ , (3) development of a request for proposal, (4) proposal evaluation, and (5) vendor selection.

2. _____ are sample programs or test jobs that represent at least a part of the buyer's primary computer workload.

3. The _____ of a computer system is its ability to add capacity or components to the system.

4. There are three basic ways to finance computer systems: purchase, rental, and _____ .

5. The _____ documents the requirements for the equipment and software, and serves as a communication tool between the potential buyer and computer-system vendors.

6. One traditional technique of performance evaluation is the _____ , which is a small sample program executed on each proposed computer.

7. _____ are computer programs that

accurately represent the buyer's planned computer workload.

8. General criteria to be evaluated when selecting computer systems include vendor support, _____ , and modularity.

9. _____ are companies that provide computer processing services on an as-needed basis.

10. _____ provide the user with access to a computer through a remote terminal, located at the user's place of business.

Multiple-Choice Questions

1. Which of the following techniques has been used extensively to evaluate complex alternative systems where an analytical evaluation is not possible?
   a. benchmark programs
   b. simulation techniques
   c. workload models
   d. kernel programs
   e. none of the above

2. Which of the following is true of monitors?
   a. There are only hardware monitors.
   b. They are primarily used in the selection of new systems.
   c. They can indicate where the bottlenecks occur within a system.
   d. Two of the above.
   e. All three of the above.

3. The evaluation criteria in selecting computer hardware include:
   a. primary-storage size
   b. multiprogramming capabilities
   c. availability of utility programs
   d. job-management features
   e. two of the above

4. Compatibility:
   a. concerns only hardware
   b. concerns only software
   c. concerns only operating systems
   d. concerns only peripheral devices
   e. concerns both hardware and software

5. Which of the following is *not* an area where vendor support is crucial to the success of a computer system?
   a. personnel training
   b. repair and maintenance

c. installation
d. software backup arrangement
e. preinstallation testing

6. Which of the following is *not* a disadvantage of purchased software?
   a. It may not meet the needs of the users.
   b. It is not well documented.
   c. The expertise is outside the user company.
   d. Certain uncontrollable risks are assumed.
   e. All of the above are disadvantages.

7. Which of the following is (are) true of rental as a financing alternative?
   a. It is the most costly approach in terms of overall cash flow.
   b. It is the most flexible alternative.
   c. The responsibility for maintenance is borne by the manufacturer.
   d. Two of the above.
   e. All three of the above.

8. Which of the following is not true of timesharing services?
   a. The user has immediate and continuous access to the computer.
   b. Timesharing is cheaper than service-bureau processing.
   c. The potential for loss of data or unauthorized access is increased.
   d. Small jobs are often feasible.
   e. All of the above are true.

9. Which of the following is true of service bureaus?
   a. They provide the opportunity to test programs prior to installing a computer.
   b. They can provide backup services for a company that owns its own computer.
   c. The user has immediate access to the computer.
   d. Two of the above.
   e. All three of the above.

10. Purchasing as a financing alternative:
   a. allows the purchaser to avoid the risk of obsolescence.
   b. may reduce overall cost in the long run.
   c. places maintenance responsibility on the seller.
   d. two of the above
   e. all three of the above

Answers

Completion

1. system analysis
2. Benchmark programs
3. modularity
4. lease
5. request for proposal
6. kernel program
7. Workload models
8. compatibility
9. Service bureaus
10. Timesharing services

Multiple Choice

1. b
2. c
3. a
4. e
5. d
6. b
7. e
8. b
9. d
10. b

Appendix A: BASIC

Introduction

BASIC is a widely used programming language that has been implemented on virtually every type of computer, from the smallest personal computer to the largest super computers. It is designed as an easy-to-learn, easy-to-use, interactive language with no particular application area targeted.

There are many versions of BASIC available. In this appendix we will use the ANSI standard for Minimal BASIC. Any departures from this standard will be explained. You should use the language reference manual supplied by the vendor as a supplement to this appendix. Most vendor versions of BASIC will not strictly adhere to the ANSI standard. They will incorporate various enhancements and limitations of the standard.

In this appendix we will utilize the following features to illustrate BASIC programming:

1. formats of the BASIC statements
2. comparisons of valid and invalid examples of the BASIC statements
3. sample BASIC programs
4. structure charts, pseudocode, and flowcharts of the sample BASIC programs
5. general discussion of the BASIC features

All programming examples used here have been written and executed on an IBM personal computer using Microsoft BASIC. These programming examples will execute on any IBM-compatible personal computer, such as the Compaq and the Tandy 1000. Comparisons will be made between IBM/Microsoft BASIC and the following other versions of BASIC:

1. Apple's Applesoft BASIC
2. Hewlett-Packard's version of BASIC
3. VAX/VMS
4. Radio Shack's TRS-80 Level II BASIC
5. Commodore's PET/CBM/Commodore-64 BASIC
6. Apple Macintosh BASIC

The following format notation will be used when presenting the BASIC statement formats:

Symbol	Example	Meaning
Uppercase letters	LET	Required keyword
Lowercase letters	variable	User-supplied entry
Brackets	[expression]	Optional entry
Brace	$\left\{ \begin{array}{c} \text{REMARK} \\ \text{REM} \end{array} \right\}$	Alternative choices

In Topic 1 we will present techniques for designing and coding simple computer programs. Then, in Topic 2, we will discuss the commands used to boot (start) the different computers for which BASIC is covered in this text. Topics 3 through 9 deal with the BASIC language. Finally, alphabetic references are provided in Topics 10 and 11. You should use these as a quick reference for BASIC statements and functions.

Topic 1: Designing and Coding Simple BASIC Programs

Introduction

In chapter 6 we discussed structured program design in terms of the system-development life cycle. The concepts of structured program design can also be applied when you are writing small programs. As you will recall the essence of structured design is to hierarchically decompose complex systems into simple modules. Students sometimes have difficulty getting started with writing even a simple program. Therefore it is an excellent idea to use structured design techniques even with simple programs. They will help you a great deal.

INPUT

NAME	HOURS WORKED	PAY RATE PER HOUR
I.M.FIRST	40	5.00
SHARON SHARALIKE	25	3.35
T. TOTTLER	33	5.00
MATT TRESS	42	4.51
HELEN HIGHWATER	17	3.35
TAYLOR MAID	25	4.51
BUD ERDBUNS	40	5.00
I.M. LAST	32	4.51
END	-999	-999

OUTPUT

PAYROLL REPORT   07-31-1985

EMPLOYEE NAME	HOURS WORKED	RATE PER HOUR	GROSS PAY	FEDERAL TAX	STATE TAX	FICA TAX	NET PAY
I.M. FIRST	40.00	5.00	200.00	24.00	6.00	14.00	156.00
SHARON SHARALIKE	25.00	3.35	83.75	10.05	2.51	5.86	65.33
T. TOTTLER	33.00	5.00	165.00	19.80	4.95	11.55	128.70
MATT TRESS	42.00	4.51	189.42	22.73	5.68	13.26	147.75
HELEN HIGHWATER	17.00	3.35	56.95	6.83	1.71	3.99	44.42
TAYLOR MAID	25.00	4.51	112.75	13.53	3.38	7.89	87.95
BUD ERDBUNS	40.00	5.00	200.00	24.00	6.00	14.00	156.00
I.M. LAST	32.00	4.51	144.32	17.32	4.33	10.10	112.57

TOTAL EARNINGS: $898.71

Figure A-1.1   Payroll Input and Output

To illustrate the designing and coding of a simple BASIC program we will use a payroll example. The input and output from our program is shown in Figure A-1.1. The input contains employee names, hours worked, and hourly pay rate. From the input a payroll report is produced.

Structured Program Design

Structure Charts   As with complex programs, the first step in designing a simple program is to draw a structure chart. All programs and therefore their structure charts, have at least a main module and three second-level modules, an input module, a processing module, and an output module. In addition, most programs also need an initialization module and a termination module. **Initialization modules** do things that must be done at the start of the program, such as setting contents of storage to zero or setting other starting values. **Termination modules** do the things that must be done at the end of a program, such as outputing totals. Figure A-1.2 illustrates a structure chart for our payroll program. We have drawn a circular arrow around the input, process, and output modules. This arrow indicates that these modules will be within a loop and therefore executed multiple times. They will be executed one time for each employee time-card input. The payroll program module at the top of the structure chart is often called the main control module. Its function is to call or cause to be executed each of the modules below it.

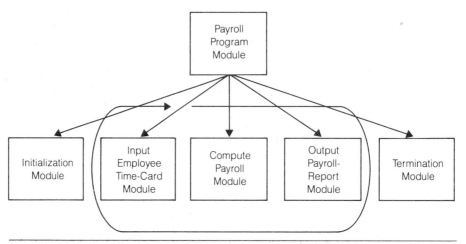

Figure A-1.2   Structure Chart for the Payroll Program

With this structure chart we have drawn a hierarchical structure of our program and broken it in such a way that each module has a relatively simple task to do. In coding our program, our intent is to write code to do the task in each of these modules and then combine the modules into a program. If each independently does its job properly they should together perform the requirements of our payroll program.

Pseudocode   The next step in designing a program is to write pseudocode or draw a program flowchart for each module in the structure chart. As you will recall from chapter 6, there are four control patterns that are used in pseudocode and structured program flowcharts. We have reproduced these in Figure A-1.3. All pseudocode and structured flowcharts can be constructed from these four basic patterns.

Figure A-1.4 contains the pseudocode for the payroll program. Note that this pseudocode is organized by the six modules that were on our structure chart shown in Figure A-1.2. The payroll program module or main control module is shown first. This module controls the calling and execution of each lower-level module. First we do the initialization module, then we loop through the input, compute, and output modules repeatedly while there are more time cards to be input. After all time cards are input, we end the loop and do the termination module. As you can see, the organization of this main control module is very similar to the structure chart. The main control module in effect summarizes the major steps that the program must perform.

Each of the second-level modules, which the main control module calls, are listed next in the pseudocode. Note that the pseudocode statements within each of these modules is just a simple sequence of statements. One of the goals of a structured approach to program design is to make each module simple. Structuring your programs as we have done here not only will help you in organizing your approach to writing a computer program, but will also make the program much more understandable so that later changes to the program will be easier to do.

Program Flowcharts   An alternative to pseudocode is the program flowchart. The symbols used in program flowcharting are illustrated in Figure A-1.5. Figure A-1.6 illustrates the program flowcharts for each module within the payroll program. Note that the structures used in these flowcharts are the same as in the structured control patterns in Figure A-1.3.

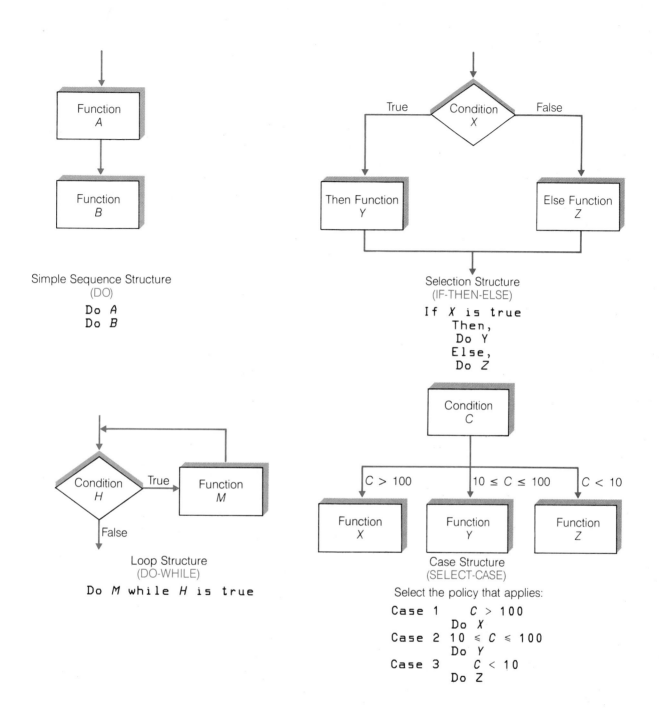

Figure A-1.3 Structured Control Patterns

```
Pseudocode
    Payroll Program (Main Control) Module
        Do initialization module
        Do While there are more time cards
            Do input employee time-card module
            Do calculate-pay module
            Do output payroll-report module
        End Do
        Do termination module
        End

    Initialization Module
        Set total earnings to 0
        Assign the literal "Payroll Report" to the variable AS
        Output header to the payroll register
        Return

    Input Employee Time-Card Module
        Input employee data
        Return

    Compute Payroll Module
        Compute gross pay
        Compute federal tax
        Compute state tax
        Compute FICA
        Compute net pay
        Add net pay to total earnings
        Return

    Output Payroll-Report Module
        Output above data for individual employee
        Return

    Termination Module
        Output total earnings
        Return
```

Figure A-1.4   Pseudocode for the Payroll Program

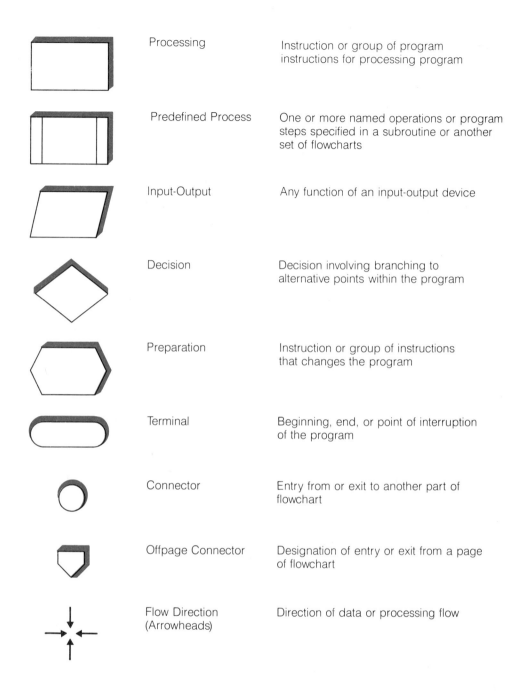

	Processing	Instruction or group of program instructions for processing program
	Predefined Process	One or more named operations or program steps specified in a subroutine or another set of flowcharts
	Input-Output	Any function of an input-output device
	Decision	Decision involving branching to alternative points within the program
	Preparation	Instruction or group of instructions that changes the program
	Terminal	Beginning, end, or point of interruption of the program
	Connector	Entry from or exit to another part of flowchart
	Offpage Connector	Designation of entry or exit from a page of flowchart
	Flow Direction (Arrowheads)	Direction of data or processing flow

Figure A-1.5   Program Flowcharting Symbols

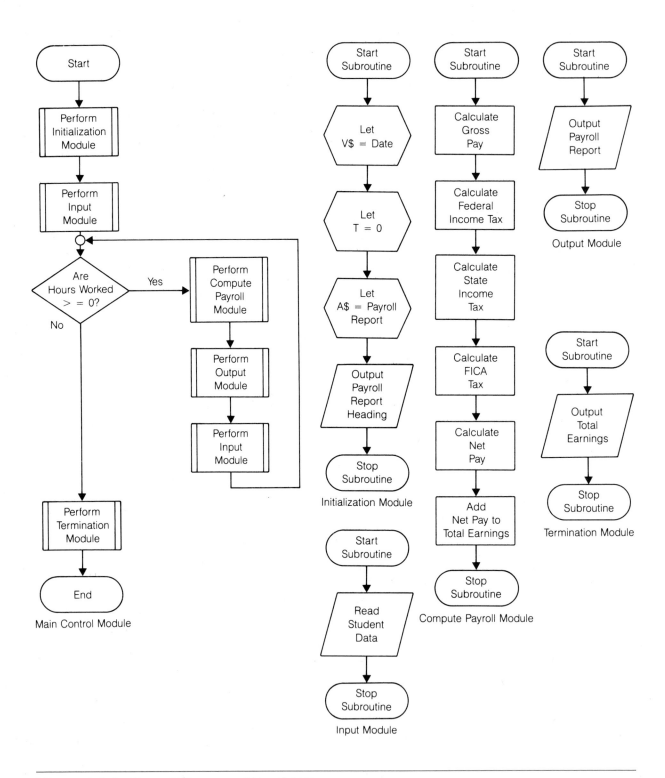

Figure A-1.6 Payroll Program Flowcharts

Some people find program flowcharts easier to understand than pseudocode. This is probably because they are graphical in nature. I like pseudocode better because it can be easily put on a word processor. This allows you to easily make changes to it. Drawing program flowcharts and making changes to these drawings can be time consuming. You should use whichever of the two helps you to better understand a program.

Writing the Program Code

The next step in developing a program is to write the program code. BASIC program code for our payroll program is illustrated in Figure A-1.7. At this point it is not important that you understand what each of the statements mean. We will cover the format BASIC statements later in this appendix. However, you should make a comparison between this BASIC program and the previously explained pseudocode and program flowcharts. Notice how closely this program corresponds to the pseudocode and the flowchart. The pseudocode or the flowchart is in effect a blueprint for writing the program.

Notice also the liberal use of the REM statements to document the program. In BASIC the REM statement is not an executable statement. It is used for documentation or to remember items within the program. The liberal use of documentation assists greatly in making a program understandable.

Testing and Debugging the Program

After the program code has been written, the program should be tested. Test data should be comprehensive, covering every possible type of valid and invalid input that could occur when the program is operational.

Almost all programs when they are run the first time have bugs (errors) in them. So don't be surprised if your program does not run correctly. BASIC has certain techniques to help you find the bugs in your program. One very useful debugging technique is the TRACE ON (TRON) command. This command causes BASIC to display on the screen the line numbers of each BASIC statement as it is executed in a run of the program. Figure A-1.8 illustrates the output from the TRACE ON command for a simple program. For the IBM PC and compatibles, the trace is turned on by pressing function key 7 and turned off by pressing function key 8. TRACE ON is useful in debugging because it allows you to see the sequence with which the program is executing statements. Quite often when a program is not executing properly, tracing through the sequence of statement execution will isolate the program bug.

Another useful debugging technique is to insert PRINT statements into the program to display the status of program variables as the program is executing. When you examine the values that are displayed for these program variables you will often find that the values are not what you expected. This usually leads to the identification of program bugs.

In addition, every computer provides error messages to aid in debugging programs. A few examples of these messages provided by IBM/Microsoft BASIC are:

FOR without NEXT—a FOR was encountered without a matching NEXT.
File not found—a LOAD references a file that does not exist on the disk in the specified drive.
Division by Zero—In an expression, you tried to divide by zero. Invalid in that mode.

Consult your user and BASIC manuals for a complete list of error codes.

```
LIST
10   REM    FIGURE A-1.7
20   REM
30   REM
40   REM
50   REM    ********************************************************************
60   REM    * This program reads employee records calculating gross pay,    *
70   REM    * taxes, and net pay.  When the end of the data block is        *
80   REM    * reached, the total net pay is calculated.  The final result   *
90   REM    * is the generation of the payroll report.                      *
100  REM    ********************************************************************
110  REM
120  REM              Variable definitions
130  REM              ********************
135  REM              V$- current date
140  REM              T - total earnings
150  REM              A$- literal
160  REM              N$- employee name
170  REM              H - hours worked
180  REM              R - rate per hour
190  REM              G - gross pay
200  REM              N - net pay
210  REM              F1- federal income tax
220  REM              S - state income tax
230  REM              F2- FICA tax
240  REM
250  REM    **********************
260  REM    * main control module *
270  REM    **********************
280  GOSUB 370
290  GOSUB 520
300  WHILE H>=0
310     GOSUB 570
320     GOSUB 670
330     GOSUB 520
340  WEND
350  GOSUB 730
360  END
370  REM    ************************
380  REM    * initialization module *
390  REM    ************************
400  LET V$-DATE$
410  LET T-0
420  LET A$ - "PAYROLL REPORT"
430  PRINT "                              ";A$;
440  PRINT "                   ";V$
450  PRINT
460  PRINT "EMPLOYEE          HOURS     RATE      GROSS   FEDERAL";
470  PRINT "    STATE     FICA     NET"
480  PRINT "  NAME          WORKED  PER HOUR    PAY      TAX   ";
490  PRINT "    TAX      TAX      PAY"
500  PRINT
510  RETURN
520  REM    ****************
530  REM    * input module *
540  REM    ****************
550  READ N$,H,R
560  RETURN
570  REM    *****************
580  REM    * process module *
590  REM    *****************
600     LET G= H*R
610     LET F1- G*.12
620     LET S- G*.03
630     LET F2- G*.07
640     LET N- G - (F1+S+F2)
650     LET T- T+N
660  RETURN
670  REM    ****************
680  REM    * output module *
690  REM    ****************
700     PRINT USING "\             \  ###.##   ###.##   ####.##    ";N$,H,R,G;
710     PRINT USING "###.##   ###.##   ###.##   ####.##";F1,S,F2,N
720  RETURN
```

Figure A-1.7 A BASIC Program to Compute Payroll

```
730 REM     **********************
740 REM     * termination module *
750 REM     **********************
760 PRINT
770 PRINT TAB(56);"TOTAL EARNINGS:    ";
780 PRINT USING "$###.##";T
790 DATA I.M. FIRST,40,5.00
800 DATA SHARON SHARALIKE,25,3.35
810 DATA T. TOTTLER,33,5.00
820 DATA MATT TRESS,42,4.51
830 DATA HELEN HIGHWATER,17,3.35
840 DATA TAYLOR MAID,25,4.51
850 DATA BUD ERDBUNS,40,5.00
860 DATA I.M. LAST,32,4.51
870 DATA END,-999,-999
```

Comparisons to Other Versions of BASIC	
Applesoft	Needs extra space after colon in input; no PRINT USING facility
HP	PRINT USING statements should have semicolon before the argument list
VAX	No differences
TRS-80	No PRINT USING facilities
PET/CBM/Commodore 64	No differences
Macintosh	Needs extra space after colon in input; no PRINT USING facility

Figure A-1.7 (continued)

```
LIST
10   REM    FIGURE A-1.8
20   REM
30   REM
40   REM
50   REM    ************************************************************
60   REM    * This program performs a simple gross-pay calculation *
70   REM    ************************************************************
80   REM
90   REM              Variable definitions
100  REM              ********************
110  REM              R - rate per hour
120  REM              H - number of hours worked
130  REM              G - gross pay
140  REM
150  REM    ****************
160  REM    * input R and H *
170  REM    ****************
180  LET R - 4.78
190  LET H - 40
200  REM    **********************
210  REM    * calculate gross pay *
220  REM    **********************
230  LET G - R*H
240  REM    ***********************************
250  REM    * output rate, hours, and gross pay *
260  REM    ***********************************
270  PRINT "    RATE    HOURS   GROSS PAY"
280  PRINT USING "######.##";R,H,G
290  END
Ok
TRON
Ok
Ok
RUN
[10][20][30][40][50][60][70][80][90][100][110][120][130][140][150][160][170][180
][190][200][210][220][230][240][250][260][270]    RATE    HOURS   GROSS PAY
[280]    4.78    40.00    191.20
[290]
Ok
```

Figure A-1.8   Output from the TRACE ON Command in BASIC

Summing Up

☐ The first step in designing a program is to draw a structure chart.

☐ All programs have at least a main module and three second-level modules—an input module, a processing module, and an output module. Most programs also need an initialization and a termination module.

☐ The program logic within each module is designed with pseudocode or program flowcharts.

☐ The program is coded (written) using the pseudocode or program flowchart as a blueprint or guide.

☐ All programs should be tested and errors removed from them.

☐ TRACE ON and PRINT statements are useful debugging tools.

☐ All versions of BASIC provide error messages to aid in debugging programs.

Topic 2: BASIC System Commands

Introduction

Here we will look at the BASIC **system commands** which are most commonly used by programmers for creating, editing, and running BASIC programs. These commands will be examined within the context of the six computers that we will be discussing throughout this appendix.

IBM PC and Compatibles' (Microsoft) BASIC Commands[1]

The DOS disk must be inserted into disk drive A (the left drive) before the system is turned on. Once the system is started up, you are prompted for the date and time:

```
Current date is Tue 1-01-1980
Enter new date: 2-20-1986
Current time is 0:00:17.90
Enter new time: 2:29

The IBM Personal Computer DOS
Version 1.10 (c)copyright IBM Corp. 1981, 1982, 1983

A>
```

The IBM banner message will appear with the DOS prompt A>. To enter the BASIC mode you must then type BASIC (or BASICA for advanced BASIC) and press the enter key. On the IBM-PC keyboard the enter key is designated by this symbol ◄─┘. Once in BASIC mode

---

[1]If you are not familiar with DOS, you should read Topic 1, The Disk-Operating System, in Appendix B before reading this section. The IBM PC keyboard is also explained in Topic 1 of Appendix B.

another banner message is shown which also displays the number of bytes that are free and unused in RAM memory:

```
The IBM Personal Computer BASIC
Version D2.10 Copyright IBM Corp. 1981, 1982, 1983
40959 Bytes Free
Ok
```

The BASIC prompt "Ok" then appears. When the "Ok" prompt appears, type in the following program:

```
10 LET A$=" HELLO MY NAME IS "
20 LET N$=" JUSTIN THYME. "
30 PRINT A$; N$
40 END
```

To run the program, press function key 2. The following should appear on the screen:

```
                    HELLO MY NAME IS JUSTIN THYME
```

To save this program for future reference, use the SAVE command:

```
SAVE"filename
```

Using a filename without a disk-drive identifier will cause the computer to save the program on the default drive (usually the A drive). Normally, you will want to save your programs on drive B. Therefore when you use a filename, precede it with a B:. For example, use SAVE"B:filename. Be sure that you have a formatted disk in drive B before entering this command. After saving the program you can retrieve it by using the LOAD command:

```
LOAD"filename
```

To display a listing of the program statements, use the LIST command:

```
LIST [line #s]
```

You can also display a range of program statements. For example, LIST 10–30 will display statements 10 through 30. Instead of typing the commands SAVE", LOAD", and LIST, pressing function keys 4, 3, and 1 respectively will place the command on the screen.

Basic allows you to modify and delete statements in the program. To modify statements, use the EDIT command:

```
EDIT [line #]
```

To insert a line between two statements, say lines 20 and 30, simply make sure that the line number of the inserted line is betwen 20 and 30. The command RENUM will renumber your statements in increments of 10.

IBM/Microsoft BASIC also has a program editor for modifying programs. See The BASIC Program Editor in chapter 2 of IBM/Microsoft's BASIC manual. To delete statements, use the DELETE command:

DELETE [line #]

The following list contains several key combinations that you will find useful in BASIC. When using a two-key combination, hold down the first key and then press the second key. When using a three-key combination, hold down the first two keys and then press the third key. (See Topic 1 of Appendix B if you are unfamiliar witht he IBM PC and compatibles' keyboard.)

Caps Lock: Locks the alphabetic characters on the keyboard to all caps.

←   :   The backspace key for correcting typing errors.

⇧ /PrtSc: Prints whatever is currently displayed on the screen.

Alt/Any Alphabetic Character: Holding the Alt key down and pressing an alphabetic character allows easy entry of BASIC statement keywords. For example, Alt-P is the same as typing PRINT. Try every alphabetic key on the keyboard. This could save you some typing time.

Ctrl/Break: Interrupts the execution of a BASIC program.

Ctrl/NumLock: Puts the computer into a pause state. This could be used to temporarily halt printing. Press any key to resume execution.

Alt/Ctrl/Del: This is similar to turning the power off and then back on. Caution: When you do this you will lose anything stored in RAM. Be sure your program is stored on the disk before doing an Alt-Ctrl-Del.

Ctrl/PrtSc: Acts as a switch to turn the printer on and off. When the printer is on, all output displayed on the screen is also printed.

To exit from BASIC mode, type SYSTEM and press enter.

VAX-11 BASIC Commands

Once logged on to the VAX/VMS system, you must type the command BASIC to enter the BASIC "environment." Once in the BASIC environment, the system will respond with "Ready".

```
Username:  BANDYMW
Password:
          Welcome to VAX/VMS version V3.0
          Virginia Tech Computing Center

$ basic

VAX-11 BASIC V1.4

Ready
```

Anything that is typed will be considered a BASIC language statement unless recognized by the system as a BASIC system command.

To create a new program, use the NEW command:

NEW [filename]

If the filename is not specified, BASIC will prompt with:

```
New file name--
```

and the filename should then be entered (if the filename is omitted, the system will name the file NONAME.BAS). An example is:

```
Ready

new
New file name--myprog

Ready

10 PRINT "What is your name";
20 INPUT N$
30 PRINT
40 PRINT "Hi ";N$;", my name is VAX."
50 END
```

Once typed in, the program can be run immediately using the RUN command. For example:

```
run
MYPROG          20-FEB-1986 10:57

What is your name? Mike

Hi Mike, my name is VAX.
Ready
```

This program is currently in primary memory. While in memory the contents of the program can be listed when you use the LIST command:

LIST [line #s]

The header will be displayed, followed by the BASIC statements. The LIST command will also list a specified range of statements, as follows:

```
list 10-30

MYPROG          20-FEB-1986 10: 59

10 PRINT "What is your name";
20 INPUT N$
30 PRINT

Ready
```

To modify statements, use the EDIT command:

```
EDIT [  line #  ] [  options  ]
```

For example:

`edit 30/PRINT/REM`

will replace PRINT with REM in line 30. To enter a line between lines 20 and 30, make sure that the line number of the inserted line is between 20 and 30. To delete a line, use the DELETE command:

```
DELETE [  line #  ]
```

Omission of the line number will result in the deletion of the current line.

To save the program for future reference, use the SAVE command:

```
SAVE [  filename  ]
```

This command stores the program that is currently in memory. Once the program is stored, modifications to the program or execution of the program are not possible until the program is retrieved or brought back into memory. This is done using the OLD command:

```
OLD [  filename  ]
```

As with the NEW command, if the filename is not specified, the prompt:

`Old file name--`

is displayed where the filename should then be entered.

To return from the BASIC environment to the VAX system level, use the EXIT command, as illustrated:

```
Ready
exit
$
```

where the dollar sign is the system prompt.

Hewlett-Packard—85 BASIC Commands

The HP–85 is essentially a BASIC machine. When the machine is turned on, the system comes up in BASIC mode. Anything typed is considered either a BASIC language statement or a BASIC system command. Any other commands are generally system maintenance (for example, the CAT command, which lists the names of all files in the catalog). Since the system is geared toward BASIC, there are several keys on the keyboard that are used for program control and execution. To run a program in memory, depress the RUN key, which executes the program immediately.

Editing each BASIC statement is done by positioning the cursor within the statement at the desired position and typing in the changes. A statement can be deleted by depressing the DEL key which will display the command DELETE on the screen. The line number(s) to be deleted must then be typed in. The DEL key, as with several others, is a typing aid; therefore, the command is not executed until the ENDLINE key is depressed.

To list the current program, depress the LIST key which immediately lists the program on the screen. Among the typing aid keys are the STORE and LOAD keys. The STORE key displays the STORE command which must be followed by the filename within quotes. The STORE command stores the current program onto the tape cassette. The LOAD key displays the LOAD command which must also be followed by a filename in quotes. The LOAD command loads the specified file into memory from the tape. As with the DEL key, to execute the STORE and LOAD commands you must depress the ENDLINE key.

TRS–80 Model III Disk BASIC Commands

When starting the TRS–80, insert the diskette with the BASIC DOS disk monitor and the machine should then be powered on. A banner message concerning copyright appears, and you are prompted for the date and time:

```
Enter Date (MM/DD/YY)? 02/20/83
Enter Time (HH:MM:SS)? 09:15:00

TRSDOS Ready
```

Then, type the word BASIC to enter the BASIC mode:

```
BASIC
how many files? 1
memory size: press enter
TRS-80 Model III Disk BASIC Rev 1.2
(c)(p)1980 Tandy Corp. All rights reserved.
Created 5-Jul-80
39348 Free Bytes  1 Files
READY
>
```

You are now ready to type in a program. Let's create and run a simple BASIC program:

```
10 PRINT "This is fun."
20 PRINT
30 END
RUN
```

The LOAD command has the following syntax:

```
LOAD "filename"
```

and the SAVE command has the following syntax:

```
SAVE "filename"
```

To exit from BASIC, type the expression CMD"A" which will return control to the operating system:

```
READY
>CMD"A"
Operation Aborted

TRSDOS Ready
```

Applesoft BASIC Commands

Before powering up the system, insert the DOS diskette in the disk drive. Then turn on the system—the switch is on the left rear of the machine. Be sure to also turn on the monitor. There will be no banner message unless the owner of the disk has created a "greeting" program. In this example, "Applesoft Floating-point BASIC" is generated by a greeting program.:

```
Applesoft Floating-point BASIC
]
```

The "]" is the prompt for the Applesoft BASIC. A flashing cursor also appears on the screen beside the prompt. As with HP–85, anything typed is considered either BASIC language statements or BASIC commands. As with the other systems, you type a BASIC command by typing the line number and then the command, and then pressing RETURN. To change a command, retype it with the same line number. Commands are inserted by using a line number for the new command that is between the line numbers of the lines between which the new command is to be inserted. For example, if the new command is to be inserted between lines 15 and 17, the new command should have a line number of 16.

To delete a single line, simply enter the line number. To delete a block of code, use the following:

DEL   begline#,endline#

To transfer files to and from disk, use the SAVE and LOAD commands with the filename. The filename is not contained in quotes as with the TRS–80. A sample session follows:

```
Applesoft Floating-point BASIC
]10 PRINT "Applesoft BASIC is easy to learn."
]20 PRINT
]30 END
]RUN
Applesoft BASIC is easy to learn."

]LIST

10 PRINT "Applesoft BASIC is easy to learn."
20 PRINT
30 END

]
```

To list only certain lines, separate the line numbers in the LIST command with commas. For example, LIST 20,50 will list lines 20 through 50. The LOAD command has the following syntax:

```
LOAD    filename
```

and the SAVE command has the following syntax:

```
SAVE    filename
```

To exit from the BASIC mode, turn off the system or remove the diskette.

Commodore's PET/CBM BASIC Commands

When powering on the Commodore system, the following banner message appears:

```
***commodore basic 4.0***

31743 bytes free
READY.
```

The system is in "direct mode" (the BASIC environment); therefore, to enter a program just begin typing. Editing is similar to the other systems. To delete a line of code, you need to enter only the line number; then depress the RETURN key. To modify a line, position the cursor on the screen and begin typing the change.

To store the program on disk, the DSAVE command is used:

```
DSAVE "filename"
```

To retrieve the program from disk, use the DLOAD command:

```
DLOAD "filename"
```

In both the DSAVE and DLOAD commands, the filename must be contained within quotes. To exit from direct mode, either turn off the system or remove the diskette. The following is a sample session:

```
ready.
10 PRINT "The Commodore PET/CBM BASIC"
20 PRINT
30 END
RUN
The Commodore PET/CBM BASIC
READY.
DSAVE "MYPROG"
READY.
```

In the session just described, the program was created, run, and then stored for future reference under the name MYPROG.

Summing Up

☐ System commands are used to help in the creation, editing, and execution of BASIC programs.

☐ IBM PC and TRS–80 systems require that you enter the BASIC environment before you can do any programming. Applesoft BASIC automatically enters the BASIC environment if the diskette containing the BASIC compiler is inserted before power is turned on.

☐ The VAX–11 system requires that you enter the BASIC environment before creating a program.

☐ The HP–85 and PET/CBM systems directly enter a BASIC environment when the computer is turned on.

Topic 3: Programming in BASIC

Introduction

When most people think of BASIC, they think of timesharing or interactive processing. BASIC has never been considered a batch-oriented language even though it is adaptable to such a system. BASIC was designed by John Kemeny and Thomas Kurtz at Dartmouth College as an easy-to-learn, easy-to-use programming language for nonscientific programmers working with the college's timesharing system. BASIC, therefore, is a user-oriented language that can be learned in a very short time period. Being user-oriented, the language is easy to code and debug. It features clear and simple error messages, which combined with strong editing capabilities, greatly facilitate programming.

Program Structure

The Character Set   The elementary unit of a BASIC program is the **statement** constructed with the BASIC language elements which are composed of the following:

1. The letters A through Z (lowercase letters are automatically translated to uppercase by most BASIC compilers)
2. The numbers 0 through 9
3. Special symbols, of which the following are the most common:

   + − * / = < > ¢
   . , ;
   ( )
   " $
   and the blank.

Special symbols may vary among different versions.

Line Format   In BASIC the format of a line is as follows:

line#   KEYWORD   operand(s)

where **keyword** is any BASIC reserved word. **Operand(s)** may be any allowable numeric or alphabetic expression. Often the word **argument** is used synonymously with operand. An example would be as follows:

```
100    LET   a = i + j
```

where

100 is the line number,
LET is the keyword, and
a = i + j is the operand.

Blanks are ignored by BASIC; therefore, BASIC statements are "free-format" and may be indented for readability.

Line Numbers   When coding a BASIC program, you must precede each statement with a unique line number. The line numbers must be positive—ranging from 1 to the limit set by the particular system. The line numbers serve several functions:

1. Line numbers are used as statement labels for program control.
2. Line numbers specify the order in which statements are executed.
3. Line numbers are used as an editing tool for changing program statements.

BASIC statements are generally executed in ascending order according to the line numbers; therefore, the ordering of the line numbers is important.

Summing Up

☐ BASIC is an easy-to-use, interactive computer language.
☐ All BASIC statements are made up of a set of alphabetic, numeric, and special characters.
☐ A BASIC statement includes a line number, a keyword, and one or more operands.

Topic 4: Elements of a BASIC Program

A Simple BASIC Program

To illustrate the elementary features of BASIC, we will "walk through" several sample programs beginning with a simple computational program, and gradually expand the programs to include each new feature discussed. A structure chart, pseudocode, and a program flowchart are included with each program listing. The first program averages a student's midterm and final test scores, printing the student's name and final grade average. The program is shown in Figure A-4.1.

Statements   **Statements** consist of keywords, variables, constants, or expressions. Expressions are composed of constants and variables joined by operators. Examples of valid statements are as follows:

```
100    LET   a = x + 1
110    PRINT  "This is a print statement"
120    REM   ... This is a remark statement.
```

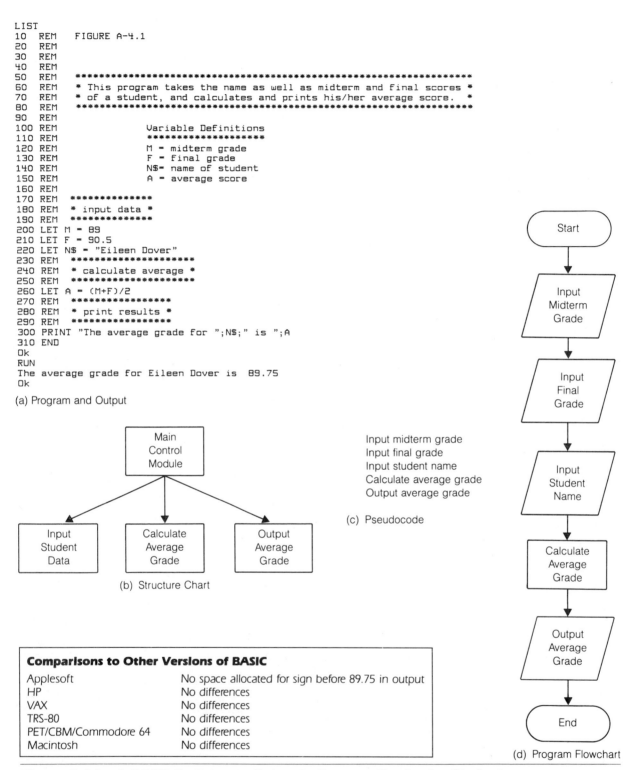

```
LIST
10   REM    FIGURE A-4.1
20   REM
30   REM
40   REM
50   REM    ****************************************************************
60   REM    * This program takes the name as well as midterm and final scores *
70   REM    * of a student, and calculates and prints his/her average score.  *
80   REM    ****************************************************************
90   REM
100  REM                  Variable Definitions
110  REM                  *******************
120  REM                  M - midterm grade
130  REM                  F - final grade
140  REM                  N$- name of student
150  REM                  A - average score
160  REM
170  REM    **************
180  REM    * input data *
190  REM    **************
200  LET M - 89
210  LET F - 90.5
220  LET N$ - "Eileen Dover"
230  REM    *********************
240  REM    * calculate average *
250  REM    *********************
260  LET A - (M+F)/2
270  REM    ****************
280  REM    * print results *
290  REM    ****************
300  PRINT "The average grade for ";N$;" is ";A
310  END
Ok
RUN
The average grade for Eileen Dover is  89.75
Ok
```

(a) Program and Output

Main Control Module

Input Student Data

Calculate Average Grade

Output Average Grade

(b) Structure Chart

Input midterm grade
Input final grade
Input student name
Calculate average grade
Output average grade

(c) Pseudocode

Start

Input Midterm Grade

Input Final Grade

Input Student Name

Calculate Average Grade

Output Average Grade

End

(d) Program Flowchart

Comparisons to Other Versions of BASIC

Applesoft	No space allocated for sign before 89.75 in output
HP	No differences
VAX	No differences
TRS-80	No differences
PET/CBM/Commodore 64	No differences
Macintosh	No differences

Figure A-4.1   A BASIC Program to Compute Average Grades for Students

Constants, Variables, and Expressions **Constants** are values that do not change during the course of execution of the BASIC program. There are three types of constants in BASIC:

1. Real (floating-point) constants
2. Integer (fixed-point) constants
3. String constants (literals)

   Real or **floating-point** constants are numbers that may contain a decimal point with or without a fractional part. The floating-point constant may be represented in two forms:

1. Decimal form
2. Exponential form

Valid examples of floating-point constants are as follows:

Decimal	Exponential
10	1.00E+01
100.	1.00E+02
−12.3	−1.23E+01
.123	1.23E−01
20.0	2.00E+01

where the *E* in the exponential form represents "times ten to the power of" the value following. The *E* notation actually positions the decimal point. For example,

> 1.00E+02 will move the decimal point two places to the right, giving the value 100.

> 1.00E−02 will move the decimal point two places to the left, giving the value 0.01.

There are certain restrictions that must be followed when using floating-point constants:

1. Embedded commas are not allowed. Examples of valid and invalid floating-point constants are as follows:

Valid	Invalid
1200	1,200
52E+01	52,E+01
35212	35,212

2. Floating-point must not exceed the minimum or maximum range established by the particular system. For example, the Applesoft BASIC allows a floating-point constant to range from 1.0E−38 to 1.0E+38.

In Figure A-4.1, statements 200 and 210 contain floating-point constants which are the numbers 89.0 and 90.5, respectively.

   Integer or **fixed-point** constants are numbers that do not contain a decimal point or a fractional part. In other words, they are whole numbers. Examples of valid and invalid fixed-point constants are as follows:

Valid	Invalid
10	.01
−20	1.23
3211	10.01E+11
25	1,600
100	

Fixed-point constants also have certain restrictions associated with their use:

1. As with floating-point constants, embedded commas are not allowed.
2. Fixed-point constants also have a system-dependent range. For example, IBM/Microsoft BASIC and Applesoft BASIC allow fixed-point constants to range between -32768 and $+32767$.

In Figure A-4.1, statement 260 contains a fixed-point constant, which is the numeral 2.

String constants, also known as **literals,** are compositions of alphanumerics (consisting of both alphabetic and numeric characters) and special characters enclosed within double quotes. The maximum number of characters allowed for a string varies from system to system. For example, DEC's BASIC–PLUS–2 allows a range of 0 to 255 characters. Examples of valid literals and their lengths are as follows:

Literal	Length
"TEXT"	4
"ABCDEFghijklMNOPQRstuvwxyz0123456789"	36
"$@#!"	4
"" (a null)	0
" " (a blank)	1
"This is a literal."	17

In Figure A-4.1, statement 300 contains literals. They are "The average grade for" and "is", respectively.

Variables are names (created by the programmer) that represent data. A variable is not the actual data, but it does represent the data and become the name of the storage area that is reserved to hold those data. The value of a variable may change during the execution of the program, although the name of the variable stays the same. The values of variables are changed by the use of the LET statement (discussed in Topic 5) and the input statements INPUT and READ (discussed in Topic 6). The two types of variables are:

1. Numeric variables
2. String variables

A standard **numeric variable** name consists of at most two characters where the first character must be a letter and the second character, which is optional, must be numeric. This is the standard; however, some versions of BASIC (such as IBM/Microsoft, Radio Shack, Apple, and DEC) allow any number of characters up to the system limit. Caution must be taken in choosing variable names when this feature is available. When creating variable names, remember that in some of these systems only the first few characters are considered significant. If two variable names are similar (such as name1 and name2), they may both be treated as the same because the first four characters are common to them. This could lead to program errors. However, in IBM/Microsoft BASIC, the first forty characters are significant. Examples of valid standard numerical variable names are shown here with invalid variable names:

Valid	Invalid (explanation)
a	.8 (Includes a decimal as the first character)
m1	2 (Includes a numeric as the first character)
f2	f* (Includes a special symbol as the second character)
c3	3c (The characters are reversed)

Some implementations differentiate between types of numeric variables. For example, the DEC version BASIC–PLUS–2 allows for a real variable name and an integer variable name which contains an alphabetic for the first character followed by a percent sign (%).

A standard **string variable** name consists of two characters, which must be an alphabet letter followed by a dollar sign ($). Omission of the dollar sign will result in an error. Examples of both valid and invalid string variable names are as follows:

Valid	Invalid (explanation)
a $	. $ (The first character must be an alphabetic)
m $	$ (Has no alphabetic as the first character)
f $	$ 2 (The first character must be an alphabetic followed by a dollar sign)
c $	d (Does not have an ending dollar sign)
	c 1 (A valid numeric variable name that will cause a data typing error)

In Figure A-4.1 the variable N$ contains the literal "Eileen Dover." Again, some systems allow for more descriptive string variable names, and the previous caveat still holds regarding the use of only the first few characters to identify a variable.

Expressions can be variables, constants, and functions or any combination of these elements separated by arithmetic operators or relational operators. **Arithmetic operators** facilitate arithmetic computation in BASIC. The following are standard arithmetic operators in order of precedence:

Precedence	Operator
1	** or ^ or ↑ (exponentiation)
2	− (the unary minus or negation)
3	/ (division)
3	* (multiplication)
4	+ (addition)
4	− (subtraction)

Examples of valid arithmetic expressions are as follows:

```
5               (A constant)
x               (A variable)
TAN(x)          (A function)
x + y / 3
2 * (x + y)
```

Operator precedence must be considered when evaluating arithmetic expressions. The evaluation of the expression is from left to right; the arithmetic operators are performed first, then the relational operators are evaluated. Evaluation, again, is dependent on operator precedence; however, this precedence may be altered by the use of parentheses. Parentheses are used in BASIC for grouping. For example, the expression:

```
a * b + c           where    a = 2
                             b = 5
                             c = 4
```

will be evaluated as follows:

2 is multiplied by 5 giving the value 10 which is then added to 4, resulting in the value 14.

Now, if the expression were altered as follows:

```
a * (b + c)
```

then evaluation would be as follows:

> 5 is added to 4 giving the value 9 which is then multiplied by 2, resulting in the value 18.

Parentheses may also be nested as follows:

```
c *((b + c)/a)
```

The evaluation of this expression is as follows:

> 5 is added to 4 giving 9 which is divided by 2 giving 4.5 which is then multiplied by 4, resulting in 18.

If you want an expression performed first, enclose it in parentheses. It is a good habit to make liberal use of parentheses in arithmetic expressions. They make the expression more readable and you do not have to be concerned with operator precedence.

Relational operators perform comparisons between variables and constants of like data type. Relational operators are symbols used to perform the comparison and are as follows:

Operator	Meaning
<> , ><	Is not equal to
<= , =<	Is less than or equal to
>= , =>	Is greater than or equal to
<	Is less than
>	Is greater than
=	Is equal to

An example of the use of a relational operator follows:

```
10 IF X>Y THEN PRINT "GREATER"
```

It should be noted that all relational operators are equal in precedence. Relational expressions, unlike arithmetic expressions, can assume only two logical values: true or false. Comparisons can be made between numeric expressions, and string values can be compared with other string values. However, a direct comparison between numeric expressions and string values is not possible.

Comments and the REMARK Statement

A very important programming practice is for programmers to thoroughly document their work. BASIC provides a convenient vehicle for internally documenting programs. This is the use of the REMARK statement, which has the following format:

line#	REMARK	[comments]
	REM	

where the comments may be anything typed by the programmer.

In Figure A-4.1, statements 10 through 190, 230 through 250, and 270 through 290 are REMARK statements. Remarks should be concise and informative. Superfluous remarks only hinder the readability of the program and use up valuable memory if you are using a small machine.

The Required END Statement

The END statement has the following format:

line#   END

The END statement terminates the program and closes any data files that were processed during execution. The END statement is required in the standard version of BASIC. However, the statement is optional for most versions and only required when subroutines are used. For all the versions discussed in this appendix, the END statement is optional. The line number associated with the END statement should be the highest in value of all line numbers within the program.

Summing Up

☐ A BASIC program is made up of sets of instructions called statements. A statement is in turn made up of keywords, constants, variables, or expressions.

☐ Constants may be real, integer, or of string type. Variables are either numeric or literal (string). Expressions are combinations of constants, variables, and functions, separated by arithmetic or relational operators.

☐ Arithmetic expressions that include more than one operator are evaluated according to an order of precedence or based on parentheses.

☐ The REMARK statement is used to insert comments at various points in the program, which describe the processing being performed.

☐ The END statement is required in some versions of BASIC to signal the end of the program.

Debugging Exercises

Find and remove the bugs in the following program segments:

```
1. 10 LET A = 1,300

2. LET B = 500

3. 10 "This program prints an integer and a string constant"
   20 LET A = "A STRING CONSTANT"
   30 LET B$ = 1.54
   40 PRINT A$, B

4. 10 LET A* = 50

5. 200 LET 5C = 500

6. 30 LET $4 = 4.00

7. 50 LET A$ = THIS IS A STRING
```

```
8. 10  IF  X$  >  A  THEN  PRINT  "GREATER THAN"

9. 20  LET  A  =  X  +  3Y

10. 30  LET  B  =  Y  ×  3
```

Topic 5: The Assignment of Values

The LET Statement

BASIC assigns values to variables through the LET statement. The format of the LET statement is as follows:

line#   LET   variable = expression

where the result of the expression must be of the same data type as the variable.

The function of the LET statement is to "assign" a value. Therefore, the symbol $"="$ does not specify mathematical equality, but is an assignment operator. The value of the variable is assigned or replaced by the value of the expression to the right of the assignment operator. This assignment is a **destructive process.** The value previously held by that variable is written over by the new value assigned. Values are assigned from right to left. A variable must be to the left of the assignment operator, and an expression must be to the right. The following are examples of valid assignments:

```
10  LET  a = 2          (Assignment of a constant)
20  LET  b$ = "yes"     (Assignment of a literal)
30  LET  f = TAN(x)     (Assignment of the results of a function)
40  LET  a = b + c      (Assignment of the results of an expression)
```

The following are examples of invalid assignments, including the reasons why they are invalid:

```
10  LET  a + b = d / 2   (There is an expression to the left of the
                          assignment operator)
20  LET  c + b = 12      (A constant cannot be assigned to an expression)
30  LET  12 = a + b      (The results of an expression can not be assigned
                          to a constant)
```

The two types of assignment in BASIC are:

1. arithmetic assignment
2. character string assignment

Arithmetic Assignment   **Arithmetic assignment** allows the results of an arithmetic expression to be assigned to a variable. For example, the following sequence of statements:

```
10   LET   a = 2.0
20   LET   b = 12.0
30   LET   c = a * b
```

will result in the variable c containing the value 24.0. BASIC performs the following steps when executing the above statements:

1. assigns the constant 2.0 to the variable a,
2. assigns the constant 12.0 to the variable b, and
3. computes the results of the expression a * b, then assigns that value to c.

An assignment that most novice programmers have difficulty visualizing is the following:

```
40   LET   a = a + 1
```

This example is a good illustration of the difference between a mathematical equation and an arithmetic assignment. If a = a + 1 were an arithmetic equation, it would be invalid. The variable a will never equal itself plus 1, according to current mathematical theorems. However, this is a valid assignment statement in BASIC language. It is interpreted as follows:

Take the value in a and add 1 to it, then assign the result of that computation to a.

This assignment is commonly used for counting the number of times a process has been performed. A few considerations must be noted:

1. A variable must have a defined value before it can be used in an expression or an error will occur. For example

```
i = i + 1
```

is meaningless if the variable i is not previously defined, and

```
y = g * 0.9
```

is meaningless if the variable g is not defined beforehand.

BASIC will not initialize variables automatically. A variable does not have any value unless a value is assigned one somewhere in the program. Common practice is to initialize variables, especially those used as counters, to zero. For example:

```
10 LET i = 0
20 REM ...a counting loop
30 LET i = i + 1
40 PRINT i
50 IF i <= 10 THEN 20
60 END
```

If the variable i had not been initialized to zero, then a logical error may occur such as the nonexecution of the loop or abnormal termination of the program because the "garbage" in the variable i may not be a numeric.

2. Arithmetic operators cannot be contiguous; that is, they cannot be beside each other. For example,

```
a = b * - c
```
is invalid,

however,

```
a = b * (-c)
```

is valid.

```
LIST
10   REM   FIGURE A-5.1
20   REM
30   REM
40   REM
50   REM   *********************************************
60   REM   * This program demonstrates the assignment of  *
70   REM   * literals to string variables                 *
80   REM   *********************************************
90   REM
100  REM   **************
110  REM   * Input data *
120  REM   **************
130  LET A$ - "FIRST WORD"
140  LET B$ - "SECOND WORD"
150  REM   ******************
160  REM   * print literals *
170  REM   ******************
180  PRINT A$;",";B$
190  END
Ok
RUN
FIRST WORD,SECOND WORD
Ok
```

(a) Program and Output

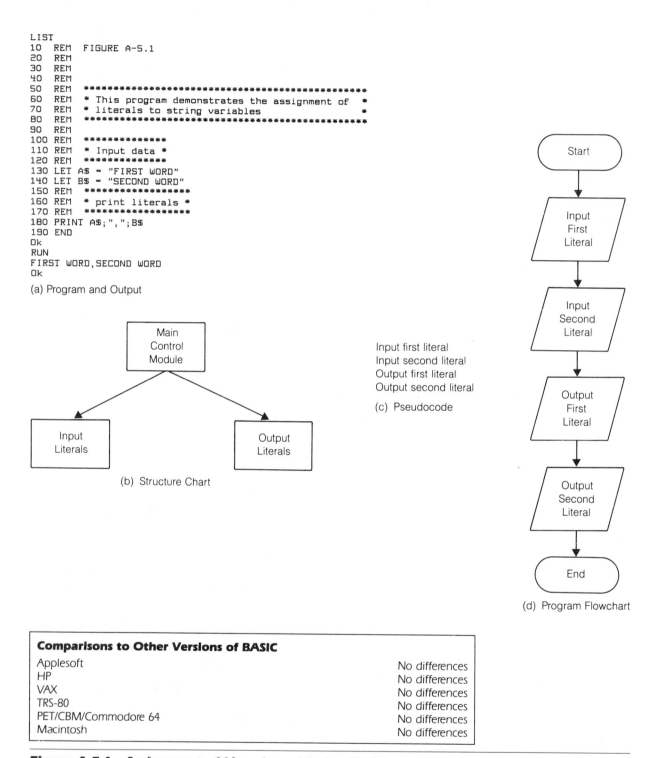

(b) Structure Chart

Input first literal
Input second literal
Output first literal
Output second literal

(c) Pseudocode

(d) Program Flowchart

Comparisons to Other Versions of BASIC	
Applesoft	No differences
HP	No differences
VAX	No differences
TRS-80	No differences
PET/CBM/Commodore 64	No differences
Macintosh	No differences

Figure A-5.1   Assignment of Literals and String Variables

Some versions of BASIC, although not standard, allow the omission of the keyword LET when coding an assignment statement. For all versions discussed in this appendix, this is true. However, it is recommended that the LET statement not be omitted, to avoid confusion and enhance portability.

Character String Assignment   The previous examples illustrate arithmetic assignment. The LET statement may also be used for character string assignment. When assigning a literal, you must enclose the string within quotation marks, and the literal may only be assigned to a string variable (denoted by a dollar sign). Statements 130 and 140 in Figure A-5.1 are valid examples of string assignment.

A numeric variable or constant cannot be assigned to a string variable or vice versa, because of the rule that like data types must be on both sides of the assignment operator. The PRINT statement in Figure A-5.1 will display the following:

first word,second word

Notice that there are no spaces before or after the comma. This effect is known as **concatenation.**

Summing Up

☐ The LET statement is used to assign a value to a variable. Since assignment is a destructive process, any previous value of the variable is destroyed when a new value is assigned to it.
☐ Arithmetic assignment is used to place the value of a constant, variable, function, or expression in the variable on the left of the assignment operator.
☐ A literal value may be assigned to a string variable through character string assignment.

Debugging Exercises

Find and remove the bugs in the following program segments:

```
1. 10 LET A*B = C + 5
2. 10 LET 15 = A + F
3. 10 LET A = A + 5
4. 10 REM "THIS IS THE FIRST STATEMENT IN A COUNTING LOOP"
   20 LET I = I + 1
   30 PRINT I
   40 IF I < = 10 THEN 10
   50 END
5. LET Z = X * - 5
```

Topic 6: BASIC Input and Output Statements

Supplying Data

We have discussed the primary building blocks for writing a BASIC program. We will now discuss how to make the program interact with the user. BASIC is a conversational language. A program can be written that will prompt the user for data, accept the data, process it, and then display the results. These functions are performed through the use of input/output statements.

BASIC offers two methods of input to a program:

1. User interaction with the program as it runs
2. Batch processing using groups of data known as **data blocks.**

The INPUT Statement   User interaction that occurs while the program is executing is facilitated by the use of the INPUT statement. The INPUT statement in conjunction with the PRINT statement (to be discussed later) gives BASIC its "conversational" characteristics. With this knowledge, we can revise Figure A-4.1 so that the program now communicates with its user. Figure A-6.1 demonstrates the use of the INPUT and PRINT statements.

Statement 180 is a PRINT statement which prompts the user for the required input data; statement 190 is the INPUT statement which accepts the data; and statement 270 is the subsequent PRINT statement which displays the results of processing (the student's name and average grade). The INPUT statement has the following format:

line#	INPUT	list of variables

where the variables in the list are separated by commas.

The INPUT statement allows data to be entered at the terminal as the program executes, creating the interactive environment. When an input statement is encountered, a prompt symbol will be displayed. On most systems, the prompt symbol is a question mark (?) or colon (:). It is good programming practice to prompt the user for the information by using a PRINT statement preceding the INPUT statement. In Figure A-6.1, for example, the prompt is:

```
"What is the name, midterm and final grades";
```

Note that this PRINT statement has a semicolon as a trailing separator. This will cause the prompt (the question mark) to be placed immediately after the question. After the prompt symbol is displayed the user enters the data values, separated by commas.

The INPUT statement performs a function similar to the LET statement, that is, the INPUT statement assigns values to variables. However, the LET statement assigns values internally (within the program) whereas the INPUT statement assigns values that are external to the program.

The variables used in the INPUT statement's variable list may be of any data type. The number of values supplied must be equal to the number of variables listed. If fewer values are supplied than variables listed, another prompt symbol is displayed until sufficient values are entered. If too many values are supplied, then the excess is ignored. Data types must match between values and variables, or else an error will occur.

```
LIST
10   REM  FIGURE A-6.1
20   REM
30   REM
40   REM  ************************************************************
50   REM  * This program accepts the name, midterm, and final grades *
60   REM  * of a student and calculates and prints his/her average   *
70   REM  ************************************************************
80   REM
90   REM                Variable definitions
100  REM                *******************
110  REM                N$ - students name
120  REM                M  - midterm grade
130  REM                F  - final grade
140  REM                A  - average grade
150  REM  *******************
160  REM  * user inputs data *
170  REM  *******************
180  PRINT "WHAT IS THE NAME, MIDTERM, AND FINAL GRADES ";
190  INPUT N$,M,F
200  REM  ****************************
210  REM  * calculate average grade *
220  REM  ****************************
230  LET A - (M+F)/2
240  REM  ****************
250  REM  * print results *
260  REM  ****************
270  PRINT "THE AVERAGE GRADE FOR ";N$;" IS ";A
280  END
Ok
RUN
WHAT IS THE NAME, MIDTERM, AND FINAL GRADES ? EILEEN DOVER,89,90,.5
THE AVERAGE GRADE FOR EILEEN DOVER IS  89.75
Ok
```

(a) Program and Output

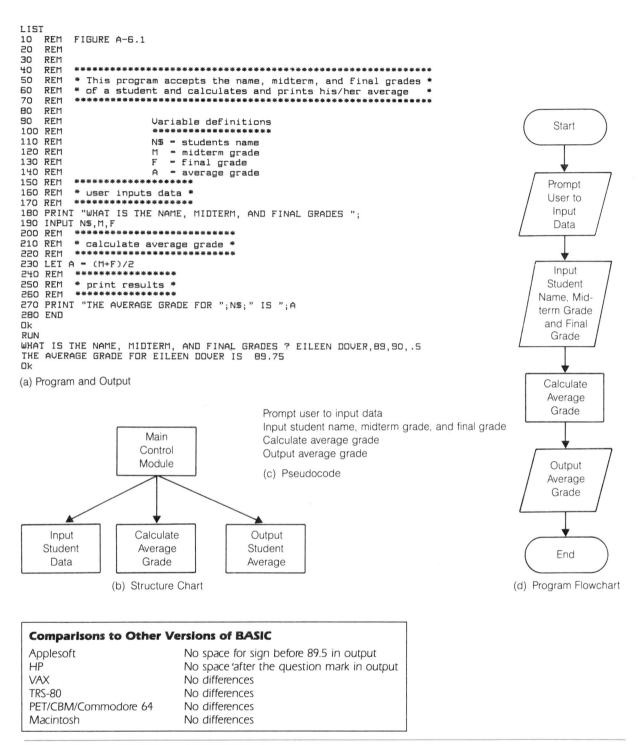

Prompt user to input data
Input student name, midterm grade, and final grade
Calculate average grade
Output average grade

(c) Pseudocode

(b) Structure Chart

(d) Program Flowchart

Comparisons to Other Versions of BASIC

Applesoft	No space for sign before 89.5 in output
HP	No space 'after the question mark in output
VAX	No differences
TRS-80	No differences
PET/CBM/Commodore 64	No differences
Macintosh	No differences

Figure A-6.1   INPUT and PRINT Statements

The READ, DATA, and RESTORE Statements   The second method of supplying data to a program is to build a data block to be accessed during execution. Using this method, the user does not interact with the program as it executes, but supplies a block of data before the program is run. Under this method data are accessed by using the READ statement in conjunction with one or more DATA statements. The format of the READ statement is as follows:

---

line#   READ   list of variables

---

where the variables are separated by commas.

The format of the DATA statement is as follows:

---

line #   DATA   list of constants

---

where the constants are numeric or string constants separated by commas.

The READ statement allows transmission of data into a BASIC program. The input data are contained within a data block consisting of one of more DATA statements. In Figure A-6.2 our data block consists of only one DATA statement.

Like the INPUT statement, the READ and DATA statements assign values that are external to the program and therefore have characteristics similar to the INPUT statement. They are as follows:

1. The variables listed in the READ statement may be of any data type.
2. These variables in the READ statement must correspond in type with the values in the DATA statement that they represent.
3. There must be at least as many values in the DATA block as there are variables in the READ statement. If there are less, an error will occur. If more, then the extra values are ignored.

The limit on the size of the data block (the number of DATA statements) depends on the system used. However, when a READ statement is used, there must be at least one DATA statement. An attempt to read data when the end of the block is reached will generate an error message.

Figure A-6.2 is a simple grade-report program, an application that lends itself to processing data in batches. The illustration demonstrates the use of the DATA and READ statements. The program terminates normally because no attempt is made to read after the end of data is reached.

The RESTORE statement is used to read the same data more than once. It has the following format:

---

line#   RESTORE

Once the DATA have been read, a RESTORE will allow the program to begin reading from the initial point of the data block (the first DATA statement in the program).

```
LIST
10   REM  FIGURE A-6.2
20   REM
30   REM
40   REM
50   REM  ****************************************************
60   REM  * This program reads in a student record which     *
70   REM  * consists of the name, midterm, and final scores, *
80   REM  * and calculates the student's average             *
90   REM  ****************************************************
100  REM
110  REM              Variable definitions
120  REM              ********************
130  REM              N$ - student name
140  REM              M  - midterm grade
150  REM              F  - final grade
160  REM              A  - average grade
170  REM
180  REM  *************
190  REM  * input data *
200  REM  *************
210  DATA JUAN MOREFORE DERHODE,95,85
220  READ N$,M,F
230  REM  *********************
240  REM  * calculate average *
250  REM  *********************
260  LET A = (M+F)/2
270  REM  ******************
280  REM  * print results *
290  REM  ******************
300  PRINT "THE AVERAGE GRADE FOR ";N$;" IS ";A
310  END
Ok
RUN
THE AVERAGE GRADE FOR JUAN MOREFORE DERHODE IS  90
Ok
```

(a) Program and Output

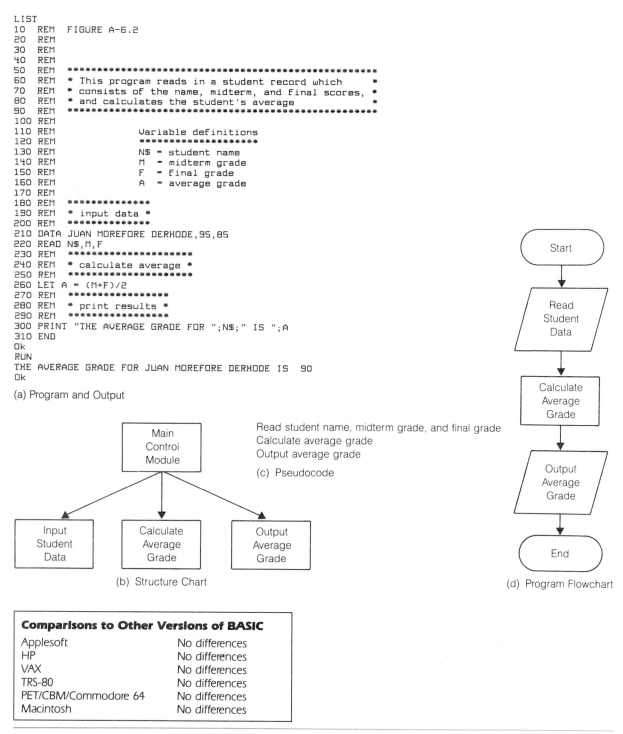

Main
Control
Module

Input
Student
Data

Calculate
Average
Grade

Output
Average
Grade

(b) Structure Chart

Read student name, midterm grade, and final grade
Calculate average grade
Output average grade

(c) Pseudocode

Start

Read
Student
Data

Calculate
Average
Grade

Output
Average
Grade

End

(d) Program Flowchart

Comparisons to Other Versions of BASIC

Applesoft	No differences
HP	No differences
VAX	No differences
TRS-80	No differences
PET/CBM/Commodore 64	No differences
Macintosh	No differences

Figure A-6.2   DATA and READ Statements

Displaying Information

The Simple PRINT Statement   We have discussed how to access input data and process the data to obtain results. Now we will consider how to display these results to the user at the terminal. The PRINT statement is used for this purpose. It has the following format:

line#	PRINT	[list of expressions]

where the expressions are separated by commas or semicolons. The list of expressions is also called an **argument list.**

The PRINT statement displays specified information on the user's terminal while the BASIC program is executing. The PRINT statement is a useful statement for:

1. Checking the results of processing
2. Communicating the results of the processing to the user

Unlike the input or reading of data, the printing of data is not destructive. The contents of a memory location are simply reproduced for display on the user's terminal.

The information displayed may be the contents of a variable, the value of an arithmetic expression, or constants (floating-point, fixed-point, and literals). Figure A-6.3 is a program that displays constants. There are fundamental rules that must be followed when printing numeric constants and literals:

1. BASIC precedes negative numbers with the minus sign, and positive numbers with a space (the Apple computer omits this space).
2. Numeric constants need not be enclosed in quotation marks.
3. Note the results of statement 130. This statement illustrates an important point about how BASIC prints numeric constants. Depending on the system, BASIC will print the decimal form of a number if it is within a specific range. If the magnitude is outside the range, the "E-notation" is used.

When printing literals, remember that the character string must be enclosed in quotation marks ("). The string will be printed exactly as it is typed, with no leading or trailing blanks. Examples are statements 100, 120, and 140 in Figure A-6.3.

The PRINT statement may also be used for displaying the values of variables and the results of expressions, which makes the PRINT statement a useful debugging tool. When printing the values of a variable, do not use quotation marks.

When an expression appears within the argument list of a PRINT statement, the PRINT statement evaluates the expression and then displays the results. Again, the expressions should not appear in quotation marks. For example, the following sequence:

```
10   LET a = 1
20   LET b = 2
30   PRINT "a+b"
40   END
```

will result in the following:

```
a+b
```

```
LIST
10    REM    FIGURE A-6.3
20    REM
30    REM
40    REM
50    REM    **********************************************************
60    REM    * This program displays a fixed-point constant, a      *
70    REM    * floating-point constant, and a literal.               *
80    REM    **********************************************************
90    REM
100   PRINT "THE FOLLOWING IS A FIXED-POINT CONSTANT:"
110   PRINT 3
120   PRINT "THE FOLLOWING ARE FLOATING-POINT CONSTANTS:"
130   PRINT 3.15,.0099
140   PRINT "THIS IS A LITERAL"
150   END
Ok
RUN
THE FOLLOWING IS A FIXED-POINT CONSTANT:
 3
THE FOLLOWING ARE FLOATING-POINT CONSTANTS:
 3.15        .0099
THIS IS A LITERAL
Ok
```

(a) Program and Output

Output fixed-point constant
Output floating-point constants
Output literal

(b) Pseudocode

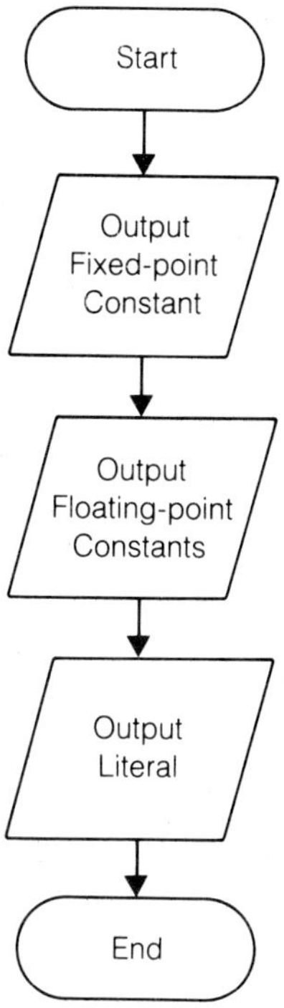

Comparisons to Other Versions of BASIC

Applesoft	Print zone width is 16
HP	Print zone width is 21
VAX	No differences
TRS-80	No differences
PET/CBM/Commodore 64	Print zone width is 10
Macintosh	No differences

Start

Output
Fixed-point
Constant

Output
Floating-point
Constants

Output
Literal

End

(c) Program Flowchart

Figure A-6.3   Displaying Constants and Literals

where the following set of statements

```
10    LET a = 1
20    LET b = 2
30    PRINT a+b
40    END
```

displays the following:

```
3
```

The standard output format is the **default format.** The user does not specify this format; it is automatically assigned by the computer. The standard output format is divided into five print zones. The width of the print zones may vary among different versions. For example, the IBM/Microsoft BASIC default format has 5 print zones, each 14 spaces wide, producing a 70-character output line. The following example shows a simple PRINT statement.

```
10    PRINT "This","line","has","five","parts."
20    END
```

resulting in:

```
This           line          has           five          parts.
```

If there are more than five elements within the PRINT statement argument list, BASIC will begin printing the sixth output element in the first print zone on the next line (on VAX, however, a sixth "print zone" begins in column 71). For example, the following statements:

```
10   PRINT   "Hello","There","My","Name","Is","MUFFY."
20   END
```

produce:

```
Hello          There         My            Name          Is
MUFFY.
```

The argument list is optional for the PRINT statement, so when the following is executed:

```
10   PRINT   "This is line one"
20   PRINT
30   PRINT   "This is line three"
40   END
```

a blank line will be printed with statement 20. Therefore, the PRINT statement without arguments may be used for printing blank lines.

Note in our illustrations that the arguments are separated with commas. When commas are used, BASIC will print each output element at the beginning of a print zone. Sometimes this is an undesirable feature. For example, if statement 320 in Figure A-6.4 contained commas instead of semicolons, the following would be printed:

```
The average grade for        Ed Settera   is                          82
```

To solve this problem, BASIC allows the use of the semicolon (;) as a legal separator of the argument list. When the semicolon is used, BASIC prints the next output element immediately following the previous element, resulting in a compressed format of the output line. For example, the following statements:

```
10   PRINT   "Hello";"There";"My";"Name";"Is";"MUFFY."
20   END
```

produce:

```
HelloThereMyNameIsMUFFY.
```

Therefore, the PRINT statement argument list may incorporate either the comma (,) or the semicolon (;) as legal separators, thereby controlling the placement of output within the print zones.

Before continuing on with other formatting techniques available, let's consider the following examples:

```
10   LET v$ = "MUFFY"
20   PRINT "My Name is ";
30   PRINT v$;
40   PRINT "."
50   END
```

This sequence of statements produces the following:

```
My Name is MUFFY.
```

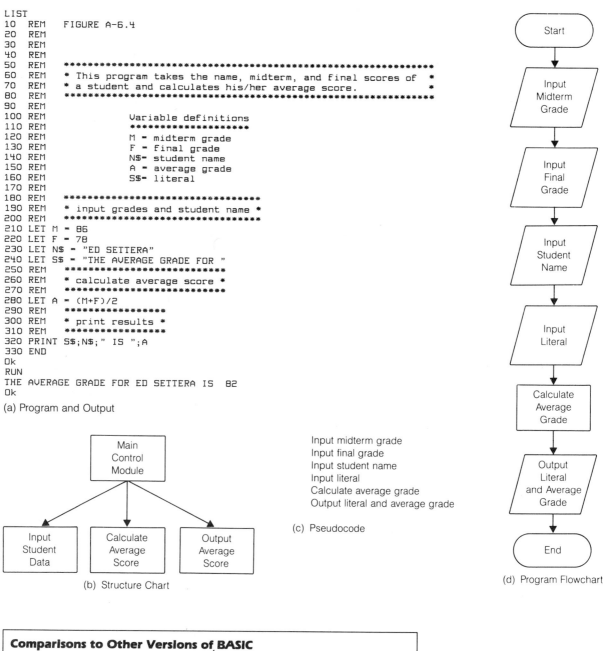

```
LIST
10   REM    FIGURE A-6.4
20   REM
30   REM
40   REM
50   REM    *******************************************************
60   REM    * This program takes the name, midterm, and final scores of  *
70   REM    * a student and calculates his/her average score.            *
80   REM    *******************************************************
90   REM
100  REM               Variable definitions
110  REM               *******************
120  REM               M - midterm grade
130  REM               F - final grade
140  REM               N$- student name
150  REM               A - average grade
160  REM               S$- literal
170  REM
180  REM    *******************************
190  REM    * input grades and student name *
200  REM    *******************************
210  LET M - 86
220  LET F - 78
230  LET N$ - "ED SETTERA"
240  LET S$ - "THE AVERAGE GRADE FOR "
250  REM    ***************************
260  REM    * calculate average score *
270  REM    ***************************
280  LET A - (M+F)/2
290  REM    ****************
300  REM    * print results *
310  REM    ****************
320  PRINT S$;N$;" IS ";A
330  END
Ok
RUN
THE AVERAGE GRADE FOR ED SETTERA IS   82
Ok
```

(a) Program and Output

Main Control Module

Input Student Data

Calculate Average Score

Output Average Score

(b) Structure Chart

Input midterm grade
Input final grade
Input student name
Input literal
Calculate average grade
Output literal and average grade

(c) Pseudocode

Start
Input Midterm Grade
Input Final Grade
Input Student Name
Input Literal
Calculate Average Grade
Output Literal and Average Grade
End

(d) Program Flowchart

Comparisons to Other Versions of BASIC

Applesoft	No space allocated for sign before 89.75 in output
HP	No differences
VAX	No differences
TRS-80	No differences
PET/CBM/Commodore 64	No differences
Macintosh	No differences

Figure A-6.4   Variables Separated by Semicolons in a PRINT Statement

How did three separate PRINT statements produce one single compressed line of output? This is done by a **hanging separator** (in this case, the semicolon). When hanging separators are used, output from two or more PRINT statements are printed on one line. If no hanging separators are used, as in the following program:

```
10   LET v$ = "MUFFY"
20   PRINT "My Name Is "
30   PRINT v$
40   PRINT "."
50   END
```

we would have this result:

```
My Name is
MUFFY
```

A hanging separator may be either of the two legal separators, the comma or semicolon. When the comma is used, the default format is in effect.

The PRINT Statement with the TAB Function

At times it is necessary for a program to display a matrix or table, since some information is best scrutinized in tabular form. An example is a sales report or an income-tax table. BASIC offers the TAB function for this purpose.

The TAB function accepts an integer as a **parameter** which indicates the desired print position. For example,

```
PRINT TAB(15); "This is my favorite book"
```

prints the literal `This is my favorite book` beginning with print position 15. The TAB function prints a series of blank spaces. The number of spaces is determined by subtracting the current print position from the integer parameter of the TAB function. If the current print position is greater than the parameter specified to the TAB function, then the null string (no spaces) is printed. The following sequence of statements illustrates this characteristic:

```
10PRINT"columnone";TAB(15);"column15";TAB(20);"column20"
20 END
```

The result is:

```
column one    column 15column 20
```

In IBM/Microsoft BASIC the TAB(20) would go to position 20 on the next line as follows:

```
column one    column 15
              column 20
```

The use of the semicolon as a separator with the TAB function is recommended for more compact formatting. Use of the comma may cause the current print position to be greater than the argument specified, causing the TAB to have an undesirable effect. The following sequence of statements demonstrates this problem:

```
10 PRINT "10",TAB(5),"20",TAB(10),"30"
20 END
```

The result is:

```
10                      20                      30
```

The TAB function can never move the current print position to the left; therefore, if a tab stop is passed the TAB function will perform as in the examples just presented.

The columns may be numbered from zero to the maximum print position (as with VAX-11, PET/CBM, TRS–80, and IBM/Microsoft versions of BASIC), or from one to the maximum print position (as with Apple).

The PRINT USING Statement

Another feature that allows the programmer to **edit** or format output is the PRINT USING statement. (This statement, however, is not considered an element of the ANSI standard minimal BASIC.) Even though some versions of BASIC do not have PRINT USING facilities, this statement will be discussed since it is such a powerful formatting tool.

The PRINT USING statement may refer to an image line by giving the line number of the image line. The format is as follows:

---

line#   PRINT USING   image line#, expression list

---

where image line# is the line number of the statement that formats the output. The expressions are separated by commas.

The statement referenced in the PRINT USING statement is known as the IMAGE statement. The IMAGE statement specifies how the data are to be arranged when printed. The format of the IMAGE statement is as follows:

---

line#:   unquoted control character string

---

where the unquoted control character string consists of special characters to be used to control the display. An example of this type of PRINT USING statement follows:

```
10 PRINT USING 20, A, B
20:     #####.##     $######.##
```

The PRINT USING statement is implemented in some versions (such as IBM/Microsoft and Apple Macintosh BASIC) as one statement which includes the string format instead of a line number. This implementation has the following format:

---

line# PRINT USING "control character string"; list of items

---

where the control character string must be enclosed in quotation marks. The display items in the list are separated by commas. The statements in Figure A-6.5 demonstrate this format.

The PRINT USING statement is a very powerful output editing tool. The following formats can be designated easily with this statement:

1. For numeric output

    a. The field width of the number
    b. Automatic rounding
    c. The location of decimal point (alignment)
    d. Insertion of symbols (positive/negative signs, dollar signs, commas, etc.)
    e. Right justification of numbers

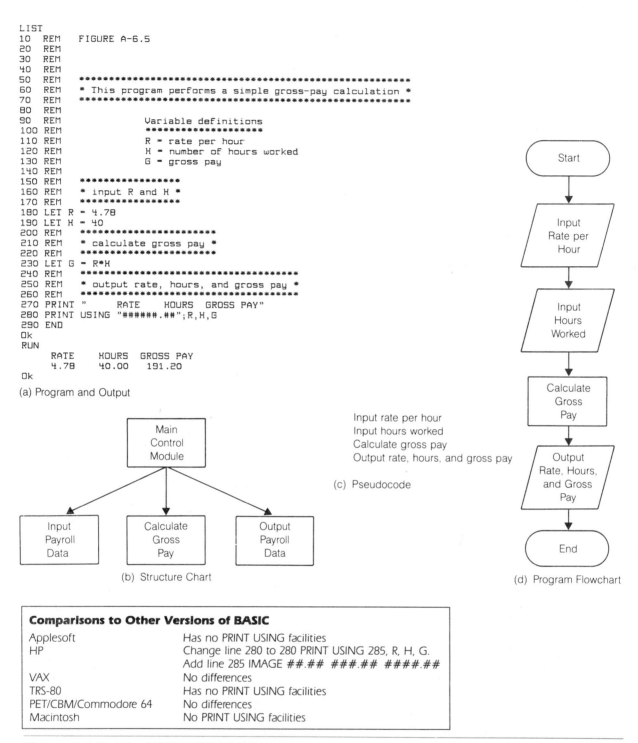

```
LIST
10   REM     FIGURE A-6.5
20   REM
30   REM
40   REM
50   REM     *******************************************************
60   REM     * This program performs a simple gross-pay calculation *
70   REM     *******************************************************
80   REM
90   REM                 Variable definitions
100  REM                 ********************
110  REM                 R = rate per hour
120  REM                 H = number of hours worked
130  REM                 G = gross pay
140  REM
150  REM     ****************
160  REM     * input R and H *
170  REM     ****************
180  LET R = 4.78
190  LET H = 40
200  REM     ************************
210  REM     * calculate gross pay *
220  REM     ************************
230  LET G = R*H
240  REM     ***************************************
250  REM     * output rate, hours, and gross pay *
260  REM     ***************************************
270  PRINT "    RATE    HOURS   GROSS PAY"
280  PRINT USING "######.##";R,H,G
290  END
Ok
RUN
      RATE    HOURS   GROSS PAY
      4.78    40.00    191.20
Ok
```

(a) Program and Output

Main Control Module

Input Payroll Data   Calculate Gross Pay   Output Payroll Data

(b) Structure Chart

Input rate per hour
Input hours worked
Calculate gross pay
Output rate, hours, and gross pay

(c) Pseudocode

Start

Input Rate per Hour

Input Hours Worked

Calculate Gross Pay

Output Rate, Hours, and Gross Pay

End

(d) Program Flowchart

Comparisons to Other Versions of BASIC

Applesoft	Has no PRINT USING facilities
HP	Change line 280 to 280 PRINT USING 285, R, H, G.
	Add line 285 IMAGE ##.## ###.## ####.##
VAX	No differences
TRS-80	Has no PRINT USING facilities
PET/CBM/Commodore 64	No differences
Macintosh	No PRINT USING facilities

Figure A-6.5   The PRINT USING Statement

2. For character strings
    a. Field width of the string
    b. Left justification
    c. Right justification
    d. Centering of string

These formats are executed through the use of **control characters.** For editing numeric output, use the following control characters:

Character	*Purpose*
#	The pound sign reserves a print position for each digit in the number.
.	The decimal point reserves a print position for the decimal point.
,	The comma reserves a print position for a comma within the number.
*	The asterisk is used for check protection where leading zeros of the number are replaced by asterisks. The asterisk reserves a print position for either a digit or an asterisk.
$	The dollar sign reserves a print position for the dollar sign. If n dollar signs are specified, print positions are reserved for at least one dollar sign and at most n-1 digits.
^^^^	The sequence of four ^^^^ causes the number to be displayed in *E*-notation. The up-arrows reserve print positions for the *E*-notation.
−, +	These signs reserve print positions either before or after the number for the specified sign.

Using these control characters, we can achieve the above designations. For example,

1. The field width is defined by a sequence of pound signs:

```
10    PRINT USING "##.#"; 12.36
20    PRINT USING "##.##"; 13.4
30    PRINT USING "###"; 1234
```

The results are:

```
12.4
13.40
% 1234
```

In line 30, the number was too large for the field width. To point this out to the user, BASIC responds with the percent sign (%) and the number to be printed.

2. This example also illustrates the automatic rounding of numbers (line 10). Least significant digits are dropped and rounding occurs if the decimal field is too small. Also note that if the decimal field is too large, the number is padded with zeros (line 20).

3. The PRINT USING statement will also cause automatic alignment, as follows:

Print statements without the USING clause:

```
10   PRINT    1
20   PRINT    20
30   PRINT    1.345
40   PRINT    2500000
50   PRINT    .00000234
```

Produce these results:

```
1
20
1.345
.25E+07
.234E-05
```

```
10   PRINT USING "#######.##"; 1
20   PRINT USING "#######.##"; 20
30   PRINT USING "#######.##"; 1.345
40   PRINT USING "#######.##"; 2500000
50   PRINT USING "#######.##"; .00000234
```

The results are:

```
      1.00
     20.00
      1.35
2500000.00
      0.00
```

Note that the numbers are more comparable when the PRINT USING statement is used. Also illustrated is the use of the decimal point for alignment. The PRINT USING statements provide for the right justification of numbers as well.

4. The following example illustrates the use of special symbols:

```
10   PRINT USING "##,###.##"; 1234.5
20   PRINT USING "######.##-"; -12.345
30   PRINT USING "$$,$$#.##"; 12.345
40   PRINT
50   PRINT USING "#.####    "; 1234.5
```

The results are:

```
1,234.50
   12.35-
  $12.35

1.2345E+03
```

Statement 10 illustrates the use of the decimal point and the comma. Statement 30 illustrates the use of the dollar sign.

Figure A-6.6 is a comprehensive example of several of the control characters used by the PRINT USING statements.

```
LIST
10    REM     FIGURE A-6.6
20    REM
30    REM
40    REM
50    REM     *********************************************************
60    REM     * This program reads employee records calculating gross pay,  *
70    REM     * taxes, and net pay.  When the end of the data block is      *
80    REM     * reached, the total net pay is calculated.  The final result *
90    REM     * is the generation of the payroll report.                    *
100   REM     *********************************************************
110   REM
120   REM                 Variable definitions
130   REM                 ********************
135   REM                 V$- current date
140   REM                 T - total earnings
150   REM                 A$- literal
160   REM                 N$- employee name
170   REM                 H - hours worked
180   REM                 R - rate per hour
190   REM                 G - gross pay
200   REM                 N - net pay
210   REM                 F1- federal income tax
220   REM                 S - state income tax
230   REM                 F2- FICA tax
240   REM
250   REM     *********************
260   REM     * main control module *
270   REM     *********************
280   GOSUB 370
290   GOSUB 520
300   WHILE H>=0
310      GOSUB 570
320      GOSUB 670
330      GOSUB 520
340   WEND
350   GOSUB 730
360   END
370   REM     ************************
380   REM     * initialization module *
390   REM     ************************
400   LET V$=DATE$
410   LET T=0
420   LET A$ = "PAYROLL REPORT"
430   PRINT "                            ";A$;
440   PRINT "                    ";V$
450   PRINT
460   PRINT "EMPLOYEE          HOURS    RATE      GROSS   FEDERAL";
470   PRINT "    STATE       FICA       NET"
480   PRINT "  NAME            WORKED  PER HOUR   PAY      TAX   ";
490   PRINT "    TAX        TAX        PAY"
500   PRINT
510   RETURN
520   REM     ****************
530   REM     * input module *
540   REM     ****************
550   READ N$,H,R
560   RETURN
570   REM     ****************
580   REM     * process module *
590   REM     ****************
600      LET G= H*R
610      LET F1= G*.12
620      LET S= G*.03
630      LET F2= G*.07
640      LET N= G - (F1+S+F2)
```

Figure A-6.6   A Comprehensive Example of the PRINT USING Statement (See Figures A-1.2, A-1.4, and A-1.6 for the structure chart, pseudocode, and flowchart for this program)

```
650     LET T= T+N
660 RETURN
670 REM    ******************
680 REM    * output module *
690 REM    ******************
700     PRINT USING "\              \ ###.##    ###.##    ####.##    ";N$,H,R,G;
710     PRINT USING "###.##    ###.##    ###.##    ####.##";F1,S,F2,N
720 RETURN
730 REM    *********************
740 REM    * termination module *
750 REM    *********************
760 PRINT
770 PRINT TAB(56);"TOTAL EARNINGS:    ";
780 PRINT USING "$###.##";T
790 DATA I.M. FIRST,40,5.00
800 DATA SHARON SHARALIKE,25,3.35
810 DATA T. TOTTLER,33,5.00
820 DATA MATT TRESS,42,4.51
830 DATA HELEN HIGHWATER,17,3.35
840 DATA TAYLOR MAID,25,4.51
850 DATA BUD ERDBUNS,40,5.00
860 DATA I.M. LAST,32,4.51
870 DATA END,-999,-999
Ok
RUN
                          PAYROLL REPORT              10-14-1985

EMPLOYEE         HOURS     RATE      GROSS   FEDERAL   STATE    FICA      NET
  NAME          WORKED   PER HOUR     PAY      TAX      TAX     TAX       PAY

I.M. FIRST       40.00     5.00     200.00    24.00    6.00    14.00   156.00
SHARON SHARALIKE 25.00     3.35      83.75    10.05    2.51     5.86    65.33
T. TOTTLER       33.00     5.00     165.00    19.80    4.95    11.55   128.70
MATT TRESS       42.00     4.51     189.42    22.73    5.68    13.26   147.75
HELEN HIGHWATER  17.00     3.35      56.95     6.83    1.71     3.99    44.42
TAYLOR MAID      25.00     4.51     112.75    13.53    3.38     7.89    87.95
BUD ERDBUNS      40.00     5.00     200.00    24.00    6.00    14.00   156.00
I.M. LAST        32.00     4.51     144.32    17.32    4.33    10.10   112.57

                                           TOTAL EARNINGS:    $898.71
Ok
```

Comparisons to Other Versions of BASIC

Applesoft	Needs extra space after colon in input; no PRINT USING facility
HP	PRINT USING statements should have semicolon before the argument list
VAX	No differences
TRS-80	No PRINT USING facilities
PET/CBM/Commodore 64	No differences
Macintosh	Needs extra space after colon in input; no PRINT USING facility

Figure A-6.6   (continued)

Summing Up

☐ Data may be input to a BASIC program in two ways. Under interactive input, the computer prompts the user to enter data while the program is executing. Under batch processing, data are entered into data blocks before the program is executed.

☐ The PRINT statement is used when data are to be output in an unformatted manner. It can make use of a default format which lines up output data in a fixed number of columns. If the default format is not used, all output data are compressed and printed without any blank spaces between data items.

☐ The use of the TAB function allows you to print out data in the form of a table. You may define the number of columns and the width of each column with the help of the TAB facility.

☐ The PRINT USING statement is a powerful data-editing facility. It gives you a number of data-formatting capabilities, including the following:

Setting field width.
Rounding off numeric values.
Alignment of columns on a decimal point.
Insertion of symbols such as dollar sign, commas, et cetera.

Debugging Exercises

Find and remove the bugs in the following program segments:

```
1. 10 REM THE USER INPUTS DATA
   20 INPUT A$, H, Z, X

2. 10 READ X, Y, N$
   20 DATA JOHN SMITH, 50, -.538

3. 50 PRINT "THE PAY RATE IS, B$

4. 10 LET A = 15
   20 LET B = 20
   30 PRINT "A", "B"

5. 30 REM PRINT THE VALUE OF THE SUM OF A + B
   40 PRINT "A + B"

6. 10 PRINT TAB(10), "10", TAB(15), "15", TAB(8), "8"

7. 10 PRINT USING "####", 25394

8. 10 PRINT USING "$$,$$#.##", A$
```

Hands-on Exercises

1. Write a program using DATA statements that will read the following payroll data and produce the report shown. Be sure to document your program well.

Input data:

Name	Pay Rate	Hours Worked
JAY HARDWICK	$3.95	40
TOM SMITH	$4.50	35
RAY ROBERTS	$8.35	45

Output Report:

	Pay	Hours	Total
	Rate	Worked	Pay
Name			
JAY HARDWICK	$3.95	40	$158.00
TOM SMITH	$4.50	35	$157.00
RAY ROBERTS	$8.35	45	$375.75

Write three versions of this program: one using the PRINT statement, one using the PRINT USING statement, and one using the TAB function to format the output. Draw a structure chart of your program and prepare pseudocode or a program flowchart. Document your program internally with REM statements.

2. Write a program using the INPUT statement that will interactively prompt a user for five numbers, calculate the average of these numbers, and print the average. Draw a structure chart of your program and prepare pseudocode or a program flowchart. Document your program internally with REM statements.

Topic 7: Program-Control Statements

Back to Basics

Most of the illustrations previously discussed execute statements in sequential order according to line number. It would be unrealistic to assume that strict sequential processing can offer a viable solution to all problems. Many problems require a **decision-making** process or step-by-step **iterations** before a solution can be reached. Therefore, the idea of program control is necessary to alter the order of execution within a program.

Program control can be described by the four basic structured control patterns we discussed in Topic 1 of this appendix. These are reviewed here with examples written in BASIC.

1. The **simple sequence construct.** Two or more operations are performed, passing control from one operation to the next in a serial fashion.

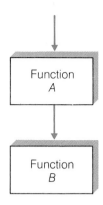

Simple Sequence Structure

```
Do A
Do B
```

An example is:

```
10   REM ... begin
20   LET a = 4
30   LET b = 2
40   LET c = a + b
50   REM ... end
```

2. The **IF-THEN-ELSE selection structure.** A test is to be made and one of two alternative paths are taken depending on the results of the test.

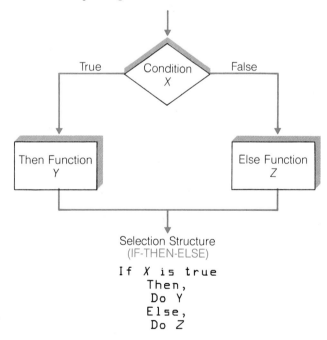

Selection Structure
(IF-THEN-ELSE)

```
If X is true
    Then,
    Do Y
    Else,
    Do Z
```

In this case, if the condition, *X* is true, the function *Y* is performed, else function *Z* is performed. An example is:

```
10   REM ... if a > b
20   IF a <= b THEN 60
30   REM ... then
40   LET c = b - a
50   GOTO 80
60   REM ... else
70   LET c = a - b
80   REM ... end if
```

Note that the condition is not tested as a "less than" but as a "greater than or equal to". Testing the opposite condition is necessary to make the loop work correctly as defined in the REM statement and is used commonly in BASIC programming.

3. The **DO-WHILE LOOP STRUCTURE.** A test of a condition is evaluated. If the result of the test is true, the function is performed repeatedly until the test evaluates to false.

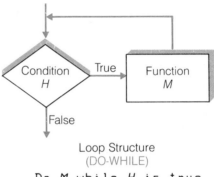

Loop Structure
(DO-WHILE)

Do *M* while *H* is true

In this case, if the condition *H* is true, the function *M* is performed repeatedly, testing the condition each time until it evaluates to false. An example is:

```
10   REM ... do while a < b
20   IF a => b THEN 50
30   LET a = a + 1
40   REM ... end the loop
50   GOTO 10
```

Note that the opposite condition is tested again, creating the loop in accordance with the REM statement. Some versions of BASIC, such as IBM/Microsoft, support a DO-WHILE statement. In IBM/Microsoft BASIC, the WHILE/WEND statement should be used for coding the DO-WHILE structure. It would be coded as follows:

```
10   REM ... do while a < b
20   WHILE a < b
30   LET a = a + 1
40   REM ... end the loop
50   WEND
```

The WHILE/WEND program-control structure is substantially easier to understand, since you do not need to test the opposite condition.

4. The **case structure.** A test is made of a condition that can have multiple values. The program branches to one of multiple functions depending on the evaluation of the condition.

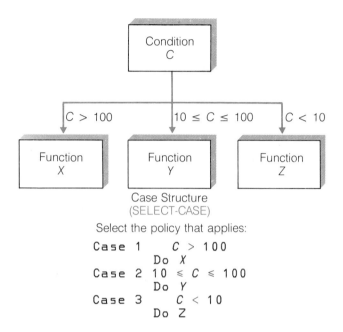

Case Structure
(SELECT-CASE)

Select the policy that applies:

```
Case 1     C > 100
           Do  X
Case 2  10 ≤ C ≤ 100
           Do  Y
Case 3     C < 10
           Do  Z
```

In this case, condition C is evaluated as follows:

If $C > 100$, then function X is executed
If $10 < = C < = 100$, then function Y is executed
If $C < 10$, then function Z is executed

One of the more important uses of the case structure is in writing menu-driven programs. These programs are discussed in Topic 9 of this appendix.

Transfer Statements

The transfer of execution to nonsequential statements is known as **branching.** There are two types of branching:

1. unconditional
2. conditional

The GOTO Statement Unconditional branching is implemented in BASIC by the GOTO statement, which has the following format:

```
line#    GOTO     destination line#
```

where the destination line# is the number of the statement to be executed next.

As an example, the program in Figure A-7.1 will accept a set of numbers, compute the sum, and print the results. This process is repeated each time a set of numbers is accepted.

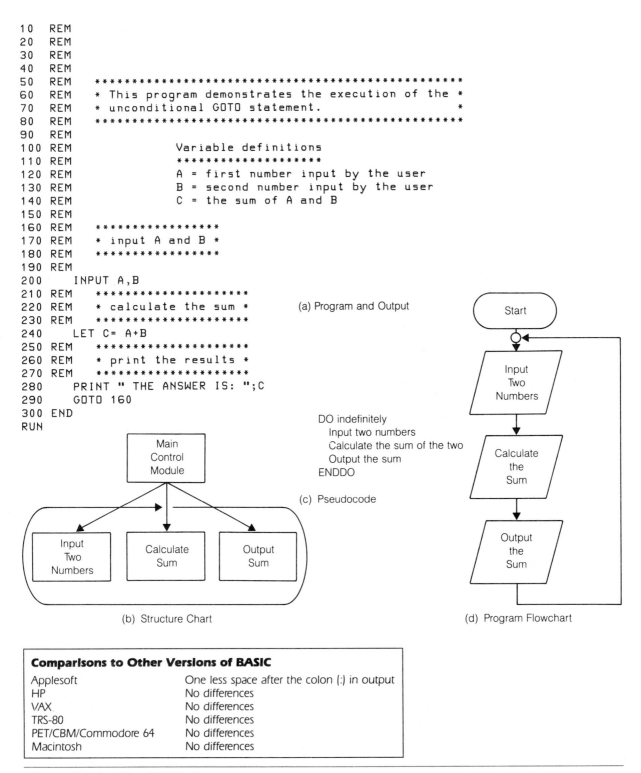

```
10  REM
20  REM
30  REM
40  REM
50  REM     ************************************************
60  REM     * This program demonstrates the execution of the *
70  REM     * unconditional GOTO statement.                  *
80  REM     ************************************************
90  REM
100 REM                Variable definitions
110 REM                *********************
120 REM                A = first number input by the user
130 REM                B = second number input by the user
140 REM                C = the sum of A and B
150 REM
160 REM     ******************
170 REM     * input A and B *
180 REM     ******************
190 REM
200    INPUT A,B
210 REM     *********************
220 REM     * calculate the sum *
230 REM     *********************
240    LET C= A+B
250 REM     *********************
260 REM     * print the results *
270 REM     *********************
280    PRINT " THE ANSWER IS: ";C
290    GOTO 160
300 END
RUN
```

(a) Program and Output

(b) Structure Chart

(c) Pseudocode

```
DO indefinitely
   Input two numbers
   Calculate the sum of the two
   Output the sum
ENDDO
```

(d) Program Flowchart

Comparisons to Other Versions of BASIC

Applesoft	One less space after the colon (:) in output
HP	No differences
VAX	No differences
TRS-80	No differences
PET/CBM/Commodore 64	No differences
Macintosh	No differences

Figure A-7.1   The GOTO Statement

Line 290 unconditionally branches to line 160, forming a loop. In this case, we have an **infinite loop.** The program will run indefinitely if it is not terminated externally. This situation may be corrected by establishing a condition to test for the end of data. We will discuss conditional branching when we introduce the IF-THEN statement.

The use of the GOTO statement should be avoided if possible. Structured programming does not allow its use. If your version of BASIC has FOR/NEXT and WHILE/WEND statements, there is no reason for using the GOTO.

The ON-GOTO and ON-GOSUB Statement Multiple conditional branching is possible with the ON-GOTO or ON-GOSUB statement. These statements allow a more discriminating form of branching, and are used to code a case structure. They have the following format.

$$\text{line\#} \quad \text{ON} \quad \text{num exp} \left\{ \begin{array}{l} \text{GOTO} \\ \text{GOSUB} \end{array} \right\} \text{list of destination line\#s}$$

where "num exp" is any legal numeric expression. The list of destination line numbers is the list of line numbers separated by commas.

The ON-GOTO or ON-GOSUB statements allow the programmer to specify several line numbers as alternatives, depending on the value of the numeric expression. Standard BASIC truncates the value of the expression to an integer (some versions round it). Often if the result is less than one or greater than the number of arguments in the line-number list, one of two events occurs:

1. The program is terminated and an error message is printed
2. The ON-GOTO or ON-GOSUB is ignored and execution continues with the next sequential statement

An example of the implementation of the ON-GOTO is as follows:

```
10 ON a GOTO 20,70,120
```

This statement is evaluated as follows:

```
If a = 1 GOTO line 20
If a = 2 GOTO line 70
If a = 3 GOTO line 120
```

Any other value results in one of the above events occurring. We will examine the ON-GOSUB statement in more depth in Topic 9 under Creating Menus.

The IF-THEN Statement The IF-THEN statement is used to code the selection structure, which is a type of conditional branching. It has the following format:

$$\text{line\#} \quad \text{IF} \quad \text{cond exp} \left\{ \begin{array}{l} \text{THEN} \\ \text{GOTO} \end{array} \right\} \text{destination line\#}$$

where "cond exp" is any conditional expression that evaluates to either true or false.

A conditional expression has the following format:

expression	relational symbol	expression

```
LIST
10   REM     FIGURE A-7.2
20   REM
30   REM
40   REM
50   REM     *************************************************************
60   REM     * This program demonstrates the execution of the IF-THEN   *
70   REM     * and the GOTO statements to perform iterative operations  *
80   REM     *************************************************************
90   REM
100  REM                Variable definitions
110  REM                *******************
120  REM                A$= continuation prompt
130  REM                A = first number input by the user
140  REM                B = second number input by the user
150  REM                C = product of A and B
160  REM
170  REM     *********************
180  REM     * input A$,A, and B *
190  REM     *********************
200      LET A$ = "Y"
210      IF A$ <> "Y" THEN 360
220      PRINT "WHAT ARE THE VALUES FOR A AND B: ";
230      INPUT A,B
240  REM     ***************
250  REM     * calculate C *
260  REM     ***************
270      LET C= A*B
280  REM     *****************
290  REM     * output results *
300  REM     *****************
310      PRINT "THE ANSWER IS: ";C
320      PRINT
330      PRINT "DO YOU WISH TO CONTINUE (Y/N)";
340      INPUT A$
350      GOTO 210
360 END
Ok
RUN
WHAT ARE THE VALUES FOR A AND B: ? 2,3
THE ANSWER IS:   6

DO YOU WISH TO CONTINUE (Y/N)? Y
WHAT ARE THE VALUES FOR A AND B: ? 1,2
THE ANSWER IS:   2

DO YOU WISH TO CONTINUE (Y/N)? N
Ok
```

(a) Program and Output

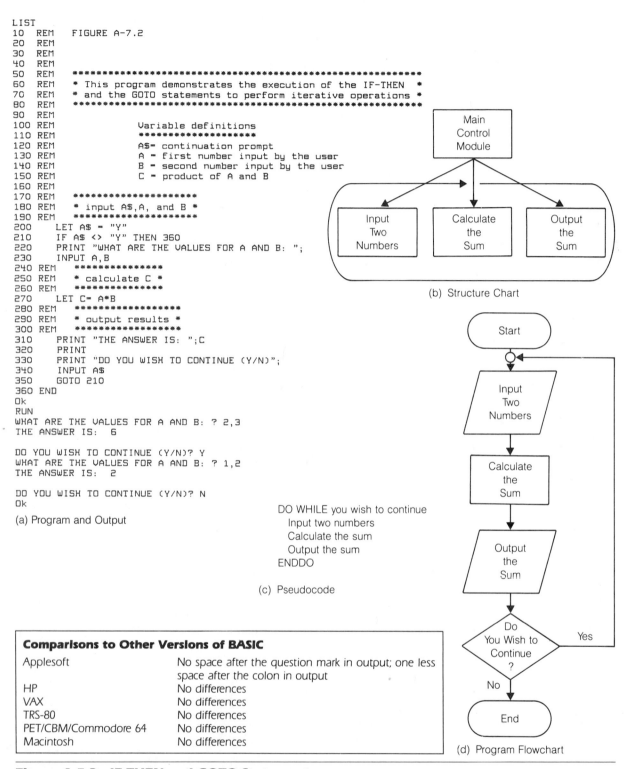

(b) Structure Chart

```
DO WHILE you wish to continue
   Input two numbers
   Calculate the sum
   Output the sum
ENDDO
```

(c) Pseudocode

(d) Program Flowchart

Comparisons to Other Versions of BASIC

Applesoft	No space after the question mark in output; one less space after the colon in output
HP	No differences
VAX	No differences
TRS-80	No differences
PET/CBM/Commodore 64	No differences
Macintosh	No differences

Figure A-7.2 IF-THEN and GOTO Statements

For example, in `10 IF X + 4 < = Y THEN 115`, the `X + 4 < = Y` is the conditional expression.

The IF-THEN statement is used for conditional branching. If the value of the logical condition evaluates to true, control is transferred to the specified line, otherwise the next sequential statement is executed. The IF-THEN is a powerful programming tool. Recall in our discussion of the GOTO the problem of the infinite loop. The solution to that problem using IF-THEN is shown in Figure A-7.2.

This program illustrates how BASIC can "converse" with you. The program prompts you for values for *a* and *b,* performs the calculations, and displays the final results. You may continue with the session by answering *Y* to the prompt. Any other character will terminate the session.

Some versions of BASIC, such as IBM/Microsoft and Apple Macintosh, allow the use of the IF-THEN-ELSE statement, which has the following format:

line#   IF   cond exp THEN clause ELSE clause

where "clause" is any valid BASIC statement or sequence of statements (separated by colons); or it may be the number of a line to branch to.

Using the IF-THEN-ELSE statement can produce programs that are more understandable. Examples of its use follow:

```
80 IF a = b THEN m = 10 ELSE m = 15
60 IF a = b THEN m = 10 ELSE m = 15 : p = 5
30 IF a = b THEN 40 ELSE 60
40 LET m = 10
50 GOTO 80
60 LET m = 15
70 LET p = 5
80 PRINT m, p
```

Programming Loop Structures

Control of a Loop   An important consideration in the construction and execution of loops is control of the loop. We will examine this topic before discussing the various BASIC statements used in writing loop structures. If a loop is "uncontrolled," there is no mechanism to stop the repetitive execution. The loop is infinite, and as seen earlier, this is an undesirable feature in a program.

The previous example illustrated one of several ways to control the execution of loops. The GOTO statement was used to create the loop by branching from the end of the loop to the beginning, and the IF-THEN statement was used to branch out of the loop upon a specified condition.

Loops may be classified as:

1. Input loops
2. Processing loops
3. Counting loops

An input loop is executed each time a new set of data is accepted, and is controlled by the use of special input data known as the **trailer value.** Trailer values, also known as **sentinel**

values, are special end markers. Each time input is read, the program tests to see whether this marker has been read. If so, the program branches out of the loop. Figure A-6.6 made use of the trailer value where the program used a loop to read in employee data. When the employee's hours become negative, the program branches to a PRINT USING statement to print totals. When creating a trailer value, be sure that it is outside the normal range of values for those data. For example, no employee works negative hours; therefore, it is a good trailer value. A simple example of the use of trailer values is Figure A-7.3. Note that the trailer value is negative since it is not possible to make a score lower than zero. The trailer-value test immediately follows the READ statement because the value should not be processed if it is the trailer.

The trailer value is used for batch processing. If the program is designed for interaction with the user, control over the loop can still be exercised in much the same fashion. The method is **user affirmation;** that is, each time data are accepted the user is asked if he or she wishes to continue. Figure A-7.2 is an example of user affirmation. Trailer values may also be used for interactive processing where the user enters the values to signify the end of data input.

Often a processing loop is not controlled by an input value, but rather by some condition on the data that are being processed. Each time the loop is executed the data are tested for the condition. Figure A-7.4 is an example of this. This program determines the number of years it will take for an initial investment to double if invested at 6 percent (compounded annually).

The data to be tested for control of the loop is the future value of the investment: Is it double the initial value? If so, then branch out of the loop; otherwise continue calculations.

A counting loop is a kind of processing loop where execution of the loop is controlled by a counter variable. When the value of the counter reaches a desired value, the loop execution terminates. Before the loop is entered, the counter must be initialized. The counter should not be initialized within the loop or the value will never change. Upon each execution of the loop, the counter is modified (that is, incremented or decremented) and a test is performed to determine whether the counter has reached the desired value. The following partial program illustrates the basic concept:

```
10    n = 1
20    REM ... test counter
30    IF n > 10 THEN 100

   (loop)

80    n = n + 1
90    GOTO 20
100   REM ... end loop
```

Again, note that the counter *n* is initialized outside the loop (line 10) and incremented upon each execution of the loop.

So that more flexibility is added to a program, a **header value** can be read by the program. The header specifies how many data items are to be processed. This concept can be demonstrated by amending Figure A-7.3, as shown in Figure A-7.5.

In Figure A-7.5 note that the counter c will increment to 1 + n; therefore, be careful when using this counter in a later statement. For example, if the counter were used in line 340 to determine the average, the answer would be incorrect unless the statement was modified to:

```
130   LET a = t / (c - 1)
```

The implementation of a loop so far has been with the IF-THEN and GOTO statements. However, BASIC provides a set of statements specially designed for iterative looping: the FOR and NEXT statements.

```
LIST
10   REM      FIGURE A-7.3
20   REM
30   REM
40   REM
50   REM      *************************************************************
60   REM      * This program reads in a set of test scores and calculates the *
70   REM      * average score, demonstrating the use of the trailer value.    *
80   REM      *************************************************************
90   REM
100  REM              Variable definitions
110  REM              *******************
120  REM              S =individual test score
130  REM              T =sum of all test scores
140  REM              N =number of test scores
150  REM              A =average test score
160  REM
170  REM      *******************
180  REM      * input T,N,and S *
190  REM      *******************
200  LET T= 0
210  LET N= 0
220  DATA 90, 89.5,75,66.7,-99
230      READ S
240      IF S<0 THEN 310
250  REM      ***********************
260  REM      * calculate T,N, and A *
270  REM      ***********************
280      LET T= T+S
290      LET N= N+1
300      GOTO 230
310  LET A= T/N
320  REM      *******************
330  REM      * print the result *
340  REM      *******************
350  PRINT "THE AVERAGE SCORE IS: ";A
360  END
Ok
RUN
THE AVERAGE SCORE IS:  80.3
Ok
```

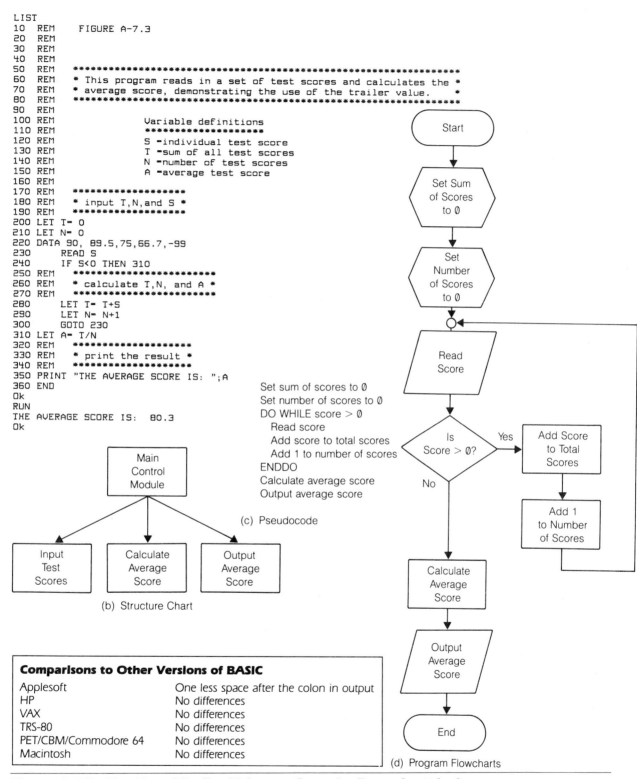

```
Set sum of scores to 0
Set number of scores to 0
DO WHILE score > 0
    Read score
    Add score to total scores
    Add 1 to number of scores
ENDDO
Calculate average score
Output average score
```

(c) Pseudocode

(b) Structure Chart

(d) Program Flowcharts

Comparisons to Other Versions of BASIC

Applesoft	One less space after the colon in output
HP	No differences
VAX	No differences
TRS-80	No differences
PET/CBM/Commodore 64	No differences
Macintosh	No differences

Figure A-7.3   The Use of Trailer Values to Stop the Execution of a Loop

```
LIST
10  REM    FIGURE A-7.4
20  REM
30  REM
40  REM
50  REM    **************************************************************
60  REM    * This program calculates the future value of an investment *
70  REM    * and displays the number of years it takes for the invest- *
80  REM    * ment to double.                                           *
90  REM    **************************************************************
100 REM
110 REM                Variable definitions
120 REM                ********************
130 REM                P - present value of the investment
140 REM                F - future value of the investment
150 REM                Y - years it takes for investment to double
160 REM                I - interest on investment each year
170 REM
180 REM    ***********
190 REM    * input P *
200 REM    ***********
210 PRINT "WHAT IS THE PRESENT VALUE OF THE INVESTMENT ";
220 INPUT P
230 LET F=P
240 LET Y=0
250 REM    ********************
260 REM    * calculate F and Y *
270 REM    ********************
280     IF F>=2*P THEN 330
290     LET I= F * .06
300     LET F=F+I
310     LET Y=Y+1
320     GOTO 280
330 REM    ***********
340 REM    * output Y *
350 REM    ***********
360 PRINT "THE NUMBER OF YEARS TO DOUBLE IS: ";Y
370 END
Ok
RUN
WHAT IS THE PRESENT VALUE OF THE INVESTMENT ? 1000
THE NUMBER OF YEARS TO DOUBLE IS:  12
Ok
```

(a) Program and Output

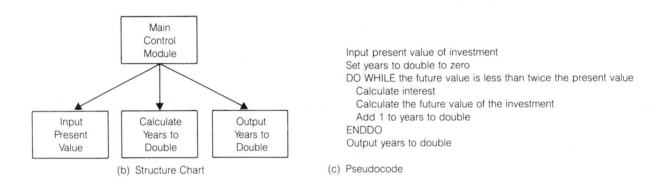

(b) Structure Chart

Input present value of investment
Set years to double to zero
DO WHILE the future value is less than twice the present value
    Calculate interest
    Calculate the future value of the investment
    Add 1 to years to double
ENDDO
Output years to double

(c) Pseudocode

Figure A-7.4 The Use of Data Being Processed to Stop the Execution of a Loop

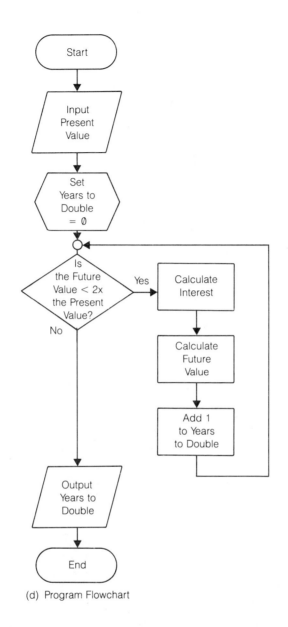

(d) Program Flowchart

Comparisons to Other Versions of BASIC

Applesoft	One less space after the colon in output
HP	No differences
VAX	No differences
TRS-80	No differences
PET/CBM/Commodore 64	No differences
Macintosh	No differences

Figure A-7.4 (continued)

```
LIST
10   REM    FIGURE A-7.5
20   REM
30   REM
40   REM
50   REM    ***********************************************************************
60   REM    * This program reads in the header value which controls the           *
70   REM    * processing loop. When the counter value equals the header, the      *
80   REM    * loop terminates and the average score is displayed.                 *
90   REM    ***********************************************************************
100  REM
110  REM                 Variable definitions
120  REM                 ********************
130  REM                 T =sum of all scores
140  REM                 N =number of scores (this is the header value)
150  REM                 C =counter
160  REM                 S =individual test score
170  REM                 A =average score
180  REM
190  REM    *****************
200  REM    * input N and S *
210  REM    *****************
220  LET T=0
230  LET C=1
240  DATA 4,90,89.5,75,66.7
250  READ N
260      IF C>N THEN 340
270      READ S
280  REM    *********************
290  REM    * calculate average *
300  REM    *********************
310      LET T=T+S
320      LET C=C+1
330      GOTO 260
340  LET A=T/N
350  REM    *****************
360  REM    * output result *
370  REM    *****************
380  PRINT "THE AVERAGE SCORE IS: ";A
390  END
Ok
RUN
THE AVERAGE SCORE IS:  80.3
Ok
```

(a) Program and Output

(b) Structure Chart

```
Set sum of scores to 0
Set counter to 1
Input header value and scores
Read header value
DO WHILE counter ≤ header value
   Read score
   Add score to sum of scores
   Add 1 to counter
ENDDO
Calculate average score
Output average score
```

(c) Pseudocode

Comparisons to Other Versions of BASIC

Applesoft	One less space after the colon in output
HP	No differences
VAX	No differences
TRS-80	No differences
PET/CBM/Commodore 64	No differences
Macintosh	No differences

Figure A-7.5   The Use of Header Value to Stop the Execution of a Loop

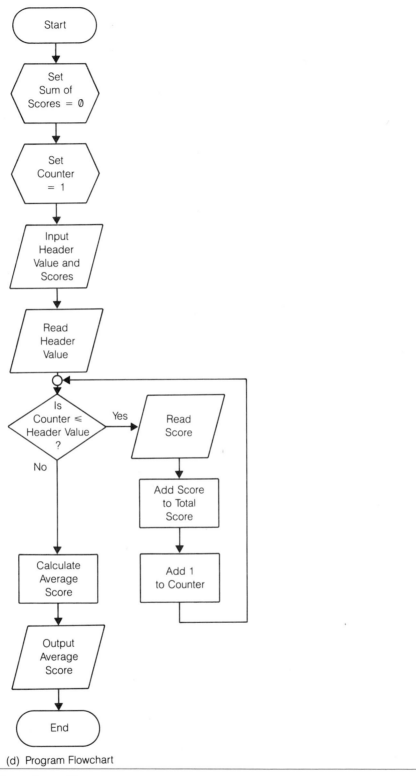

(d) Program Flowchart

Figure A-7.5 (continued)

The FOR and NEXT Statements   One way of coding a loop structure is to use FOR and NEXT statements. These statements allow for the controlled repetition of a set of statements. The FOR statement has the following format:

line#   FOR variable = initial value TO terminal value [STEP size]

where variable is the loop variable. Initial value is the starting value for the variable and terminal value is the ending value.

The STEP size is optional. If the step size is omitted it is assumed to be +1. The FOR and NEXT statements surround the set of statements composing the loop. The program will execute this loop until the loop variable becomes greater than (or less than, if a negative step size is used) the terminal value, upon which the program branches to the statement immediately following the NEXT statement. The NEXT statement has the following format:

line#   NEXT variable

where the variable must be the same as in the FOR statement.

The loop created by the FOR and NEXT statements is in effect a counting loop. A simple loop follows:

```
FOR c = 1 to 5   STEP 1
  PRINT c
NEXT c
```

The result would be:

```
1
2
3
4
5
```

Suppose we want to decrement the variable **c**. We can do this by using a negative step size:

```
FOR c = 5 to 1   STEP -1
  PRINT c
NEXT c
```

The result would be:

```
5
4
3
2
1
```

There are a few rules to remember when using the step size:

When the step size is positive, the initial value must be less than the terminal value.

When the step size is negative, the initial value must be greater than the terminal value.

A step value of zero may never be used.

The FOR-NEXT loop performs a pretest, that is; the value of the loop variable is tested before the loop is executed. If the value is outside the range defined by the initial and terminal values, the loop is ignored.

The program in Figure A-7.5 has been modified using FOR and NEXT statements, as shown in Figure A-7.6. The loop within the program (lines 250-280) will execute until the loop variable *i* has exceeded the header value *n*. Line 250 initializes the loop variable to 1 and tests to see whether the value of the loop variable exceeds the header value. In this case it does not, so the loop is executed. When the NEXT statement is encountered, the index variable is incremented by 1 (the default step size since the STEP option was not specified) and branches back to the FOR statement (line 250).

FOR-NEXT Loops and Transfer of Control   Certain factors must be remembered when using FOR-NEXT loops with transfer statements. Any of the forms of branching discussed earlier can be made from one statement to another statement within the FOR-NEXT loop, or from a statement within the loop to another statement outside the loop. Branching into loops from an outside statement cannot be made. In other words, the previously discussed transfer statements (GOTO, IF-THEN, ON-GOTO) cannot transfer control to any statement within a loop of which the transfer statements are not a part. For example:

```
200   GOTO 500

400   FOR i = 1 TO 5
500       a = a + 1

900   NEXT i
```

is invalid. However, the following are valid:

```
 300   REM ...transfer to outside of the loop
 400   FOR i = 1 TO 5
 500       a = a + 1
 600       IF a = 3 GOTO 1000
 900   NEXT i
1000   PRINT i

 200   REM ...transfer within the outer loop
 300   FOR i = 1 TO 5
 400     IF i = 2 THEN 800
 500     FOR j = 1 TO 3
 600         PRINT "i=";i,"j=";j
 700     NEXT j
 800   NEXT i
 900   END
```

Nested Loops   A loop may contain one or more loops within it; however, caution must be exercised by the programmer. The inner loop must be completely contained within the outer loop. Loops may not overlap. Also, each loop must contain unique loop variables. Figure A-7.7 demonstrates a valid nesting. Note the indentation of loops for readability. The inner loop will execute three times for every one time the outer loop executes.

```
LIST
10  REM    FIGURE A-7.6
20  REM
30  REM
40  REM
50  REM    ************************************************************
60  REM    * This program reads in a header value which controls the  *
70  REM    * number of times the processing loop executes. When the loop *
80  REM    * terminates, the average score is displayed.               *
90  REM    ************************************************************
100 REM
110 REM              Variable definitions
120 REM              ********************
130 REM              T =sum of all scores
140 REM              N =number of scores
150 REM              S =individual scores
160 REM              I =counter
170 REM              A =average score
180 REM
190 REM    ****************
200 REM    * input N and S *
210 REM    ****************
220 LET T=0
230 DATA 4,90,89.5,75,66.7
240 READ N
250 FOR I=1 TO N
260     READ S
270     LET T=T+S
280 NEXT I
290 REM    ********************
300 REM    * calculate average *
310 REM    ********************
320 LET A=T/N
330 REM    ****************
340 REM    * output result *
350 REM    ****************
360 PRINT "THE AVERAGE SCORE IS:  ";A
370 END
Ok
RUN
THE AVERAGE SCORE IS:  80.3
Ok
```

(a) Program and Output

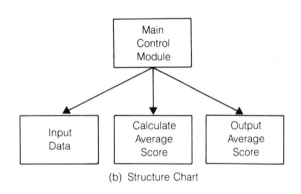

(b) Structure Chart

```
Set sum of scores to 0
Read header value
DO WHILE I < header value
   Read score
   Add score to sum of scores
   Next I
ENDDO
Calculate average score
Output average score
```

(c) Pseudocode

Figure A-7.6   The Use of FOR and NEXT Statements to Control a Loop

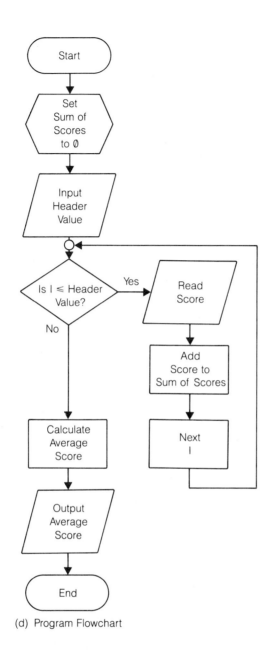

(d) Program Flowchart

Comparisons to Other Versions of BASIC	
Applesoft	One less space after the colon in output
HP	No differences
VAX	No differences
TRS-80	No differences
PET/CBM/Commodore 64	No differences
Macintosh	No differences

Figure A-7.6   (continued)

```
*LIST
10  REM    FIGURE A-7.7
20  REM
30  REM
40  REM
50  REM    *************************************************
60  REM    * This program displays the number of times     *
70  REM    * a loop is executed.                            *
80  REM    *************************************************
90  REM
100 REM                Variable definitions
110 REM                ********************
120 REM                I -first counter
130 REM                J -second counter
140 REM
150 FOR I-1 TO 2
160    FOR J-1 TO 3
170 REM    *********************
180 REM    * output I and J *
190 REM    *********************
200        PRINT "I-";I,"J-";J
210    NEXT J
220    PRINT
230 NEXT I
240 END
Ok
RUN
I- 1            J- 1
I- 1            J- 2
I- 1            J- 3

I- 2            J- 1
I- 2            J- 2
I- 2            J- 3

Ok
```

(a) Program and Output

```
For I = 1 to 2
   For J = 1 to 3
      Output I and J
   Next J
Next I
```

(b) Pseudocode

(c) Program Flowchart

Comparisons to Other Versions of BASIC	
Applesoft	No spaces after equal sign
HP	No differences
VAX	No differences
TRS-80	No differences
PET/CBM/Commodore 64	No differences
Macintosh	No differences

Figure A-7.7   Nested FOR and NEXT Statements

The following is an example of invalid nesting, which results in an execution error:

```
10    FOR i = 1 TO 2
20       FOR j = 1 TO 3
30          PRINT "i=";i,"j=";j
40       NEXT i
50       PRINT
60    NEXT j
```

A common application of loops, nested loops, and specifically the FOR-NEXT construction is the manipulation of arrays (which will be discussed in Topic 8).

The WHILE and WEND Statements   Often when coding a program you may wish to tell the computer to process certain statements repeatedly while a specific condition is true. Some versions of BASIC, such as the IBM/Microsoft version, provide this capability with the WHILE and WEND statements. Their format is as follows:

WHILE expression
- •
- •
- •
(loop statements)
- •
- •
- •
WEND

where expression is any numeric expression. The loop statements are executed repetitively while the expression is true. For example, the use of a trailer value to control an input loop as illustrated in Figure A-7.3 could be coded as follows:

```
 10 LET T = 0
 20 LET N = 0
 30 DATA 90, 89.5, 75, 66.7, -99
 40 READ S
 50 WHILE  S = > 0
 60    LET  T = T + S
 70    LET  N = N + 1
 80    READ S
 90 WEND
100 LET A = T/N
110 PRINT "THE AVERAGE SCORE IS: ";A
```

The WHILE and WEND statements are very useful. You should use them whenever possible to control loops. They improve the clarity of programs.

Summing Up

☐ Program control may be described in terms of four components: the simple sequence structure, the selection structure, the loop structure, and the case structure.

☐ Control is transferred from one point in a program to another through the use of branching. In BASIC, unconditional branching is written with the GOTO statement.

☐ An unconditional branching statement transfers control whenever it is encountered.

☐ A conditional branch is executed only if a certain logical condition is satisfied. In BASIC, conditional branching is written with the IF-THEN-ELSE and ON-GOTO statements.

☐ A loop is a set of statements that are performed repeatedly. The loop may be terminated either when all existing data are processed, or after a fixed number of iterations.

☐ The FOR and NEXT statements are one method used to control a program loop. They automatically increment a counter and test whether the desired number of iterations have been completed. The counter may be incremented in every iteration by any desired value, positive or negative.

☐ The WHILE and WEND statements are available on some versions of BASIC. They are used to control a loop that is to continue its repetition while a certain condition is true.

Debugging Exercises

Find and remove the bugs in the following program segments:

```
1. 10 ON F$ GOSUB 20, 70, 110
2. 30 IF (A < 10) AND (10 < A) THEN 80
3. 10 IF X = Y THEN C = 5
   20 ELSE C = 10
4. 10 FOR C = 5 TO 1 STEP 1
   20 PRINT C
   30 NEXT C
5. 10 FOR C = M TO E
   20 PRINT C
6. 10 FOR C = M TO Z STEP 0
   20 PRINT C
   30 NEXT M
7. 10 FOR C = 1 TO 5 STEP -1
   20 PRINT C
   30 NEXT C
8. 100 GOTO 300
   290 FOR I + 1 TO N
   300 B = B + 2
   310 NEXT I
9. 10 FOR J = 1 TO 5
   20     FOR K = 1 TO 8
   30         PRINT J, K
   40     NEXT J
   50 NEXT K
```

Hands-on Exercises

1. Write a program that will compute the compounded value of a sum of money invested at compound interest. The program should assume that the interest is compounded yearly. So that any initial investment, interest rate, and number of years to compound (length of the investment) can be used, you should design the program to accept these variables interactively with the INPUT statement. The program should ask you if you want to compute more compounded values and ask for more input values if you respond with a yes. Draw a structure chart of your program and prepare pseudocode or a program flowchart. Document your program internally with REM statements.

2. Write a program that allows your computer to act as a cash register. The program should accept the price for each item that a customer is buying and then compute a total for the sale, including 4 percent sales tax. Next, the program should accept the amount the customer gives to the sales clerk and compute the amount of

change to be returned to the customer. After each sale, the program should be able to display the total amount of sales for all customers processed. This total sales amount should only be displayed if the sales clerk asks the computer to do so. Draw a structure chart of your program and prepare pseudocode or a program flowchart. Document your program internally with REM statements.

Topic 8: Arrays

Array Elements and Subscripts

An **array** is a group of related data items identified by a single name. An array is used when it is necessary to process a large amount of information more than once. In a sense, the array is a storage area containing data to be referenced each time the program needs to operate on those data. An array can be visualized as a table or list of data items where each entry in the table is an array element. The array element is indexed by a unique identifier that references the element by position. This is done through the use of **subscripts.** In previous discussions every variable used was unsubscripted. The following are unsubscripted variables and their values:

Variable	Value
A	11
B	2
C	12
D	5
E	4

Each value has its own unique name. Looking at this example we see that these values can be put into a table as follows:

Table A

11
2
12
5
4

In BASIC, this table is called an array with a single name—in this case, A. Now we need a way to identify each element in the array. This is done with subscripted variables. A subscripted variable is of the form:

$A(i)$

where A is the array name and i is the subscript enclosed in parentheses. The subscript can be any numeric expression, where the value of the expression will be truncated to an integer. Therefore, the following are valid:

A(i)
A(l)
A(i*2)
A(i/3)

Another name for a subscript is an **index** because its function is to index (or reference by position) an array element.

Looking at the table again we can assign unique names to each element:

A(1)	11
A(2)	2
A(3)	12
A(4)	5
A(5)	4

where A(1) references the first element, A(2) references the second element, and so on. Therefore, the subscripted variables have the following values:

A(1) = 11
A(2) = 2
A(3) = 12
A(4) = 5
A(5) = 4

The DIM Statement

The DIM statement is used by the programmer to specify the dimensions or bounds of the array so that BASIC can reserve storage for the array. The DIM statement has the following format:

line#	DIM	list of subscripted variables

where the subscripted variables are separated by commas.

Each subscripted variable represents an array name in which the program may specify the number of subscripts and the magnitude of each subscript (the subscript must be a numeric or integer constant). For example:

```
10   DIM A(20),B(3,4)
```

declares the arrays A and B. A has 1 column and up to 21 rows (counting from 0). The array B is a two-dimensional array and may have up to 4 rows and 5 columns.

Because BASIC allows subscripts of an array to range from zero (not one) to the system limit, the array B in the DIM statement just presented may hold up to 20 elements:

B(0,0)	B(0,1)	B(0,2)	B(0,3)	B(0,4)
B(1,0)	B(1,1)	B(1,2)	B(1,3)	B(1,4)
B(2,0)	B(2,1)	B(2,2)	B(2,3)	B(2,4)
B(3,0)	B(3,1)	B(3,2)	B(3,3)	B(3,4)

An important note is that BASIC automatically reserves storage for arrays with a maximum of 11 elements for one-dimensional arrays and 121 elements for two-dimensional arrays;

that is A(10) and B(10,10). Therefore, the DIM statement should be used if the arrays are to exceed this maximum amount of storage. If an array is referenced with a subscript not within the bounds declared, BASIC will print an error message.

BASIC provides an OPTION BASE statement, which allows the programmer to set the lower boundary of arrays in the program. If the programmer does not wish to have arrays with zero as the lower boundary, the OPTION BASE provides a vehicle to adjust it. The OPTION BASE statement has the following format:

```
line#    OPTION BASE    lbound
```

where lbound is the desired lower boundary for the arrays used in the program. For example:

```
10 OPTION BASE 1
20 DIM A(10),B(5)
```

causes both arrays A and B to have a lower boundary of 1.

Input/Output of Arrays

Input and output of arrays may be done explicitly or through the use of looping techniques. For example, the following explicitly reads in each element array:

```
10   READ   A(1),A(2),A(3),A(4),A(5)
```

whereas the following uses a looping technique to perform the same operation:

```
10   FOR i = 1 TO 5
20      READ A(i)
30   NEXT i
```

The FOR-NEXT construct is a useful tool for processing arrays. The looping technique can also be used for printing the array. For example, the following displays the array just read:

```
40   FOR i = 1 to 5
50      PRINT A(i)
60   NEXT i
```

Two-dimensional arrays are handled in a similar fashion, but nested loops are needed to read and print two-dimensional arrays. Figure A-8.1 demonstrates the I/O of two-dimensional arrays. This array can be visualized as a table:

10	15
7	2
9	8

The program in Figure A-8.2 reads in the name and four exam scores for each student, calculates the average for each student, and calculates the class average for each exam as well as the total class average. This figure makes use of several arrays. The arrays displayed in the output are as follows:

1. The name array, n$(10), which is a character string array
2. The scores array, s(10,4), which is a two-dimensional numeric array

```
LIST
10   REM    FIGURE A-8.1
20   REM
30   REM
40   REM
50   REM    *****************************************************
60   REM    * This program demonstrates the input and output of *
70   REM    * two-dimensional arrays.                           *
80   REM    *****************************************************
90   REM
100  REM              Variable definitions
110  REM              ********************
120  REM              I -row number
130  REM              J -column number
140  REM              A -array name
150  REM
160  REM    **************
170  REM    * input data *
180  REM    **************
190 DATA 10,7,9,15,2,8
200 FOR J-1 TO 2
210    FOR I-1 TO 3
220       READ A(I,J)
230    NEXT I
240 NEXT J
250 REM    ****************
260 REM    * output array *
270 REM    ****************
280 FOR J-1 TO 2
290    FOR I-1 TO 3
300       PRINT "A(";I;",";J;")=";A(I,J)
310    NEXT I
320 NEXT J
330 END
Ok
RUN
A( 1 , 1 )= 10
A( 2 , 1 )= 7
A( 3 , 1 )= 9
A( 1 , 2 )= 15
A( 2 , 2 )= 2
A( 3 , 2 )= 8
Ok
```

(a) Program and Output

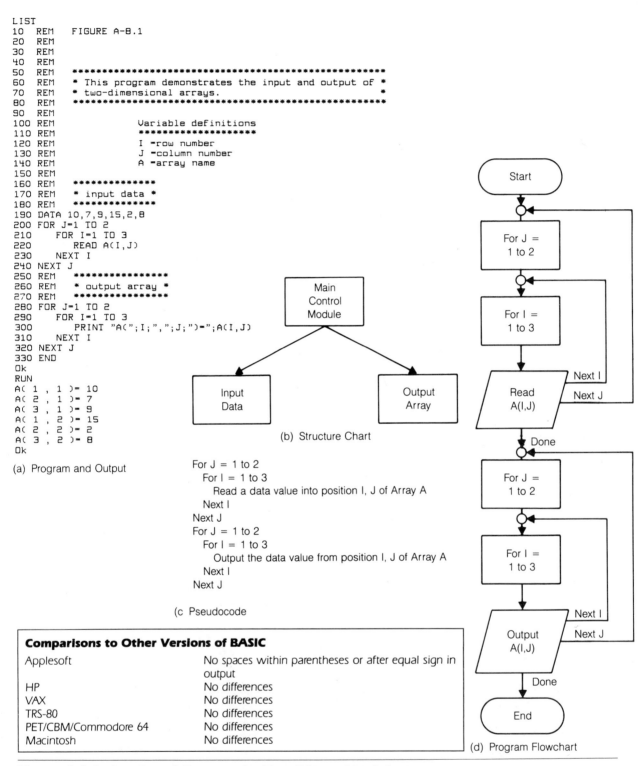

(b) Structure Chart

```
For J = 1 to 2
   For I = 1 to 3
      Read a data value into position I, J of Array A
   Next I
Next J
For J = 1 to 2
   For I = 1 to 3
      Output the data value from position I, J of Array A
   Next I
Next J
```

(c Pseudocode

(d) Program Flowchart

Comparisons to Other Versions of BASIC

Applesoft	No spaces within parentheses or after equal sign in output
HP	No differences
VAX	No differences
TRS-80	No differences
PET/CBM/Commodore 64	No differences
Macintosh	No differences

Figure A-8.1   Input and Output of a Two-Dimensional Array

```
LIST
10   REM    FIGURE A-8.2
20   REM
30   REM
40   REM
50   REM    ***********************************************************************
60   REM    * This program reads in the name and four exam scores for each        *
70   REM    * student, and calculates the averages for each student and the       *
75   REM    * class.                                                              *
80   REM    ***********************************************************************
90   REM
100  REM                 Variable definitions
110  REM                 ********************
120  REM                 N -number of students
130  REM                 I -row number
140  REM                 J -column number
150  REM                 N$-student names
155  REM                 S -scores for each test for all students
160  REM                 T1-sum of scores for each student
170  REM                 T2-sum of scores for each test
180  REM                 T3-total sum of all scores
190  REM                 S -scores for each test for all students
200  REM                 A1-average for each student
210  REM                 A2-class average for each test
220  REM                 A3-overall class average
230  REM
240  REM    *************************
250  REM    * main control module *
260  REM    *************************
270   GOSUB 330
280   GOSUB 380
290   GOSUB 490
300   GOSUB 590
310   GOSUB 730
320  END
330  REM    *************************
340  REM    * initialization module *
350  REM    *************************
360  DIM S(20,20)
370  RETURN
380  REM    ****************************
390  REM    * input student data module *
400  REM    ****************************
410  READ N
420  FOR I-1 TO N
430     READ N$(I)
440     FOR J-1 TO 4
450        READ S(I,J)
460     NEXT J
470  NEXT I
480  RETURN
490  REM    ***********************************
500  REM    * calculate student averages module *
510  REM    ***********************************
520  FOR I-1 TO N
530     FOR J-1 TO 4
540        LET T1(I)-T1(I) + S(I,J)
550     NEXT J
560     LET A1(I)-T1(I)/4
570  NEXT I
580  RETURN
590  REM    *********************************
600  REM    * calculate class averages module *
610  REM    *********************************
```

Figure A-8.2   The Use of Arrays to Calculate Student and Class Averages

```
620 FOR I=1 TO N
630     FOR J=1 TO 4
640         LET T2(J)=T2(J) +S(I,J)
650     NEXT J
660     LET T3=T3+A1(I)
670 NEXT I
680 FOR J=1 TO 4
690     LET A2(J)=T2(J)/N
700 NEXT J
710 LET A3=T3/N
720 RETURN
730 REM    *****************************
740 REM    * output grade report module *
750 REM    *****************************
760 PRINT TAB(25);"GRADE REPORT"
770 PRINT
780 PRINT "NAME            TEST1    TEST2    TEST3    TEST4    AVERAGE"
790 PRINT
800 FOR I=1 TO N
810     PRINT USING"\                \    ###      ###      ";N$(I),S(I,1),S(I,2);
820     PRINT USING "###     ###     ###";S(I,3),S(I,4),A1(I)
830 NEXT I
840 PRINT
850 PRINT USING "CLASS AVERAGE      ###      ###      ###      ";A2(1),A2(2),A2(3);
860 PRINT USING "###     ###";A2(4),A3
870 RETURN
880 DATA 10,JB ANTHONY,90,92,89,100,RS BROWN,80,86,90,92
890 DATA JM CHRISTIAN,100,98,97,99,FL HARRIS,85,84,92,95
900 DATA BR MARTIN,62,72,59,82,RA MEADOWS,47,62,50,70
910 DATA JJ PATRICK,75,82,78,60,SR SMITH,59,85,72,80
920 DATA TW TURNER,89,94,90,93,KH WONG,100,100,99,100
Ok
RUN
                          GRADE REPORT

NAME              TEST1     TEST2     TEST3     TEST4     AVERAGE

JB ANTHONY          90        92        89       100        93
RS BROWN            80        86        90        92        87
JM CHRISTIAN       100        98        97        99        99
FL HARRIS           85        84        92        95        89
BR MARTIN           62        72        59        82        69
RA MEADOWS          47        62        50        70        57
JJ PATRICK          75        82        78        60        74
SR SMITH            59        85        72        80        74
TW TURNER           89        94        90        93        92
KH WONG            100       100        99       100       100

CLASS AVERAGE       79        86        82        87        83
Ok
```

(a) Program and Output

(b) Structure Chart

Figure A-8.2 (continued)

Main control module
    Do initialization module
    Do input student data module
    Do calculate student averages module
    Do calculate class averages module
    Do output grade report module

Initialization module
    Specify dimensions for array S

Input student data module
    For I = 1 to N
      read student name
      For J = 1 to 4
        read student score
      Next J
    Next I

Calculate student average module
    For I = 1 to N
      For J = 1 to 4
        Add score to sum of scores
      Next J
      Calculate student average
    Next I

Calculate class average module
    For I = 1 to N
      For J = 1 to 4
        Add scores to sum of scores for each test
      Next J
      Add sum of scores to total score
    Next I
    For J = 1 to 4
      Calculate class average for each test
    Next J
    Calculate overall class average

Output grade report module
    For I = 1 to N
      Output student name, score 1, score 2, score 3, score 4, average
    Next I
      Output class average for each test and overall class average

(c) Pseudocode

Comparisons to Other Versions of BASIC	
Applesoft	No PRINT USING facility
HP	PRINT USING statements should have semicolon before argument list
VAX	No differences
TRS-80	No PRINT USING facility
PET/CBM/Commodore 64	No differences
Macintosh	No differences

Figure A-8.2 (continued)

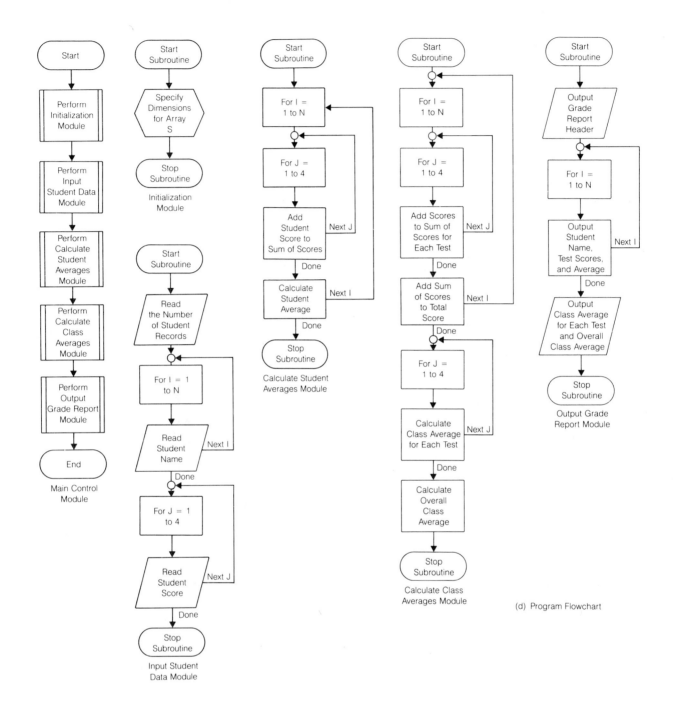

Main Control
Module

Initialization
Module

Input Student
Data Module

Calculate Student
Averages Module

Calculate Class
Averages Module

Output Grade
Report Module

(d) Program Flowchart

3. The student average array, a1(10), which contains the average score for each student
4. The class average array, a2(4), which contains the average of each test

The figure demonstrates that any information displayed in tabular form (such as reports, statements, registers, and journals) can be stored in arrays. Processing of these data is simplified because the data can be referred to several times without having to be reread.

Processing Arrays

Arrays are very powerful tools in BASIC, and with efficient methods such as looping techniques for searching, sorting, copying and so on, programming can be minimal and effective. This section looks at two common techniques in array processing: searching and sorting.

Searching Arrays   In most applications it is necessary to search an array to locate a desired value. Discussed here are two types of searches: linear and binary.

A **linear search** is similar to a table look-up; that is, the search begins by looking at the first element of the array. If this element is not the value desired, the second element is examined. The search continues in a serial fashion until the value desired is found or the end of the array is encountered. Figure A-8.3 demonstrates a linear search. The search would be visualized as follows:

a(1)	7	— 1st look
a(2)	3	— 2nd look
a(3)	5	— 3rd look
a(4)	2	— 4th look
a(5)	6	

A **binary search** requires that the elements be in ascending or descending order. The search begins by looking at the middle element in the array. In effect, the array is divided in half, hence the name *binary*. The search determines whether the value is in the lower half (that is, the value desired is less than the value of the middle element) or in the upper half. The appropriate half of the array is then searched by looking at the middle element of that half, again dividing the array into equal parts. The search continues until the value is found or it is determined that the value does not exist in the array. Figure A-8.4 demonstrates a binary search.

The search would be visualized as follows:

a(1)	1	
a(2)	2	— 2nd look
a(3)	4	— 3rd look
a(4)	9	— 4th look
a(5)	11	— 1st look
a(6)	15	
a(7)	16	
a(8)	20	
a(9)	23	
a(10)	25	

```
LIST
10  REM    FIGURE A-8.3
20  REM
30  REM
40  REM
50  REM    *******************************************************
60  REM    * This program demonstrates a linear search technique. *
70  REM    *******************************************************
80  REM
90  REM              Variable definitions
100 REM              ******************
110 REM              V =the value to be searched for
120 REM              N =number of values in array
130 REM              I =row number
140 REM              A =array name
150 REM
160 REM    ****************
170 REM    * input values *
180 REM    ****************
190 DATA 7,3,5,2,6
200 LET V=2
210 LET N=5
220 FOR I= 1 TO N
230    READ A(I)
240 NEXT I
250 REM    ****************
260 REM    * search for V *
270 REM    ****************
280 FOR I=1 TO N
290    IF A(I)=V THEN 320
300 NEXT I
310 PRINT "VALUE";V;"IS NOT IN THE ARRAY."
320 PRINT "A(";I;") CONTAINS THE VALUE ";V
330 END
Ok
RUN
A( 4 ) CONTAINS THE VALUE  2
Ok
```

(a) Program and Output

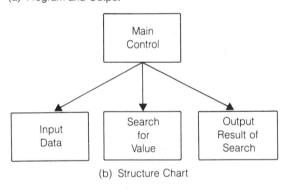

(b) Structure Chart

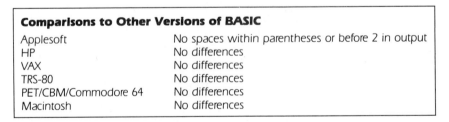

Comparisons to Other Versions of BASIC	
Applesoft	No spaces within parentheses or before 2 in output
HP	No differences
VAX	No differences
TRS-80	No differences
PET/CBM/Commodore 64	No differences
Macintosh	No differences

Figure A-8.3   A Linear Search

Input the data value to be searched for
Input the number of data values in the array
DO WHILE there are more data values to be read
    Read a data value into an array position
ENDDO
Do for each position in the array
    If the data value being searched for is in this array position
        Output the array position of the data value
    ENDIF
ENDDO
If the data value being searched for is not found
    Output a message saying the value is not in the array
ENDIF

(c) Pseudocode

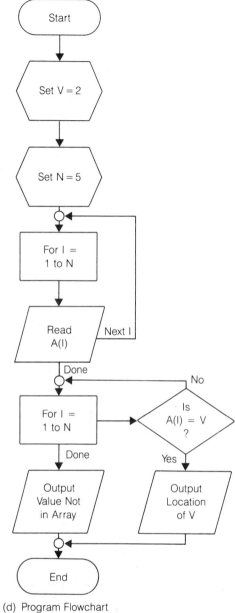

(d) Program Flowchart

Figure A-8.3 (continued)

```
LIST
10   REM FIGURE A-8.4
20   REM
30   REM
40   REM
50   REM   *********************************************
60   REM   * This program demonstrates a binary search. *
70   REM   *********************************************
80   REM
90   REM                Variable definitions
100  REM                ********************
110  REM        M =the subscript of the array value currently being
120  REM            searched
130  REM        T =the subscript of the highest value in the range current-
112  rem            ly being searched
140  REM        B =the subscript of the lowest value in the range current-
150  REM            ly being searched
160  REM        N =number of values to be searched
170  REM        V =value to be searched for
180  REM        A =array name
190  REM
200  REM    ****************
210  REM    * input values *
220  REM    ****************
230  DATA 1,2,4,9,11,15,16,20,23,25
240  LET B=1
250  LET N=10
260  LET T=N
270  LET V=9
280  FOR I=1 TO N
290     READ A(I)
300  NEXT I
310  REM    ****************
320  REM    * search for V *
330  REM    ****************
340     LET M=INT((B+T)/2)
350     IF A(M)=V THEN 450
360     IF B>T THEN 470
370     IF V<A(M) THEN 400
380     LET B=M+1
390     GOTO 310
400     LET T=M-1
410     GOTO 310
420  REM    *****************
430  REM    * output results *
440  REM    *****************
450  PRINT "A(";M;")CONTAINS THE VALUE";V
460  GOTO 480
470  PRINT "VALUE";V;"IS NOT IN THE ARRAY."
480  END
Ok
RUN
A( 4 )CONTAINS THE VALUE 9
Ok
```

(a) Program and Output

Comparisons to Other Versions of BASIC

Applesoft	No spaces within parentheses or before 9 in output
HP	No differences
VAX	No differences
TRS-80	No differences
PET/CBM/Commodore 64	No differences
Macintosh	No differences

Figure A-8.4   A Binary Search

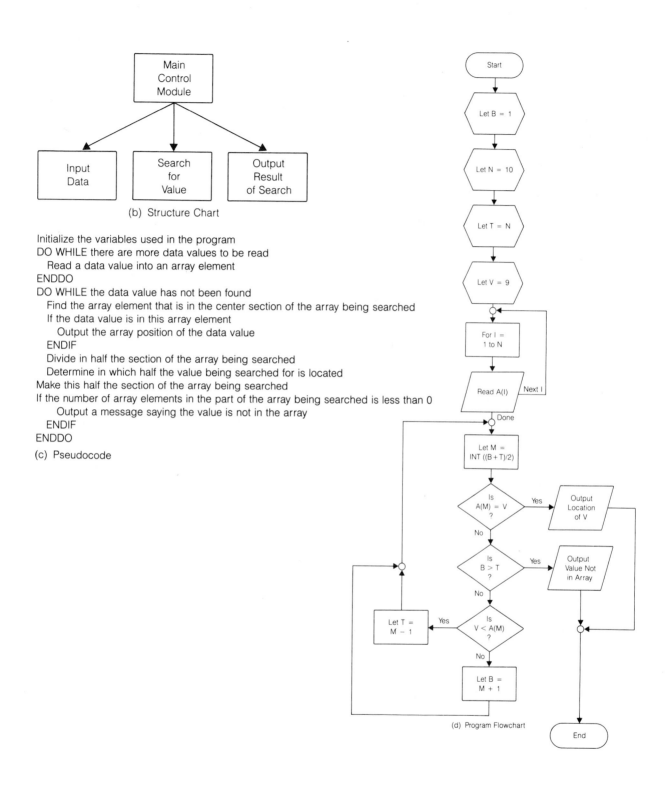

(b) Structure Chart

Initialize the variables used in the program
DO WHILE there are more data values to be read
　Read a data value into an array element
ENDDO
DO WHILE the data value has not been found
　Find the array element that is in the center section of the array being searched
　If the data value is in this array element
　　Output the array position of the data value
　ENDIF
　Divide in half the section of the array being searched
　Determine in which half the value being searched for is located
Make this half the section of the array being searched
If the number of array elements in the part of the array being searched is less than 0
　　Output a message saying the value is not in the array
　ENDIF
ENDDO

(c) Pseudocode

(d) Program Flowchart

If the array is in ascending or descending sequence, binary searches are much more efficient for searching large arrays than are linear searches. Linear searches must look at every value in the array until the value sought is found. Binary searches use far fewer looks to find the value. For example, a binary search using only 12 looks can find a single value in an array containing 4,000 elements!

Sorting Arrays   Another useful processing technique is the sorting of arrays. There are many techniques for sorting where the technique chosen depends on some characteristic of the array (such as size).

The **bubble sort** is a simple technique used to sort array data into ascending or descending order. The sort begins with the first array element being compared to the second. If the elements are out of order, then they are switched. If the array is to be sorted in ascending order, then the largest element is pushed to the bottom, letting the smaller elements "bubble" to the top. Figure A-8.5 demonstrates the bubble sort.

The sorting process is as follows:

11	2	2	2
2	11	5	4
12	5	4	5
5	4	11	11
4	12	12	12

| j = 1 | j = 2 | j = 3 | j = 4 |

Line 280 optimizes the technique. Since this sort pushes the largest value to the bottom of the array during the first pass through the j loop, it is not necessary to look at the last element. Each time the largest remaining element is pushed down to its proper position, the number of elements to be compared decreases by one. Therefore, fewer comparisons are made in the i loop with each execution of the j loop.

Summing Up

☐ An array may be used to reference a series of similar variables. Each of these variables is referenced by using the array name and a subscript number.
☐ The DIM statement is a nonexecutable statement that defines the boundaries (size) of an array.
☐ Many useful array operations are easily performed in BASIC; common ones are array searches and sorting.

Debugging Exercises

Find and remove the bugs in the following program segments:

```
1. 10 DIM B(-4)
2. 10 DIM M(40)
   20 FOR K = 1 TO 60
   30    READ M(K)
   40 NEXT M
```

```
LIST
10   REM    FIGURE A-8.5
20   REM
30   REM
40   REM
50   REM    **********************************************
60   REM    * This program demonstrates the bubble sort. *
70   REM    **********************************************
80   REM
90   REM              Variable definitions
100  REM              ********************
110  REM              N =number of values
120  REM              A =array name
130  REM              I =row number
140  REM              J =column number
150  REM
160  REM    *****************
170  REM    * input values *
180  REM    *****************
190  DATA 11,2,12,5,4
200  LET N=5
210  FOR I=1 TO N
220     READ A(I)
230  NEXT I
240  REM    *****************
250  REM    * sort the array *
260  REM    *****************
270  FOR J=1 TO N-1
280     LET M=N-J
290     FOR I=1 TO M
300        IF A(I)<A(I+1) THEN 340
310        T=A(I)
320        A(I)=A(I+1)
330        A(I+1)=T
340     NEXT I
350  NEXT J
360  REM    **********************
370  REM    * output sorted array *
380  REM    **********************
390  FOR I=1 TO N
400     PRINT "A(";I;")=";A(I)
410  NEXT I
420  END
Ok
RUN
A( 1 )= 2
A( 2 )= 4
A( 3 )= 5
A( 4 )= 11
A( 5 )= 12
Ok
```

(a) Program and Output

Comparisons to Other Versions of BASIC

Applesoft	No spaces within parentheses or after equal sign in output
HP	No differences
VAX	No differences
TRS-80	No differences
PET/CBM/Commodore 64	No differences
Macintosh	No differences

Figure A-8.5   A Bubble Sort

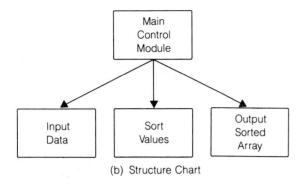

(b) Structure Chart

Set number of data values = 5
DO WHILE there are more data values to be read
   Read a data value into an array element
ENDDO
Do for each element in the array
   Do for each element in the array
      If the next value in the array is smaller than the current value
         Swap the next value with the current value
      ENDIF
   ENDDO
ENDDO
DO WHILE there are more data values to be output
   Output an array value
ENDDO

(c) Pseudocode

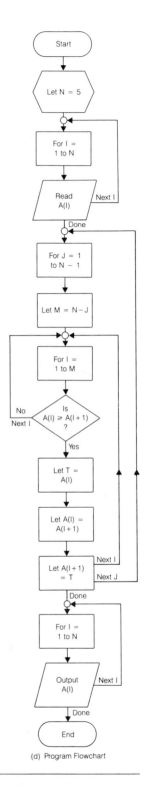

(d) Program Flowchart

Figure A-8.5 (continued)

Hands-on Exercises

1. Write a program that displays a multiplication table for even numbers 2 through 10. The rows and columns of this table should be labeled 2, 4, 6, 8, and 10. The intersection of a specific row and column will show the product of the numbers on the row and column labels. Draw a structure chart of your program and prepare pseudocode or a program flowchart. Document your program internally with REM statements.

2. Write a program that will accept as input the monthly utility costs for one year for natural gas, electricity, telephone, and water/sewer. Have the program compute the average monthly cost for each utility, the actual total monthly cost for all utilities, and the total yearly cost for each utility and all utilities together. Draw a structure chart of your program and prepare pseudocode or a program flowchart. Document your program internally with REM statements.

Topic 9: Subroutines and Creating Menus

Subroutines

A **subroutine** performs an operation (that is, does some work for the calling program) as well as accepts arguments and returns values. An **argument** is a constant or variable passed between a calling and a called program. The subroutine may return more than one value or perhaps no value at all to the calling program. In the case of no value returned, the subroutine has an "effect" on the program state. For example, the subroutine may display the data it has passed and return no value.

A subroutine also provides **modularity.** All programs that are complex should be coded in a modular form using subroutines. As a general rule, program modules or routines should:

1. Perform only one function (have one purpose)
2. Not be unduly complex (be less than one page in length)

These characteristics enhance the operation and readability of programs, thereby making program maintenance easier and more effective. BASIC implements the concept of a subroutine or module with the GOSUB and RETURN statements.

The GOSUB and RETURN Statements

The GOSUB and RETURN statements establish the link between the program and the subroutine to be invoked. The GOSUB statement has the following format:

```
line#    GOSUB    destination line#
```

where destination line# is the label of the first statement (or entry point) of the subroutine.

The GOSUB transfers control from the current line in the calling program to the entry point of the subroutine. This also establishes a link which allows the subroutine to return control to the statement immediately following the GOSUB statement. The transfer of control from the subroutine back to the calling program is done only when the RETURN statement is encountered. The RETURN statement has the following format:

```
line#    RETURN
```

The RETURN statement causes the transfer of control back to the statement immediately following the GOSUB statement. Figure A-9.1 demonstrates the concept of modularity and the use of the GOSUB/RETURN statements.

This program has a subroutine which accepts the input value and tests to see whether it is greater than zero. If not, an error message is printed and the user is asked for another value. The program also has a routine for displaying the results. Even though this program may seem too elaborate for such a simple operation (determining the square root of a number), it illustrates the basic concept of a modular program in which every routine performs only one operation and is easily readable. For more complex applications, this concept is essential for well-structured, error-free programs.

You may also want to refer to Figures A-1.7 and A-8.2 in this appendix. These two programs are examples of more complex programs that have been written in a modular form using subroutines.

Creating Menus

A menu-driven application is one in which the user is given a choice of actions to be taken or a choice of routines to be executed. A **menu** is simply a display of selections. For example:

```
          MENU
1.  Add students to the file
2.  Change student grades
3.  Delete students from the file
4.  Erase the complete student file
5.  Exit to DOS

YOUR SELECTION?
```

In this sample menu, if the user enters selection 1, a subroutine that allows students to be added to a file would be executed. If the user enters selection 2, then he or she could change student grades.

Menus are most important to the user-friendliness of software. All good interactive software packages use menus. Integrated packages such as Ability, Framework, and Symphony make extensive use of menus.

Menus can be easily created through the use of the ON-GOSUB command. The format of the ON-GOSUB command is as follows:

```
line#    On var GOSUB destination line# [,destination
              line#, destination line# ....]
```

```
LIST
10   REM    FIGURE A-9.1
20   REM
30   REM
40   REM
50   REM    ***********************************************************
60   REM    * This program demonstrates the use of subroutines.       *
70   REM    * The program is designed to accept a positive number,    *
80   REM    * find the square root, and display the results.          *
90   REM    ***********************************************************
100  REM
110  REM              Variable definitions
120  REM              ********************
130  REM              A -any value input by the user
140  REM              S -square root of A
150  REM              R$-continuation prompt
160  REM
170  REM    **********************
180  REM    * main control module *
190  REM    **********************
200  GOSUB 310
210  REM    *************************************
220  REM    * calculate the square root of A *
230  REM    *************************************
240  LET S=SQR(A)
250  GOSUB 400
260  PRINT
270  PRINT "DO YOU WISH TO CONTINUE (Y/N)";
280  INPUT R$
290  IF R$="Y" THEN 170
300  END
310  REM    **********************************************
320  REM    * subroutine to accept and test input *
330  REM    **********************************************
340      PRINT "WHAT IS THE POSITIVE VALUE FOR A";
350      INPUT A
360      IF A>0 THEN 390
370      PRINT "VALUE MUST BE POSITIVE, TRY AGAIN."
380      GOTO 340
390      RETURN
400  REM    ************************************************
410  REM    * subroutine to display value and results *
420  REM    ************************************************
430      PRINT
440      PRINT "THE SQUARE ROOT OF ";A;" IS ";S
450      RETURN
Ok
RUN
WHAT IS THE POSITIVE VALUE FOR A? -4
VALUE MUST BE POSITIVE, TRY AGAIN.
WHAT IS THE POSITIVE VALUE FOR A? 4

THE SQUARE ROOT OF  4  IS  2

DO YOU WISH TO CONTINUE (Y/N)? Y
WHAT IS THE POSITIVE VALUE FOR A? 85

THE SQUARE ROOT OF  85  IS  9.219544

DO YOU WISH TO CONTINUE (Y/N)? N
Ok
```

(a) Program and Output

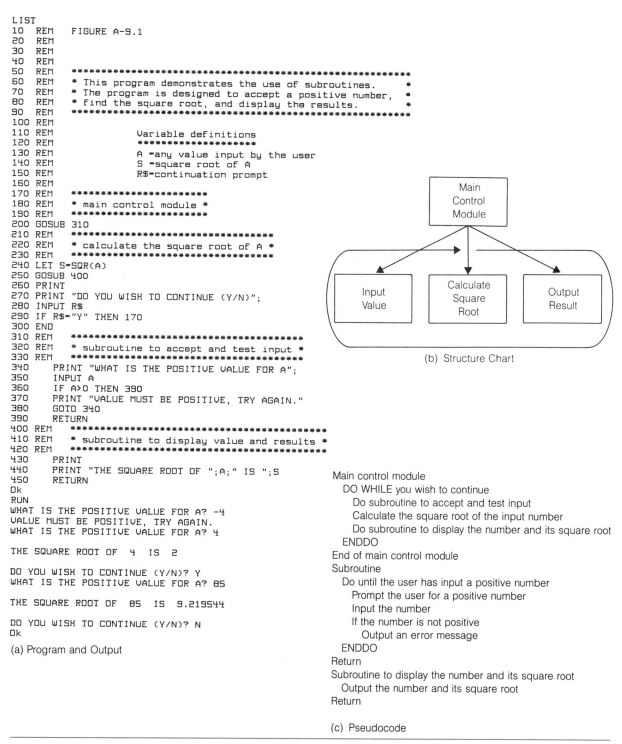

(b) Structure Chart

Main control module
  DO WHILE you wish to continue
    Do subroutine to accept and test input
    Calculate the square root of the input number
    Do subroutine to display the number and its square root
  ENDDO
End of main control module
Subroutine
  Do until the user has input a positive number
    Prompt the user for a positive number
    Input the number
    If the number is not positive
      Output an error message
  ENDDO
Return
Subroutine to display the number and its square root
  Output the number and its square root
Return

(c) Pseudocode

Figure A-9.1   The Use of Subroutines

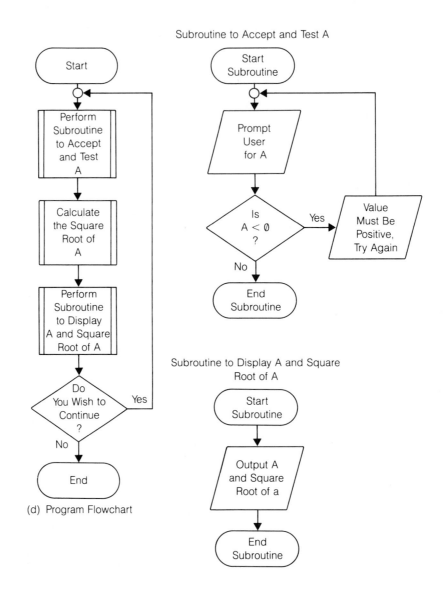

Subroutine to Accept and Test A

(d) Program Flowchart

Subroutine to Display A and Square Root of A

Comparisons to Other Versions of BASIC	
Applesoft	No space after the question mark or colon in output
HP	No differences
VAX	No differences
TRS-80	No differences
PET/CBM/Commodore 64	No differences
Macintosh	No differences

Figure A-9.1   (continued)

where destination line# is the first line number of the subroutine to be executed. The value of the variable (var) determines which subroutine will be executed. For example, if the value of the variable is 2, the second line number in the list will be the destination of the branch. As with the GOSUB statement, the list of statements in the subroutine must be followed by a RETURN statement. Figure A-9.2 demonstrates the use of the ON-GOSUB statement. In the figure, statements 350–400 contain the first routine and statements 440–490 contain the second routine.

Summing Up

☐ Subroutines are processes that may have to be repeated at multiple places within a program. They may be coded once and used many times with the help of subroutine calls.

☐ The RETURN command causes transfer of control back to the statement immediately following the GOSUB statement.

☐ A menu-driven application is one in which the user is given a choice of actions to be taken or routines to be executed. Menus can be created through the use of the ON-GOSUB statement.

Debugging Exercises

Find and remove the bugs in the following program segments:

```
1.   10 REM**THIS IS THE MAIN PROGRAM**
     20 GOSUB 40
     30 GOSUB 70
     40 REM**SUBROUTINE 1**
     50 READ A, B, X
     60 LET  C = B * X
     70 REM**SUBROUTINE 2**
     80 READ M$, F
     90 END
2.   10 INPUT X
     20 ON X GOSUB 90, 40, 70
     30 END
     40 REM**SUBROUTINE 2**
     50 PRINT "SUBROUTINE 2 HAS BEEN CALLED"
     60 RETURN
     70 REM**SUBROUTINE 3**
     80 PRINT "SUBROUTINE 3 HAS BEEN CALLED"
     90 REM**SUBROUTINE 1**
    100 PRINT "SUBROUTINE 3 HAS BEEN CALLED"
    110 END
```

```
LIST
10  REM     FIGURE A-9.2
20  REM
30  REM
40  REM
50  REM     ************************************************************
60  REM     * This program demonstrates the use of the ON-GOSUB command by *
70  REM     * displaying a simple menu-driven application.               *
80  REM     ************************************************************
90  REM
100 REM                 Variable definitions
110 REM                 *******************
120 REM                 S =menu selection input by the user
130 REM
140 REM     ****************
150 REM     * display menu *
160 REM     ****************
170 PRINT "          MENU"
180 PRINT "1. DISPLAY STUDENT NAME"
190 PRINT "2. DISPLAY STUDENT GRADE"
200 PRINT "3. EXIT FROM PROGRAM"
210 PRINT
220 PRINT "YOUR SELECTION ";
230 REM     ************************
240 REM     * input menu selection *
250 REM     ************************
260 INPUT S
270 REM     **************************
280 REM     * execute menu selection *
290 REM     **************************
300 ON S GOSUB 360,450,320
310 GOTO 170
320 END
330 REM     *********************************
340 REM     * display result of selection 1 *
350 REM     *********************************
360 PRINT
370 PRINT "THE STUDENT'S NAME IS MARCO DESTINKSHUN"
380 PRINT
390 PRINT
400 PRINT
410 RETURN
420 REM     *********************************
430 REM     * display result of selection 2 *
440 REM     *********************************
450 PRINT
460 PRINT "THE STUDENT'S GRADE IS 96"
470 PRINT
480 PRINT
490 PRINT
500 RETURN
Ok
RUN
          MENU
1. DISPLAY STUDENT NAME
2. DISPLAY STUDENT GRADE
3. EXIT FROM PROGRAM

YOUR SELECTION ? 1

THE STUDENT'S NAME IS MARCO DESTINKSHUN
```

(a) Program and Output

Figure A-9.2   A Menu-Driven Program

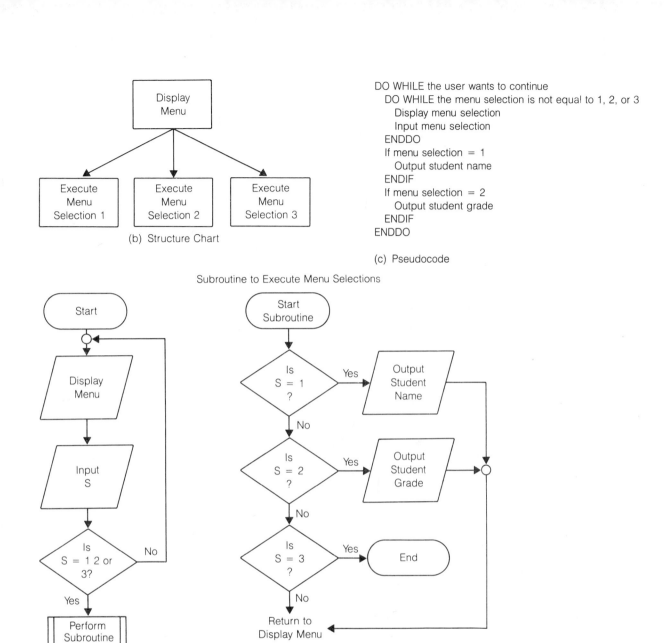

(b) Structure Chart

DO WHILE the user wants to continue
    DO WHILE the menu selection is not equal to 1, 2, or 3
        Display menu selection
        Input menu selection
    ENDDO
    If menu selection = 1
        Output student name
    ENDIF
    If menu selection = 2
        Output student grade
    ENDIF
ENDDO

(c) Pseudocode

Subroutine to Execute Menu Selections

(d) Program Flowchart

Comparisons to Other Versions of BASIC

Applesoft	No differences
HP	No differences
VAX	No differences
TRS-80	No differences
PET/CBM/Commodore 64	No differences
Macintosh	No differences

Figure A-9.2 (continued)

Topic 10: Alphabetic Reference of BASIC Statements

DEF FN

---
line#   DEF FNa (arglist) = expression

---

where:

a is any letter from A to Z, allowing a maximum of 26 function names.

arglist contains any numeric variable names separated by commas.

expression is any valid numeric expression.

The DEF statement is provided by BASIC as a vehicle for programmers to define their own functions. Some versions, although not standard, provide multiple-line DEF statements with the following format:

---
line#   DEF FNa (arglist)

         BASIC statements needed for calculations

line#   FEND

DIM

---
line#   DIM   list of subscripted variables

---

where:

the subscripted variables in the list are separated by commas.

The DIM statement is a nonexecutable statement used by the programmer to specify the dimensions or boundaries of the array so that BASIC can reserve storage for the array. Each subscripted variable represents an array name in which the program may specify the number of subscripts (up to 2) and the magnitude of each subscript. (The subscript must be a numeric or integer constant.) See Figure A-8.2 for an example of the DIM statement.

---
line#   END

The END statement terminates the program and closes any files that were processed during execution without any diagnostic messages. The END statement is required in the standard BASIC version, but is optional for most versions, and only required when subroutines are used. The line number associated with the END statement should be the highest in value of all line numbers within the program.

FOR/NEXT

line#   FOR variable = initial exp TO term exp [STEP inc exp]

where:

variable is the index variable for the loop.

initial exp is an expression that evaluates to the initial value of the index.

term exp is an expression that evaluates to the terminal value of the index.

inc exp is an expression that evaluates to the incremental value of the index.

The STEP size is optional. The FOR and NEXT statements encompass the set of statements composing the loop. The program will execute this loop until the variable becomes greater than the terminal value of the index upon which the program branches to the statement immediately following the NEXT statement.

line#   NEXT variable

where:

the variable must be the same as in the FOR statement.

The loop created by the FOR and NEXT statements is a special counting loop. See Figure A-7.6 for an example of FOR and NEXT statements.

GOSUB/RETURN

line#   GOSUB   destination line#

where:

destination line# is the label of the first statement (or entry point) of the subroutine.

The GOSUB and RETURN statements establish the link between the program and the subroutine to be called. The GOSUB transfers control from the current line in the invoking program to the entry point of the subroutine. A link is now established that allows the subroutine to return control to the statement immediately following the GOSUB statement. The transfer of control from the subroutine back to the invoking program is done only when the RETURN statement is encountered.

line#   RETURN

The RETURN statement causes the transfer of control back to the statement immediately following the GOSUB statement. See Figure A-9.1 for an example of GOSUB/RETURN statements.

GOTO

line#   GOTO   destination line#

where:

the destination line# is the number of the statement to be executed next.

Unconditional branching is performed in BASIC by the GOTO statement. See Figure A-7.1 for an example of the GOTO statement.

IF-THEN

line#   IF   cond exp $\begin{Bmatrix} \text{THEN} \\ \text{GOTO} \end{Bmatrix}$ destination line#

where:

cond exp is any expression which evaluates to either true or false.

The IF-THEN statement provides a means for conditional branching. If the value of the expression evaluates to true, control is transferred to the specified line; otherwise the next sequential statement is executed. See Figure A-7.2 for an example of the IF-THEN statement.

INPUT

line#   INPUT   list of variables

where:

the variables in the list are separated by commas.

The INPUT statement allows data to be entered at the terminal as the program executes; this creates an interactive environment. When an input statement is encountered, a prompt symbol is displayed. On most systems, the prompt symbol is a question mark (?) or colon (:). See Figure A-6.1 for an example of the INPUT statement.

LET

line#   LET   variable = expression

where the result of the expression must be of the same data type as the variable. The function of the LET statement is to assign a value to a variable. See Figure A-5.1 for an example of the LET statement.

ON-GOSUB

```
line#   ON   num exp   GOSUB   list of destination line #s
```

where:

num exp is any legal numeric expression or variable.

the list of destination line #s is the list of line numbers separated by commas.

The ON-GOSUB allows the programmer to specify several line numbers as alternatives, depending on the value of the numeric expression. The standard version of BASIC truncates (or rounds) the result of the expression to an integer. In some versions of BASIC this statement is ON-GOTO rather than ON-GOSUB. For an example of the ON-GOSUB statement see Figure A-9.2.

OPTION BASE

```
line#   OPTION BASE   lbound
```

where:

lbound is the desired lower boundary for the arrays used in the program.

BASIC provides the OPTION BASE statement which allows the programmer to set the lower boundary of arrays in the program. Thus if the programmer does not wish to use arrays with zero as the lower boundary, the OPTION BASE provides a vehicle to adjust it.

PRINT

```
line#   PRINT   [list of expressions]
```

where:

the expressions are separated by commas or semicolons.

The PRINT statement displays specified information to the user's terminal while the BASIC program is executing. See Figures A-6.3 and A-6.4 for examples of the PRINT statement.

PRINT USING/IMAGE

```
line#   PRINT USING   image line#, expression list
```

where:

image line# is the line number of the statement that formats the output, and the expressions are separated by commas.

The statement referenced in the PRINT USING statement is known as the IMAGE statement. The IMAGE statement is a nonexecutable statement that specifies how the data are to be arranged when printed. The format of the IMAGE statement is as follows:

line#:   unquoted control character string

where:

the unquoted control character string is a special string that formats the output.

The PRINT USING is also implemented on some versions as one statement.

line# PRINT USING "control character string"; list of items

where:

the control character string must be enclosed in quotation marks.

the display items in the list are separated by commas.

See Figure A-6.6 for an example of the PRINT USING statement.

READ/DATA

line#   READ   list of variables

where:

the variables are separated by commas.

The format of the DATA statement is as follows:

line#   DATA   list of values

where:

the values are numeric or string constants separated by commas.

The READ statement allows transmission of data into a BASIC program. The input data are contained within a data block consisting of one or more DATA statements. See Figure A-6.2 for an example of the READ/DATA statements.

REMARK

line#   (REMARK)   [comments]
         (REM)

where:

the comments may be anything typed by the programmer.

These comments are ignored by the computer, but help the programmer understand the program better.

RESTORE

> line#   RESTORE

The RESTORE statement is used to read the same data more than once. Once the DATA have been read, a RESTORE will allow the program to begin reading from the initial point of the data block (the first DATA statement in the program).

WHILE AND WEND

> line#   WHILE
> line#   WEND

The WHILE and WEND statements execute a series of statements in a loop as long as a given condition is true. The format of these statements is:

        WHILE expression
           •
           •
           •
        (loop statements)
           •
           •
           •
        WEND

The loop statements are executed repeatedly as long as (while) the expression is true. When the expression is false, execution continues with the first statement after the WEND. See Figure A-1.7 for an example of these statements.

Topic 11: Alphabetic Reference of Built-in BASIC Functions

Function	Description
ABS(exp)	Returns the absolute value of the expression specified.
ASCII(x$)	Returns the ASCII representation of the first character of the string specified.
ATN(exp)	Returns the arctangent of the expression specified.
CHR$(exp)	Returns the string representation of the ASCII code specified.

COS(exp)	Returns the cosine of the expression specified.
EXP(exp)	Returns the value *e* raised to the power of the expression specified.
INT(exp)	Returns the greatest integer less than or equal to the expression specified.
LEFT$(x$,exp)	Returns the leftmost substring of the length specified, of the string.
LEN(x$)	Returns the number of characters in the string specified.
LOG(exp)	Returns the natural logarithm of the expression specified.
MID$(x$,exp1,exp2)	Returns the substring beginning at position exp1 with the length specified by exp2.
RIGHT$(x$,exp)	Returns the rightmost substring of the length specified by exp.
RND	Returns a pseudorandom number between 0 and 1.
SGN(exp)	Returns +1 if the exp is positive, −1 if the exp is negative, 0 if the exp is zero.
SIN(exp)	Returns the sine of the expression specified.
SQR(exp)	Returns the square root of the expression specified.
STR$(exp)	Returns the string representation of the value of the expression specified.
TAN(exp)	Returns the tangent of the expression specified.
VAL(x$)	Returns the numeric literal represented by the string specified.
x$ + y$	Concatenation: joins the string x$ with the string y$.

Topic 12: Comprehensive Hand-on Exercises

1. Write a program that will keep track of your program of study. You can use DATA statements containing all the courses you plan to take in your degree program. Each DATA statement should have fields for the course number, course name, the semester or quarter hours of the course, the term you plan to take the course, the term you actually took the course, the grade you plan to make in the course, and the actual grade you made in each course. The program should print your name at the top and all the data fields for each course in order by when you plan to take or actually took the course. At the bottom of the printout, print values for the following:

Total hours planned

Total hours taken

Total hours yet to take

Planned overall grade point average

Actual overall grade point average

Planned grade point average in your major

Actual grade point average in your major

Use this program during your academic career. Change and improve it as you use it. Draw a structure chart of your program and prepare pseudocode or a program flowchart. Document your program internally with REM statements.

2. Using DATA statements for input, write a personal budgeting program. The program should accept up to thirteen weeks of budgeted and actual expenses for a variable number of expense categories, such as rent, gasoline, books, tuition, and so on. Design your output so that it will be most helpful to you. As a minimum, you should show the differences (over and under budget) for each budget category for each week and in total for each four-week and thirteen-week period. Use this program to plan your budget. Change and improve it as you use it. Draw a structure chart of your program and prepare pseudocode or a program flowchart. Document your program internally with REM statements.

3. Create a computer program that will accept as input an employee's name, wage rate, and hours worked for the period (week). Several employee records will be inputted. The output of the program should include a report showing:

Name

Gross pay

Income tax deduction

Social-security deduction

Take-home pay

For simplification, assume the tax rate is 15 percent on a weekly gross pay of $200 or less. For gross pay of $200 to $300, the income tax equals $30 + 20 percent of gross pay exceeding $200. For gross pay of $300 and up, income tax equals $50 + 25 percent of gross pay exceeding $300. Assume social security is taxed on 7.5 percent of gross pay.

Subroutines should be used for the computation of gross pay and for the computation of income taxes (two different subroutines). Any hours over forty per week are paid at 1.5 times the normal hourly rate. The following is a table of data to be input.

Employee Name	Wage Rate	Hours Worked
John Haskell	$ 4.00	40
Paul Duncan	5.50	37
Alfred Martin	12.00	45
Joanne Wesley	9.00	40
Mary Smith	6.75	40

This information should be input using the DATA statement. Draw a structure chart of your program and prepare pseudocode or a program flowchart. Document your program internally with REM statements.

4. Create an interactive inventory program that will accept as input:

Item name

Unit cost

Actual quantity on hand (QOH)

QOH according to records

Prompts should be used to make the program more user-friendly. For example, when it is time to enter the item name, your CRT screen should display a message similar to:

PLEASE ENTER ITEM NAME

After each record, the program should ask you whether more records are to be added.

A report is to be generated as output. This report will have the following columns:

1. Item name
2. Cost per item
3. Actual quantity-on-hand (QOH)
4. Actual total cost of QOH
5. Recorded quantity-on-hand
6. Recorded total cost of QOH
7. Surplus QOH (actual minus recorded)
8. Surplus cost
9. Shortage QOH (actual minus recorded)
10. Shortage cost

A sum of surplus cost and shortage cost should be printed at the bottom of the report. The format should be as follows:

				Differences	
Item Name	Cost/ Item	Actual QOH Total Cost	Recorded QOH Total Cost	Shortage QOH Total Cost	Surplus QOH Total Cost

Sum of Surplus Cost
Sum of Shortage Cost

You should test your program using the following intput data:

Item Name	Unit Cost	Actual QOH	Recorded QOH
Pencils	1.05	7,000	6,593
Paper	2.13	1,025	1,200
Pens	4.35	739	739
Notebooks	1.12	325	340
Rulers	.38	10,100	10,328

Draw a structure chart of your program and prepare pseudocode or a program flowchart. Document your program internally with REM statements.

Appendix B: Hands-on Use of the Personal Computer

Topic 1: The Disk-Operating System

An operating system is a special kind of program written to "manage" the resources of a computer and to perform certain tasks for other programs. For example, operating systems often handle the job of reading and writing files to disks, a common job required by most application programs. The operating system used by IBM-PCs and other similar personal computers is called the **disk-operating system (DOS).** The purpose of this section is to provide an introduction to DOS.

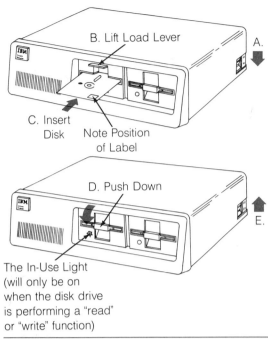

B. Lift Load Lever

A.

C. Insert Disk   Note Position of Label

D. Push Down

E.

The In-Use Light (will only be on when the disk drive is performing a "read" or "write" function)

A. Set the system unit's power switch to Off.
B. Lift the load lever.
C. Insert the disk until the rear stop is felt.
D. Push the load lever down and it will latch closed.
E. Set the system unit's power switch to On.

FIGURE B-1.1   Inserting a Disk into Drive A and Booting the Computer

You must first open the drive lid, then insert the disk with your thumb on the label, and finally close the lid.

Getting Started with DOS

The best way to learn DOS is to use it! You will need the following materials:

1. An IBM-PC or compatible machine
2. A disk containing DOS[1]
3. A blank disk

To begin, take the DOS disk and place it in the left disk drive, as shown in Figure B-1.1. As a matter of convention the left drive is called the A drive and the right drive is called the B drive. When putting the disk into the machine, insert the exposed portion first, with the disk label facing up. If you have never used floppy disks you may want to refer to Figures 8-21 and 8-22 in chapter 8 and the discussion that accompanies them. These figures present the components of floppy disks and disk terminology.

Once you have placed the disk in the machine, close the disk drive door. Now turn on your computer and the monitor. It will take a moment for the machine to run some start-up diagnostic tests. Then, the computer will read a file from the A drive and you will be prompted to enter the date. Starting up your computer in this fashion is called a **cold boot.** If your computer is already on, you can use a **warm boot.** To do this, hold down the [Ctrl] and [Alt] keys and strike the [Del] key. The machine will skip the diagnostics this

[1]All the material in this topic will be based on PC-DOS version 2.1 from Microsoft Corporation. However, earlier versions of PC-DOS as well as other DOS products are very similar.

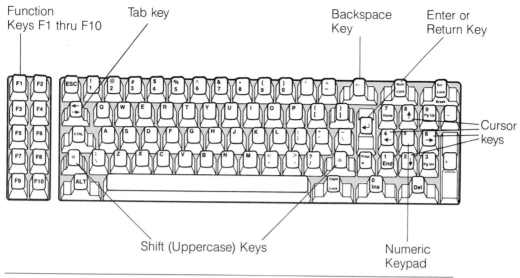

Figure labels:
- Function Keys F1 thru F10
- Tab key
- Backspace Key
- Enter or Return Key
- Cursor keys
- Shift (Uppercase) Keys
- Numeric Keypad

FIGURE B-1.2   The IBM-PC Keyboard

time, but again read a file from the disk in drive A and prompt you for a date. The date prompt will look like this:

```
Current date is Tue 1-01-1980
Enter new date:
```

Before you enter the date, refer to Figure B-1.2 and locate the following keys on the keyboard:

1. The enter [⏎] key. It is located on the right side of the keyboard where the "Return" key is normally located on a typewriter.
2. The backspace [←] key. This key is located on the right side of the top row on the keyboard.
3. The shift [⬆] keys. There are two shift keys just like on a typewriter. They are located on both sides of the keyboard. Each has a wide arrow pointing to the top of the keyboard. If you need uppercase for any key, hold the shift key down while pressing that key.

In this application we will refer to the three keys by their names: the enter, backspace, and shift keys. You should remember that on the IBM-PC and most compatibles they are labeled with the symbols just shown.

Now back to DOS. At this point the computer is requesting that you enter the date. Type in the date using digits for the month, day, and year. You should separate the month, day, and year with a hyphen (-), as follows: 8-15-85. If you make a mistake keying any command, you can correct it by using the backspace key and retyping. After you have typed in the complete date, press the [enter] key. Next the computer will prompt you for the time. The computer uses a 24-hour clock so if it is 1:42 P.M., type in 13:42. You should separate the hours and minutes with a colon (:) and press [enter] when you are finished. If you have entered this information properly your screen should look like Figure B-1.3. The A> is called the **DOS prompt.** It tells you that Drive A is the *default* disk drive and that DOS is ready to receive your next command. When is the default disk drive used? Any

default
A value, attribute, or option that is assumed when none has been specified.

```
Current date is Tue  1-01-1980
Enter new date: 7-09-1985
Current time is  0:00:31.36
Enter new time: 1:30:32.20


The IBM Personal Computer DOS
Version 2.10 (C)Copyright IBM Corp 1981, 1982, 1983

A>
```

FIGURE B-1.3   The DOS Screen after You have Entered the Date and Time

If your computer has a clock/calendar installed and the necessary software to use it is on your DOS disk, the date and time will be picked up automatically. Also, notice that DOS allows you to enter the time in terms of hours, minutes, seconds, and hundreds of seconds. Usually only the hours and minutes are entered. DOS will accept the year as 85 instead of 1985.

time your computer needs to read or write to a disk it will use the default (assumed) drive unless you specify that a different disk drive is to be used.

The next step is to find out what files are stored on your disk. Type DIR, for directory (use uppercase or lowercase), and press [enter]. In response, the PC will show you all the files that are on the disk in Drive A. Try this several times. Figure B-1.4 shows the directory displayed on the screen.

You probably noticed that some information that appeared after you requested the directory did not stay on the screen. This is because there are more than a screen full of files on the disk. To see all the files on the disk, type DIR/W and press [enter]. This time you will be able to see all the files at once. Notice that you see the file names only. Before, you saw the file names, file sizes, and the date the files were created. Another format of the DIR command is DIR/P. Type this. With DIR/P the scrolling of the directory will pause when the screen is full. This gives you the opportunity to inspect every file without having to give up the information on file size and date.

The DIR command can also be used in conjunction with a "wild card" specifier to list files with similar names. To understand how this feature works, you need to know what file names are acceptable to DOS. A filename consists of two parts—the name and the extension (see Figure B-1.5). Optionally you can specify a disk drive the file is located on. The name can be any combination of up to eight letters and/or numbers or certain special characters such as $, #, &, @, !, and %. The filename cannot contain blanks. The extension can be any combination of up to three numbers, letters, or special characters. The name must be separated from the extension by a period. As you work on the personal computer, it is a good habit to try to use filenames and extensions that help you identify what is in a file. Extensions are particularly useful for grouping similar files together. Figure B-1.6 illustrates some commonly used extensions.

How can you produce a directory of similar files? The wild-card specifier in DOS is the asterisk (*). It is interpreted to mean any string of characters. The way you use the asterisk is best understood by some examples. Type the command DIR *.COM and then press the [enter] key. The directory listing that is produced includes any file with the file extension COM. Now try DIR D*.* and see what is displayed. DOS has interpreted this request as "give a directory listing with any file extension where the file name is a D followed by any other characters." Try some other DIR commands on your own. You will use the DIR (directory) command often, so make sure you understand what it does before you proceed.

```
dir

     Volume in drive A has no label
     Directory of A:\

COMMAND   COM   17792   10-20-83   12:00p
ANSI      SYS    1664   10-20-83   12:00p
FORMAT    COM    6912   10-20-83   12:00p
CHKDSK    COM    6400   10-20-83   12:00p
SYS       COM    1680   10-20-83   12:00p
DISKCOPY  COM    2576   10-20-83   12:00p
DISKCOMP  COM    2188   10-20-83   12:00p
COMP      COM    2534   10-20-83   12:00p
EDLIN     COM    4608   10-20-83   12:00p
MODE      COM    3139   10-20-83   12:00p
FDISK     COM    6369   10-20-83   12:00p
BACKUP    COM    3687   10-20-83   12:00p
RESTORE   COM    4003   10-20-83   12:00p
PRINT     COM    4608   10-20-83   12:00p
RECOVER   COM    2304   10-20-83   12:00p
ASSIGN    COM     896   10-20-83   12:00p
TREE      COM    1513   10-20-83   12:00p
GRAPHICS  COM     789   10-20-83   12:00p
SORT      EXE    1408   10-20-83   12:00p
FIND      EXE    5888   10-20-83   12:00p
MORE      COM     384   10-20-83   12:00p
BASIC     COM   16256   10-20-83   12:00p
BASICA    COM   26112   10-20-83   12:00p
        23 File(s)      28672 bytes free
```

FIGURE B-1.4   The DOS Directory

A very good use of this directory is to print it and place it with the disk in the jacket. If you have several disks, the procedure of printing the directory will save you time in finding a particular file, since you can see immediately what is on a disk without having to call up the directory on the computer. To print the directory at the same time as it is being displayed on the screen, turn on your printer and then hold down the [Ctrl] key and press the [PrtSc] key. This causes the printer to print the same information that is being displayed on the screen. Next, display a directory by typing DIR and pressing [enter].

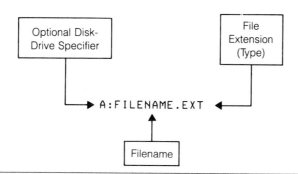

FIGURE B-1.5   The Parts of a File's Name

A file's name is made up of a filename and an extension. The combination of filename and extension must be unique for each file stored on a disk. A good name for a file will be descriptive of the data or program contained in the file.

```
.COM    A DOS Program File
.EXE    A DOS Program File
.BAT    A Set of Program Files or Statements Strung Together for Sequential Execution
.BAS    A BASIC Program File
.WKS    A LOTUS 1-2-3 Worksheet File
.PIC    A LOTUS 1-2-3 Picture (Graph) File
.DBF    A dBASE II or III Data Base File
.NDX    A dBASE II or III Index File
.PRG    A dBASE II or III Program File
.FRM    A dBASE II or III Report Form
.LBL    A dBASE II or III Label Form
.MEM    A dBASE II or III Memory Variable File
```

FIGURE B-1.6 Commonly Used File Extensions

Many software packages such as Lotus 1-2-3 and dBASE III automatically assign extensions to filenames. Others such as WordStar allow the user to assign any extension.

Moving Along with DOS

The next step is to learn how to format a disk. The format command prepares a disk for storing data or programs. Before you can store data or programs for the first time on a disk, the disk must be formatted. Once again request a directory of the DOS disk by using the DIR/W command. Observe that there is a file called FORMAT.COM on the DOS disk. This file contains a program that can format a disk. When you format a disk, anything stored on that disk will be permanently erased. *Never* format a disk that contains files you want to keep. (At this point you do not need to be concerned about erasing any files, but you will need to know this in the future.) To format your disk, type FORMAT/S B: and press [enter]. Be sure to put a space between FORMAT/S and B: and include the colon or the command will not work properly. The B: tells DOS that it is the disk in drive B that you wish to format. If you omit this drive specifier, the computer will assume you want to format the disk in the default drive, which is currently drive A.

In response to your command, the following will be shown on the screen.

```
A>format/s b:

Insert new diskette for drive B:
and strike any key when ready
```

Place the disk you want to format in the right disk drive with the exposed portion going in first, and the label side up. Then close the disk-drive door and press any key. After a little while the PC will respond with:

```
Formatting . . . Format complete
System transferred

     362496 bytes total disk space
      40960 bytes used by system
     321536 bytes available on disk

Format another (Y/N)?
```

Unless you want to format another disk, press the [N] key. Congratulations—you have just run your first DOS program! Good work!

Now that your disk has been formatted it can be used to store files of data and programs. Since some of the files on the DOS disk are useful, the next step will be to copy files. At this point you should have the DOS disk in drive A and a formatted disk in drive B. Copying files from one disk to another is simple with DOS. Let's copy the file TREE.COM from the

DOS disk to the newly formatted disk. To do this type `COPY A:TREE.COM B:` and press [`enter`]. Remember to put one space after the word `COPY` and before the word `B:`. When the PC has finished copying the file TREE.COM onto the disk in drive B, it will respond with:

```
1 File(s) copied
```

To practice copying files, copy the files FORMAT.COM and CHKDSK.COM from the DOS disk to your formatted disk using the procedures just described. Have you copied two files? Now, let's make use of the wild-card specifier (*) that you learned about earlier. Type `COPY D*.* B:` to copy all of the files on the default (A:) drive that start with the letter D, onto the B drive.

hidden files
Files that do not appear on the directory of the disk.

bootable
A disk is bootable if it has the necessary DOS system files on it to start up (boot) the computer.

Have you copied these files onto your disk? Do you wonder if it really worked? You can check to see. You first need to tell DOS that you want some information from the B drive. The way to do this is to type `B:` and press [`enter`]. Notice that the DOS prompt is now B> instead of A>, which means the default drive is the B or the right drive. Now you can request a directory (`DIR`) from the B drive. Try it. You should see that the disk in drive B now has the files you copied onto it. Additionally, the file COMMAND.COM is now on your disk. This system file was copied there automatically, along with two *hidden files* that are not listed on the directory, when you formatted the disk. The COMMAND.COM file and the two hidden files are necessary to make your disk *bootable*.

Gaining Speed with DOS

You already know what the file FORMAT.COM does, so let's consider the other files. The file CHKDSK.COM contains a useful program that displays how much of the disk's storage and computer's memory are available. Type `CHKDSK` and press [`enter`]. The PC will respond with:

```
362496 bytes total disk space
22528 bytes in 2 hidden files
40960 bytes in 6 user files
299008 bytes available on disk

327680 bytes total memory
303104 bytes free
```

The first four lines of the CHKDSK (check disk) listing give information concerning the disk. The last two lines refer to the computer's memory. The numbers on the last two lines will not be the same for all computers, as they depend on how much primary memory each computer has installed. The numbers on the first four lines may also vary based on which version of DOS you are using. You can use the CHKDSK command anytime you want to see how much storage is available. CHKDSK will also tell you when there are damaged portions of the disk that cannot be used.

You have already used some of the programs in the COMMAND.COM file. Remember when you turned the PC on you had to wait a few seconds before you were asked to enter the date and time. One of the things that happened while you were waiting was that the file COMMAND.COM was loaded from the disk. It was a part of COMMAND.COM that asked for the date and time. The DIR program, which you have also used, is in the COMMAND.COM file as well. Two other programs in the COMMAND.COM file that are useful to learn are RENAME and ERASE. The RENAME program allows you to rename a file already stored on the disk. Before you try this program, make sure that the default drive is set to B:. You can check this by observing that the DOS prompt is B>. Also, check to verify that the disk in drive B is your disk with the files that were copied to it earlier.

To try the RENAME command, rename the file TREE.COM to BUSH.COM. This can be done by typing `RENAME TREE.COM BUSH.COM` and pressing [`enter`]. Be sure to put one space after the word RENAME and before BUSH.COM. Use the DIR command to verify that you renamed the file.

Now change the file named BUSH.COM back to TREE.COM. You can do this by using the same command, RENAME, but you must type BUSH.COM first and TREE.COM second. You can see that the general form of the RENAME command is old filename and extension, followed by new file name and extension. You should not change the name of the COM-MAND.COM file. If you do, it will not execute properly when the PC is turned on.

The last command is the ERASE command. A word of warning—be careful not to erase files before you are certain that you will not need them anymore. Since the TREE.COM file is not used frequently, you probably will not want to keep in on your disk. To erase this file, type: ERASE TREE.COM and press [enter]. Use the DIR command to verify that the TREE.COM file has been erased.

This concludes the introduction to DOS. All of the commands and uses of DOS have not been presented, but you should know enough now to begin to work with many of the programs written for the IBM PC. Figure B-1.7 is a summary of useful DOS key combinations and commands.

Summary of Useful Key Combinations in DOS

[Alt] & [Ctrl] & [Del] Same as turning the computer off-on. You lose everything stored in RAM when you use this command.
[Ctrl] & [Break] Cancels the current operation. For example, you may use it to stop the execution of a program.
[Ctrl] & [S] An alternative to [Ctrl] & [Break] to stop screen scrolling. It works like a toggle switch to turn scrolling on and off.
[Ctrl] & [PrtSc] Turns the printer echo on and off. It works like a toggle switch.
[Esc] Cancels the current line.

Summary of DOS Commands

A: Changes default drive to A.
B: Changes default drive to B.
BACKUP Backs up a hard disk to floppy disks.
CHKDSK Checks disk and reports status.
CLS Clears the display screen.
COMP Compares files.
COPY Copies files.
DATE Permits you to change the date known to the system.
DIR Lists a directory of filenames.
DISKCOMP Compares disks.
DISKCOPY Copies disks.
ERASE Deletes files.
FORMAT Formats disks.
PRINT Queries and prints data files.
RECOVER Recovers files from a disk that has developed a defective sector.
RENAME Renames files.
RESTORE Restores one or more files from floppy disks to a hard disk.
TIME Permits you to change the time of day known to the system.
TYPE Displays the contents of a specified file on the screen.
VER Displays the DOS version number you are working with on the screen.

FIGURE B-1.7 Summary of DOS Key Combinations and Commands

The exact format and explanations on how to use these DOS commands can be found in chapter 6 of the *Disk Operating System* reference manual.

If you would like to learn more about DOS, I suggest the *Disk Operating System User's Guide* by Microsoft Corporation. This booklet comes with DOS. You can also refer to the *Disk Operating System* reference manual (which also comes with DOS) for a detailed explanation of DOS commands. If you are in a PC lab, both of these books will probably be available there. If you would like to learn DOS in depth, I suggest reading:

Norton, Peter. *MS-DOS and PC-DOS: User's Guide.* Bowie, Maryland: Brady Communications Company, Inc., 1984.

For readers who want to learn even more about the IBM-PC and DOS, I recommend:

Norton, Peter. *Inside the IBM PC, Access to Advanced Features and Programming.* Bowie, Maryland: Brady Communications Company, Inc., 1984.

Hands-on Exercises

1. Try each of the useful key combinations in Figure B-1.7. For some of them, you will have to have an operation executing in order to interrupt it. For example: do a directory with the DIR command, and cancel it with the [Ctrl] and [Break] keys while it is executing. The [Break] key is underneath the [Scroll Lock] key. You can also use the DIR command to test the other key combinations.

2. Place the DOS disk in drive A and try the following DOS commands from Figure B-1.7:
   CLS
   DATE
   TIME
   VER
   B:
   A:
   CHKDSK
   DIR
   DIR/P
   DIR/W

3. Place the DOS disk in drive A and any disk in drive B. Try the following command from Figure B-1.7:
   A:
   CHKDSK B:
   DIR B:
   DIR/P B:
   DIR/W B:

   As you can see, placing a B: after the command causes the PC to use drive B when executing the command. Now type B: and press [enter]. This changes the default drive to B. Now try each of the commands without the B:. The PC now defaults to drive B and the results of the commands are the same as they were when you executed them before.

4. Place the DOS disk in drive A and a blank unformatted disk in drive B. Type DISKCOPY A: B:, press [enter], and then follow the instructions on the screen. (The source diskette is the disk you are copying from and the target disk is the one you are copying to.) This command formats the disk in drive B and copies the entire contents of the disk in drive A onto the disk in drive B. Actually, the disk in drive B does not have to be a blank unformatted disk, but one whose files you do not want to keep, as the DISKCOPY command will erase everything on the disk. After executing a diskcopy, answer [N] to the question, copy another (Y/N)?. By executing the DISKCOMP command, you can make sure the disk in drive B is identical to the one in drive A. Type in DISKCOMP A: B:, press [enter], and then follow the instructions on the screen.

5. Complete exercise 4 before doing this exercise. Do a CHKDSK on the disk you copied to in exercise 4 (the one in drive B). Type CHKDSK B: and press [enter]. Notice that the number of bytes of total disk space is not 362496 (360K in DOS 2.1). On my PC it is 179712 bytes. On yours it may be something different; in fact, it may be 362496. The number of total bytes for the disk in drive B is completely dependent on how the disk in drive A was formatted. One of the disadvantages of the DISKCOPY command is that it formats the target disk exactly the way the source disk is formatted. This may produce a disk that will not hold the maximum number of bytes (360K) that DOS is capable of putting on a disk. Let's see how you can get around this problem. First format the disk in drive B. Type FORMAT B: and press [enter]. Notice that the bytes of total disk space is the maximum (362496 for DOS 2.1). Answer [N] to the question format another (Y/N)? Type the command COPY *.* B: and press [enter] to copy the files from drive A to B. Now, do a checkdisk on both disks by typing

CHKDSK B: and pressing [enter] and typing CHKDSK and pressing [enter]. The number of bytes of total disk space for the disk in drive B is still the maximum, leaving you with much more free space on the disk than when you used DISKCOPY. (This, of course, may not be true if your DOS disk in drive A is formatted for the maximum number of bytes.) Notice though that there are two hidden files on disk A that were not copied onto disk B. These are the system files IBMBIO.COM and IBMDOS.COM. (See Figure 10-3 and the discussion of these files in chapter 10.) The COPY command does not copy hidden files, whereas DISKCOPY does. This is not a problem if you do not want the disk in drive B to be bootable. A disk is bootable if it contains the necessary system files to start the computer. Let's see whether the disk in drive B will boot the computer. Remove the DOS disk from drive A. Insert the disk that is now in drive B into drive A. Do a warm boot by holding down the [Alt] and [Ctrl] keys and pressing the [Del] key. Since the disk does not contain the necessary system files (IBMBIO.COM and IBMDOS.COM), it will not boot. You get the message:

Non-System disk or disk error

Replace and strike any key when ready

Now take the disk from drive A, replace it with the DOS disk, strike any key, enter the date, and enter the time. However, there is still a problem. What if you want your new disk to be bootable and be able to hold the maximum number of bytes, as would be the case if you wanted to store the new files you are creating on disk drive A? This is often a convenience even if you have two disk drives (since you will need only one disk) and is a necessity when you have only one disk drive. A good example is when you are writing BASIC programs. The next exercise shows you how to do this.

6. This exercise demonstrates how to create a bootable disk that contains the BASICA interpreter and holds the maximum number of bytes that DOS allows (360K for DOS 2.1). This will allow you the convenience of using only one disk when storing and executing your BASIC programs. First place the DOS disk in drive A and a blank disk in drive B. Type FORMAT B:/S,

press [enter], and follow the directions on the screen. The /S on the FORMAT command causes the following DOS system files to be copied to disk B as it is being formatted:

> IBMBIO.COM
> IBMDOS.COM
> COMMAND.COM

These files are necessary to make the disk bootable. Answer [N] to the question, format another (Y/N)? Now type CHKDSK B: and press [enter]; then type DIR B: and press [enter]. Notice that disk B is formatted for the maximum number of bytes. It contains one user file (COMMAND.COM) and two hidden files (IBMBIO.COM and IBMDOS.COM). The disk is now bootable. To copy the BASIC interpreter onto it, type COPY BASICA.COM B: and press [enter]. You now have a disk that is bootable, contains the BASICA interpreter, and has a large amount of free space for storing BASIC programs. Do a DIR B: to verify this. With this disk, you will not be able to execute the DOS commands that are stored outside of COMMAND.COM, such as CHKDSK and DISKCOPY. If you want all of the DOS capabilities on your new disk, repeat the procedure starting with the FORMAT B:/S command and change the COPY command to COPY *.* B:. This causes DOS to copy all the files (except the hidden ones) from drive A to B. You should also place the new disk in drive A and do a warm boot (hold down the [Alt] and [Ctrl] keys while striking the [Del] key) to verify that the disk is bootable. After you enter the date and time, type BASICA and press [enter] to go into BASIC. At this point either enter and save a BASIC program or return to DOS by typing SYSTEM and pressing [enter].

7. Place the DOS disk in drive A and a disk in drive B that has tape covering the write-protect notch. Type DISKCOPY A: B:, press [enter], and then follow the instructions on the screen. As you can see, the computer will not write onto the write-protected disk. To change this situation, either press the [Ctrl]-[Break] key combination or take out the disk in drive B and replace it with a blank disk that is not write protected.

Topic 2: Using WordStar for Word Processing

This introduction to word processing will be based on WordStar, a menu-driven word-processing program marketed by Micropro International Corporation. Although word-processing programs differ in their implementation, they have in common a basic set of functions—text creation, text deletion, text insertion, and text centering, just to name a few. These common functions make this introduction a valuable learning tool even if the word-processing software you eventually use is not WordStar.

Entering the WordStar Software

To start WordStar, you first boot up your personal computer by using DOS. After you have responded to the DOS date and time inquiries and have the DOS A> prompt, remove your DOS diskette and place your WordStar diskette in the left (A:) disk drive. Now type WS and press [enter]. A copyright message will appear on the screen for several seconds. It will then disappear and the WordStar opening menu will appear. This menu is shown in Figure B-2.1.

From the opening menu you can control all the files in the disk drive(s) of the computer in use. A directory of the files on one of these drives appears below the menu. Files (the letters, reports, memos, and other documents that have been created) can be printed, copied, renamed, and erased from this menu. This menu is also the point at which you can open and enter an existing or a new document. Any task shown on the opening menu can be initiated by pressing the letter next to the task description. You will come back to this menu later to do some printing, but right now let's open a new document and explore the features available there.

```
         not editing
                    < < < O P E N I N G   M E N U  > > >
    ---Preliminary Commands---  ¦ --File Commands--  ¦ -System Commands-
L  Change logged disk drive     ¦                    ¦ R  Run a program
F  File directory     off (ON)  ¦ P  Print a file    ¦ X  EXIT to system
H Set Help Level
   ---Commands to open a file---  ¦ E  RENAME a file  ¦ -WordStar Options-
    D  Open a document file       ¦ O  COPY   a file  ¦ M  Run MailMerge
    N  Open a non-document file   ¦ Y  DELETE a file  ¦ S  Run SpellStar
DIRECTORY of disk A:
```

FIGURE B-2.1 WordStar Opening Menu

From the opening menu, you can open any file for editing, printing, renaming, or special manipulations.

Opening a Document

You need to open a document, so press the [D] key. WordStar responds with:

```
NAME OF FILE TO EDIT?
```

If you give WordStar the name of an existing document it will open that file and you can make changes to (edit) it. If you give WordStar a new document name it will create a blank document with that name, on which you can enter text. Type in CAESAR (the name for our new document) and then press the [enter] key.

The screen that now appears is split into two areas and looks like the one shown in Figure B-2.2.

The top of the screen displays the WordStar main menu. The bottom of the screen is a blank work area for you to enter the text. Above the menu is a status line that looks like this:

```
A:CAESAR  PAGE 1 LINE 1 COL 1        INSERT ON
```

The status line tells you that you are editing a file named CAESAR from the A drive. It tells you that you are on the first page of the document and that your cursor is positioned on the first column (character) of the first line of that page. The status line also indicates that you are in insert mode.

At the bottom of the menu is a ruler line which looks like the one shown here:

```
L----!----!----!----!----!----!----!----!----!----!----!---R
```

The ruler line shows you where the left and right margins are set (the L and R) and where tabs (!) are currently set.

Go ahead and enter the following short line of text:

```
Caesar is well named.
```

Now, back up your cursor (using one of the four arrow keys on the numeric pad) until it is on the *w* in *well*. Key in the words a dog so that your text will look like this:

```
Caesar is a dog well named.
```

You just used the insertion feature of word processors. All word processors have the ability to be in insert mode or strikeover mode. Let's turn the insertion feature of WordStar off so

```
    A:CAESAR  PAGE 1 LINE 1 COL 01            INSERT  ON
                < < <     M A I N    M E N U    > > >
     --Cursor  Movement--   ! -Delete- !  -Miscellaneous-  !  -Other  Menus-
 ^S char left ^D char right !^G  char  ! ^I Tab   ^B Reform ! (from Main only)
 ^A word left ^F word right !DEL chr lf! ^V INSERT ON/OFF   !^J Help  ^K Block
 ^E line up   ^X line down  !^T word rt!^L Find/Replce again!^Q Quick ^P Print
    --Scrolling--           !^Y  line  !RETURN End paragraph!^O Onscreen
 ^Z line up   ^W line down  !          ! ^N Insert a RETURN !
 ^C screen up ^R screen down!          ! ^U Stop a command  !
 L----!----!----!----!----!----!----!----!----!----!--------R
```

FIGURE B-2.2 WordStar Main Menu

The main menu appears when a document is opened. The commands in it will act on the file currently being keyed or edited. From the main menu, five other edit menus can be accessed.

that you can use the strikeover feature. Press the [Ins] key in the lower right-hand corner of your keyboard. Notice that your status line no longer displays the INSERT ON message. Press the [Ins] key two more times and watch as the INSERT ON message reappears and then disappears again.

With the insert feature turned off, any text you insert will type over the preexisting text. Let's try this by typing the word *cat* over the word *dog*. Simply move your cursor to the *d* in *dog* and type cat. Your text should now look like this:

```
Caesar is a cat well named.
```

It is more convenient to keep the insert feature off and do the majority of your editing in the overstrike mode.

Deleting Text

One of the most common and useful features of a word processor is the ability to delete text. The most frequently deleted part is the single character. Turn your insert mode on and insert an extra *a* in the word *cat*. Then turn the insert feature off again. Your document should now look like this:

```
Caesar is a caat well named.
```

Now move your cursor to one of the two *a*'s in *caat*. Hold down the control key (the key marked [Ctrl] and strike the [G] key one time. This will delete the character. The [Ctrl]-[G] key sequence appears in the main menu at the top of your document under the Delete heading. The "^" symbol represents the [Ctrl] key. Let's use the ^T and ^Y commands to delete a word and then a line of text. Place your cursor on the *n* in the word *named*. Hold down the [Ctrl] key and strike the [T] key once. The word disappears. Once again hold down the [Ctrl] key, but this time press the [Y] key once (it doesn't matter where you locate the cursor on the line). The line is deleted.

Word Wrap

One of the nicest features of word processors is word wrap. This means you don't have to press the enter key at the end of a line as is necessary with the carriage return key on a typewriter. When you get to the end of a line, just keep on typing and the WordStar software will automatically advance you to the next line when you type past the margin. Test this feature by typing the paragraph in Figure B-2.3. Don't forget to use the features you have already learned to make corrections as you go along.

Reforming Paragraphs and the Hard Carriage Return

After entering and editing the first paragraph of your document, it might not look much like a paragraph. The right margin may be jagged, and text may run off the page in some

---

Caesar is a cat well named. One might think that a pet cat exists for the pleasure of its owner, but the reverse is true in Caesar's case. Washing, meal preparation, and kindly stroking are a few of the ammenities that Caesar enjoys. Her favorite entertainment, however, is to hide behind a bush or chair and then leap out and startle me just when I've started to worry about where she is.

FIGURE B-2.3   Your First Paragraph

places. When using WordStar you may occasionally need to reform your paragraphs. To do this, use your cursor to move the first character of the paragraph. Now, while holding down the [Ctrl] key, press the [B] key one time. Your paragraph will have been reformed and the cursor placed at the end of the paragraph. If this does not occur, one of two things has probably happened. First, WordStar may have stopped in the middle of reforming to ask you whether you would like to hyphenate a word. Follow the instructions of the message by pressing ^B again if you do not want to insert a hyphen or by pressing the hyphen if you do. There is a way to turn this hyphenation feature off, which we will discuss later.

The second reason your paragraph may not have reformed is that you inadvertently placed one or more hard carriage returns in your paragraph. This means that you pushed the enter key at the end of a line instead of continuing to type and letting the word-wrap feature take the words you typed to the next line. You can easily tell whether or not you have done this by looking at the right margin of your text. Any hard carriage return will appear as a < symbol. If you have one of these symbols, place your cursor just to the right of any text on the line where the hard carriage return is located and use the ^G (delete character) feature until you see the < symbol disappear. Then use the ^B key combination to reform your paragraph again. You can use the reform command from any cursor location in the paragraph. Doing so will reform the paragraph, starting with the current line (the line where your cursor is located) and continuing until a hard carriage return is encountered.

Saving Your Work

So far, all of your work has been done in the random-access memory (RAM) of the computer. This is volatile memory which would be lost if the power were to be interrupted. For your work to be permanently saved, you must write your document from RAM to your floppy disk. This saving process is done at the end of short word-processing sessions as part of exiting the document. When long sessions occur, it is wise to periodically save the work you have typed so far, while remaining in the document to continue entering and editing text.

To use the save features available in WordStar, you must move to another menu. The main menu currently at the top of your document has an area on the right side with the heading -Other Menus-. The save commands are available from the block menu. Use the ^K key combination to move to this menu (see Figure B-2.4). Notice the area of the menu labeled -Saving Files-. Any of these options can be selected by pressing the corresponding letter. The first option is Save & resume. This writes your document to the disk but leaves you within the document. The next option is Save--done. This writes

```
^K        A:CAESAR   PAGE 1 LINE 1 COL 01            INSERT ON
                        < < <    B L O C K   M E N U    > > >
 -Saving  Files- ! -Block Operations- ! -File  Operations- !   -Other   Menus-
 S Save & resume ! B  Begin  K  End   ! R  Read  P  Print   ! (from Main only)
 D Save--done    ! H  Hide / Display  ! O  Copy  E  Rename  ! ^J Help  ^K Block
 X Save & exit   ! C  Copy   Y  Delete! J  Delete           ! ^Q Quick ^P Print
 Q Abandon file  ! V  Move   W  Write ! -Disk  Operations-  ! ^O Onscreen
 -Place Markers- ! N  Column  on (OFF)!L Change logged disk! Space Bar returns
 0-9 set/hide 0-9!                     !F Directory on (OFF)! you to Main Menu.
 L----!----!----!----!----!----!----!----!----!----!--------R
```

FIGURE B-2.4 WordStar Block Menu

From the block menu, sections of text can be moved, copied, saved, or otherwise manipulated. File operations such as renaming and printing can also be performed from this menu.

Now and again Caesar does treat me with some compassion. If I go for a walk Caesar will come along. She stays about ten yards back, however, so as not to give anyone the impression that she is too awfully fond of me. She'll also give a soft rub on my shin occasionally, even though the occasion is usually dinner.

All things considered, there is still something about this mistress of the household that is irresistible. So, I think we'll continue our acquaintance . . . if she agrees.

FIGURE B-2.5   *The Remaining Paragraphs of Your Text*

your document to the disk and moves you out of the document, back to the opening menu. The third option is `Save & exit`. This writes your document to the disk, stops the WordStar software, and returns you to the DOS A> prompt. The last option under the `-Saving Files-` section is to `Abandon file`. This would remove you from the document without saving any work that had been done since the last time the file was written to the disk. You would choose this option if you decided that the changes you have made to the file are not desirable.

Let's use the `Save--done` feature by pressing the [D] key. WordStar needs a few seconds to save your file. While this task is being done, the following message is displayed:

```
^Kd          WAIT
 SAVING FILE A:CAESAR
```

You will also notice that the light on the left disk drive glows, indicating your document is being written to the disk.

After the document has been saved, the system presents the WordStar opening menu. A directory of the files on the A disk is displayed below the menu. Your CAESAR document should now be a part of that directory listing. Now open the CAESAR document again so that you can explore some more features of WordStar.

Your document is starting to get larger so let's take a look at some of the cursor-movement commands. On an IBM PC or compatible the numeric keypad offers a number of cursor movement features. The arrows on the 4 [←] and 6 [→] keys move the cursor one character to the left and to the right, respectively. The up [↑] and down [↓] arrows on the 8 and 2 keys move the cursor up or down one line of text. The [Pg Up] and [Pg Dn] keys move you up or down one screen of text. The home key moves your cursor to the top of the current screen and the end key moves the cursor to the bottom of the current screen. In addition to these cursor movements, you can move to the right one word by using ^F and left one word by using ^A (as shown at the -Cursor Movements- section of the main menu). Some personal computers do not have cursor arrow keys; thus you have to use the cursor-movement key combinations displayed on the main menu. There are some additional cursor commands available on the `Quick` menu. The Quick menu is accessed from the Main menu by using the ^Q key combination. Practice moving around your document until you feel comfortable with the techniques available. Now type the paragraphs in Figure B-2.5. Don't forget to put a hard carriage return at the end of each paragraph.

Onscreen and Print Formatting

You've got the basics down. Now let's get fancy. Move up to the top of your file so that your cursor is on the very first character in the text. Now use the ^N key combination to insert a blank line at the top of your text. Use ^N two more times until there are three blank lines at the top of your document. You've just made room for a title. On the top line at the left margin, type in the title CAESAR. Now you will use a WordStar formatting command to center the title. Centering is one of the formatting features found on the `Onscreen` menu. Access this menu by using ^O. Now press a [c] for center. Your title will have moved to the center of your ruler line and WordStar will have simultaneously brought you back to the main menu.

Let's look at some of the other onscreen abilities of WordStar. Use the ^O key combination to enter the onscreen menu again. Notice under the -Line Functions- heading there is a line-spacing option. Select it by pushing an [S]. WordStar should now be prompting you for the line-spacing option you desire. Enter a 2. Note that the status line now displays this added piece of information. If you're wondering why nothing changed on the screen it is because none of the paragraphs have been reformed. Move to the beginning of each paragraph and reform it. This will cause double spacing to appear. If your paragraph re-forming is being held up by the hyphenation feature, you may want to turn this feature off by using ^OH.

Some formatting functions are not available on the screen but are available during printing. Underlining is an example of such a feature. It is found on the Print menu. First, be sure that your cursor is on the first letter in your title and then obtain the print menu by using ^P. Then press an [S] to mark the beginning of the underscore. Notice that your title now has a ^S in front of it. Move your cursor to the first blank space after the title and use the ^PS combination again. Your title should now look like this:

^SCaesar^S

The symbols before and after the title are control symbols and will *not* be printed by the printer. The printer will interpret them to mean "turn the underline on and then turn the underline off."

For the final part of this introduction, let's print out your document. First, take a moment to correct any errors in your document. Then, exit the document by using ^KD ([Ctrl] [K] takes you to the block menu; and the D, you will recall, is for Save--done). You should now be back at the opening menu. One of the options here is to print a file. Select this option by pressing the [P] key. WordStar responds with:

NAME OF FILE TO PRINT?

Type in CAESAR, the name of our file. WordStar now responds:

For default press ENTER for each question:
   DISK FILE OUTPUT (Y/N):

WordStar is providing you with various print options. You will be asked to respond to six questions (see Figure B-2.6). If you are unsure about how to respond to a question, press the [enter] key. WordStar is programmed to assume the most common answer, which is set up as the "default" value. Explanations for the six inquiries are presented in Figure B-2.6. After you have answered all the questions, make sure the printer is turned on and then press the [enter] key. If you need to stop the printer during a printing job, simply press the [P] key which is now labeled Stop PRINT on the opening menu.

Most word processors, including WordStar, have hundreds of features that make it easier to input, edit, format, and print documents. Learning to use all of them will take some time, but in the long run your hard work will pay off. The key to learning the features is continued regular use and experimentation. Each time you use your word processor, explore the options it has to offer.

If you would like to explore WordStar further, there are some good paperback books that cover this software in depth. I would suggest Micro Workshop of Cambridge, *WordStar for the IBM PC: A Self-Guided Tutorial*. Bowie, Maryland: Brady Communications Company, Inc., 1984.

```
P        editing no file
```

```
NAME OF FILE TO PRINT? CAESAR
For default press RETURN for each question:
    DISK FILE OUTPUT (Y/N): N
    START AT PAGE NUMBER (RETURN for beginning)? 1
    STOP AFTER PAGE NUMBER (RETURN for end)? 1
    USE FORM FEEDS (Y/N): N
    SUPPRESS PAGE FORMATTING (Y/N): N
    PAUSE FOR PAPER CHANGE BETWEEN PAGES (Y/N): N
Ready printer, press RETURN:
```

DISK FILE OUTPUT (Y/N):
    A Y response sends your output to a file instead of to the printer. Default is N.

START AT PAGE NUMBER (RETURN for beginning)?
    Gives you the option of beginning the print function at a specified page number of your text. Default is page 1.

STOP AFTER PAGE NUMBER (RETURN for end)?
    Gives you the option of stopping the print function at a specified page number of your text. Default is the last page of your document.

USE FORM FEEDS (Y/N):
    Answer Y when you are using a cut-sheet feeder instead of a tractor feed. Default is N.

SUPPRESS PAGE FORMATTING (Y/N):
    A Y answer suppresses margins, footers, and headers. Default is N.

PAUSE FOR PAPER CHANGE BETWEEN PAGES (Y/N):
    Answer Y to this question if you have neither a cut-sheet feeder or a tractor feed. WordStar will give you time to insert a new piece of paper after each page of your text is printed. Default is N.

cut-sheet feeder
A mechanism that automatically inserts individual pages (cut sheets) into a printer.

tractor feed
A sprocket mechanism that feeds continuous-form paper through a printer. Continuous-form paper is perforated between the individual sheets.

FIGURE B-2.6 WordStar Print Options

If you are unsure how to answer any of the WordStar print inquiries, just press the [enter] key. WordStar is programmed to use (default to) the most likely response.

Another inexpensive approach to obtaining word-processing software is to get PC-Write. PC-Write is published by Quicksoft and is a complete word-processing package (not a crippled version which is often provided for student use). For ten dollars, Quicksoft will send you a disk containing the software and an instruction manual on the disk. You can print the manual from the disk and learn to use the package. Quicksoft also encourages you to give copies of the disk to your friends. So several students can obtain the software for a fraction of the shared ten-dollar cost, plus the cost of a disk. If you want a more complete bound manual as well as program updates, send seventy-five dollars to Quicksoft. You can write Quicksoft at 219 1st N., Box 224, Seattle, WA 98109 or phone 206-282-0452.

Hands-on Exercises

1. Write, save, and print a short business letter thanking a customer for an order.
2. Write, save, and print a short business letter asking for more time to pay a bill.
3. Retrieve the letter you created in the first exercise, change the address, and add a sentence in the middle of a paragraph. After making these changes, save and print the new letter.
4. Write, save, and print a short summary (not more than two pages) of the advantages and disadvantages of using word-processing software as compared to using a typewriter.

Topic 3: Using Lotus 1-2-3 and SuperCalc3 to Build Electronic Spreadsheets

Accountants and other business people have been using columnar paper for many years to organize their work. Accompanying the advent of personal computers, electronic spreadsheets appeared. This introduction to spreadsheet programs has three sections. First will be a discussion on the common characteristics of all spreadsheets, followed by introductions to Lotus 1-2-3 and SuperCalc3, two frequently used spreadsheets.

Spreadsheet Concepts

Although there are many spreadsheet programs available today, virtually all of them have a similar fundamental design. The basic design of an electronic spreadsheet is the same as its paper counterpart—the columnar pad (see Figure B-3.1). The spreadsheet pictured has four vertical lines separating the spreadsheet into **columns.** The columns are labeled A, B, C, D, and E. The horizontal lines separate the spreadsheet into **rows.** They are labeled 1 through 5 in the example. The intersection of a row and a column is called a **cell.** Each cell has an **address,** which is the combination of the column letter and row number that form the cell. Thus the top left-hand corner in the example is cell A1. The bottom right-hand corner is cell E5. One of the advantages of electronic spreadsheets over their paper counterpart is size. For example, Lotus 1-2-3 has 256 columns and 2,048 rows. Thus there are 524,288 cells! To get an idea of how big this is, consider the following: if each cell was ¾-inch wide and ¼-inch high, the size of the paper represented by the spreadsheet would be 16 feet wide and 43 feet high! Obviously you could not view all of these cells on the screen of your computer at once. Your screen is like a movable window; you view small portions of the spreadsheet at a time. If you want to see another part, you move the window to that section. This movement is called **scrolling.**

Now that you understand the basic design of the spreadsheet, how does it work? Although some features are unique to a particular spreadsheet, several items are quite common.

Most spreadsheets are designed so that cells will hold text, **labels,** numbers, or formulas. (Numbers and formulas are often called **values.**) Cells that hold text can be used for titles, explanations, or descriptions. Cells that hold numbers allow you to input the numerical data that is needed for calculations. Finally, formulas are used to compute additional numbers, based on some specified relationship between the cells of the worksheet. Any particular cell may hold either text, labels, numbers, or formulas.

A brief example will clarify these terms. Suppose you have a small spreadsheet used to calculate the total sales for a company with three divisions (see Figure B-3.2). This spread-

	A	B	C	D	E	...
1						
2						
3						
4						
5						
.						
.						
.						

FIGURE B-3.1   A Spreadsheet

A spreadsheet is also called a worksheet. The electronic spreadsheet has been a primary factor in the popularity of personal computers. Of the computer software that allows you to create your own tailor-made applications, spreadsheets are perhaps the easiest to learn and use.

sheet uses two columns (A and B) and five rows (1 through 5). Cell A1 has text in it (the word *division*). Cells A2, A3, A4, and A5 also have text. Cell B1 is blank. Cells B2, B3, and B4 all have numbers in them. These numbers represent the sales for each division. At first glance it appears that cell B5 also has a number in it, just like the cells above it, but this number is different. This number is the **result** of adding the numbers in cells B2, B3, and B4. Cell B5 actually contains a formula. However, it is the result of the formula, not the formula itself, that is displayed on the screen. This formula would be provided at the time

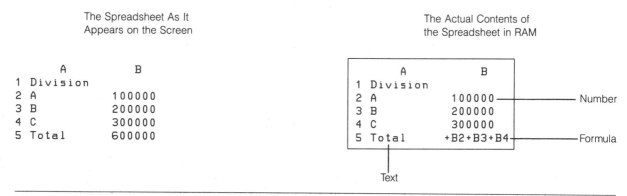

FIGURE B-3.2   The Contents of a Spreadsheet

You can place any number, text, or formula in any cell of a spreadsheet. The essence of the power of an electronic spreadsheet is the ability to place formulas in cells that reference other cells, as shown in cell B5 of this figure. These formulas may be as complex as your courage will allow.

the worksheet is prepared. If any of the numbers in cells B2, B3, and B4 are changed, the number in B5 changes also. It is the ability of spreadsheets to perform these computations easily and quickly that has led to the widespread use of this type of software.

Another common feature of spreadsheets is that frequently used computations are pre-programmed into the software and may be accessed by key words or symbols in the formula. Some common functions available are average, present value, and total or sum.

A Note Before You Proceed

In the following introduction to Lotus 1-2-3 and SuperCalc3, a common example will be provided. The example is a business that is applying for a bank loan. The loan officer has requested that the firm prepare, in addition to financial statements, a three-year projection of its net income. The following numbers have been obtained from the firm's management:

Expected Sales
Year 1	$300,000
Year 2	$350,000
Year 3	$375,000

Cost of goods sold is approximately 60 percent of the total sales. Other expenses are estimated at $100,000 per year.

The task is to provide management with the projected net income each year for the three-year period. This process will be described separately for Lotus 1-2-3 and SuperCalc3.

Before you proceed, you should be familiar with DOS, the Disk Operating System, which is discussed in Topic 1 of this appendix. You should now have (1) an IBM-PC or compatible computer, (2) a copy of either Lotus 1-2-3 or SuperCalc3, and (3) a formatted floppy disk. If you are missing any of these items, please stop until you have them all.

Lotus 1-2-3

Accessing Lotus 1-2-3   To begin, place the Lotus 1-2-3 disk in drive A and your formatted disk in drive B. Turn the computer on. After entering the date and time you will see the initial screen for Lotus 1-2-3, as shown in Figure B-3.3. (This depends on how your Lotus 1-2-3 disk has been set up. You may have to type LOTUS and press [enter] before you get the screen shown in Figure B-3.3.) At the top of the screen you will see a horizontal menu of commands which begins with the command 1-2-3 (see Figure B-3.3). Notice that 1-2-3 is highlighted with the cursor. Press the right cursor key and move the cursor (the highlighted area) across from 1-2-3 to the other commands on that line.

```
Lotus Access System  V.1A  (C)1983 Lotus Development Corp.            MENU
--------------------------------------------------------------------------
1-2-3  File-Manager  Disk-Manager  PrintGraph  Translate  Exit
Enter 1-2-3 -- Lotus Spreadsheet/Graphics/Database program
==========================================================================
```

FIGURE B-3.3   The Lotus 1-2-3 Access Menu

Lotus 1-2-3 is a good example of a menu-driven program. You communicate with the software by choosing commands on a menu rather than by keying in commands as you would with a command-driven program. The dBASE II and III are examples of command-driven programs.

Notice that each time the cursor moves to a new command, the text in the area immediately below the command menu line changes. This text is intended to be an explanation of the highlighted command. This method of highlighted commands with explanations will be used throughout the Lotus 1-2-3 package, and it will become quite familiar to you after a short while. Since the command 1-2-3 is the one that actually accesses the worksheet (Lotus 1-2-3 uses the term *worksheet* instead of spreadsheet), move the cursor over to 1-2-3 and press the [enter] key. In a moment you will see a screen appear with the Lotus 1-2-3 copyright notice on it. Press any key to leave this screen and to begin working.

Using the HELP Screens   The first thing to understand about Lotus 1-2-3 is how to access its HELP screens. One of the many features of this software is that help is easily available. The way to get it is to press the [F1] key. (Remember the keys [F1] through [F10] are the function keys located on the left side of the keyboard.) When you press the [F1] key, the worksheet temporarily disappears and a page of information appears, as shown in Figure B-3.4.

There are hundreds of pages of HELP text available. You can move from page to page within HELP by moving the cursor and highlighting the topic you are interested in. Then press the [enter] key. Try this by moving the cursor to How to Use "Help" and then pressing the [enter] key. After reading this HELP screen, move the cursor to Help Index and again press the [enter] key.

Any topic on this HELP index that you can highlight with the cursor can be chosen by moving the cursor to it and pressing the [enter] key. Try one. Move your cursor to Modes and Indicators and press [enter]. After reading this screen choose ERROR by highlighting it and pressing [enter]. Look over this information and then select Fixing Typing Mistakes. After reading this page return to the HELP index by selecting Help

```
A1:                                                                              HELP


═══════════════════════════════════════════════════════════════ 41;81 ═══════
  Ready Mode      The mode indicator "Ready" in the upper right corner of the screen
  ══════════      means 1-2-3 is ready for you to issue a command or type a cell
                  entry.  The first key you press determines your action:

  FORMULA OR NUMBER ... if you press a digit (0..9)      ┌─────────────────────┐
                        or one of these characters. ───→ │  +    -    .     (  │
                                                         │  @    #    $        │
                                                         └─────────────────────┘
  LABEL ... if you press a letter (A..Z, a..z) or most   ┌─────────────────────┐
        other characters. Start with a "label-prefix"    │ '    left-aligned   │
  character to create a label of a particular type. ───→ │ "    right-aligned  │
                                                         │ ^    centered       │
  COMMAND ... if you press "slash" (/).                  │ \    repeating.     │
                                                         └─────────────────────┘
  SPECIAL FUNCTION ... if you press a function key: F1, F2, .. F10.

        ┌──────────────────────────────────────────────────────────────┐
        │ Don't remove the 1-2-3 System Disk -- this "Help" facility will│
        │ cease to work! To learn more about "Help", press [End], then ↵.│
        └──────────────────────────────────────────────────────────────┘

  Further Help ->    Cell Entries        Erasing Cell Entries      Mode Indicators
         Topics ->   Special Keys        Help Index                How to Use "Help"
```

FIGURE B-3.4   A Lotus 1-2-3 HELP Screen

I n d e x. As you just did, you can move around the HELP screen and then move back to the HELP index and choose other topics. You should practice doing this until you are familiar with moving through the HELP screens. At this point do not attempt to understand the text of the HELP screens in depth. You only need to understand how to use the HELP facility.

Lotus 1-2-3 cuts down on the amount of "page turning" that you have to do in the HELP system by keeping an eye on what you are attempting to do in the worksheet at all times. When you go for help, Lotus 1-2-3 has an idea of the topic you need help on and will present you with the appropriate screen. If you were building a graph, for example, and you pressed the [F1] key, Lotus 1-2-3 would present you with a HELP screen containing graph-related information. Lotus 1-2-3 aids in your HELP needs in one other convenient way. At the upper right corner of every HELP screen are page-number references to the Lotus 1-2-3 user's manual. Those pages of the manual will give you even more detailed information on the topic you're investigating. To return to your worksheet from any section of the HELP system, just press the escape key [Esc]. If the HELP information is still on the screen, press the [E s c] key now. Use the HELP system often; you will be able to learn many of the options that are available in Lotus 1-2-3 by referring to it.

Interpreting the Control Panel   The next thing to learn is the information on the screen in the area above the worksheet, which is called the **control panel** (see Figure B-3.5). First, notice that in the top left corner of the screen the address of the current cell is shown. The current cell is the one that is highlighted. Move the highlighted cell around by using the cursor keys located on the number pad, and see how the control panel changes. In the upper right corner of the spreadsheet is a **mode indicator.** It should now display a READY **mode.** This indicates Lotus 1-2-3 is ready for you to enter information into the worksheet. We'll talk about other messages or modes when we need to use them.

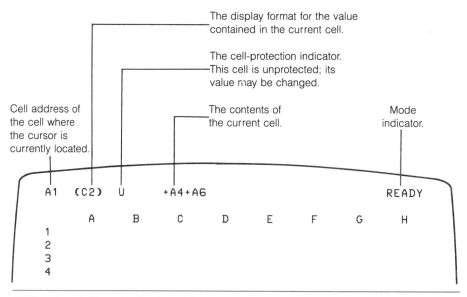

FIGURE B-3.5   The Lotus 1-2-3 Control Panel

On your computer screen you probably do not see the display format, the cell-protection indicator, or the contents of the current cell. As you enter values in the worksheet, you will begin to understand these components of the control panel.

Moving Around the Worksheet   As noted earlier, the Lotus 1-2-3 spreadsheet is 256 columns across and 2,048 rows down. The columns are specified by alphabetic characters. The first column is A, the twenty-sixth is Z, the twenty-seventh is AA, and so on until column IV, the 256th column. The rows are numbered consecutively from 1 to 2,048. With a spreadsheet this large, it is important to be comfortable with the various ways to move the cell pointer around the spreadsheet. The cell pointer can be moved a cell at a time, a page at a time, and by direct addressing.

By this time you probably have moved the cell pointer from one cell to another by using the cursor keys on the right side of your keyboard. This is moving one cell at a time, and is the best way to move the cell pointer short distances. However, if you had to move from cell B1 to cell Y400, this would not be the best way to move. You can move an entire screen up or down by using the [PgUp] and [PgDn] keys. Try this. You can also move a screen at a time to the left or to the right by using the [TAB] key. The [TAB] key on the IBM PC is on the left side of the keyboard and is marked with one arrow pointing left and one pointing right. Pressing the [TAB] key will move one screen on the worksheet to the right. Holding the [SHIFT] key down and pressing the [TAB] key will move one screen to the left. Try this a few times. If you have strayed a long way from the A1 cell, there is a quick method for getting back. Simply press the [Home] key (located on the 1 key of the numeric keypad) and you will be taken back to cell A1.

Another way to move around the spreadsheet is by direct addressing. Press the [F5] key on the left side of your keyboard. A message appears on the top of your screen asking for a cell address to go to. You can enter the coordinates of any cell and Lotus 1-2-3 will instantly move the cell pointer to that location. Type any cell address, enter it, and then use the [Home] key to return to the upper left corner of the spreadsheet.

Accessing the Command Line   The last general item to understand before preparing the worksheet is how to access the **command line.** This can be done by pressing the slash key [/] which is on the bottom of the right side of the keyboard with the question mark. Try it. When you press this key a list of command choices appears at the top of the screen, as shown in Figure B-3.6. The first command choice is Worksheet. Once again, you can move the cursor from one command to the next by using the cursor control keys. As the cursor is moved the words beneath the menu line change. Instead of being explanations of the command itself, these words are actually lists of **subcommands** that are available if you choose the highlighted command by pressing [enter]. For example, move the cursor to the word File. The second line should contain the following words: Retrieve, Save, Combine, Xtract, Erase, List, Import, Directory. You can return to the worksheet by pressing [Esc]. However, if you have selected a subcommand or sub-sub-command, you may need to press the Escape key more than once to return to the worksheet. Notice that while the command lines are on the screen, the mode indicator in the upper right corner of the spreadsheet shows MENU. You can tell that you are out of the command mode when the indicator is back to READY. Try calling

```
A1:                                                              MENU
┌─────────┐
│Worksheet│ Range  Copy  Move  File  Print  Graph  Data  Quit
└─────────┘
    Global, Insert, Delete, Column-Width, Erase, Titles, Window, Status
```

FIGURE B-3.6   The Main Command Menu

This is the top-level Lotus 1-2-3 command menu. As you use 1-2-3, you will see that it has many levels of menus.

up the command list and returning to the worksheet a few times until you feel comfortable with it. You will do this quite frequently as you work with Lotus 1-2-3.

So far in this discussion of Lotus 1-2-3 commands you have always used the cursor control keys to move the cursor from one command to the next. Once the desired command is reached you press the [enter] key to choose that particular command. There is a quicker way to do this, however. Once again call up the command line by pressing the slash key [/]. Move the cursor over to the word Graph and press [enter]. Now press the [Esc] key and move the cursor back to the word Worksheet. This time, instead of moving the cursor to graph and pressing enter, just press the G key [G]. As you can see, the same result occurs. So you have two ways to select a command. You can either move the cursor to that command and press [enter] or press the first letter of the command's name. This will work with all Lotus command lines. Press the [Esc] key twice before you move on.

label
Text data that are not used in calculations.

value
A number or formula that is used in calculations.

Building a Worksheet   It is finally time to begin. Move the cursor to cell A2. Type Sales and press [enter]. Notice that while you are typing the mode indicator shows LABEL. When you input data into a spreadsheet cell, Lotus 1-2-3 always interprets it as either a *label* or a *value*. The importance of the distinction between the two types of cell contents will become apparent as you continue with the example. In cell A3 type Cost of Goods Sold. In cell A4 type Gross Profit. Make sure you press [enter] after each time you type an entry into a cell. If you make a mistake, move the cursor to the correct cell and retype it. In A5 type Other Expenses and in cell A6 type Net Income. Now in cells B1, C1, and D1 type in the years 1986, 1987, and 1988. When you have finished, the worksheet should look something like the one shown in Figure B-3.7.

As you can see, the labels entered into column A are much wider than column A itself. This does not appear at the moment to be a problem, since the adjacent cells are empty. However, it will not work well later when you insert information into column B. Therefore it will be useful to make column A wider. This can be done by following a command sequence. First, move the cursor to cell A3. Next, press the slash key [/] to indicate that you would like to enter a command. Move the cursor to Worksheet on the main command line and press [enter]. Now, either move the cursor to the Column-Width command and press [enter] or type C to choose the Column-Width command. In order to change an existing column width select the Set command or type S. Using the right cursor key on the number pad, expand the column width one character at a time until the column is wide enough to contain the phrase Cost of Goods Sold. Then press [enter] to complete the operation. Column A should now be about nineteen spaces wide.

The next step is to enter the expected sales. Move the cursor to cell B2 and type 300000. Note that you should *not* enter in dollar signs or commas as you type in numbers. You will see how this is handled a little later. Continue by entering the expected sales for 1987 and 1988—350000 and 375000 in cells C2 and D2, respectively.

```
         A              B         C         D
1                       1986      1987      1988
2 Sales
3 Cost of Goods Sold
4 Gross Profit
5 Other Expenses
6 Net Income
7
```

FIGURE B-3.7   A Partially Completed Worksheet

Entering Formulas The cost of goods sold is 60 percent of sales. So for 1986, the cost of goods sold is $180,000. However, it is *not* wise to enter $180,000 into cell B3. If you did this, the cost of goods sold would have to be reentered if the sales estimate were to change. This is called **hardwiring** a spreadsheet, which means that a number specific to a certain situation was entered, instead of a formula which could handle a variety of situations. Hardwiring should be avoided whenever possible. As an alternative, you could enter a formula into cell B3. Since costs of goods sold are always 60 percent or .6 of sales, and sales are located in cell B2, the formula +B2*.6 will properly compute the cost of goods sold. Lotus 1-2-3 uses the * to indicate multiplication. The + is not mathematically necessary, but it is necessary to keep Lotus 1-2-3 from confusing the formula with a label (a word starting with the letter B). As soon as you type the +, the mode indicator will show VALUE, indicating that Lotus 1-2-3 is expecting a number or formula. Go ahead and type +B2*.6 and press [enter]. You should see the result of your formula in cell B3. Good work!

Using the Copy Command It really would not be too much trouble to type in a similar formula in cells C3 and D3; however, there is a faster way. Instead of retyping the formula, you can copy it. Remember as you go through choices in the command menu that if you make a mistake you can press [Esc]. Lotus 1-2-3 will return to the point in the menu where you were before you made the error. Don't be afraid to press the keys in 1-2-3. Generally the [Esc] key will allow you to escape from errors. To copy the formula, first move the cursor to cell B3. Press the slash key [/] to select a command, then choose the Copy command. Next you will be asked which cell or range of cells you wish to copy FROM. Lotus 1-2-3 guesses that you want to copy the cell where the cursor presently resides, which is correct, so press [enter]. Then Lotus 1-2-3 wants to know where to copy the formula TO. Since you would like the formula to be copied to cells C3 and D3, tell Lotus 1-2-3 this by moving the cursor to cell C3, pressing the period key [.] to pin the cursor down, and then stretching the cursor over to cell D3. Now both cells C3 and D3 should be highlighted on the screen. To finish the copy command press [enter]. On the screen you should be able to see the computed cost of goods sold for all three years.

Let's see the result of a copy command. Move the cursor to cell B3 if it is not already there. In the top left corner (control panel) of the screen, you can see the formula +B2*0.6 for cell B3. Move the cursor across to cells C3 and D3 while you look at the formula. You will see that Lotus 1-2-3 copied the formula, adjusting it as it was copied. Copying formulas can save a great deal of time; use it often.

Now let's complete the rest of the projections. The next number you want to compute is gross profit. The formula for gross profit for 1986 is +B2-B3. Type this in cell B4 and press [enter]. Using the steps just listed, copy this formula to cells C4 and D4. Next, enter in the other expenses of $100,000 into cell B5. Remember, you do not enter the dollar sign ($) or the comma (,). Copy the 100000 to cells C5 and D5. Finally, in cells B6 through D6 enter a formula for net income—it should be +B4-B5. Again copy this formula to cells C6 and D6. If you make any mistakes, you can either move to the incorrect cell and type over the entry or move to the cell and press the [F2] key. This will give you the opportunity to edit (change) the cell contents. Notice that the mode indicator shows EDIT when you do this. After pressing the [F2] key, change the cell's contents by using the left and right arrow and the [Del] keys for moving around and deleting. If you want to erase a cell completely, use the command Range Erase. To find out how to use this command, go to the help system. (Press [/], select Range, and then press [F1].) After you have used the [Esc] key to return from HELP, your worksheet should look like Figure B-3.8.

Saving Worksheets on Disk Since you are probably beginning to get comfortable with entering commands, you can start using a shorter form of commands. Instead of saying "Type the slash key [/] and select the copy command" we will use a shortcut and say type

	A	B	C	D
1		1986	1987	1988
2	Sales	300000	350000	375000
3	Cost of Goods Sold	180000	210000	225000
4	Gross Profit	120000	140000	150000
5	Other Expenses	100000	100000	100000
6	Net Income	20000	40000	50000

FIGURE B-3.8   Another Partially Completed Worksheet

This worksheet is functional (useful), because you can change some of the numbers and the rest will recalculate. You will dress it up later.

/Copy. This does not mean to type a slash and then the word *Copy*. Type only the first letter of the words in a command sequence. Lotus 1-2-3 knows that when you press the C key after pressing the slash key that you want the copy command. So for /Copy you type only /C.

Usually you will want to save the spreadsheet that you are working on for later use or reference. Let's save the spreadsheet that you have created so far. Type /File Save. (Remember, you only need to type the first letter of each word.) Lotus 1-2-3 now requests the filename. A filename can be any combination of one to eight letters or letters and numbers. Let's use the filename EXAMPLE. Type EXAMPLE and press [enter]. The light on the B disk drive will come on as Lotus 1-2-3 saves the file. Check to see whether the file was properly saved. First erase the existing worksheet. To do this type /Worksheet Erase Yes. To retrieve the file, type /File Retrieve. Lotus 1-2-3 then provides you with a list of all the worksheet files on your disk. Move the cursor over to select the file EXAMPLE and press [enter]. The file you saved just a minute ago is loaded in and now you are ready to continue your work.

Making a Worksheet Look Good   The worksheet you have created so far is good, but its appearance can be improved. As you may know, it is typical in financial reports to put commas between the 000's and to put a dollar sign in front of the first and last items in a column. Let's do this in the EXAMPLE spreadsheet, beginning with the sales figures. In order to format the sales figures properly, first move the cursor to cell B2 and type /Range Format Currency 0. Then press [enter]. Next, stretch the cursor over the range B2..D2 by pressing the right cursor [→] key twice. Finish the command by pressing [enter]. All the sales figures should now have dollar signs and commas. Following the same steps, format the net-income figures. Then format the remaining numbers (not with dollar signs but with commas). To do this, type /Range Format , 0 [enter] B3..D5 [enter]. The report is beginning to take shape. Notice that this time you typed in the cell range B3..D5 instead of pointing with the cursor.

Move your cell pointer to cell A9. Type Total Projected 3 Year Income. Now move your cell pointer to cell D9. You want the total of cells B6, C6, and D6 (the individual annual net incomes) in cell D9. You could use the formula +B6+C6+D6, but there is a more powerful way. Type the formula @sum(B6..D6) and press the [enter] key. The @SUM formula tells Lotus 1-2-3 to sum up the values in the cells within the range from cell B6 to cell D6. In this case not a lot of time was saved, but it is easy to see how this could save time if a column or a row of a hundred numbers needed to be added together. Lotus 1-2-3 has many @ formulas like the @sum formula that operate on a range of cells. Some of the more commonly used ones are shown in Figure B-3.9.

@ Formulas That Work on Ranges

`@SUM(range)`	Gives the sum of a range of cells.
`@AVG(range)`	Gives the average (mean) of a range of cells.
`@VAR(range)`	Gives the variance of a range of cells.
`@STD(range)`	Gives the standard deviation of a range.
`@MIN(range)`	Gives the minimum value of a range of cells.
`@MAX(range)`	Gives the maximum value of a range of cells.
`@COUNT(range)`	Counts the number of entries in a range (will not count an empty cell).

@ Formulas That Work on a Single Cell Address

`@ABS(cell address)`	Gives the absolute value of specified cell.
`@SIN(cell address)`	Gives the sine of specified cell.
`@COS(cell address)`	Gives the cosine of specified cell.
`@TAN(cell address)`	Gives the tangent of specified cell.
`@ASIN(cell address)`	Gives the arc sine of specified cell.
`@ACOS(cell address)`	Gives the arc cosine of specified cell.
`@LN(cell address)`	Gives the log base e of specified cell.
`@LOG(cell address)`	Gives the log base 10 of specified cell.
`@ROUND(cell addr, n)`	Gives the value of specified cell rounded to nearest n decimal places.
`@INT(cell address)`	Gives only the integer part of specified cell.
`@SQRT`	Gives square root of specified cell.

Financial @ Formulas

`@IRR(guess,range)`	Gives internal rate of return for the sequence in range.
`@NPV(x,range)`	Gives net present value of range based on interest rate x; x can be a cell address.
`@FV(prn,int,term)`	Gives future value of principle (prn) after (term) periods at interest rate (int) per period; prn, int, and term can all be cell addresses.
`@PV(pmt,int,term)`	Gives the present value of an ordinary annuity of payments (pmt) for (term) periods at interest rate (int); pmt, int, and term can be cell addresses.
`@PMT(prn,int,term)`	Gives the per-period payment for borrowing (prn) dollars for (term) periods at interest rate (int); prn, int, and term can be cell addresses.

FIGURE B-3.9 Frequently Used Lotus 1-2-3 @ Formulas

These are often called functions, but Lotus 1-2-3 treats them the same as formulas.

Go ahead and format this cell as you did for sales and net income, except use two decimal places. After being sure the cursor is on cell D9, type `/Range Format Currency 2` `[enter][enter]`. The D9 cell has suddenly filled with asterisks. Lotus 1-2-3 does not allow a value to spill into the next cell. After you formatted it, the number was too large for the cell. Use the `/Worksheet Column-Width Set` Command sequence and the right cursor [→] key to set columns B, C, and D to a width of 12.

Next, put on a heading. Most reports have the company name, title of the schedule, and the date at the top of each page. However, we have not left any room for this information. The Move command will be useful here. First put the cursor in cell A1. Next type `/ Move` `A1..D9 [enter] A6 [enter]`. This moves the whole range down five rows, adjusting the formulas as necessary. Put the following heading in Cells B1, B2, and B3.

```
Lotus Example, Inc.
 Schedule of Income
For 1986, 1987, 1988
```

The last change will be to insert several rows with the spreadsheet to separate the subtotals. Move the cursor to cell A9. Type `/ Worksheet Insert Row [enter]`. This inserts

```
                  A                    B             C             D
        1                        Lotus Example, Inc.
        2                        Schedule of Income
        3                        For 1986, 1987, 1988
        4
        5
        6                              1986          1987          1988
        7      Sales               $300,000      $350,000      $375,000
        8      Cost of Goods Sold   180,000       210,000       225,000
        9                          --------------------------------------
       10      Gross Profit         120,000       140,000       150,000
       11      Other Expenses       100,000       100,000       100,000
       12                          --------------------------------------
       13      Net Income           $20,000       $40,000       $50,000
       14                          ======================================
       15
       16      Total Projected 3 Year Income                $110,000.00
       17                                                    ===========
```

FIGURE B-3.10   A Completed Worksheet

With the cell formats set and a few other aesthetic touches your worksheet takes on an appealing look.

a blank row between the cost of goods sold and gross profit. Move the cursor to cell A12 and type the same keystrokes to insert a row before net income. In the blank rows you have just created, put a string of dashes to separate the figures. This can be done by placing your cursor on cell B9, typing [\] key and the [-] key, pressing [enter], and then copying this to the other cells in the row. In the cells below net income put a string of equal signs to underline these figures. Put your cursor on cell A14 and type \= [enter]. Then copy this across the row. Finally, put a string of equal signs in cell D17 by entering \= in the cell. Your spreadsheet should now look like the one in Figure B-3.10.

Before going any further, let's save this file again. Just like before, use /File Save to begin this process. Since this file's original name was EXAMPLE, Lotus 1-2-3 proposes that that name be used again. Press [enter] to select this name. Lotus 1-2-3 now reminds you that there is already a file on the disk with the name EXAMPLE. By selecting Replace, tell Lotus 1-2-3 to replace that file with your new version.

It is useful to get a printed copy of a file. This can be done by using the print command. If you have a printer connected to your PC, try printing your worksheet. Begin this command by typing:

/Print Printer Range A1..D17 [enter] Go

When you have finished printing, select Quit to end the print command.

Producing Graphs with Lotus 1-2-3   The last feature to be discussed is the graph. Graphing is one of the many features that make Lotus 1-2-3 such an outstanding product. To begin the graphing procedure, type /Graph. The first thing to do is to select the type of graph you wish to produce. We will prepare a bar graph of the net income on your worksheet, so select the Type command and choose the Bar setting. Next, the data for the graph should be indicated. The X range will be the year, located in cells B6 through D6, so choose X and indicate the range B6..D6. Conclude this by pressing the [enter]

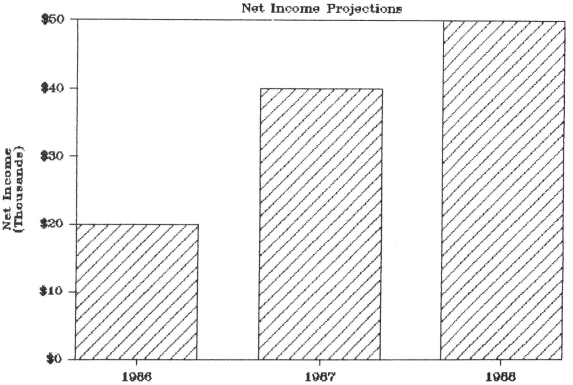

FIGURE B-3.11   A Graph Prepared with Lotus 1-2-3

key. The A range, cells B13 through D13, should be indicated in a similar fashion. If you have a color monitor or a graphics monochrome monitor you can see the graph by choosing the View command. If not, you must save it and then print it later. When you are finished viewing the graph you can return to the spreadsheet by pressing the [Esc] key. Many options can be added to the graph. Figure B-3.11 illustrates a printed graph from Lotus 1-2-3.

This concludes the introduction to Lotus 1-2-3. Many features have not been discussed, such as the data command and macros. These will be left for you to discover as you use Lotus 1-2-3. Some of the more useful Lotus 1-2-3 commands are listed in Figure B-3.12 for your reference. If you would like to explore LOTUS 1-2-3 further, I recommend either of the two following paperback books:

LeBlond, Geoffrey T. and Cobb, Douglas Ford. *Using 1-2-3.* Indianapolis: Que Corporation, 1983.

Bolocan, David. *LOTUS 1-2-3 Simplified.* Blue Ridge Summit, PA: Tab Books, Inc., 1984.

/ Worksheet Erase	Erase the current worksheet.
/ Worksheet Delete Row	Remove a row from the current worksheet.
/ Worksheet Delete Column	Remove a column from the current worksheet.
/ Worksheet Column-width	Change the width of the column where cell pointer is.
/ Range Erase	Erase a cell's contents or erase the contents of a range of cells.
/ Range Format	Set the display format of a cell or range of cells.
/ Copy	Copy the contents of a cell or range of cells.
/ Move	Move the contents of a cell or range of cells.
/ File Save	Save the current worksheet.
/ File Retrieve	Load an old worksheet from the disk (erases current wks).
/ File Erase	Erase a file from the disk.
/ File List	List the files that are on the default disk.
/ File Directory	Change the default disk.
/ Print Printer	Send a worksheet or part of a worksheet to the printer.
/ Graph	Create a graph based on data in the worksheet.
/ Data Fill	Fill a range of cells with a set of sequential values.
/ Data Sort	Sort rows of information based on the contents of a specified column.
/ Quit	Leave the worksheet and return to the LOTUS 1-2-3 access system (save your work first).

FIGURE B-3.12   Commonly Used Lotus 1-2-3 Command Sequences

SuperCalc3

Accessing SuperCalc3   The first step in using SuperCalc3 is to put the SuperCalc3 disk in drive A and put a formatted disk in drive B. Turn the computer on. Depending on how your disk is set up, you will go directly to SuperCalc3 or you will type SC3 and press [enter]. (You may need to load in DOS before typing SC3, check with your instructor.) At this point you will see a message on the screen stating that you're working with SuperCalc3. If you press any key, you will actually begin. Go ahead and press a key.

Using the Answer Screens   You should now see a blank SuperCalc3 spreadsheet on your screen. One of the first things you need to learn about SuperCalc3 is how to access its help system. The help system in SuperCalc3 is called answer screens. If you want to see an answer screen, press the [F1] key. (Remember the [F1] through [F10] keys are the function keys on the left side of the keyboard.) Try it. When you press the [F1] key, the spreadsheet temporarily disappears and a page of information appears, as shown in Figure B-3.13.

There is a great deal of information available to you through the answer screens. SuperCalc3 even helps out by sensing what you are trying to do (for example, what command you are trying to use) and then providing a screen of related information. So if you need help, try the answer screens before turning to the manual. Well, let's get back to work. Press any key to leave the answer screen and return to the spreadsheet, as shown in Figure B-3.14.

Interpreting the Control Panel   Look down toward the bottom of the screen shown in Figure B-3.14. The last four lines display important control information. The bottom line explains the meaning assigned to four of the function keys. Notice that [F1] is the help key. We just saw what it did. The keys labeled [F2], [F9], and [F10] have all been assigned functions. We will cover them later. The second line up from the bottom of the screen has a blinking cursor. This is where information typed in from the keyboard will appear until you press [enter], at which time it will be moved into the current cell. The third line up from the bottom shows information about the width of the current column, the amount of memory left, and other information. The fourth line up shows the present location of the active cell as well as any information that has already been typed into that cell.

```
SuperCalc3    AnswerScreen Initial Character Meanings:

 /  -- Starts a command entry.

 "  -- Starts entry of Text which otherwise would be formula.

 '  -- Starts Repeating Text entry.

 =  -- Specifies a cell to jump to.

 !  -- Forces recalculation.

 ;  -- Puts cursor in other window.

 &  -- Resumes Execute (.XQT) file control.

Four arrow keys move the Spreadsheet Cursor.
F1 or ? - Displays current AnswerScreen.
F2 or Ctrl-Z - Erase Entry Line/Return to spreadsheet.
F9 or Ctrl Y - Plots current graph.
F10 or Ctrl T - Displays current graph.
Any other character starts formula or text entry.

    Press any key to continue
F1 = Help; F2 = Erase Line/Return to Spreadsheet; F9 = Plot; F10 = View
```

FIGURE B-3.13 The Initial Answer Screen in SuperCalc3

```
    |  A  ‖  B  ‖  C  ‖  D  ‖  D  ‖  E  ‖  F  ‖  G  ‖  H  |
  1|
  2|
  3|
  4|
  5|
  6|
  7|
  8|
  9|
 10|
 11|
 12|
 13|
 14|
 15|
 16|
 17|
 18|
 19|
 20|
> A1
Width:  9  Memory:126 Last Col/Row:A1    ?  for  HELP
  1>
F1 = Help; F2 = Erase Line/Return to Spreadsheet; F9 = Plot; F1-10 = View
```

FIGURE B-3.14 A Blank SuperCalc3 Spreadsheet

Moving Around the Spreadsheet   The SuperCalc3 spreadsheet is 63 columns wide and 254 rows deep. (If you are using the Apprentice Series Version the spreadsheet has been restricted to 26 columns and 40 rows.) The columns are lettered A to BK. The rows are numbered 1 to 254. If you take time to figure it out, you will find that your spreadsheet has 16,000 cells! With a spreadsheet this big, you need to know how to move around. There are two ways to move in SuperCalc3: a cell at a time or by direct addressing.

By this time you have probably already figured out how to move a cell at a time. You use the arrow cursor keys on the right side of the keyboard. If you haven't tried this yet, go ahead. Notice that as you push the arrow keys a bright cell moves in the direction of the arrow. This bright cell is called the current, or active, cell and indicates the cell into which text, numbers, or formulas will be entered.

As you can see, this works pretty well, as long as you don't have too far to go. When you do want to move a larger distance there is a faster way—direct addressing. To move directly to a specific cell first press the [=] key. SuperCalc3 then asks you what cell you would like to move to. Type Z40 and press [enter]. One last technique—anytime you want to get back to cell A1 just press the [Home] key. Try this now before you move on.

Accessing the Command Line and Data Entry   SuperCalc3 recognizes three kinds of information to be stored in its cells: numbers, formulas, and text. Numbers can be typed directly into a cell. Formulas include references to cells that contain numbers or other formulas. Text is any other information entered into a cell. The only other type of input recognized by SuperCalc3 is a command. A special key is used to initiate a command. Press the [/] key. As you can see, when the slash key is pressed the third line from the bottom of the screen is changed. It now has the word Enter followed by a series of letters. The letters represent the commands available to you in SuperCalc3 (see Figure B-3.15). Some of these commands will be covered later. For the moment, let's get back to the spreadsheet. To do this, press the [F2] key. Use the [F2] key any time you want to return to the starting position.

Building a Spreadsheet   Now let's begin to prepare a spreadsheet. First move the cursor to cell A6. Type the word Sales and press [enter]. Next type Cost of Goods Sold in cell A7. Continue down the column, typing Gross Profit, Other Expenses, and Net Income into cells A8, A9, and A10. As you can see, several of these phrases are wider than column A. This is not a problem yet because nothing is in the cells of column B. However, you will want to use column B later, so you must make column A wider. Use the format command, which you access by pressing the [/] key. Next press F for format and then C for column, since that is what you want to widen. SuperCalc3 then requests that the column range be entered. Type A for column A and press [enter]. Finally, enter 19 and press [enter] to make the column 19 spaces wide.

Let's develop the rest of the spreadsheet. Move the cursor to cell B1, type SuperCalc Example, Inc., and press [enter]. Next move to cell B2 and type Projected Income Statements. In cell B3 type For 1986, 1987, and 1988. In cells B5, C5, and D5 enter the years 1986, 1987, and 1988. In cells B6 through D6 enter the sales estimates for those years (as shown earlier in Topic 3 under A Note Before You Proceed). Do not put in the commas or dollar signs; you will do this later. Since the cost of goods sold is always going to be 60 percent of the sales figure, you can enter it as a formula. Move the cursor to cell B7. Type the formula B6*.6 and press [enter]. With this formula, any time the sales estimate is changed, the cost of goods sold will be appropriately updated. Put similar formulas in cells C7 and D7. Remember to adjust the formula to cells C6 and D6. A formula can also be used to calculate the gross profit. Move the cursor to cell B8 and type B6-B7 and [enter].

This time, however, don't retype the formulas for 1987 and 1988. They can be replicated: type /R. In response to the question "From?" enter B8, since that is where the formula

A(rrange)	Sorts cells in ascending or descending order.
B(lank)	Removes (empties) contents of cells or graphs.
C(opy)	Duplicates graphs or contents and display format of cells.
D(elete)	Erases entire rows or columns.
E(dit)	Allows editing of cell contents.
F(ormat)	Sets display format at Entry, Row, Column, or Global levels.
G(lobal)	Changes global display or calculation options.
I(nsert)	Adds empty rows or columns.
L(oad)	Reads spreadsheet (or portion) from disk into the workspace.
M(ove)	Inserts existing rows or columns at new positions.
O(utput)	Sends display or cell contents to printer, screen, or disk.
P(rotect)	Prevents future alteration of cells.
Q(uit)	Ends the SuperCalc3 program.
R(eplicate)	Reproduces contents of partial rows or columns.
S(ave)	Stores the current spreadsheet on disk.
T(itle)	Locks upper rows or left-hand columns from scrolling.
U(nprotect)	Allows alteration of protected cells.
V(iew)	Shows data as Pie, Bar, S-Bar, Line, Area, X-Y, or Hi-Lo graph.
W(indow)	Splits the screen display.
X(eXecute)	Accepts commands and data from a .XQT file.
Z(ap)	Erases spreadsheet and format settings from workspace.
/	Additional commands(//D accesses Data Management options).

FIGURE B-3.15 SuperCalc3 Commands

is that you would like to replicate. Press [enter] next. In response to the question "To?" type C8:D8 which is the range to which the formula should be replicated. Finish by pressing [enter]. As you can see the formula was properly replicated to cells C8 and D8 from B8. In cells B9 through D9 enter 100000 for the other expenses. In cells B10 through D10 input a formula to calculate net income. For example, in cell B10 the formula would be B8-B9. Once this cell's formula has been entered try to replicate it for the remaining two years. When you have finished all of this your spreadsheet should look like Figure B-3.16.

This is a good point to take a break, but first you must save the file by using the save command. Type /S. Then type B: and the filename. Use EXAMPLE. So type B:EXAMPLE and press [enter]. Next, by pressing the [A] key, tell SuperCalc3 that you want to save all of the file. To end this session, type /Q and the Y to exit from SuperCalc3.

After your break you will want to start working where you left off. First load SuperCalc3 and get the blank spreadsheet in front of you. Next type /L for the load command. If you recall you saved the file on the B disk with the filename EXAMPLE, so type B:EXAMPLE and press [enter]. Finally, type A to indicate that you would like all of the file loaded. You should now be back to where you were before the break.

Making the Spreadsheet Look Good The file looks okay now, but you can do a few things to jazz it up. First let's format the numbers so that the first and last number in each column has a dollar sign in front and all numbers have commas separating the thousands from the hundreds. To do this you will use the format command. One of the unique features of SuperCalc3 is that is has user-definable formats. To set up the formats, type /F D for format define. You should now have a grid on the screen with eight columns, one for each of the user-definable formats as shown in Figure B-3.17.

Set up format 1 so that it allows for a floating dollar sign, embedded commas, and no decimal places. Since format 1 already has a floating dollar sign and embedded commas, you don't need to make changes there. Move the cursor to Decimal Places and type a 0. Set up format 2 with no floating dollar sign, with comma separators, and with no decimal places. Then press [F2] to enter the worksheet.

```
   |          A           ||    B   ||   C   ||    D     |
 1|                        SuperCalc Example, Inc.
 2|                        Projected Income Statements
 3|                        For 1986, 1987, and 1988
 4|
 5|                            1986      1987      1988
 6|Sales                      300000    350000    375000
 7|Cost of Goods Sold         180000    210000    225000
 8|Gross Profit               120000    140000    150000
 9|Other Expenses             100000    100000    100000
10|Net Income                  20000     40000     50000
```

FIGURE B-3.16   A Partially Completed Spreadsheet

Now format the numbers. Once again type /F for the format command. Next press R for row, type 6 for row 6, and press [enter]. Then, type U for user define and 1 for the user-defined format selected. Complete the process by pressing the [enter] key. As you can see, all the sales numbers are now formatted as you requested. Follow the same steps, changing the row number to 10 to format the net income row.

All of the remaining numbers will be formatted using the user-defined format 2. To save time, type /F and then press E for entry. Then SuperCalc3 prompts you for the range of the entries to format. Type B7:D9 and press [enter]. Now, type U2 and press [enter] for format 2, which we defined earlier.

The last thing you need to do is put in some spaces and lines between subtotals and at the end of each column. Since you did not originally include spaces for this purpose, they must be inserted. Type /I for insert. Next, type R to tell SuperCalc3 that you want to insert a row. Then, respond that you would like to insert a row above row 8, so type 8 and press [enter]. Do this again, except this time insert a row above row 11, net income.

```
                          User-defined formats
                          1   2   3   4   5   6   7   8

Floating $                Y   Y   Y   Y   Y   Y   Y   Y

Embedded Commas           Y   Y   Y   Y   Y   Y   Y   Y

Minus in ( )              N   N   N   N   N   N   N   N

Zero as Blank             N   N   N   N   N   N   N   N

%                         N   N   N   N   N   N   N   N

Decimal Places            2   2   2   2   2   2   2   2

Scaling factor            0   0   0   0   0   0   0   0

F2 to return to worksheet.

> A1
Y(es) or N(o)?
 15>/Format,Define
F1 = Help; F2 = Erase Line/Return to
Spreadsheet; F9 = Plot; F10 = View
```

FIGURE B-3.17   SuperCalc3 Screen for User-Defined Formats

```
      |        A        ||    B    ||    C    ||    D        |
  1|                     SuperCalc Example, Inc.
  2|                     Projected Income Statements
  3|                     For 1986, 1987, and 1988
  4|
  5|                         1986      1987      1988
  6|Sales                  $300,000  $350,000  $375,000
  7|Cost of Goods Sold      180,000   210,000   225,000
  8|                       ------------------------------
  9|Gross Profit            120,000   140,000   150,000
 10|Other Expenses          100,000   100,000   100,000
 11|                       ------------------------------
 12|Net Income             $20,000   $40,000   $50,000
 13|                       ==============================
```

FIGURE B-3.18   A Completed Spreadsheet

There is no direct way to format a number so that it is underlined in SuperCalc. However, this can be accomplished by inserting the rows as you have done, and putting a string of minus signs, or hyphens, in the blank cell. Move your cursor to cell B8 and type - - - - - - - - -. After you press [enter] you will see that the desired effect is achieved. Do this again in cells C8 and D8. After inserting a blank row in row 11 also put a string of hyphens in cells B11 through D11. Use a string of equal marks in cells B13 to D13 to double-underscore the net income. To keep from confusing SuperCalc, place a quotation mark (") before the first equal sign in each cell. After all of these changes have been made, your spreadsheet should look like Figure B-3.18.

Saving and Printing Files   Before you print this file, it is a good idea to save it. Just like before, type /S for save. Again use the filename EXAMPLE. Don't forget to indicate that you want to save the file on the disk in drive B, so type B:EXAMPLE and press [enter]. Finish the command by typing B to create a backup of the old version, and then type A since you want to save all of the file.

Once the file has been saved, you can print it. Note that it is not necessary to save a file before you print it; however, it is a good idea. If you have a printer, get it ready before proceeding. (If you don't, just read this section without typing commands.) To print, type /O for output. Next, SuperCalc3 gives you a choice of whether to print a display or a contents report. A display lists what you see on the screen. A contents report lists the cell formulas in the spreadsheet. Choose display by pressing D. Now type in the range that is to be printed. We would like to print the whole schedule, so the range is A1:D13. Then press [enter]. Select P to send the report to the printer. As you can see, the report is printed just as it appears on the screen.

Producing Graphs with SuperCalc3   The last feature to be discussed is graphing. Earlier versions of SuperCalc did not have the extensive graphing capabilities now available in SuperCalc3. To begin the graphing commands, type /V (V stands for view). Then tell SuperCalc3 what data to use in preparing the graph. To do this, press D for data and then type the range of the data. In our example you want to graph net income so type the range B12:D12 and press [enter]. Next type G for graph-type and select the bar graph-type by pressing a B. If you have a color display or a monochrome display with a graphics card, you will be able to see the graph on the screen by pressing [F10]. When you have finished viewing the graph, press any key to go back to the spreadsheet. If you would like to print this graph, and a dot-matrix printer is connected to your PC and turned on, then just press

[F9] and the graph will be printed. Note that you can create up to nine different graphs from the same spreadsheet file, and when you save the spreadsheet all of the graph settings such as data ranges and graph type will also be saved. With a little practice you will be able to make professional-looking graphs. Figure B-3.19 is an example of the type of graph that SuperCalc3 can create.

One more important command needs to be mentioned. Before a new spreadsheet file is loaded into SuperCalc3, it is important to remove any old spreadsheet files presently loaded. This is done by the zap command. Just for practice, zap the existing spreadsheet. To do this, type /Z for zap and Y for yes. Now you are finished. Type /QY to end the SuperCalc3 session.

There are many, many features available in SuperCalc3 which have not been included in this introduction. For example, you can create graphs such as the one in Figure B-3.19 and can perform basic data-management functions. These features are fully documented in the user's guide as well as through the help screens. Explore these features as soon as you can.

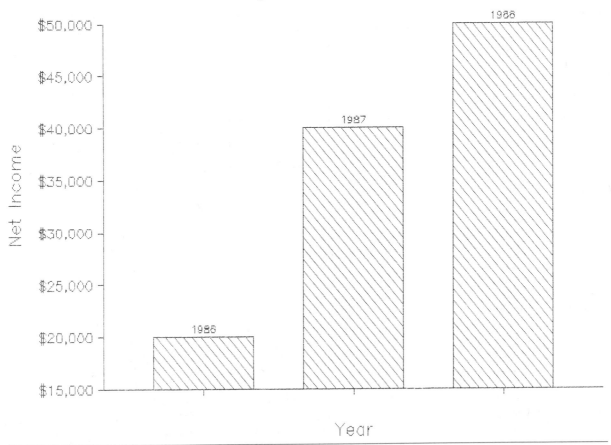

FIGURE B-3.19 A SuperCalc3 Graph

Hands-On Exercises

1. Using Lotus 1-2-3 or SuperCalc, design a worksheet that computes the value of the inventory for a hypothetical fruit stand. After you complete the worksheet, it should look like this:

```
TYPE OF FRUIT      QUANTITY    UNIT PRICE           AMOUNT
APPLES                 400        $0.30      $    120.00
ORANGES                600        $0.40      $    240.00
GRAPES                1200        $0.65      $    780.00
PEARS                  500        $0.80      $    400.00
CHERRIES               700        $1.20      $    840.00
                                             -----------
TOTAL                                        $2,380.00
                                             ===========
```

2. Insert dollar signs before each price and amount in exercise 1. Now try moving the "amount" column over to the right by two columns.

3. Budgeting and planning your expenditures is the first step in successful personal financial planning. In this exercise you should prepare a financial budget for one semester (or quarter) of school. Outlined here is a general format for your budget:

```
INPUT SECTION

NAME:       Paula Baynett

ADDRESS:    3007 Campus Row
            Blacksburg, VA

SCHOOL:     Virginia Tech      BEGINNING BALANCE             $1,300

TERM:       Fall               FIRST DAY AT SCHOOL ----> 08-Sep
```

```
                    CASH RECEIPTS

SOURCE                  AMOUNTS          PERIODICITY*
-------------           -------          -------------
PARENTS                   $600       FIRST OF MONTH
PART-TIME JOB             $40        WEEKLY
SCHOLARSHIPS             $500        FIRST OF TERM
LOANS                               AS NEEDED
INVESTMENTS             $200        MONTHLY, AT FIRST OF MONTH
OTHER                   $300        END OF TERM
```

```
                 CASH DISBURSEMENTS
EXPENDITURES            AMOUNTS          PERIODICITY*
-------------           -------          ------------
RENT                     $300       MONTHLY, FIRST OF MONTH
FOOD                     $75        WEEK
TUITION                $1,000       FIRST OF TERM
BOOKS                   $300        FIRST OF TERM
OPERATION OF CAR
    AT SCHOOL            $25        WEEK
CAR TRIPS HOME          $40         END OF MONTH
ENTERTAINMENT           $30         WEEK
CLOTHING               $100         TERM, AVERAGE PER WEEK
OTHER                  $500         TERM, AVERAGE PER WEEK
```

*Note a term is assumed to be thirteen weeks. Change this to fit your school.

This format should be in the input section of your spreadsheet. When you are using the spreadsheet, all of your input will be in this section.

The output section of your spreadsheet follows:

Output Section

BUDGET ITEMS WEEK BEGINNING	08-Sep	15-Sep	22-Sep	29-Sep	06-Oct	13-Oct	20-Oct	27-Oct	03-Nov	10-Nov	17-Nov	24-Nov	01-Dec
							RECEIPTS						
PARENTS	600				600				600				600
PART-TIME JOB	40	40	40	40	40	40	40	40	40	40	40	40	40
SCHOLARSHIPS	500												
LOANS													
INVESTMENTS	200				200				200				200
OTHER													
BEGINNING BALANCE	1300	870	740	610	440	810	680	550	380	1050	920	790	620
CASH AVAILABLE	2640	910	780	650	1280	850	720	590	1220	1090	960	830	1460
							EXPENDITURES						
RENT	300				300								
FOOD	75	75	75	75	75	75	75	75	75	75	75	75	75
TUITION	1,000												
BOOKS	300												
OPERATION OF CAR AT SCHOOL	25	25	25	25	25	25	25	25	25	25	25	25	25
CAR TRIPS HOME				40				40					
ENTERTAINMENT	30	30	30	30	30	30	30	30	30	30	30	30	30
CLOTHING	7	7	7	7	7	7	7	7	7	7	7	7	7
OTHER	33	33	33	33	33	33	33	33	33	33	33	33	33
CASH AVAILABLE END OF MONTH	$870	$740	$610	$440	$810	$680	$550	$380	$1,050	$920	$790	$620	$1,290

Your spreadsheet should compute all of the numbers in this output section from the input section. No input should be made in the output section. Most of the labels for the output section of the budget can be copied from the input section. Once the formulas are in place for the first week, the formulas for the remaining weeks can be copied from the first. Remember to use cell referencing whenever possible. The rule is to enter a number only once in the input section. Each time thereafter, use cell referencing.

If your instructor has asked you to turn in this exercise you may want to put dummy data in it for privacy. However, after you have built this spreadsheet put real data in it and use it. The secret to learning how to use computers is to use them for something that you find useful. (This exercise is used with permission from Samuel A. Hicks.)

4. Think of a spreadsheet application that is useful to you or your family. Build the spreadsheet and use it.

Topic 4: Using dBASE II and dBASE III

DBASE II and dBASE III are relational data-base systems marketed by Ashton-Tate. You will recall from chapter 12 that a relational data base uses flat files, where the columns of the file represent the fields and the rows represent the individual records. Two flat files are shown in Figure B-4.1. The first one is a generic file with no defined fields and the second is an example of a file containing field definitions and information.

THE GENERAL FORM OF A FLAT FILE

	field1	field2	field3	field4	...
record1					
record2					
record3					
. . .					

AN EXAMPLE OF A FLAT FILE

	last name	first name	phone number
record1	Smith	Samuel	555-1212
record2	Davis	Richard	444-1234
record3	Travis	Jennifer	123-4567

FIGURE B-4.1   Flat Files

The two files show the columnar format of a relational data-base flat file.

A set of files, once created, can be used as a complete information-management facility for storing, processing, updating, retrieving, and reporting information. DBASE II and dBASE III (Ashton-Tate's most recent release) are management systems for such a set of files. The main text of this introduction will be based on dBASE II, although most of the commands will work with dBASE III as well. Any significant differences between the commands presented and the proper dBASE III commands will be indicated in the text or highlighted within each figure.

Loading the dBASE II Software

Entering the dBASE II software is easy. First, boot your computer using DOS and enter the date and time. (If you have not done this previously, refer to Topic 1 of this appendix and go through the tutorial on the disk-operating system.) You should now have the DOS A> prompt. Remove your DOS disk and replace it with the dBASE II disk. Place a formatted disk in drive B of your computer. Type DBASE. After you type a dBASE command you must press [enter]. In the remainder of this tutorial we will assume that you know to press [enter]. The dBASE software should load and you will be presented with a copyright message and then a dot. The dot, like the A> in DOS, is the software's way of telling you that it is awaiting your next command. It is called the **dBASE prompt.** The next step is to type SET DEFAULT TO B. This command tells dBASE to assume that the files you are using are stored on the disk in drive B. Therefore you will not need to type B: in front of the filenames you use. DBASE recognizes the difference between a lowercase letter and an uppercase letter, so for consistency type everything in capitals. You can do this by pressing the [Caps Lock] key one time. If you decide to quit dBASE while you are going through this tutorial, be sure to enter the command QUIT prior to turning your computer off. Failure to do so may cause you to lose data that you have typed in. When you enter dBASE again, be sure to type and enter SET DEFAULT TO B and press the [Caps Lock] key (Figure B-4.2).

dBASE III

If you are using dBASE III type the command SET MENU ON before starting. There won't be any effect at this point; but, as you need them, menus will be produced on the top half of the screen to remind you of the commands available.

FIGURE B-4.2 dBASE III HELP Menus

Creating Files

The first thing you need to know about dBASE is how to create files. You must have some way of defining the structure of the file, which requires defining the fields (columns) that your flat file will have. In dBASE, you start this definition process by issuing the **CREATE** command. Type `CREATE`. DBASE II will respond by asking for a filename. The file you are going to build is a personnel file; it will contain information about the employees of a company. A filename is limited to eight characters, so let's call the file `EMPLOYEE`. Type in this name in response to dBASE's inquiry. Your screen should now look like Figure B-4.3.

DBASE is prompting you to enter the definition for the first field (column) of this file. It has requested that four pieces of information (name, type, width, and decimal places) be entered, separated by commas. The field type defines the kind of data that can be put into a field. Valid field types under dBASE II are C (for character), N (for numeric), and L (for logical). If a field is classified as a character type, then dBASE will accept any string of characters including letters, numbers, and special symbols. Numeric data fields are stored such that mathematical operations can be performed on them. Logical fields contain a T for true or an F for False.

The field width is expressed in a number of characters. DBASE II will allow up to 254 characters in a single field, although the width of most fields is considerably smaller. The number of decimal places requested need only be entered if a numeric field type has been declared. The absence of a specified number of decimal places from a numeric field is interpreted by dBASE as a request for zero significant figures after the decimal point.

The first field in our employee file will hold the employee's last name. Enter the following definition for field 001 and then press the [`enter`] key:

```
LASTNAME,C,15
```

DBASE should now be requesting information for field 002. Continue typing field definitions, as shown in Figure B-4.5.

dBASE II

```
ENTER RECORD STRUCTURE AS FOLLOWS:
FIELD    NAME,TYPE,WIDTH,DECIMAL  PLACES
001
```

dBASE III

```
  field  name  type        width  dec
1 [          ] [Char/text] [    ] [    ]
```

FIGURE B-4.3 File Structure Entry Screen

At this point dBASE is requesting that you define the fields of the file. Although the entry screens are slightly different for dBASE II and dBASE III, both require the same information (name, type, width, and decimal places) for each field.

dBASE III

In addition to the three field types allowed in dBASE II, dBASE III offers a DATE field type and a MEMO field type. The DATE field type allows for date arithmetic to be performed (i.e. 12/31/85 − 09/15/85 = 107 days). Memo fields are meant to handle long strings of character information, such as recipes, more efficiently than the character field type.

When defining your file structure, choose field types by pressing the space bar. Each time you press the space bar, the field type of the field you are currently defining will change to another acceptable field type. A corresponding explanation of the field type will be shown on the bottom of the screen.

FIGURE B-4.4 Acceptable dBASE III Field Types

After you have typed the definition for the fifth field, dBASE will display `006`, indicating it is awaiting information for another field. Press the [`enter`] key without entering any information. This completes the definition process. DBASE now asks whether you would like to input data (records) at this point. Answer `N` for no.

Displaying the Structure of a File

You have just created an empty file. It has a defined set of fields, or structure, but it contains no records. This is synonymous with having labeled the columns of a flat file without placing any information in these columns. Let's take a look at the structure (or nutshell, as it is sometimes called) of the file. First, however, since there could be a number of files on the disk, you must identify the file you wish to use by telling dBASE to `USE EMPLOYEE`. You can then examine the structure by asking dBASE to `DISPLAY STRUCTURE`. As you can see, the field names, field types, and field lengths that you previously defined are displayed.

dBASE II

```
ENTER RECORD STRUCTURE AS FOLLOWS:
FIELD     NAME,TYPE,WIDTH,DECIMAL PLACES
001       LASTNAME,C,15
002       FIRSTNAME,C,10
003       EMPNO,N,4,0
004       DEPT,C,5
005       SALARY,N,8,2
006
```

dBASE III

	field name	type	width	dec
1	LASTNAME	Char/text	15	
2	FIRSTNAME	Char/text	10	
3	EMPNO	Numeric	4	0
4	DEPT	Char/text	5	
5	SALARY	Numeric	8	2
6		Char/text		

FIGURE B-4.5 Your Completed File Structure

When you finish entering the field definitions for the EMPLOYEE file, your screen should look like this.

```
┌──────────────────────────────────────────────────────────────────────────┐
│                                  dBASE III                                 │
│                                                                            │
│  In dBASE III you do not have to temporarily copy the records to another   │
│  file, since it is done automatically. Be careful, however, because you    │
│  can still lose data if you change a field name or delete a field entirely.│
└──────────────────────────────────────────────────────────────────────────┘
```

FIGURE B-4.6   A dBASE III Improvement

You may make an error while entering the field definitions, or you may want to change a field definition or add a new field to an existing file. DBASE II allows you to make corrections and additions to the file's structure through the command MODIFY STRUC-TURE. Whether you have corrections to make or not, go ahead and issue this command. DBASE II responds with a warning that the requested modification will destroy all existing records in the file. When modifying the structure of a file that is not empty, you must first copy any existing records to a temporary file (see Figure B-4.6). These records can then be re-added to the original file after it has been modified. Your file does not contain any data, so you can answer [Y] for yes, signaling that you would like to proceed with the modification. The file structure appears on the screen once again. This time, however, you are free to move the cursor to the various definitions and change them. Make any necessary changes so that your file is identical to the one shown in Figure B-4.7. After you have made all the changes you want, save the new structure with the [Ctrl] [W] key combination (hold down the [Ctrl] key and strike the [W] key one time). You should now be back at the dot prompt.

```
                          dBASE II

                     NAME        TYP  LEN   DEC
      FIELD 01    :LASTNAME       C   015   000   :
      FIELD 02    :FIRSTNAME      C   010   000   :
      FIELD 03    :EMPNO          N   004   000   :
      FIELD 04    :DEPT           C   005   000   :
      FIELD 05    :SALARY         N   008   002   :
```

```
    ┌────────────────────────────────────────────────┐
    │                     dBASE III                    │
    │                                                  │
    │     field name  type        width    dec         │
    │   ╺━━━━━━━━━━━━━━━━━━━━━━━━━━━━━━━━━━━━━━━━━━━━╸   │
    │   1  LASTNAME    Char/text     15               │
    │   2  FIRSTNAME   Char/text     10               │
    │   3  EMPNO       Numeric        4      0        │
    │   4  DEPT        Char/text      5               │
    │   5  SALARY      Numeric        8      2        │
    │                                                  │
    └────────────────────────────────────────────────┘
```

FIGURE B-4.7   Full Screen Editing of a File Structure
Modify the structure in your file so that it agrees with the file structure shown here.

```
RECORD # 00001
LASTNAME   :PHILLIPS      :
FIRSTNAME :WILMER    :
EMPNO      : 110:
DEPT       :ACCT :
SALARY     :34000.00:
```

FIGURE B-4.8   The First Data Record

Shown here on five lines, the information you put into record number 00001 will make up the first line of the EMPLOYEE file.

Inputting Data

The next thing you need to do is add data records to your currently empty file. Do this by using the APPEND command. The APPEND command causes dBASE to insert new records at the end of the file. DBASE presents you with an empty-record screen. Notice that the input screen is labeled RECORD # 00001. This tells you that the information from this screen will be kept in the first row or record of that flat file named EMPLOYEE. Using the cursor keys to move from field to field, fill in the information for the first record so that it looks like Figure B-4.8. After you enter the salary into the salary field by pressing the [enter] key, dBASE will present you with a new entry screen, this time labeled RECORD # 00002. Continue entering information into the file using the data provided in Figure B-4.9. Don't worry about having a few errors in your data; you'll have a chance to correct them later.

After you have entered the data for the fifteenth record, dBASE will present you with an entry screen for record sixteen. To stop the entry process, press the [enter] key without entering any information into the lastname field. This will return you to the dot prompt. Congratulations—you've successfully completed building the EMPLOYEE file.

			LASTNAME	FIRSTNAME	EMPNO	DEPT	SALARY
			=========	==========	=======	======	========
RECORD	#	00001	PHILLIPS	WILMER	110	ACCT	34000
RECORD	#	00002	JOHNSON	JAY	140	MKT	28000
RECORD	#	00003	JONES	THELMA	132	ADMIN	43000
RECORD	#	00004	TIETZ	LISA	124	ACCT	18000
RECORD	#	00005	KARWACKI	MARK	125	MKT	22000
RECORD	#	00006	LAUMANN	JOHN	128	ADMIN	31000
RECORD	#	00007	SMITH	GEORGE	134	ADMIN	19000
RECORD	#	00008	DAVIS	ELIZABETH	113	MKT	22000
RECORD	#	00009	TULLY	EARL	115	ACCT	34000
RECORD	#	00010	BELL	JEFF	105	ACCT	23450
RECORD	#	00011	BUCKINGHAM	DAVE	131	MKT	26700
RECORD	#	00012	VOLZ	DOUGLAS	119	ADMIN	45000
RECORD	#	00013	LYTLE	JOE	130	MKT	30000
RECORD	#	00014	DIAL	DAVID	112	MKT	20000
RECORD	#	00015	KENWORTHY	MARK	123	ACCT	19500

FIGURE B-4.9   Input Data

The fifteen records shown here make up the data that you should enter into the EMPLOYEE file. Don't be too concerned with typing errors; you'll have a chance to fix those later.

Listing a File

Now that you have a file containing useful information, let's see how you can access that information. By entering the command L I S T, you instruct dBASE to list the records of the file. Your file listing should look like the one in Figure B-4.10.

Notice that each record is preceded by its record number. You can view the same list without the record numbers by typing L I S T O F F. Go ahead and try it. If you have a printer connected to your personal computer, you may want to use the S E T P R I N T O N command followed again by the L I S T command. If your printer is turned on, a copy of the file listing will be sent to the printer. You'll need to S E T P R I N T O F F after your listing is done printing. Figure B-4.11 shows you how to correct errors you may make in typing dBASE commands.

The list command is very powerful and has many options. We'll talk about these options a little later, but first let's learn how to make corrections to the records in your file. Corrections to existing records are necessary when information has been incorrectly input or when information about an individual or other entity has changed. For instance, if one of the employees transferred from one department to another, you would need to change the contents of the DEPT field for that employee's record.

Directly changing the contents of a record is known as editing. The most common way of editing in dBASE is through the edit command. L I S T your file again and note the record number of a record that has an error. If you do not have an error in your file, pick a record number at random. Type E D I T n, where n is the record number of the record in which you need to make corrections or changes. DBASE II will bring the requested record onto

```
00001    PHILLIPS      WILMER        110 ACCT     34000.00
00002    JOHNSON       JAY           140 MKT      28000.00
00003    JONES         THELMA        132 ADMIN    43000.00
00004    TIETZ         LISA          124 ACCT     18000.00
00005    KARWACKI      MARK          125 MKT      22000.00
00006    LAUMANN       JOHN          128 ADMIN    31000.00
00007    SMITH         GEORGE        134 ADMIN    19000.00
00008    DAVIS         ELIZABETH     113 MKT      22000.00
00009    TULLY         EARL          115 ACCT     34000.00
00010    BELL          JEFF          105 ACCT     23450.00
00011    BUCKINGHAM    DAVE          131 MKT      26700.00
00012    VOLZ          DOUGLAS       119 ADMIN    45000.00
00013    LYTLE         JOE           130 MKT      30000.00
00014    DIAL          DAVID         112 MKT      20000.00
00015    KENWORTHY     MARK          123 ACCT     19500.00
```

---

dBASE III

DBASE III has improved on the basic LISTing by providing column or field headings at the top of all requested fields. You can turn the headings feature off or on by using the command:

SET HEADINGS ON/OFF

FIGURE B-4.10   The Employee File Listing

The result of the LIST command, shown here, is the quickest way to retrieve information from a dBASE file.

dBASE II

CORRECTING COMMAND ERRORS

When you type in a command that dBASE II does not recognize, you will be presented with the following option:

```
CORRECT AND RETRY (Y/N)?
```

If you answer N (for no), you will be returned to the dot prompt and can retype the command correctly. If you answer Y (for yes) you will be given the opportunity to change the incorrect section of the command you typed. The following short dialogue shows how this would be done.

```
. set prnt off
*** SYNTAX ERROR ***
      ?
set prnt off
CORRECT AND RETRY (Y/N)? Y
CHANGE FROM :prnt
CHANGE TO   :print
set print off
MORE CORRECTIONS (Y/N)? N
```

---

dBASE III

DBASE III responds to an incorrect command entry by asking if you would like some help. If you type a [y] for yes, dBASE III tries to locate help information on the command it suspects you are trying to use. If you type a [n] for no, dBASE III will return you to the dot prompt.

FIGURE B-4.11 Correcting Errors

the screen. You can then make the necessary changes. The list of control combinations shown in Figure B-4.12 are helpful when you use the edit function. In each case, you should hold down the [Ctrl] key and strike the corresponding lettered key one time.

You can move from the current record to the next record by moving your cursor with the down-arrow key past the last field of the current record. Likewise, you can move to the previous record by moving your cursor with the up-arrow key past the first field of the current record. Record to record movement can also be done by using the [Ctrl][C] and [Ctrl][R] key combinations, as shown in Figure B-4.12. When you have finished making changes, use [Ctrl][W] to save the changes and end the editing session.

Another way of directly editing a file is to use the dBASE BROWSE command. Before entering this command, type GO TOP. Then issue the command BROWSE. DBASE II is now displaying the entire file. You can make changes to any of the fields in any of the records. The same key combinations hold true for BROWSE as for EDIT. In addition, the four control key combinations in Figure B-4.13 are helpful.

The pan control combinations are necessary when a file has so many fields that they will not all fit on the screen at the same time. In these cases the monitor's screen acts like a window over the flat file, the same way an electronic spreadsheet works. You may have to move, or "pan," the window up and down to see all the rows, and left and right to see all the columns. Once again use [Ctrl][W] to save any changes you have made, and return to the dot prompt.

`Ctrl-G` Deletes the character above the cursor.
`Ctrl-Y` Erases all characters in the field to the right of the cursor.
`Ctrl-V` Turns the insert function on and off.
`Ctrl-W` Saves the changes made and returns to "." prompt.
`Ctrl-Q` Ignores changes made and returns to "." prompt.
`Ctrl-U` Marks/unmarks record for deletion.
`Ctrl-C` or `Pg Up` Saves the changes and advances to next record.
`Ctrl-R` or `Pg Dn` Saves the changes and moves back to the previous record.

---

dBASE III

`Del`   Deletes the character above the cursor.
`Ctrl-Y`   Erases all characters in the field to the right of the cursor.
`Ins`   Turns the insert function on and off.
`Ctrl-Home`   Saves the changes made and returns to "." prompt.
`Esc`   Ignores changes made and returns to "." prompt.
`Ctrl-U`   Marks/unmarks record for deletion.
`Pg Dn`   Saves the changes and advances to next record.
`Pg Up`   Saves the changes and moves back to the previous record.

All of the [`Ctrl`] combinations shown for dBASE II also work for dBASE III. In addition, dBASE III offers more logical key combinations, as shown here. These more fully make use of the IBM-PC keyboard.

FIGURE B-4.12 Key Combinations for Editing Records

These key combinations also are used with the MODIFY STRUCTURE and BROWSE commands. To initiate any of the editing or cursor-movement functions in this list, hold down the [Ctrl] key and strike the indicated letter key once.

---

dBASE II

`Ctrl-X` Move cursor right one field.
`Ctrl-E` Move cursor left one field.
`Ctrl-B` Pan window right one field.
`Ctrl-Z` Pan window left one field.

---

dBASE III

`End`   Move cursor right one field.
`Home`   Move cursor left one field.
`Ctrl-→`   Pan window right one field.
`Ctrl-←`   Pan window left one field.

FIGURE B-4.13 Cursor Movement When Using Browse

To initiate any of these cursor-movement functions, hold down the [Ctrl] key and strike the indicated letter key once.

Currency

In order to understand many of the dBASE commands, you must understand the concept of *currency.* Any time a data-base file is in use, the data-base software has a pointer directed at one of the records in the file. This pointer is called the **currency pointer.** When you first open a file by issuing the USE command, the currency pointer is on the first record in the file. To find out what record number you are currently pointing at, type DISPLAY. This will cause the current record (the record the currency pointer is aimed at) to be displayed. Now type GO TOP and then DISPLAY again. Record # 00001 should be displayed. You can move the currency pointer directly to any record you want by telling dBASE to GO n, where n is the record number you wish to make the current record. You can also move a given number of records by using the SKIP n command. Try these two commands a few times, then use the GO TOP or GO 1 command to get back to the top of the file. The concept of currency is important because some dBASE commands act on the current record. Currency is also important in sequential processing of a file where records are accessed one at a time.

Indirect Editing

Now that you understand the concept of currency, you can make use of another method of editing records. Records can be edited indirectly by using the dBASE replace and change commands. First we'll look at the replace command. Let's assume that Joe Lytle moves from the marketing department to the administration department. Instead of editing his record, type GO 13. DBASE should now be pointing at Joe Lytle's record. Enter DISPLAY to be sure. Now type REPLACE DEPT WITH "ADMIN". Then LIST the file to see the change. You could also have typed REPLACE DEPT WITH "ADMIN" FOR EMPNO=130. This would have eliminated the need to first make record 13 the current record. The replace command also gives you the ability to make a series of replacements simultaneously. Suppose you want to give everyone in the accounting department a 10 percent raise. You could say REPLACE ALL SALARY WITH SALARY*1.10 FOR DEPT="ACCT". Type this command and then LIST the file to see the effect.

The change command prompts you one record at a time for any requested field changes. Suppose you wanted to give everyone in the marketing department a raise based on our own scrutiny. Type the command CHANGE ALL FIELD SALARY FOR DEPT="MKT". DBASE would prompt you for a new salary for each person in the marketing department. Go ahead and change the salaries as you see fit.

More on the List Command

Now that you have finished making corrections and changes to the personnel file, let's continue with our discussion of the list command. Previously, you listed the entire personnel file when using the list command. More often, however, you will want to access only a portion of a file at any one time. This may not be as obvious with your file since it conveniently fits onto one screen; but imagine a file with hundreds of records. It would be difficult to locate the one or two records you are really interested in if you are presented with hundreds to scan. Similarly, many files have more fields than you may need to see at any one time. Limiting the number of fields (columns) listed is known as a **projection.** Limiting the records (rows) retrieved is known as a **selection.** You can make a selection, projection, or both a selection and a projection of your personnel file by using the dBASE list command.

Suppose you want to list only the last name, first name, and department fields of the personnel file. You can obtain such a list by typing LIST LASTNAME, FIRSTNAME, DEPT. The output for this command is shown in Figure B-4.14. Although you used the same field order as in your file structure, you are not limited to this. For instance, you could

```
00001    PHILLIPS      WILMER      ACCT
00002    JOHNSON       JAY         MKT
00003    JONES         THELMA      ADMIN
00004    TIETZ         LISA        ACCT
00005    KARWACKI      MARK        MKT
00006    LAUMANN       JOHN        ADMIN
00007    SMITH         GEORGE      ADMIN
00008    DAVIS         ELIZABETH   MKT
00009    TULLY         EARL        ACCT
00010    BELL          JEFF        ACCT
00011    BUCKINGHAM    DAVE        MKT
00012    VOLZ          DOUGLAS     ADMIN
00013    LYTLE         JOE         ADMIN
00014    DIAL          DAVID       MKT
00015    KENWORTHY     MARK        ACCT
```

FIGURE B-4.14 A dBASE Projection

This figure shows the subset of the whole EMPLOYEE file which is listed when the LIST LASTNAME, FIRSTNAME, DEPT query is made. Note that only the requested fields or columns are listed.

LIST FIRSTNAME, LASTNAME, DEPT. Neither are you limited to only the fields in the data base. You can produce "virtual" fields which are modifications or products of existing fields. Suppose, for example, that you are interested in monthly instead of annual salaries. You can LIST LASTNAME, FIRSTNAME, DEPT, SALARY/12. Here you have produced a listing that includes a column of monthly salaries, even though that information is not directly contained as a field in your file.

Let's look at some examples of how select records are retrieved. DBASE makes selections through the use of the "for" clause in the list command. If you want information about employees in the accounting department only, you can retrieve those records by telling dBASE to LIST FOR DEPT="ACCT". The output for this command is shown in Figure B-4.15. If you want to look only at the record for JONES, you could LIST FOR LASTNAME="JONES". Only the record for THELMA JONES would be retrieved. In a large file there may be dozens of Joneses listed. You could be more specific by using the dBASE .AND. operator. You could LIST FOR LASTNAME="JONES" .AND. FIRSTNAME="THELMA". Go ahead and try some of your own selections. Remember that you must use a valid field name and that character fields must be in quotations. Also keep in mind that some queries will not return any data at all. This obviously occurs with a request

```
00001    PHILLIPS      WILMER      110 ACCT    37400.00
00002    TIETZ         LISA        124 ACCT    19800.00
00009    TULLY         EARL        115 ACCT    37400.00
00010    BELL          JEFF        105 ACCT    25795.00
00015    KENWORTHY     MARK        123 ACCT    21450.00
```

FIGURE B-4.15 A dBASE Selection

The figure shows the subset of the whole EMPLOYEE file which is listed when the LIST FOR DEPT="ACCT" query is made. Only the requested records or rows are listed.

```
00001    110    PHILLIPS    37400.00
00003    132    JONES       43000.00
00009    115    TULLY       37400.00
00012    119    VOLZ        45000.00
```

FIGURE B-4.16   A dBASE Projection and Selection

When only specific fields and specific records are requested, the result is the intersection of a projection and a selection. Only the data fields and records shown in this figure will be listed when the dBASE query LIST EMPNO, LASTNAME, SALARY FOR SALARY>35000 is made.

like LIST FOR LASTNAME="GREMLIN". There is no record in the file that satisfies the FOR clause. Look at the following query:

```
LIST FOR DEPT="ACCT" .AND. DEPT="MKT"
```

Can you figure out why this query fails to return any data? What was the issuer of this query probably seeking? What would be the correct query? Would replacing the AND with OR work?

By using selection and projection together, you can access even smaller portions of the file. For instance, let's list the employee number, last name, and salary for all those employees with salaries greater than $35,000. The correct query would be LIST EMPNO, LASTNAME, SALARY FOR SALARY>35000. This returns a listing that is only a small subset of the original file (see Figure B-4.16). It actually represents the intersection of the rows and columns you have requested through your selection and projection. This is shown in Figure B-4.16.

Additional Query Functions

Besides the selection, projection, and other options of the list command, there are additional functions available for accessing information about a file. One such function is the sum command. This produces a total for numeric fields. You can find the total of all the yearly salaries in your payroll file by typing SUM SALARY. You could find out totals for monthly salaries by typing SUM SALARY/12. The FOR selection clause is also available, so you can obtain the sum of a particular field for only certain records. By requesting SUM SALARY FOR DEPT="ACCT", for example, you get the sum of the salaries in the accounting department.

Another useful function is the count command. You can count the number of employees in your file by simply typing COUNT. Again, you can use the FOR clause, such as COUNT FOR DEPT="MKT", which would give you the number of employees in the marketing department.

Sorting

Go ahead and list the employee file again by using the LIST command. Notice that the employee records are in a random order. It is often desirable to have the file in some logical order. One way you can accomplish this in dBASE is to sort the data base.

Before you sort the employee data base, use the dBASE help facility to learn how to do the sort. Press the [F1] function key. Pressing the [F1] key is the same as entering the help command. Read through the help screens that are now on your monitor. As you can see, there are many dBASE commands. The one you now want to learn about is SORT, so first

> SORT ON <field> TO <file> [ASCENDING / descending] -- writes a
> new copy of the database in use with all records arranged
> in order. Uses ASCII values to determine the order (gener-
> ally Spaces, Numbers, Uppercase, Lowercase, then Symbols).
> SORT will not copy records marked for deletion. Default
> order is ASCENDING.

      Example: . USE MAILLIST
                . SORT ON ZIP TO MAILZIP DESCENDING

```
                              dBASE III

                               SORT
                               ====

Syntax       : SORT TO <new file> [ASCENDING/DESCENDING]
                    ON <field> [/A] [/D] [,<field2> [/A] [/D]]...
                    [<scope>] [FOR <condition>]

Description : SORT copies all or part of a database (.dbf) to a new
              database file. The contents of the new file are ordered
              chronologically, alphabetically, or numerically by the
              key field list.
              Individual field sorting can be done in ascending order
              (the default option/A) or in descending order (option/D).

See also     : INDEX

  PgUp=previous screen, Esc=exit Help, ^Home=previous menu, or enter command.

          ENTER  >   [                    ]
```

FIGURE B-4.17 The Sort Help Message

A help message, like the one shown here for the SORT command, can be obtained for any dBASE command. Just type HELP COMMAND-NAME.

press the [ESC] key one time and then enter the command HELP SORT. You should have gotten a message like the one in Figure B-4.17. If you didn't, then you are using an early version of dBASE, or the help file (dbasemsg.txt) is missing from your diskette.

The sort help message gives you the general form of the sort command. You must specify a field name (do you want to sort by salary, last name, et cetera?) and a destination file name. DBASE II actually puts the sorted records into a new file which you name in the sort command. You may specify ascending (A to Z) or descending (Z to A) order. If you do not specify, then dBASE will present it in ascending order. Let's sort your personnel file by department. Issue the command SORT ON DEPT TO SORTPAY.

If you issue a LIST command now, you will see the employee records in their original order. This is because you are currently "using" the EMPLOYEE file and not the SORTPAY file. Type USE SORTPAY so that you are now using the new sorted file. Now LIST the file. The records in this file are listed by department.

If any records are added after the file has been sorted, it will have to be resorted unless the dBASE INSERT command is used. This allows a record to be inserted anywhere in a file instead of just at the end. The insert command is limited in usefulness, however, because it is very slow. Fortunately, the makers of dBASE provide an alternative which is discussed in the section on indexing later in this appendix.

The dBASE Report Generator

As you learned in an earlier section, the LIST command provides a great deal of flexibility. You can turn the record number column on or off by using the OFF option. You can select only particular records by using a FOR clause. You can project only certain columns (including virtual fields), and put those columns in any order. Finally, you can send any list to the printer by using the SET PRINT ON command before the LIST command. Even so, a report printed in this fashion is missing some fundamental formatting capabilities: control over margins, page breaks, column headings, page headings, page numbering, column totals, column subtotals, column widths, and so on. In order for you to have these formatting abilities, dBASE has a built-in report generator. The generator uses dialogue and prompts to request information from you about the report's content and format. Let's use the generator to produce a report for your SORTPAY file.

Start the report generator by typing REPORT and pressing [enter]. Call the report EMPREP in response to dBASE's request for a name. Next, dBASE gives you the option of selecting the width of the left margin, the number of lines per page, and the width of the page. DBASE has standard settings (called default settings) that it will use if you do not specify any of these attributes. The standard settings are fine for this report so just press the [enter] key to move on. From this point follow the questions and appropriate answers provided in Figure B-4.18.

When you get to column 006, press the enter key without entering any information. If the report scrolled by too quickly for you to see it, don't worry. You can run the report again by typing REPORT FORM EMPREP. Still too quick? You can do two things about that. First, you can obtain a hard copy of the report form from the printer; just type REPORT FORM EMPREP TO PRINT. Second, you can stop the scrolling of the report on the screen by holding down the [Ctrl] key and striking the [Num Lock] key when the report is at the section you would like to examine. Striking any key restarts the report. You can start and stop the scrolling of a report on the screen as many times as you like.

If you made a mistake in entering the answers to the report-form questions shown in Figure B-4.18, you can correct them by entering the command MODIFY COMMAND EMPREP.FRM. Enter this command now. You should see on your screen the answers you typed in response to the report questions. Using the cursor keys, move around the answers, correcting those which are in error. The [Ctrl][W] key combination will save your corrected report form or the [Ctrl][Q] key combination will take you back to the dot prompt without saving any changes you made to the report form.

It should be pointed out that the report you created is not static. The authors of dBASE refer to it as a report "form" because it contains the format of the report and not the report itself. The report is actually regenerated every time the report form is invoked. This means that if data in the file change, so does the report. If you change a salary or add an employee, you will not get the same report when you run the report form. It is important, then, that you produce a hard copy of the report on a timely basis since the report form does not save this information.

```
. REPORT
ENTER REPORT FORM NAME: EMPREP
ENTER OPTIONS, M=LEFT MARGIN, L=LINES/PAGE, W=PAGE WIDTH
PAGE HEADING? (Y/N) Y
ENTER PAGE HEADING: EMPLOYEE SALARY REPORT
DOUBLE SPACE REPORT? (Y/N) N
ARE TOTALS REQUIRED? (Y/N) Y
SUBTOTALS IN REPORT? (Y/N) Y
ENTER SUBTOTALS FIELD: DEPT
SUMMARY REPORT ONLY? (Y/N) N
EJECT PAGE AFTER SUBTOTALS? (Y/N) N
ENTER SUBTOTAL HEADING: DEPARTMENT:
COL     WIDTH,CONTENTS
001     7,EMPNO
ENTER HEADING: EMP NO.
ARE TOTALS REQUIRED? (Y/N) N
002     15,LASTNAME
ENTER HEADING: LAST NAME
003     9,FIRSTNAME
ENTER HEADING: FIRST NAME
004     10,SALARY
ENTER HEADING: ANNUAL SALARY
ARE TOTALS REQUIRED? (Y/N) Y
005     10,SALARY/12
ENTER HEADING: MONTHLY SALARY
ARE TOTALS REQUIRED? (Y/N) Y
006
```

---

dBASE III

DBASE III uses the command **CREATE REPORT** to start the report form defining process. Although the format is different, dBASE III requests the same information that dBASE II does. Give the same answers to the report as in dBASE II and note any problems with the report. The report can then be modified by using the command:

```
MODIFY REPORT EMPREP
```

FIGURE B-4.18   Report Generator Dialogue

By answering this list of simple questions, a complete report form is created and stored on the disk. You may use this report form at any time in the future by entering REPORT FORM EMPREP.

Deleting Records and Files

So far you have learned how to create files, change those files by modifying their structure, add records to a file, make changes to those records, produce reports, and query data from the files. Another common need for information processing is to delete files or to delete records in a file. Let's start by learning how to delete records in a file.

Make record #00002 the current record by using the GO 2 command. *Issue a DISPLAY to see that this record is the record for Lisa Tietz. Now tell dBASE DELETE. DBASE responds 1 deletion. The current record, which was record #00002, has been deleted. LIST the file to see the effect of this deletion. There is now an asterisk next to record #00002. DBASE has marked the record as deleted but has not removed it from the file. You can hide any deleted records from view by issuing the command SET DELETED ON. Try this and then LIST the file again. The file listing now does not show the deleted record. SET DELETED OFF will allow you to once again view any records marked for deletion. There are two advantages to not immediately removing a requested deletion. First, it is sometimes desirable to maintain information about an inactive employee. For example, in a payroll file you would want to delete employees as they leave the company. However, you would need to hold on to the employees' data until the current year was over so that you would have adequate tax records. By using SET DELETED OFF, you can have that information available even though the employees' records would not show up in reports run when DELETED is ON.

A second advantage is that you sometimes change your mind about deleting a record or you accidentally delete the wrong record. Having a two-step deletion process gives you a safety catch. You can "undelete" a record by using the recall command (with DELETED set OFF). Issue the command RECALL ALL. Now LIST the file again. Lisa has been reinstated. If you want to permanently remove records currently marked for deletion, use the pack command. This removes any marked records for good and renumbers the remaining records.

There are a number of ways to mark a record for deletion. To delete Lisa Tietz you could have used DELETE RECORD 2. That would have kept you from first having to make record #00002 the current record. Records can also be deleted by using the FOR clause as it was used in the list command. You could have said DELETE FOR LASTNAME = "TIETZ" .AND. FIRSTNAME = "LISA". The FOR clause also gives you the power to delete a number of records at once, such as DELETE ALL FOR DEPT="ACCT". This would mark everyone in the accounting department for deletion. One final way to mark a record for deletion is to use the [Ctrl][U] key combination when editing a specific record. This toggles the deletion mark (*) on and off. Try this by first typing EDIT 6 and then using the [Ctrl][U] combination.

Let's make a copy of the file you are currently using, SORTPAY, so that you have a file to delete. Type COPY TO TEMPFILE FOR DEPT="MKT". DBASE will respond 5 RECORDS COPIED. You have just created a file with the same structure as your employee and sortpay files. However, this file only contains records for marketing personnel. Issue a USE TEMPFILE command and then a LIST to see the new file. It is not a good practice to delete an open file, so type CLEAR (CLEAR ALL in dBASE III). This closes all open files. Now type DELETE FILE TEMPFILE.DBF.DBASE will respond FILE HAS BEEN DELETED.

The dBASE Programming Language

DBASE comes complete with its own programming language that is similar to BASIC. There are three major uses for the language. First, it allows for the production of custom reports (such as mailing labels) that cannot be produced by the report generator. Second, it provides a method for sequential processing of files. If you routinely have need to systematically

---

*If you are using dBASE III, use GO 3. Because of a sorting difference between dBASE II and dBASE III, the record we want to go to, Lisa Tietz, will be record 3 if you are using dBASE III. Also, if you are using dBASE III, the references to record #00002 on this page should be read as record #00003.

```
*NAME TAG PROGRAM

SET TALK OFF  *KEEPS DBASE MESSAGES FROM BEING INCLUDED IN OUTPUT
GO TOP        *MOVES THE CURRENCY POINTER TO THE FIRST RECORD
ERASE
USE EMPLOYEE
?"                              NAME TAG PROGRAM"
?
?
ACCEPT "SHOULD OUTPUT BE SENT TO THE PRINTER (YES/NO)" TO ANSWER

* IF THE QUESTION ABOVE IS ANSWERED YES THEN THE PRINTER IS TURNED ON
IF ANSWER="YES"
   SET PRINT ON
ENDIF

* CONTINUE LOOPING FROM HERE TO "ENDDO" STATEMENT UNTIL END OF FILE IS
* ENCOUNTERED (UNTIL THE CURRENCY POINTER IS ON THE LAST RECORD)
DO WHILE .NOT. EOF()

   * BASED ON WHICH DEPT ABBREVIATION IS PRESENT IN THE CURRENT RECORD, STORE
   * THE FULL NAME TO THE VARIABLE DEPART
   DO CASE
      CASE DEPT="ACCT"
        STORE "ACCOUNTING" TO DEPART
      CASE DEPT="ADMIN"
        STORE "ADMINISTRATION" TO DEPART
      CASE DEPT="MKT"
        STORE "MARKETING" TO DEPART
      OTHERWISE                         *IF DEPT IS NOT ACCT, ADMIN OR MKT
        STORE DEPT TO DEPART            *STORE WHATEVER IT IS TO DEPART
   ENDCASE

   *SKIP TWO LINES, PRINT THE FIRST NAME (TRIMMED OF ANY BLANKS) FOR THE CURRENT
   *RECORD, PRINT THE LAST NAME FOR THE CURRENT RECORD, SKIP TWO MORE LINES
   ?
   ?
   ? TRIM(FIRSTNAME),LASTNAME
   ? DEPART
   ?
   ?

   *MOVE THE CURRENCY POINTER TO THE NEXT RECORD IN THE FILE (SKIP ONE RECORD)
   SKIP

ENDDO    * LOOP BACK TO THE BEGINNING OF THE DO WHILE LOOP

SET PRINT OFF  *TURN THE PRINTER OFF
SET TALK ON    *TURN DBASE MESSAGES BACK ON
RETURN
```

For this program to run on dBASE III, change ERASE to CLEAR in the fourth line.

FIGURE B-4.19   dBASE NAMETAGS Program Listing

The NAMETAGS program generates a nametag or label for each employee. This simple program should give you a feel for the dBASE programming language.

dBASE III

One of the most significant improvements between dBASE II and dBASE III was the addition of the ASSIST command. The ASSIST command turns dBASE III into a menu-driven system instead of a prompted, comand-based system. It is an excellent feature to use while you are mastering the dBASE III commands. One command worth learning is the LABEL command. This command allows labels (like the ones generated by the NAMETAGS program) to be created very quickly.

Use the ASSIST feature to learn the LABEL command. Type `ASSIST`. Then make selections from the menus and watch while dBASE builds the equivalent command at the bottom of your screen.

FIGURE B-4.20 The ASSIST Command: A Powerful dBASE III Help Tool

move through a file, performing some operation on each record, the dBASE programming language gives you the ability to automate the task. Last, the programming language allows you to build menus, input screens, and other interfaces for users of dBASE II.

Let's write a program that uses the data in your employee file to generate some name tags for the company picnic. To create your program file, type `MODIFY COMMAND NAMETAGS`. DBASE now gives you a blank screen on which to enter the program code. Type the code as it is shown in Figure B-4.19. Three [`Ctrl`] combinations are helpful when inputting a program. [`Ctrl`][`T`] will erase the line where your cursor is located. [`Ctrl`][`Y`] will erase everything on a line to the right of your cursor. [`Ctrl`][`N`] will insert a blank line at your current cursor location. The lines in the program listing marked with an asterisk are documentation lines that are not necessary for the program to run. They are there to help you understand the logic of the program. When you have finished entering the lines of code, use the [`Ctrl`][`W`] key combination to save the program.

To run the program, type `DO NAMETAGS`. If your program doesn't run correctly then use the `MODIFY COMMAND NAMETAGS` command again and carefully check to see whether you made any errors when typing the lines of the program. Figure B-4.20 points out a significant improvement in dBASE III over dBASE II.

Indexing

One of the most powerful features of dBASE is indexing. An index is essentially a map that shows how to proceed from record to record in some predetermined order. Like sorting, indexing must be done on a key field. Let's index your employee file and then examine the advantages of indexing over sorting. First, make sure you are using the `EMPLOYEE` file by typing `USE EMPLOYEE`. Type the command `INDEX ON EMPNO TO EMPINDEX`. DBASE responds with `15 records indexed`. Now `LIST` the file. Your file, like the one shown in Figure B-4.21, should be in order by employee number. Notice that unlike sorting, the original record numbers have not been changed. The file is listed in a user-defined order instead of in record-number order.

One advantage that indexing has over sorting is that there is only one occurrence of each record in a single data-base file, rather than the same record appearing in several different files. Often you need to view your file in more than one order. Sometimes you may want to look at it in departmental order, and other times you may want to look at it in employee number order. Still other times you may want to look at it in alphabetic order by last name. It would be too slow to re-sort the file into a different order each time. To get by this you could have three files, each sorted in a different order. However, this is called redundancy and it causes several problems. First, it would be a waste of secondary-storage space to have three files with the same information in it. Second, if you had to make a change to an employee's record you would have to be careful to make it in all three places. At best this would be bothersome and at worse it could cause an inconsistency in the data if the change were made in one place and not another.

Indexing overcomes these problems because no matter how many different ways you index the file, there is still only one occurrence of each record in the data-base file. You can switch from index to index, viewing the records in a different order, but it is always the same records and the same file you are working with.

Another, and perhaps more important, advantage to indexing is that when you append records to a file you don't have to reindex the file like you have to resort when you add a record to a sorted file. Try it by appending a new employee to your file. Type APPEND. DBASE should respond with a blank input screen for record #00016. Fill in your own name and salary and give yourself the employee number 121. After you have filled in record 16, dBASE II will present you with an input screen for record 17. Press [enter] without entering any information and you will be placed back at the dot prompt. Now, go ahead and LIST the file. Your record (#00016) has been placed right after Douglas Volz, in proper employee-number order.

Having a file indexed gives you the ability to use a very powerful search function called FIND. Type FIND 130. Now type DISPLAY. DBASE has made the record where the employee number is 130 the current record. DBASE can "find" an indexed record very quickly, even in large files. In an unindexed file, if you were interested in finding the same information, you could use LIST FOR EMPNO=130 or LOCATE FOR EMPNO=130. You have used the list command before. The locate command is like the find command; that is, it makes the employee 130 the current employee but does not display the record unless requested. In both the list and locate command, dBASE looks at every record in the file, one by one, and compares the EMPNO field contents to the requested employee number to see whether a match occurs. In an indexed file, since the requested field is in order, dBASE can track down the correct record just as you would look up a word in a dictionary, skipping large chunks of data at a time instead of looking at every word. In small files the difference in speed is not noticeable, but in files with several hundred records, it would take several minutes to locate a record compared with less than a second to find it.

00010	BELL	JEFF	105	ACCT	25795.00
00001	PHILLIPS	WILMER	110	ACCT	37400.00
00014	DIAL	DAVID	112	MKT	20000.00
00008	DAVIS	ELIZABETH	113	MKT	22000.00
00009	TULLY	EARL	115	ACCT	37400.00
00012	VOLZ	DOUGLAS	119	ADMIN	45000.00
00015	KENWORTHY	MARK	123	ACCT	21450.00
00004	TIETZ	LISA	124	ACCT	19800.00
00005	KARWACKI	MARK	125	MKT	22000.00
00006	LAUMANN	JOHN	128	ADMIN	31000.00
00013	LYTLE	JOE	130	ADMIN	30000.00
00011	BUCKINGHAM	DAVE	131	MKT	26700.00
00003	JONES	THELMA	132	ADMIN	43000.00
00007	SMITH	GEORGE	134	ADMIN	19000.00
00002	JOHNSON	JAY	140	MKT	28000.00

FIGURE B-4.21 An Indexed File Listing

This indexed listing displays the records in a logical, user-defined order instead of in record-number order.

Practice Makes Perfect

The last part of this introduction provides you with a list of the more common dBASE II and III commands (see Figure B-4.22). Using the HELP facility and some trial and error, you should be able to learn to use any of them. Remember, the best way to learn about software is to use it.

If you would like to explore dBASE II in more depth, I recommend the following paperback book: Simpson, Alan. *Understanding dBASE II*. Berkeley, CA: Sybex, Inc., 1984.

Hands-On Exercises

1. Using dBASE II or III, create a payroll file. Start by typing the following:

```
CREATE
ENTER FILENAME:
ENTER RECORD STRUCTURE AS FOLLOWS:
 FIELD   NAME,TYPE,WIDTH,DECIMAL PLACES
 001     DEPT,C,2
 002     EMPNO,C,4
 003     LNAME,C,20
 004     FNAME,C,20
 005     POSITION,C,3
 006     SALARY,N,9,2
 007
 INPUT DATA NOW?
```

Point to the new payroll file by entering the USE command:

```
USE B:PAYROLL
```

Use the APPEND command to enter the following data into the file:

```
APPEND
17 6010 FIRST          I.M.              211      5947.84
17 5698 DERHODE        JUAN MOREFORE     569      1794.92
17 3312 SHARALIKE      SHARON            531      2123.87
17 2515 LEAVES         T.                231      4943.19
```

Use the LIST command to look at the data:

```
LIST
00001  17 6010 FIRST       I.M.            211     5947.84
00002  17 5698 DERHODE     JUAN MOREFORE   569     1794.92
00003  17 3312 SHARALIKE   SHARON          531     2123.87
00004  17 2315 LEAVES      T.              231     4943.19
```

Let us assume that Ms. leaves marries Mr. Tottler. Use the EDIT command to change her last name:

```
EDIT 4
```

dBASE II

APPEND Appends information from another dBASE II data base or files in Delimited or System
Data format.
BROWSE Full-screen window viewing and editing of data base.
CHANGE Non-full-screen edit of fields of data base.
CLEAR Closes data bases in use and releases current memory variables.
CONTINUE Continues the searching action of a LOCATE command.
COPY Creates a copy of an existing data base.
COUNT Counts the number of records that meet some criteria in a file.
CREATE Creates a new data base.
DELETE Deletes a file or marks records for deletion.
DISPLAY Display files, data base records or structure, memory variables, or status.
DO Executes command files or structured loops in same.
EDIT Initiates edit of records in a data base.
ERASE Clears the screen.
FIND Positions to record corresponding to key in index file.
GO or GOTO Positions to specific record or place in file.
HELP Accesses help file overview or specific help-file entry.
INDEX Creates an index file.
INSERT Inserts new record in data base.
JOIN Joins output of two data bases.
LIST Lists files, data base records or structure, memory variables, and status.
LOCATE Finds a record that fits a condition.
MODIFY Creates and/or edits command file or modifies structure of existing data base.
PACK Erases records marked for deletion.
QUIT Exits dBASE and returns to operating system.
RECALL Erases mark for deletion.
REINDEX Updates existing index file.
RENAME Renames a file.
REPLACE Changes information in record(s) or entire data base field by field.
REPORT Formats and displays a report of information.
SET Sets dBASE control parameters.
SKIP Positions forward or backward in data base.
SORT Writes copy of data base sorted on one of the data fields.
SUM Computes and displays the sum of data-base field(s).
USE Specifies data base to USE until next USE command is issued.

Differences with dBASE III

CLEAR Erases the screen.
CLEAR ALL Closes all open files.
ERASE Erases a specified file. (Must include a file extension.)
REPORT FORM Generates a report.
CREATE REPORT Creates a new report.
MODIFY REPORT Modifies an existing report.

FIGURE B-4.22 Frequently Used dBASE Commands

Use the arrow keys to move around and CTR-W to exit
the edit. Then LIST the file to see the change:

```
LIST
00001  17 6010 FIRST       I.M.               211    5947.84
00002  17 5698 DERHODE     JUAN MOREFORE      569    1794.92
00003  17 3312 SHARALIKE   SHARON             531    2123.87
00004  17 2315 TOTTLER     T.                 231    4943.19
```

2. Using the payroll file in exercise 1, create a report
showing monthly salaries. This can be done by typing
the following:

```
REPORT
ENTER REPORT FORM NAME: B:DEPTSAL
ENTER OPTIONS, M=LEFT MARGIN, L=LINES/PAGE, W=PAGE WIDTH
PAGE HEADINGS? (Y/N) Y
ENTER PAGE HEADING: MONTHLY DEPARTMENTAL SALARIES
DOUBLE SPACE REPORT? (Y/N) N
ARE TOTALS REQUIRED? (Y/N) Y
SUBTOTALS IN REPORT? (Y/N) Y
ENTER SUBTOTALS FIELD: DEPT
SUMMARY REPORT ONLY? (Y/N) N
EJECT PAGE AFTER SUBTOTALS? (Y/N) N
ENTER SUBTOTAL HEADING: DEPARTMENT
COL      WIDTH, CONTENTS
001       5,EMPNO
ENTER HEADING: EMP #
002      15,LNAME
ENTER HEADING: LAST NAME
003      15, FNAME
ENTER HEADING: FIRST NAME
004       9,SALARY
ENTER HEADING: SALARY
ARE TOTALS REQUIRED?          Y
005
```

The following report should appear:

```
PAGE NO. 00001
06/30/84

                MONTHLY DEPARTMENTAL SALARIES

EMP #    LAST NAME        FIRST NAME      SALARY

* DEPARTMENT 17
6010   FIRST             I. M.            5947.84
5698   DERHODE           JUAN MOREFORE    1794.92
3312   SHARALIKE         SHARON           2123.87
2315   TOTTLER           T.               4943.19
** SUBTOTAL **
                         14809.82
```

To see the report again, simply enter the following:

```
REPORT FORM B:DEPTSAL
```

If you want to stop the report from scrolling off the top of the screen, use the `Ctrl-Num Lock` keys. After producing the above report, change the department for two employees by using the `EDIT` command. Produce the report again by entering: `REPORT FORM B:DEPTSAL`.

3. Using dBASE II or III, change the function of the F2 key so that the report created in exercise 2 will be shown when the F2 key is pressed. This can be done in dBase II by typing `SET F2 TO 'REPORT FORM B:DEPTSAL'`. In dBase III, you should type `SET FUNCTION 2 TO 'REPORT FORM B:DEPTSAL'`. Press the F6 key to see the change in the setting, then press F2 to test the change.

Glossary

Sources

Gaining familiarity with information-system terms is important to your understanding of information systems. The many different definitions of these terms are often a barrier to your understanding of the subject. The American National Standards Institute (ANSI) has attempted to standardize the definitions of the terms through publication of the *American National Dictionary for Information Processing Systems*. Where possible we will use definitions from this book. Definition sources are identified as follows:

1. ANSI definitions are preceded by an asterisk. An asterisk to the left of the term indicates that the entire entry is reproduced with permission from American National Standards, Committee X3, Technical Report, *American National Dictionary for Information Processing Systems*, X3/TR-1-82, copyright 1982 by the Computer and Business Equipment Manufacturers Association (CBEMA), copies of which may be purchased from CBEMA, 311 First Street NW, Washington, DC 20001. Where definitions from other sources are included in the entry, ANSI definitions are identified by an asterisk to the right of the item number. The symbol (ISO) at the beginning of a definition indicates that it has been discussed and agreed upon at meetings of the International Organization for Standardization, Technical Committee 97/Subcommittee 1, and has been approved by ANSI for inclusion in the *American National Dictionary for Information Processing Systems*. The symbol (SC1) at the beginning of a definition indicates that it is reprinted from an early working document of ISO Technical Committee 97/Subcommittee 1 and that agreement has not yet been reached among its members.
2. Definitions from *Vocabulary for Data Processing, Telecommunications, and Office Systems*, IBM Publication C-20-1699-6 (July 1981), are indicated by (IBM) prior to the definition.

access: To read, write, or update information, usually on secondary storage such as a disk.

*access arm: A part of a magnetic-disk storage unit that is used to hold one or more reading and writing heads.

access controls: The controls that limit access to program documentation, program and data files, and computer hardware.

*access time: (ISO) The time interval between the instant at which an instruction control unit initiates a call for data and the instant at which delivery of the data is completed.

accounts-payable system: A computer system that helps provide control over payments to suppliers, issues checks to these suppliers, and provides information necessary for effective cash management.

accounts-receivable system: A computer system used for billing customers, maintaining records of amounts due from customers, and generating reports on overdue amounts.

*accuracy: 1. (ISO) A quality held by that which is free of error. 2. (ISO) A qualitative assessment of freedom from error, a high assessment corresponding to a small error.

acoustic coupler (IBM): A type of data-communication equipment that permits use of a telephone handset as a connection to a telephone network for data transmission by means of sound transducers. See modem.

action construct: A construct in a program where a single action is performed.

*address: 1. (ISO) A character or group of characters that identifies a register, a particular part of storage, or some other data source or destination. 2. (ISO) To refer to a device or an item of data by its address.

algorithm: Synonym for program.

alphabetic character (IBM): A letter or other symbol, excluding digits, used in a language.

*alphanumeric: Pertaining to a character set that contains letters, digits, and usually other characters, such as punctuation marks. Synonymous with alphameric.

American National Standards Institute (ANSI) (IBM): An organization for the purpose of establishing voluntary industry standards.

*analog computer: 1. (ISO) A computer in which analog representation of data is mainly used. 2. A computer that operates on analog data by performing physical processes on these data. 3. Contrast with digital computer.

anticipation check: A control based on the fact that certain fields in an input record should always be nonblank or that an input record is expected for each master-file record.

APL: (SC1) A programming language with an unusual syntax and character set, primarily designed for mathematical applications, particularly those involving numeric or literal arrays.

application: A specific use of a computer to perform a business task.

application controls: Controls applied directly to the individual computer application: (1) input controls, (2) processing controls, and (3) output controls.

application development by users: The development of application programs by users, with only limited support from programmers and system analysts.

application generator: A software system that generates computer programs based on the user's needs. An application generator consists of a large number of pre-coded modules that perform various functions. The user merely specifies the functions needed for his or her application and the system invokes the appropriate modules and runs them.

application program (IBM): A program that is written for or by a user and that applies to a particular application.

application programmer: A programmer who writes and maintains application programs. Contrast with system programmer.

application software: Programs that are written for or by a user and that apply to a particular application of the computer. For example, a payroll program is application software.

application systems: Computer programs written to perform specific business tasks.

archival storage: Storage, not under direct control of the computer, on which backup information and old records are kept.

arithmetic assignment: The assignment of the results of an arithmetic operation to a numeric variable.

*arithmetic logic unit: (ISO) A part of a computer that performs arithmetic operations, logic operations, and related operations.

arithmetic operator: A symbol that represents the performance of an arithmetic operation such as addition, subtraction, multiplication, or division.

arithmetic proof checks: A control that verifies the results of mathematical operations.

array: An arrangement of elements in one or more dimensions.

*artificial intelligence: The capability of a device to perform functions that are usually associated with human intelligence, such as reasoning, learning, and self-improvement.

*ASCII (American National Standard Code for Information Interchange): The standard code, using a coded character set consisting of seven-bit coded characters (eight bits, including parity check), used for information interchange among data-processing systems, data-communication systems, and associated equipment. The ASCII set consists of control characters and graphic characters.

*assemble: To prepare a machine-language program from a symbolic-language program by substituting absolute operation codes for symbolic operation codes, and absolute or relocatable addresses for symbolic addresses.

*assembler: (ISO) A computer program used to assemble. Synonymous with assembly program.

*assembly language: A computer programming language whose statements may be instructions or declarations. The instructions usually have a one-to-one correspondence with machine instructions.

assignment: Placing a certain value in a variable.

assignment statement: A program statement that performs some computations and assigns the resulting value to a variable.

asynchronous transmission: A data transmission method in which each byte is transmitted separately.

attribute: A characteristic or property that an entity has.

audit trail: The capability to reconstruct processing steps and trace information back to its origins.

backup copy: A duplicate of data or programs used to restore the original if it is lost or destroyed.

backup file: A file containing redundant copies of programs and data that are used to reconstruct current files in case current files are partially or totally destroyed.

backup procedure: A control procedure that provides additional evidence about the integrity of stored information.

base register: A register in the CPU which is used as a reference point to specify all other storage locations for the program.

BASIC (Beginner's All-Purpose Symbolic Instruction Code): (SC1) A programming language with a small repertoire of commands and a simple syntax, primarily designed for numerical applications.

batch (IBM): An accumulation of data to be processed.

batch-direct: The processing method where changes and inquiries to the file are batched and processed periodically under a direct-access file organization method.

*batch processing: 1. The processing of data or the accomplishment of jobs accumulated in advance in such a manner that each accumulation thus formed is processed or accomplished in the same run. 2. The processing of data accumulated over a period of time. 3. The execution of computer programs serially. 4. Pertaining to the technique of executing a set of computer programs such that each is completed before the next program of the set is started.

batch-sequential processing: The processing method where changes and inquiries to the file are batched and processed periodically under a sequential-file access method.

batch-serial execution: A method of data processing where each program is executed in the order in which it was read into the system; only one program is executed at a time.

batch total: The sum resulting from the addition of a specified numeric field from each record in a batch of records; it is used for control and checking purposes. See control total and hash total.

*baud: A unit of signaling speed equal to the number of discrete conditions or signal events per second. Synonymous with bits per second (bps).

benchmark program: A sample program that is representative of at least part of the buyer's primary computer workload and that is executed on various computer configurations to provide information useful to the buyer making a computer acquisition decision.

bidirectional printing: The ability of a printer to print onto the paper when the carriage is moving either to the right or to the left. This speeds up printing because it eliminates carriage returns, during which no printing can take place.

binary: 1. A condition that has two possible values or states. 2. A number system whose base is two.

*binary digit (Bit): 1. (ISO) Synonym for bit. 2. In binary notation, either 0 or 1.

binary representation: A number system that uses only the digits 0 and 1, rather than the ten digits in the decimal system. This system is used to depict electronic computer design since its two digits represent the two conditions (on and off) present in electronic components.

binary search: A method of searching for a value in an array which is in ascending or descending order. The array is split in two, and one half is searched for the value. The half, in turn, splits into two parts. This process continues until the required element is found.

*bit: 1. (ISO) In the pure binary numeration system, either 0 or 1. Synonymous with binary digit. 2. (ISO) Synonymous with binary element.

bit mapped: A system in which each possible dot of a CRT display is controlled by a single bit of memory.

*block: 1. (ISO) A string of records, a string of words, or a character string formed for technical or logic reasons to be treated as an entity. 2. A collection of contiguous records recorded as a unit. Blocks are separated by interblock gaps and each block may contain one or more records.

block format: The format of each individual message sent through a communication system. This includes control characters to mark the beginning and end of the message, and error-detection characters.

bootstrap: A program used to start (or "boot") the computer, usually by clearing the primary memory, setting up various devices, and loading the operating system from secondary storage or ROM.

bottleneck: A slowdown in one part of the system that can cause the whole system to operate below capacity.

boundary: The area that separates one system from another.

bpi (IBM): Bits per inch.

bps: Bits per second.

*branch: 1. (ISO) In the execution of a computer program, to select one from a number of alternative sets of instructions. 2. A link between a parent node and a child node in a tree structure.

branching: The transfer of execution to nonsequential statements.

break: A key on most keyboards that is used to tell the computer that the current operation is to be aborted.

bubble sort: A method of sorting the elements of an array. Each element is compared with the next element, and if they are out of the intended order, they are switched.

bubble storage: A nonvolatile memory device that stores data by polarizing microscopic bubbles in a crystalline substance.

buffer area: An area in primary memory where information is stored temporarily after it is retrieved from secondary storage or before it is placed in secondary storage. The information may be modified by a program while it is in the buffer.

*bug: A mistake or malfunction.

bundling: The selling of hardware and software together as a package.

*burst: 1. In data communication, a sequence of signals counted as one unit in accordance with some specific criterion or measure. 2. To separate continuous-form paper into individual sheets.

bus: A communication link that connects the CPU to its peripheral devices.

byte: 1.* (ISO) A binary character string operated on as a unit and usually shorter than a computer word. 2. (IBM) The representation of a character.

CAD: An acronym for computer-aided design or computer-assisted design. The term covers a wide range of systems that function as tools to expedite mechanical and electronic design.

calculate: To perform one or more arithmetic functions, including addition, subtraction, multiplication, and division.

*calculator: (ISO) A data processor, especially suitable for performing arithmetical operations, that requires frequent intervention by a human operator.

call: To cause a module to begin execution.

CAM: An acronym for computer-aided manufacturing or computer-assisted manufacturing.

capacity: The amount of data that can be stored on a disk, most often expressed in kilobytes or megabytes (1,024 and 1,048,576 bytes, respectively). Because most disks use some area for storing format and location information, capacities are usually given as both unformatted and formatted.

*card punch: 1. A device that punches holes in a card to represent data. 2. (ISO) Synonym for keypunch.

*card reader: 1. (ISO) A device that reads or senses the holes in a punched card, transforming the data from hole patterns to electrical signals. 2. An input device that senses hole patterns in a punched card and translates them into machine language. Synonymous with punched-card reader.

card sorter: (ISO) A device that deposits punched cards in pockets selected according to the hole patterns in the cards.

cartridge: For tape, one of the ways that recording tape is packaged. Cartridges include two tape reels and a set of guide rollers inside a shell that looks like a fat audio cassette. For disks, cartridges are plastic shells that hold removable hard disks.

cassette: A package for magnetic tape similar in appearance to a standard audio cassette, but filled with tape optimized for digital recording.

cathode ray tube (CRT) (IBM): An electronic vacuum tube, such as a television picture tube, that can be used to display graphic images or data.

*central processing unit (CPU): (ISO) A unit of a computer that includes circuits controlling the interpretation and execution of instructions. Synonymous with central processor.

chaining (IBM): A system of storing records in which each record belongs to a list or group of records and has a linking field for tracing the chain.

channel: 1.* A path along which signals can be sent; for example, data channel or output channel. 2. (IBM) A device that connects the processing unit and main storage with the I/O control units. 3. The individual magnetic tracks along the length of a tape.

*character: A letter, digit, or other symbol that is used as part of the organization, control, or representation of data. A character is often in the form of a spatial arrangement of adjacent or connected strokes.

character data: Data on which arithmetic calculations will not be done.

*character printer: (ISO) A device that prints a single character at a time, such as a typewriter. Synonymous with character-at-a-time printer and serial printer. Contrast with line printer.

*character set: An ordered set of unique representations called characters; examples include the 26 letters of the English alphabet, Boolean 0 and 1, the set of symbols in the Morse code, and the 128 ASCII characters.

character string assignment: The assignment of a literal value to a string variable.

*check bit: A binary check digit, such as a parity bit.

checkpoint: 1.* (ISO) A place in a computer program at which a check is made or at which a recording of data is made for restart purposes. 2. (IBM) A point at which information about the status of a job and the system can be recorded so that the job step can be later restarted.

chief programmer team: An organizational structure often used for programming projects. A small group consisting of a chief programmer, assistant programmers, a librarian, and a backup programmer works independently, with very little supervision, on a programming task.

*chip: 1. A minute piece of semiconductive material used in the manufacture of electronic components. 2. An integrated circuit on a piece of semiconductive material.

circuit board: See printed circuit board.

classify: The identification of an item of data with a certain category. For instance, a sales transaction may be classified as cash or credit.

clock/calendar: A hardware and software feature that automatically sets the time and date when the computer is started or rebooted.

clustered system: A data-entry system in which several keyboards are connected to one or two magnetic tape drives.

*COBOL (Common Business-Oriented Language): A programming language designed for business data processing.

CODASYL (IBM): Conference of Data Systems Languages.

code: 1.* (ISO) A set of unambiguous rules specifying the manner in which data may be represented in a discrete form. Synonymous with coding scheme. 2. *A set of items, such as abbreviations, representing the members of another set. 3. (IBM) One or more computer programs, or part of a computer program. 4. (ISO) To represent data or a computer program in a symbolic form that can be accepted by a data processor. 5. (IBM) To write a routine.

code inspection: A review of program code by a review team. The programmer walks the reviewers through the code; the reviewers check the code for compliance with design specifications.

*column: A vertical arrangement of characters or other expressions. Contrast with row.

*command: 1. A control signal. 2. An instruction. 3. A mathematical or logic operator. 4. Synonym for instruction.

communication processor: A device that converts information to a standard protocol before transmitting it over communication lines, and decodes received data for the computer's own use.

communication protocol: A set of rules governing the flow of data through a communication system.

compare: To examine two pieces of data to determine whether they are equal or one is greater than the other.

compatible (IBM): Pertaining to computers on which the same computer programs can be run without appreciable alteration.

*compile: 1. (ISO) To translate a computer program expressed in a problem-oriented language into a computer-oriented language. 2. To prepare a machine-language program from a computer program written in another programming language.

*compiler: (ISO) A computer program used to compile. Synonymous with compiling program.

compiler diagnostics: Errors detected in a computer program during its compilation.

compile-time diagnostics: Error diagnostics that are produced when a program is compiled.

compressed format: A data format that eliminates unnecessary blanks between data values.

compressed printing: By reducing the horizontal distance between dots in a dot-matrix printer, characters can be made to print narrower (although they remain same height) so that there are more characters per inch and thus a compressed format.

*computer: (ISO) A data processor that can perform substantial computation, including numerous arithmetic or logic operations, without intervention by a human operator during the run.

computer-assisted instruction (CAI) (IBM): A data-processing application in which a computing system is used to assist in the instruction of students. The application usually involves a dialogue between the student and a computer program that informs the student of mistakes as they are made.

computer fraud: Illegal use of computer facilities to misappropriate corporate resources. This includes unauthorized changes to both software and hardware systems.

computer graphics: (SC1) That branch of science and technology concerned with methods and techniques for converting data to or from graphic display via computers.

computer operator: An employee who monitors the performance of the CPU and storage devices. He or she performs most of the human functions necessary to keep the system running.

*computer output microfilm (COM): 1. (ISO) Microfilm that contains data that are received directly from computer-generated signals. 2. To place computer-generated data on microfilm.

*computer program: A series of instructions or statements, in a form acceptable to a computer.

computer service technician: A trained technician who is responsible for the repair and maintenance of hardware devices.

concatenation: The process of joining together two or more literals to form a single literal.

concentric tracks: Circular tracks that have a common center.

*concurrent: 1. (ISO) Pertaining to the occurrence of two or more activities within a given interval of time. 2. Contrast with consecutive, sequential, and simultaneous.

connection: A link between two modules showing which module calls the other.

*consecutive: 1. (ISO) Pertaining to the occurrence of two sequential events without the intervention of any other such event. 2. Contrast with concurrent, sequential, and simultaneous.

*console: A part of a computer used for communication between the operator or maintenance engineer and the computer.

constant: (IBM) A fixed or invariable value or data item.

consultant: An EDP information-system expert who assists users in developing and debugging their own applications.

control: The process of comparing actual results to planned results.

control data: Data that are used by the program solely for making processing decisions.

control group: The group of personnel (separated from computer operations) that maintains input-output controls and reviews output prior to distribution to users.

*control program: (ISO) A computer program designed to schedule and supervise the execution of programs of a computing system. See operating system.

Control Program for Microcomputers (CP/M): A popular operating system for personal computers.

control statement: A statement that regulates the order of execution in a program; for example, an IF statement.

control total (IBM): A sum, resulting from the addition of a specified field from each record in a group of records, that is used for checking machine, program, and data reliability.

control unit: 1. A subsystem contained within the transformation process of every information system. A control component selects, interprets, and executes programmed instructions so that the system can function. In total, it controls the actions of a system. 2. That part of the central processing unit that decodes program instructions and directs the other components of the computer system to perform the task specified in the program instruction.

conversion (IBM): 1. The process of changing from one method of data processing to another. 2. The process of changing from one form of representation to another; for example, to change from decimal representation to binary representation.

copy protected: Disks or tapes that have been recorded in a way that is supposed to prevent the information on them from being copied, although it can be read and used.

core storage: 1.* A magnetic storage in which the data medium consists of magnetic cores. 2. Synonym for primary storage.

counter: A variable used to keep track of the number of times a loop has been executed. Its value is increased (or decreased) by one every time the loop is traversed.

couple: A data item that moves from one module to another.

CPU time (IBM): The amount of time devoted by the processing unit to the execution of instructions. Synonymous with CPU busy time.

*CRT display: See cathode ray tube.

cursor (IBM): A movable spot of light on the screen of a display device, usually indicating where the next character will be entered.

cursor key: A key that, when pressed, causes the cursor to move in a designated direction. Arrows on the keys indicate direction of cursor movement: up, down, right, left, or home (top left corner of screen).

*cycle: An interval of space or time in which one set of events or phenomena is completed.

cylinder: 1. (ISO) In a disk pack, the set of all tracks with the same nominal distance from the axis about which the disk pack rotates. 2. (IBM) The tracks of a disk storage device that can be accessed without repositioning the access mechanism.

daisy wheel: A print element for several popular printers consisting of a plastic or metal disk with spokes radiating from the center portion (like the petals on a daisy). At the end of each spoke is a circular area with a typeface impression on it.

DASD (IBM): Direct-access storage device.

*data: 1. (ISO) A representation of facts, concepts, or instructions in a formalized manner suitable for communication, interpretation, or processing by humans or automatic means. 2. Any representations such as characters or analog quantities to which meaning is, or might be, assigned.

*data base: 1. (ISO) A set of data consisting of at least one file, that is sufficient for a given purpose or for a given data-processing system. 2. A collection of data fundamental to a system. 3. A collection of data fundamental to an enterprise. The terms *data base* and *data bank* are often used interchangeably.

data-base administrator: The person responsible for coordinating the data base, including provisions for data security.

data-base machine: A computer dedicated entirely to the use of a data-base management system.

data-base management system: A computer program that stores, retrieves, and updates data that are stored on one or more files.

data block: A set of data values processed as a whole.

data cartridge (IBM): The storage medium of the mass-storage system, consisting of a container with magnetic media wound around a spool inside it. All data cartridges within the mass-storage facility are on-line.

data communication: 1.* The transmission and reception of data. 2. The transfer of data from one device in an information system to another. 3. The transmission of data from one physical location to another.

*data definition: A program statement that describes features of, specifies relationships of, or establishes context of data.

data-definition language: A language that is used to define the relationship between the logical and physical views of a data base.

data dictionary: A dictionary that defines the meaning of each data item stored in a data base, and describes interrelationships among them.

data editing: Synonymous with editing.

data entry: The process of entering data into a computer system in order to communicate with it.

data-entry operator: An employee who keys data from source documents into computer-readable form such as disk or tape.

data-flow diagram: A graphic representation of the movement and transformations of data within an organization.

data independence: A lack of dependence between the physical structure of data storage and the structure of application programs.

data item: The smallest element of data stored or used by a program.

*data management: The function of controlling the acquisition, analysis, storage, retrieval, and distribution of data.

data-manipulation language: A language that is used to define data-base operations, such as retrieval, sorting, and updating of records.

data processing: The capture, storage, and processing of data to transform it into information that is useful for decision making.

data redundancy: The situation where identical data are stored in two or more files.

data set (IBM): The major unit of data storage and retrieval in the operating system, consisting of a collection of data in one of several prescribed arrangements and described by control information to which the system has access. Synonymous with file. See file.

data-structure diagram: A graphical representation of the logical relationships between various data files.

data switch: A device similar to a telephone exchange, which can establish a data-communication link between any two devices connected to it.

data type: The category that a data item belongs to, such as numeric or alphabetic.

*debug: (ISO) To detect, trace, and eliminate mistakes in computer programs or in other software.

decimal number system: A number system whose base is ten; that is, it represents numbers in terms of the powers of ten (for example, units of tens, hundreds, and so on). This is the number system we use in our everyday lives.

decision-making: The process of selecting one course of action from two or more alternatives, based on the value(s) of one or more variable(s).

decision model: A set of rules that are used in making a choice between two or more alternatives.

*decision table: 1. (ISO) A table of all contingencies that are to be considered in the description of a problem, together with the actions to be taken. 2. A presentation in either matrix or tabular form of a set of conditions and their corresponding actions.

decision tree: A graphic representation of all contingencies to be considered, together with the actions that must be taken for each one of them.

default format: A data format automatically assigned by the computer, if the programmer does not specify one.

*default option: An implicit option that is assumed when no option is explicitly stated.

demand listing: A report generated only when a user requests it. Typically used to fill irregular needs for information.

*density: See recording density.

destructive process: A process that destroys the existing value of a variable it is operating on.

device controller: A part of the CPU that manages communications between the CPU and peripheral devices.

diagnostics: A set of routines used to detect program errors, to discover system malfunctions, or to carry out standard performance tests. Errors and failures are detected by comparing the results with known correct results.

dial-up terminal: 1. (IBM) A terminal that is connected to the computer by dialing the computer system over a telephone line. See hardwired terminal.

*digital computer: (ISO) A computer in which discrete representation of data is mainly used.

digitize: To convert voice or other patterns to digital signals so they can be processed and stored by a digital computer.

DIP switches: A collection of small switches on a Dual In-line Package (DIP), used to select options on circuit boards without having to modify the hardware.

direct access: 1. (ISO) The facility to obtain data from a storage device, or to enter data into a storage device in such a way that the process depends only on the location of those data and not on a reference to data previously accessed. 2. (IBM) Contrast with sequential access. 3. The file organization that enables a record to be located and retrieved by the CPU without a large amount of searching.

direct-access storage device (DASD) (IBM): A device in which the access time is effectively independent of the location of the data. Synonymous with immediate-access storage.

direct conversion: A method of converting to a new information system, such that the old system is discontinued one day and the new system is started the next day.

direct file organization: A file organization that allows direct access to a record without sequentially examining a large number of other records.

disaster controls: Controls that minimize the risk of loss owing to natural disasters such as flooding and hurricanes.

*disk: A flat, circular plate with a magnetizable surface layer on which data can be stored by magnetic recording.

disk-controller card: A printed circuit board that interfaces disk storage drives to the CPU of a personal computer.

disk drive: A device that houses a disk or diskette that is in use. It contains a motor and one or more magnetic heads to read and write data on the disk.

diskette: Synonymous with floppy disk.

display: 1.* (ISO) A visual presentation of data. 2. (IBM) To present a display image on a display surface. 3. (IBM) Deprecated term for display device.

distributed data base: A data base that resides on two or more separate computers simultaneously. The data base may either be partitioned between the two computers or replicated at both locations.

distributed data processing: The concept of distributing the load of data processing through the installation of minicomputers at a company's remote locations, so the local data-processing needs are handled by the remote location's own local computer.

document: 1.* (ISO) A data medium and the data recorded on it; it generally has permanence and can be read by people or computers. 2. To record information in order to provide support or proof of something.

documentation: 1.* (ISO) The management of documents; it may include the actions of identifying, acquiring, processing, storing, and disseminating them. 2. A collection of documents that support and explain a data-processing application.

documentation standards: Specific procedures for system documentation, including flowcharting conventions, coding conventions, and documentation-revision procedures.

DOS: disk-operating system.

***dot-matrix printer:** (ISO) A printer in which each character is represented by a pattern of dots.

double-density diskette: A diskette manufactured with technology that allows it to hold twice as much data as diskettes manufactured at the standard density.

double-sided diskette: A disk that provides two surfaces on which data may be written by the computer.

DO-WHILE construct: A construct in a program where an operation is repeatedly performed as long as a certain logical condition remains true.

downloading: The process by which information from within a data base, stored in a remote mainframe or minicomputer, is brought "down" to a personal computer for manipulation.

DP operations department: MIS personnel who are responsible for managing the day-to-day operations of data-processing facilities.

***drum printer:** A line printer in which the type is mounted on a rotating drum that contains a full character set for each printing position.

***dump:** 1. (ISO) Data that have been dumped. 2. (ISO) To write the contents of a storage, or part of a storage (usually from an internal storage to an external medium) for a specific purpose—such as to allow other use of the storage as a safeguard against faults or errors, or in connection with debugging.

***duplex:** In data communication, pertaining to a simul-taneous two-way independent transmission in both directions. Synonymous with full duplex.

***duplication check:** A check based on the consistency of two independent performances of the same task.

***EBCDIC (Extended Binary-Coded Decimal Interchange Code):** A coded character set consisting of eight-bit coded characters.

echo check: 1.* A method of checking the accuracy of transmission of data in which the received data are returned to the sending end for comparison with the original data. 2. A hardware control that verifies that a device has been activated to carry out an operation which it has been instructed to perform.

edit: 1.* (ISO) To prepare data for a later operation. Editing may include the rearrangement or the addition of data, the deletion of unwanted data, format control, code conversion, and the application of standard processes such as zero suppression. 2. To examine data for error conditions. 3. To modify the output of a program in a way that improves its readability.

edit-directed I/O: Input or output of formatted data.

editor: A program through which text can be entered into the computer memory, displayed on the screen, and manipulated as the user chooses. An editor is an aid for writing a program. It is also the central component of a word processor.

EDP auditor: An auditor who specializes in auditing computer-based information systems.

***electronic data processing (EDP):** (ISO) Data processing largely performed by electronic devices.

electronic disk: Software that permits extra primary memory to be used as if it were a disk drive by simulating disk drives within the system's RAM.

electronic funds transfer system: A computerized system that can transfer money from one point to another immediately, using data-communication lines.

electronic mail: The transmittal of messages between computer users via a data-communication network.

electronic shopping: Selecting merchandise and ordering it through a remote terminal installed in your home.

embedded pointer: A field within a record which contains the address of a related record.

encoding: Storage of data in coded form; the data cannot be accessed by a user who does not know the code.

encryption: To convert programs or data into a secret code or cipher.

end users: Persons who ultimately use application software.

entity: A subject on which data are kept in an information system.

entry controls: Control measures regarding entry to areas where computer equipment such as CPUs and storage devices are installed.

*erasable storage: 1. (ISO) A storage device whose contents can be modified. 2. Contrast with read-only storage.

ergonomics: The science of designing computer hardware and software to make them more easy and comfortable for people to use them.

error handling: Procedures for detecting errors in input data, and ensuring that they are corrected before the data are processed.

error message: An indication that an error has been detected.

error recovery: The ability of a system to continue operating normally after the user has made an input error.

exception report: A report generated only if an activity or system gets out of control and requires human attention.

executable statement: A program statement that instructs the computer to perform a certain action.

execution: To run a computer program.

execution path: The specific set of program instructions used by the computer.

execution time (IBM): The time during which an instruction is decoded and performed.

execution-time diagnostics: Error diagnostics that are produced when a program is executed.

expansion board: A printed circuit board that accommodates extra components for the purpose of expanding the capabilities of a computer.

expansion slot: A slot for installing additional expansion boards that perform functions not provided by the computer's standard hardware.

expert systems: Systems that possess artificial intelligence.

expression: A variable, constant, function, or any combination of these elements separated by arithmetic or relational operators.

extract: 1.* (ISO) To select and remove from a set of items those items which meet some criteria. 2. (IBM) To remove specific items from a file.

facilities management vendor: A firm that specializes in managing, staffing, and operating computer installations for its customers.

feasibility study: The first step in the system-development life cycle. At this step the system analyst identifies the objectives of the present system and determines whether an attempt to develop a new system would be cost-effective.

fiber optics: A laser-based data-communication technique that transmits data over glass fibers by means of light waves; photonic (light-based) mode of data transmission.

*field: (ISO) In a record, a specified area used for a particular category of data, for example, a group of card columns in which a wage rate is recorded.

file: 1. (ISO) A set of related records treated as a unit; for example, in stock control, a file could consist of a set of invoices. 2. A collection of related records.

file activity ratio: The proportion of master-file records that are actually used or accessed in a given processing run of the file or during a given period of time.

file area: The area on the disk available for storage of files containing data or programs.

file directory: The disk area allocated to hold a directory that names and indicates the area occupied by each file and the available space on the disk.

*file layout: (ISO) The arrangement and structure of data or words in a file, including the order and size of the components of the file.

file-maintenance inputs: All file changes that are not originated by transactions.

file protected (IBM): Pertaining to a tape reel with the write-enable ring removed.

file-protection ring: A plastic ring that must be inserted into a reel of magnetic tape before the tape can be written on. (An alternative is a no-write ring, which when inserted, prevents the file-protection ring from being inserted and therefore prevents files from being written on.)

file-protect notch: The cut-out area in the upper right corner of a floppy disk; it is used to prevent accidental destruction of data.

file query: The retrieval of some specific information from a file.

file volatility ratio: The proportion of additions and deletions to a file in a given period of time.

fine tuning: Removing bottlenecks and reallocating work among system resources, in order to obtain maximum output from the given resources.

fire controls: Controls that minimize the risk of losses from fire. These include both emergency procedures and preventive measures.

fixed disk: A disk that is permanently mounted in its disk drive.

fixed-length record (IBM): A record having the same length as all other records with which it is logically or physically associated. Contrast with variable-length record.

fixed-point constant: Synonymous with integer constant.

*flag: 1. Any of various types of indicators used for identification, such as a word mark. 2. A character that signals the occurrence of some condition, such as the end of a word. 3. (ISO) Synonym for mark.

flat file: A file containing only fixed-length records of equal length.

floating parameter: A variable within the definition of a user-defined function. It has no meaning outside the function definition.

floppy disk: A data storage medium that is a 3½-, 5¼-, or 8-inch disk of polyester film covered with a magnetic coating.

flowchart: 1.* (ISO) A graphical representation for the definition, analysis, or method of solution of a problem, in which symbols are used to represent operations, data flow, equipment, et cetera. 2. See data flow diagram, program flowchart and system flowchart.

*font: A family or assortment of characters of a given size and style; for example, nine-point Bodoni Modern.

format: To put the magnetic track and sector pattern on a disk, which is needed before the disk can store any information. Formatting completely erases any previously stored data.

*FORTRAN (Formula Translation): A programming language primarily used to express computer programs by arithmetic formulas.

fourth-generation language: A flexible application development tool such as electronic spreadsheets, query languages, and application generators that allow you to develop applications by describing to the computer what you want rather than programming it in a how-to, step-by-step fashion.

front-end processor: A minicomputer that processes the minor jobs or communication tasks for a large CPU.

function: A preprogrammed set of statements that can be called by a one-line reference, and that returns one single value to the calling program.

functional area: An organizational unit of a business corresponding to its major duty or activity, such as engineering or finance.

functional information system: A set of application systems that satisfies the information needs within a functional area of the business.

functional primitive: The lowest level of a data-flow diagram, where the actual processing of data is described.

functional reference: A call to a function at some point in the program. This is done simply by giving the function name and a value for its parameter(s).

Gantt chart: A graph where activities are plotted as bars on a time scale.

general controls: Overall managerial controls applied to all software, hardware, and personnel involved in the information system.

generalized module: A precoded module that performs some commonly used function. It may be used by many users for a variety of purposes.

giga (G) (IBM): When referring to storage capacity, two to the thirtieth power (1,073,741,824 in decimal notation).

gigabyte: One billion bytes.

grandparent-parent-child backup: A file backup system in which the current version of the file and the two previous versions are always retained.

graphics (IBM): See computer graphics.

graphics language: A computer language that may be used to retrieve data from files or data bases and display it graphically.

*half-duplex: 1. In data communication, pertaining to an alternate, one-way-at-a-time, independent transmission. 2. Contrast with duplex.

half-inch tape: The big reels of tape used with mainframes and minicomputers.

hanging separator: A symbol used at the end of a PRINT statement which causes the next PRINT statement to continue writing on the same output line.

hard copy: 1. (SC1) In computer graphics, a permanent copy of a display image that can be separated from a display device; for example, a display image that is recorded on paper. 2. (IBM) A printed copy of machine output in a visually readable form; for example, printed reports, listings, documents, and summaries. Contrast with soft copy.

hard error: An error in disk data that persists when the disk is reread.

*hardware: (ISO) Physical equipment as opposed to programs, rules, and associated documentation.

hardware monitor: A machine device that monitors usage and performance of various computer-system devices.

hardware study: An analysis of hardware requirements for an information system. It usually leads to a tentative selection of equipment.

hardwired terminal: A terminal that is directly wired to the computer. See dial-up terminal.

*hash total: The result obtained by applying an algorithm to a set of data for checking purposes; for example, a summation obtained by treating data items as numbers.

*head: A device that reads, writes, or erases data on a storage medium.

header: 1. The top part of a report, including the column headings. 2. In a file, the first record which contains descriptive information concerning the file.

header label (IBM): A file or data set label that precedes the data records on a unit of recording media.

header value: A special value specified before a loop is executed. It tells the program how many times the loop is to be performed.

hexadecimal representation: A number system whose digits represent powers of sixteen. The hexadecimal system is used to make printouts of the binary contents of computer memory more readable.

hierarchical network: A distributed system design where a superior/subordinate relationship exists between distributed computer installations.

*Hollerith card: A punch card characterized by eighty columns and twelve rows of punch positions.

horizontal network: A distributed system design where each local installation is equal and has the capability of communicating with all other installations (synonymous with ring network).

host computer (IBM): 1. The primary or controlling computer in a multiple computer operation. 2. The primary or controlling computer in a data communication system.

human factors: The positive and negative behavioral implications of introducing EDP systems into the workplace.

hybrid network: A ring-structured communication network where each node on the ring is also the center of a star network.

IF-THEN-ELSE construct: A construct in a program where one of two possible courses of action is taken, depending on whether a certain logical condition is true or false.

immediate-direct processing: The immediate processing of transactions and inquiries with direct-access files.

immediate mode: A mode of processing under which transactions are processed to update the master file shortly after the transactions occur.

*impact printer: (ISO) A printer in which printing is the result of mechanical impact.

implementation: A phase in the system development cycle when coding, testing, and manual-procedure development are done.

index: A list used to indicate the address of records stored in a file. An index is much like an index to a book.

index file: A file that indicates the address of records stored on secondary-storage devices.

indexed sequential access method (ISAM): A file organization where records are stored sequentially, yet direct access can be made to individual records in the file through an index of the records' absolute addresses.

infinite loop: A loop in a program that has no exit. The computer will keep performing the loop indefinitely unless some external action is taken to stop the program.

information: 1.* (ISO) The meaning that a person assigns to data by means of the known conventions used in their representation. 2. Data processed by people to reduce uncertainty.

information center: In an organization, a service department that assists users in developing their own computer applications.

*information retrieval (IR): 1. (ISO) The action of recovering specific information from stored data. 2. (ISO) Methods and procedures for recovering specific information from stored data.

information-system consultant: An individual who assists users with various problems, ranging from simple troubleshooting to complete system design and implementation.

information-system manager: An MIS professional who is responsible for managing the entire EDP department or some part of it.

information-system master plan: An outline of the overall strategy for implementation of the information system.

information workers: People who create, process, and use substantial amounts of information as a normal part of their jobs.

in-house development: When a firm produces its own application software.

initial program load (IPL) (IBM): The initialization procedure that causes an operating system to commence operation.

initialize: To assign an initial value to a variable, before beginning a specific process. Counter variables are often initialized to zero before they start counting the number of loops executed.

ink-jet printer (IBM): A nonimpact printer in which the characters are formed by the projection of a jet of ink onto paper.

input controls: Controls that ensure that all inputs are authorized, accurate, and properly converted to machine-readable format.

*input data: 1. (ISO) Data being received or to be received into a device or into a computer program. Synonymous with input. 2. Data to be processed.

input mask: A form displayed on a CRT to guide the keying of input.

input/output statement: A program statement that causes the computer to either read input data or produce output.

*input unit: (ISO) A device in a data-processing system by which data can be entered into the system.

inquiry (IBM): A request for information from storage; for example, a request for the number of available airline seats, or a machine statement to initiate a search of library documents. Synonym for query.

*instruction: (ISO) In a programming language, a meaningful expression that specifies one operation and identifies its operands, if any.

integer constant: A constant number that does not contain a decimal point or a fractional part.

integrated circuit: A device containing transistors that are deposited photochemically onto a chip of silicon material. These devices have greatly increased the speed of computers while sharply reducing their size.

integrated package: A personal-computer package that typically includes the functions of electronic spreadsheet, word processing, data-base management, and communications.

intelligent terminal: 1. (IBM) Synonym for programmable terminal. 2. A terminal that contains a microprocessor and is therefore capable of performing some data processing by itself, without recourse to the central computer.

interactive (IBM): Pertaining to an application in which each entry calls forth a response from a system or program, as in an inquiry system or an airline-reservation system. An interactive system may also be conversational, implying a continuous dialogue between the user and the system.

interactive data entry: The process of entering data directly into the computer through a data-entry terminal.

*interface: 1. A shared boundary. An interface might be a hardware component to link two devices or it might be a portion of storage or registers accessed by two or more computer programs. 2. The inputs and outputs that move from one module to another in a software system.

internal storage: 1. (ISO) Storage that is accessible by a computer without the use of input/output channels. 2. (IBM) Synonym for main storage, primary storage, and RAM.

international data transfer: The movement of data across national boundaries through data-communication networks.

interpreter: A program that translates a high-level language, such as BASIC, into a machine language so it can be used in the computer. It is slower and less efficient than a compiler, but easier for programmers to use.

*interrupt: (ISO) A suspension of a process, such as the execution of a computer program, caused by an event external to that process, and performed in such a way that the process can be resumed.

*inverted file: 1. A file whose sequence has been reversed. 2. In information retrieval, a method of organizing a cross-index file in which a keyword identifies a record; the items, numbers, or documents pertinent to that keyword are indicated.

*I/O: input/output.

*ISO: International Organization for Standardization.

job: 1.* A set of data that completely defines a unit of work for a computer. A job usually includes all necessary computer programs, linkages, files, and instructions to the operating system. 2. (IBM) A collection of related programs.

*job-control language (JCL): A problem-oriented language designed to express job statements that are used to identify the job or describe its requirements to an operating system.

job queue: A line of programs awaiting their turn for execution.

kernel program: A small sample program executed on various computer configurations to provide information useful to a person making a computer-acquisition decision.

key: 1.* (ISO) Within a set of data, one or more characters that contain information about the set, including its identification. 2. (IBM) To enter information from a keyboard.

key-to-disk data entry: The process of recording information on disks before inputting it to the computer.

key-to-diskette data entry: The process of recording information on diskettes before inputting it to the system.

key-to-tape data entry: The process of recording information on magnetic tape before inputting it to the computer.

key verifier: A machine verifying that data which were keypunched, were keypunched correctly.

keyword: A special word in a programming language that tells the computer which operation to perform.

kilobyte: 1,024 bytes of memory which will store 1,024 characters of data or programs. Kilobyte is usually abbreviated as K. 256K of memory will hold 256 times 1,024 (or 262,144) characters of data. In contexts other than computers, the word *kilo* or the symbol K indicates 1,000. In terms of computers, K is a power of 2 (it is 2^{10} or 1,024) because of the binary nature of computer memory.

label: 1.* (ISO) One or more characters, within or attached to a set of data, that contains information about the set, including its identification. 2.* (ISO) In computer programming, an identifier of an instruction. 3. (IBM) An identification record for a tape or disk file. (External labels are written on paper on the outside of a physical volume. Internal labels are stored in computer-readable form on the storage medium itself.)

language: In relation to computers, any unified, related set of commands or instructions that the computer can accept. Low-level languages are difficult to use but closely resemble the fundamental operations of the computer. High-level languages resemble English.

language translator (IBM): A general term for any assembler, compiler, or other routine that accepts statements in one language and produces equivalent statements in another language.

laser printer: A high-quality nonimpact printer that is capable of producing a wide variety of type fonts.

laser storage: A memory device that makes use of laser beams for storing data. These laser beams form microscopic patterns to represent characters on various surfaces.

leasing: A contract arrangement that binds a user to rent a system over a relatively long period of time. It usually costs less than a rental arrangement.

left justify: To line up characters such that the first non-blank character in each line is on the left margin.

letter quality: Printed output that appears to have been typed on a typewriter.

leveled data-flow diagram: A hierarchically partitioned data-flow diagram. Each level describes in more detail the data flows shown in the level above it. Increased partitioning at lower levels keeps the diagrams of manageable size.

librarian: An MIS employee who is responsible for the storage of program and data files. These files are usually stored on tape or disk.

*library: 1. A collection of related files. For example, one line of an invoice may form an item, a complete invoice may form a file, the collection of inventory-control files may form a library, and the libraries used by an organization are known as its data bank. 2. A repository for demountable recorded media, such as magnetic-disk packs and magnetic tapes. 3. A set of prewritten subprograms that may be called by the programmer simply with a one-line reference to the subprogram name.

*library routine: A proven routine that is maintained in a program library.

light pen: An input device that allows the console operator to choose among alternatives. When a menu is presented on the screen, for instance, the operator gets a number of choices, each with a box next to it. The operator positions the light pen to a box representing his or her choice and then presses the entry button on the pen. The pen contains a light sensor that returns a signal indicating to the computer which choice the operator has made.

limit/reasonableness check: See reasonableness checks.

linear search: A sequential search of the elements of an array for the purpose of locating a particular value.

line feed: The action of advancing the paper in a printer or the cursor on a screen to the next line.

*line printer: 1. (ISO) A device that prints a line of characters as a unit. Synonymous with line-at-a-time printer. 2. Contrast with character printer and page printer.

*linkage editor: (ISO) A computer program used to create one load module from one or more independently translated object modules or load modules by resolving cross references among the modules.

link edit (IBM): To create a loadable computer program by means of a linkage editor.

linking: Synonymous with link editing.

*list: 1. (ISO) An ordered set of items of data. 2. To print or otherwise display items of data that meet specified criteria. 3. (ISO) Synonym for chained list.

literal: Synonymous with string constant.

lithium battery: An easily removable battery that lasts from twelve to eighteen months and is usually used to power clock/calendars in personal computers.

load: 1. (ISO) In computer programming, to enter data into storage. 2. (IBM) To bring a program from secondary storage into primary storage for execution.

load module: (ISO) A program that is suitable for loading into main storage for execution.

local data: Data that are used by only one computer in a distributed data-processing environment.

logical file: 1. A file independent of its physical environment. 2. A file in a format that is meaningful to the application programmer and end user.

logical model: A system model that emphasizes what is to be done, rather than who or what does it.

logical record: 1.* A record independent of its physical environment. Portions of the same logical record may be located in different physical records, or several logical records or parts of logical records may be located in one physical record. 2. (IBM) A record from the standpoint of its content, function, and use rather than its physical attributes; that is, a record that is defined in terms of the information it contains.

logical view: Representation of the data in a data base in a format that is meaningful to the application programmer and end user.

logoff (IBM): The procedure by which a user ends a terminal session.

logon (IBM): The procedure by which a user begins a terminal session.

loop: A set of statements that are repeatedly performed during program execution. (Also used as a verb.)

loop variable: A variable used as a counter in a FOR-NEXT loop. It keeps track of the number of times the loop has executed.

machine cycle: The time required by the CPU to perform one machine operation.

*machine language: A language that is used directly by a machine.

machine operation: The smallest unit of processing done by a computer; for example, adding 0 to 1.

macro instruction: A set of program statements that can be invoked simply by issuing a one-line reference to the set.

mag tape: Magnetic tape.

magnetic core storage: See core storage.

*magnetic disk: (ISO) A flat, circular plate with a magnetic surface layer. Synonymous with disk.

*magnetic drum: (ISO) A circular cylinder with a magnetizable surface layer on which data can be stored by magnetic recording.

*magnetic-ink character recognition (MICR): 1. Character recognition of characters printed with ink that contains particles of a magnetic material. 2. Contrast with optical character recognition.

*magnetic storage: A storage device that utilizes the magnetic properties of certain materials.

magnetic tape: 1. (ISO) A tape with a magnetizable surface layer on which data can be stored by magnetic recording. 2.* (ISO) A tape with a magnetic surface layer. 3.* A tape with magnetic material used as the constituent in some forms of magnetic cores.

mainframe: 1.* Synonym for central processing unit. 2. A large computer system.

*maintainability: (ISO) The ease with which maintenance of a functional unit can be performed in accordance with prescribed requirements.

maintenance: Correcting errors discovered in programs, and updating the programs to satisfy changed requirements.

man-machine boundary: The line of demarcation between manual operations and computerized functions.

management controls: Control mechanisms that ensure proper management of EDP facilities in accordance with organizational objectives.

management information system (MIS): 1.* (ISO) Management performed with the aid of automatic data processing. 2.* An information system designed to aid in the performance of management functions. 3. A system for providing information for decision making; an automated system that uses a computer to process data.

*manual input: 1. The entry of data by hand into a device. 2. The data entered by hand into a device.

mass storage: (ISO) Storage having a very large storage capacity.

*master file: (ISO) A file that is used as an authority in a given job and that is relatively permanent, even though its contents may change. Synonymous with main file.

*matrix printer: (ISO) A printer in which each character is represented by a pattern of dots. Synonymous with dot-matrix printer.

megabyte: 1,048,576 bytes of memory. A megabyte is often thought of as one million bytes, but more accurately it is 1,048,576 bytes, since it is 2^{20} bytes.

*memory: (ISO) Synonym for primary storage.

memory dump: To print the contents of primary storage.

memory module: Extra memory chips that may be added to the basic hardware of a personal computer in order to expand primary storage.

*MICR: Magnetic-ink character recognition.

microcoding (microprogramming): The technique of placing programs in hardware devices (like ROM). This is often used for system programs such as operating systems.

microcomputer: The smallest of computer systems.

*microfiche: A sheet of microfilm capable of containing microimages in a grid pattern, usually with a title that can be read without magnification.

microfilm: (SC1) Microform whose medium is film, in the form of rolls, that contains microimages arranged sequentially.

microform: (SC1) Any medium that contains microimages; for example, microfiche and microfilm.

microprocessor chip: The microprocessor chip contains the circuitry of the CPU—the portion of the computer that does the calculating and executes the program. It is mounted in one socket of the CPU board of a personal computer.

microsecond (IBM): One-millionth of a second.

millisecond (IBM): One-thousandth of a second.

minicomputer: A medium-sized computer generally used in midsize or smaller organizations by several users at the same time.

minimal BASIC: A basic set of commands recommended by the ANSI for inclusion in any version of the BASIC language.

*MIS: Management information system.

*mnemonic symbol: (ISO) A symbol to assist the human memory; for example, an abbreviation such as *mpy* for multiply.

modem (modulator-demodulator): (SC1) A functional unit that modulates and demodulates signals. One of the functions of a modem is to enable digital data to be transmitted over analog transmission facilities.

*modularity: The extent to which a system is composed of modules.

*module: 1. A program unit that is discrete and identifiable with respect to compiling, combining with other units, and loading; for example, the input to or output from an assembler, compiler, linkage editor, or executive routine. 2. A packaged functional hardware unit designed for use with other components.

monitor: 1. (ISO) A functional unit that observes and records selected activities within a data-processing system for the purpose of analysis. 2. (IBM) Software or hardware that observes, supervises, controls, or verifies the operations of a system. 3. A CRT for viewing computer output.

*monitor program: (ISO) A computer program that observes, regulates, controls, or verifies the operations of a data-processing system. Synonymous with monitoring program.

motherboard: A printed circuit board onto which other printed circuit boards connect.

MS-DOS (Microsoft Disk-Operating System): An operating system used in personal computers, especially the IBM PC and its compatibles.

*multiplexing: (ISO) In data transmission, a function that permits two or more data sources to share a common transmission medium such that each data source has its own channel.

multiprocessing: 1. (ISO) A mode of operation that provides for parallel processing by two or more processors of a multiprocessor. 2. The processing of a single program by two or more CPUs.

multiprogramming: 1.* A mode of operation that provides for the interleaved execution of two or more computer programs by a single central processing unit. 2. The capability of a computer CPU to execute two or more programs concurrently.

nanosecond (IBM): One-thousand-millionth of a second.

*nest: 1. (ISO) To incorporate a structure or structures of some kind into a structure of the same kind. For example, to nest one loop (the nested loop) within another loop (the nesting loop); or to nest one subroutine (the nested subroutine) within another subroutine (the nesting subroutine). 2. To embed subroutines or data in other subroutines at a different hierarchical level such that the different levels of routines or data can be executed or accessed recursively.

network (IBM): In data communication, a configuration in which two or more terminal or processor installations are connected.

network data structure: The data structure that allows a many-to-many relationship among the nodes in the structure.

*node: 1. The representation of a state or an event by means of a point on a diagram. 2. In a tree structure, a point at which subordinate items of data originate. 3. A CPU, terminal, or other device on a communication network.

nonexecutable statement: A statement that does not cause the computer to perform any action. It merely informs the computer or a human reader about the format, characteristics, and nature of various data and processes.

nonimpact printer: (ISO) A printer in which printing is not the result of mechanical impacts; for example, thermal printers, electrostatic printers, and photographic printers.

nonrecurring costs: The initial costs which are not expected to arise in years subsequent to the initial installation of a computer system.

nonprogrammable decision: A decision related to an ill-defined or unstructured problem.

nonvolatile storage: Primary or secondary storage that does not lose the data stored in it when the electrical power is interrupted or turned off.

*numeric: (ISO) Pertaining to data or to physical quantities represented by numerals. Synonymous with numerical.

numeric/alphabetic checks: A control that assures that input record fields that should contain only numeric characters do not contain alphabetic characters or vice versa.

numeric data: Numbers on which arithmetic calculations will be performed.

numeric variable: A variable that can assume only numeric values.

nybble: Four bits.

object code: A machine language program that has been produced from a higher-level language through the compilation process. It is called object code since its production is the *objective* of compilation or translation.

object module (IBM): A program that is the output of an assembler or a compiler and is suitable for input to a linkage editor.

object program: Synonymous with object code.

office automation: The use of EDP systems to perform routine office chores and improve productivity.

off-line: Data or a device that are not under direct control of the computer. Usually a person must place an off-line reel of tape on a tape drive before the computer can access data stored on it.

*off-line storage: Storage not under control of the central processing unit.

on-line: 1. (ISO) Pertaining to the operation of a functional unit that is under the continual control of a computer. The term *on-line* is also used to describe a user's access to a computer via a terminal. 2. A computer system, peripheral device, or file, such as a terminal or disk drive, that is in direct communication with the CPU.

on-line direct-access system: A computer system that has several terminals in direct communication with the CPU that in turn is in direct communication with direct-access files.

on-line storage: Storage under the control of the central processing unit.

on-line system (IBM): A system in which the input data enter the computer directly from the point of origin or in which output data are transmitted directly to where they are used.

*operand: 1. (ISO) An entity to which an operation is applied. 2. That which is operated upon. An operand is usually identified by an address part of an instruction.

*operating system: (ISO) Software that controls the execution of computer programs and that may provide scheduling, debugging, input/output control, accounting, compilation, storage assignment, data management, and related services.

operational decision: A decision on how to carry out specific tasks effectively and efficiently.

operator: A symbol that indicates the performance of a mathematical operation such as division, multiplication, addition, or subtraction.

opscan: Synonymous with optical scanner.

*optical character recognition (OCR): The machine identification of printed characters through use of light-sensitive devices.

optical disk: A disk that records information and reads it back using light (laser beams).

optical reader (IBM): A device that reads handwritten or machine-printed symbols into a computing system.

*optical scanner: (ISO) A scanner that uses light for examining patterns and reading them into a computing system.

order-processing system: A computer system that initiates shipping orders, keeps track of back orders, and produces various sales-analysis reports.

origination: The creation of raw data as a result of a business event or transaction.

output: The information produced by a computer.

output controls: Controls that help assure the accuracy of computer results and proper distribution of output.

*output unit: (ISO) A device in a data-processing system by which data can be received from the system.

packed decimal (IBM): Representation of a decimal value by two adjacent digits in a byte. For example, in packed decimal, the decimal value 23 is represented in one eight-bit byte by 00100011.

packaged software: A program designed for a specific application of broad, general usage, unadapted to any particular installation.

page: (ISO) In a virtual-storage system, a fixed-length block that has a virtual address and that can be transferred between real primary storage and auxiliary storage.

page printer (IBM): 1. A device that prints one page as a unit; for example, a cathode-ray-tube printer, film printer, and zerographic printer. Synonymous with page-at-a-time printer. 2. Contrast with character printer and line printer.

paging: 1. (ISO) The transfer of pages between real storage and auxiliary storage. 2.* A time-sharing technique in which pages are transferred between primary storage and auxiliary storage. Synonymous with page turning.

paint: To draw directly on a video screen, as opposed to writing programs that create images.

palette: The overall selection of colors or shades available in a graphics-display system.

parallel conversion: A method of converting to a new system whereby both the old and the new systems operate concurrently until management is satisfied that the new system will perform satisfactorily.

parallel port: A connection, through which data are transmitted eight bits at a time (or in parallel). Generally used with printers.

*parallel processing: The simultaneous execution of two or more processes in a single unit.

parameter: A constant value supplied by the user to the program. The execution of the program is in some way modified, based on the value of this parameter.

parameterized application package: Prewritten application programs that the user can modify to suit his or her own requirements. The modification is done simply by specifying values for certain parameters.

*parity bit: A check bit appended to an array of binary digits to make the sum of all the binary digits, including the check bit, always odd or always even.

*parity check: A check that tests whether the number of ones (or zeroes) in an array of binary digits is odd or even. Synonymous with odd-even check.

partitioning: Decomposing a data-flow diagram into smaller, more detailed diagrams.

PASCAL: A block-structured, high-level computer language named after the pioneer computer scientist Blaise Pascal.

password (IBM): 1. A unique string of characters that a program, computer operator, or user must supply to meet security requirements before gaining access to data. 2. In systems with time sharing, a one-to-eight character symbol that the user may be required to supply at the time he or she logs on the system. The password is confidential, as opposed to the user identification, which is not confidential.

*patch: To modify a routine in a rough or expedient way.

payroll program: A computer program that prepares checks to pay employees and maintains payment information.

payroll register: A report that provides a recap of payment transactions for each employee and serves as an important part of the audit trail of the system.

payroll system: A computer system that assists in the preparation of salary checks, maintains payment records, and provides management reports related to payroll activities.

*peripheral equipment: (ISO) In a data-processing system, any equipment, distinct from the central processing unit, that provides the system with outside communication, storage, input/output, or additional facilities.

personal computer: A computer small enough to be placed on a desktop and designed to be used by one person who possesses very little, if any, programming knowledge.

PERT-CPM: Scheduling methods that use graphic networks to depict the activities and time that are necessary to complete a project. These methods compute the minimum amount of time in which a project can be completed. They also highlight those activities whose completion are most critical to the completion of the project.

phased conversion: A method of converting to a new system whereby the old system is gradually phased out, and the new gradually phased in at the same time.

physical file: A collection of records that are physically located contiguous to one another. Contrast with logical file.

physical implementation: The way a system is actually performed in the real world. Manual systems and automated systems, such as computers, are different types of physical implementation.

physical record: 1. (ISO) A record whose characteristics depend on the manner or form in which it is stored, retrieved, or moved. A physical record may consist of all or part of a logical record. 2. Records that physically exist. Contrast with logical record.

physical view: In a data base, representation of the data in terms of physical characteristics such as location, field length, and access method.

picosecond (IBM): One trillionth of a second. One thousandth of a nanosecond.

pie chart: A chart that shows the relative values of various quantities as arc-shaped sections of a circle.

pilot conversion: A method of converting to a new system whereby the new system is introduced in selected departments. If it functions satisfactorily, then it is extended to the whole organization.

pixel: The smallest dot that can be displayed on a screen. The word is derived from a contraction of *picture element*. All screen images, including both text and graphics, are made up of combinations of pixels. The more pixels per screen, the finer the images that can be drawn.

planning: Planning is part of the process of management decision making. Planning involves identifying the alter-

natives, selecting the criteria to be used in choosing an alternative, and selecting the plan of action to be implemented for the problem.

platter: The actual metal (or other rigid material) disk that is mounted inside a fixed-disk drive.

plotter: An output device (driven by the computer) that moves a pen across a sheet of paper to create a multiple-line pattern.

plug-compatible: A hardware unit produced by one manufacturer that can directly replace units produced by another manufacturer.

*pointer: An identifier that indicates the location of a data item.

point-of-sale (POS) data entry: Immediate entry of sales transactions to the computer through a cash register that is connected to the computer.

polarize: To cause a magnetic substance to contain a positive or negative charge.

polling: A process by which the CPU addresses different terminals in turn to check whether they have any input data for transmission to the CPU. A single line links all these terminals to the CPU.

port: An input/output (I/O) connection for interfacing peripherals and computers.

portability: 1. (IBM) The ability to use data sets or files with different operating systems. Volumes whose data sets or files are listed in a user catalog can be demounted from storage devices of one system, moved to another system, and mounted on storage devices of that system. 2. The ability to move programs from one computer to another without modification.

post-implementation audit: Usually consists of two steps: (1) an evaluation of a new system, using the objectives stated during the system's investigation phase, and (2) a review and evaluation of the system development cycle.

power controls: Controls that prevent the system from being damaged by voltage fluctuations and power breakdowns.

precision: The number of digits that a number is allowed to have.

prespecified computing: EDP applications for which processing requirements can be determined ahead of time and programmed in the conventional manner.

primary key: In a record, a field whose value uniquely identifies the record. For instance, identification number may be a primary key for a file or data base pertaining to students at a university.

primary storage: Within a central processing unit, the area that stores the program while it is being executed, the data which the program is using, and all or part of the operating system. Primary storage is often also called memory, internal storage, core storage, and RAM (random access memory).

printed circuit board: A laminated plastic board, about a sixteenth of an inch thick, onto which wiring is electroplated. This wiring connects components and sockets which are fastened to the board. The sockets receive chips.

print spooler: Software that allows a memory area to hold output to be printed, enabling the user to simultaneously perform other tasks on the personal computer.

printer (IBM): A device that writes output data from a system onto paper.

*procedure-oriented language: (ISO) A problem-oriented language that facilitates the expression of a procedure as an explicit algorithm. Examples include FORTRAN, ALGOL, COBOL, and PL/I. Synonymous with procedural language.

*process: 1. A course of events that occurs according to an intended purpose or effect. 2. A systematic sequence of operations used to produce a specified result. 3. To perform operations on data.

*process control: Automatic control of a process in which a computer is used for the regulation of usually continuous operations or processes.

process description: A description of the data transformations that occur within the most detailed processes on a data-flow diagram.

processing controls: Controls that increase the integrity of processing.

production: Refers to the jobs, programs, or files that are used in the daily tasks of an information system.

program: A set of instructions for the computer to follow.

program bug: An error in a computer program.

program code: The instructions used in a computer program.

program documentation: The documentation relating to individual programs.

*program flowchart: (ISO) A flowchart representing the sequence of operations in a computer program. Synonymous with program flow diagram.

program library: 1.* (ISO) An organized collection of computer programs that are sufficiently documented to allow them to be used by persons other than their authors. 2.* A collection of available computer programs and routines. 3. (IBM) Synonym for partitioned data set. 4. A file containing the production copy of both application and system programs.

program module: A small, identifiable unit of program statements that performs one program task.

program stubs: Dummy modules that are called by the parent module during the testing phase. This allows testing of the parent module before the lower-level modules are written.

programmable decision: A decision that is made within the guidelines of an established policy.

programmable read-only memory: A read-only memory into which data or programs can be written by an external programming device.

*programmer: A person who designs, writes, and tests computer programs.

programmer/analyst: An MIS professional who performs both programming and system-analysis functions.

*programming: (ISO) The designing, writing, and testing of computer programs.

*programming language: (ISO) An artificial language established for expressing computer programs.

*Programming Language One (PL/I): A programming language designed for use in a wide range of commercial and scientific computer applications.

prompt: A symbol presented on the CRT screen to tell you that the operating system or program is ready to accept a new command or line of text.

proprietary: That which is exclusively owned by an individual or corporation, such as a patent.

protect: To safeguard data from unauthorized changes or destruction.

protocol: A set of codes that must be transmitted and received in the proper sequence to guarantee that the desired terminals or computers are hooked together and can "talk" as desired.

prototype: An experimental version of a computer application.

pseudocode: A description of program logic using English-language sentences instead of the statements of a computer language.

*punched card: 1. A card punched with hole patterns. 2. See Hollerith card.

QUBE system: A combination of cable TV and a computer system that allows viewers to respond, through a keyboard, to broadcast messages.

queries: Requests for information from a file.

query language: A high-level computer language used to retrieve specific information from a data base.

RAM: See random-access memory.

RAM disk: See electronic disk.

random: Something that occurs in no particular order.

random access: (ISO) Synonym for direct access.

random-access memory (RAM): Storage whose contents can be read and modified directly, without searching. RAM is usually used for primary storage.

random addressing: Synonymous with randomizing.

randomizing (IBM): A technique by which the range of keys for an indirectly addressed file is reduced to smaller ranges of addresses by some method of computation until the desired address is found. Synonymous with hashing.

read-after-write: A mode of operation that has the computer read back each sector written to the disk, checking that the data read back are the same as recorded. This slows down disk operations, but increases reliability.

read-only memory (ROM): (ISO) Synonym for read-only storage.

read-only storage (ROS): (ISO) A storage device whose contents cannot be modified, except by a particular user, or when operating under particular conditions; for example, a storage device in which writing is prevented by a lockout. Synonymous with fixed storage.

read/write head: (ISO) A magnetic head capable of reading and writing.

real constant: A constant that may contain a decimal point with or without a fractional part.

real storage: (ISO) The main storage in a virtual-storage system. Physically, real storage and main storage are identical.

realtime information: Information about ongoing events that reflects the status of these events in a completely up-to-date manner.

*realtime processing: (ISO) The manipulation of data that are required or generated by some process while the process is in operation; usually the results are used to influence the process, and perhaps related processes, while it is occurring.

realtime system: A computer system with the capability of immediately capturing data concerning ongoing events or processes and providing information necessary to manage these ongoing events.

reasonableness checks: Program controls that monitor the values of input data and make sure that they are within proper limits. For instance, a reasonableness check would trap a time card that showed 150 hours worked in one week.

record: 1.* (ISO) A collection of related data or words, treated as a unit; for example, in stock control, each invoice could constitute one record. 2. A collection of adjacent data fields relating to some specific entity. Analogous to a file folder in a manual file.

*record layout: (ISO) The arrangement and structure of data or words in a record, including the order and size of the components of the record.

*recording density: The number of bits in a single linear track, measured per unit of length of the recording medium.

recurring costs: The costs expected to continually arise throughout the life of the computer's installation.

redundancy check: 1. (ISO) A check using extra (redundant) data systematically inserted for that purpose. 2. A control imposed by the performance of a task by two hardware units independent of each other.

*register: (ISO) In a computer, a very fast storage device, usually intended for some special purpose, capable of storing a specified amount of data such as a bit or a word.

*relative address: (ISO) An address expressed as a difference with respect to a base address.

relational data model: A logical view of a data base which treats all data as if they were stored in the form of tables.

relational operator: A symbol that represents the performance of a comparison operation between two quantities or values. For instance, *is greater than* is a relational operator.

relevance: The usefulness of data for decision making.

reliability: A quality held by that which is dependable and can be trusted.

remote (IBM): In data communication, pertaining to devices that are connected to a data-processing system through a data link.

remote job entry (RJE): (ISO) Submission of a job through an input unit that has access to a computer through a data link.

removable disk: A disk drive where the disk itself can be removed; in particular, a hard disk drive using disks mounted in cartridges.

report: Management information printed on a hard-copy medium such as paper.

report generation: To produce information output.

report generator: A high-level language that can be used to produce reports in almost any format.

Report Program Generator (RPG) (IBM): A programming language that can be used to generate object programs that produce reports from existing sets of data.

request for proposal: A document that specifies the requirements for equipment and software to be purchased.

reserved words: In a program, words that have a special meaning for the compiler. The user cannot use them for any other purpose.

resident: (ISO) Pertaining to computer programs that remain on a particular storage device.

resident supervisor: That part of the operating system which is used most often, and is continuously stored in primary storage.

resolution: How fine the detail appears on a display. Resolution for computer displays is usually stated as the number of possible lines across the image, and the maximum number of possible dot positions in each line. The IBM PC has a maximum screen resolution of 640 dots across by 200 lines.

resource (IBM): Any facility of the computing system or operating system required by a job or task, and including main storage, input/output devices, the processing unit, data sets, and control of processing programs.

resource allocation: (ISO) The assignment of the facilities of a data-processing system for the accomplishment of jobs; for example, the assignment of main storage, input-output devices, and files.

resource management: Synonymous with resource allocation.

response time: 1.* (ISO) The elapsed time between the end of an inquiry or demand on a data-processing system and the beginning of the response; for example, the length of time between an indication of the end of an inquiry and the display of the first character of the response at a user terminal. 2. The elapsed time between submission of a command on a remote terminal and the completion of that command as evidenced by a message on the terminal screen or printer.

retrieve: To move data from secondary storage to the CPU in order to be processed.

right justify: To line up characters such that the last nonblank character in each line is on the right margin.

rigid disk: A hard, flat, circular plate coated with magnetic material, used as a secondary-storage device.

ring-network configuration: A communication network in which several CPUs are connected in a circular pattern. Each computer can communicate with either one of its neighbors in the circle.

*RJE: (ISO) See remote job entry.

ROM: See read-only memory.

rounding: The process of replacing a number with the closest possible number, after dropping some of its decimal digits.

routine: 1.* (ISO) An ordered set of instructions that may have general or frequent use. 2. A computer program.

*row: 1. A horizontal arrangement of characters or other expressions. 2. Contrast with column.

RPG: See Report Program Generator.

RS-232C (serial) port: A personal computer I/O port through which data are transmitted and received serially, one bit at a time. It can be used in conjunction with modems, printers, or other serial devices.

*run: (ISO) A single performance of one or more jobs.

sabotage controls: Controls that reduce the risk of sabotage in EDP operations.

*scan: To examine sequentially, part by part.

schema: The logical structure of a data base.

scheduled listing: A report that is produced at a regular interval, such as a week, a month, or a year.

scratch (IBM): To erase information on a tape or disk or delete its identification so that the tape or disk can be used for another purpose.

scratch file (IBM): A file used as a work area.

*search: (ISO) The examination of a set of items for one or more having a given property.

secondary storage: 1.* (ISO) A storage device that is not primary storage. 2.* Storage that supplements another storage. 3. (IBM) Data storage other than primary storage; for example, storage on magnetic tape or direct-access devices. Synonymous with external storage and secondary storage. 4.* Contrast with primary storage.

*sector: (ISO) That part of a track or band on a magnetic drum, a magnetic disk, or a disk pack that can be accessed by the magnetic heads in the course of a predetermined rotational displacement of the particular device.

seek: A movement of the disk read/write head in or out to a specified track.

segment: A term often used as a synonym for record in a data-base management system.

segregation of functions: Dividing up the workload among employees such that the work of one becomes a check on the work of others.

self-documenting: A characteristic of a computer language whose statements are easy enough to understand that English descriptions of the program steps are not necessary.

semantic gap: A lack of correspondence between a problem definition and the computer code written to solve it.

semantic error: An error in the logic of the program, as opposed to a syntax error.

*semantics: 1. (ISO) The relationships of characters or groups of characters to their meanings, independent of the manner of their interpretation and use. 2. The relationships between symbols and their meanings.

semiconductor: A solid crystalline substance, such as silicon, that has a conductivity greater than good insulators but less than good conductors such as metal.

semiconductor storage: Storage that uses integrated electronic circuits on semiconductor material to represent bits of data. See chip.

sentinel value: Synonymous with trailer value.

sequence check: A control that verifies that input records are in ascending order by record-key field.

*sequential: 1. Pertaining to the occurrence of events in time sequence, with no simultaneity or overlap of events. 2. Contrast with concurrent, consecutive, and simultaneous.

sequential access (IBM): 1. An access mode in which records are obtained from, or placed into, a file in such a way that each successive access to the file refers to the next subsequent record in the file. The order of the records is established by the programmer when creating the file. 2. Contrast with direct access.

sequential construct: A construct in a program where two or more operations are performed in sequence.

sequential file organization: A file organization with all records usually ordered in ascending order by record key.

*serial processing: 1. Pertaining to the sequential or consecutive execution of two or more processes in a single device such as a channel or processing unit. 2. Contrast with parallel processing.

service bureau: A company that provides batch computer processing service on an as-needed basis and charges for the service according to an hourly rate.

shared data: Data that are used by two or more computers concurrently in a distributed data-processing system.

*sign bit: (ISO) A bit or a binary element that occupies a sign position and indicates the algebraic sign of the number represented by the numeral with which it is associated.

*simplex transmission: (ISO) Data transmission in one preassigned direction only.

simulate: To build a model or imitation of something that occurs in the real world, such as a business, weather system, or aircraft. Simulations that are built on computers are mathematical models.

*simulation: (ISO) The representation of certain features of the behavior of a physical or abstract system by the behavior of another system; for example, the representation of physical phenomena by means of operations performed by a computer or the representation of operations of a computer by those of another computer.

*simultaneous: 1. (ISO) Pertaining to the occurrence of two or more events at the same instant of time. 2. See also concurrent, consecutive, and sequential.

skeleton application program: A simple program developed as a model for an actual application. The skeleton program includes only the most essential capabilities needed in the actual application. Synonymous with prototype.

soft copy: An image on a video or other electronic screen, as opposed to hard copy on paper.

soft error: An error found when reading data (from the disk) that does not recur if those same data are reread.

soft-sectored: Disks that mark the beginning of each sec-

tor of data within a track by a magnetic pattern rather than by a physical hole in the disk.

*software: (ISO) Computer programs, procedures, rules, and possibly associated documentation concerned with the operation of a data-processing system.

software directory: A reference book that lists a large number of software packages and describes their major characteristics.

software monitor: A software system that monitors the performance of various system devices.

*sort: 1. The operation of sorting. 2. (ISO) To segregate items into groups according to specified criteria. Sorting involves ordering, but need not involve sequencing, for the groups may be arranged in an arbitrary order. 3. To arrange a set of items according to keys which are used as a basis for determining the sequence of the items; for example, to arrange the records of a personnel file into alphabetical sequence by using the employee names as sort keys.

*sort key: A key used as a basis for determining the sequence of items in a set.

sound synthesizer: An acoustic device that, when connected to a computer, can produce many different musical sounds.

source code: A program written in a higher-level language than machine language. It is called source code because it is the starting point or *source* in the compilation process to produce object code.

source-data automation: The capture of data, in computer-readable form, at the place and time of an event.

source document: A form containing data that are being keyed into a computer system.

*source language: (ISO) A language from which statements are translated.

*source program: 1. (ISO) A computer program expressed in a source language. 2. Contrast with object program.

specification statement: In a program, a passive statement that describes data characteristics to the computer but does not make it perform any action.

specification form: A form used to specify computations, input-file format, and report format in RPG.

spindle: The center shaft of a disk.

spooling (simultaneous peripheral operation on-line): (ISO) The use of auxiliary storage as a buffer storage to reduce processing delays when transferring data between peripheral equipment and the processors of a computer.

spreadsheet: A program that allows the user to create a large, two-dimensional table on the computer's screen, and to manipulate the data in the table in many different ways.

stand-alone: Computer hardware or software that operates in an independent and separate manner.

standard: An acknowledged guideline or norm against which performance is measured.

star-network configuration: A communication network in which several microcomputers are connected to one central CPU.

*statement: 1. (ISO) In a programming language, a meaningful expression that may describe or specify operations and is complete in the context of that programming language. 2. In computer programming, a symbol string or other arrangement of symbols. 3. (ISO) Synonym for instruction.

statistical multiplexor: A multiplexing device that allocates transmission time to different terminals in proportion to their volume of data input/output.

storage: The process of retaining data, program instructions, and output in machine-readable form.

*store: 1. (ISO) To enter data into a storage device or to retain data in a storage device. 2. (ISO) In computer programming, to copy data from registers into internal storage.

stored program: A set of instructions, residing in the computer's memory, that can be executed without human intervention.

strategic decision making: Involves making decisions at the upper or strategic level of the organization. These decisions affect the future of the organization and are made in an environment of uncertainty. Strategic decisions involve establishing goals, policies, and long-term resource allocations.

streaming tape: A tape-recording method used only to make backup copies of information from hard disks. Streaming tapes record data blocks close together, leaving too little room to be able to start and stop between blocks.

*string: (ISO) A linear sequence of entities such as characters or physical elements.

string constant: A constant composed of alphabetic, numeric, and special characters, enclosed within double quotes.

string variable: A variable that can take on as a value any string of alphabetic, numeric, and special characters.

structure chart: A graphic representation of the hierarchical relationships between various modules.

structured: That which is highly organized.

structured analysis: A system-analysis methodology used in structured system development. A structured analysis moves from a study of the existing system to its logical model. Then the logical model of the new system is created and developed into a new physical system.

structured design: Development of the logic of program modules and their interfaces.

structured English: A tool used for describing program logic in English-like terminology. It uses the vocabulary of English combined with the logical constructs of a programming language to make the logic understandable to people.

structured programming: An approach to computer programming that restricts the flow of control to three basic constructs: sequence, loop, and conditional.

structured system development: A system-development methodology based on three major principles: partitioning into small modules, specification of interfaces between modules, and specification of processes within the modules.

*subroutine: 1. (ISO) A sequenced set of statements that may be used in one or more computer programs and at one or more points in a computer program. 2. A routine that can be part of another routine.

subschema: The logical view of that part of a data base which is of interest to a particular application.

subscript: A variable whose values uniquely identify individual elements of an array. Synonymous with index.

substrate: The material the disk is made of beneath the magnetic coating. Hard disks are generally made of aluminum or magnesium alloys (or glass, for optical disks), whereas the substrate on floppy disks is usually Mylar.

subsystem: 1. (IBM) A secondary or subordinate system, usually capable of operating independently of, or asynchronously with, a controlling system. 2. A part of the total system. All subsystems combine to comprise the system.

summary file: A file containing data extracted and summarized from other files.

*supervisory program: (ISO) A computer program, usually part of an operating system, that controls the execution of other computer programs and regulates the flow of work in a data-processing system. Synonymous with executive program and supervisor.

surface: The top or bottom side of a disk platter.

*symbolic language: A programming language that expresses addresses and operation codes of instructions in symbols convenient to people rather than in machine language.

synchronous transmission: A data-transmission method in which a long stream of bytes is transmitted without interruption. This method is economical for complex, high-speed equipment that processes large volumes of data.

*syntax: 1. (ISO) The relationship among characters or groups of characters, independent of their meanings or the manner of their interpretation and use. 2. The structure of expressions in a language. 3. The rules governing the structure of a language.

*system: (ISO) In data processing, a collection of people, machines, and methods organized to accomplish a set of specific functions.

system analysis: 1. (IBM) The analysis of an activity to determine precisely what must be accomplished and how to accomplish it.

system analyst: A person whose responsibility is to analyze, design, and develop information systems.

system command: Operating-system commands issued by the user to facilitate the creating, editing, and execution of programs.

system-development life cycle: The different phases that a typical computer-based information system goes through in its development and use.

system-development controls: Control procedures to manage the system development, system documentation, and program-maintenance functions.

system documentation: The documentation that provides an overview of the system's features.

system flowchart: A flowchart providing an overall view of the inputs, processes, and outputs of a system.

system maintenance: Correcting errors discovered in programs and changing the programs to satisfy modified user requirements or conditions.

system network architecture (SNA): A data-communication system used to connect various IBM devices.

system and programming group: MIS personnel who develop or acquire application software systems.

system programmer (IBM): A programmer who plans, generates, maintains, extends, and controls the use of an operating system with the aim of improving the overall productivity of an installation. Contrast with application programmer.

system unit: The part of a personal computer that contains the central processing unit.

system software: A set of programs that controls the use of hardware and software resources. These programs allocate system resources to application programs, based on the application programs' needs and priorities.

table: 1. A two-dimensional data structure used as a logical model in relational data-base management systems. 2.* (ISO) An array of data, each item of which may be unambiguously identified by means of one or more arguments.

tactical decision-making: Involves making decisions at the middle or coordinating level of the organization. The decisions are made primarily to reach the current goals of the organization. A common decision on this level involves resource allocation for the current needs of the organization.

*tape drive: 1. (ISO) A mechanism for controlling the movement of magnetic tape. This mechanism is generally used to move magnetic tape past a read head or write head, or to allow automatic rewinding. Synonymous with tape deck and tape transport. 2. (ISO) Synonym for tape unit.

technical support staff: MIS personnel who are responsible for hardware maintenance and establishing data-processing standards.

telecommunications: Any communication between two computers, or devices with embedded computers, in various locations. It differs from networks in that this communication takes place over long distances and is usually carried out over phone lines, radio waves, or a satellite-transmission apparatus.

*temporary storage: In computer programming, storage locations reserved for intermediate results. Synonymous with working storage.

terminal: 1.* A point in a system or communication network at which data can either enter or leave. 2. (IBM) A device, usually equipped with a keyboard and some kind of display, capable of sending and receiving information over a communication channel.

test data: Hypothetical data used to test a new program for errors. Test data should be comprehensive enough to cover all possible types of valid and invalid inputs so that program performance can be observed under all circumstances.

third-generation language: A programming language such as FORTRAN, COBOL, PASCAL, or BASIC which requires that the user instruct the computer in a procedural, step-by-step fashion.

third party: A company other than the user or the computer manufacturer.

thrashing (IBM): In virtual-storage systems, a condition in which the system can do little useful work because of excessive paging.

throughput: (ISO) A measure of the amount of work performed by a computer system over a given period of time (for example, jobs per day).

timeliness: The speed with which data are provided to the user for decision-making purposes.

timesharing: 1. (ISO) A mode of operation of a data-processing system that provides for the interleaving in time of two or more processes in one processor. 2. (IBM) A method of using a computing system that allows a number of users to execute programs concurrently and to interact with the programs during execution. 3. (ISO) Synonym for conversational mode.

timesharing service: A service firm that rents out computer time to its customers. The customer typically accesses the CPU through a remote terminal located at its place of business.

top-down approach: A system-development approach that calls for the development of an integrated information system based on the objectives of the business.

trace: 1.* A record of the execution of a computer program; it exhibits the sequences in which the instructions were executed. 2. (IBM) To record a series of events as they occur.

track: An invisible magnetic circle pattern written on a disk as a guide to where to store and read the data.

track density: How closely the tracks are packed on a disk. The number is specified as tracks per inch (tpi), with most fixed disks in the hundreds or thousands.

tractor feed: A mechanism with a train of feed pins on each side that fit into the pinholes of continuous paper stock. Line-advance commands from the computer then cause the paper to advance.

trailer label: The last record in a file on magnetic tape; the record contains control information such as the total number of records in the file.

trailer value: A special data value that signals the end of a set of data. Synonymous with sentinel value.

transaction: A business event, such as a sale to a customer. In information systems, the term *transaction* often refers to any change made in a computer file.

transfer rate: For a disk or other peripheral device, the rate at which information is transferred from the device to memory, or vice versa.

transform description: A description, at the lowest levels of a data-flow diagram, of how data are to be processed.

translation: Generation of object code from source code.

***translator:** (ISO) A computer program that translates from one language into another language, and in particular from one programming language into another programming language. Synonymous with translating program.

tree data structure: A hierarchical data structure, characterized by a top node called a root, and nodes having a one-to-many relationship.

turn-around document: A document that can be sent out to people and is also readable by the computer when it is returned. The punched card containing remittance advice that often comes with utility bills is a common example of a turn-around document.

turn-around time: 1. (ISO) The elapsed time between submission of a job and the return of the complete output. 2. The elapsed time between submission of a batch job and the availability of output.

turnkey system: A complete system in which all hardware and software have been installed and debugged. In theory, all the user has to do is turn a key.

two-dimensional: Allowing only rows and columns.

universal product code (UPC): A bar-coded symbol printed on the package of a consumer product. This is detected by an optical reader and is used by the computer to identify and price the product.

update (IBM): To modify a master file with current information, according to a specified procedure.

user (IBM): Anyone who requires the services of a computing system.

user affirmation: The process of a program asking the user whether he or she will enter further data. This is used when executing programs that require interactive data entry.

user-defined function: A function that a programmer defines, as opposed to a built-in function.

user-defined words: Words that the programmer assigns specific meanings in a program.

user-driven computing: EDP applications for which users do not always know what information they will need and when. It is often necessary to modify the programs on short notice in such systems.

user-friendly systems: Software systems that make it easy for noncomputer-oriented people to use computers.

***utility program:** 1. (ISO) A computer program in general support of the processes of a computer; for instance, a diagnostic program, a trace program, and a sort program. Synonymous with service program. 2. A program designed to perform an everyday task, such as copying data from one storage device to another.

vacuum tubes: Glass-covered instruments that were used to regulate the flow of electrons through the circuits of early computer systems.

***validation:** The checking of data for correctness, or for compliance with applicable standards, rules, and conventions.

validity checks: A hardware control that monitors the bit structure of bytes to determine whether the combination of the on and off bits represent a valid structure within the character set of the computer.

***variable:** A quantity that can assume any of a given set of values.

variable-length record: 1. (IBM) A record having a length independent of the length of other records with which it is logically or physically associated. Contrast with fixed-length record. 2.* Pertaining to a file in which the records are not uniform in length.

vendor support: Services provided by the seller of a hardware or software system. These typically include training, repair and maintenance, installation, testing, consulting, and backup arrangements.

verifiability: The ability to confirm the accuracy of data. Accuracy may be confirmed by comparing the data with other data of known accuracy, or by tracing back to the original source.

virtual drive: The use of a drive name (a letter of the alphabet on the personal computer) to refer to part of a disk drive. Virtual drives are often used for large-capacity hard disks.

virtual storage: (ISO) The storage space that may be regarded as addressable main storage by the user of a computer system in which virtual addresses are mapped into real addresses. The size of virtual storage is limited by the addressing scheme of the computing system and by the amount of auxiliary storage available, and not by the actual number of main-storage locations.

voice-recognition system: A hardware or software device that can interpret the patterns of an individual's speech, thereby enabling voice input to a computer.

volatile storage: (ISO) A storage device whose contents are lost when power is removed.

walkthrough: A step-by-step review of the documentation or other work produced by a system analyst or programmer.

Winchester disks: Hard disks that use a technology similar to an IBM model that had the Winchester code name. These disks use the read/write heads that ride just above the magnetic surface, held up by the air dragged by the turning disk. When the disks stop turning, the heads land on the surface, which has a specially lubricated coating. Winchester disks must be either sealed or have a filtration system, since ordinary dust particles are large enough to fit between the head and the disk.

window: (SC1) In computer graphics, a bounded area within a display image.

*word: 1. (ISO) A character string or a binary-element string that is convenient for some purpose to consider as an entity. 2. A character string or a bit string considered to be an entity.

word-processing system: A computer system that stores and processes text data. These systems typically include powerful editing and text-formatting capabilities.

word size: A measure of the amount of data the CPU can process simultaneously.

*working storage: (ISO) Synonym for temporary storage and working space.

workload model: A set of one or more computer programs that are representative of the buyer's planned computer workload. These are typically executed on various computer configurations to provide information useful to the person making an acquisition decision.

*write: (ISO) To make a permanent or transient recording of data in a storage device or on a data medium.

write-enable ring (IBM): A device that is installed in a tape reel to permit writing on the tape. If a tape is mounted without the ring in position, writing cannot occur, and the file is protected.

write-protect notch: A cut-out in one corner of a diskette that is optically scanned to allow writing on a disk. If the notch is covered with tape, the drive will not write on the diskette; thus it is write-protected.

write-read checks: A control similar to redundancy checks. As information is written on magnetic tape or disk, it passes through a read head, which reads the information and compares it to the information that should have been written.

write-once: As applied to optical disks, technologies that allow the drive to store information on a disk and read it back, but not to erase it.

INDEX

Data processing operations, personnel for, 438–439
Data processing operations department, 402
Data representation, 294–301
Data storage, 10–16
    logical vs physical views of, 331–332, 333t, *334*
Data switch, for computer communications, 359–360, *360*
Data-switching networks, 367
Data transfers, international, 426–427
Data transmission. *See* Transmission.
Data type, 493
    in Pascal, 508
Datapro Reports on Microcomputer Software, 58
dBase II, 25
Debug process, 298
Decimal number system, 201, 294
Decision making,
    automated, 87
    levels of, 74–76, *76*
        characteristics, 77t
        information required by, 77t
Decision-support systems, 84–85, 522–535
    building, 530–533, *531*
    components, *525,* 525
    defined, 57, 524–525
    functions of, 526–528
    need for, 529
    organization for, 529
    software for, 525–526
Decision-support tools, 178
    examples of, 180t
Decision tables, 134, 136, *136*
Decision trees, 136, *138*
Default, defined, 504
Demand reports, 81
Dependent variables, 527
Desk check, as module test, 161
Device, vs medium, 236
Difference engine (Babbage), 459, *460*
Digital computers, vs analog computers, 200–202
Digital signals, conversion of analog signals, *365*
Digitize, defined, 383
Direct file organization, 307–309
    disadvantage of, 309
    overview, *308*
Direct-access, defined, 318–319
Direct-access file, 15–16
Directory, defined, 303
Disk pack, *219, 221*
Diskettes. *See* Floppy disks.
Display, as output in data processing, 108
Distributed data processing, 212–213, 355–390, 472
    data decentralization, 377, 379–380
    hardware distribution, 371–373
    need for, 371

software distribution, 373–374, 376–377
Division/remainder method of hashing, 308, *308*
Documentation,
    for Fortran, 494
    in system development, 163
Dot-matrix printers, 45, *46,* 251
    character set for, *256*
    mechanism in, *47*
    varied fonts for, 253
Download, defined, 66
    Dumb terminals, 357–358, *358*

EBCDIC representation of data, 296, 297t
    with even parity, 300t
EDP auditors, 438
EDP Auditors Foundation, 441
EDSAC, 465
EDVAC, 465
ENIAC, *464,* 464–465
EPROM (Erasable programmable read-only memory), 207, 210
Eckert, J. Presper, Jr., 464, 465
Editing of data, 106
Educate Ability Student Manual, 38
Educational Privacy Act, 425
Electromechanical computers, 463
Electronic bulletin boards, defined, 64
Electronic computers, history, 464–465
Electronic funds transfer system, 423
Electronic mail, 382–383
Electronic spreadsheets. *See* Spreadsheet software.
Embedded pointer, 342
End users, 172
    application development by, 171–191
Entity, defined, 11
Entry control, to MIS, 411
Environment, of system, 98–99
Environmental disaster control, for MIS, 412
Erasable programmable read-only memory (EPROM), 207, 210
Ergonomics, defined, 479
Error detection, with parity bit, 299–300
Error reports, 81
Exception reports, 81
Executable statements, in Fortran, 494
Execution, defined, 6
Execution cycle, 211
Execution path, defined, 6
Execution-time diagnostics, defined, 517
Executive programs, 273
Expansion boards, on PCs, 42
Expert systems, 422–423
Extended Binary Coded Decimal Interchange Code (EBCDIC), 296, 297t
    with even parity, 300t

Facilities-management vendor, 553
Fair Credit Reporting Act (1970), 424
Feasibility study, 126

Feedback, 101–102
    systems with and without, *103*
Field, 11–12
Fifth-generation computers, 478–479
File-access methods, summary, *314*
File activity, 314
File activity ratio, 302
File directories, *305*
    organization of, 306
File organization, 302–315
    overview, *307*
    selection of, 314–315
File query, defined, 314
File volatility, defined, 314
Files, 12–13
    accidental erasure, 345
    locating data in, 14–16
    manual, components of, *15*
    types of, and processing, 18
    user tips for naming, 14
Financial functions, with decision-support systems, 527
Financial management software, 54, *56*
Financial modeling tools, 178
    examples of, 180t
Fire control, for MIS, 412
Firmware, 207
Fixed disks, 220, *220,* 221
    back up copies for, 313
Flat-panel display, 250, *254*
Floppy disks, 44, 220, 222, *224*
    back ups for, 22
    causes of data loss on, *226*
    defined, 9
    formatting process, 78
    handling and care, 50
    keying to, for data entry, 237
    terminology, 225
Floppy-disk drives, *45*
Flowcharts, 95
Font, defined, 246
Formulas, in spreadsheets, 20
Fortran, 469, 489–494
    program sample, *492–493*
    selection of, 517
Fourth-generation language,
    categories and examples of, 176–180, *177,* 180–181t
    characteristics of, 176
    defined, 142, 172
Freedom of Information Act (1970), 424–425
Front-end processors, 287, 368, *369*
Full-duplex channel, 364
Fully indexed files, 310, *310*
Functional area, defined, 82
Functional information systems, 82–83, *84*
Functional primitives, 134

Gantt charts, 155, 403, 404–405, *407*
Gigabyte, defined, 213
GOTO-less programming, 152

MICR (Magnetic ink character recognition), 244–245, *248*
Machine languages, 466–467, 486–487, *490*
Macro, defined, 100
Macro commands, 514
Magnetic cores, as primary storage, 203, *205*
Magnetic disks, 9, 218–224, 469, *469*
Magnetic ink character recognition, 244–245, *248*
Magnetic tape, 468
  as storage, 215–218, *216*
Magnetic tape drive, *217*
Mail-order supplier, as source of PC Purchase, 60
Mailing lists, 384, *385*
Mainframe computers, 38, 213, *214*
  data communication link with PC, 361
  storage of operating system for, *274*
Maintainability, of system, defined, 141
Management,
  of corporate data in computers, 65
  understand of data communications, 356
  uses of information, 77–79
Management by exception, 81
Management decisions, vs objectives and information needs, 75
Management information needs,
  and computers, 10
  vs objectives and decisions, 75
Management information systems, 71–91
  components of, *84*
  data-processing operations, 408–409
  defined, 72
  impact on business, 86–88
  internal structure, 401–403, *404–405*
  organizational location, 400–401, *401, 402*
  physical security, 410–412
  relation to DBMS, *85*
  relationships within, *97*
  vs data processing, *73*
Management objectives, vs decisions and information needs, *75*
Management-science models, with decision-support systems, 527
Manufacturers, 550
Mark I electromechanical computer, *463*, 463–464
Martin, James, 174
Mass-storage devices, 227, *227*
Master file, *14*
Master-slave relationship, 357, 358
Mauchly, John W., 464, 465
Mechanical calculators, 457
Medium, vs device, 236
Megabyte, defined, 42
Memory dump, defined, 298
Memory expansion boards, on PCs, 42, *43*

Memory modules, 42
Memory. *See* Primary storage.
Message envelope, 360–361, *362*
Metcalfe, Henry, 459–460
Micro, defined, 100
Microcoding, 207
Microcomputers, 38, 211-212, *212. See also* Personal computers.
Microfiche, computer-output, 255, 257, *260*
Microprocessor chips, *468*
Microprocessors, 39, 203
  speed of, 40–41
Microprogramming, 207
Minicomputers, 38, 212, *213,* 471
Model building, with decision-support systems, 526
Modems, 48–49, *51,* 365, *366,* 375
Modularity, of computer system, 544
Modules, 148, 152
  design of, 155–156
  in ADA, 511
Monitor programs, 273
Monitors, *8,* 542
  for PC, 42, 44, *44*
Monochrome graphics cards, 178
Mouse, 47, *49*
Multi-user systems, 284
Multifunction memory board, 228, *229*
Multiplexors, 366-367, *367*
Multiprocessing, 286-287, *288*
Multiprogramming, 241, 279–282
Multitasking. *See* Multiprogramming.

Natural disaster control, for MIS, 412
Near-letter-quality printers, 46
Network, defined, 360
Network structures, for data-bases, 342–343, *344*
Node, defined, 342
Nonexecutable statements, in Fortran, 492–493
Nonimpact printers, 251–252
Nonprocedural language, 525
Nonprogrammable decisions, 75–76
Nonvolatile storage, defined, 45, 206
Normative models, 532
Norton Utilities, 345
Numeric data, defined, 25

Object code, 486
Office automation, 383–384, 422
  human factors, 385–387
Offline, 213
On-line, defined, 318
On-line direct-access system, 319, *320*
On-line realtime systems, 471
Operands, 210, 334
Operating systems, 469
  compatibility, 411
  defined, 268
  DOS, 475

for IBM-PC, *271*
for mainframe, storage of, *274*
functions of, in loading application software, *272–273*
multiprogramming, 471
types of, 278–279
virtual-storage, 472–473
Operation code, 210
Operational decisions, 75
Optical character recognition, 246, 248, *250*
Optical mark recognition equipment, 246
Organic computers, 479
Origination of data, 106
Output devices, 9, 11
Output step, in data processing, 107–108
Outputs, 7, 99

PC Magazine, 60
PC Week, 60
PERT (Program evaluation and review technique), 155, 402, 403
PL/1 (Programming Language/1), 471, 501, *502–503,* 504
  selection of, 517
POS (Point-of-sale) equipment, 244, *246*
PROM (Programmable read-only memory), 207, 210
Packages, as module in ADA, 511
Packed decimal data representation, 296
Page printers, 251
Parallel transmission, 362, *363,* 364
Parity bits, 299–301
Partitioning, 122–123, *123*
  in structure chart, *150*
  of data bases, *379,* 379-380
Pascal, Blaise, 457
Pascal, 506, 508, *509–510,* 510
  selection of, 516
Password, defined, 64
Payroll program, defined, 6
Performance monitors, 276–277
Peripheral devices, 236
  link with computer, 357–358
  manufacturers, 553
Personal Computer Disk-Operating System, for IBM-PC, *271*
Personal computers, *8,* 37–69, *39,* 211–212, *212,* 472
  American Express use of, 192–195
  application tools for, 176–177
  autoexec.bat files, 495
  cooperatives, 547
  coordination group for, 406
  data communication link with mainframe, 361
  defined, 7
  expansion boards on, 42
  expansion slots, 544
  hardware, *40*
  hardware industry for, 51–53
  history, 473, 475–476

PC USER TIP INDEX

INTEXT PHOTO CREDITS *(continued)*

Fig. 2–4, 2–6 Courtesy of Quadram Corporation. **Fig. 2–8** Courtesy of Epson America, Inc. **Fig. 2–11** Illustration by Yukio Kondo, reprinted from "Meet the Mouse," by Phil Lopiccola, published in the March 1983 issue of "Popular Computing" magazine. Copyright © 1983 by McGraw-Hill, Inc., NY 10020. All rights reserved. **Fig. 2–12** Photo Courtesy of Hewlett-Packard Company. **Fig. 2–14** Courtesy of Hayes Microcomputer Products, Inc. **Fig. 2–17** Courtesy of "InfoWorld," 2-11-85, p. 28. **Fig. 2–18** Courtesy of Mesa Technology Corporation. **Fig. 2–20** Courtesy of International Business Machines Corporation. **Fig. 2–21** Reprinted with permission of Dunsplus, Inc. **Fig. 2–22** Reprinted with permission of Price Waterhouse from "MICROCOMPUTERS: Their use and Misuse in Your Business." Copyright © 1983, Price Waterhouse. All rights reserved. **Chapter 3 Opening Photo** Courtesy of General Electric Company. **Chapter 4 Opening Photo** Courtesy of Hewlett-Packard Company. **PART II Opening Photo** Courtesy of NCR Corporation. **Chapter 5 Opening Photo** Courtesy of Calcomp. **Chapter 6 Opening Photo** Bill Gallery/Stock, Boston. **Chapter 7 Opening Photo** Courtesy of Information Builders Inc. **Fig. 7–3** James Martin, *Application Development Without Programmers,* pp. 55. Copyright © 1982. Reprinted by permission of Prentice-Hall, Inc. Englewood Cliffs, NJ. **Fig. 7–4** Reprinted from *The James Martin Report on High-Productivity Languages,* published by High-Productivity Software, Inc. **Fig. 7–5** Courtesy of Dataplotting Services, Inc. 255 Duncan Mill Road, Don Mills, Ontario, M3B 3X9, 416/441-4163. **Table 7–1** Reprinted from *The James Martin Report on High-Productivity Languages,* published by High-Productivity Software, Inc. **Table 7–2** James Martin, *Application Development Without Programmers* Copyright 1982, pp. 66–67. Reprinted by permission of Prentice-Hall, Inc. Englewood Cliffs, NJ. **Fig. 7–9** James Martin, *Application Development Without Programmers* Copyright 1982, p. 306. Reprinted by permission of Prentice-Hall, Inc. Englewood Cliffs, NJ. **PART III Opening Photo** Courtesy of NCR Corporation. **Chapter 8 Opening Photo** Courtesy of NCR Corporation. **Fig. 8–5** Courtesy of NCR Corporation. **Fig. 8–6** Courtesy of NCR Corporation. **Fig. 8–7** Courtesy of NCR Corporation. **Fig. 8–8** Courtesy of Intel Corporation. **Fig. 8–9** Photo Courtesy of Apple Computer, Inc. **Fig. 8–10** Photo Courtesy of Prime Computer, Inc. **Fig. 8–11** Courtesy of IBM Corporation. **Fig. 8–12** Courtesy of Cray Research, Inc. **Fig. 8–14** Courtesy of IBM Corporation. **Fig. 8–15** Photo Courtesy of Tecmar, Inc. **Fig. 8–17** Courtesy of IBM Corporation. **Fig. 8–18** Courtesy of NCR Corporation. **Fig. 8–20** IDEA disk is a product of IDEAssociates, Inc. IDEA disk is a trademark of IDEAssociates, Inc. **Fig. 8–21, 8–22, 8–23** Publishing permission granted by Verbatim Corporation, 1985. **Fig. 8–24** Courtesy of 3M Optical Recording Project. **Fig. 8–25** Courtesy of IBM Corporation. **Fig. 8–26** Courtesy of AT&T Bell Laboratories. **Fig. 8–27** Courtesy of Quadram Corporation. **Chapter 9 Opening Photo** Courtesy of Sperry Univac Corporation. **Fig. 9–2** Courtesy of REI/INFOREX. **Fig. 9–4** Courtesy of REI/INFOREX. **Fig. 9–5** Courtesy of Northern Telecom, Inc. **Fig. 9–9** Courtesy of NCR Corporation. **Fig. 9–11** Courtesy of IBM Corporation. **Fig. 9–13** Courtesy of NCR Corporation. **Fig. 9–15** Courtesy of AT&T. **Fig. 9–16** Courtesy of Texas Instruments. **Fig. 9–17** Courtesy of AT&T Bell Laboratories. **Fig. 9–18** Photo Courtesy of Epson America Inc. **Fig. 9–20** Photo Courtesy of Xerox Corporation. **Fig. 9–22** Courtesy of IBM Corporation. **Fig. 9–26** Courtesy of NCR Corporation. **Fig. 9–27** Photo Courtesy of 3M Corporation. **Fig. 9–28** Photo provided by NICOLET'S Computer Graphics Division. **Fig. 9–29** Courtesy of Sperry Univac Corporation. **Chapter 10 Opening Photo** Courtesy of NCR Corporation. **Chapter 11 Opening Photo** Courtesy of TRW, Inc. **Chapter 12 Opening Photo** Courtesy of Information Builders, Inc. **Fig. 12–9** James Martin, *An End User's Guide to Data Base.* Copyright © 1981, p. 33. Reprinted by permission by Prentice-Hall, Inc., Englewood Cliffs, NJ. **Fig. 12–10** Courtesy of Britton Lee Inc. **Chapter 13 Opening Photo** Courtesy of Teltone Data Carrier Systems. **Fig. 13–11** Courtesy of Hayes Microcomputer Products, Inc. **PART IV Opening Photo** Courtesy of Cincinnati Milicron. **Chapter 14 Opening Photo** Courtesy of Sperry Univac Corporation. **Chapter 15 Opening Photo** Courtesy of Digital Equipment Corporation. **Fig. 15–1** Courtesy of DIALOG Information Services, Inc. **Fig. 15–2** Courtesy of United States Robots. **Chapter 16 Opening Photo** Courtesy of Micrografx, Inc. **Fig. 16–2** From *The DPMA Model Curriculum for Undergraduate Computer Information Systems.* Copyright © and reprint permission granted 1985. Data Processing Management Association. All rights reserved. **Module A Opening Photo** Courtesy of Sperry Univac Corporation **Fig. A–1** Courtesy of IBM Corportation. **Fig. A–2** Courtesy of IBM Corporation. **Fig. A–3** Courtesy of IBM Corporation. **Fig. A–4** Courtesy of IBM Corporation. **Fig. A–5** Courtesy of IBM Corporation. **Fig. A–6** Courtesy of IBM Corporation. **Fig. A–7** Photo Courtesy of Sperry Univac Corporation. **Fig. A–8** Photo Courtesy of Sperry Univac Corporation. **Fig. A–9** Courtesy of IBM Corporation. **Figure A–10** Courtesy of IBM Corporation. **Fig. A–11** Courtesy of Texas Instruments. **Fig. A–12** Photo Courtesy of Apple Computer, Inc. **Figure A–15** Reprinted from the June 10, 1985 issue of *Business Week* by special permission, Copyright © 1985 by McGraw-Hill, Inc. **Module B Opening Photo** Courtesy of NCR Corporation. **Module C Opening Photo** Courtesy of Inforex, Inc. **Module D Opening Photo** Courtesy of Hewlett-Packard Company.

GALLERY CREDITS

Frontmatter Photos: p. i. Courtesy of AT & T Bell Laboratories. **p. ii.** Courtesy of TRW, Inc. **p. iii.** Courtesy of AT & T Bell Laboratories. **p. iv,** *bottom left.* Courtesy of International Business Machines Corporation. *Top right.* Courtesy of TRW, Inc. **Gallery 1: Buying and Setting Up a PC.** Introductory photo and photo 2. Photographs furnished courtesy of Entre' Computer Centers, Inc. Copyright 1985 Entre' Computer Centers, Inc. All rights reserved. Photos 1 & 3 through 35 by Scott Hamilton. Courtesy of Barton J. Wilner, Entre' Computer Center, Roanoke, Virginia. **Gallery 2: Using a Fourth Generation Language to Develop an Application.** All photos courtesy of Applied Data Research Corporation. **Gallery 3: The Making of a Chip.** Introductory photo. Courtesy of TRW, Inc. Photos 1 and 2. Courtesy of Hewlett-Packard Company. Photo 3. Courtesy of National Semiconductor Corporation. Photos

4, 5, and 6. Courtesy of Hewlett-Packard Company. Photo 7. Courtesy of AT & T Bell Laboratories. Photos 8, 9, and 10. Courtesy of Hewlett-Packard Company. Photo 11. Courtesy of AT & T Bell Laboratories. Photos 12, 13, and 14. Courtesy of TRW, Inc. Photo 15. Courtesy of Hayes Microcomputer Products, Inc. Photo 16. Courtesy of AT & T Bell Laboratories. Photo 17. Courtesy of Honeywell, Inc. **Gallery 4: A Tour of a Large Computer Center.** Introductory photo. Courtesy of Norfolk Southern Corporation. All other photos by Scott Hamilton. Courtesy of Norfolk Southern Corporation. **Gallery 5: Human/Computer Interaction.** Introductory photo. Courtesy of Whirlpool Corporation. Photo 1. Copyright Steve Uzell, III, Planning Research Corporation. Photo 2. Courtesy of MSI Data Corporation. Photos 3 and 4. Courtesy of Hewlett-Packard Company. Photos 5 and 6. Courtesy of Interstate Voice Products. Photo 7. Courtesy of Polytel. Photo 8 by Scott Hamilton. Photo 9. Courtesy of Apple Computer. Photo 10. Courtesy of National Semiconductor Corporation. Photos 11 and 12. Courtesy of International Business Machines Corporation. Photo 13. Courtesy of Fran Heyl Associates. Photo by Dan McCoy. Photo 14. Courtesy of Houston Instruments. Photo 15. Courtesy of International Business Machines Corporation. Photo 16. Courtesy of Xerox Corporation. Photo 17. Courtesy of Houston Instruments. Photo 18. Courtesy of Hewlett-Packard Company. Photo 19. Courtesy of Houston Instruments. Photos 20 and 21. Courtesy of ISSCO. Photo 22. Courtesy of Polaroid. Photo 23. Courtesy of General Electric. Photo 24. Courtesy of General Motors Corporation. Photo 25. Courtesy of Ramtek Corporation. Photo 26. Courtesy of International Business Machines Corporation. **Gallery 6: Telecommunications.** Introductory photo, photos 1 and 2. Courtesy of AT & T Bell Laboratories. Photo 3. Courtesy of Motorola. Photo 4. Courtesy of International Business Machines Corporation. Photo 5. Courtesy of Paradyne. Photo 6. Courtesy of Hayes Microcomputer Products, Inc. Photos 7, 8, and 9. Courtesy of AT & T Bell Laboratories. Photo 10. Courtesy of International Business Machines Corporation. Photo 11. Courtesy of AT & T Bell Laboratories. Photo 12. Courtesy of Motorola. Photo 13. Courtesy of AT & T Bell Laboratories. Photos 14, 15, 16, and 17. Courtesy of COMSAT. Photo 18. Courtesy of NASA. **Gallery 7: Computer Security.** Introductory Photo by Scott Hamilton. Photo 1. Courtesy of Interstate Voice Products. Photo 2. Courtesy of On-Line Software International, Inc. Photo 3 by Scott Hamilton. Photo 4. Courtesy of American Locker Security Systems. Photo 5. Courtesy of TACT Technology. Photo 6. Courtesy of Paradyne. Photo 7 by Scott Hamilton. Photo 8. Courtesy of Stellar Systems. Photo 9. Courtesy of Maynard Electronics. Photos 10 and 11. Courtesy of Diebold, Inc. Photos 12a and 12b. Courtesy of Tecmar, Inc. Photo 13. Courtesy of Diebold, Inc. Photo 14. Courtesy of TRW, Inc. Photo 15. Courtesy of Diebold, Inc. **Gallery 8: The Blue Collar Computer: Robots and Industrial Automation.** Introductory photo and photos 1 and 2. Courtesy of Cincinnati Milicron. Photo 3. Courtesy of TRW, Inc. Photo 4. Courtesy of Hewlett-Packard Company. Photo 5. Courtesy of Cincinnati Milicron. Photo 6. Courtesy of General Motors Corporation. Photo 7. Courtesy of Whirlpool Corporation. Photo 8. Courtesy of National Semiconductor Corporation. Photo 9. Courtesy of TRW, Inc. Photo 10. Courtesy of Electro Scientific Industries, Inc., Portland, OR. Photos 11 and 12. Courtesy of International Business Machines Corporation. Photo 13. Courtesy of Hewlett-Packard Company. Photos 14, 15, and 16. Courtesy of International Business Machines Corporation. Photos 17 and 18. Courtesy of Odectics, Inc., Anaheim, CA. Chapter 1 Courtesy of AT & T Bell Laboratories. Chapter 2 Courtesy of International Business Machines Corporation. Chapter 3 Courtesy of International Business Machines Corporation. Chapter 4 Courtesy of TRW, Inc. Chapter 5 Courtesy of CAP Gemini. Chapter 6 Courtesy of TRW, Inc. Chapter 7 Courtesy of AT & T Bell Laboratories. Chapter 8 Courtesy of Hewlett-Packard Company. Chapter 9 Courtesy of RAMTEK Corporation. Chapter 10 Courtesy of AT & T Bell Laboratories. Chapter 11 Courtesy of International Business Machines Corporation. Chapter 12 Courtesy of Information Builders, Inc. Chapter 13 Courtesy of AT & T Bell Laboratories. Chapter 14 Courtesy of SAS/GRAPH Institute, Inc. Chapter 15 Courtesy of International Business Machines Corporation. Chapter 16 Courtesy of Hayes Microcomputer Products. Module A Courtesy of Harris Company. Module B Courtesy of SAS/GRAPH Institute, Inc. Module C Courtesy of Cullinet. Module D Courtesy of Intel.